Essential Study Skills

EIGHTH EDITION

LINDA WONG

CENGAGE
Learning®

Australia • Brazil • Mexico • Singapore • United Kingdom • United States

Essential Study Skills, Eighth Edition

Linda Wong

Product Director: Annie Todd

College Success Senior Product Manager:
Shani Fisher

Senior Content Developer: Judy Fifer

Content Coordinator: Rebecca Donahue

Senior Media Developer: Amy Gibbons

Marketing Manager: Lydia LeStar

Market Development Manager: Josh Adams

Content Project Manager: Cathy Brooks

Senior Art Director: Pam Galbreath

Rights Acquisitions Specialist:
Shalice Shah-Caldwell

Manufacturing Planner: Sandee Milewski

Production Service: Cenveo Publisher Services

Cover and appendix title page photo montage:
©Africa Studio/Shutterstock.com;
with additional elements from
© gjergji kolonja/Shutterstock.com,
© Maxx-Studio/Shutterstock.com,
© Seyyahil/Shutterstock.com,
© Skylines/Shutterstock.com,
© Betacam-SP/Shutterstock.com,
© Bryan Solomon/Shutterstock.com, and
© Gilmanshin/Shutterstock.com

For product information and technology assistance, contact us at
Cengage Learning Customer & Sales Support, 1-800-354-9706
For permission to use material from this text or product,
submit all requests online at **www.cengage.com/permissions.**
Further permissions questions can be emailed to
permissionrequest@cengage.com.

Library of Congress Control Number: 2013940695

ISBN-13: 978-1-285-43009-6

ISBN-10: 1-285-43009-3

Cengage Learning
200 First Stamford Place, 4th Floor
Stamford, CT 06902
USA

Cengage Learning is a leading provider of customized learning solutions with office locations around the globe, including Singapore, the United Kingdom, Australia, Mexico, Brazil, and Japan. Locate your local office at: **international.cengage.com/region.**

Cengage Learning products are represented in Canada by Nelson Education, Ltd.

For your course and learning solutions, visit **www.cengage.com.**

Purchase any of our products at your local college store or at our preferred online store **www.cengagebrain.com.**

Instructors: Please visit **login.cengage.com** and log in to access instructor-specific resources.

Printed in the United States of America
1 2 3 4 5 6 7 17 16 15 14 13

Contents

CHAPTER 5

Processing Information into Your Memory   134

CHAPTER 6

Rehearsing and Retrieving Information from Memory   166

CHAPTER 7

Preparing for Upcoming Tests   194

CHAPTER 8

Selecting a Reading System   230

CHAPTER 9

Strengthening Reading and Notetaking Skills   264

APPENDIX A

Essential Test-Taking Skills   A1

APPENDIX B

Answer Keys   B1

APPENDIX C

Exercises, Inventories, and Checklists   C1

APPENDIX D

Excerpts   D1

Preface

Welcome to the new edition of *Essential Study Skills*. As in the Seventh Edition, the Eighth Edition empowers students to excel by using a metacognitive, multisensory approach throughout the textbook to provide them with essential study skills to increase their academic performance. Changing behaviors occurs most successfully when students understand *how* they learn, *what* skills they need to learn to use to perform specific tasks, and *which* strategies work most effectively to achieve desired outcomes. In the new world of ever-increasing technological distractions, the Eighth Edition of *Essential Study Skills* specifically shows students how to refocus on student-oriented strategies that work and how to consider ways to use technology to their advantage when studying. The textbook is designed to encourage all students—freshmen, nontraditional, and returning—to take greater responsibility for their learning, increase their self-confidence and motivation, discover strategies that work for them as individuals, and implement plans of action to achieve their academic and personal goals. The majority of students *want* to learn! This Eighth Edition provides students with exciting tools to turn *wants* and *desires* into reality and academic success.

Helping Students Study and Learn

Essential Study Skills, Eighth Edition, is a student-friendly textbook that builds a strong foundation of essential study skills strategies designed to boost memory, integrate skills and concepts, and excel in the classroom. The following chart highlights the book features in the Eighth Edition that make this edition unique, engaging, appealing—and most important of all—highly effective.

Book Features to Help Students

Features to Help Students Grasp Key Concepts and Main Ideas in Chapters	• Clear chapter Learning Objectives • Chapter Outline • Chapter Visual Mapping to expand with details of topics • Concise Learning Objectives Review
A Wealth of Step-by-Step Approaches	• Direct, easy–to-read and learn strategies • Clear steps for using memory tools • Concise bulleted points to clarify important concepts • Clear examples to explain new concepts
Features to Enhance Learning	• List of chapter terminology to learn • Marginal notes with definitions of terms to know • Visually appealing charts that summarize strategies • Multicolor format showing levels of information • Exercises that reinforce learning strategies

(continued)

Book Features to Help Students *(continued)*

Self-Assessment Tools	• Chapter Profiles to examine attitudes and behaviors • Checklists in the textbook to assess skills and progress • Concept Checks to strengthen comprehension • Self-correcting Check Points to verify understanding • End-of-the-chapter Review Questions
Activities to Engage Students	• Textbook exercises • Textbook Case Studies • Group Processing activities • Reflective Writing assignments • Critical Thinking activities
Appendix A	A comprehensive Essential Test-Taking Skills guide with fifty-two test-taking strategies and tips to apply to all kinds of test questions and test-taking situations
Appendix B	Answer keys for Chapter Profiles, Check Point quizzes, and Chapter Review Questions
Appendix C	Inventories and checklists to self-assess performance and skill levels
Appendix D	Textbook excerpts from a variety of content areas to reinforce skills used throughout the textbook

Online Features to Help Students

The Eighth Edition recognizes that technology motivates many students and provides them with multisensory approaches for working with course materials and skills. Many online materials and options are available for students to use to enhance the learning process. Students will be delighted to see the following online materials available for the *Essential Study Skills,* Eighth Edition textbook:

- The **online textbook** in the student College Success CourseMate
- Self-correcting **Chapter Profile** questions
- Printable **Chapter Visual Mapping** to expand with details
- An **expanded Chapter Outline** to use for studying and reciting
- Complete **list of Concept Check questions** to use for self-quizzing
- **Textbook Case Studies** and **Reflective Writing assignments**
- **Topics In-Depth** that present information that is only available online
- **Practice Quizzes** available only online for each chapter Check Point
- **Enhanced Quizzes** that link to sections of the online textbook
- **Flashcards** and an **online glossary** of terminology
- New **Chapter Study Guides** for each chapter

Helping Instructors Teach with Resources

Essential Study Skills, Eighth Edition, is an instructor-friendly textbook that provides the pedagogy and resources to help students build a strong foundation of essential study skills strategies, heighten their understanding of the learning process, and increase their performance and excellence in the classroom. The Eighth Edition recognizes instructors' needs to have a wealth of resources available at their fingertips to use to create a dynamic, engaging, and highly effective study skills course. The following chart highlights the book features in the Eighth Edition that make this edition ideal for instructors who want a textbook packed with resources and instructional options oriented to active learning.

Book Features to Help Instructors

Chapter Sequencing	• Flexible format allows you to select the most effective order of chapters to teach • Instructor options for best time to teach Appendix A, Essential Test-Taking Skills
Structured Chapters	• Color-coded headings related to the chapter Learning Objectives • Clear subheadings to identify specific topics • Bulleted points to identify important details and steps • Consistent chapter format with Concept Checks, Check Points, definitions in margins, and types of chapter exercises
Ready-to-Use Classroom Activities	• A variety of exercises in the textbook that you can use for class activities for which only you have the answer keys • Concept Check questions in margins for small group or class activities, writing assignments, or short pop quizzes • List of Terms to Know for partner vocabulary drills and quizzing • Group Processing activities designed to use with small groups • Critical Thinking activities for homework assignments, small group activities, or whole class discussions
Ready-to-Use Self-Assessment Tools	• Checklists within chapters for students to engage in the topics • Self-scoring Checklists in Appendix C for students to complete, reflect on, and discuss in class • Inventories for students to analyze their behaviors and skills
Instructor Resource Manual (IRM)	• A printed version and an online version available • Suggestions for organizing your course and grading system • Step-by-step teaching tips • Answer keys for chapter exercises • Reduced images of PowerPoint slides • Reduced images of transparency masters that you can use in class or as handouts

(continued)

Book Features to Help Instructors *(continued)*

Excerpts in Appendix D to Use for Instructional Purposes	Use the following excerpts to practice reading, annotating, notetaking, and test-taking skills: • Excerpt 1: Understanding Stress and Stressors • Excerpt 2: Practice Visualization • Excerpt 3: Adopting a Healthy Lifestyle • Excerpt 4: Semantic Networks • Excerpt 5: Building Blocks of Medical Language • Excerpt 6: Professional Leadership • Excerpt 7: The Scientific Method • Excerpt 8: How to Listen Critically
Self-Scoring Activities	• Students have answer keys to score Chapter Profiles • Students have answer keys to score Check Point quizzes • Students have answer keys to score chapter Review Questions

Online Features to Help Instructors

The **Instructor Website** is a comprehensive website that puts teaching tools and resources at your fingertips. By logging in at *CengageBrain.com*, you will find the following valuable instructor resources:

- The complete **Instructor Resource Manual** online, which includes teaching tips, answer keys to chapter exercises, and ready-to-use tests. (A printed version is also available upon request.)
- The **transition guide** that helps you move from the Seventh Edition to the Eighth Edition
- **Expanded Chapter Outlines** and **Lists of Concept Checks**
- **Ready-to-use tests** and **answer keys** for each chapter
- **Grading rubrics** to use for inventories, writing assignments, and homework exercises
- Full-size **transparency masters and PowerPoint slides** to download for classroom lectures, presentations, and handouts for each chapter
- The twelve new **Chapter Study Guides** to print for students, make available on your class website, or request students to download and print from the College Success CourseMate
- **Answer Keys for the new Chapter Study Guides**
- The **Cognero Online Testing Program** is the flexible online testing system that allows you to author, edit, and manage test bank content. You can create multiple test versions instantly and deliver them through your Learning Management System from your classroom, or wherever you may be, with no special installs or downloads required.

What's New in the Eighth Edition of *Essential Study Skills*

The Eighth Edition has a new chapter on technology (Chapter 12); a revised chapter organization that puts earlier emphasis on self-management or self-regulatory skills; new pairings and integration of related topics; new topics in chapters; and more comprehensive coverage of high-demand topics.

Reorganized Chapters

As you examine the full table of contents for the Eighth Edition, you will discover the new lineup of chapters, topics, and study strategies:

- **Chapters 1 through 4 Focus on Personal Preferences and Self-Management Skills**
  - Working with learning style and personality preferences and multiple intelligences
  - Developing a powerful mindset that includes attitudes and beliefs
  - Strengthening critical thinking skills
  - Managing time and increasing concentration
  - Achieving goals and increasing motivation
  - Reducing stress and procrastination

- **Chapters 5 and 6 Focus on Strengthening Memory**
  - Exploring how memory works in the Information Processing Model
  - Learning how to use new memory processes and strategies
  - Understanding ways to combat six kinds of forgetting
  - Applying the Twelve Principles of Memory
  - Using mnemonics effectively

- **Chapter 7 Focuses on Preparing for Tests**
  - Organizing materials and time to prepare for upcoming tests
  - Understanding different kinds of test questions
  - Using Appendix A, the Essential Test-Taking Skills pull-out guide
  - Managing test anxiety

- **Chapters 8 through 11 Focus on Reading, Notetaking, and Listening Skills**
  - Improving textbook reading skills by understanding the reading process
  - Using different reading systems for different kinds of textbooks
  - Learning skills for reading online (digital) e-textbooks
  - Working with paragraph-levels skills, such as vocabulary and organizational patterns
  - Annotating (highlighting, marking, and making marginal notes) in textbooks
  - Using a variety of notetaking systems to take textbook and lecture notes
  - Adjusting reading strategies for reading in a variety of content areas
  - Creating and using visual notes to learn course content
  - Strengthening listening skills and developing effective lecture notes

- **NEW: Chapter 12 Focuses on Using Technology**
  - Understanding basic computer concepts and computer literacy skills
  - Learning about the structure, requirements, bulletin boards, and etiquette for online courses

- Exploring the Internet and websites; using online resources and research skills

- Evaluating online materials

- Avoiding intentional and unintentional plagiarism

- Exploring new digital devices and apps (applications) for tablets, iPads, and smartphones

New Topics in the Eighth Edition

The following topics are new for the Eighth Edition, so taking time to familiarize yourself with the topics is recommended.

- **Eight Personality Types:** Chapter 1 now includes descriptions and checklists to estimate individual personality preferences that result in eight possible personality types based on the Myers-Briggs Type Indicator® assessment. A personality preference refers to a way of doing or responding that feels more natural, automatic, or comfortable, and which produces better results in the following four categories: (1) where you focus your attention, (2) how you take in information, (3) how you make decisions, and (4) how you approach or structure your life. Understanding the basic characteristics of the following eight personality preferences provides insight about oneself, friends, and classmates: Extraversion–Introversion, Sensing–Intuition, Thinking–Feeling, and Judging–Perceiving.

- **Time Management and Personality Preferences:** Chapter 2 discusses ways the personality preference styles of Sensing, Intuition, Judging, and Perceiving affect the way students perceive and use time-management strategies.

- **GPS Strategy for Setting Goals:** Chapter 4 introduces a new, simplified strategy for setting goals or creating plans of action. This strategy consists of three steps:

  1. G = Goal   Set a specific, realistic goal with target dates and times.

  2. P = Purpose   Identify the purpose, intention, or significance of the goal.

  3. S = Steps   Identify specific steps to achieve the goal.

- **Twelve Memory Processes:** Chapter 5 identifies twelve specific memory processes that play an active role in developing memory. The twelve processes summarize important information, but do not need to be memorized or learned as a set of twelve processes. These processes include: selective attention, deeper levels of encoding, immediately working with stimuli, Magic 7 ± 2 Theory, schemas, factual and procedural information, elaborative rehearsal, multisensory strategies, selectivity, feedback, associations and retrieval cues, and not rushing the learning process.

- **Six Forgetting Theories:** Chapter 6 includes information that explains why forgetting sometimes occurs in our information processing system and memory. The seventh edition had one excerpt in Appendix D that discussed five forgetting theories; for the Eighth Edition, the Emotional Blocks Theory has been added to explain why some learned information cannot be accessed or located in long-term memory.

- **Outline Reading System:** In Chapter 8, students learn to use an outline reading system by creating informal outline notes during the reading process. These notes become excellent guides for reciting information, writing summaries, and using as review tools.

- **Organizational Patterns and Graphic Materials:** Chapter 10 uses an integrative skills approach with the organizational patterns. After reading the new paragraph examples, students annotate and create diagrams to show the details. In the graphic materials section, new graphics to analyze are followed by comprehension and discussion questions.

- **An Effective Listening Plan:** Chapter 11 introduces students to a listening plan that helps increase the quality of listening experiences. The steps include: (1) attitude, (2) purpose, (3) image, (4) depth, (5) notes, (6) refocus, (7) feedback, and (8) open-ended, closed, probing, and leading questions.

- **Top Twenty Technology Picks:** Lucy MacDonald, an expert in online education and digital materials, offers her top twenty technology picks for students to explore. This resource in Chapter 12 provides students with a variety of applications, videos, and comprehensive websites to enhance the use of technology.

- **Online Chapter Study Guides:** Comprehensive Chapter Study Guides (available only online) require students to return to the chapter to use the "cloze reading technique" that requires students to locate specific words to complete statements. The Study Guides also include closed and open-ended questions for topics throughout the chapter. These study guides provide a thorough review of chapters.

What's Revised in the Eighth Edition
of *Essential Study Skills*

Examples, exercises, and excerpts are updated with more current topics to engage students in the study skills processes and to better prepare them for a broader range of academic challenges that they will encounter in their classes. More details about revisions are available on the **Instructor Website, Transitioning to the Eighth Edition**. The following chart summarizes major revisions.

Revisions to the Eighth Edition

Early Introduction of Critical Thinking Skills and New Activities	*Teaching students to think on higher levels, to interpret, to evaluate, and to apply what they are learning to other content areas as well as to their personal lives is emphasized in each chapter.* • Critical thinking now introduced in Chapter 2 • New Critical Thinking activities for each chapter

Transfer These Skills Activities	*Teaching students to transfer skills to other courses is valuable and essential for meaningful, long-term learning. New exercises to transfer skills include:* • Chapter 1: Using the See-Say-Do Strategy • Chapter 2: Personalizing the Self-Efficacy Cycles • Chapter 3: Prioritizing and Creating a Task Schedule • Chapter 4: Planning a Term-Long Project • Chapter 5: Drawing Semantic Networks and Schemas • Chapter 6: Using The Loci Method • Chapter 7: Developing Summary Notes and a 5-Day Study Plan • Chapter 8: Surveying a Chapter and Applying SQ4R • Chapter 9: Applying Vocabulary Skills • Chapter 10: Creating a Visual Mapping • Chapter 11: Developing Two-Column Notes and PowerPoint Notes • Chapter 12: Conducting Internet Searches
Appendix A: Essential Test-Taking Skills	*Being prepared for tests and knowing how to perform well on tests are valuable skills for all college students.* • Appendix A has been condensed to fifty-two strategies. • The strategies in Appendix A are reinforced throughout the textbook. Each Check Point quiz and Chapter Review quiz refers students to specific strategies in Appendix A for responding to the type of question posed in the quiz.
The Information Processing Model	*Metacognition involves understanding the basic processes involved in learning and developing memory.* • The memory model has been condensed and is now presented in a more direct, easy-to-understand model. • Twelve memory processes reinforce the processes used in the Information Processing Model and working memory.
Bloom's Taxonomy	*Understanding and using the six cognitive levels in Bloom's Taxonomy is a foundation for critical thinking skills.* • Emphasis in Chapter 2 is on the six revised levels in Bloom's Taxonomy: Remembering, Understanding, Applying, Analyzing, Evaluating, and Creating. • A website appears in the Twenty Top Technology Picks for students to explore descriptions and prompt words for questions.

Revised Critical Thinking Activities

Each chapter ends with a Critical Thinking activity that you can use for class or small group discussions or for homework writing assignments. These activities are open-ended and engage students in the process of paying closer attention to the integration of concepts, to relationships beyond those stated in the textbook, and to analysis of information they are studying.

- **Chapter 1 Critical Thinking:** Examine the fairness of employers using personality tests to find applicants who fit specific jobs. A new excerpt, "Personality Tests Help Employers Find Applicants Who Fit," is included.
- **Chapter 2 Critical Thinking:** Discuss relationships among cognitive learning styles, multiple intelligences, and personality types described in Chapter 1.
- **Chapter 3 Critical Thinking:** After reading a new excerpt, "The Power of Chunking," define the term and compare and contrast the processes of *chunking up* and *chunking down*.
- **Chapter 4 Critical Thinking:** Use Excerpt 3 in Appendix D, "Adopting a Healthy Lifestyle," for writing long-term, intermediary, short-term, and immediate goals applicable to the content of the excerpt.
- **Chapter 5 Critical Thinking:** Select one of several multisensory options to *create* a product that shows understanding of the Twelve Principles of Memory.
- **Chapter 6 Critical Thinking:** Identify relationships between the Twelve Principles of Memory and the three memory centers introduced in Chapter 5; identify ways each principle of memory activates other principles of memory.
- **Chapter 7 Critical Thinking:** Write practice test questions using all six levels in Bloom's Taxonomy. Questions may be discussed in class, presented as a review activity, or used on an upcoming test.
- **Chapter 8 Critical Thinking:** Locate an online news article. Use the criterion provided to evaluate the article in terms of reliability, quality, and usefulness.
- **Chapter 9 Critical Thinking:** Apply and create a set of two-column notes for their choice of subject matter.
- **Chapter 10 Critical Thinking:** Apply different forms of test-taking questions to the information in Excerpt 7 in Appendix D, "The Scientific Method."
- **Chapter 11 Critical Thinking:** Read Excerpt 8 in Appendix D, "How to Listen Critically" and the table "Guidelines for Critical Listening," and then compile key words and key actions used in critical reading, critical listening, and critical thinking processes.
- **Chapter 12 Critical Thinking:** Optional activities are designed by the instructor to interact with online discussion boards, Internet research, forums, wikis, blogs, tweets, and mobile device applications.

Features Retained from the Seventh Edition

Instructors who have used previous editions of *Essential Study Skills* will find many familiar features that continue to be an essential part of this student-oriented textbook:

- **Chapter Learning Objectives and Chapter Outlines** provide students with the "big picture" of a chapter before they begin more in-depth reading.
- **Your Chapter Mapping** is a study tool that students expand by adding important details for each heading of the chapter that appears on the visual mapping.
- **Chapter Profiles** provide students with a self-correcting series of ten questions to assess their current attitudes and behaviors at the beginning and at the end of the term.
- **Essential Strategies Charts** that appear throughout each chapter highlight and summarize essential strategies presented in the chapter.

- **Concept Checks** in the margins provide students with questions to assess their understanding of concepts discussed in the adjacent paragraphs.

- **Definitions in the Margins** provide students with course-specific definitions for all the key terms that appear in bold colored print.

- **Case Studies** in every chapter present students with real-life student situations to analyze and then suggest strategies to address the problems posed in the case studies.

- **Reflective Writing assignments** provide students with opportunities to personalize the chapter content, discuss their current skills and attitudes, and integrate the chapter's skills with other study skills and personal experiences.

- **Group Processing: A Collaborative Learning Activity** in each chapter provides a small-group activity that enhances student interest and creates a forum for student interaction, brainstorming, discussion, problem-solving, critical thinking, and cooperative work.

- **Student exercises** reinforce skills that appear throughout each chapter. Instructors may select appropriate exercises to use for homework assignments, class discussions, or for small-group activities in the classroom. Answer keys appear in the Instructor Resource Manual; students do not have access to answer keys for exercises.

- **Check Points at the end of each main heading** provide students with several questions to assess how well they comprehended the textbook information. Students can refer to Appendix A if they need help answering specific kinds of questions. Students self-correct by using the answer keys in Appendix B.

- **Practice and Enhanced Quizzes in the College Success CourseMate** provide students with additional practice working with course content and test-taking skills. Quizzes are scored online and can be repeated multiple times.

- **Learning Objectives Review** at the end of each chapter uses bulleted points to summarize the most important points for each of the chapter's objectives.

- **Terms to Know** identify the key terms in the chapter that students need to be able to define.

- **Chapter Review Questions** provide students with a tool to assess their understanding and recall of essential concepts, skills, and strategies discussed in the chapter. Answer keys appear in Appendix B.

- **Appendix A** provides students with a comprehensive resource for developing test-taking skills. The direct, step-by-step approach for true-false, multiple-choice, matching, fill-in-the-blanks, listing, definition, short answer, math, and essay test questions is easy to use.

- **Appendix B** provides students with answers to their Profile Charts, a Master Profile Chart to record their results, and answer keys for Check Point quizzes and Chapter Review questions.

- **Appendix C** provides students with an array of exercises and self-assessment inventories or checklists to use to assess their strengths and weaknesses and adjust their strategies.

- **Appendix D** gives students the opportunity to apply critical thinking and study skills to materials that originated in a variety of textbooks from across the curriculum.

Dedication

I dedicate this new edition to the thousands of educators who demonstrate an endless commitment to providing high-quality, valuable educational experiences for their students, and to all students who strive to excel and benefit from their educational opportunities.

Acknowledgments

My appreciation is extended to the following reviewers who dedicated their time and expertise to contribute ideas to enrich this textbook and further strengthen the effectiveness of this instructor-friendly and student-friendly textbook. Thank you all for your contributions: Melanie Abst, Cynthia Avery, Judith Colson, Valerie Cunningham, Karen Fenske, SusAnn Key, Lucy MacDonald, Pamela Moss, Janet Moynihan, Amanda Nimetz, Brenda Wallace, and Alice Warner.

I extend my sincere appreciation for the outstanding editorial and production staff that has worked diligently with me through all the phases of creating the Eighth Edition of *Essential Study Skills*. Most readers of this textbook are unaware of the high degree of coordination, teamwork, time commitment, and resources required to produce a new edition of a textbook and all its companion resources. The process is extensive and requires the utmost attention to details. I acknowledge your level of dedication and your utmost commitment to the development of this Eighth Edition. I appreciate and value you for your contributions. Thank you!

To the Student

Essential Study Skills, Eighth Edition is a valuable resource designed to provide you with an array of study skills strategies that will unlock your learning potential and empower you to improve your academic performance. Reading the following section carefully will provide you with important information that explains how to get the most out of *Essential Study Skills,* Eighth Edition.

Quick Start Checklist

Go to the College Success CourseMate for a Quick Start Checklist to use to prepare for an upcoming term. Look for the Quick Start Checklist link on the left side of the home page screen. Click on it to learn about the following topics:

- Creating class schedules
- Familiarizing yourself with your campus
- Organizing your notebooks
- Selecting a system to record homework assignments
- Getting off to a good start on the first day of class
- Planning sufficient study time for your classes
- Other suggestions and tips for getting off to a good start

Steps to Access the College Success CourseMate
Go to *CengageBrain.com* to access these resources, and look for this icon to find resources related to your textbook in College Success CourseMate. You will be prompted to enter the required CourseMate access code. If you do not have an access code, you will be able to purchase one at *CengageBrain.com.*

Starting the Term: Getting an Overview

As soon as you purchase this book, begin familiarizing yourself with the textbook. Read through the **Preface** and this introductory **To the Student** section carefully, examine the **Table of Contents**, and familiarize yourself with the end matter that follows Chapter 12: **Appendix A:** Essential Test-Taking Skills; **Appendix B:** Master Profile Chart and Answer Keys; **Appendix C:** Exercises, Inventories, and Checklists; **Appendix D:** Excerpts; and the textbook **index**.

   Essential Study Skills, Eighth Edition, has a College Success CourseMate to enhance your learning experience and strengthen your understanding of course materials. Each time you see this icon in your textbook, visit the College Success CourseMate for interactive quizzes and online materials. Your instructor may assign these activities, or you may complete the activities independently to strengthen your comprehension and learn content more thoroughly. Take time now to familiarize yourself with the wealth of online resources available to assist you throughout the term. As you click on the main menu for each chapter, you will see the following categories of your online materials:

- Chapter E-Book
- Chapter Profile
- Chapter Visual Mapping
- Expanded Chapter Outline

- Chapter Concept Checks
- Reflective Writing Assignments
- Textbook Case Studies
- Topics In-Depth
- Practice and Enhanced Quizzes
- Chapter Study Guide
- Glossary
- Flashcards

Essential Study Skills E-Book

The College Success CourseMate for *Essential Study Skills,* Eighth Edition, has an interactive e-book for you to use with this textbook. If you have not yet experienced using an e-book, you are in for an exciting new learning experience! You can go to Chapter 8, pages 255–258 to learn about reading e-books and the Chapter 8 online Topics In-Depth to learn more about this book's e-textbook and the online features associated with it.

Starting Each Chapter

Surveying is an effective study strategy that provides you with an overview of a chapter before you begin the process of careful reading. Surveying familiarizes you with the topic, creates a mindset for studying, and prepares your memory to receive new information. Use the following steps for surveying a new chapter:

1. Read the *Chapter Objectives* that list learning goals or objectives for the chapter. The chapter objectives clearly indicate the skills you will learn and will be able to demonstrate when you finish studying the chapter. The color-coding used for the chapter objectives correlates with the color-coded headings throughout the chapter.

2. Read through the *Chapter Outline* for an overview of the organization and content of the chapter. You will find an expanded chapter outline on CourseMate.

3. Glance at the main topics in the *Your Chapter Mapping* to get a clear, visual image of the main headings in the chapter. After reading the chapter information under a heading, return to your visual mapping. Attach key words to show subheadings and important details for each heading on the visual mapping.

4. Complete the *Chapter Profile* before continuing to survey the chapter. This is not a graded assignment; answer the questions honestly. The profiles are designed to examine your current attitude and habits in specific skill areas. These scores will be compared to end-of-the-term scores to show your progress and growth. You can complete the profile in the textbook, or you can complete it online in the College Success CourseMate.

5. Survey or skim through the chapter by examining the following items and features:

   - All of the bold *headings* and *subheadings*
   - The *information in the margins,* which includes Concept Check questions and definitions of terminology

- *Terminology* that appears in bold colored print in paragraphs
- *Graphic materials,* which include figures and charts
- *Check Point questions* at the end of information under each main heading

6. Read the *Learning Objectives Review* at the end of the chapter. Key points for each of the objectives provide you with additional insights about the content of the chapter.

7. Read through the *Terms to Know* that lists the course-specific terminology. The definitions for these terms appear in the margins of the chapter.

8. Read through, but do not answer, the *Chapter Review Questions*. Plan to answer these questions after you have read the chapter carefully. For immediate feedback, you will be able to check your answers with the answer keys in Appendix B.

Using Chapter Features

The following chapter features are designed to increase your comprehension and reinforce key concepts and skills in each chapter. Using these features consistently facilitates the process of mastering the concepts and skills in the chapter.

Your Chapter Mapping shows you the basic skeleton or topic and the main headings used in the chapter. To create a visual study tool, expand the chapter visual mapping by connecting key words to show important details for each of the main headings. Chapter visual mappings also appear in the College Success CourseMate.

Definitions in the margins provide a quick view of key terminology and definitions to learn. Review these definitions when you study for tests. Practice reciting the full definition without looking at the textbook, and then check the accuracy of your definition.

Concept Checks in the margins provide you with study questions to assess your comprehension and promote critical thinking skills. For each Concept Check, answer the questions on paper, mentally, or out loud to yourself. At times, your instructor may ask you to write responses, or these questions may be used for short pop quizzes or on chapter tests. Return to these questions when you prepare for tests.

Check Points in each chapter provide you with short assessment tools to check your comprehension of information presented under each main heading in the chapter. Refer to the Appendix A strategies to review answering specific kinds of questions. Answer keys in Appendix B provide you with immediate feedback.

Exercises appear throughout each chapter. Your instructor will assign some, but usually not all, of the exercises in the chapter. Notice that some exercises appear in the chapter, and other longer exercises appear in Appendix C. For practice and enrichment, you may complete any of the exercises that your instructor does not assign you to complete.

Case Studies are exercises that describe student situations or problems. After reading a case study, identify the key issues or problems that appear in the case study. Answer the question at the end of each case study by providing specific answers or suggestions that deal with the problem. Use specific strategies and terminology from the chapter in your answers. Case studies use open-ended questions, meaning there are many possible answers. They can be completed on paper or in your College Success CourseMate.

Practice Quizzes in the College Success CourseMate consist of self-correcting quizzes that provide you with additional practice and reinforcement of the skills in the chapter. You can complete these quizzes as many times as you wish. You will receive feedback and brief explanations with each answer.

Essential Strategy Charts highlight key strategies to use to improve the way you study, process information, and master course content. Applying the essential strategies in these charts will increase your performance and academic success. Refer to these charts when you want to brush up on essential study skills or review for tests.

Terms to Know list the course-specific vocabulary terms that you should know how to define. Practice defining these terms. You can go to the College Success CourseMate to practice flashcards and to review the online glossary.

Chapter Review Questions provide you with practice test questions to assess your memory or recall of chapter concepts and key terms. Refer to the Appendix A strategies to review answering specific kinds of questions. Complete the Chapter Review Questions without referring to your textbook pages or your notes. Check your answers with the answer keys in Appendix B.

Enhanced Quizzes in the College Success CourseMate provide you with additional practice answering objective test questions and assessing your level of comprehension of chapter skills and concepts. The Enhanced Quizzes link you to the heading in the e-textbook that covers the content of the quiz question.

Chapter Study Guides in the College Success CourseMate provide you with a detailed study guide to complete for a thorough review of each chapter.

Appendix A: Essential Test-Taking Skills

Many college students feel overwhelmed and underprepared for the variety of test-taking situations and test questions that they encounter in their courses. Do you experience any of the following test-taking issues or concerns?

- *Do you sometimes struggle with taking tests because you have never really learned how to take tests?* Appendix A provides you with a direct, step-by-step approach as well as clear explanations and examples for learning fifty-two essential test-taking strategies.
- *Do you sometimes have difficulty answering certain kinds of test questions?* Easy-to-use strategies provide you with the skills to answer true-false, multiple-choice, matching, fill-in-the-blanks, listing, definition, short-answer, math, and essay test questions.
- *Do you sometimes have difficulty understanding or interpreting questions?* Through easy-to-read bulleted points, Appendix A teaches you strategies for reading, understanding, and interpreting objective, recall, math, and essay test questions.

- *Do you sometimes get confused and waste valuable test-taking time trying to figure out how to move through a test?* In Appendix A, you will learn the value of using systematic approaches for answering questions. These approaches increase your accuracy rates and lead to higher grades on tests.

Appendix A, the Essential Test-Taking Skills guide, is a valuable resource that provides a flexible format for acquiring essential test-taking skills whenever the need arises. You can use this pull-out guide for independent study at any time during the present or future terms to prepare for upcoming tests. You may go directly to a specific section in Appendix A to prepare for a specific kind of test or to answer questions in the textbook's **Check Points** and **Chapter Review Questions.**

Your instructor will provide you with additional information about using Appendix A. Your instructor may choose to discuss Appendix A in conjunction with Chapter 7, "Preparing for Upcoming Tests," or your instructor may choose to discuss Appendix A at a different time during the term. Refer to your course syllabus or list of chapters and topics for the term.

Appendix B: Answer Keys

Use **Appendix B** to score and chart your **Chapter Profile** questions, and use the chapter answer keys for all **Check Points** and **Chapter Review Questions.**

Appendix C: Exercises, Inventories, and Checklists

For some exercises in the textbook chapters, you will be directed to **Appendix C.** Follow the directions for completing the exercises, inventories, and checklists. Use these self-assessment tools to strengthen your study skills strategies and improve your approaches to learning.

Appendix D: Excerpts

For some exercises, you will be directed to **Appendix D** to use excerpts from a variety of content areas to practice reading, annotating, notetaking skills, and other textbook study skills.

A Note to You from the Author

Your goal is not to learn *about* study skills, but to learn to *use* powerful study skills to consistently achieve your goals and experience success. Learning is a lifelong process. Each time you are faced with a new learning situation—whether at school, at home, or at work—you can draw upon the skills you have learned in this textbook. By applying the skills of time management, goal setting, concentration, processing information, strengthening memory, test taking, reading comprehension, and an array of additional strategies in this textbook, you will be prepared to experience the rewards of success ... again and again and again. May my commitment to you, belief in you, and support of you in the learning process be reflected in the pages of this textbook.

—Linda Wong

1 Discovering Your Learning Styles and Preferences

© Digital Vision/Getty Images

D o you know your learning style preference, your strongest intelligences, and your personality type? In this chapter, you will gain insights about yourself as a learner. You will learn skills that empower you and utilize your personal preferences so learning feels more natural and effective. By identifying your learning style preference, you are able to select powerful multisensory strategies to increase academic performance. As you explore multiple intelligences, you will realize that you already have skills and abilities in all eight intelligences. Finally, as you explore your personality type, you will gain insights about where you focus your attention and how you take in information, make decisions, and structure your life. After completing this chapter, you will understand more about yourself and about people you encounter at school, at work, and in your personal life.

1 THREE COGNITIVE LEARNING STYLES

Learning Style Preferences

Characteristics and Essential Strategies

Multisensory Learning Strategies

2 MULTIPLE INTELLIGENCES

Subintelligences

Linguistic Intelligence

Logical-Mathematical Intelligence

Musical Intelligence

Bodily-Kinesthetic Intelligence

Spatial Intelligence

Interpersonal Intelligence

Intrapersonal Intelligence

Naturalist Intelligence

3 PERSONALITY TYPES

Eight Personality Preferences of MBTI Personality Types

Four Core Building Blocks of MBTI Personality Types

Sixteen Personality Types

Extraversion and Introversion

Sensing and Intuition

Thinking and Feeling

Judging and Perceiving

Understanding Yourself and Others

 Access Chapter 1 Expanded Chapter Outline in your College Success CourseMate, accessed through *CengageBrain.com.*

YOUR CHAPTER MAPPING

After reading information under each heading, return to the chapter visual mapping below. Add key words to show subheadings and important details related to each heading.

 Access Chapter 1 Visual Mapping in your College Success CourseMate, accessed through *CengageBrain.com.*

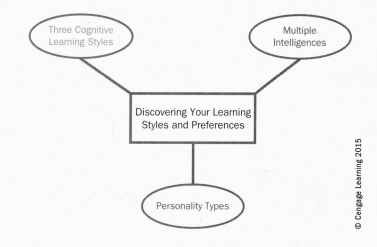

© Cengage Learning 2015

LEARNING OBJECTIVES

1 *Identify your preferred cognitive learning style and describe learning strategies you can use to utilize your preferred learning style and strengthen your other modalities.*

2 *Define the term* intelligences *and describe the common characteristics of each of Howard Gardner's eight intelligences.*

3 *Identify the eight personality preferences defined by Myers and Briggs and discuss the use of opposite preferences in their theory.*

Discovering Your Learning Styles and Preferences

ANSWER each profile question honestly. Your answers should reflect what you do, not what you wish to do. Check YES if you do the statement always or most of the time. Check NO if you do the statement seldom or never.

Access Chapter 1 Profile in your College Success CourseMate, accessed through *CengageBrain.com.*

SCORE the profile. To get your score, give yourself one point for every answer that matches the answer key on page B2 in the back of your book. If you complete the profile online, the profile will be scored for you.

RECORD your score on the Master Profile Chart on page B1 in the column that shows the chapter number.

ONLINE: You can complete the profile and get your score online in this textbook's College Success CourseMate.

	YES	NO
1. I am aware of my learning style preference as a visual, auditory, or kinesthetic learner.	X	
2. I can describe the modality involved in four or more learning strategies that I use on a regular basis.		X
3. Instead of using a multisensory learning strategy such as the See-Say-Do Strategy, I select one learning activity or process and use that to study material in all of my courses.		X
4. I usually study new information in a straightforward manner without spending time making creative study or review tools.	X	
5. I recognize which of Howard Gardner's eight intelligences are my strongest.		X
6. I have the potential to acquire new skills that will increase my abilities in the eight intelligences.	X	
7. I understand the differences between Extraversion and Introversion personality preferences, and I know which preference is mine.		X
8. I understand how my "Thinking" personality preference or my "Feeling" personality preference affects the way I make decisions.		X
9. I understand basic ways in which different personality preferences can affect people's attitudes, behaviors, and decision-making processes.		X
10. I am confident that I can adjust my learning strategies to meet the demands of new learning situations or tasks.	X	

QUESTIONS LINKED TO THE CHAPTER LEARNING OBJECTIVES:

Questions 1–4: objective 1   Questions 7–9: objective 3

Questions 5–6: objective 2   Question 10: all objectives

Three Cognitive Learning Styles

1 Identify your preferred cognitive learning style and describe learning strategies you can use to utilize your preferred learning style and strengthen your other modalities.

Learning is an individualized process; different educational and background experiences, personality traits, levels of motivation, and numerous other variables affect the way you learn. The term *cognitive* refers to thinking and reasoning processes, so **cognitive learning styles** refers to the general ways people *prefer* to have information presented in order to problem solve, process, learn, and remember new information. Three commonly recognized cognitive learning styles, or **learning modalities**, are *visual, auditory,* and *kinesthetic.* **Figure 1.1** shows these three main cognitive learning styles.

> **Cognitive learning styles** refers to the general ways people *prefer* to have information presented in order to problem solve, process, learn, and remember new information.

> **Learning modalities** refers to cognitive learning styles such as visual, auditory, and kinesthetic.

Learning Style Preferences

Most people have a **learning style preference**, which is a tendency to use a visual, auditory, or kinesthetic modality when there is a choice of ways to learn and process new information. For example, a *visual learner* may prefer to read a manual or a textbook or learn from pictures, charts, or graphs. An *auditory learner* may prefer to be told how a new process or piece of equipment works. A *kinesthetic learner* may prefer to be given an opportunity to perform each step as he or she learns a new process or operation of equipment.

> **Learning style preference** indicates a tendency to use a visual, auditory, or kinesthetic modality when there is a choice of ways to learn and process new information.

Your learning style preference started in your childhood. As you matured, entered into the educational system, and were exposed to new learning situations, you learned to use, strengthen, and integrate all of your modalities. The childhood modality preference may still be dominant, but as an adult with broadened skills, in most situations, you are able to learn even when information is presented in a form that is not based on your preferred method of learning. Your learning style preference is just that—a preference—and not a limitation as to your ability to process information.

Understanding your cognitive learning style preference can guide your selection of effective learning strategies that capitalize on your strengths, boost your memory, and strengthen your ability to recall information. As you take in and process information, your brain uses visual, auditory, and kinesthetic (motor) codes to accept

---

FIGURE 1.1   Cognitive Learning Styles

1. **Visual learners** learn and remember best by *seeing* and *visualizing* information.

2. **Auditory learners** learn and remember best by *hearing* and *discussing* information.

3. **Kinesthetic learners** learn and remember best by using large and small body *movements* and *hands-on experiences.*

© 2015 Cengage Learning.

and move the information into different locations in your memory system. The following points are important to understand:

- When you use your strongest modality or your preferred learning style to take in and process information, learning can occur more efficiently and recalling information at a later time may occur more smoothly.

- Many learning strategies involve the use of more than one modality. In other words, more than one kind of coding into memory occurs. Multisensory strategies, such as the *See-Say-Do Strategy* (page 13), utilize all three modalities to process information into memory.

- When you use more than one sensory channel to process information, you create a stronger imprint or impression of the information in your memory, so recalling information often occurs more rapidly and accurately.

- Situations that require you to learn information using one of your less developed learning modalities may be more difficult than anticipated and may require you to activate a modality that does not use your preferred learning style.

Learning Styles Inventory

DIRECTIONS: Go to the Learning Styles Inventory in Appendix C, pages C1–C3, to identify your learning style preference and strength of your modalities. After reading each statement carefully, you will select a YES or a NO answer. Directions for scoring your inventory are included. **Return to this page to write your scores on the following lines:**

_8_ VISUAL   _7_ AUDITORY   _18_ KINESTHETIC

ANALYZING YOUR SCORES:

Highest Score   =   Preferred modality and way to process new information

Lowest Score   =   Weakest or least frequently used modality

Scores > 10   =   Frequently used modality

Scores < 10   =   Less frequently used modality

- If your two highest scores are the same, you use both modalities equally well.
- Your weakest modality and any modalities with scores lower than 10 may be the result of limited experiences that utilize this modality.
- Your weakest modality and any modalities with scores lower than 10 may be due to physical or neurological impairments, which may include learning disabilities.

EXERCISE 1.1

Characteristics and Essential Strategies

As you read through the following common characteristics for each of the three types of learners or learning style preferences, relate this information to what you learned about yourself in the Learning Styles Inventory (**Exercise 1.1**). Do you have the same or similar characteristics? Note that a person does not necessarily possess abilities or strengths in all of the characteristics but may instead demonstrate strengths in specific characteristics. Your strengths may reflect your educational or personal background. For example, an auditory learner may be strong in the area of language skills but may not have had the experience or the opportunity to develop skills with a foreign language or music. Finally, pay close attention to the variety of essential learning strategies that you can incorporate into your approach to learning. **Figure 1.2** summarizes essential strategies for each modality.

Visual Learners

Visual learners are learners who prefer to process and learn information in visual forms such as pictures, charts, lists, paragraphs, or other printed formats. They learn and remember best by *seeing* and *visualizing* information. The following are additional characteristics of visual learners:

- Can easily recall information in the form of numbers, words, phrases, or sentences
- Can easily understand and recall information presented in pictures, charts, or diagrams

Visual learners are learners who prefer to process and learn information in visual forms such as pictures, charts, lists, paragraphs, or other printed formats.

FIGURE 1.2	Essential Strategies for Visual, Auditory, and Kinesthetic Learners
VISUAL	Highlight textbooks and notes. Write notes in textbooks. Create movies in your mind. Create visual study tools. Use color coding. Visualize information. Add pictures. Write to remember. Make writing a habit. Be observant.
AUDITORY	Participate in discussions. Paraphrase and summarize. Ask questions. Verbalize. Recite frequently. Tape lectures. Create study tapes or recordings. Create rhymes, jingles, or songs. Use technology.
KINESTHETIC	Use hands-on learning. Create hands-on study tools. Get out of the chair. Work standing up. Use action-based activities. Create action-oriented games. Use creative movement. Use a computer or electronic devices.

© Cengage Learning 2015.

- Have strong visualization or visual memory skills and can look up (often up to the left) and "see" information
- Make "movies in their minds" of information they are reading
- Have strong visual–spatial skills that involve sizes, shapes, textures, angles, and dimensions
- Have a good eye for colors, design, visual balance, and visual appeal
- Pay close attention and learn to interpret body language (facial expressions, eyes, stance)
- Have a keen awareness of aesthetics, the beauty of the physical environment, and visual media

Visual learners often favor creating and using visual strategies when they study. Having something that they can *see*, examine for details, and memorize as a mental image is important and effective for visual learners. The following essential strategies for visual learners strengthen and utilize visual skills. Check YES if you already use the strategy. Check TRY if you are willing to try using this strategy. Check NO if the strategy does not interest you. **Check a response for each bulleted point.**

CONCEPT CHECK   1.2

Visual learners can easily recall which kinds of visual information? What other abilities do visual learners exhibit?

	YES	TRY	NO
Highlight textbooks and notes. Use colored highlighter pens to create a stronger visual impression of important facts, definitions, formulas, and steps.	X		
Write notes in textbooks. Write questions in the margins, highlight the answers, and then picture the answers as you review the questions.		X	
Create movies in your mind. Use your visual memory as a television screen with the information that you read (and hear) moving across the screen as a "movie with the cameras rolling." Practice reviewing or replaying the movie in your mind.			X
Create visual study tools. Create visual mappings, hierarchies, and comparison charts to show levels of detail. Practice visualizing and recalling the images of the study tools.	X		X
Use color coding. Color-code different levels of information in your visual tools, your textbook highlighting, your time management schedules, and your notes. Using different colors facilitates the process of memorizing and recalling visual images.	X		
Visualize information. Visually memorize pictures, graphs, study tools, or small sections of printed information. Practice looking away, visualizing, and then checking the accuracy and details of your visual images.		X	

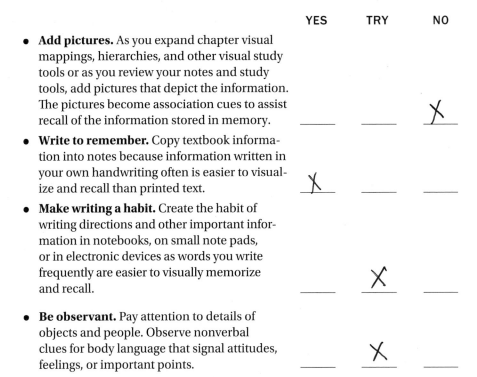

	YES	TRY	NO
Add pictures. As you expand chapter visual mappings, hierarchies, and other visual study tools or as you review your notes and study tools, add pictures that depict the information. The pictures become association cues to assist recall of the information stored in memory.	___	___	X
Write to remember. Copy textbook information into notes because information written in your own handwriting often is easier to visualize and recall than printed text.	X	___	___
Make writing a habit. Create the habit of writing directions and other important information in notebooks, on small note pads, or in electronic devices as words you write frequently are easier to visually memorize and recall.	___	X	___
Be observant. Pay attention to details of objects and people. Observe nonverbal clues for body language that signal attitudes, feelings, or important points.	___	X	___

Auditory Learners

Auditory learners are learners who prefer to process and learn by hearing and discussing information. They prefer to have information presented to them verbally instead of, or in addition to, in writing. They learn by listening to others explain, debate, summarize, or discuss information about topics they are studying. Auditory learners, however, are not passive. Auditory learners like to *talk* and *listen* as they learn. The following are additional characteristics of auditory learners:

- Often engage in discussions and enjoy the process of communication
- Learn by explaining information in their own words, expressing their understanding or opinions, and providing comments and feedback to other speakers
- Can accurately remember details or specific information heard in conversations, lectures, movies, or music
- Have strong language and vocabulary skills and an appreciation of words, their meanings, and their etymology (word history)
- Have strong oral and expressive communication skills and are articulate
- Have "finely tuned ears" and may find learning a foreign language relatively easy
- Have above average ability to hear tones, rhythms, and notes of music, and often excel in areas of music
- Have keen auditory memories

Auditory learners often select learning strategies that code or process information through their auditory channel into memory. The following essential strategies for auditory learners strengthen and utilize auditory skills. Check YES if you already

> **Auditory learners** are learners who prefer to process and learn by hearing and discussing information.

use this strategy. Check TRY if you are willing to try using this strategy. Check NO if the strategy does not interest you. **Check a response for each bulleted point.**

	YES	TRY	NO
• **Participate in discussions.** Actively engage in group activities, discussions, study groups, and in tutoring sessions.		X	
• **Paraphrase and summarize.** Express your ideas to others, paraphrase speakers, and summarize what you learn from lectures, conversations, and discussions.			X
• **Ask questions.** Show your interest and clarify information by asking questions. Practice recalling information and answers that you hear.	X		
• **Verbalize.** Read out loud to activate your auditory channel or auditory processes. For difficult materials, read with exaggerated expression as the natural rhythm and patterns of language tend to group words into units of meaning when spoken.			X
• **Recite frequently.** Reciting involves stating information out loud, in your own words, in complete sentences, and without referring to printed information. Reciting provides you with feedback to gauge how well you remember and understand information.		X	
• **Tape lectures.** In difficult classes, request permission to tape lectures. Use the tapes to review and complete your notes after class.			X
• **Create study tapes or recordings.** Tape yourself reading or reciting main ideas, facts, details, or lists. Use your study tapes or recordings to review information and prepare for tests. Your ability to recall information from tapes that have your own voice may strengthen your auditory memory and recall abilities.			X
• **Create rhymes, jingles, or songs.** Short, catchy sayings or tunes that contain information you need to remember are effective study tools for recalling information. Original rhymes, jingles, or songs work as mnemonics or memory tools and associations to recall information. To increase accuracy, practice the rhymes, jingles, or songs multiple times.		X	
• **Use technology.** Check with your learning labs, library, Internet resources, and electronic applications for audio materials and products to use to reinforce learning.	X		

Kinesthetic Learners

Kinesthetic learners are learners who prefer to process and learn information through large and small muscle movements and hands-on experiences. Large and small muscles hold memory, so involving movement in the learning process creates muscle memory. The following are additional characteristics of kinesthetic learners:

> **Kinesthetic learners** are learners who prefer to process and learn information through large and small muscle movements and hands-on experiences.

- Learn best by working with physical objects and engaging in hands-on learning that involves feeling, handling, using, manipulating, sorting, assembling, and experimenting with concrete objects

- Can recall information by duplicating the movement or hand motions involved in the learning process

- Learn well by using large muscle or full body movements, such as movements used when working at large charts, working at a chalkboard or white board, role-playing, dancing, or performing

- Work well with their hands in areas such as repair work, sculpting, and art

- Are well coordinated, with a strong sense of timing and body movements

- Have a strong awareness of their need or interest to add movement to study and work situations

- Are able to focus better when they can engage in movement, which may include wiggling, tapping hands or feet, or moving legs when sitting

Kinesthetic learners often prefer to use strategies that engage their small and large muscles in the learning process. The following essential strategies for kinesthetic learners strengthen and utilize kinesthetic skills. Check YES if you already use this strategy. Check TRY if you are willing to try using this strategy. Check NO if the strategy does not interest you. **Check a response for each bulleted point.**

	YES	TRY	NO
Use hands-on learning. Handle objects, tools, or machinery that you are studying. For processes such as computer applications, repeat the hands-on learning applications several times to create muscle memory.	X		
Create hands-on study tools. Create flashcards that you can shuffle, spread out, sort, categorize, and review. Copy charts, diagrams, visual mappings, or hierarchies; cut them apart and practice reassembling the pieces.	X		
Get out of the chair. When you study, engage large muscles by using exaggerated hand expressions or body movements. Pace or walk with study materials in hand.		X	
Work standing up. Work at a chalkboard, white board, or flip chart to list, draw, practice, or rework problems. Use poster paper to create study tools, such as large visual mappings, charts, or timelines.			X

	YES	TRY	NO

- **Use action-based activities.** Create ways to add action to the learning process; for example, if you are studying perimeters, tape off an area and walk the perimeter. — X —

- **Create action-oriented games.** Convert information you are studying into a game such as Twenty-One Questions, Jeopardy, or Concentration. Review the information by playing the game with another student or group. X — —

- **Use creative movement.** When feasible, incorporate drama, dance, pantomime, or role-playing into your study sessions. — X —

- **Use a computer or electronic devices.** Type information and create notes, tables, and charts on the computer. Enter or access information on electronic devices. Keyboard strokes help create muscle memory that you can use to simulate the actions and recall information. X — —

CONCEPT CHECK   1.3

Define the terms visual learner, auditory learner, *and* kinesthetic learner. *Describe the characteristics of each type of learner.*

GROUP PROCESSING

A Collaborative Learning Activity

DIRECTIONS:

Form groups of three or four students. Then complete the following directions. Create a chart with three columns. Label the columns *Visual, Auditory,* and *Kinesthetic.* As a group, brainstorm different learning strategies or "things you can do when you study" that capitalize on each of the learning modalities. Use your own experiences and ideas for study strategies as well as ideas presented in this textbook. You may use the following examples to begin your chart.

Visual	Auditory	Kinesthetic
Use colored pens to highlight.	*Talk out loud to study.*	*Make wall charts to review.*

Multisensory Learning Strategies

Now that you are aware of your learning style and learning preference, you can begin the process of exploring new learning strategies; select some that utilize your strengths and some that help you "stretch" and strengthen your other modalities. As you experiment with the various essential learning strategies, strive to design *multisensory strategies*, strategies that combine two or more

Multisensory strategies are learning strategies that combine two or more modalities.

modalities. The incorporation of multisensory strategies benefits you in the following ways:

- You boost your memory by coding information in more than one way or with more than one sensory channel.
- You create stronger sensory paths into long-term memory so information is more clearly imprinted in your long-term memory.
- You create multiple ways to access and recall information at later times. If one recall process does not produce results, you have another process to use to search for information in memory.
- You add motivation and interest to the learning process, and you remind yourself on a regular basis that there is always more than one way to process information.

When you strive to design multisensory learning strategies, frequently you will use the following four common sensory-related processes:

1. *Visualizing* is the process of creating mental images of pictures and colors. Once you memorize or place the images in memory, you must then take time to recall, practice, and rehearse the images.

2. *Verbalizing* is the process of speaking or reading out loud to activate the auditory channel and build auditory memory. Verbalizing involves vocalizing information that you are looking at or reading. Verbalizing is less demanding on memory than reciting.

3. *Reciting* is the process of explaining information out loud, in complete sentences, and in your own words without looking at printed information. Reciting provides immediate feedback as to how well you do or do not understand and remember information. When you are not able to explain information out loud and in your own words, restudy the printed material before repeating the process of reciting.

4. *Developing muscle memory* is a kinesthetic process that involves performing multiple repetitions of steps or actions until the actions become automatic. Copying, assembling, constructing, or performing problem-solving steps are hands-on processes that create automatic muscle memory when practiced repeatedly.

The See-Say-Do Strategy

The *See-Say-Do Strategy* is a multisensory learning strategy that involves visual, auditory, and kinesthetic actions or processes. Using this strategy involves making a conscious effort to create learning combinations that help you *see* the information in new ways, *say* the information you are learning, and *do* some type of movement or hands-on activity. The following example shows how easily you can encode information into memory using three sensory channels.

To learn a process to solve a difficult math problem:

- **See:** Read the math problem and examine the significant details.
- **Say:** Verbalize the steps for a solution.
- **Do:** Copy the steps into your notes.
- **See:** Color-code each step.
- **Say:** Recite the problem-solving steps for the problem.
- **Do:** Rework the problem multiple times. Check your accuracy.

Visualizing is the process of creating mental images of pictures and colors.

Verbalizing is the process of speaking or reading out loud to activate the auditory channel and build auditory memory.

Reciting is the process of explaining information out loud, in complete sentences, and in your own words without looking at printed information.

Developing muscle memory is a kinesthetic process that involves performing multiple repetitions of steps or actions until the actions become automatic.

See-Say-Do Strategy is a multisensory learning strategy that involves visual, auditory, and kinesthetic actions or processes.

CONCEPT CHECK   1.4
Why are multisensory strategies so effective? Give an example of using a See-Say-Do approach for a specific learning task.

Transfer These Skills: Using the See-Say-Do Strategy

DIRECTIONS:

1. Look at the following examples of students using the See-Say-Do Strategy.

Mark reviews a section of a chapter by:

Visual: looking at the ceiling to mentally recall textbook pictures and graphs

Auditory: reciting information about each visual image

Kinesthetic: redrawing diagrams from memory and checking his accuracy

Lisa uses the following strategies to write reports and essays:

Visual: creates an outline or organizational chart for her writing assignment

Auditory: reads her work out loud or asks someone to read it to her

Kinesthetic: types her papers

2. **Transfer These Skills:** On separate paper, describe a learning process or activity that you have to do for one of your classes. Then identify how you can use the See-Say-Do Strategy. What can you do that is visual? Auditory? Kinesthetic? Describe your process.

3. **BONUS CHALLENGE:** Solve the following problem. Pay attention to the approach you use to find the answer.

A parent and a child are standing together on the sidewalk. They both start walking at the same time. Each person begins the first step with the right foot. The child must take three steps for every two steps the parent takes. How many steps must the child take until they both land again on the same foot?

- How many steps did the child need to take?
- Did they both land on the right foot or the left foot?
- How did you solve this problem?

Diverse Learners in the Classroom

In every one of your classrooms, you can be assured that you are a member of a diverse group of learners. Students with visual, auditory, and kinesthetic learning style preferences sit side by side, taking in and processing information differently. Different learning styles and learning preferences partially explain why some students seem to grasp information more readily while other students struggle with making sense of new information.

Instructors' teaching styles often reflect their own individual learning styles and preferences. Historically, the American approach to education favored visual learners. As instructors learned new teaching methods and perhaps even modified their learning style preferences, many instructional approaches became more multisensory and better suited to meeting the needs of those with different learning styles. However, at some point, you will find yourself in a classroom with an instructor whose teaching style differs from your learning style preferences. To do well in such classes, you will need to vary your learning strategies to adjust to the instructor, the classroom approach, and the materials. Your goal as an adult learner is to increase your ability to perform well in a wide range of learning situations.

When you have the option, consider the following suggestions for identifying courses and instructors that are compatible with your learning style preferences:

1. Before enrolling in a course that offers several sections with different instructors, talk to other students, instructors, and counselors to learn more about the teaching and classroom styles of each instructor. *If you have a choice,* enroll in the section with the instructor who seems most compatible with your learning styles and preferences.

2. Find out what support services are available for the course. Are there study guides, study groups, supplemental computer instruction, videos, or tutors available? If so, use them.

3. Find out what forms of assessment are used in the course. Are grades based solely on tests or do grades include group or individual projects, assignments, or portfolios?

CHECK POINT 1.1

Answers appear on page B2.

True or False? See Test-Taking Strategies 1–9 in Appendix A.

 1. The term *cognitive* refers to people's awareness of their surroundings.

 2. To be considered a "visual learner," one must possess all the characteristics of a visual learner, have strong visualization skills, and make movies in his or her mind during the reading process.

 3. To some degree, a person's learning style preference reflects his or her personal background and educational experiences.

 4. Having a learning style preference means that a person is strong in only one of the three cognitive learning styles.

5. Multisensory learning strategies include some form of learning that involves two or all three learning modalities.

 6. The three cognitive learning styles are hands-on, visual, and kinesthetic.

 7. The See-Say-Do Strategy is a multisensory approach that seldom incorporates more than two cognitive learning styles or modalities.

 8. *Reciting* and *verbalizing* are two terms used for the same process that basically means a person talks out loud.

 Access Chapter 1 Practice Quiz 1 in your College Success CourseMate, accessed through *CengageBrain.com.*

EXERCISE 1.3

Textbook Case Studies

DIRECTIONS:

1. Read each case study carefully. Respond to the question at the end of each case study by using *specific* strategies discussed in this chapter. Answer in complete sentences.

2. Write your responses on paper or online in this textbook's College Success CourseMate, Textbook Case Studies. You will be able to print your online response or e-mail it to your instructor.

CASE STUDY 1: Elaine is an outgoing person who does not know anyone on campus. Consequently, she usually studies alone in the library. She knows that she is an auditory learner. Her midterm grades confirmed that she is having difficulty retaining information. Her motivation and interest in her classes are declining. What learning strategies can Elaine use to combat the problems she has encountered in the first half of this term?

CASE STUDY 2: Conor is enrolled in a poetry class to complete one of his program requirements. He has never enjoyed poetry, but this class is even more challenging for him because there is little activity or interaction in class. Students take turns reading verses, and then individual students are called on to answer questions posed by the instructor. Conor is an athlete and is not used to sitting in what seems to be an inactive environment. One student suggests that he switch to a different section with a different instructor. What type of classroom environment and teaching approach would be better suited for this kinesthetic learner?

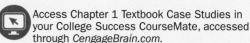
Access Chapter 1 Textbook Case Studies in your College Success CourseMate, accessed through *CengageBrain.com.*

© Cengage Learning 2015

Multiple Intelligences

2 *Define the term* intelligences *and describe the common characteristics of each of Howard Gardner's eight intelligences.*

Traditional intelligence, or IQ (intelligence quotient), tests basically measure linguistic, logical-mathematical, and spatial abilities. The Stanford-Binet Intelligence Scale is an intelligence test that consists of verbal and nonverbal questions for different age groups. The results of the test provide a single IQ score for the individual. The Wechsler Intelligence Scale is another test used to measure intelligence and yields a general intelligence score. IQ scores are derived by comparing a person's mental age to his or her chronological age. An IQ of 100 (an average IQ) means that chronological age equals mental age.

In 1983, Howard Gardner, a noted Harvard University psychologist, presented a new theory of cognitive development in his book *Frames of Mind: The Theory of Multiple Intelligences.* Gardner's **Theory of Multiple Intelligences** (MI) is a cognitive theory that proposes that individuals have at least eight kinds of intelligences. According to Gardner, an **intelligence** is the potential to take in and process information that can then be used or activated to solve problems or create products that are valued in a specific culture. Gardner established specific scientific criteria to identify seven intelligences; however, in 1996, Gardner used the same criteria

Theory of Multiple Intelligences is a cognitive theory that proposes that individuals have at least eight kinds of intelligences.

An **intelligence** is the potential to take in and process information that can then be used or activated to solve problems or create products that are valued in a specific culture.

FIGURE 1.3   The Eight Intelligences in Gardner's MI Theory

- Linguistic
- Musical
- Logical-mathematical
- Spatial
- Bodily-kinesthetic
- Intrapersonal
- Interpersonal
- Naturalist

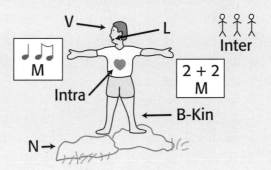

© Cengage Learning 2015.

---

to identify and add an eighth intelligence, *naturalist*. He contends that additional intelligences could be identified in the future. **Figure 1.3** shows Howard Gardner's eight intelligences. In the Theory of Multiple Intelligences, people have the potential to be wise or "smart" in eight areas: *words, numbers, music, body, pictures, people, self,* and *nature.*

Gardner's MI theory of eight kinds of intelligence challenges traditional IQ theory that basically measures intellectual abilities in three areas: verbal, visual–spatial, and logical mathematics. Gardner's MI theory differs from the IQ theory in other ways as well. **Figure 1.4** shows the major differences between traditional IQ theory and Gardner's MI theory.

Howard Gardner's Theory of Multiple Intelligences has opened new doors to understanding and acknowledging individual differences, skills, abilities, and interests. The MI theory recognizes that most people have some degree of each of the

CONCEPT CHECK   1.5

What abilities does Gardner's Theory of Multiple Intelligences (MI) include that are not directly assessed in traditional IQ theory? In what other ways does MI theory differ from traditional IQ theory?

FIGURE 1.4   Traditional IQ and Multiple Intelligences

Traditional Intelligence Quotient	Gardner's Multiple Intelligences
• Intelligence involves problem-solving, memory, reasoning, and cognitive skills.	• Intelligence involves more than problem-solving, memory, reasoning, and cognitive skills; it involves the ability to solve problems and create products of value.
• IQ measures ability in three areas: verbal, visual-spatial, and logical mathematics.	• MI theory recognizes eight intelligences: linguistic, musical, logical-mathematical, spatial, bodily-kinesthetic, intrapersonal, interpersonal, and naturalist.
• IQ tests may be culturally biased and not recognize impact of cultural values, languages, and experiences.	• MI theory recognizes the significance of cultural settings and that different skills are valued in different cultures.
• The level of ability is summed up in one number or score.	• Intelligences are *potentials* and cannot be summed up in one number or score.
• Intelligence level is established and static.	• Intelligences may be strengthened by opportunities and experiences.
• IQ theory is established by empirical evidence and standardized forms of assessment.	• MI theory is not established by traditional empirical evidence or standardized forms of assessment.

© Cengage Learning 2015.

You possess interests, abilities, and learning styles unique to you. Learning to use your strengths and apply your abilities increases your academic performance. How do you use your talents, interests, and learning styles in your courses?

intelligences and that some intelligences are more developed than others. By making a conscious effort to activate your potential, capitalize on new experiences, and engage in new opportunities, you can strengthen your intelligences as you problem solve and create products of value.

Subintelligences

> **Subintelligences** are core abilities that are part of a larger individual intelligence.

Gardner states that **subintelligences** are *core abilities* that are part of a larger individual intelligence. Each of the eight intelligences has subintelligences. For example, people can exhibit many different talents and abilities under the category of musical intelligence. Due to lack of opportunity, experiences, or training, a person with a high musical intelligence at a given time may not demonstrate a high level of all of the subintelligences of music. Singing, playing different instruments, composing, conducting, critiquing, and appreciating a variety of music require different skills, abilities, and processes. The level of accomplishment or mastery of subintelligences will vary among individuals, but the *potential* exists to activate, develop, and strengthen the various subintelligences of each intelligence. In the following sections, you will have the opportunity to examine which core abilities you feel are well developed in you.

Linguistic Intelligence

> **Linguistic intelligence** is the ability to use verbal and written language effectively.

Linguistic intelligence is the ability to use verbal and written language effectively. Following are common subintelligences (core abilities) of this intelligence. **Check the core abilities you believe are well developed in you.**

____Have a love of language—a curiosity, fascination, and sensitivity to words, their meanings, their ability to evoke feelings, and their usages (semantics)

____Have an interest in the structure of language (syntax)

____Appreciate and show interest in the sounds used in a language (phonology)

____ Have sharp, detailed, and vivid memories about written or spoken language

____ Excel in word games such as crossword puzzles, Words with Friends, or Scrabble

_X_ Show an ability to create, recite, and remember puns, jingles, or poetry

____ Show an ability to learn and speak foreign languages

____ Express ideas well in public (presentations, storytelling, or debates)

_X_ Express ideas well in writing (novels, articles, journals, prose, or poetry)

> Following are common career options for people with strong linguistic intelligence:
>
> author, journalist, editor, blogger, poet, newscaster, television announcer, motivational speaker, playwright, politician, consultant, lawyer

Logical-Mathematical Intelligence

Logical-mathematical intelligence is the ability to use logic, problem solving, analysis, and mathematical calculations effectively. Following are other subintelligences (core abilities) for logical-mathematical intelligence. **Check the core abilities you believe are well developed in you.**

> Logical-mathematical intelligence is the ability to use logic, problem solving, analysis, and mathematical calculations effectively.

_X_ Use logic and sound reasoning to problem solve

____ Use pattern identification and sequential thinking

_X_ Think both concretely and abstractly

____ Understand and apply abstract numerical symbols and operations

____ Perform complex calculations

_X_ Use systematic, logic-based, sequential problem-solving techniques

____ Use scientific methods to measure, hypothesize, test, research, and confirm results

> Following are common career options for people with strong logical-mathematical intelligence:
>
> mathematician, math or business teacher, scientist, computer programmer, accountant, tax expert, banker, researcher

Musical Intelligence

Musical intelligence is the ability to show an acute sensitivity and appreciation of musical patterns and elements, such as pitch, timbre, and harmony. People with these developed abilities may use vocal or instrumental music to express creativity, imagination, and the gamut of human emotions. Following are other

> Musical intelligence is the ability to show an acute sensitivity and appreciation of musical patterns and elements, such as pitch, timbre, and harmony.

subintelligences (core abilities) for musical intelligence. **Check the core abilities you believe are well developed in you.**

X Are able to read and write (compose) music

____ Understand music theory and symbols in music

X Have a passion for different types and structures of music

____ Have a strong auditory memory for verbal information

____ Have a strong auditory memory for musical information and lyrics

X Appreciate various forms of musical expression: singing, chanting, humming, or drumming

____ Exhibit the ability to sing

X Exhibit the ability to play musical instruments

> Following are common career options for people with strong musical intelligence:
>
> music teacher, composer, conductor, performer, sound engineer, filmmaker, music, marketing, or advertising director

Bodily-Kinesthetic Intelligence

Bodily-kinesthetic intelligence is the ability to use precise body rhythms and movements, motor coordination skills, and other skills such as timing, balance, and flexibility.

Bodily-kinesthetic intelligence is the ability to use precise body rhythms and movements, motor coordination skills, and other skills such as timing, balance, and flexibility. People with high bodily-kinesthetic intelligence often prefer hands-on or activity-oriented tasks. Following are other subintelligences (core abilities) for bodily-kinesthetic intelligence. **Check the core abilities you believe are well developed in you.**

____ Possess dexterity and possibly above average strength or speed

X Have well-developed gross (large) motor skills

____ Are able to judge how their bodies will respond to certain situations

____ Are able to fine-tune and train their bodies to perform at higher levels

____ Have well-developed fine (small) motor skills

X Engage in activity-oriented or hands-on activities

X Work well with their hands to create, modify, or fix objects

____ Have an acute sensitivity "through their hands"; for example, a mechanic unable to see inside an engine is able to locate and fix a problem using only touch

X Enjoy physical exercise, sports, dancing, drama, role-playing, inventing, building, and repairing things

Following are common career options for people with strong bodily-kinesthetic intelligence:

dancer, athlete, actor, musician, instrumentalist (guitarist, drummer, pianist), dance teacher, choreographer, photographer, mime artist, painter, sculptor, surgeon, inventor, craftsperson

Spatial Intelligence

Spatial intelligence is the ability to use keen perceptions of patterns, shapes, textures, and visual skills. People with developed spatial intelligence often demonstrate strong visual memory skills. Following are other subintelligences (core abilities) for spatial intelligence. **Check the core abilities you believe are well developed in you.**

> **Spatial intelligence** is the ability to use keen perceptions of patterns, shapes, textures, and visual skills.

____Perceive sizes, geometric forms, lines, curves, and angles accurately and with precision

____Possess strong visual imagery or visualization skills

_X_ Show creativity and active imagination

____Able to present ideas graphically in the form of pictures, blueprints, or charts

____Visualize abstract concepts; for example, a gifted chess player can play a challenging game of chess blindfolded or an architect can picture the floor plans of a building before drawing them

_X_ Show interest and abilities in the areas of fine arts, such as painting, sculpting, drawing, drafting, or photography

Following are common career options for people with strong spatial intelligence:

architect, designer, interior decorator, artist, painter, sculptor, fashion designer, landscaper, carpenter, contractor, graphic artist, advertiser, cartographer, inventor, pilot, surgeon

Interpersonal Intelligence

Interpersonal intelligence is the ability to use effective communication, social, leadership, and cooperative teamwork skills. Individuals with strong interpersonal intelligence relate well to a diversity of people in a variety of situations. Following are other subintelligences (core abilities) for interpersonal intelligence. **Check the core abilities you believe are well developed in you.**

> **Interpersonal intelligence** is the ability to use effective communication, social, leadership, and cooperative teamwork skills.

____Enjoy actively participating in groups

_X_ Create bonds with diverse groups of people

____Feel a sense of global responsibility toward others

_X_Are able to interpret nonverbal clues (facial expressions, gestures, or general body language)

_X_Are able to interpret the behavior, motivation, and intentions of others

____Enjoy and skilled at socializing

____Enjoy helping others, sharing their skills, tutoring or teaching others

____Contribute to the development of positive group dynamics

> Following are common career options for people with strong interpersonal intelligence:
>
> parent, tutor, teacher, therapist, counselor, healer, social activist, motivational speaker, workshop leader, mentor, religious leader, sociologist, actor, political organizer, salesperson

Intrapersonal Intelligence

Intrapersonal intelligence is the ability to use skills related to personal growth, self-understanding, and self-motivation and to use intuition and spirituality.

Intrapersonal intelligence is the ability to use skills related to personal growth, self-understanding, and self-motivation and to use intuition and spirituality. Individuals with strong intrapersonal intelligence use a variety of skills to achieve personal goals and potential. Following are other subintelligences (core abilities) for intrapersonal intelligence. **Check the core abilities you believe are well developed in you.**

____Use self-reflection and self-motivation

_X_Enjoy exploring feelings, values, goals, strengths, weaknesses, and personal history

____Show ability to interpret life experiences as lessons and as guides to change aspects of their lives or to give their lives meaning

____Show an ability to project a sense of pride, self-esteem, confidence, self-responsibility, control, and empowerment

____Demonstrate self-regulating, self-motivating, and goal-oriented behaviors

_X_Adapt well to a wide variety of situations and circumstances

CONCEPT CHECK **1.6**
What are the main differences between interpersonal intelligence and intrapersonal intelligence?

> Following are common career options for people with strong intrapersonal intelligence:
>
> psychiatrist, spiritual or personal counselor, self-help writer, motivational speaker, guidance counselor, life coach, philosopher, blogger, biographer

Naturalist Intelligence

Naturalist intelligence is the ability to show a sensitivity to cycles and patterns in the physical world.

Naturalist intelligence is the ability to show a sensitivity to cycles and patterns in the physical world. Following are other subintelligences (core abilities) for naturalist intelligence. **Check the core abilities you believe are well developed in you.**

____ Observe keenly nature's elements—such as daily, seasonal, and cyclical changes

X Feel sensitivity to and understand the relationships in nature, which include the balance of plants, animals, and the environment

X Demonstrate detailed knowledge and expertise in recognizing and classifying plants and animals

____ Show ability to organize, classify, arrange, or group items and ideas into logical units or categories

X Show ability to apply strong pattern-recognition talents to areas outside of the plant–animal world, such as with artists, poets, laboratory scientists, and social scientists

CONCEPT CHECK 1.7
Which intelligences do you believe require more "mental activity" than "physical activity"?

Following are common career options for people with strong naturalist intelligence:

meteorologist, geologist, botanist, herbologist, horticulturist, biologist, naturopath, holistic healer, medicine man, gardener, landscaper, farmer, environmentalist

Recognizing Intelligences

EXERCISE 1.4

DIRECTIONS: Work with a partner or in a small group to analyze specific tasks and the intelligences activated and used in each task. Discuss which of the eight intelligences is actively being used in each activity: linguistic (words), logical-mathematical (numbers), musical (music), bodily-kinesthetic (body), spatial (picture), interpersonal (people), intrapersonal (self), or naturalist (nature). You may identify more than one intelligence per activity. You may be asked to share your answers with the class.

1. Work as a group to create a student handbook for incoming freshmen.

2. Perform a scene from a book in a literature class.

3. Interview four people who work in a career field of interest to you, and then compile the results of the four interviews you conducted.

4. Collect and organize samples of music from five cultural or ethnic groups.

5. Use a computer graphics program to create an eye-catching presentation about your heritage or cultural ties.

6. Construct a 3-D model that shows your idea for making better use of an existing space on campus.

7. Keep a daily journal or log to record your progress in reaching a specific goal.

© Cengage Learning 2015

CHECK POINT 1.2

Answers appear on page B2.

True or False? See Test-Taking Strategies 1–9 in Appendix A.

__F__ 1. The Theory of Multiple Intelligences proposes that there are eight kinds of intelligences, each with core abilities called subintelligences.

__T__ 2. To be considered intellectually strong in a specific intelligence, a person must exhibit well-developed abilities in all of the core abilities for that intelligence.

__T__ 3. Standardized testing can give individuals specific IQ and MI scores that compare them to people within the same age range.

__F__ 4. A person with a well-developed interpersonal intelligence may demonstrate leadership skills and work well with others.

__T__ 5. In the MI Theory, an intelligence does not refer to the potential to solve problems or create products that have value in a culture.

Fill-in-the-Blanks See Test-Taking Strategies 21–24 in Appendix A.

1. In MI theory, subintelligences are also referred to as _____ _____.

2. In Gardner's MI theory, the _____ intelligence includes the ability to look for patterns within and outside of nature; the _____-_____ intelligence includes the ability to look for and use numerical patterns.

3. Authors, journalists, poets, playwrights, and lawyers often demonstrate strength and abilities in _____intelligence.

 Access Chapter 1 Practice Quiz 2 in your College Success CourseMate, accessed through *CengageBrain.com.*

CHAPTER 1 REFLECTIVE WRITING 1

 On separate paper, in a journal, or online in this textbook's College Success CourseMate, complete the following directions.

1. What academic major or career path interests you? How does your choice of careers reflect or not reflect your abilities or perceived intelligences as defined by Gardner?

2. What did you learn about your preferred cognitive learning style that will help you perform well in your courses? How will understanding your learning style preference impact the learning strategy choices you intend to use this term in school?

 Access Chapter 1 Reflective Writing 1 in your College Success CourseMate, accessed through *CengageBrain.com.*

Personality Types

3 *Identify the eight personality preferences defined by Myers and Briggs and discuss the use of opposite preferences in their theory.*

The personality assessment instrument and personality preferences in this section do not evaluate your modalities, skill levels, or abilities. Instead, the Myers-Briggs Type Indicator® (MBTI®) instrument is a personality assessment tool developed in the 1940s by Isabel Briggs Myers and Katharine Cook Briggs. The *Myers-Briggs Type Indicator® assessment* is an inventory test that identifies sixteen personality types. Following are important points about the personality types identified by the Myers-Briggs assessment:

- *Personality types* are sixteen combinations comprising four personality preferences. The four letters in each personality type represent four specific preferences. (See Figure 1.5 next page.)

- A *personality preference* refers to a way of doing or responding that feels more natural, automatic, or comfortable and that produces better results.

- Being aware of your personality preferences and personality type helps you understand many facets of yourself, including your behavior, your decision-making processes, your motivation, and your values.

- One value of knowing your type is being able to choose to do things that come more naturally most of the time, which will take less energy and will be easier for you to do. This also includes selecting effective study skills that feel more natural and require less effort to use.

- As you better understand your personality preferences and type, you will gain insights about other people, understand and appreciate them more, and become aware of different ways to interact more effectively.

- All personality types are of value and importance. One personality preference or personality type is not superior or more desirable than another.

- Even though you may prefer to approach situations or processes using your personality preferences, you will encounter situations in which you may need to use strategies that are opposite of your preferred methods. You may feel somewhat uncomfortable or awkward in such situations, but that does not mean that you will be incapable of performing or functioning effectively.

Eight Personality Preferences of MBTI Personality Types

As previously stated, a personality preference refers to a way of doing or responding that feels more natural, automatic, or comfortable, and that produces better results. To demonstrate how preferences work, place a pen in your hand and write your first name. Now, place the pen in your other hand and write your first name. You were able to write your name with both hands, but which hand produced the better results and felt more natural to use? The hand you used with greater ease is your preferred hand for writing. Following are important points about personality preferences:

- When you are using your personality preference, what you are doing requires less effort or struggle.

- When you are not using your personality preference but instead are using the opposite pole, you may feel more stress, frustration, discomfort, or dissatisfaction with the results.

- In some situations, you may choose to use the opposite of your personality preference; you may not feel as comfortable or confident, but you will be able to respond or perform.

Myers-Briggs Type Indicator® assessment is an inventory test that identifies sixteen personality types.

Personality types are sixteen combinations comprising four personality preferences.

Personality preference refers to a way of doing or responding that feels more natural, automatic, or comfortable and that produces better results.

CONCEPT CHECK 1.8

How do personality preferences differ from learning style preferences? What do they have in common?

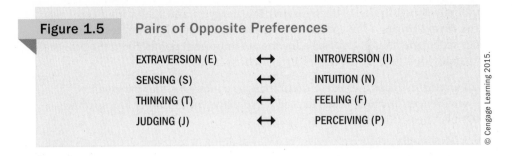

| Figure 1.5 | Pairs of Opposite Preferences |

EXTRAVERSION (E)   ↔   INTROVERSION (I)
SENSING (S)   ↔   INTUITION (N)
THINKING (T)   ↔   FEELING (F)
JUDGING (J)   ↔   PERCEIVING (P)

© Cengage Learning 2015.

● We all use the eight personality preferences, but four of the preferences will work more comfortably and more effectively as our personal preferences.

   Figure 1.5 shows the eight personality preferences that are the building blocks of personality types. Notice the letters used to represent the eight preferences: E, I, S, N, T, F, J, and P. The preferences appear as sets of opposites, referred to as *poles* of each personality building block. One personality preference in each pair of opposites is your personality preference. You can use only one of the two preferences at any given time. In other words, you cannot use Extraversion and use Introversion at the same time.

Four Core Building Blocks of MBTI Personality Types

The four core building blocks identified by the MBTI instrument are the foundation pillars to understanding personality types. These building blocks are also referred to as *scales*. Each core building block (or scale) has a pair of opposite personality preferences that represent where you focus your attention, how you take in information, how you make decisions, and how you structure your life. (For a visual mapping of this information, go to **Figure 10.13** on page 326.) Notice which personality preferences belong to each of the core building blocks.

1. Core Building Block: **Where do you focus your attention?**
   *Do you prefer Extraversion (**E**) or Introversion (**I**)?*

2. Core Building Block: **How do you take in information?**
   *Do you prefer Sensing (**S**) or Intuition (**N**)?*

3. Core Building Block: **How do you make decisions?**
   *Do you prefer Thinking (**T**) or Feeling (**F**)?*

4. Core Building Block: **How do you approach or structure your life?**
   *Do you prefer Judging (**J**) or Perceiving (**P**)?*

Sixteen Personality Types

The only way to verify your MBTI type is to take the MBTI assessment test, which may be administered on your college campus or place of employment. However, without taking the formal MBTI assessment test, in the next section you may estimate your personality type by selecting characteristics or traits of each personality preference that seem to describe you the best and reflect ways to do things that are easier, more comfortable, or feel more natural for you.

| FIGURE 1.6 | Sixteen Personality Types |

ISTJ	ISFJ	INFJ	INTJ
ISTP	ISFP	INFP	INTP
ESTP	ESFP	ENFP	ENTP
ESTJ	ESFJ	ENFJ	ENTJ

© Cengage Learning 2015.

Selecting your preferences from the pairs of opposites for each of the core building blocks results in four letters that represent your personality type. **Figure 1.6** shows the sixteen possible combinations of personality types. Communication styles, social and learning behaviors, values, focus of attention, decision-making processes, self-regulatory skills (managing time, change, and conflict), relationship dynamics, and other characteristics vary for each personality type. These sixteen personality types are all of equal value or importance; one type is not better or more desirable than the others.

CONCEPT CHECK 1.9
What are the sixteen personality types? Translate the four letters in Figure 1.6 to the words they represent to name each personality type. For example, the first personality would be Introversion-Sensing-Thinking-Judging.

Extraversion and Introversion

Where do you focus your attention? Do you get energized by the outside world of people and activities or the inner world of ideas, thoughts, and reflections? Does your focus turn outward to people and the world or inward with self-reflection? Answers to these questions may be indicators of your natural personality preference of *Extraversion* (E) or *Introversion* (I).

The *Extraversion personality preference (E)* tends to focus attention on the outer world of people and things. The *Introversion personality preference (I)* tends to focus attention on the inner world of ideas, thoughts, and reflection. Keep in mind that we do both *E* and *I*, but one will be easier—the one we instinctively do more often and with the more comfort. **Exercise 1.5** provides you with the opportunity to estimate your personality preference for Extraversion or Introversion.

Extraversion personality preference (E) tends to focus attention on the outer world of people and things.

Introversion personality preference (I) tends to focus attention on the inner world of ideas, thoughts, and reflection.

Where You Focus Your Attention

EXERCISE 1.5

DIRECTIONS: Check the descriptions or characteristics that seem to be most closely related to you, are easier for you to do, or reflect how you perceive yourself to be. For each pair of opposite characteristics, check only one of the items in the pair—either in the left column or the right column. After completing the list, which column has the most checks? Circle the word **Extraversion** or **Introversion** at the top of the list to indicate which personality preference best describes you.

WHERE YOU FOCUS YOUR ATTENTION

Extraversion

X **1.** Focus attention and get energized by people and experiences in the world

Introversion

_____ **1.** Focus attention and get energized by inner world of thoughts and ideas

(continued)

Exercise 1.5 (continued)

Extraversion

_____ **2.** Tend to think out loud and share ideas comfortably and freely with others

X **3.** Prefer to communicate and work ideas out with others by talking

X **4.** Learn best by moving around, talking, and discussing

X **5.** May get bored if it's too quiet

X **6.** Sociable, expressive, outgoing

_____ **7.** Active, enthusiastic

_____ **8.** Fairly easy to get to know

Introversion

X **2.** Tend to think things through privately before telling a few selected others

_____ **3.** Prefer to communicate in writing

_____ **4.** Learn best by reflection, mental rehearsal, reading, and listening

_____ **5.** May feel drained if setting is too noisy

_____ **6.** Private, reserved, reflective

X **7.** Quiet, calmer nature, contemplative

X **8.** Known personally only by a few close friends

Sources: Adapted from I. B. Myers, *Introduction to Type*, 6th ed. (Mountain View, CA: CPP, 1998); MBTI® Complete assessment

Students with Extraversion and Introversion Preferences

Now that you are aware of the opposite characteristics of people with an Extraversion personality preference and people with an Introversion personality preference, you are better equipped to understand classroom dynamics that occur when students with opposite personality preferences interact. As you read the following descriptions of students with Extraversion personality preferences and students with Introversion personality preferences, you will likely recognize the personality preference for yourself and other students in your classes.

Students in the Classroom	
Students with **Extraversion preference** tend to	Students with **Introversion preference** tend to
• liven up the class with enthusiasm and energy.	• be quiet and reserved.
• talk freely and are eager to share information.	• refrain from volunteering information or comments.
• welcome discussions and class questions.	• prefer to have questions provided in advance to allow time to formulate responses.
• enjoy group activities.	• not enjoy participating in group activities.
• possibly dominate conversations or overwhelm students with Introversion preference.	• appreciate when questions or conversations slow down or even pause so they do not feel too overwhelmed.
• respond quickly to questions.	• appreciate time to contemplate and then respond to question cautiously.
• get restless or impatient if the classroom pace is slow or they are not engaged.	• feel uncomfortable if classroom pace is too fast for them to feel confident participating.

CONCEPT CHECK **1.10**

How would people with Introversion and Extraversion personality preferences react differently to: a group project, an ongoing journal writing assignment, a study group, and working with a tutor?

Friends with Extraversion and Introversion Preferences

Friendships may feel more comfortable and less stressful with individuals who have the same or similar personality preferences. However, understanding the differences between personality preferences may help you better understand your friends; create stronger, more sincere friendships; and encourage compromises and adjustments to accommodate each other's interests and preferences. For example, friends with the Extraversion personality preference may prefer to plan a party or go out to a place with a lot of people or activities because they tend to meet people readily and engage in immediate conversations. They may dominate conversations, talk endlessly about whatever comes to mind, or speak too quickly without sufficient thought. These friends may be easier to get to know because they openly share information, thoughts, experiences, and opinions.

Friends who have the Introversion personality preference may prefer a quiet dinner together, a movie at home, or a small gathering as they do not tend to reach out immediately to meet new people or begin the process of forming new friendships. They tend to listen and comment only after having contemplated an appropriate answer. These friends may be more difficult to get to know, but they often are genuine and become good friends when, over time, they let another person into their more private world. They are not likely to share a friend's stories or information with others; they value and can be trusted with confidence. On the other hand, friends with the Extraversion personality preference may need to heighten their awareness of the need to maintain confidentiality and trust by refraining from sharing private aspects of a friend's life.

Sensing and Intuition

How do you take in information about yourself and about the world? What kind of information do you trust and find easier to work with or value more? Answers to these questions may be indicators of your natural personality preference of *Sensing* (S) or *Intuition* (N).

The *Sensing personality preference (S)* tends to take in information through the five senses: sight, sound, touch, taste, and smell. The *Intuition personality preference (N)* tends to take in information by noting patterns, relationships, and sometimes hunches or possibilities beyond the five senses. **Exercise 1.6** provides you with the opportunity to estimate your personality preference for Sensing or Intuition.

> **Sensing personality preference (S)** tends to take in information through the five senses: sight, sound, touch, taste, and smell.

> **Intuition personality preference (N)** tends to take in information by noting patterns, relationships, and sometimes hunches or possibilities beyond the five senses.

EXERCISE 1.6

How You Take In Information

DIRECTIONS: Check the descriptions or characteristics that seem to be most closely related to you, are easier for you to do, or reflect how you perceive yourself to be. For each pair of opposite characteristics, check only one of the items in the pair—either in the left column or the right column. Not all of your checks need to appear in only one column. After completing the list, which column has the most checks? Circle the word **Sensing** or **Intuition** at the top of the list to indicate which preference best describes you.

HOW YOU TAKE IN INFORMATION

Sensing

_____ **1.** Focus and rely on information that comes through the senses

__X__ **2.** Oriented to present realities, realistic, literal

Intuition

__X__ **1.** Focus on meanings, relationships, patterns, and big pictures

_____ **2.** Oriented to future possibilities, imaginative, figurative, symbolic

(continued)

Exercise 1.6 (continued)

Sensing

X **3.** Trust factual, concrete information and accurate details

X **4.** Interested in accuracy of details

X **5.** Move carefully and thoroughly to reach conclusions

____ **6.** Start at the beginning and work step by step

X **7.** Tend to follow instructions

X **8.** Enjoy, value, and trust experiences, traditions, and tried-and-true ways

Intuition

____ **3.** Trust hunches, creativity, inspiration, and thinking outside the box

____ **4.** Interested in big-picture ideas, concepts, or patterns

____ **5.** Move quickly to conclusions and follow hunches or intuition

X **6.** Begin anywhere in a task and skip over steps

____ **7.** Tend to create own instructions and be inventive

____ **8.** Enjoy, value, and respect new experiences, and original, innovative ways

Sources: Adapted from I. B. Myers, *Introduction to Type*, 6th ed. (Mountain View, CA: CPP, 1998); MBTI® Complete assessment

CONCEPT CHECK 1.11

Do you have a Sensing or an Intuition personality preference? How does your way of taking in information differ from the personality preference opposite of yours?

Students with Sensing and Intuition Preferences

Personality preferences in many ways are also learning style preferences as they reflect ways students can learn best by selecting strategies that may be easier and more comfortable or natural to use. The Sensing and the Intuition preferences are the opposites or poles for the building block "How You Take In Information."

As you read the following descriptions of students with the Sensing personality preference and students with the Intuition personality preference, ponder how these different personality preferences impact classroom instruction and activities designed to help students take in new course information.

Students in the Classroom	
Students with **Sensing preference** tend to	Students with **Intuition preference** tend to
• favor step-by-step instruction.	• favor approaches with opportunities to explore new, innovative ways to receive and express information.
• like direct, to-the-point presentations of information.	• enjoy brainstorming.
• prefer receiving concrete facts and theories with practical applications and conclusions.	• enjoy experimenting with alternative ways to develop creative solutions or reach conclusions.
• see specific details before seeing the total picture.	• see the "big picture" before focusing on details.
• find comfort in established, proven methods and traditional approaches.	• not always be able to explain how conclusions were reached.

Friends with Sensing and Intuition Preferences

Because Sensing and Intuition personality preferences are opposites, some differences in behaviors will occur. For example, differences may appear in *traditional* verses *novel* or *new* choices of activities, opinions, or ways to take in information. Friends with the Sensing personality preference may feel most comfortable taking in new information by engaging in activities or topics that involve personal experiences, things that are familiar, and an established way of doing things. On the other hand, friends with the Intuition personality preference may prefer taking in new information by experimenting, changing methods or strategies, seeking newness, and thinking outside the box. As with all opposite characteristics and personality types, each can help balance the other. In other words, friends with the Sensing personality preference will benefit from the uniqueness and new opportunities provided by friends with the Intuition personality preference. Friends with the Intuition personality preference will benefit from the consistency, predictability, and value of traditions from friends with the Sensing personality preference.

CHAPTER 1
REFLECTIVE WRITING 2

 On separate paper, in a journal, or online in this textbook's College Success CourseMate, complete the following directions.

1. What intrigued you as you learned about personality preferences? Which personality preferences immediately reminded you of yourself and which reminded you of specific family members or close friends?

2. After reading about all the personality preferences, which personality type in Figure 1.6 shows your estimated or self-perceived personality type? Use the information about your personality type to write one or more paragraphs that describe your overall personality characteristics.

 Access Chapter 1 Reflective Writing 2 in your College Success CourseMate, accessed through *CengageBrain.com*.

Thinking and Feeling

How do you make decisions? What do you most often rely on to help you decide on the best answer, solution, or route to take? Answers to these questions may indicate your natural personality preference of *Thinking* (T) or *Feeling* (F). Your preferred way of making decisions will be the way that feels most natural, is easier, and is the way you depend on most often.

A person with the ***Thinking personality preference (T)*** tends to make decisions based on logical analysis and cause-effect reasoning. The person with the ***Feeling personality preference (F)*** tends to make decisions based on personal values, harmony, and compassion for others. **Exercise 1.7** provides you with the opportunity to estimate your personality preference for Thinking or Feeling. Remember, however, that in order to make the best decisions, you need to develop skills that use both personality preferences. In some situations, you may need to make adjustments in order to work cooperatively and productively to solve problems or make decisions.

> **Thinking personality preference (T)** tends to make decisions based on logical analysis and cause-effect reasoning.

> **Feeling personality preference (F)** tends to make decisions based on personal values, harmony, and compassion for others.

Students with Thinking and Feeling Preferences

In the classroom, students prefer using different processes to make decisions. Decision-making for students with the Thinking personality preference is based on logic and cause-effect thinking. Decision-making for students with the Feeling personality preference is based on how decisions or outcomes will affect other people. As you read the following descriptions, ponder how these different approaches to decision-making affect classroom dynamics.

> **CONCEPT CHECK 1.12**
>
> *In a decision-making situation, what adjustments might a person with a Thinking personality preference and a person with a Feeling personality preference have to make to work cooperatively and productively together?*

How You Make Decisions

DIRECTIONS: Check the descriptions or characteristics that seem to be most closely related to you, are easier for you to do, or reflect how you perceive yourself to be. For each pair of opposite characteristics, check only one of the items in the pair—either in the left column or the right column. Not all of your checks need to appear in only one column. After completing the list, which column has the most checks? Circle the word **Thinking** or **Feeling** at the top of the list to indicate which preference best describes you.

HOW YOU MAKE DECISIONS

Thinking	**Feeling**
_____ **1.** Analytical, objective, logical, impartial	_X_ **1.** Empathetic, subjective, understanding, personal values
_____ **2.** Use cause-effect reasoning to solve problems with logic	_X_ **2.** Guided by individual needs, impact of decisions on others
_X_ **3.** Skeptical, critical, wanting proof, challenge accuracy of information	_____ **3.** Approve, agree, trust accuracy of other's information
_____ **4.** Focus on established principles, rules	_X_ **4.** Focus on harmony, positive interactions, cooperation
_____ **5.** Focus on the task	_X_ **5.** Focus on the people
_____ **6.** Reasonable, firm, assertive, direct, "lay-it-on-the-line"	_X_ **6.** Compassionate, gentle, agreeable, indirect, round-about approach
_____ **7.** Can be seen as "tough-minded"	_X_ **7.** Can be seen as "tender hearted"
_____ **8.** Want everyone treated fairly	_X_ **8.** Want everyone treated as individuals

Sources: Adapted from I. B. Myers, *Introduction to Type*, 6th ed. (Mountain View, CA: CPP, 1998); MBTI® Complete assessment

Students in the Classroom	
Students with **Thinking preference** tend to	Students with **Feeling preference** tend to
• make decisions based on logic, known or proven details, and established procedures.	• place less emphasis on facts and more emphasis on how decisions or outcomes will affect other people.
• use cause-effect thinking and an analytical approach to argue or debate ideas.	• use personal values to argue or debate ideas and strive to create win-win situations.
• appreciate recognition for logical decision-making skills and competency.	• appreciate being recognized as individuals and understood based on personal values and convictions.

Friends with Thinking and Feeling Preferences

Thinking and Feeling personality preferences belong to the building block that focuses on how you make decisions. Your friends with the Thinking personality preference may tend to make decisions based on logic and reason after weighing the pros and cons of different options and after considering the consequences. They make decisions in a matter-of-fact manner based on the task or situation, not based on individual values, benefits, or concerns. Your friends with the Feeling personality preference tend to make decisions based on personal meaning and personal values. They may weigh the pros and cons of different options, but with emphasis on how the final decision would affect other people, how friends or co-workers would respond, or how it would be compatible with their personal values. Decisions tend to reflect a sense of compassion, commitment, and concern for the well-being of self and others.

Judging and Perceiving

How do you approach or structure your life? How much order or structure do you like in your daily life? How do you tackle tasks that need to be done? Answers to these questions may be indicators of your natural personality preference of *Judging* (J) or *Perceiving* (P).

The *Judging personality preference (J)* tends to approach and structure life in an orderly, structured, and systematic way. The *Perceiving personality preference (P)* tends to approach and structure life in a flexible, spontaneous, and more open-ended way. **Exercise 1.8** provides you with the opportunity to estimate your personality preference for Judging or Perceiving.

> **Judging personality preference (J)** tends to approach and structure life in an orderly, structured, and systematic way.

> **Perceiving personality preference (P)** tends to approach and structure life in a flexible, spontaneous, and more open-ended way.

How You Approach or Structure Your Life

DIRECTIONS: Check the descriptions or characteristics that seem to be most closely related to you, are easier for you to do, or reflect how you perceive yourself to be. For each pair of opposite characteristics, check only one of the items in the pair—either in the left column or the right column. Not all of your checks need to appear in only one column. After completing the list, which column has the most checks? Circle the word **Judging** or **Perceiving** at the top of the list to indicate which preference best describes you.

HOW YOU APPROACH OR STRUCTURE YOUR LIFE

Judging	Perceiving
1. Scheduled, organized, structured, orderly, systematic, methodical	X 1. Spontaneous, flexible, relaxed, open-ended, adaptable
2. Perform best through steady progress	X 2. Perform best with bursts of action or energy
X 3. Dislike diversions or getting sidetracked	3. Enjoy diversions and changes in direction
X 4. Appreciate planned details, like schedules	4. Inhibited by too many details, constrained by schedules
5. Make short- and long-term plans	X 5. Prefer not to have short-term or long-term plans
X 6. Make lists to organize days, try to avoid last-minute stresses	6. Stay open to unexpected, welcome change
X 7. Plan for the future, make things happen	7. Stay in the present, go with the flow, react to things that happen
8. Motivated by self-discipline	X 8. Motivated by last-minute pressure

Sources: Adapted from I. B. Myers, *Introduction to Type*, 6th ed. (Mountain View, CA: CPP, 1998); MBTI® Complete assessment

CONCEPT CHECK 1.13

If you are assigned to complete a complex group project within a four-week period, what challenges or possible conflicts might occur if the group has people with strong Judging and strong Perceiving personality preferences?

Students with Judging and Perceiving Preferences

Personality preferences for Judging and Perceiving students are quite obvious in the classroom as they tend to approach or structure their lives quite differently. Individuals with the Judging personality preference may tend to label individuals with the Perceiving personality preference as disorganized or as procrastinators, but such is not the case. Individuals with the Perceiving personality preference tend to use energy in a different way, which leads to misperceptions. As you read the following descriptions, notice the two opposite ways to approach and structure life.

Students in the Classroom	
Students with **Judging preference** tend to	Students with **Perceiving preference** tend to
• favor organization, structure, and routines. • appreciate structure provided by the instructor. • work best with clear expectations, deadlines, and schedules. • create plans to complete assignments on time. • work steadily on an assignment until it is done to satisfaction. • pride themselves on being exact and following guidelines. • be goal-oriented.	• feel stifled by too much structure. • prefer to use their own methods and not the structure provided by the instructor. • dislike using schedules. • think about and mull over options to do an assignment but do not start immediately working on it. • work best with bursts of energy and gain momentum and motivation when working under pressure and closer to deadlines. • prefer a more open-ended, less structured, more flexible, and spontaneous way of doing things. • be open to new experiences and the unexpected.

Friends with Judging and Perceiving Preferences

The opposite characteristics of friends with Judging and Perceiving preferences can easily impact friendships. Friends with the Judging personality preference tend to want to schedule and organize the details of social get-togethers well in advance. They may feel anxious or annoyed when a social activity is not scheduled on a calendar or planned ahead of time. Friends with the Judging personality preference feel comfortable being in control and without having to deal with any surprises or last-minute changes. Friends with the Perceiving personality preference tend not to want to be locked into a schedule, arrange a specific time to get together that is not in the immediate future, or commit to a specific activity. They feel more comfortable deciding what to do closer to the time of the get-together, or even at the last minute, thus allowing a change of plans or a greater sense of spontaneity. Friends with the Perceiving personality preference are comfortable getting together without a plan, going with the flow, or being open to surprises or unexpected events.

CHECK POINT 1.3

Matching See Test-Taking Strategies 16–20 in Appendix A.

Match the items on the left to the items on the right. Write only one letter answer on each blank line. Answers cannot be used more than one time.

_____ 1. Thinking and Feeling

_____ 2. Feeling preference

_____ 3. Extraversion preference

_____ 4. Intuition preference

_____ 5. Judging preference

_____ 6. Sensing and Intuition

_____ 7. Perceiving preference

_____ 8. Scales of MBTI

a. opposite personality preference of Sensing

b. personality preference that tends to be orderly, structured, and systematic

c. the four building blocks in MBTI

d. the scale that shows how you tend to approach or structure life

e. personality preferences for "How You Take In Information"

f. opposite personality preference of Thinking

g. personality preferences for "How You Prefer to Make Decisions"

h. opposite personality preference of Introversion

i. personality preference that tends to be flexible, spontaneous, and open-ended

Access Chapter 1 Practice Quiz 3 in your
College Success CourseMate, accessed through
CengageBrain.com.

Chapter 1 Critical Thinking

PURPOSE: Critical thinking involves a wide range of cognitive or thinking skills. Throughout this textbook, you will learn more about critical thinking skills, which include the following:

- examining ideas carefully and forming meaningful questions
- gathering, understanding, and utilizing relevant information to reach conclusions or problem solve
- using processes such as applying, analyzing, evaluating, and creating

DIRECTIONS:

1. Read the excerpt "Personality Tests Help Employers Find Applicants Who Fit" on the next page.

2. Answer the following questions:

   a. Does it seem fair, justified, or acceptable to you that some employers use both interviews and objective personality tests to make hiring decisions? Explain your answer.

   b. What are some objections to or disadvantages of using personality tests in the hiring process?

   c. How do you think managers should handle a situation in which a person gives an impressive, strong interview but has some personality trait identified by a personality test that does not match the job position?

   d. Have you ever been subjected to a personality test as a part of an interview process? What was your reaction to this kind of testing? What were the results?

Critical Thinking (contnued)

Personality Tests Help Employers Find Applicants Who Fit

More and more job applicants are being required to take personality tests. Already, at least one-third of employers, ranging from governments to hospitals, retail stores to restaurants, and airlines to maufacturing plants, use personality tests in their hiring and promotion process.

There are many personality tests, and each measures something different. For instance, the Myers-Briggs measures personality traits necessary for leadership and teamwork and is used by 89 of the Fortune 100 companies. The Minnesota Multiphasic Personality Inventory measures an individual's tendency toward substance abuse and psychopathology and is used by 60% of police departments as a way to screen applicants. Personality tests look at a variety of other characteristics, such as thought processes, sociability, motivation, self-awareness, emotional intelligence, stress management, dependability, and work style.

Some experts believe personality tests are overused and overinterpreted, and they caution employers about the potential negative impact of the tests on minority applicants. Others believe personality tests have an important place in the hiring process because the tests can predict how well an applicant "fits" with the job description. For instance, when hiring a salesperson, a company can have a list of the personality traits of successful salespeople and then match an applicant's test results against that standard.

Many companies that have used personality tests showed a decrease in absenteeism and turnover, which means big savings for the company. By using personality tests, one California theme park increased levels of employee retention and customer satisfaction, and reduced levels of absenteeism and theft. Also, a bottling company in Milwaukee reduced the number of sick days in half, and an airline reduced tardiness by one-third.

Personality tests are increasingly being used in the hiring process to supplement interviews and a resumé review. So how should you respond to test questions to be sure you get the job? Although ideal responses vary by job position and company, experts suggest that you not falsify your responses, as many personality tests have a sophisticated way of knowing if you're lying. Luis Valdes, an executive consultant, explains, "For any given character trait, say independence, there's an optimal amount. If a person seems to be really extreme, well, most people aren't that extreme, so it suggests they tried to answer all the questions in a positive but not very realistic way" (Valdes, 2006). In the case of personality tests, it appears that honesty is the best policy. (Adapted from Cha, 2005; Cullen, 2006; Frieswick, 2004; Gladwell, 2004; Gunn, 2006; Smith, 1997; Valdes, 2006; Wessel, 2003)

From Plotnik/Kouyoumdjian, *Discovery Series: Introduction to Psychology* (with Psychology CourseMate with eBook Printed Access Card), 1E. © 2013 Cengage Learning.

Understanding Yourself and Others

The primary goal of this chapter is to present information that will encourage you to become more aware of who you are, what makes you "tick," what works most effectively for you and ways to strengthen your understanding about the people who surround you in your everyday life. An ultimate goal for you involves expanding and strengthening skills and strategies compatible with your own preferences as well as skills and strategies associated with your nonpreferred learning style or personality type.

Learning Objectives Review

① *Identify your preferred cognitive learning style and describe learning strategies you can use to utilize your preferred learning style and strengthen your other modalities.*

- Visual, auditory, and kinesthetic are modalities related to three cognitive learning styles or learning preferences.

- Learning preferences reflect how individuals prefer to have information presented in order to problem solve, process, learn, and remember new information. Learning occurs more efficiently and effectively and with less stress when students use their preferred learning styles.

- Effective study strategies for each modality preference as well as the See-Say-Do multisensory strategy are available to use during the learning process. Many of the strategies include visualizing, verbalizing, reciting, and developing muscle memory.

② *Define the term* intelligences *and describe the common characteristics of each of Howard Gardner's eight intelligences.*

- Howard Gardner's Theory of Multiple Intelligences differs in a variety of ways from traditional IQ theory, skills or abilities, and test scores. No standardized tests are available to assess a person's multiple intelligences.

- Gardner identifies eight intelligences: linguistic, logical-mathematical, musical, bodily-kinesthetic, spatial, interpersonal, intrapersonal, and naturalist. Naturalist was added more than a decade after Gardner identified the original seven intelligences.

- General characteristics, skills, and career tendencies exist for each intelligence.

- Gardner's definition of intelligence involves having the potential to solve problems or create products that are of value in a culture.

- Each of the eight intelligences has subintelligences (core abilities). A person may not exhibit well-developed abilities in all of the subintelligences.

③ *Identify the eight personality preferences defined by Myers and Briggs and discuss the use of opposite preferences in their theory.*

- The Myers-Briggs Type Indicator (MBTI) inventory identifies sixteen personality types, which are the result of combinations of eight personality preferences: *Extraversion–Introversion, Sensing–Intuition, Thinking–Feeling,* and *Judging–Perceiving.* Each has its own set of opposite characteristics.

Terms to Know

By yourself or with a partner, practice reciting or writing definitions for the following terms. You may also practice defining these terms by using the online flashcards or comparing your answers to the online glossary.

cognitive learning styles p. 5

learning modalities p. 5

learning style preference p. 5

visual learners p. 7

auditory learners p. 9

kinesthetic learners p. 11

multisensory strategies p. 12

visualizing p. 13

verbalizing p. 13

reciting p. 13

developing muscle memory p. 13

See-Say-Do Strategy p. 13

Theory of Multiple Intelligences p. 16

an intelligence p. 16

subintelligences p. 18

linguistic intelligence p. 18

logical-mathematical intelligence p. 19

musical intelligence p. 19

bodily-kinesthetic intelligence p. 20

spatial intelligence p. 21

interpersonal intelligence p. 21

intrapersonal intelligence p. 22

naturalist intelligence p. 22

Myers-Briggs Type Indicator® assessment p. 25

personality types p. 25

personality preference p. 25

Extraversion personality preference (E) p. 27

Introversion personality preference (I) p. 27

Sensing personality preference (S) p. 29

Intuition personality preference (N) p. 29

Terms to Know
continued

Thinking personality preference (T) p. 31

Feeling personality preference (F) p. 31

Judging personality preference (J) p. 33

Perceiving personality preference (P) p. 33

 Access Chapter 1 Flashcards and Online Glossary in your College Success CourseMate, accessed through *CengageBrain.com.*

- Personality preferences appear as pairs of opposites that fit into four core building blocks: *Where You Focus Your Attention, How You Prefer to Take In Information, How You Prefer to Make Decisions,* and *How You Prefer to Approach and Structure Your Life.*

- A personality preference refers to one of two opposite personality preferences that is more natural, comfortable, and automatic and that produces better results for the individual.

- Understanding Myers-Briggs personality types leads to better understanding of yourself and other people in situations at home, at work, and at school.

Chapter 1   Review Questions

Answers appear on page B2.

True or False? See Test-Taking Strategies 1–9 in Appendix A.

F 1. Cognitive learning styles refer to the way people interact in group settings.

T 2. Learning style preferences and personality types both reflect people's preferred ways of doing a variety of tasks and processing information.

F 3. The See-Say-Do Strategy is not a multisensory strategy that uses three learning modalities.

T 4. Howard Gardner's Theory of Multiple Intelligences claims that eight intelligences reflect potential abilities that individuals can develop and strengthen.

T 5. The core building blocks for understanding personality types discuss where you focus your attention, how you take in information, how you make decisions, and how you use your values to communicate with friends.

Multiple Choice See Test-Taking Strategies 10–15 in Appendix A.

_____ 1. Which of the following is *not* true about multisensory learning?

     a. It involves selecting strategies that utilize two or more modalities.

      b. It always requires both verbalizing and reciting to process information.

     c. It provides multiple ways to access and recall information later.

     d. It may focus on strategies that use a combination of *see, say,* and *do* processes.

_____ 2. In the Theory of Multiple Intelligences,

     a. the definition of *intelligence* is broader and differs from traditional definitions of intelligence and IQ levels.

     b. three of the intelligences have the same name or label as three of the Myers-Briggs personality types.

     c. the sixteen kinds of intelligence can be measured with standardized tests.

     d. intrapersonal intelligence is defined as the ability to use a kinesthetic approach to work on projects by yourself without the help of others.

_____ 3. Which statement is *not* true about Myers-Briggs personality types?

    a. Pairs of opposites or poles are used for personality preferences and characteristics for each building block.

    b. When a person makes decisions or takes in information using his or her personality preference, the process is easier and more natural than if that person used a nonpreferred personality preference.

    c. The ISTJ and the ENTP personality types function more effectively in a work environment, with children, and in the area of academics than any of the other personality types.

    d. Understanding personality types helps individuals understand themselves better and understand other people, their behaviors, and the way they think.

_____ 4. A person with a well-developed naturalist intelligence may exhibit

    a. strong pattern-recognition skills.

    b. the ability to organize and classify objects in the plant and animal world.

    c. a sensitivity to the cycles and balances in nature.

    d. all of the above.

Definitions See Test-Taking Strategies 29–31 in Appendix A.

On separate paper, define each of the following terms:

1. The See-Say-Do Strategy
2. Reciting
3. Subintelligences
4. A personality preference

 Access Chapter 1 Enhanced Quiz and Chapter 1 Study Guide in your College Success CourseMate, accessed through *CengageBrain.com.*

Access all Chapter 1 Online Materials in your College Success CourseMate, accessed through *CengageBrain.com.*

2 Creating a Powerful Mindset

Chris Schmidt/E+ /Getty Images

Throughout your college or university years, you will face many challenges and frustrations, as well as accomplishments and feelings of pride, jubilation, and competency. Each student's journey is unique; however, successful journeys often share common elements that contributed to success. Knowing and using effective study skills is one of the elements that improves academic performance and completion of academic goals. Another element, equally important, involves creating a mindset that helps you work through the difficult times, emerge with positive outcomes and achievements, and develop more sophisticated critical thinking skills. In this chapter, you will learn ways to create a powerful mindset to succeed in school, in a work environment, and in your personal life with family, friends, and relationships.

1 **ATTITUDES AND BELIEFS**

Self-Talk

Affirmations

Focus on the Present

Fear of Failure

Locus of Control

2 **SELF-ESTEEM AND SELF-EFFICACY**

Self-Esteem

Self-Efficacy

3 **CRITICAL THINKING**

Critical Thinkers

Bloom's Taxonomy

 Access Chapter 2 Expanded Outline in your College Success CourseMate, accessed through *CengageBrain.com*.

YOUR CHAPTER MAPPING

After reading information under each heading, return to the chapter visual mapping below. Add key words to show subheadings and important details related to each heading.

 Access Chapter 2 Visual Mapping in your College Success CourseMate, accessed through *CengageBrain.com*.

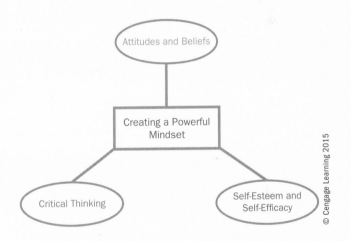

© Cengage Learning 2015

LEARNING OBJECTIVES

1 *Discuss strategies, such as self-talk, affirmations, managing fear of failure, and locus of control, to adjust attitudes and beliefs to create a powerful mindset for success.*

2 *Define self-esteem and self-efficacy and explain how to strengthen each to create a more powerful mindset for learning.*

3 *Define critical thinking; discuss critical thinking behaviors and the six levels of Bloom's Taxonomy.*

Creating a Powerful Mindset

ANSWER, SCORE, and RECORD your profile before you read this chapter. If you need to review the process, refer to the complete directions given in the profile for Chapter 1 on page 4.

ONLINE: You can complete the profile and get your score online in this textbook's College Success CourseMate.

 Access Chapter 2 Profile in your College Success CourseMate, accessed through *CengageBrain.com*.

	YES	NO
1. I strive to develop a strong mindset to better control my situations, performance, and outcomes.	X	
2. I am often discouraged or frustrated by my "inner voice" or inner self-talk, which tends to be negative.	X	
3. I recognize when I have a fear of failure and know strategies to use to overcome the fears.		X
4. Other factors or people control most of the situations in my life.		X
5. Overall I see myself as having a high self-esteem.		X
6. I can identify at least one activity, task, or set of skills in my life where I have the confidence in my ability to perform at a specific level and do well.	X	
7. I tend to rush to conclusions with confidence.		X
8. I think about the way I think and evaluate the quality of my thinking.		X
9. I make a conscious effort to apply what I learn to new situations, and I analyze and evaluate information when I read.		X
10. I am confident in my ability to learn strategies to create a stronger mindset for learning.		X

QUESTIONS LINKED TO THE CHAPTER LEARNING OBJECTIVES:

Questions 1–4: objective 1   Questions 7–9: objective 3

Questions 5–6: objective 2   Question 10: all objectives

Attitudes and Beliefs

 Discuss strategies, such as self-talk, affirmations, managing fear of failure, and locus of control, to adjust attitudes and beliefs to create a powerful mindset for success.

What is a mindset? A mindset is a set of concepts people establish that shows how they see the world and how they see themselves. A mindset is a mental tendency or

habit that affects goals, attitudes, intentions, and self-image. The mindset you carry with you or hold onto dearly can work to your benefit or to your detriment. The attitudes you exhibit without giving them much thought may affect your performance, outcomes, and interactions with other people. Intentionally and purposefully creating a powerful mindset puts you better in control of your situations, choice of actions, and outcomes. Creating a powerful mindset requires a willingness to examine attitudes, beliefs, and personal patterns as well as a willingness to make changes or adjustments. Notice the attitude and beliefs reflected by the following statements:

1. Do you see the glass as half empty or as half full?

2. A negative mind sees everything as problems; a positive mind sees everything as opportunities.

3. Failure is not falling down—it's refusing to get up.

4. A motivated, persistent person does not stop; an unmotivated, indifferent person does not start.

5. What you can see, you can achieve.

6. If you believe it is going to be bad, it will be bad.

7. A positive attitude enhances the experience; a negative attitude hinders it.

8. Success breeds success; motivation breeds motivation.

9. If you want to change your life, change your thoughts.

This process of creating a powerful mindset can be done only by you, for yourself. Staying in your comfort zone is always easier than stretching or reaching for higher, greater, or more demanding ways of thinking and doing things in your life. However, the work, effort, and determination to create a powerful mindset lead to rewards that enrich and empower you as an individual. **Figure 2.1** summarizes strategies to use to begin to create a powerful mindset.

Self-Talk

As you strive to create a powerful mindset, you will find yourself paying attention to your attitudes and beliefs and willingly examining how your mind works and

---

FIGURE 2.1 Strategies to Begin Creating a Powerful Mindset

1. Use positive self-talk on a regular basis or to replace negative self-talk.
2. Use and repeat affirmations.
3. Learn from the past, but focus on the present.
4. Select appropriate strategies to deal with the fear of failure.
5. Develop an internal locus of control.
6. Develop a strong sense of self-esteem and sense of self-efficacy.
7. Strengthen your skills to think critically.
8. Strengthen your ability to formulate and respond to higher-level questions.

© Cengage Learning 2015

Self-talk is that ever-busy inner voice that monitors, critiques, and comments on what you are doing.

Positive self-talk is the internal conversation that focuses on positive qualities and words of encouragement.

Negative self-talk is the internal conversation that is critical and focuses on negative qualities.

CONCEPT CHECK 2.1

What are the differences in the way positive self-talk and negative self-talk affect a person's behavior, choice of actions, and confidence level?

Affirmations are short, positive statements used as motivators to make changes or promote thinking, behaving, or performing in positive ways.

what approaches are available for you to use. One approach that you can immediately begin to use is to practice listening to and responding to self-talk. *Self-talk* is that ever-busy inner voice that monitors, critiques, and comments on what you are doing. Self-talk ultimately affects your behavior, choice of actions, self-esteem, level of confidence, and motivation. The following points about self-talk are important to understand:

- *Positive self-talk* is the internal conversation that focuses on positive qualities and words of encouragement. Positive self-talk is supportive, uplifting, and motivating; it reflects high self-esteem and confidence. Positive self-talk helps a person push on, persevere, and stay on course even when the going gets tough.

- *Negative self-talk* is the internal conversation that is critical and focuses on negative qualities. Negative self-talk involves words of discouragement, belittlement, frustration, lower self-image, and greater self-doubt. Negative self-talk may tell you that you can't do something, don't have the ability, are not worthy of the reward, are not "smart" enough, or will not succeed. Negative self-talk drags a person down, hinders progress, encourages quitting, and reduces the sense of self-confidence or self-worth.

- Motivation quickly dwindles when negative self-talk takes over. Motivation quickly gains momentum when positive self-talk takes over.

- Instantly when you hear negative self-talk, take action quickly to turn negative self-talk into constructive, powerful, positive self-talk. Use positive self-talk statements, such as the following:

  - *I have the ability to do this.*
  - *I can focus on the steps and figure this out.*
  - *This is important and I can do this.*
  - *I am willing to work hard to reach this goal.*
  - *I am worthy of receiving this.*

Affirmations

Affirmations are short, positive statements used as motivators to make changes or to promote thinking, behaving, or performing in positive ways. Affirmations help change your basic belief systems, your self-image, and the direction you are moving to make changes in your life. Use the following suggestions for writing and using affirmations:

- **Use positive words and tones.** Avoid using words such as *no, never,* or *won't.* Say, for instance, "I complete my written work on time," rather than "I will never turn in a paper late again."

- **Write affirmations in the present tense.** Using present tense verbs in your affirmations creates a belief system that a specific behavior already exists. Actions or behaviors can change to match the beliefs stated in the affirmations. Say, for example, "I eat healthy food," rather than "I will stop eating junk food soon"; or "I complete assignments on time," rather than "I will get better at completing my assignments on time."

- **State your affirmation with certainty and conviction.** Avoid using words such as *want to, try to,* or *hope to.* Say, for instance, "I exercise for thirty minutes every day," rather than "I want to exercise more each day"; or "I manage my time well," rather than "I hope I can use my time-management schedule."

- **Keep the affirmation short and simple; repeat it often**. Brief, simple affirmations are easier to remember and repeat. Reinforce the affirmation by repeating frequently. You can place your affirmation on cards around your house or inside your notebook.

CONCEPT CHECK   2.2

What is the purpose of affirmations? Create an affirmation that is meaningful to you.

Focus on the Present

In many ways, we are the reflection of our past. Past experiences are strong influencing factors of who we are today, and understanding those influencing factors is important for self-understanding and growth. The expression "Let it go" is often easier said than done, but it merits our attention. The past is done and can't be changed. You can learn from it, but do not dwell on it. What you *can* change is what you do right now, in the present moment. Choose to shift your attention to the present and accentuate the positive elements that you are creating in your life at this very moment.

Fear of Failure

An attitude and belief pattern that may surface as a response to unfamiliar or stressful experiences is the fear of failure. *Fear of failure* is a belief pattern that can hinder progress or action because the person fears the outcome or consequences will be negative. One might say, "It's better to not try than to try and fail." When dealing with a fear of failure, a person may procrastinate starting a task or may give up on completing a task. In addition to triggering procrastination, this fear may trigger anger or anxiety, or may cause a person to shift blame for the situation to other people. The following statements reflect "fear of failure" thinking:

Fear of failure is a belief pattern that can hinder forward progress or action because the person fears the outcome or consequences will be negative.

- *I lack the skills to do this right.*
- *I can't do it because I don't understand it.*
- *I feel overwhelmed and already know I'll fail at this.*
- *I don't want to look stupid to other people.*
- *I don't want to be embarrassed in front of others.*
- *I know I can't do well because I am not prepared and I didn't do the work.*
- *I am not as smart, talented, and educated as the other students.*

Strategies to Deal with Fear of Failure

Fear of failure usually is based on false beliefs or images you have of yourself as a learner. When you find yourself fearing to take on a project or a task because you predict failure, take charge of the situation by following the steps to create a positive mindset. Try one or more of the following strategies:

- Refocus your mind on your positive traits. On a piece of paper, list the qualities and skills you have to tackle the new task.

- Plan to succeed. Identify previous tasks that were similar to the specific task that triggered the fear of failure. List the steps or processes you used that brought good results. Make a new list of the steps or a plan of action you will use to lay the foundation for successful completion of the task that you no longer fear.

- Negate self-doubt and self-criticism. Activate positive self-talk.
- Engage suggestions or assistance from other people who can help you work through the processes or steps to complete the task.
- Do what needs to be done in terms of clarifying the assignment, planning adequate time to complete the task, and gathering the required materials you will need.
- To boost your self-confidence, visualize or mentally rehearse the steps of the task several times before you actually begin the work. Envision yourself succeeding, not failing.

CONCEPT CHECK   **2.3**

What are several specific examples of ways to turn "fear of failure" statements into positive self-talk statements or affirmations?

Fear of Failure and Tests

Have you ever studied for a test and thought you were prepared, but when the test came back, you were disappointed and discouraged by the grade? Have you ever made statements such as the following?

- *I never get decent grades on tests*, or *I never do well on tests.*
- *I am not a good test-taker, so I know I won't do well on this next test.*
- *I shouldn't have bothered to study because it made no difference.*
- *Instructors write tricky tests designed to flunk most students.*
- *Tests make me feel stupid and embarrassed.*

Negative test-taking experiences can affect a person's mindset. Unless constructive steps are taken to understand what happened, followed by a plan of action to try a new approach, the experience may leave that person with a negative self-image, a fear to face a similar situation again, a lack of motivation, and a developing habit of negative self-talk, self-doubt, and low self-confidence.

A student who is committed to creating a positive mindset examines the situation, analyzes what went wrong, designs a plan to improve, and learns from the situation without hanging on to the negative feelings. For example, the student might decide to:

- Discuss the test with the instructor, tutor, or other students.
- Identify which study strategies worked and which ones did not.
- Use a test-taking inventory (**Exercise 7.1**) to self-assess the test-preparation and test-taking processes.
- If possible, rework or redo sections of the test to imprint the correct answers in memory.
- Create a different plan of action to prepare for the next test by identifying strategies that were not used previously but that could be effective.
- Replace negative self-talk with positive self-talk and affirmations.
- Immediately stop or change the direction of conversations that dwell on negative aspects of the test, the grade, or the content. In other words, stop adding fuel to the fire by contributing or repeating negative emotions and comments.

Test anxiety is excessive stress that hinders a person's ability to perform well before or during a test.

Fear of Failure and Test Anxiety

Ignoring this fear of failure and not taking steps to improve the situation may lead to a more complex problem: *test anxiety*. **Test anxiety** is excessive stress that hinders a person's ability to perform well before or during a test. Students whose test anxiety stems from a fear of failure tend to fear the negative consequences of poor grades. There is a tendency to exaggerate or overstate the outcomes or the negative consequences. The following student comments reflect test anxiety triggered by the fear of failure:

- *I am so worried that my grades will disappoint my parents.*
- *I am so concerned that my grades will affect my scholarship.*
- *If I don't pass this test with a good grade, my GPA for the term is ruined.*
- *A bad grade on this test will prove that I am in way over my head and shouldn't even be taking this class.*
- *If I don't pass the course, I could lose my scholarship or get kicked off the team.*

Notice how the fear of failure tends to focus on disappointing someone else or not fulfilling some type of expectation. Also notice how implementing the previous strategies could have helped the student avoid test anxiety. You will learn more about test-taking strategies and test anxiety in Chapter 7.

Textbook Case Studies

EXERCISE 2.1

DIRECTIONS:

1. Read each case study carefully. Respond to the question at the end of each case study by using *specific* strategies discussed in this chapter. Answer in complete sentences.

2. Write your responses on paper or online in this textbook's College Success CourseMate, Textbook Case Studies. You will be able to print your online response or e-mail it to your instructor.

CASE STUDY 1: Paul often schedules time to work with Blake, his math tutor, to discuss problems he has with his math course. Paul often begins the session with comments such as the following: *I gave up trying to understand this. I decided to wait until I could work with you. I really need your help. I just can't figure any of this out by myself. I have never been good at math. I am going to flunk this class no matter what I do. You've got to save me.* Blake explained to Paul the importance of changing his attitude toward learning math. What strategies could the tutor teach Paul to help him adjust his attitude and increase his confidence and performance?

CASE STUDY 2: Julia is excited about her courses this term. Even though her confidence level is high, she knows that sometimes as the term progresses she has a tendency to start doubting her abilities. A nagging inner voice seems to pop into her head and dampen her optimism. She decides she needs to learn some positive strategies to keep herself on track and motivated. What strategies would work well to help Julia achieve her goals of maintaining a positive attitude?

 Access Chapter 2 Textbook Case Studies in your College Success CourseMate, accessed through *CengageBrain.com*.

FIGURE 2.2   Locus of Control

External Locus of Control	Internal Locus of Control
• I did not do well because my instructor does not like me. • This test is totally unfair. • I could not study because of my children. • All the questions were trick questions. • I failed the test because it was poorly written. • My instructor did not even take the time to try to understand what I wrote. • My instructor did not understand my situation. • The textbook didn't explain this clearly.	• I need to adjust my attitude—quickly. • I take full responsibility; I was not prepared for this test. • I forgot to study the charts. • I need to find more time to myself to study. • I am going to talk to the tutor about my test-taking strategies. • I am going to use more ongoing review every week. • I am going to work to improve my writing skills. • I can learn from this experience.

© Cengage Learning

Locus of Control

Locus of control is a belief pattern that shows whether a person believes external or internal forces control circumstances in his or her life.

An **internal locus of control** occurs when individuals feel that they have the power to control most situations or circumstances in their lives.

An **external locus of control** occurs when individuals relinquish control and see other people or other situations as having power or control over their circumstances.

CONCEPT CHECK   2.4

Explain the relationship you see between intrapersonal intelligence and the problem-solving skills used by a person with an internal locus of control.

Locus of control is another belief pattern that reflects attitudes and beliefs that have the power to affect behavior. **Locus of control** is a belief pattern that shows whether a person believes external or internal forces control circumstances in his or her life. **Figure 2.2** shows the different attitudes expressed by individuals with two different locus of control beliefs in response to receiving test results that were lower than anticipated or desired.

An **internal locus of control** occurs when individuals feel that they have the power to control most situations or circumstances in their lives. They exhibit self-confidence and experience stress or anxiety less frequently than students with an external locus of control. When individuals with an internal locus of control do not do as well as expected, they accept responsibility for outcomes and use problem-solving techniques to create plans for improvement.

An **external locus of control** occurs when individuals relinquish control and see other people or other situations as having power or control over their circumstances. They blame others for their personal shortcomings instead of accepting personal responsibility. They tend to have low confidence in their abilities and high levels of frustration, self-doubt, and possibly fear of failure.

As soon as individuals hear themselves laying blame on others, making excuses for disappointing performance, or not stepping up and accepting responsibility for disappointing outcomes, they can shift gears to create a more powerful mindset by:

- **Listening to their self-talk and paying attention to their thought patterns:** Acknowledging an external locus of control is the first step to accepting responsibility for the situation and to making changes.

- **Reversing their self-talk and their thought patterns:** Turn the negative self-talk into positive self-talk. Notice in **Figure 2.2** the opposite ways to express feelings, thoughts, and attitudes.

- **Writing affirmations and focusing on positive qualities:** Writing statements that begin with "I" and listing plans of action that begin with "I" shifts the focus and responsibility back onto the individual to create an internal locus of control.

EXERCISE 2.2

External and Internal Statements

DIRECTIONS: Figure 2.2 shows opposite statements, "justifications," or excuses used by students after receiving a test score lower than anticipated or desired. On your own paper, create a new chart that shows at least six sets of opposite statements that might be made by a person using an external locus of control and a person using an internal locus of control for a different situation. For example, your sets of statements may be in response to applying for a job, getting fired from a job, missing an important deadline, problems working on a group project, losing something important, or an issue in a personal relationship.

Describe the situation: _____

External Locus of Control	Internal Locus of Control

CHECK POINT 2.1

Answers appear on page B2.

Multiple Choice See Test-Taking Strategies 10–15 in Appendix A.

_____ 1. A mindset is not a
   a. set of concepts that shows how people see themselves.
   b. narrow-minded, rigid way of looking at and interpreting the world.
   c. mental habit or way of thinking that affects attitudes and self-image.
   d. way of thinking that can help a person control situations and outcomes.

_____ 2. Self-talk refers to
   a. a term that is limited to describing a behavior that occurs when a person is under pressure to perform.
   b. negative self-talk that may portray frustration or self-doubt.
   c. positive self-talk that may portray high self-esteem.
   d. internal conversations that may positive or negative.

_____ 3. Affirmations are not
   a. positive statements that can alter a person's beliefs.
   b. short, positive statements written in the present tense.
   c. effective if they are long or include words that reflect uncertainty or wishful thinking.
   d. repeated or stated out loud more than one time.

_____ 4. A person with an internal locus of control
   a. does not blame other people for his or her shortcomings or situations.
   b. feels in control of his or her circumstances.
   c. is willing to use problem-solving techniques to improve.
   d. demonstrates all of these characteristics.

(continued)

Listing See Test-Taking Strategies 25–28 in Appendix A.

List any four strategies a student could use to combat test anxiety caused by a fear of failure.

1. _____

2. _____

3. _____

4. _____

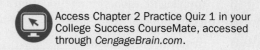

Access Chapter 2 Practice Quiz 1 in your College Success CourseMate, accessed through *CengageBrain.com*.

Self-Esteem and Self-Efficacy

2 *Define self-esteem and self-efficacy and explain how to strengthen each to create a more powerful mindset for learning.*

> **Self-esteem** is the perception you have of yourself as a human being.

> **Self-efficacy** is the belief in your abilities to accomplish a specific task or to demonstrate a set of related skills at a specific level of performance.

Striving to use positive self-talk and affirmations, focusing on action plans for the present time, confronting fear of failure, and developing an internal locus of control all contribute to creating a positive mindset that is ready and able to handle challenges and achieve many successes. *Self-esteem* is the perception you have of yourself as a human being. *Self-efficacy* is the belief in your abilities to accomplish a specific task or to demonstrate a set of related skills at a specific level of performance. Strengthening your self-esteem and your sense of self-efficacy also help create a strong, positive mindset, which benefits you in many ways:

- Increases motivation, effort, and drive to achieve goals
- Strengthens persistence and perseverance
- Increases academic resilience (persist or persevere despite difficulties, setbacks, or negative outcomes)
- Improves performance and results in more achievements
- Reduces stress and negative emotional responses
- Increases self-confidence and sense of well-being

Self-Esteem

Self-esteem is the result of the way you interpret or remember past experiences, choices, behaviors, decisions, and consequences. This self-perception also reflects your memory of past reactions of acceptance or rejection from family members, friends, teachers, or coworkers. An individual's self-esteem, sense of worthiness, and degree of personal pride may be high or low depending on these self-perceptions or memories of the past.

In the following lists of characteristics, notice that the characteristics of high self-esteem and of low self-esteem appear as opposite characteristics. Development of a strong, high self-esteem leads to positive outcomes and achievements. After reading the following two lists, return to the list of characteristics for high self-esteem. **Circle all the characteristics in the High Self-Esteem list that reflect the way you perceive yourself.**

High Self-Esteem	Low Self-Esteem
• High motivation	• Low motivation or unmotivated
• Positive results for effort	• Negative results for lack of effort
• Willing to try new ways	• Rigid and prefer established ways
• Able to adjust to change	• Resistant and unwilling to change
• Courage to take risks, to try something new	• Avoid taking risks to try something new
• Optimism helps make changes	• Pessimism makes change unlikely
• Self-confident in many situations	• Lack of self-confidence
• Make plans of action	• Do not make plans of action
• Perceive "failures" as lessons	• Perceive "failures" as more of the same
• Willing to seek help or advice	• Uncomfortable asking for help or advice
• Can overcome obstacles	• Obstacles stop forward progress
• Control events in life	• Lack control of events in life
• Use positive approaches	• Use negative approaches
• Use positive self-talk	• Use negative self-talk

Figure 2.3 provides additional characteristics of the self-esteem cycles for individuals with low and individuals with high self-esteem.

Self-Efficacy

Self-efficacy is the belief in your abilities to accomplish a *specific* task or to demonstrate a *set of related skills* at a specific level of performance. A person with high self-efficacy in one area will exhibit a sense of self-confidence and motivation to succeed at new tasks *related to that area*. However, the same person may have a

CONCEPT CHECK 2.5

How does the high self-esteem cycle differ from the low self-esteem cycle? How might these differences affect individuals' mindsets?

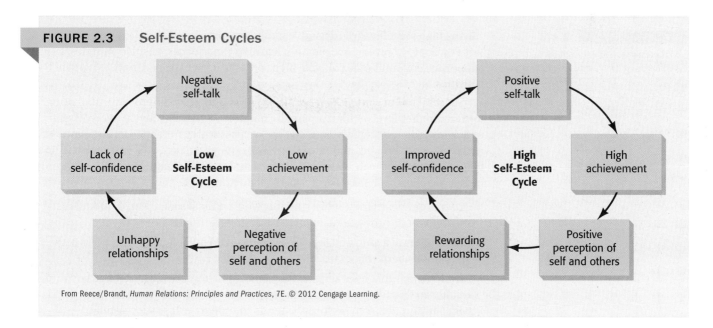

FIGURE 2.3   Self-Esteem Cycles

From Reece/Brandt, *Human Relations: Principles and Practices*, 7E. © 2012 Cengage Learning.

low sense of self-efficacy for an unfamiliar area or for a task that is outside of his or her realm of successful experiences, comfort zone, or achievements. For example, a concert pianist may have a strong sense of self-efficacy when on stage performing, auditioning, or recording music. The same pianist, however, may have a low sense of self-efficacy speaking publicly, solving math equations, or running marathons. In another example, a student may have a high sense of self-efficacy for mastering coursework in math, science, and computer classes, but the student may not have a high sense of self-efficacy for composition, speech, or performing arts classes.

Highly successful or productive people tend to have a strong sense of self-efficacy for their area or areas of expertise. They carry themselves with confidence and have a mindset that believes they can tackle projects or tasks in specific areas and be successful. Individuals with a high sense of self-efficacy often demonstrate the following characteristics:

- Set goals to achieve and aim high
- Work hard and diligently on goals
- Persist longer and harder to reach a desired level of performance
- Seek new or alternative ways when there is a need to improve performance

When an individual tackles a task in which self-efficacy is low, the person tends to believe that he or she is not going to do well before even starting. In other words, the person expects to fail. The following may also occur:

- The negative self-talk or negative attitude kicks in and affects the outcome.
- To try to compensate for the lack of confidence or drive, the person may set lower goals or avoid setting goals at all.
- The person's under-performance is discouraging and frustrating, so perseverance and motivation falter.
- The result is a feeling of incompetence, failure, and lack of ability to perform the task adequately. However, in many cases, the lack of effective strategies, not ability, is the reason for not achieving the goal or completing the task.

CONCEPT CHECK   **2.6**

What behaviors show a high sense of self-efficacy and a low sense of self-efficacy?

Having high self-efficacy is desirable, but how does one go about strengthening self-efficacy? Achievements, pleasant learning experiences, positive attitudes, and supportive environments cultivate high self-efficacy for specific tasks or types of activities.

Success and accomplishment push a person to grow, improve further, or perform on higher levels. When a person completes a task effectively, receives praise or acknowledgment, enjoys teaching the process with confidence to someone else, and feels good, excited, and motivated while doing the task, self-efficacy rises. The following strategies can boost self-efficacy and the belief that you can perform on higher levels for specific tasks or sets of related skills:

- Observe and learn from other students who are mastering the task. Model their strategies and try new ways to increase your performance.
- Create plans of action and follow them so you do not fall behind and set yourself up to under-perform or fail.
- Develop plans that have series of steps that lead to success. Break large goals into smaller goals or steps. As you achieve each step, you build your confidence and belief in your ability to perform better or complete the task successfully.

- Reach out for suggestions or assistance. Your goal is to experience success, so be willing to explore new avenues to learn the required skills or techniques. Work with tutors or a study group. Watch instructional videos. Create stronger communication with other students and your instructor.

EXERCISE 2.3

Transfer These Skills: Self-Efficacy Cycles

BACKGROUND: Self-efficacy refers to your belief in your abilities to perform a specific task or set of related skills at a specific level of performance or quality. Self-efficacy, for example, may be high or it may be low in one or more of the following areas.

• athletic skill	• painting, sculpting, designing	• formal social events
• interviewing for jobs	• public speaking	• writing editorials
• leadership skills	• mentoring someone	• writing essay tests
• teaching something	• debating on a debate team	• dancing, performing
• computer repairs	• car maintenance	• scrapbooking

DIRECTIONS: Below each self-efficacy cycle, identify a specific task or set of related skills in which you feel a high sense of self-efficacy and a task in which you feel a low sense of self-efficacy. Within the five boxes in each self-efficacy cycle, write characteristics that describe what happens to you when you are in the high and in the low self-efficacy cycles. Choose descriptions that do not appear in Figure 2.3

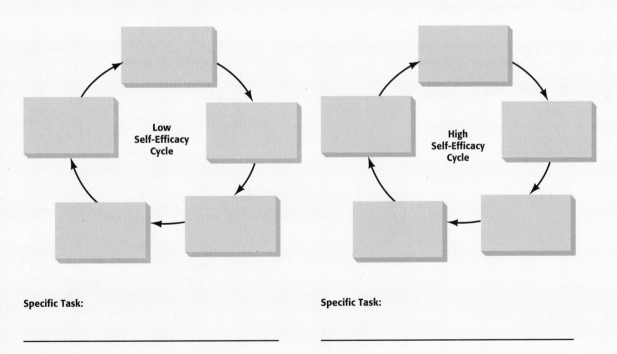

Specific Task:

_____

Specific Task:

_____

CHECK POINT 2.2

Answers appear on page B2.

True or False? See Test-Taking Strategies 1–9 in Appendix A.

_____ 1. Self-esteem refers to a perception someone has of himself or herself.

_____ 2. Self-esteem stems from a negative self-image or external locus of control.

_____ 3. A person with high self-esteem tends to demonstrate stronger academic resilience.

_____ 4. A person's self-esteem never reflects negative past experiences but often reflects positive memories from the past.

_____ 5. Self-efficacy is another word that basically means self-esteem.

_____ 6. A person with high self-efficacy shows confidence and ability in everything he or she does.

_____ 7. High self-esteem and high self-efficacy both affect a person's level of performance, persistence, and attitude.

 Access Chapter 2 Practice Quiz 2 in your College Success CourseMate, accessed through _CengageBrain.com_.

CHAPTER 2 REFLECTIVE WRITING 1

 On separate paper, in a journal, or online in this textbook's College Success CourseMate, complete the following directions.

1. A person's attitudes and beliefs affect performance, outcomes, and achievements. Discuss specific ways you can use the information about self-talk, affirmations, focus on the present, fear of failure, and locus of control to modify, change, or improve your attitudes and beliefs to create a more powerful mindset.

2. What important insights did you discover when reading about self-esteem and self-efficacy? How will you use this information to create a more powerful mindset?

 Access Chapter 2 Reflective Writing 1 in your College Success CourseMate, accessed through _CengageBrain.com_.

Critical Thinking

3 _Define critical thinking; discuss critical thinking behaviors and the six levels of Bloom's Taxonomy._

A mindset is an attitude that you can adopt, implement, and accept as a part of the image or perception you have of yourself. As a college student, you can strive to become a critical thinker—to see yourself activating a wide range of cognitive behaviors and skills that show your intellect, abilities, and inquisitiveness to learn new information.

In an age of information overload, we often feel the need to remember and understand a vast amount of information, yet research continually changes information already learned and provides us with new information that was previously unknown or undiscovered. As we earnestly strive to remember and understand new information, to be an effective thinker we must first learn the lower-order cognitive skills and then push ourselves to think more deeply, more seriously, and more critically about the information we encounter. With access to the Internet and endless databases, we easily can locate information, but to understand, use, and evaluate the information effectively requires us to know how to think critically.

Critical thinking is a higher-order, purposeful, skillful thinking that focuses on gathering, understanding, and utilizing relevant information to reach logical, trustworthy conclusions about what to believe, what to do, or what decisions to make in everyday life. Critical thinking involves carefully examining ideas, questioning the truth or validity of information, and analyzing personal thinking processes. Because critical thinking is an important element in creating a powerful mindset, more in-depth information about critical thinking and critical thinking exercises will appear throughout this textbook.

> **Critical thinking** is a higher-order, purposeful, skillful thinking that focuses on gathering, understanding, and utilizing relevant information to reach logical, trustworthy conclusions about what to believe, what to do, or what decisions to make in everyday life.

Critical Thinkers

Critical thinking involves a wide range of cognitive and behavioral skills. The more you practice and train your mind to think critically, the more you will grow as a critical thinker. Use the following basic guidelines to become a more powerful critical thinker:

> **CONCEPT CHECK** 2.7
> *Define critical thinking. Why is critical thinking important in today's world?*

- **Be inquisitive and ask meaningful questions.**
  - Ask questions, such as *Why? Is this factual? Is this a generalization? Does this show opinion or bias? Is this reasonable? Does this make sense with other information I already know? Is this credible? Can you explain it further? Where is the proof?*

  - Seek out information that relates to topics of interest. Expand your background knowledge by acquiring factual details to support your point of view or statements.

  - Question statements, generalizations, theories, and beliefs before accepting them as trustworthy, accurate, or useful.

  - Ask questions to clarify information you do not understand or that seems contradictory or incomplete.

- **Think independently and reflectively.**
  - Scrutinize statements. Look for faulty thinking, assumptions, or distorted facts. Avoid automatically accepting what you hear or read as being accurate or true.

  - Examine how you define specific terms, such as *honest, valuable, fair,* or *best*. Carefully listen to others to understand more clearly how they define key terms being used in discussions or arguments.

  - Recognize that emotionally charged, controversial topics often are based on faulty thinking, exaggerated statements, or inaccurate broad generalizations.

  - Identify generalizations or broad statements that are not supported by factual information.

  - Analyze statements that show opinions, bias, or promotion of a specific agenda or point of view.

- Carefully examine writers' words and ideas. Form conclusions, not based on your personal opinions, but based on the evidence that is provided and can be verified as true.

- Evaluate the credibility of sources of information. Ask, *Is the information reliable? Does the information come from a person of authority or expertise? Is the source reputable? Is the information unbiased? Is the information updated and complete?*

- **Evaluate the quality of your thinking.**
  - Think about and examine the way you think and process information.
  - Look for weaknesses in your thought processes, such as jumping to conclusions based on opinions or personal beliefs.
  - Identify ways to adjust the way you think and respond to information you hear or read.

- **Show open-mindedness.**
  - Be willing to explore or examine an opposite point of view.
  - Examine whether you have preconceived ideas or opinions that limit your ability to listen critically.
  - Be willing to reconsider your stance or change your point of view after hearing, reading, or discovering new information.
  - Avoid getting defensive or argumentative when listening to or reading someone else's opposite point of view.

- **Understand and identify facts and opinions.**
  - A *fact* is an idea or statement that can be verified to be true or accurate. Facts are objective, which means they are not based on personal feelings, attitudes, or opinions.
  - Studies, reports, experts, scientific research, or polls may be used to present information as facts.
  - When analyzing something you read or hear, strive to identify what information is factual (that is, can be verified). Ask questions. Look for proof of factual information before accepting it as true.
  - An *opinion* is a subjective, personal thought or idea that reflects the feelings, beliefs, or point of view of one person or a group of people.
  - An opinion may include factual information to use as reasons to support or justify the opinion, but the opinion itself cannot be verified as being true.
  - For nearly any opinion, the opposite opinion or point of view also exists. A person may show a *bias*, or a strong preference or commitment, to one specific point of view.
  - Descriptive language, such as emotionally laden words or adjectives (words that describe nouns), frequently appear in statements of opinion. One cannot verify statements as true when words such as *deplorable, brainless, unfair, incompetent, greedy,* or *common sense* are used in statements that express opinions.

A **fact** is an idea or statement that can be verified to be true or accurate.

An **opinion** is a subjective, personal thought or idea that reflects the feelings, beliefs, or point of view of one person or a group of people.

- **Evaluate your decision-making skills.**
  - Recognize problems and analyze the dynamics involved. Ask questions, such as *What needs to be done, fixed, or changed? Why? What details are important? What are the desired results? Why are they important?*
  - Examine and evaluate possible new solutions or conclusions to use to solve problems. Ask questions, such as *What are some ways to go about this? What are the pros and the cons of the options? What could go wrong? What assumptions am I making with this decision?*
  - Modify your problem-solving strategies by trying new approaches or processes to make decisions about what to think or what to do.

CONCEPT CHECK **2.8**
Which of the guidelines could you use to become a stronger critical thinker? Explain with specific details.

CHAPTER 2
REFLECTIVE WRITING 2

On separate paper, in a journal, or online in this textbook's College Success CourseMate, complete the following directions.

1. You have read a formal definition of critical thinking, and you have read characteristics of critical thinkers. Without referring to the printed information, write a short paragraph explaining what "critical thinking" means to you. Use your own words, examples, or explanations.

2. As you read your textbooks and engage in class discussions, you can demonstrate a powerful critical thinking mindset by asking meaningful questions that probe for higher levels of information. Make a list of ten important questions you could use in a variety of situations to show your critical thinking mindset. Use the questions as you read or engage in classroom discussions. Summarize the results in which you applied these critical thinking questions.

Access Chapter 2 Reflective Writing 2 in your College Success CourseMate, accessed through *CengageBrain.com*.

GROUP PROCESSING

A Collaborative Learning Activity

DIRECTIONS: Work with a group of three or four students, with a partner, or by yourself to answer the following questions. Go to Excerpt 2: Practice Visualization in Appendix D in the back of your textbook. Read the excerpt carefully, one paragraph at a time. Then answer the following questions.

1. What is *visualization* and how does it work?

2. Excerpt 2 explains how to use the process of visualization to prepare for a public speaking situation. In what other situations could you use this process of visualization?

3. What is *self-fulfilling prophecy* and how is it related to the topics discussed in this chapter for creating a powerful mindset?

4. Does it take long for a clear visualization to affect your mindset? How do you know this to be true?

5. Other than visualization, what other strategies can you use to replace negative images with positive ones?

Bloom's Taxonomy

Critical thinking involves a wide range of thinking or cognitive skills. ***Bloom's Taxonomy*** is a classification system with six levels of thinking or cognitive processes. The first three levels, *remembering*, *understanding*, and *applying*, involve lower-level thinking skills. The last three levels, *analyzing*, *evaluating*, and *creating*, are the higher-level critical thinking skills. To perform on the higher levels, you must have learned to use the lower-level skills first. You can strengthen your critical thinking skills by understanding and using Bloom's levels of cognitive skills when you ask questions, examine information, and make decisions.

In 1956, a psychologist named Benjamin Bloom, along with several colleagues, developed *Bloom's Taxonomy*, a model for educators to use to identify educational goals and objectives, design curriculum, and promote higher-level thinking and questioning skills. In the mid-1990s, a group of educators revised the levels for Bloom's Taxonomy. **Figure 2.4** shows the revised levels in Bloom's Taxonomy and question words associated with each level.

Bloom's Taxonomy is a classification system with six levels of thinking or cognitive processes.

CONCEPT CHECK   **2.9**

The term "taxonomy" means "classification." What does Bloom's Taxonomy classify? What are the six levels of classification in Bloom's Taxonomy?

FIGURE 2.4   **Bloom's Taxonomy**

LEVEL	NAME	BASICS	QUESTION WORDS
6	Creating	Use creativity, originality, and synthesis.	*combine, compile, collaborate, compose, construct, create, design, develop, devise, elaborate, formulate, generalize, hypothesize, invent, integrate, modify, plan, prepare, rearrange, revise, solve, substitute, synthesize, validate, what if?, write*
5	Evaluating	Use criteria to judge or critique.	*appraise, argue, assess, compare, conclude, convince, critique, debate, decide, defend, determine, discriminate, evaluate, explain, grade, interpret, judge, justify, measure, persuade, prioritize, rank, rate, recommend, select, summarize, support, test, validate*
4	Analyzing	Examine and analyze parts.	*analyze, arrange, classify, categorize, compare, contrast, connect, diagram, differentiate, dissect, divide, examine, experiment, explain, illustrate, infer, interpret, investigate, order, outline, relate, select, separate, subdivide, survey*
3	Applying	Apply to new problem, task, or situation.	*apply, calculate, chart, classify, collect, complete, compute, construct, demonstrate, determine, develop, discover, examine, graph, illustrate, modify, plan, practice, predict, produce, project, select, show, solve, use, utilize*
2	Understanding	Comprehend.	*associate, calculate, classify, compare, contrast, describe, differentiate, discuss, estimate, explain, generalize, illustrate, interpret, organize, outline, paraphrase, predict, restate, translate, sequence, summarize, trace*
1	Remembering	Recall facts.	*choose, define, describe, enumerate, find, identify, label, list, locate, match, name, quote, relate, select, show, spell, tell, what, when, where, who*

Based on Benjamin Bloom, along with several colleagues, developed Bloom's Taxonomy (1956).

Being aware of the levels of thinking in Bloom's Taxonomy will benefit you in the following ways:

- **Understand the levels of textbook and test questions:** Some questions will require lower-level answers, while other questions will demand responses based on higher-order critical thinking. You will feel more confident and in control by understanding the level of the questions.

- **Create effective questions about topics and concepts:** You can use Bloom's Taxonomy levels to ask questions about information you read, ask questions in class or in discussions, or predict and practice writing your own test questions to review course information and prepare for tests.

- **Realize that every course has basic learning and more complex learning:** The different levels of learning require you to be aware of your thinking processes and to push yourself to learn more thoroughly and think more deeply.

- **Become comfortable working on all six levels:** You do not need to feel intimidated by the higher levels of critical thinking skills. With an increased awareness of levels of critical thinking and practice using the levels, you will become more comfortable working on all six levels. (For more information on Bloom's levels and question prompts, see **Figure 12.3**, No. 19 Bloom's Taxonomy and website.)

Remembering Level

The *Remembering Level* (originally called the Knowledge Level) is the lowest, most basic level of thinking in Bloom's Taxonomy. When you use the Remembering Level to question, think about, or learn information, you are able to do the following:

- Remember and recall specific, previously learned information that answers the questions *Who? What? Why? When? Where? How?*

- Learn the basic factual information, such as dates, people, places, events, vocabulary terms, key ideas, and information from diagrams or charts

- Complete worksheets, recite definitions, read charts and diagrams, or remember lists of information

- Define, describe, identify, label, list, match, and use the other question words shown in **Figure 2.4**

> The **Remembering Level** (originally called the Knowledge Level) is the lowest, most basic level of thinking in Bloom's Taxonomy.

Understanding Level

The *Understanding Level* (originally called the Comprehension Level) is the second level in Bloom's Taxonomy. When you use the Understanding Level to question, think about, or learn information, you are able to do the following:

- Follow, grasp, and comprehend ideas and information
- Explain meanings and information to someone else
- Restate, paraphrase, or recite the information in your own words
- Demonstrate your understanding through some type of activity, such as drawing, illustrating, demonstrating, or teaching someone else
- Interpret information, graphs, or charts
- Show relationships, such as cause and effect, and provide examples
- Classify, compare, contrast, estimate, explain, interpret, organize, outline, summarize, and use the other question words shown in **Figure 2.4**

> The **Understanding Level** (originally called the Comprehension Level) is the second level in Bloom's Taxonomy.

Applying Level

The **Applying Level** (originally called the Application Level) is the third level in Bloom's Taxonomy.

The *Applying Level* (originally called the Application Level) is the third level in Bloom's Taxonomy. To work on this level requires that you already have the necessary knowledge and skills from the Remembering and Understanding Levels. When you use the Applying Level to question, think about, or learn information, you are able to do the following:

- Apply previously learned information, rules, models, prototypes, facts, steps, or processes to new learning tasks or new problems to solve
- Apply the information to activities, such as build a model, role play, conduct interviews, use steps to complete a process
- Compute, construct, demonstrate, illustrate, graph, project, solve, complete an experiment, or use the other question words shown in **Figure 2.4**

Analyzing Level

The **Analyzing Level** (originally called the Analysis Level), a complex, higher-order thinking level, is the fourth level in Bloom's Taxonomy.

The *Analyzing Level* (originally called the Analysis Level), a complex, higher-order thinking level, is the fourth level in Bloom's Taxonomy. To think and respond on the Analyzing Level, one needs to have the skills of the Remembering, Understanding, and Applying Levels. In other words, it would be difficult, perhaps impossible, to think on the Analyzing Level about a subject when the learner has no background knowledge, understanding, or experience. When you use the Analyzing Level to question, think about, or learn information, you are able to do the following:

- Break down information or material into its smaller parts to examine or analyze
- Explain how the parts fit together, such as the thesis, main ideas, and supporting details in reading materials, or individual steps in an equation to solve a math problem
- Identify and examine the organizational structure of the material, such as an essay or a musical arrangement
- Identify and examine patterns and relationships, such as cause and effect
- Analyze information for faulty assumptions, facts versus opinions, biases, and lack of sufficient details to support a point of view
- Complete activities such as analyzing a questionnaire, spreadsheet, organizational structure, data, diagrams, and charts
- Analyze, categorize, classify, infer, compare, contrast, differentiate, or use the other question words shown in **Figure 2.4**

Evaluating Level

The **Evaluating Level** (originally called Evaluation Level), a higher level of critical thinking, is the fifth level in Bloom's Taxonomy.

The *Evaluating Level* (originally called the Evaluation Level), a higher level of critical thinking, is the fifth level in Bloom's Taxonomy. To use this level effectively requires skills on the previous four levels. When you use the Evaluating Level to question, think about, or learn information, you are able to do the following:

- Identify a specific set of criteria as well as personal values to judge or critique the value, importance, accuracy, or worthiness of information

- Use a defined set of standardized criteria to judge or evaluate information or a piece of work
- Ask questions, such as *Does this make sense? Are statements backed by facts? Do the author's affiliations slant the point of view? Are there too many broad generalizations? Is the source of the information credible?*
- Evaluate the soundness or accuracy of differing opinions or sources of information on a given topic
- Defend a position or point of view by providing strong proof or support
- Complete activities, such as evaluating a product report, making recommendations for a project, judging a performance, evaluating information based on its source, relevancy, and accuracy, or conducting a self-evaluation
- Appraise, assess, convince, persuade, critique, grade, judge, debate, defend, rank, recommend, or use the other question words shown in **Figure 2.4**

Are the levels in Bloom's Taxonomy arranged in a sequential order or a random order? Discuss how the sequential or random order is important for developing critical thinking skills.

Creating Level

The *Creating Level* (originally called the Synthesis Level) is the sixth and the highest level in Bloom's Taxonomy. The Creating Level involves more complex thinking skills and involves creativity and originality to put parts together to create something new. When you are using the Creating Level to question, think about, and learn information, you are able to do the following:

The **Creating Level** (originally called the Synthesis Level) is the sixth and the highest level in Bloom's Taxonomy.

- Draw a conclusion or present alternative solutions
- Creatively integrate and show new patterns or relationships
- Predict test questions or create your own questions for reading materials
- Create or design a new product, process, or way to solve a problem
- Organize and explain ideas in a project, speech, or research paper
- Use information from several sources to create an original way to show, classify, or group information
- Combine and integrate information from several sources
- Respond to "What if…?" statements
- Complete activities, such as design a brochure, design a new product, or develop a multimedia presentation
- Compile, compose, construct, design, develop, hypothesize, revise, integrate, or use the other question words shown in **Figure 2.4**

Monkey Business Images/Shutterstock.com

Creating a powerful mindset includes developing higher-level critical thinking skills. How can you apply the basic guidelines for becoming a critical thinker when you communicate and interact with your classmates?

Bloom's Original and Revised Taxonomy

BACKGROUND: The original Bloom's Taxonomy developed in 1956 was a model for educators to use to identify educational goals and objectives, design curriculum, and promote higher-level questioning skills. In the mid-1990s, a group of educators revised the taxonomy to show a more active form of thinking.

DIRECTIONS: Examine the details in the following chart. Answer the questions that follow the chart.

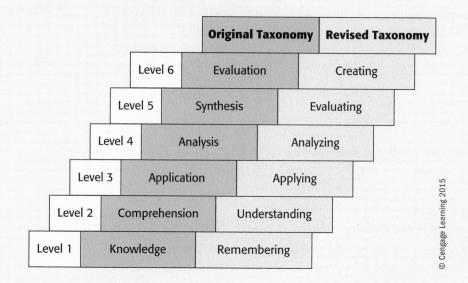

	Original Taxonomy	Revised Taxonomy
Level 6	Evaluation	Creating
Level 5	Synthesis	Evaluating
Level 4	Analysis	Analyzing
Level 3	Application	Applying
Level 2	Comprehension	Understanding
Level 1	Knowledge	Remembering

© Cengage Learning 2015

QUESTIONS:

1. What are the major differences between the original taxonomy and the revised version?

2. What is the meaning of *synthesis*? How does it relate to the process of creating?

3. What are possible reasons educators chose to revise the taxonomy?

CHECK POINT 2.3

Answers appear on page B2.

Definition Questions See Test-Taking Strategies 29–31 in Appendix A.

1. On your own paper, define the term *critical thinking*.

2. On your own paper, define the term *taxonomy*.

3. On your own paper, define the term *Applying Level* in Bloom's Taxonomy.

Listing and Short-Answer Questions See Test-Taking Strategies 25–28 and 32–36 in Appendix A.

1. On your own paper, list in order the six levels of thinking skills in Bloom's Taxonomy.

2. On your own paper, briefly describe three characteristics of critical thinkers.

 Access Chapter 2 Practice Quiz 3 in your College Success CourseMate, accessed through *CengageBrain.com*.

Chapter 2 Critical Thinking

DIRECTIONS: Use your critical thinking skills to ponder and respond to the following questions focused on the relationships between learning styles and topics in this chapter. Your instructor may use some or all of these questions for discussion or for writing assignments.

COGNITIVE LEARNING STYLES

1. Which strategies in the section "Attitudes and Beliefs" utilize the strength of auditory learning?

2. What is the cause-and-effect relationship between using a preferred learning style to master coursework and self-esteem and self-efficacy?

3. Critical thinking involves constructing meaningful questions to examine information on deeper levels. How might visual learners differ from auditory learners in ways they create and use meaningful questions?

MULTIPLE INTELLIGENCES

1. Which strategies in the section "Attitudes and Beliefs" require the use of intrapersonal intelligence skills and abilities?

2. The definition of *intelligences* includes the notion of having the *potential* to develop skills and abilities. Why is having *potential* important to the process of strengthening one's sense of self-efficacy?

3. How are critical thinking skills an essential part of the logical-mathematical, spatial, and naturalist intelligences?

PERSONALITY TYPES

1. Which personality preferences would feel natural and comfortable using the strategies in the "Attitude and Beliefs" section? Which personality preferences might resist or feel uncomfortable using skills such as positive self-talk, affirmations, or strengthening internal locus of control?

2. What differences might be observed between the way people with an Extraversion personality preference and people with an Introversion personality preference focus their attention on issues related to self-esteem and self-efficacy?

3. How would people with a Sensing personality preference differ from people with an Intuition personality preference in terms of ways they would work on the Analyzing Level of Bloom's Taxonomy?

Terms to Know

By yourself or with a partner, practice reciting or writing definitions for the following terms. You may also practice defining these terms by using the online flashcards or comparing your answers to the online glossary.

self-talk p. 44

positive self-talk p. 44

negative self-talk p. 44

affirmations p. 44

fear of failure p. 45

test anxiety p. 46

locus of control p. 48

internal locus of control p. 48

external locus of control p. 48

self-esteem p. 50

self-efficacy p. 50

critical thinking p. 55

fact p. 56

opinion p. 56

Bloom's Taxonomy p. 58

Remembering Level p. 59

Understanding Level p. 59

Applying Level p. 60

Analyzing Level p. 60

Evaluating Level p. 60

Creating Level p. 61

 Access Chapter 2 Flashcards and Online Glossary in your College Success CourseMate, accessed through *CengageBrain.com*.

Learning Objectives Review

1 *Discuss strategies, such as self-talk, affirmations, managing fear of failure, and locus of control, to adjust attitudes and beliefs to create a powerful mindset for success.*

- Attitudes and beliefs are key factors in the formation of a person's mindset, which is how people see the world and see themselves. One's mindset affects performance, outcomes, and interactions with other people.

- Using positive self-talk and affirmations, focusing on the present, dealing with fear of failure, and developing an internal locus of control can strengthen a person's mindset.

- *Positive self-talk* and *negative self-talk* have opposite effects on individuals' mindset. *Affirmations*, which are positive statements used as motivators, reinforce positive self-talk.

- Placing a focus on the present shifts attention to making changes now.

- *Fear of failure* is a belief pattern that hinders progress. A variety of strategies exists to deal with the fear of failure and excessive fear of failure that may lead to test anxiety.

- *Locus of control* is a belief pattern that reflects whether a person believes external or internal forces control circumstances in personal life. Strategies can be used to develop or strengthen the internal locus of control

2 *Define self-esteem and self-efficacy and explain how to strengthen each to create a more powerful mindset for learning.*

- *Self-esteem* is the perception a person has of himself or herself as a human being. Characteristics differ between individuals with high self-esteem and individuals with low self-esteem.

- *Self-efficacy* is an individual's belief in his or her abilities to accomplish a specific task or to demonstrate a set of related skills at a specific level of performance. Using strategies to create a stronger sense of self-efficacy contributes to improved performance, increased self-confidence, and greater motivation.

3 *Define critical thinking; discuss critical thinking behaviors and the six levels of Bloom's Taxonomy.*

- *Critical thinking* is a higher-order, purposeful, skillful thinking that focuses on gathering, understanding, and utilizing relevant information to reach logical, trustworthy conclusions about what to believe, what to do, or what decisions to make in everyday life.

- Critical thinkers display a variety of characteristics and skills. Six basic guidelines help individuals become more critical thinkers.

- *Bloom's Taxonomy* is a classification system with six levels of thinking or cognitive processes. Each level represents different levels of difficulty or complexity of thinking. Specific kinds of activities and question words appear for each level.
- The six levels in Bloom's Taxonomy, arranged from most basic to most complex, are the following: Remembering, Understanding, Applying, Analyzing, Evaluating, and Creating.

Chapter 2   Review Questions

Answers appear on page B2.

True or False? See Test-Taking Strategies 1–9 in Appendix A.

_____ 1. A mindset is defined as a stubborn way of viewing the world.

_____ 2. Creating a powerful mindset requires a willingness to examine attitudes and to adjust or change beliefs.

_____ 3. Positive self-talk, affirmations, and self-efficacy reflect positive attitudes and beliefs about oneself.

_____ 4. The high and the low self-esteem cycles show opposite characteristics for the use of self-talk, self-confidence, relationships, achievement, self-perception, economic level, and form of employment.

_____ 5. Critical thinking always leads to critiquing and criticizing the work of others.

_____ 6. Bloom's Taxonomy proves that a person can work effectively on the Evaluating Level before working on the Understanding and the Remembering Levels.

_____ 7. Asking questions and questioning the validity or accuracy of information are ways to improve critical thinking skills.

_____ 8. Critical thinkers tend to be inquisitive, think reflectively, evaluate their thinking and decision-making skills, and show awareness of different levels of thinking skills.

_____ 9. To examine opposite points of view, a person needs to be open-minded and willing to put his or her personal beliefs and opinions to the side.

_____ 10. Facts are objective; opinions are subjective.

Multiple Choice See Test-Taking Strategies 10–15 in Appendix A.

_____ 1. Creating a powerful mindset does not involve
   a. a willingness to examine personal attitudes and beliefs.
   b. using critical thinking skills in academic and personal situations.
   c. limiting personal growth or taking away your ability to control situations.
   d. a willingness to examine patterns or levels of thinking.

_____ 2. Self-talk
   a. is not always positive or encouraging.
   b. is the ever-busy inner voice that can affect your behavior, self-esteem, level of confidence, and motivation.
   c. may be positive or negative.
   d. is all of the above.

_____ 3. Well-written, effective affirmations

    a. restate the negative behaviors you do not wish to continue.

    b. are short, in the present tense, and positive.

    c. are short, in the future tense, and avoid using the word _I_.

    d. have all of the above characteristics.

_____ 4. Which of the following statements would not be made by a person with a fear of failure for an upcoming test?

    a. I have studied but I already know I don't test well so I probably won't pass.

    b. I am going to lose my scholarship if I fail this test.

    c. I have an internal locus of control so I take responsibility for the results.

    d. I don't want to be in class when the graded tests are returned.

_____ 5. Students can create a more powerful mindset about taking tests by

    a. mentally rehearsing the process of taking tests successfully.

    b. creating a plan of action to succeed.

    c. changing negative self-talk to positive self-talk.

    d. creating a plan of action to succeed, which includes using a variety of study strategies and test-taking skills.

_____ 6. Which of the following statements is not true?

    a. Self-efficacy is the overall perception you have of yourself in social situations.

    b. Improved self-esteem has a direct effect on creating a positive mindset.

    c. Having high self-esteem and a strong sense of self-efficacy increases academic resilience, persistence, and motivation.

    d. A person who is willing to try new ways, perceives "failures" as lessons, uses positive approaches, and is willing to seek advice shows characteristics of having high self-esteem.

_____ 7. Which statement is true about locus of control?

    a. Students with an external locus of control experience less stress and higher self-esteem than students with an internal locus of control.

    b. Reversing self-defeating thought patterns and learning to take more control and responsibility for situations are two ways to move from an external locus of control to an internal locus of control.

    c. When a student with an internal locus of control performs poorly on a test or a task, he or she tends to become angry and frustrated.

    d. Learning to use the locus of control strengthens a person's ability to control the behavior of people in groups or in personal relationships.

_____ 8. Critical thinking involves

    a. learning to use lower-order cognitive skills, such as the skills in Bloom's Taxonomy, before tackling higher-order thinking skills.

    b. striving to utilize relevant information to draw conclusions about what to do or what to believe.

    c. questioning, analyzing, and validating information.

    d. doing all of the above.

_____ 9. The three higher-order, more advanced critical thinking levels in Bloom's Taxonomy are

    a. understanding, applying, and creating.

    b. analyzing, evaluating, and applying.

    c. analyzing, evaluating, and creating.

    d. remembering, understanding, and applying.

_____ 10. Which statement about Bloom's Taxonomy is inaccurate?

    a. The question words used often indicate the difficulty level of thinking according to Bloom's Taxonomy.

    b. The question words *construct, invent, compile, critique,* and *interpret* are higher-order question words than the words *identify, label, list, name,* and *compare.*

    c. All skilled readers can work on the analyzing, evaluating, and creating levels in Bloom's Taxonomy even when they are not able to recall facts or demonstrate an understanding of the basic concepts.

    d. Performing adequately on the first two levels of Bloom's Taxonomy is usually required before effectively using the levels of applying, analyzing, evaluating, and creating.

 Access Chapter 2 Enhanced Quiz and Chapter 2 Study Guide in your College Success CourseMate, accessed through *CengageBrain.com*.

Access all Chapter 2 Online Materials in your College Success CourseMate, accessed through *CengageBrain.com*.

3 Using Time Effectively

© iStockphoto.com/Viorika

Time management is perhaps the most essential of all study skills because it lays the foundation for you to have adequate time and structure to utilize all other study skills. Knowing how to maintain a focus and concentrate on tasks leads to greater productivity, more successes, and less stress. Time management skills paired with concentration strategies result in taking better control of time and your ability to balance the academic, work, and leisure areas of your life. Time is a precious commodity, and you will benefit by managing time effectively.

1 SKILLFUL TIME MANAGERS

Time Management with Personality Types

The Pie of Life

Strategies for Skilled Time Managers

2 SCHEDULES AND STRATEGIES

Term Schedules

Weekly Schedules

Daily Schedules

3 FOCUS AND CONCENTRATION

An Ideal Study Area

Essential Concentration/Focusing Strategies

Manage Distractors

 Access Chapter 3 Expanded Chapter Outline in your College Success CourseMate, accessed through *CengageBrain.com*.

YOUR CHAPTER MAPPING

After reading information under each heading, return to the chapter visual mapping below. Add key words to show subheadings and important details related to each heading.

 Access Chapter 3 Visual Mapping in your College Success CourseMate, accessed through *CengageBrain.com*.

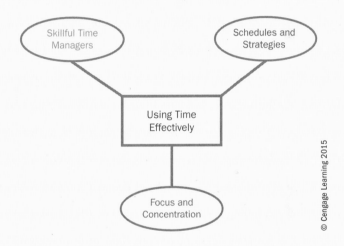

© Cengage Learning 2015

LEARNING OBJECTIVES

1 *Discuss how skillful time managers create balance, prioritize tasks, and use task schedules in their approaches to managing time.*

2 *Create and use effective term, weekly, and daily schedules to manage your time.*

3 *Explain how to create an ideal study area, use time effectively by maintaining a focus and concentrating, and manage internal and external distractions.*

Using Time Effectively

ANSWER, SCORE, and **RECORD** your profile before you read this chapter. If you need to review the process, refer to the complete directions given in the profile for Chapter 1 on page 4.

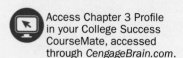 Access Chapter 3 Profile in your College Success CourseMate, accessed through *CengageBrain.com*.

ONLINE: You can complete the profile and get your score online in this textbook's College Success CourseMate.

	YES	NO
1. I use strategies to create a comfortable balance in my school, work, and leisure life.	_____	_____
2. I make a list of things I need to do and then start with the tasks that seem the easiest or most interesting to do.	_____	_____
3. I create a specific task schedule or list of steps to use to work on a task or project during a specific period of time.	_____	_____
4. I organize my activities and my time by making and following a weekly time-management schedule.	_____	_____
5. I usually study for two or three hours during the week for every class.	_____	_____
6. I often study for three hours or more in a row so I can stay current with my reading and homework assignments.	_____	_____
7. I have little control over the people or things that break my concentration or disrupt my study time.	_____	_____
8. I use effective strategies to concentrate and block out internal and external distractors when I study.	_____	_____
9. The places where I study have a low noise level, at least two sources of lighting, and an uncluttered workspace.	_____	_____
10. I am confident that I have the skills necessary to manage my time effectively and maintain a focus and concentrate on the work that I am doing.	_____	_____

QUESTIONS LINKED TO THE CHAPTER LEARNING OBJECTIVES:

Questions 1–3: objective 1   Questions 7–9: objective 3

Questions 4–6: objective 2   Question 10: all objectives

Skillful Time Managers

1 *Discuss how skillful time managers create balance, prioritize tasks, and use task schedules in their approaches to managing time.*

Everyone faces demands on their time. Students, parents, professors, secretaries, delivery drivers, CEOs, accountants, researchers, and anyone else you can name face demands on time. Our lives are busy, and for many people responsibilities and expectations are high. To use time the most effectively, to get the most out of each day, and to manage daily obligations and still enjoy free time require taking control of the hours so your days are meaningful and rewarding. By becoming an effective time manager, you experience or do the following:

- Increase awareness of time and how you use it
- Gain sense of control by identifying what needs to be done and making time to do it
- Gain more time by not wasting time, floundering or spinning aimlessly in circles
- Get started more quickly on projects or tasks and procrastinate less
- Increase productivity by setting time aside to do what needs to be done
- Boost confidence and self-esteem each time you complete goals on time
- Increase motivation when you begin to see progress and results
- Become more punctual, meet deadlines, and complete goals
- Establish structure for your daily routines
- Take responsibility by valuing your time and that of others
- Learn faster and more efficiently during focused, specific study blocks
- Improve grades by making more time available to study and review
- Meet obligations and commitments with less stress and frustration
- Recognize and stop unproductive use of time when you have time pressures
- Enjoy and appreciate social, family, and recreational time and events
- Organize priorities and show results
- Increase confidence in your ability to take charge of your life in an orderly way
- Strengthen time-management skills valued in the world of work

With so many advantages and benefits of managing time, why would anyone not want to improve time-management skills? Some people are resistant to time management for a variety of reasons, such as not wanting to be "controlled by a schedule" or "bound to something that takes away spontaneity." Often times, however, people resist becoming time managers due to a lack of time-management strategies or lack of know-how to change well-established personal patterns and routines. They are comfortable with the way they move through the days and the weeks and are not all that interested in changing what is familiar. Use **Exercise 3.1** to self-assess your time-management skills and the need for new strategies.

Time Management with Personality Types

As you recall from Chapter 1, the Myers-Briggs Type Indicator instrument discusses eight different personality preferences that combine in various ways to represent sixteen personality types. Four of these personality preferences may affect the

Time-Management Inventory

DIRECTIONS:

To assess your time-management skills or need for new time-management strategies, go to Exercise 3.1: Time-Management Inventory in Appendix C, page C4.

manner in which a person views time and time-management strategies: Sensing, Intuition, Judging, and Perceiving.

Sensing and Intuition: How You Prefer to Take In Information

Students with the *Sensing personality preference* tend to display the following characteristics related to time-management concepts and strategies:

- Prefer factual, concrete, and realistic approaches to take in information
- Show interest in the accuracy of details
- Value established, proven methods
- Work in a logical, sequential way
- Take in information through the senses; for time management, prefer to see a schedule or a plan that shows how they intend to use time

Students with a Sensing personality preference tend to accept and even embrace creating and following time-management schedules. They use specific blocks of time to complete assignments, and they use the guidelines to schedule sufficient study blocks to meet the requirements of their courses. They get a sense of comfort, control, and confidence knowing that they have control of their time and have created plans of action that work and create balance in their lives.

Students with the *Intuition personality preference* tend to display the following characteristics related to time-management concepts and strategies:

- Rely on hunches or guesses for how to process information
- Use imaginative, creative, or inventive ways to perform tasks
- Tend to create unique personal strategies or approaches
- Focus on big picture and develop details during a process

Students who find that the most natural or comfortable way to process information is to let details or steps unfold once they get started, or students who use hunches or intuition to figure out how to organize time or work on assignments, may find scheduling and using time-management schedules uncomfortable or difficult. This does not mean that they should forego creating a schedule. The time-management schedules or task schedules for students with the Intuition personality preference may be more "big picture" or "global" in nature. Their schedules may simply label blocks of time, but their intuitive approaches come into play when they sit down to begin working on a specific subject in a specific block of time. Their approach may be to start on the assignment and figure out how to get to the outcome as they explore various possibilities. They may choose not to create task schedules because the steps unfold as a part of the process and are not anticipated or planned in advance.

CONCEPT CHECK 3.2

How does your personality preference or learning style preference affect your attitude and approach toward time management? Be specific.

Judging and Perceiving: How You Prefer to Approach or Structure Your Life

Students with the *Judging personality preference* tend to display the following characteristics related to time-management concepts and strategies:

- Prefer organized, structured, orderly approaches
- Organize using systematic, methodical strategies
- Make short-term and long-term goals with plans of action to complete
- Use lists to plan time, projects, or assignments
- Avoid completing projects at the last minute

Students with a Judging personality preference tend to accept and even embrace creating and following time-management schedules. They work steadily to complete goals and complete assignments before the deadlines occur. They are most comfortable with clear expectations and feel that the most natural way to approach life is to be organized, goal-oriented, and structured. They experience a sense of comfort and confidence knowing that they have control over their time and have created plans of action that work. Notice that this personality preference mirrors the characteristics of the Sensing personality preference.

Students with the *Perceiving personality preference* tend to display the following characteristics related to time-management concepts and strategies:

- Prefer to be more spontaneous and flexible
- Feel constrained and even stressed by schedules
- Are energized by last-minute pressure to meet deadlines
- Perform with bursts of energy

Students with a Perceiving personality personality preference tend to be the most resistant to using time-management strategies and schedules. These students often think about or ponder their approach to assignments, but they wait to start closer to the deadlines. They are not, however, starting cold; they have thought about the assignment, but they postpone getting down to the nitty gritty details of working on the assignment itself. The productive final burst of energy close to deadlines often results in work getting done on time. This last-minute approach has its drawbacks. If the student underestimates the time needed for the assignment or gets sidetracked by other activities, the assignment may be late or not reflect the quality work that the student is capable of doing. Students with this Perceiving personality preference benefit by doing the following:

- Accept that their approach to life works for many things but not necessarily for academic requirements and performance
- Show a willingness to incorporate modified time-management strategies and schedules into their approach for dealing with commitments and obligations

- Use the earlier blocks of time on a time-management schedule to examine the topic, understand the assignment, and begin to think about how to proceed to complete the assignment
- Schedule longer or more frequent blocks of time close to the deadline to use the bursts of energy to complete the assignment on time

Learning Flexibility

Effective learners are able to adapt or modify their approaches to learning. Acquiring new skills from other learning styles or personality preferences strengthens students' abilities to handle a greater variety of learning situations, processes, and assignments. Following are examples of students acquiring skills or strategies from a different or opposite preference style:

- A student with the Extraversion personality preference can learn to become more reflective and refrain from being so open. A student with the Introversion personality preference can learn to become more sociable and comfortable discussing with others.
- A student with the Sensing personality preference can learn to become more flexible and open to more creative ways. A student with the Intuition personality preference can learn to give more attention to details and concrete information.
- A student with the Thinking personality preference can learn to be less rigid or fixed in logic and more open to compassion and feelings. A student with the Feeling personality preference can learn to use more logic and less empathy to make decisions.
- A student with the Judging personality preference can learn to be more flexible and spontaneous. A student with the Perceiving personality preference can learn to add more structure and organization by planning tasks.
- A visual learner can learn to incorporate more auditory and kinesthetic strategies. An auditory learner can learn to incorporate more visual and kinesthetic strategies. A kinesthetic learner can learn to incorporate more visual and auditory strategies.

In other words, all types of learners benefit by expanding their range of strategies and approaches. Making a conscious effort to use a variety of strategies, some of which are not from your learning style preferences, strengthens your ability to perform effectively in different situations and with various tasks, assignments, or requirements. In terms of using time-management strategies, it is important to remember that we live in a world that revolves in many ways around time. Being punctual, meeting deadlines, and organizing study or work demands reflect your character and influence the impression you make on others you encounter. Learning to manage time is essential to function in our time-oriented world.

The Pie of Life

Time management is a set of skills designed to help you monitor and use time effectively to increase performance, gain a sense of control over many aspects of your life, and achieve goals. As a student, you must continually balance three main areas in your life: school, work, and leisure. How you spend your time in these three main areas will vary term by term and will be influenced by your personal goals, needs, and interests. Imbalances in these three areas of life can lead to an array of negative consequences, including frequent frustration, low productivity, resentment, confusion, or a lack of motivation.

Time management is a set of skills designed to help you monitor and use time effectively to increase performance, gain a sense of control over many aspects in your life, and achieve goals.

CHAPTER 3
REFLECTIVE WRITING 1

 On separate paper, in a journal, or in this textbook's College Success CourseMate, respond to the following questions.

1. How do you see yourself as an effective time manager? If you are effective, what habits or processes do you use that build your confidence that you are an effective time manager? If you do not see yourself as an effective time manager, what attitudes or behaviors do you demonstrate that lead to limited or weak skills as a time manager?

2. What do you see as benefits for learning to become an effective time manager? How would it affect your performance as a student? How would it affect your personal life? How would it affect you on a job or in your career?

 Access Chapter 3 Reflective Writing 1 in your College Success CourseMate, accessed through *CengageBrain.com*.

The *Pie of Life* is a graphic that shows how much time you dedicate to each of the three main areas of your life: *school*, *work*, and *leisure*. **Figure 3.1** shows the activities, responsibilities, and commitments that are a part of each section of the Pie of Life. A balanced Pie of Life is not necessarily divided into three equal parts. The amount of time dedicated to school, work, and leisure vary according to an individual's circumstances, goals, and values. Consider the different Pies of Life for the following students:

The **Pie of Life** is a graphic that shows how much time you dedicate to each of the three main areas of your life: school, work, and leisure.

- A student who lives in a dorm and does not work while attending school
- A student who works a graveyard shift and attends college full time
- A student who lives at home and has few responsibilities other than school
- A student who attends school full time on an athletic scholarship
- A student who is a single parent and is enrolled in college part time
- A full-time student who has three children and family responsibilities

FIGURE 3.1   Three Main Areas of the Pie of Life

School	Work	Leisure
Classes	Work/Job	Family time
Homework	Parenting	Social time with friends
Study/review time	Household chores	Recreation
Tutoring	Errands, shopping	Exercise
Study groups	Volunteer work	Personal "alone" time
Test preparation	Committee work	Hobbies
Lab projects		Television, movies, music
Meetings		Computer time
Conferences		Church
Team practices/games		

© Cengage Learning

Access Chapter 3 Topics In-Depth: Interactive Pie of Life in your College Success CourseMate, accessed through *CengageBrain.com*.

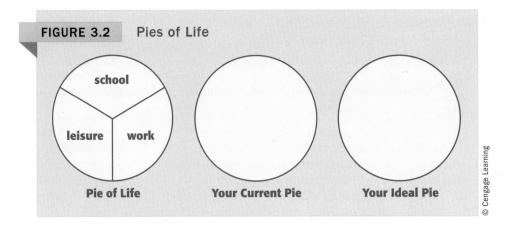

FIGURE 3.2   Pies of Life

Pie of Life — school / leisure / work

Your Current Pie

Your Ideal Pie

© Cengage Learning

CONCEPT CHECK   3.4

What does it mean to have a "balanced Pie of Life"? What would your balanced Pie of Life look like?

In **Figure 3.2**, the first circle shows a Pie of Life divided into three equal parts for school, work, and leisure. Think about your current use of time for these three main areas of the Pie of Life. Then divide the second circle to show the *estimated amount of time* you currently spend per week in each of the three areas. In the last circle, adjust the lines to show your *ideal* Pie of Life that reflects the balance that you wish to obtain.

Achieving your ideal Pie of Life requires a willingness to examine the ways you currently use time and to commit to exploring new strategies that will improve your time-management skills. Change is not always easy, but the benefits of having a more balanced life make the process rewarding and worthwhile. In **Exercise 3.2** you will have the opportunity to complete a three-day time log to examine how you use time.

How to Use Time: A Three-Day Time Log

EXERCISE 3.2

PURPOSE: Creating a more effective balance of time in your life begins with an awareness of your daily patterns, habits, and priorities for using time. Keep a log of how you spend your time for three complete days. After analyzing the results of your three-day time log, you can begin applying time-management strategies to create a more effective balance in your life. (A form for a 7-day time log is available in this textbook's College Success CourseMate.)

DIRECTIONS: Go to Exercise 3.2 in Appendix C, pages C5–C6. Complete the following steps:

1. **Step 1:** On the chart, record all your activities for three days. *Be specific.* For example, you might write: in class, met with tutor, lab work, team practice, job, laundry, television, gym, hobby, e-mail, talked on phone, commuted, napped, or ate dinner.

2. **Step 2:** After completing your three-day log, count the number of hours spent each day in the areas shown on the final chart. Some activities may fit into more than one category; however, count them only once in the most appropriate category.

3. **Step 3: Class Discussion:** How do the results of your three-day log match your ideal Pie of Life as shown in Figure 3.2? Explain.

Access Chapter 3 Topics In-Depth: 7-Day Time Log in your College Success CourseMate, accessed through *CengageBrain.com*.

What time-management strategies help you break inertia and get you moving on a productive path? What are common consequences of not using effective time-management strategies in all three areas of your life: school, work, and social settings?

© PNC/Digital Vision/Getty Images

Strategies for Skilled Time Managers

Skilled time managers demonstrate a confidence in dealing with demands on time and meeting important deadlines and obligations. Skilled time managers rely on their ability to create well-planned, balanced schedules and use the schedules to organize time and tasks. Effective time-management strategies guide you through the process to produce the desired results.

Create Better Balance

You only have so many hours in a week. If your Pie of Life is unbalanced, you have two choices:

1. **Learn more efficient ways to do things.** Explore more efficient ways to study, to avoid wasting time during study blocks, to organize tasks at school and work, and to complete daily chores. Use goal-setting strategies to organize, finish projects, and achieve goals in less time without reducing the quality of the finished product. Spend less time floundering and more time using strategies that organize you in an efficient, focused, and productive way. Become an "efficiency manager" as well as a "time manager."

2. **Use the Increase-Decrease Method to change the boundaries in your Pie of Life.** The *Increase-Decrease Method* involves increasing or decreasing time used in one area of life in order to make more time for another area of life. Begin by identifying the section of your Pie of Life that needs more time to create a better balance in your life. As you increase time in this section, you will need to decrease time allocated to one or both of the remaining sections of your pie. For example, if your goal is to increase the amount of time allocated to *school*, you will need to decrease the time you spend in the area of *work* or *leisure* or both. Do not be too quick to say, "That won't work" or "That's not possible in my situation." Finding a better balance involves a willingness to change old behaviors and routines and to give possibilities a chance to work for you.

The **Increase-Decrease Method** involves increasing or decreasing time used in one area of life in order to make more time for another area of life.

FIGURE 3.3   ABC Method to Prioritize Tasks

1. List all the tasks that you want to achieve within a specific time period.

2. Use the letter "A" to label your highest-priority tasks—the most important or the most urgent tasks on your list to complete.

3. Use the letter "B" to label the tasks of medium importance and less urgency to complete.

4. Use the letter "C" to label the tasks of lowest importance and urgency— the ones you wish to complete but only after the higher-priority A and B tasks are achieved.

5. Return to the "A" list to prioritize these tasks. Identify the order in which you plan to complete these tasks.

6. Continue prioritizing your "B" and "C" lists of tasks to complete.

7. Use goal-setting and motivational strategies to begin working on your sequenced list of tasks. As you complete one task, start on the next.

© Cengage Learning 2015

CONCEPT CHECK   3.5

In the ABC Method to prioritize tasks, what do the letters A, B, and C represent? How does this method work?

The **ABC Method** is a strategy to prioritize tasks or projects according to rank of importance or urgency.

Prioritize Tasks

Having multiple tasks to manage, goals to achieve, and projects to tackle is a situation that many people face. Sometimes multitasking is possible, but trying to multitask often results in a lack of productivity or a variety of tasks that are started but are not completed. The lack of success results in feelings of being overwhelmed, frustrated, or defeated. Skilled time managers know the importance of organizing and prioritizing what needs to be done. It takes only a few minutes to organize tasks from most important or urgent to the least important or least urgent. The result is a logically sequenced list of tasks or goals that serve as a road map for greater productivity and success. The *ABC Method* is a strategy to prioritize tasks or projects according to rank of importance or urgency. **Figure 3.3** shows the steps to use in the ABC Method.

Create Task Schedules

A *task schedule* is a step-by-step plan for completing a specific task in a specific block of time. Taking a few minutes at the beginning of a block of time to create a task schedule structures the block of time. **Figure 3.4** shows a task schedule for a study block. Task schedules help you to do the following:

A **task schedule** is a step-by-step plan for completing a specific task in a specific block of time.

CONCEPT CHECK   3.6

How can you use task schedules with your weekly schedule? What is the value of using task schedules?

- Increase your efficiency by organizing the process before your begin
- Waste less time trying to decide where to begin or what to do next
- Motivate you to identify what you need to do and to create a plan of action
- Increase motivation by planning a reward upon completion of the task
- Perform in a time-efficient and an organized, logical manner
- Set immediate goals for study blocks, job-related tasks, personal responsibilities, or household chores

FIGURE 3.4   Task Schedule for a Study Block

Step 1: Specific goal: Review math class and do math homework pp. 26–33.

Step 2: Target date and time: Wednesday, 10:00–11:00 AM

Step 3: Individual steps:

1. Review class notes and rework class problem sets.

2. Read pages 26–32. Highlight key points. Study examples.

3. Do even-numbered problems on p. 33.

4. Check answers with answer key. Study/rework any incorrect problems.

Step 4: Reward: Extrinsic: Watch my favorite show on television.

© Cengage Learning

EXERCISE 3.3

Transfer These Skills: Prioritizing and Creating a Task Schedule

PURPOSE: Using the ABC Method to prioritize important things you need to accomplish and creating task schedules to use as you work on prioritized items are effective strategies skillful time managers rely on to be productive and efficient.

DIRECTIONS: Complete the following steps to demonstrate your use of these strategies.

1. Make a list of your upcoming assignments, obligations, projects, and goals for your academic, personal, and work life.

2. Use the ABC Method. Group the tasks into A, B, C groups.

3. Within each A, B, C group, number the order or sequence you will use to tackle and complete the tasks within each group.

4. Select one item in the "A" list. Create a task schedule that shows step-by-step what you need to do to complete the task in a timely manner.

CHECK POINT 3.1

Answers appear on page B3.

True or False? See Test-Taking Strategies 1–9 in Appendix A.

_____ 1. Balance in the areas of school, work, and leisure often results in less stress, greater productivity, and a more positive lifestyle.

_____ 2. For realistic balance in one's daily life, a person should allocate equal time to school, work, and leisure activities.

_____ 3. The majority of *school* time in the Pie of Life occurs within the classroom.

_____ 4. The main goal of the Increase-Decrease Method is to decrease social and leisure time.

_____ 5. A task schedule should be used only for "A" level tasks or projects.

_____ 6. A person who attempts to begin too many tasks simultaneously would benefit from using the ABC Method.

 Access Chapter 3 Practice Quiz 1 in your College Success CourseMate, accessed through *CengageBrain.com*.

Schedules and Strategies

(2) *Create and use effective term, weekly, and daily schedules to manage your time.*

Well-designed schedules serve as road maps to guide you through the months of an academic term, through each week, and through each day. Rather than being at the mercy of time, schedules empower you with the ability to take control of time. With schedules, *you* decide and plan how you wish to spend your time. Your skills as a time manager become lifelong skills that benefit you well in school, at home, and in your chosen career.

Term Schedules

A *term schedule* is a month-by-month calendar that shows important events and deadlines for the entire term. You can use a regular calendar, a monthly planner, an electronic organizer, or a computer calendar program for each month in your current academic term. At the beginning of each term, create your term schedule; include the items that appear in **Figure 3.5**.

> A **term schedule** is a month-by-month calendar that shows important events and deadlines for the entire term.

CONCEPT CHECK   3.7

What system will you use to create a term schedule? What specific details from Figure 3.5 will appear on your term schedule?

FIGURE 3.5	Items to Include on Your Term Schedule

1. Important deadlines for special projects, reports, and writing or lab assignments that appear on your course syllabi

2. Scheduled tests, midterms, and final exams

3. Special events, meetings, workshops, or conferences

4. Holidays

5. Scheduled times for tutors, study groups, or other support services

6. Personal appointments on or off campus

© Cengage Learning

Create a Term Schedule

EXERCISE 3.4

PURPOSE: Create a term schedule that provides you with an overview of the term and serves as a guide when you create your weekly schedule.

DIRECTIONS: Gather together your campus calendar, the syllabus from each of your courses, and your personal calendar of events to create a term schedule.

1. Use a month-by-month planner or calendar. On your calendar, enter the items shown in Figure 3.5.

2. Place your month-by-month calendars in the front of your notebook, or if you are using an electronic calendar program, refer to the monthly calendar at the beginning of each week when you create your weekly schedule.

3. Update your term calendar throughout the term with deadlines for new assignments or significant events.

 Access Chapter 3 Topics In-Depth: Quick Start Forms in your College Success CourseMate, accessed through *CengageBrain.com*.

Weekly Schedules

A *weekly schedule* is a detailed plan that serves as a guide for creating a manageable plan for each day of the week. While term schedules provide you with an overview of important events and deadlines on a month-to-month basis, weekly schedules focus your attention on details and requirements for the upcoming week. Using a weekly schedule helps you to maintain a focus and to organize, monitor, and regulate your use of time.

Unlike a time log made *after* you complete activities or tasks, a weekly time-management schedule is made *before* you engage in the activities. The weekly schedule becomes your plan, your guide, and your structure for the week. **Figure 3.6** shows a well-planned weekly schedule. A well-planned weekly schedule includes the following characteristics:

- **A realistic, balanced Pie of Life for school, work, and leisure**

- **Adequate time for study blocks:** Study blocks are scheduled throughout the week so you study on a regular basis, not just when you have assignments due or an upcoming test.

- **Sufficient time for online courses:** You will need to spend time listening to or viewing lectures, watching instructional videos, working and reworking problems, submitting written work, corresponding with the instructor, or engaging in discussion boards.

- **Effective use of all blocks of time:** Tighten up your schedule to avoid wasted blocks of time, such as an hour between classes or an hour or two after dinner.

- **Blocks of time for work and for leisure activities:** Your schedule shows your hours of employment. If your work hours change weekly, your weekly schedule reflects these changes. Your weekly schedule also shows time set aside for household chores, errands, exercise, recreation, social and family time, and daily routines, such as getting ready in the morning, commuting, or preparing and eating meals.

- **Strong, consistent patterns:** Patterns, such as specific times for studying specific classes, eating meals, doing chores, or engaging in recreation help you follow your schedule to the point that it becomes routine and habitual.

- **Time allocated to work on personal goals or prioritized items:** For example, if you want to jog three times a week or spend time in the park with your children twice a week, your schedule shows time set aside for those goals. Your schedule also shows adequate time to complete the steps on a task schedule for school, work, or personal life.

- **A routine time to sleep each night:** Going to bed about the same time each night helps stabilize your internal clock and your sleep-awake patterns. Short nights occasionally followed by long nights of sleep disrupt your normal rhythm and your natural flow of energy.

Five Steps to Create a Weekly Time-Management Schedule

Using a systematic approach to create your weekly time-management schedule helps you plan sufficient time for important areas of your daily life. **Figure 3.7** explains a five-step approach for developing your weekly time-management

> A **weekly schedule** is a detailed plan that serves as a guide for creating a manageable plan for each day of the week.

CONCEPT CHECK 3.8

How do you know if your weekly schedule is effective? What criteria could you use to assess your or another student's weekly schedule?

FIGURE 3.6   Example of a Weekly Time-Management Schedule

WEEKLY TIME-MANAGEMENT SCHEDULE

For the week of _____

Time	Monday	Tuesday	Wednesday	Thursday	Friday	Saturday	Sunday
12–6 AM	SLEEP →						
6–7:00	SLEEP →						
7–8:00	Get up, get ready, eat breakfast →					SLEEP	SLEEP
8–9:00	Commute to school →					Get up	Get up
9–10:00	PE Class	Online Math Course	PE Class	Online Math Course	PE Class	Breakfast	Breakfast
10–11:00	Online Math Course		Online Math Course		Study Math with TUTOR	Career Class	Get ready
11–12 NOON		LUNCH		LUNCH		Study Career	CHURCH
12–1:00	LUNCH	Computer Class	LUNCH	Computer Class	LUNCH	ERRANDS	CHURCH
1–2:00	Reading Class	Computer Class	Reading Class	Computer Class	Reading Class	LUNCH	LUNCH
2–3:00	Study Reading	Lab-Study Computer	Study Reading	Lab-Study Computer	Study Reading	CHORES	LEISURE
3–4:00	Study Reading	Lab-Study Computer	FLEX	Lab-Study Computer	FLEX	CHORES	LEISURE
4–5:00	Commute home →					Study Math	Online Math Course
5–6:00	DINNER →						
6–7:00	LEISURE	LEISURE	LEISURE	LEISURE	WORK	WORK	DINNER
7–8:00	Study Reading	WORKOUT	Study Computer	WORKOUT	WORK	WORK	Study Math
8–9:00	Study Reading		Study Computer		WORK	WORK	Study Computer
9–10:00	LEISURE		LEISURE		WORK	WORK	FLEX
10–11:00	LEISURE	↓	LEISURE	↓	WORK	WORK	PLAN WEEK
11–12 AM	SLEEP →				WORK	WORK	SLEEP

FIGURE 3.7	Five Steps for Creating a Weekly Time-Management Schedule

1. Write in all your fixed activities.
2. Write in your fixed study blocks for each class.
3. Add two or three flexible study blocks.
4. Add time for personal goals and personal responsibilities.
5. Schedule leisure, family, and social time.

© Cengage Learning

Access Chapter 3 Topics In-Depth: Quick Start Forms in your College Success CourseMate, accessed through *CengageBrain.com*.

schedule. The following points will help you develop and use your weekly schedule effectively:

- Each Sunday spend a few minutes planning your schedule for the upcoming week.

- Keep your weekly schedule in the front of your notebook or in your electronic organizer. Refer to your weekly schedule whenever you wish to make new plans or set up appointments.

- Use your schedule for the entire term. On occasion, you may need to make minor changes in your schedule to accommodate special events or work schedules.

- Apply the strategies discussed in the following five steps for creating a weekly time-management schedule.

Step 1: Write your fixed activities. *Fixed activities* are those activities that do not vary much from week to week. On your weekly schedule, write the following fixed activities in the appropriate time blocks:

Fixed activities are those activities that do not vary much from week to week.

1. Class times

2. Work schedule (employment)

3. Daily routines: getting ready in the morning, commuting

4. Meals: breakfast, lunch, and dinner

5. Special appointments

6. Sleep

Step 2: Write your fixed study blocks. *Fixed study blocks* are well-planned blocks of time set aside to study specific subjects during the course of the week. By having effective fixed study blocks, you place a high priority on having sufficient time to complete your reading and homework assignments, create study tools, use elaborative rehearsal, and practice retrieving information through ongoing review.

Fixed study blocks are well-planned blocks of time set aside to study specific subjects during the course of the week.

Step 3: Add several flexible study blocks. *Flex study blocks* are flexible blocks of time on a weekly schedule that you use only when you need them. Flex blocks are safety nets for extra study time. Identify two or three hours each week that

Flex study blocks are flexible blocks of time on a weekly schedule that you use only when you need them.

you can hold in reserve in case you need additional time to study for a specific class, prepare for a test, or complete a special project. On your weekly schedule, write *FLEX* for these time blocks. Unlike fixed study blocks, which you should use each time they appear on your schedule, if you do not need to use the flex blocks, *convert them to free time.*

Step 4: Add time for personal goals and responsibilities. Schedule time blocks to work specifically on important goals or personal responsibilities. If you do not set aside time specifically for these important goals, tasks, or responsibilities, you may find yourself postponing or procrastinating about them or ignoring them completely.

Step 5: Schedule leisure, family, and social time. Label the remaining time on your schedule as *family*, *social*, or *leisure.* For the upcoming week, you can specify plans for time blocks, such as "swimming," "movie," or "entertaining," or you can leave the time blocks open and flexible to do whatever you decide to do on that day in that time block. Having family, social, and leisure time is important for mental and physical health as well as for strong relationships. If you do not have adequate time on your schedule for these activities, explore ways to use the Increase-Decrease Method to find more social and leisure time.

CONCEPT CHECK 3.9

What are the five steps to use to create a weekly schedule? Why are the first three steps important to you as a student?

Five Basic Time-Management Strategies

The following five strategies provide additional guidelines for organizing your study blocks and using your time wisely for academic success.

1. **Use the 2:1 ratio to schedule fixed study blocks.** The *2:1 ratio* is a time-management technique that involves studying two hours for every one hour in class. For example, if your writing class meets for three hours each week, schedule six hours of studying *for the writing class* each week. Studying in college means more than just doing homework. The 2:1 ratio provides you, in most cases, with sufficient time not only to read, take notes, memorize, and elaborate on course work, but also to rehearse or review to keep information in long-term memory fresh and accessible.

   The **2:1 ratio** is a time-management technique that involves studying two hours for every one hour in class.

2. **Use the 3:1 ratio for independent study or online courses.** The *3:1 ratio* is a time-management technique that involves studying nine hours a week for three-credit independent study or online courses. Even though independent study and online courses offer students flexibility, they often require a higher level of self-discipline and time commitment to complete successfully. For three-credit independent study or online courses that have few or no in-class hours, you need to schedule a minimum of *nine hours* per week for coursework. Use the course syllabus to create a term schedule and your personal week-by-week schedule of assignments to ensure that you complete the course in a timely manner.

   The **3:1 ratio** is a time-management technique that involves studying nine hours a week for three-credit independent study or online courses.

3. **Use spaced practice.** *Spaced practice*, also known as *distributed practice*, is a time-management strategy that involves making multiple contacts with new information and spreading this contact over several days or weeks. Spaced practice limits the length of a study block and spreads study blocks out over time. Using spaced practice increases comprehension, retention, motivation, concentration, and productivity. You will spend less time rereading and relearning information. Following are important points to understand about spaced practice:

   Spaced practice, also known as *distributed practice*, is a time-management strategy that involves making multiple contacts with new information and spreading this contact over several days or weeks.

- You will understand and recall information better for a subject if you study it for one hour six times a week, or two hours three times a week, rather than study it for six hours on the same day.

- The breaks or rest intervals between every fifty-minute study block give your memory system time to sort, process, and connect information.

- After studying two or three hours (with short breaks between each fifty-minute study block), change to a different kind of activity, such as a leisure or social activity. Your thinking processes do not shut down when you step away from the books for a few hours. When you return to studying, you will be more alert and receptive to new information.

4. **Avoid marathon studying.** *Marathon studying*, also known as *massed practice*, occurs when you study more than three hours in a row. Three or more continuous hours of studying without a break leads to problems with productivity, concentration, and retention. Avoiding marathon studying will also help you avoid overloading your memory system.

   Marathon studying *is* acceptable in some learning situations that involve a creative flow of ideas or energy. Marathon studying may be appropriate for learning tasks such as painting, sculpting, constructing a model, or writing a research paper because tapping into the same channel of creativity and thought patterns at a later time may be more difficult to achieve. In such situations, scheduling longer study blocks is acceptable.

5. **Use trading time sparingly.** *Trading time* is a time-management technique that allows you to trade or exchange time blocks for two activities within the same day. Use this strategy when you need flexibility in your schedule to adjust to a special event. For example, if you want to participate in an unexpected social activity that will occur during your 7:00–9:00 PM study block, trade the study block with a 2:00–4:00 PM block of time you had set aside to spend with friends. Use trading time cautiously. If you trade time blocks too frequently, you will lose the sense of routine, and your self-discipline to follow your schedule may decline.

> **Marathon studying**, also known as *massed practice*, occurs when you study more than three hours in a row.

> **CONCEPT CHECK**   3.10
> *What is the difference between the 2:1 ratio and the 3:1 ratio? What is the difference between spaced practice and massed practice?*

> **Trading time** is a time-management technique that allows you to trade or exchange time blocks for two activities within the same day.

GROUP PROCESSING

A Collaborative Learning Activity

Form groups of three or four students. You will need to have a chart to record information. Select one member of your group to be the group recorder. Complete the following directions.

1. Divide a large chart into two columns. In the left column write all the problems the members of your group have encountered with managing time. List as many different ideas or problems as possible.

2. After you have a list of common problems, brainstorm possible solutions. Write the possible solutions in the right column. You may provide more than one possible solution for each problem. Be prepared to share your list of problems and possible solutions with the class.

FIGURE 3.8   Essential Strategies for Scheduling Fixed Study Blocks

- Label and use each study block for one specific subject.
- Schedule at least one study block every day of the week.
- Schedule a math study block every day.
- Study during your most alert times of the day.
- Schedule your hardest or least-liked subject early in the day.
- Schedule a study block right *before* a class that involves discussions or student participation.
- Schedule a study block right *after* a lecture or a math class.

© Cengage Learning

Essential Strategies for Scheduling Fixed Study Blocks

Learning to become a time manager involves a willingness to adjust behaviors, attitudes, and ways you use time. To succeed as a time manager, you will need to anticipate change, be willing to relax or replace your old patterns, and be patient with yourself as you make the necessary adjustments. As you learn to use your weekly schedule, you may at times recognize that you are wandering from your time-management plan. Do not be hard on yourself or discard the schedule. Instead, recognize that change requires adjustments. Return to your schedule and get yourself back on track.

Creating an effective weekly schedule helps you get off to a good start and experience the benefits of using time management. **Figure 3.8** provides you with seven essential strategies to use as you schedule your fixed study blocks.

Label and use each study block for one specific subject. Labeling a block "study" does not provide you with a specific study plan and tends to promote an ineffective habit of studying whatever feels to be of the greatest urgency. Instead, use specific labels such as *Study English*, *Study Math*, or *Study Psychology*. Plan to use the entire study block for one subject. Jumping from one subject to another within a one-hour block disrupts the process of creating a "mindset" for the subject matter. Use the entire fifty-minute study block to review previous work, complete the current assignment, make notes or other study tools, and review. At the end of fifty minutes, give yourself a ten-minute break before moving into the next hour of studying.

Schedule at least one study block every day of the week. Spreading your study times throughout the entire week is a good spaced practice strategy, and you will experience less stress and frustration. Studying long hours during the weekdays and then engaging mainly in leisure or social activities on the weekend is ineffective.

Schedule a math study block every day. Math involves working with steps and processes, the kind of knowledge that requires repetition, repetition, and more repetition. Studying math on a daily basis provides essential time for repetition and to practice increasing problem-solving speed and accuracy. When possible, schedule a math study block right after your math class; on the days of the week that you do not have a math class, schedule your math study block during your alert times of the day.

CONCEPT CHECK   **3.11**

What specific strategies or guidelines can you use to schedule study blocks for your most difficult class, a Spanish class, a math class, and a history lecture class?

Study during your most alert times of the day. Study when you feel the most mentally sharp, alert, and focused, not when you know your body and eyes are physically fatigued. Mornings, midafternoons, and early evenings are often the most productive times to study. Studying late at night or right after a meal is often less productive. Use low-energy or low-attention times for tasks that do not require high cognitive functioning.

Schedule your hardest or least-liked subjects early in the day. By placing the hardest or least-liked subjects first on your study priorities, you are able to use a more alert mind and focused attention to tackle the assignments and process new information.

Schedule a study block right before a class that involves discussion or student participation. This puts you in the mindset for the course, refreshes your memory of key concepts, and provides you with time to rehearse as needed.

Schedule a study block right after a lecture or a math class. Taking notes is your main task during a lecture class. By scheduling a study time right *after* the class, you can review your notes, compare them with other students' notes, fill in missing details, and reorganize your notes in more meaningful ways while the information is still fresh in your mind. Scheduling a study time right after a math class reinforces the processes and provides immediate practice working problem sets or applications while the class explanations or examples are fresh in your memory.

Exercise 3.5 guides you through the process of creating your weekly time-management schedule. Examine the effectiveness of your schedule during the first three weeks of using it. If you do not follow your plans for some of the scheduled blocks of time, analyze the situations to identify what happened. Adjust your schedule the following week if necessary. As you learn these skills, remember that the time-management skills you learn now are highly prized skills recognized and admired in both the work force and the academic world.

Creating a Weekly Schedule

EXERCISE 3.5

DIRECTIONS: Go to Exercise 3.5 in Appendix C, pages C7–C8, for a weekly time-management form and a Time-Management Self-Assessment Checklist. Photocopy the weekly schedule form to use for this exercise or download the form from online Chapter 3 in the Topics In-Depth: Quick Start Forms. Complete the following directions.

1. **Step 1: Use the steps diagrammed on the following page to create a weekly time-management schedule.** Use a pencil at first so you can rearrange time blocks and make adjustments as needed to create a manageable and realistic schedule.

2. **Step 2: Mentally walk through each day** on your schedule to determine that it is realistic. Make adjustments if necessary.

3. **Step 3: Complete the Time-Management Self-Assessment Checklist** on page C8 in Appendix C. Use that information to make any necessary adjustments on your schedule.

4. **Step 4: Color-code your schedule** so it is easier to see at a glance. Use one color for your classes; another for study times; and a third for leisure, family, and social time. Use a fourth color for work or leave the spaces without color coding.

(continued)

Exercise 3.5 (continued)

5. **Step 5: Make a copy of your schedule** to keep in the front of your notebook if your instructor asks you to turn in your original schedule and the Time-Management Self-Assessment Checklist.

6. **Step 6: Begin following your schedule** as soon as possible. Several times during the day, indicate on your schedule how often you followed it as planned. Create a code system such as using stars for blocks that worked as planned and checks for blocks that you did not follow according to the plan.

7. **Step 7: Use your schedule for a full seven days.** After you have used your schedule for a full week, your instructor may ask you to turn in your first schedule and the Time-Management Self-Assessment Checklist.

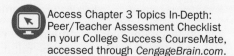

Access Chapter 3 Topics In-Depth: Peer/Teacher Assessment Checklist in your College Success CourseMate, accessed through *CengageBrain.com*.

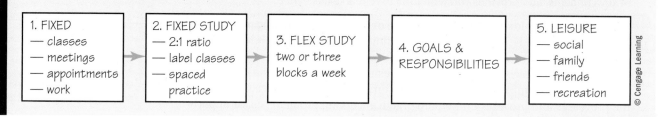

1. FIXED	2. FIXED STUDY	3. FLEX STUDY	4. GOALS & RESPONSIBILITIES	5. LEISURE
— classes — meetings — appointments — work	— 2:1 ratio — label classes — spaced practice	two or three blocks a week		— social — family — friends — recreation

© Cengage Learning

Daily Schedules

> A **daily schedule** is a specific list of tasks that you plan to achieve over the course of a day.

A *daily schedule* is a specific list of tasks that you plan to achieve over the course of a day. It is your to-do list that helps you move through the day efficiently. Use an index card, a daily planner, or an electronic organizer for your daily schedule. Each night before you go to bed, take a few minutes to prepare your daily schedule for the next day's activities. Keep the schedule in a convenient place for quick reference. **In Figure 3.9, after examining the example of the daily schedule on the left, make a daily schedule for yourself in the box on the right.**

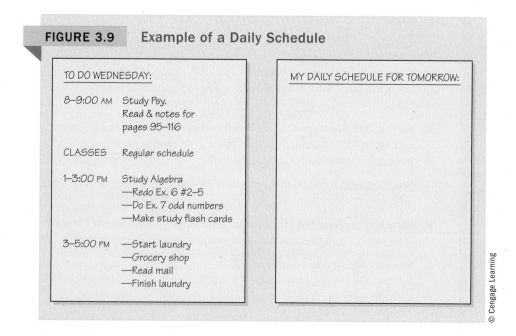

FIGURE 3.9   Example of a Daily Schedule

TO DO WEDNESDAY:		MY DAILY SCHEDULE FOR TOMORROW:
8–9:00 AM	Study Psy. Read & notes for pages 95–116	
CLASSES	Regular schedule	
1–3:00 PM	Study Algebra —Redo Ex. 6 #2–5 —Do Ex. 7 odd numbers —Make study flash cards	
3–5:00 PM	—Start laundry —Grocery shop —Read mail —Finish laundry	

© Cengage Learning

CHECK POINT 3.2

Matching See Test-Taking Strategies 16–20 in Appendix A.

Match the terms on the left with the shortened definitions or descriptions on the right. Write the letter of the definition next to the word in the left column.

_____ 1. flex blocks

_____ 2. 2:1 ratio

_____ 3. spaced practice

_____ 4. massed practice

_____ 5. trading time

_____ 6. online courses

_____ 7. lecture classes

_____ 8. speech classes

_____ 9. fixed study blocks

_____ 10. term schedule

a. often require more than the hours associated with the 2:1 ratio

b. occurs with marathon studying

c. best to schedule study block right before class

d. distributed practice

e. study blocks set to study specific courses

f. set of monthly calendars with deadlines and events

g. two or three blocks of time set aside as "safety nets"

h. best to schedule study block after class

i. a formula for allocating sufficient time to study in most courses

j. an exchange of two blocks of time within the same day

Access Chapter 3 Practice Quiz 2 in your College Success CourseMate, accessed through *CengageBrain.com*.

Textbook Case Studies

EXERCISE 3.6

DIRECTIONS:

1. Read each case study carefully. Respond to the question at the end of each case study by using *specific* strategies discussed in this chapter. Answer in complete sentences.

2. Write your responses on paper or online in the College Success CourseMate, Textbook Case Studies. You will be able to print your online response or e-mail it to your instructor.

CASE STUDY 1: Julian always seems to be caught off-guard. He is surprised when he arrives in class and hears that a specific assignment is due that day. He seldom has his assignments done on time. Sometimes he does not remember them, and other times he runs out of time. He prefers to do all his studying on the weekends, so when an assignment is due in the middle of or at the end of the week, he never has it completed. What suggestions would you give to Julian so he might modify his approach to his assignments?

(continued)

Exercise 3.6 (continued)

Case Study 2: Melissa is a very spontaneous, creative person who likes to march to her own drum. She feels that she works well under pressure and can pour on the energy to do what it takes to finish things and make deadlines. However, in reality, her work is "hit and miss." Sometimes it is creative and well done, and other times it is thrown together too quickly to show quality. A bigger problem is that she is often stressed and exhausted because she uses marathon studying to meet deadlines. What changes in attitudes and behaviors would benefit Melissa as a student?

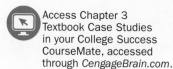 Access Chapter 3 Textbook Case Studies in your College Success CourseMate, accessed through *CengageBrain.com*.

Focus and Concentration

 Explain how to create an ideal study area, use time effectively by maintaining a focus and concentrating, and manage internal and external distractions.

Creating well-planned schedules lays the foundation for managing time effectively and accomplishing important goals and tasks. However, to make the very best use of the time you schedule to be productive involves acquiring skills and strategies to keep your mind focused—to concentrate on your intended plan of action.

Concentration is the ability to block out *external* and *internal distractors* in order to stay focused on one specific item or task. Concentration is a flighty process; you can concentrate one minute and then easily become distracted and lose that concentration. The following are important points about concentration:

- Concentration requires a concerted effort on your part to train or discipline your mind.
- Concentration involves monitoring your thoughts and emotions as well as your environment.
- External and internal distractors consume space in your memory system, disturb your brainwave patterns, and affect the flow of stimuli throughout your memory system (see Chapter 5). You can use effective strategies to train your mind and your attention to not respond to external and internal distractors.
- *External distractors* are disruptions caused by things in your physical environment. Noises, people, music, television, enticing or harsh weather, clutter, and lighting are examples of external distractors. If you are working online, e-mail, social media, and instant messaging can quickly become external distractors.
- *Internal distractors* are disruptions that occur inside you physically or emotionally. Worry, stress, anxiety, depression, sickness, hunger, pain,

Concentration is the ability to block out *external* and *internal distractors* in order to stay focused on one specific item or task.

CONCEPT CHECK   3.12

What are common external and internal distractors you encounter when you study? What effects do they have on your thought processes?

External distractors are disruptions caused by things in your physical environment.

Internal distractors are disruptions that occur inside you physically or emotionally.

daydreams, and anticipation of upcoming events are examples of internal distractors.

An Ideal Study Area

An ideal study area is a specific area designated as your place in which to concentrate and focus on studying. You should have an ideal study area on campus and one at home so you have an organized area in both locations that is conducive to learning, has few or no distractions, and helps you focus your attention on your learning tasks. Creating ideal study areas will help you do the following:

- Increase your ability to concentrate
- Promote the use of selective attention on specific tasks and goals
- Increase motivation and academic performance
- Reduce the tendency to procrastinate
- Reduce or eliminate the effects of internal and external distractors

Creating an ideal study area may require some thoughtful planning and rearranging of furniture or materials, but the time spent will bring positive results. During this process, pay careful attention to three elements in your physical environment: the noise level, the lighting, and the workspace.

CONCEPT CHECK 3.13
What constitutes an ideal study area? How do the elements in your study environment affect your thinking and memory processes?

The Noise Level

Even though people have different tolerance levels for noise, research shows that noisy environments interrupt the steady flow of thought processes and brainwave patterns, thus causing concentration to turn on and off and on and off in split-second intervals. External noise takes up space in your memory system, thus reducing the amount of memory available to process information efficiently. A noisy study environment impacts the quality of learning, so consciously increase your awareness of the noise level around you and be willing to change your study location or adjust your existing learning space. **Check the following items that describe your current study spaces at home and on your campus:**

Television is turned off.	Home:_____ Campus: _____
No music is playing.	Home:_____ Campus: _____
Little or no movement is present.	Home:_____ Campus: _____
Minimal or no noises are present.	Home:_____ Campus: _____
People refrain from interrupting you.	Home:_____ Campus: _____

The Lighting

Proper lighting is important in any study area. If you have too little light, your eyes can easily become strained and tired. Some lighting can create shadows or glare on your books or your digital monitors. To avoid many of the problems created by poor lighting, have *two* sources of light in your study area. These light sources may include overhead lights, desk lamps, or floor lamps. **Check the following items that describe your current study spaces:**

Two sources of lighting are used.	Home:_____ Campus: _____
No glare appears on textbook pages or on a monitor.	Home:_____ Campus: _____
Computer monitor is bright and easy to read.	Home:_____ Campus: _____
Computer resolution level is "easy on the eyes."	Home:_____ Campus: _____

The Workspace

Trying to study in an area that lacks sufficient space to spread out your textbooks, open your notebooks, access a computer, take notes as you read, or use other study materials and supplies creates distractions. Trying to study on the floor, in a recliner, on a couch, on a bed, or outdoors tends to create unnecessary distractions. **Check the following items that describe your current study spaces:**

No clutter to create distractions is present.	Home:_____ Campus: _____
Space has limited visual stimuli (posters or pictures).	Home:_____ Campus: _____
Space has a work surface with ample room for your notebooks, textbooks, computer, and supplies.	Home:_____ Campus: _____
Space has a comfortable chair that is an appropriate height for the table or desk and for you.	Home:_____ Campus: _____

Essential Concentration/Focusing Strategies

As you will learn in Chapter 6, concentration is a memory principle that promotes effective use of your memory in the learning process. **Figure 3.10** summarizes six essential concentration strategies for studying. After reading explanations of each strategy, return to **Figure 3.10** and recite what you remember about each strategy.

FIGURE 3.10 Essential Concentration Strategies for Studying

- Set learning goals with plans of action.
- Be an active learner.
- Chunk information.
- Create a study ritual.
- Begin with a warm-up activity.
- Use mental rehearsal.

© Cengage Learning

Set Learning Goals

Knowing *what* you plan to do and *how* you plan to achieve your goals gives you a purpose, a motivation to stay focused, and a mission to achieve. At the beginning of a study block, create a task schedule that identifies your specific intentions for your study block. Setting learning goals and creating task schedules activate your memory and initiate the plan of action to achieve the goals.

Be an Active Learner

Active learning is a process of engaging in the learning process instead of working in a detached, mechanical way. Active learning increases concentration and helps you avoid internal distractors, such as sleepiness, boredom, or disinterest. Be an active learner by studying with a pen in hand, taking notes, highlighting textbooks, writing questions, and creating study tools, such as diagrams, flashcards, and visual notes.

> **Active learning** is a process of engaging in the learning process instead of working in a detached, mechanical way.

Chunk Information

Chunking down is the process of breaking larger assignments or sections of information into smaller, more manageable units that memory can process. Trying to take in too much information too rapidly overloads your memory and results in loss of concentration and ineffective learning. When you feel distracted by the demands of an assignment, the complexity of a project, or a task such as reading a long chapter, take a deep breath and methodically identify the steps or parts that you need to complete. Breaking an overwhelming assignment, project, or task into smaller units boosts your confidence level, and you find that the task is manageable and less intimidating.

> **Chunking down** is the process of breaking larger assignments or sections of information into smaller, more manageable units that memory can process.

Create a Study Ritual

A *study ritual* is a series of steps or a consistent routine that helps you start quickly on a task. Instead of wasting time trying to decide what to do or where to begin, a study ritual moves you directly into the mindset of studying. For example, your study ritual might be to use a quick relaxation or visualization technique, create a task schedule, and do a warm-up activity.

> A **study ritual** is a series of steps or a consistent routine that helps you start quickly on a task.

> **CONCEPT CHECK** 3.14
> *What strategies can you use within the first five minutes of a study block to help you focus your mind on the assignment? Can you name all six strategies?*

Begin with a Warm-Up Activity

Warm-ups are activities at the beginning of a study block that shift thoughts and create a mindset for studying and concentrating. Warm-ups activate memory and set up frameworks, schemas, or big pictures in your memory for new information. *Previewing* (skimming through a new chapter or assignment to get an overview) and *reviewing* previous work are effective warm-up activities.

> **Warm-ups** are activities at the beginning of a study block that shift thoughts and create a mindset for studying and concentrating.

Use Mental Rehearsal

Mental rehearsal is the process of creating a picture or a movie in your mind that shows you performing effectively. The image that you hold of yourself as a learner often affects the behaviors you exhibit. Use mental rehearsal to replace any negative images of yourself as a learner with positive images of yourself as a learner who stays focused and achieves learning goals. For example, picture yourself beginning an assignment, working with ease, writing answers on a test with confidence, or studying without distractions.

> **Mental rehearsal** is the process of creating a picture or a movie in your mind that shows you performing effectively.

CHAPTER 3
REFLECTIVE WRITING 2

On separate paper, in a journal, or online in this textbook's College Success CourseMate, respond to the following questions:

1. *When* and *where* do you have the most problems concentrating when you study? How can you change the study environment so it is more conducive for concentrating and focusing on learning?

2. What concentration strategies work best for you to help you keep your mind focused when you are studying? Describe strategies with details.

Access Chapter 3 Reflective Writing 2 in your College Success CourseMate, accessed through *CengageBrain.com*.

Manage Distractors

When you find yourself distracted and unable to concentrate, the first step is to analyze the situation to determine the source of your distraction. Is it caused by an *internal distractor* or an *external distractor*? The second step is to select an appropriate technique to address the concentration problem. **Figure 3.11** summarizes six quick, easy-to-use techniques to reduce or eliminate distractors. After reading about each technique, return to **Figure 3.11** and recite what you remember about each technique. Then practice using the techniques several times to increase your ability to stay focused and manage distractors.

The *Say No Technique* involves resisting the urge to participate in an external or internal distraction. Assertively *say no* when friends or family members ask you to drop your study schedule and participate in an activity with them. Train yourself to *say no* and to stay focused when you want to get a snack, turn on the television, daydream, text friends, or check social media accounts.

The *No Need Technique* is the process of training yourself not to look up and not to break your concentration to attend to minor, familiar distractions. Wherever you

> The **Say No Technique** involves resisting the urge to participate in an external or internal distraction.

> The **No Need Technique** is the process of training yourself not to look up and not to break your concentration to attend to minor, familiar distractions.

CONCEPT CHECK **3.15**

Which of the techniques in Figure 3.11 work to reduce or eliminate external distractors? Which work to eliminate internal distractors? Which work best for you?

FIGURE 3.11 Techniques to Manage Distractors

- Say No
- No Need
- Do Not Disturb Symbol
- Check Mark
- Mental Storage Box
- Take Charge

© Cengage Learning

are studying, you know minor distractions and predictable noises will occur. Force yourself to keep your eyes and your attention on your own work. Tell yourself, "There is *no need* to look."

The *Do Not Disturb Symbol Technique* involves using a symbol, such as a sign or a red bow, to signal to others that you do not want to be interrupted or disturbed. Place this symbol on your door or in your work area to indicate to others that they should not disturb you.

The *Check Mark Technique* involves keeping a score card to record and reduce the number of distractions that you allow to disrupt your concentration. Each time you lose your concentration during a study block, make a check mark on a score card you keep on your desk. At the end of your study block, count the number of checks. Set a goal each time you study to reduce the number of check marks.

The *Mental Storage Box Technique* involves placing any internal distractors into an imaginary box, putting a lid on the box, and setting that box aside to be dealt with at a later time. Before you begin studying, identify any concerns, worries, or emotions that might interrupt your concentration. Place them inside your mental storage box. Tell yourself that you will deal with the contents of the box at a more appropriate time, and then do so later.

The *Take Charge Technique* involves taking responsibility for your environment by seeking an alternative place to study or by modifying the existing environment so it has few or no distractions. You do not want to waste your valuable time trying to study in an environment filled with distractions. Taking charge of your environment exhibits a willingness to let go of old habits and try new strategies to increase your ability to concentrate and your overall performance. Use this technique to eliminate a pattern of blaming others for your situation. You are in control by taking charge and making necessary adjustments.

> The **Do Not Disturb Symbol Technique** involves using a symbol, such as a sign or a red bow, to signal to others that you do not want to be interrupted or disturbed.

> The **Check Mark Technique** involves keeping a score card to record and reduce the number of distractions that you allow to disrupt your concentration.

> The **Mental Storage Box Technique** involves placing any internal distractors into an imaginary box, putting a lid on the box, and setting that box aside to be dealt with at a later time.

> The **Take Charge Technique** involves taking responsibility for your environment by seeking an alternative place to study or by modifying the existing environment so it has few or no distractions.

CHECK POINT 3.3

Answers appear on page B3.

True or False? See Test-Taking Strategies 1–9 in Appendix A.

_____ 1. Using concentration strategies effectively increases memory space for cognitive functions.

_____ 2. You can focus your mind more quickly on studying when you create plans of action, create a study ritual, and do a warm-up activity.

_____ 3. A person's physical environment has less of an impact on concentration than his or her emotional state of mind.

_____ 4. The Take Charge, Mental Storage Box, and the Say No techniques are designed to deal only with external distractors.

 Access Chapter 3 Practice Quiz 3 in your College Success CourseMate, accessed through *CengageBrain.com*.

Chapter 3 Critical Thinking

PURPOSE: The term "chunking down" refers to breaking larger sections of information into smaller, more manageable units of information that memory can process. The excerpt below discusses the power of chunking; however, this refers to the process of "chunking up."

DIRECTIONS: After you read the excerpt, answer the following critical thinking questions.

1. What is your definition of **chunking up**?

2. What is the purpose or value of using a **chunking up** process?

3. How do the processes of **chunking down** and **chunking up** differ?

4. What do the processes of **chunking down** and **chunking up** have in common?

5. Brainstorm applications. List ways you could apply the **chunking up** process to a variety of situations.

6. Brainstorm applications. List ways you could apply the **chunking down** process to a variety of situations.

The Power of Chunking

Chunks of information can be quite complex. If you heard someone say, "The boy in the red shirt kicked his mother in the shin," you could probably repeat the sentence perfectly. Yet it contains twelve words and forty-three letters. How can you repeat the sentence so effortlessly? The answer is that you are able to build bigger and bigger chunks of information (Ericsson & Staszewski, 1989). In this case, you might represent "the boy in the red shirt" as one chunk of information rather than as six words or nineteen letters. Similarly, "kicked his mother" and "in the shin" represent separate chunks of information.

Learning to use bigger and bigger chunks of information can improve short-term memory. In fact, children's short-term memories improve partly because they gradually become able to hold as many as seven chunks in memory and also because they get better at grouping information into chunks (Servan-Schreiber & Anderson, 1990). Adults also can greatly increase the capacity of their short-term memory by using more efficient chunking. For example, after extensive training, one college student increased his immediate memory span from seven to eighty digits (Neisser, 2000a). So although the capacity of short-term memory is more or less constant (from five to nine chunks of meaningful information), the size of those chunks can vary tremendously.

From Bernstein, *Essentials of Psychology*, 6e. © 2013 Cengage Learning.

Learning Objectives Review

1 *Discuss how skillful time managers create balance, prioritize tasks, and use task schedules in their approaches to managing time.*

- Knowing how to control and manage time has many benefits.

- Two personality preferences tend to embrace scheduling and using time-management strategies: Sensing and Judging. Two other personality preferences tend to resist and have more difficulties learning to structure time: Intuition and Perceiving.

- The Pie of Life represents three main areas of life that people need to learn to manage and balance: school, work, and leisure.

- Skilled time managers find more efficient ways to do things, use the Increase-Decrease Method, prioritize tasks by using the ABC Method, and create task schedules to be more productive.

2 *Create and use effective term, weekly, and daily schedules to manage your time.*

- Term schedules provide a method to plan for important events and deadlines month-by-month for an entire term.

- Weekly schedules serve as a guide for managing daily plans for a week.

- A variety of strategies are available to create a well-planned weekly schedule with individual blocks of time dedicated to specific subjects, tasks, or obligations.

- Five steps to create a weekly time-management schedule include identifying fixed activities, fixed study blocks, flexible study blocks, personal goals, and time for leisure, family, and social activities.

- Five important strategies for scheduling study blocks involve using the 2:1 ratio, the 3:1 ratio, spaced practice, trading time, and avoiding marathon studying.

- Daily schedules are a form of to-do lists to organize time for a day.

3 *Explain how to create an ideal study area, use time effectively by maintaining a focus and concentrating, and manage internal and external distractions.*

- Concentration is the ability to block out external and internal distractors.

- An ideal study area has little or no noise, two or more sources of lighting, and an uncluttered work area.

- A variety of concentration strategies help you focus and stay on task: setting learning goals, being an active learner, chunking information, creating a study ritual, using a warm-up activity, and using mental rehearsal.

- To maintain a focus and concentrate require using strategies to manage or eliminate internal and external distractors. Six strategies are recommended to manage distractors.

Terms to Know

By yourself or with a partner, practice reciting or writing definitions for the following terms. You may also practice defining these terms by using the online flashcards or comparing your answers to the online glossary.

time management p. 74
Pie of Life p. 75
Increase-Decrease Method p. 77
ABC Method p. 78
task schedule p. 78
term schedule p. 80
weekly schedule p. 81
fixed activities p. 83
fixed study blocks p. 83
flex study blocks p. 83
2:1 ratio p. 84
3:1 ratio p. 84
spaced practice p. 84
marathon studying p. 85
trading time p. 85
daily schedule p. 88
concentration p. 90
external distractors p. 90
internal distractors p. 90
active learning p. 93
chunking down p. 93
study ritual p. 93
warm-ups p. 93
mental rehearsal p. 93
Say No Technique p. 94
No Need Technique p. 94
Do Not Disturb Symbol Technique p. 95
Check Mark Technique p. 95
Mental Storage Box Technique p. 95
Take Charge Technique p. 95

 Access Chapter 3 Flashcards and Online Glossary in your College Success CourseMate, accessed through *CengageBrain.com.*

Chapter 3   Review Questions   Answers appear on page B3.

Multiple Choice See Test-Taking Strategies 10–15 in Appendix A.

_____ 1. A well-planned term schedule
   a. shows only midterm and final exams.
   b. reflects academic and personal timelines and commitments.
   c. states your weekly goals and shows your daily homework assignments.
   d. accomplishes all of the above.

_____ 2. When you use a fifty-minute study block effectively, you
   a. spend time reviewing each of your courses.
   b. create a mindset that focuses on only one subject.
   c. cover as many textbook pages as possible by reading fast.
   d. begin by identifying which class has an assignment due the next day.

_____ 3. An effective weekly time-management schedule includes
   a. eight hours of studying on weekends.
   b. three or more flex blocks and three times set aside for trading time.
   c. adequate time to use the 2:1 ratio, elaborative rehearsal, and spaced practice.
   d. all study blocks completed by 9:00 PM.

_____ 4. A person with an Intuition or Perceiving Myers-Briggs personality preference often does not tend to
   a. feel comfortable establishing structure, schedules, and predictable routines.
   b. prefer more creative or open-ended ways of approaching assignments.
   c. explore different ways to work through the steps of an assignment.
   d. make any effort to manage time or try to create a usable schedule.

_____ 5. The primary purpose of the Increase-Decrease Method is to
   a. help you find ways to increase your social time each week.
   b. find a more satisfying and productive balance in your Pie of Life.
   c. move you toward having a Pie of Life that shows an equal amount of time each week for school, work, and leisure.
   d. decrease the amount of time you need to study each day.

_____ 6. Concentration is
   a. the ability to block out distractions and focus on only one item or task.
   b. a process that affects memory.
   c. a mental discipline that involves training your mind to maintain a focus.
   d. all of the above.

_____ 7. Which techniques would not work well for a student who wants to stop wasting the first half hour of a study block trying to "get started" on studying?
   a. Warm-up activities and using the Take-Charge Technique.
   b. Chunking technique and mental rehearsal.
   c. Setting learning goals and creating a task schedule.
   d. Looking through assignments for each course to decide where to begin.

_____ 8. The ABC Method is used to
   a. make a single list numbered from one to ten to show things you need to do daily.
   b. learn how to recite the alphabet.
   c. identify, classify, organize, and prioritize tasks based on importance or urgency.
   d. do all of the above.

Fill-in-the-Blanks See Test-Taking Strategies 21–24 in Appendix A.

1. The 2:1 ratio and the 3:1 ratio are used to determine the amount of time on a weekly schedule to set aside for _____ .

2. Marathon studying is also known as _____ practice.

3. Spaced practice is also known as _____ practice.

4. Disruptions or distractions that occur within you are called _____ distractors.

5. The process of breaking larger assignments or sections of information into more manageable units is called the process of _____ .

6. The _____-_____ Technique involves assuming responsibility for situations, being willing to make changes, and not blaming others for your circumstances.

Access Chapter 3 Enhanced Quiz and Chapter 3 Study Guide in your College Success CourseMate, accessed through *CengageBrain.com*.

Access all Chapter 3 Online Materials in your College Success CourseMate, accessed through *CengageBrain.com*.

4 Creating and Achieving Goals

© iStockphoto.com/szefei

Learning to set goals provides you with well-defined plans of action to achieve specific results. Learning strategies to motivate and energize yourself to achieve your goals is rewarding and productive. In this chapter you will learn to become a skillful goal setter as well as learn strategies for becoming a stress manager and a procrastination manager. As you work with these skills, you will realize that goal setting involves lifelong skills that will benefit you in your academic, professional, and personal life.

Access Chapter 4 Expanded Chapter Outline in your College Success CourseMate, accessed through *CengageBrain.com*.

YOUR CHAPTER MAPPING

After reading information under each heading, return to the chapter visual mapping below. Add key words to show subheadings and important details related to each heading.

 Access Chapter 4 Visual Mapping in your College Success CourseMate, accessed through *CengageBrain.com*.

© Cengage Learning 2015

LEARNING OBJECTIVES

1 *Explain how to use the GPS Strategy, visualization, extrinsic and intrinsic rewards, and other strategies to create a plan of action for term-long projects and for immediate, short-term, intermediary, and long-term goals.*

2 *Discuss ways to achieve goals by using intrinsic and extrinsic motivation, the Incentive Theory, the Expectancy Theory, and Maslow's Hierarchy of Needs.*

3 *Explain how to become a stress manager by using coping, relaxation, and intrapersonal strategies to combat stressors.*

4 *Explain how to become a procrastination manager by using effective strategies to identify and reduce procrastination.*

CHAPTER 4 PROFILE

Creating and Achieving Goals

ANSWER, SCORE, and **RECORD** your profile before you read this chapter. If you need to review the process, refer to the complete directions given in the profile for Chapter 1 on page 4.

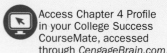

Access Chapter 4 Profile in your College Success CourseMate, accessed through *CengageBrain.com*.

ONLINE: You can complete the profile and get your score online in this textbook's College Success CourseMate.

	YES	NO
1. I use a systematic approach for planning and achieving goals.	_____	_____
2. I tend to have difficulty completing term-long projects on time.	_____	_____
3. I use goal setting for immediate tasks I need to do, but I do not use goal setting for assignments or projects that are not due for several weeks.	_____	_____
4. I am self-motivated when I have a purpose or a reason to work hard to achieve goals.	_____	_____
5. I am only motivated when I know I will receive something like a good grade, money, recognition, or some incentive for my effort and work.	_____	_____
6. I use effective strategies, such as relaxation or coping strategies, to manage my stress levels.	_____	_____
7. My level of stress often reduces my performance or ability to complete my goals.	_____	_____
8. I prolong starting on goals that relate to tasks that are difficult or unpleasant to do.	_____	_____
9. I recognize when and why I procrastinate, and then I select strategies to get back on track and moving forward.	_____	_____
10. I am confident that I have the skills necessary to become a skillful goal setter.	_____	_____

QUESTIONS LINKED TO THE CHAPTER LEARNING OBJECTIVES:

Questions 1–3: objective 1   Questions 8–9: objective 4

Questions 4–5: objective 2   Question 10: all objectives

Questions 6–7: objective 3

Skillful Goal Setters

1 *Explain how to use the GPS Strategy, visualization, extrinsic and intrinsic rewards, and other strategies to create a plan of action for term-long projects and for immediate, short-term, intermediary, and long-term goals.*

Goals are well-defined plans of action aimed at achieving specific outcomes or results.

Goals are well-defined plans of action aimed at achieving specific outcomes or results. Effective goal setting requires effective time management because you need to be aware of time and allocate sufficient time to work through the steps to complete your goals. Your goals become your road maps to guide you to your desired outcomes.

Many people have good intentions and a strong desire or motivation to succeed by achieving their goals; however, many of these same people fall short of making their goals a reality. Frequently, the inability to achieve goals begins with the lack of a sound process or strategy to write and plan effective goals. In other cases, people shy away from goal setting because of attitudes such as the following:

- *I have a fear of failure,* or *I have a fear of success.*
- *It's better not to try than to try and not succeed.*
- *I'll just get discouraged, frustrated, or embarrassed, so why bother?*
- *I've never been a goal setter and I'm doing okay.*
- *I have never learned how to set goals and don't know where to start.*

Fortunately, you can learn strategies to write effective goals and achieve those goals or desired outcomes. How effective are you as a goal setter? **Exercise 4.1** gives you an opportunity to examine your current goal-setting skills and achievements.

> **CONCEPT CHECK** 4.1
>
> *Why are some people all talk but no results? What are possible consequences for people who set goals but do not complete them?*

EXERCISE 4.1

Goal-Setting Inventory

DIRECTIONS: Go to Exercise 4.1 in Appendix C, page C9 to complete the Goal-Setting Inventory. This inventory provides the opportunity to examine your current goal-setting skills and achievements. This nongraded inventory provides you with insights about yourself as a skillful goal setter.

> A **long-term goal**, is a well-defined plan of action to achieve a specific result after two or more years.

Long-Term and Intermediary Goals

A *long-term goal* is a well-defined plan of action to achieve a specific result after two or more years. To complete a long-term goal usually involves completing a series of smaller subgoals called *intermediary goals.*

An *intermediary goal*, a subgoal or a stepping stone to a long-term goal, is a well-defined plan of action to achieve a specific result within a time period of one or two years. For example, a long-term goal to complete a four-year degree in computer science requires other, smaller steps or stepping stones, such as completing required courses as a freshman, completing a 2-year transfer degree, and then completing 2 years of course requirements to receive a bachelor of science degree. **Exercise 4.2** encourages you to think about long-term and intermediary goals important to you in several areas of your life.

> An **intermediary goal**, a subgoal or a stepping stone to a long-term goal, is a well-defined plan of action to achieve a specific result within a time period of one or two years.

> **CONCEPT CHECK** 4.2
>
> *How are intermediary goals related to long-term goals? Do long-term goals always have intermediary goals? Explain your answer.*

EXERCISE 4.2

Long-Term and Intermediary Goals

DIRECTIONS: Complete the following chart or copy the chart into a table in a computer file. For each of the following categories, identify a long-term goal for yourself. In the column on the right, jot down two or more intermediary goals that you need to complete in order to achieve your long-term goal. The intermediary goals are your *stepping stones* to get to the final outcome, the long-term goal.

Category	Long-Term Goal	Intermediary Goals
Education	•	• • •
Finances	•	• • •
Health/Physical	•	• • •
Social Life	•	• • •
Family Life	•	• • •
Other	•	• • •

© Cengage Learning 2015

CHAPTER 4
REFLECTIVE WRITING 1

On separate paper, in a journal, or online in this textbook's College Success CourseMate, respond to the following questions.

1. Based on the results of the Goal-Setting Inventory in Exercise 4.1, how effective are you as a skillful goal setter? What are your strengths and what are your weaknesses?

2. Explain specific strategies you have used to successfully complete a recent goal. Then, explain a situation in which you set a goal but did not achieve success. What happened and how could you change the situation if you were to set the goal again?

Access Chapter 4 Reflective Writing 1 in your College Success CourseMate, accessed through *CengageBrain.com*.

Short-Term and Immediate Goals

A *short-term goal* is a well-defined plan of action to achieve a specific result within a length of time ranging from 1 week to 3 months. For some short-term goals, using the *chunking down* technique you learned in Chapter 3 helps you break the short-term goal into manageable, clearly-organized steps or a series of *immediate goals*. An *immediate goal* is a well-defined plan of action to achieve a specific result within a few hours to a few days. You can then use the series of immediate goals as a checklist to keep the process moving forward. Following is an example of a short-term goal with related immediate goals.

Short-Term Goal: **Clean out the garage by 4:00 pm March 15.**
Immediate Goals:

_____ 1. Sort through the boxes on the shelf. Bag up items for recycling or donating. Discard unneeded items.

_____ 2. Organize the tools on the wall and in the drawers.

_____ 3. Recycle old newspapers, bottles, and cardboard boxes.

You will quickly realize that you can use goal-setting strategies for a variety of immediate goals or tasks that can be done within a few hours or within a few days. For example, you can tighten up your use of time, work more efficiently, and use goal-setting strategies to do a variety of tasks:

- Do laundry, chores, shopping, errands, and pay bills
- Organize an ideal study area, your notes, or your weekly schedule

Goals Based on Time and Based on Behaviors

Two ways to categorize goals are based on time and based on behaviors. Learning to manage time, stress, or procrastination are ongoing goals based on a commitment to change behaviors. They may include specific time-based goals, or they may stand alone as goals to strive continuously to strengthen to bring about the desired behaviors.

Long-term, intermediary, short-term, and immediate goals are defined by specific timelines required to achieve the goals. The four kinds of goals defined by time appear in **Figure 4.1**. Completion of long-term goals involves a clear picture of the

> A **short-term goal** is a well-defined plan of action to achieve a specific result within a length of time ranging from 1 week to 3 months.

> An **immediate goal** is a well-defined plan of action to achieve a specific result within a few hours to a few days.

> CONCEPT CHECK   4.3
> *What are the differences between short-term and immediate goals? How can you use the process of chunking down when planning goals?*

> CONCEPT CHECK   4.4
> *What are examples of behaviors a person may wish to change by setting ongoing goals to change or modify habits and patterns?*

FIGURE 4.1   A Flow Chart for a Long-Term Goal

Long-Term Goal (*2 or more years*)	Acquire a 4-year degree
Intermediary Goal (*1 to 2 years*)	Acquire a 2-year transfer degree
Short-Term Goal (*1 week to 3 months*)	Complete each course this term with a B grade or higher
Immediate Goal (*a few hours to a few days*)	Pass the math test on Friday / Complete essay draft by 8:00 PM Wednesday
	Pass biology midterm with B grade or higher / Complete group sociology project

© Cengage Learning 2015

goal and its subgoals, their importance, and a well-defined plan of action to guide the process through its many steps.

The GPS Strategy for Setting Goals

Many cars and smartphones have GPS (Global Positioning System) navigational systems to navigate roads and freeways and to find convenient, direct routes to get people to where they want to go. The *GPS Strategy* is a systematic three-step goal-setting process to create a plan of action to achieve desired outcomes or goals. This GPS Strategy is your roadmap or navigational system to use for immediate, short-term, intermediary, and long-term goals. **Figure 4.2** shows the three steps in the GPS Strategy for setting goals.

Step One: GOAL

Begin by identifying a specific, well-defined goal that is clear, realistic, and has a definite target date and time for completion. To simply say, "I will do better" or "I want something new" results in vague wishes that are not specific, meaningful, or measureable. To say, "I will be a millionaire tomorrow" is not realistic for most people. To say, "I would like to do that whenever I have some time," or "I will start but have no idea when I'll finish it" does not set a specific or definite timeline (date and time) to finish the steps and achieve the goal. A well-defined target date and time work as a form of motivation to keep you moving forward and on time.

Step 2: PURPOSE

Identifying a purpose for your goal shows that you understand the importance, relevance, and value of the outcome. Having a specific purpose in mind adds motivation, intensity, and commitment to the process of achieving your goal. Goals, especially long-term goals, can become outdated due to changes in values or life circumstances. If a goal is no longer of value to you, replace it with a new, more significant goal. After you identify a specific goal, examine its purpose by asking yourself the following questions:

- Why is this goal important to me?
- What benefits will I gain when I achieve this goal?
- Is this goal compatible with other goals of mine?
- Is this goal an intermediary goal or a step essential for a long-term goal?
- Why am I motivated to follow the steps and complete this goal?
- Do I want to complete this goal for my own satisfaction or to please someone else?
- What consequences will I encounter if I do not achieve this goal?

> **GPS Strategy** is a systematic three-step goal-setting process to create a plan of action to achieve desired outcomes or goals.

> **CONCEPT CHECK** 4.5
>
> *What does each letter in the GPS Strategy represent (G-P-S)? Why is each step important for successful goal setting?*

FIGURE 4.2   The GPS Strategy for Goal Setting

G = **GOAL** with target date and time of completion

P = **PURPOSE** stating importance, relevancy, value

S = **STEPS** to complete to achieve the outcome

© Cengage Learning 2015

When a goal is right for you, you are motivated to get started, feel a sense of excitement, anticipation, and commitment to achieve the outcome. You can vividly picture or create a vision of the desired outcome and know that the goal is important and right for you. When you acknowledge that a goal is important to you, but you need to increase motivation, select one or more of the goal-setting strategies on pages 110–112.

Step 3: STEPS

On paper, in chronological order, list the individual steps you need to work through to achieve your goal. Be specific in naming the steps and the details. Next to each step, jot down any special supplies, materials, or resources you will need to complete that step. Jotting down this information helps you organize yourself so the process does not get interrupted due to poor planning or lack of access to items you need to complete the step. For steps that are spread across different time blocks, days, weeks, or months, schedule the dates on a calendar to show when you will complete each step. Following are additional strategies to use to plan the steps in your GPS Strategy for setting goals:

- **Break larger goals into smaller subgoals.** By using the *chunking down technique*, your larger goal becomes a series of smaller, more manageable, and realistic subgoals. As you check off and complete each smaller subgoal, you gain momentum and motivation and realize you are moving toward completion of the larger goal.

- **Schedule time to complete each step.** Use your weekly schedule to identify blocks of time you can use to work on one or more steps of your goal.

- **Use a goal organizer.** A *goal organizer* is a chart that consists of six questions to help plan a course of action to achieve a specific goal. **Figure 4.3** shows the questions used in a goal organizer. As you use a goal organizer, you will find that it helps you do the following:

  - Identify a specific goal and its importance to you
  - Increase awareness and prepare you to deal with possible obstacles you may encounter as you work on your goal
  - Utilize the support of other people and resources

A **goal organizer** is a chart that consists of six questions to help plan a course of action to achieve a specific goal.

CONCEPT CHECK 4.6
What is the value of a goal organizer? How can it assist you in achieving a specific goal?

FIGURE 4.3 The Goal Organizer

1. What is your goal?
2. What benefits will you gain by achieving this goal?
3. What consequences will you experience by *not* achieving this goal?
4. What obstacles might you encounter while working on this goal?
5. How can you deal with the obstacles effectively if they occur?
6. What people or resources could help you with achieving this goal?

© Cengage Learning

EXERCISE 4.3

Achieving an Immediate Goal

PURPOSE: Select an immediate goal that you can complete within the next day or two. Use the GPS Strategy steps to tackle a small task that you would like to accomplish but keep putting off doing.

DIRECTIONS: On a separate piece of paper, complete each of the following steps.

1. **Complete the following steps of the GPS Strategy.**

    Step 1: What is your specific goal, with a specific target date and time to complete? Write a clear, specific goal complete with a completion date and time.

    Step 2: What is the purpose of this goal? Why is it important? Why do you want it done? Write a clear statement that explains your purpose for this goal.

    Step 3: What are the individual steps you must complete to achieve the goal? Are there subgoals with separate timelines? Are there specific supplies, materials, or resources you need to have available for one or more of the steps? Write the specific steps you need to work through to achieve your goal.

2. **Implement your plan of action.** Begin working to complete each step as soon as possible.

3. **After your target date and time pass, respond to the following questions:**

    Did you achieve your goal by the target date and time? If yes, explain what contributed to your success. If no, describe the obstacles that interfered with the process.

CONCEPT CHECK 4.7

What potential problems can you avoid by using all five steps to set goals and create a plan of action for a term-long project?

Goals for Term-Long Projects

Term-long projects occur when early in the term instructors assign a project, such as a research report, a group project, or a portfolio project, that is not due until later in the term. Following are situations students often face with term-long projects:

- **False sense of time:** Rather than start immediately, they believe the project will not take long, so they start on the project too close to its due date, often neglecting their other study times and classes in order to meet the deadline.

- **Procrastination:** Not sure how to manage the project, they postpone starting. Instead of identifying the steps that need to be done and beginning the project as soon as it is assigned, they wait too long to begin, and they run out of time. This creates unnecessary stress and may lower the quality of the work.

When faced with term-long projects, use the strategies in **Figure 4.4** to guide you through the steps to complete your project on time. Taking time to create and then follow your plan of action results in completion of your project on time. This process also provides you with sufficient time to produce quality work that reflects your abilities. **Figure 4.5** shows the format to use to create your plan of action for a term-long project.

FIGURE 4.4	Setting Goals for a Term-Long Project

Step 1: Break the assignment into specific tasks. Analyze the project carefully until you can identify the individual tasks involved for the entire project. List these tasks or steps on paper.

Step 2: Estimate the time needed for each task. Estimate the number of hours you think you will need to complete each task. Base this estimate on your past experiences with similar projects. Write the estimates next to each task.

Step 3: Double the estimated time needed for each task. To avoid running short on time or to counteract underestimating the time you will need, double your estimate. Doubling your estimated time also gives you a safety net to deal with any unforeseen problems. Planning too much time for a project always is better than running out of time to finish a project or having too little time to produce quality work that you are proud to turn in.

Step 4: Record target dates on your term calendar for each task. Plan target dates and times to complete each step. Identify time each week on your weekly schedule to work on specific steps for the term-long project. If you finish a task ahead of schedule, adjust your calendars and begin working on the next task.

Step 5: Begin immediately. Do not waste time or add unnecessary stress by procrastinating. Give yourself all the time possible to produce a quality project that reflects your abilities.

© Cengage Learning

FIGURE 4.5	Example of Format for Planning a Term-Long Project

STEP 1: List the tasks	STEP 2: Estimated time	STEP 3: Doubled time
1.	3 hrs.	6 hrs.
2.	3 hrs.	6 hrs.
3.	2 hrs.	4 hrs.
4.	4 hrs.	8 hrs.
5.	5 hrs.	10 hrs.
	Time Needed:	34 hrs.

STEP 4: Schedule time on your term schedule and your weekly time-management schedule to complete each task.

Weeks 1 and 2: Do Task 1 (6 hours).

Weeks 3 and 4: Do Task 2 (6 hours).

Week 5: Do Task 3 (4 hours).

Weeks 6 and 7: Do Task 4 (8 hours).

Weeks 8 and 9: Do Task 5 (10 hours).

STEP 5: Begin immediately.

© Cengage Learning

Transfer These Skills: A Term-Long Project

DIRECTIONS: In Figure 4.4, you learned five steps for setting goals for a term-long project. Complete the following steps.

1. Identify a term-long project you have in one of your classes this term. The term-long project may be a research paper, compiling a portfolio for the term, or completing some other individual or group project. If you do not have a term-long project, you can select the "Optional Term-Long Project" included here.

2. Use the five steps for setting a goal for a term-long project. Write your plan of action with these five steps. Your instructor may ask you at the end of the term to discuss your success in achieving the goal you identified.

OPTIONAL TERM-LONG GOAL: CREATE AN ESSENTIAL STUDY SKILLS STRATEGY RESOURCE NOTEBOOK

1. Create your own *Essential Study Skills Strategy Notebook* to use as a reference resource for future classes throughout your college years.

2. Throughout the term, identify essential strategies from each chapter in your textbook that are useful to you. You may photocopy any charts, forms, or lists that you would like to have in your resource notebook for future use or reference.

3. Remove the Essential Test-Taking Skills Guide in Appendix A. Include it in your notebook.

4. Organize your notebook so it is functional, useful, and easy to manage. Use dividers to label different sections of information.

Strategies to Achieve Goals

Task schedules and the GPS Strategy for setting goals are plans of action to achieve specific outcomes. Creating plans of action for any goal increases the likelihood that you will complete the goal. However, knowing *how to write or create goals* is only the first step to becoming a skillful goal setter. Knowing *how to complete or achieve goals* is the true sign of an effective, skillful goal setter. **Figure 4.6** summarizes strategies to achieve goals.

The following strategies from Figure 4.6 provide an extra boost, motivation, or direction for turning your plan of action into reality with successful completion of your goals.

- **Use positive self-talk and affirmations.** Create a positive mindset to increase motivation.

- **Use the ABC Method.** List and prioritize tasks for assignments and goals.

- **Use visualization.** *Visualizing Success* is a strategy to strengthen your self-image and belief in your abilities to behave in a specific way, perform at a desired level, and achieve specific goals. Visualizing and then experiencing the completing of goals improves self-image, increases self-confidence, and motivates you to create plans of action and make changes in your life. Use the following steps to imprint positive images of yourself into your memory:

   1. Close your eyes. Create a picture or an image of yourself, and "watch yourself" performing effectively the steps you identified for a specific goal. Acknowledge the emotions attached to performing well.

Visualizing Success is a strategy to strengthen your self-image and belief in your abilities to behave in a specific way, perform at a desired level, and achieve specific goals.

FIGURE 4.6   Strategies to Achieve Goals

- Use positive self-talk and affirmations.
- Use the ABC Method to prioritize.
- Use visualization and the Visualizing Success strategy.
- Use extrinsic and intrinsic rewards.
- Plan and expect to succeed.
- Evaluate the importance of a goal.
- Analyze your goal-setting strategies.
- Monitor your progress.
- Keep your goals in the forefront.

© Cengage Learning 2015

2. Visualize or "see" yourself receiving the rewards for your behavior, performance, and completion of the goal. Feel the sense of pride, accomplishment, or success.

3. Practice "rerunning" the visualization several times and recalling it from memory to use as a motivator.

- **Use extrinsic and intrinsic rewards.** Plan a reward to celebrate the completion of a goal. You can use that reward as an incentive—a motivator—to achieve your goal. For any rewards to work as motivators, the rewards should truly represent what you *want* and look forward to receiving. You can use two kinds of rewards in your goal-setting plan: extrinsic rewards and intrinsic rewards.

  - *Extrinsic rewards* are material things, incentives, or activities that are awarded when a goal is achieved. Buying a CD, going to a movie, going out to dinner, or planning a short trip are examples of extrinsic rewards. An extrinsic reward is a strong motivator only if you use it *after* you achieve the goal. You must also withhold the reward if you do not achieve or complete the goal.

  - *Intrinsic rewards* are emotions or feelings that a person experiences when a goal is achieved. Increased self-esteem, pride, relief, joy, confidence, or immense satisfaction are examples of intrinsic rewards.

- **Plan and expect to succeed.** Success seldom "just happens." Take the time to plan clear, specific goals and clear, specific plans of action. Develop a mindset that shows you expect to succeed and achieve your goals. Erase doubts, hesitations, negative self-talk, and lack of initiative.

- **Evaluate the importance of a goal.** Goals, especially long-term goals, can become outdated due to changes in values or life circumstances. If a goal is no longer of value to you, replace it with a new, more significant goal. Do not, however, abandon a goal because it is more difficult to achieve or requires more from you than you had originally anticipated.

- **Analyze your goal-setting strategies.** When you do not achieve a goal by a specific target date or do not get the desired outcome, turn such situations into

Extrinsic rewards are material things, incentives, or activities that are awarded when a goal is achieved.

Intrinsic rewards are emotions or feelings that a person experiences when a goal is achieved.

CONCEPT CHECK   4.8
Summarize the strategies to use to increase your likelihood of achieving specific goals. Which strategies work most effectively for you?

learning experiences. Ask yourself the following kinds of questions, and then use your responses to adjust your approach the next time you set goals:

Was the goal that I set unrealistically high or too low?

Did I feel a lack of purpose or unchallenged?

Was the goal high on my priority list of importance?

Did I think through the steps carefully when I planned the goal?

Did I allot sufficient time on my weekly schedule to work on the goal?

Was I sufficiently motivated? Were the incentives valued?

Was I motivated by intrinsic or extrinsic motivation?

Did I really apply effort and follow my plan of action?

What would I do differently if I were to set this goal again?

- **Monitor your progress.** Create an easy-to-use method, such as checkmarks or stars, to track your progress and show that you are meeting target dates and completing the steps of a goal. Using a calendar, a checklist, or a personal journal can help you monitor your progress and motivate you to stay on course to achieve your goals.

- **Keep your goals in the forefront.** If on occasion you find yourself struggling with your goal-setting plans, your motivation dwindles, your momentum temporarily stalls, or you find yourself ignoring your goals, write your goals on index cards. Place these cards around your house and in your notebook as a constant reminder to spend time each day working toward the outcome.

CHECK POINT 4.1

Answers appear on page B3.

True or False? See Test-Taking Strategies 1–9 in Appendix A.

_____ 1. Setting a specific target date to complete a goal can help reduce or eliminate procrastination.

_____ 2. Extrinsic rewards include positive feelings, a sense of pride, and relief.

_____ 3. Not all immediate and short-term goals are subgoals of long-term goals.

_____ 4. The GPS Strategy is ineffective for planning immediate or short-term goals.

_____ 5. Lack of goal-setting strategies, lack of a clear direction, and lack of procrastination are the three main reasons people do not complete goals.

_____ 6. When planning a term-long project, you should double the estimated time you anticipate needing for only the most difficult tasks on your plan of action.

Access Chapter 4 Practice Quiz 1 in your College Success CourseMate, accessed through *CengageBrain.com*.

Motivation to Achieve Goals

2 *Discuss ways to achieve goals by using intrinsic and extrinsic motivation, the Incentive Theory, the Expectancy Theory, and Maslow's Hierarchy of Needs.*

Motivation is the driving force that moves a person to take action, create plans of action, and persevere to achieve goals. Motivation is the feeling, emotion, or desire that becomes the internal driving force to help you achieve goals, change behaviors, and "push on" and not give up. The strength of your motivation to achieve a specific goal or task often determines the intensity and persistence for achieving the goal. Following are important points about motivation:

> **Motivation** is the driving force that moves a person to take action, create plans of action, and persevere to achieve goals.

- Goals motivate. When you use the GPS Strategy to set goals, you identify a purpose for achieving a specific outcome. As you focus on a goal with its desired outcomes, your desire to achieve increases. This motivation increases the likelihood of success.

- High motivation equates to success; low motivation equates to lower achievement, lower performance, and incompletion of goals.

- High motivation results in high self-esteem and self-confidence. Low motivation results in negative results, lack of effort, and low self-confidence.

- Individuals with a high sense of self-efficacy set goals, aim high, and work diligently to achieve goals. With each success, they become even more motivated to continue on a positive path of achievement and productivity.

- Individuals with a low sense of self-efficacy tend not to set goals; they feel frustrated and increasingly become unmotivated. They often feel stuck in a negative pattern without realizing there are ways to get out of the downward spiral.

Intrinsic and Extrinsic Motivation

Two forms of motivation drive people to achieve their goals: intrinsic and extrinsic motivation. *Intrinsic motivation* is the driving force to take action that comes from within oneself. Intrinsic motivation, also known as *self-motivation*, uses *intrinsic rewards* (emotions or feelings that a person experiences when a goal is achieved).

> **Intrinsic motivation** is the driving force to take action that comes from within oneself.

    Extrinsic motivation is the driving force to take action that comes from incentives outside of oneself. Extrinsic motivation uses *extrinsic rewards*: material things, incentives, feedback, or activities awarded when a goal is achieved.

> **Extrinsic motivation** is the driving force to take action that comes from incentives outside of oneself.

Intrinsic Motivation

Intrinsic motivation is the most powerful and effective form of motivation because you "own" it, give it personal meaning, importance, and conviction. The outcome is rewarding and personally fulfilling. Intrinsic motivation often provides the platform for achieving peak performance, striving for a new, meaningful experience, or embracing personal growth. The following are common sources of intrinsic motivation:

- A desire to fulfill a basic need, such as food, shelter, or financial security

- A personal commitment to take action to change and improve some area of your life that is significant and important to you

- A personal challenge to move outside your comfort zone to take on something new without a fear of failure or self-doubt

- An internal desire and personal choice to engage in behaviors or actions that bring feelings of pride, joy, victory, sense of accomplishment, increased self-esteem, or uplifting personal satisfaction (intrinsic rewards)
- A desire to affirm your self-image, live by your values, and prove your abilities to yourself

Extrinsic Motivation

CONCEPT CHECK **4.9**

How do intrinsic and extrinsic motivation differ? Why is intrinsic motivation so powerful?

The second type of motivation is extrinsic motivation. Rewards, recognition, praise, prizes, or income are typical motivators for extrinsic motivation. Another common form of extrinsic motivation is a desire to please or meet expectations of parents, family members, friends, employers, or colleagues. You look to them for approval, praise, positive feedback, and acknowledgment of your own value. For many people, work or employment is driven by the extrinsic motivation to earn an income, make money to pay bills, and acquire sufficient funds to enjoy other activities, such as entertainment or travel. Many business models use extrinsic motivation by offering incentives to encourage employees to develop specific behaviors, increase work performance, or achieve company goals. Special programs, such as acknowledging an employee of the month, awarding a prime parking space to a top performer, presenting a plaque for achievement, or providing salary increases based on performance, are all incentives designed to boost extrinsic motivation. Following are important points about extrinsic motivation:

CONCEPT CHECK **4.10**

What is extrinsic motivation? When might it be effective? What extrinsic rewards motivate you?

- To work effectively, the incentives need to be meaningful and valued. Incentives with low value or interest are not motivators. Incentives with high value are motivators that energize individuals to apply effort and perform.
- Incentives become goals as individuals strive to excel or to receive an award, recognition, praise, pay raise, promotion, or prize.
- Extrinsic rewards such as praise, positive feedback, or acknowledgment need to be sincere, honest, and based on genuine accomplishments to work as extrinsic motivators.
- Extrinsic motivation often relies on someone else to provide the motivation; consequently, individuals may focus their attention on extrinsic rather than intrinsic rewards.
- You can convert extrinsic motivation to intrinsic motivation by shifting your focus and attaching a personal value, interest, or importance to the goal. In other words, strive to convert your extrinsic motivation to intrinsic motivation so your main purpose is to achieve for yourself and for intrinsic rewards—not for the main purpose of pleasing others.

Three Theories of Motivation

Motivation is the driving force that moves a person to take action, create plans of action, and persevere to achieve goals. Positive results build self-confidence, boost self-esteem, and strengthen motivation to take on new goals. Thus, it should not be surprising that researchers, educators, corporate managers, counselors, and motivational speakers continue to explore ways to understand and tap into the power of motivation.

Three theories provide informative perspectives on motivation: The Incentive Theory, the Expectancy Theory, and Maslow's Hierarchy of Basic Needs.

Textbook Case Studies

DIRECTIONS:

1. Read each case study carefully. Respond to the question at the end of each case study by using *specific* strategies discussed in this chapter. Answer in complete sentences.

2. Write your responses on paper or online in this textbook's College Success CourseMate, Textbook Case Studies. You will be able to print your online response or e-mail it to your instructor.

CASE STUDY 1: Cary really wants to change his lifestyle. He wants to quit smoking, and he wants to manage his assignments with less stress. He says he wants to feel more in control of his life. When asked how he is going to accomplish these resolutions, he says he's going to quit smoking "cold turkey" when he's ready because his girlfriend complains about the smell and about his coughing. He's going to try using different strategies for his assignments to see if he can find ways that work better and produce less stress. He wants less chaos and more control. What advice could you give Cary to help him set and achieve his goals?

CASE STUDY 2: Amy is the first to admit that she always runs out of time to complete assignments on time. She's concerned about a research project that is due in eight weeks. She has to create a list of questions, interview four experts in the world of business, summarize findings, explain the outcomes, and relate them to textbook concepts. What strategies could Amy use to set and achieve the goal of completing this assignment on time?

Access Chapter 4 Textbook Case Studies in your College Success CourseMate, accessed through *CengageBrain.com*.

The Incentive Theory of Motivation

The *Incentive Theory of Motivation* states that incentives and rewards are the driving forces behind people's choices and behaviors. The incentive or motivation behind specific behaviors may be to receive a desired reward or a positive consequence or to avoid some type of punishment or negative consequence. The following points provide further clarification about the Incentive Theory:

> The *Incentive Theory of Motivation* states that incentives and rewards are the driving forces behind people's choices and behaviors.

- Incentives motivate people to behave in positive ways. For example, children behave in specific ways to receive a treat or praise. The incentive for many working adults is to receive a decent paycheck. The incentive for many students to study hard is to receive good grades, meet scholarship requirements, be admitted to a desired program, or earn a degree.

- Incentives also motivate people to refrain from negative behaviors that may have negative consequences. A student is motivated *not* to cheat on a test or plagiarize a research paper because of potentially severe consequences.

- Incentives become strong motivators only when the individual places a high value on the incentive and is willing to take action to obtain the reward. Effective incentives energize people and instill a desire to excel.

- To work as motivators, the incentives and rewards must be obtainable. For example, most employees would not be highly motivated by an employer's offer of a week's paid vacation (incentive) if the goal set to receive the award is unrealistically high and most likely unobtainable.

> **CONCEPT CHECK** **4.11**
> *Why do you think business models tend to use the Incentive Theory to motivate employees? What makes incentives work effectively as motivators?*

CONCEPT CHECK   4.12

Why is the self-fulfilling prophecy concept an integral part of the Expectancy Theory of Motivation? In what ways do your beliefs affect your ability to complete goals?

The **Expectancy Theory of Motivation** states that the degree of motivation is determined by a person's belief in the likelihood, desire, and ability to achieve a specific outcome or goal.

Self-fulfilling prophecy is a belief that what one thinks or believes is what will become reality.

• You use this Incentive Theory of Motivation each time you use a goal organizer or the GPS Strategy. Asking questions such as the following focus your attention on the value, importance, and consequences of striving to achieve a specific goal.

- *What benefits will I gain by achieving this goal?*
- *What is the purpose, value, or meaning of this goal?*
- *What negative consequences will I experience by not achieving this goal?*
- *Will not achieving this goal hurt me or my future opportunities in any way?*

The Expectancy Theory of Motivation

The *Expectancy Theory of Motivation* states that the degree of motivation is determined by a person's belief in the likelihood, desire, and ability to achieve a specific outcome or goal. This theory is based on the concept of *self-fulfilling prophecy*. *Self-fulfilling prophecy* is a belief that what one thinks or believes is what will become reality. In other words, "What you think is what you get." When you exhibit self-confidence to succeed, and you believe you are worthy and capable of achieving a specific goal, your attitude and expectancy to succeed motivate you to give your very best to achieve that goal. However, if you exhibit hesitancy or self-doubt, or question your ability or interest in achieving a goal, the result is lower motivation and the expectancy not to achieve the goal. The excerpt in **Figure 4.7** explains the Expectancy Theory.

FIGURE 4.7   Expectancy Theory of Motivation

Expectancy Theory, developed by Victor Vroom, is a very complex model of motivation based on a deceptively simple assumption. According to the expectancy theory, motivation depends on how much we want something and on how likely we think we are to get it. Consider, for example, the case of three sales representatives who are candidates for promotion to one sales manager's job. Bill has had a very good sales year and always gets good performance eval- uations. However, he isn't sure he wants the job because it involves a great deal of travel, long working hours, and much stress and pressure. Paul wants the job badly but doesn't think he has much

chance of getting it. He has had a terrible sales year and gets only mediocre performance evaluations from his present boss. Susan wants the job as much as Paul, and she thinks she has a pretty good shot at it. Her sales have improved significantly this past year, and her evaluations are the best in the company.

Expectancy theory would predict that Bill and Paul are not very motivated to seek the promotion. Bill doesn't really want it, and Paul doesn't think he has much of a chance of getting it. Susan, however, is very motivated to seek the promotion because she wants it *and* thinks she can get it.

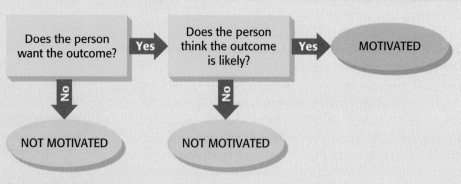

From Pride/Hughes/Kapoor, *Business,* 12E. © 2014 Cengage Learning

Maslow's Hierarchy of Needs for Motivation

In 1970, American psychologist Abraham Maslow suggested that human behavior is influenced or motivated by categories of needs. *Maslow's Hierarchy of Needs* is a theory that identifies five categories of human needs, from the most basic to the most difficult to achieve. The lowest level of needs is level 1, physiological survival needs; individuals are motivated to fulfill those needs first. According to Maslow's theory, as lower level needs are fulfilled, individuals become motivated to fulfill the needs on the higher levels. **Figure 4.8** (page 118) shows the order of needs that motivate human behavior. Following are important points about Maslow's Hierarchy of Needs:

- Even though Maslow's hierarchy has been referred to extensively in many fields of study, some critics believe the hierarchy is too simplistic and argue that one level of needs does not need to be completely fulfilled before working on higher levels of needs. For example, can a person be motivated to meet the need of love and belonging if he or she is still working on goals to feel safe and secure?

- Another point of discussion is whether the levels of needs must be satisfied in a specific order. Could it be that individuals are motivated by different levels of needs as they move from one situation to another? For example, if a person feels defeated after losing a job or after going through a divorce, could that person possibly become motivated to improve esteem needs before applying for a new position or looking for a new relationship?

- Being familiar with the levels of needs may help explain why you are motivated to achieve specific goals. When you set a goal and strive to identify the purpose of the goal, ask yourself, *Why is this important to me?* Your answer may relate directly to one of the five levels of needs in Maslow's Hierarchy.

> **Maslow's Hierarchy of Needs** is a theory that identifies five categories of human needs, from the most basic to the most difficult to achieve.

CONCEPT CHECK 4.13
Do you believe you must fulfill the needs on a specific level in Maslow's Hierarchy before you are motivated to move up to the needs on the next higher level? Explain your answer.

CHECK POINT 4.2

Answers appear on page B3.

True or False? See Test-Taking Strategies 1–9 in Appendix A.

_____ 1. Extrinsic motivation based on physical, monetary, or intrinsic rewards tends to be the most powerful form of motivation for adults.

_____ 2. As extrinsic motivators gain momentum, a person may convert them to intrinsic motivators to attach more meaning, purpose, or value to them.

_____ 3. Incentives may motivate people to behave in positive ways or refrain from behaving in negative ways with negative consequences.

_____ 4. The self-fulfilling prophecy concept reflects a person's attitudes and beliefs.

_____ 5. A person can refer to Maslow's Hierarchy of Needs to try to understand what needs he or she is trying to fulfill when striving to achieve a specific goal.

_____ 6. Setting goals, using a goal organizer, and boosting a sense of self-efficacy can work as motivators to persevere to achieve goals.

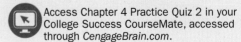 Access Chapter 4 Practice Quiz 2 in your College Success CourseMate, accessed through *CengageBrain.com*.

FIGURE 4.8   Maslow's Hierarchy of Needs

If you were very hungry and very lonely at the same time, which need would you satisfy first, your biological need (hunger) or your social need (affiliation)? One answer to this question can be found in Maslow's (1970) hierarchy of needs.

Maslow's hierarchy of needs is an ascending order, or hierarchy, in which biological needs are placed at the bottom and social needs at the top.

Level 5 Self-Actualization: Fulfillment of One's Unique Potential

According to Maslow, the highest need is self-actualization, which involves developing and reaching our full potential as unique human beings. However, Maslow cautioned that very few individuals reach the level of self-actualization because it is so difficult and challenging.

Level 4 Esteem Needs: Achievement, Competency, Approval, and Recognition

During early and middle adulthood, people are especially concerned with achieving their goals and establishing their careers. As we develop skills to gain personal achievement and social recognition, we turn our energies to Level 5.

Level 3 Love and Belonging Needs: Affiliation with Others and Acceptance by Others

Adolescents and young adults, who are beginning to form serious relationships, would be especially interested in fulfilling their needs for love and belonging. After we find love and affection, we advance to Level 4.

Level 2 Safety Needs: Protection from Harm

People who live in high-crime or dangerous areas would be very concerned about satisfying their safety needs. After we find a way to live in a safe environment, we advance to Level 3.

Level 1 Physiological Needs: Food, Water, Sex, and Sleep

People who are homeless or jobless would be especially concerned with satisfying their physiological needs above all other needs. We must satisfy these basic needs before we advance to Level 2.

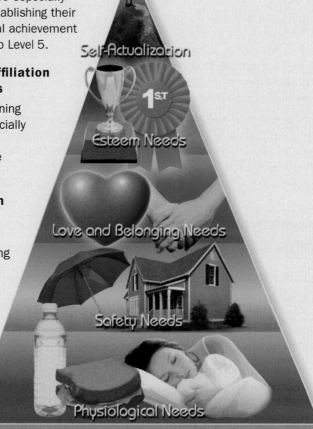

From Plotnik/Kouyoumdjian, *Discovery Series: Introduction to Psychology* (with Psychology CourseMate with eBook Printed Access Card), 1E. © 2013 Cengage Learning

Goal: Become a Stress Manager

3 *Explain how to become a stress manager by using coping, relaxation, and intrapersonal strategies to combat stressors.*

Stress is a reaction or response to events or situations that threaten or disrupt a person's normal patterns or routines. Stress is the wear and tear on our bodies due to physical, emotional, cognitive, and behavioral responses. The following are important points about stress:

- Some stress is normal as we move through life, making decisions and changing directions in our personal, work, and academic lives.

- In some situations, stress is beneficial. Stress can compel us to take action and to move in new directions. The increased adrenaline from stress can help us perform at higher levels.

- As stress increases, our ability to deal with and control the stress decreases.

- Early warning signs that stress is becoming more intense and moving into the danger level include headaches, backaches, insomnia, fatigue, anxiety attacks, mood swings, depression, forgetfulness, carelessness, and irritability.

- You can learn more about stress by reading Excerpt 1: Understanding Stress and Stressors in Appendix D.

> **Stress** is a reaction or response to events or situations that threaten or disrupt a person's normal patterns or routines.

Creating a Goal to Reduce Stress

If you experience stress on a regular basis or stress seems to increase in intensity or frequency, creating a goal to change patterns or behaviors to reduce stress is important. Learning to manage stress is a lifelong skill that affects the quality of life and longevity. It is not something you simply accomplish in one week and then set aside as a completed goal. Reducing stress is important for a variety of reasons:

- Excessive stress hinders performance and affects cognitive functions. Excessive stress affects memory processes and reduces the ability to concentrate, solve problems, and make wise decisions.

- Excessive stress from unresolved issues has physical consequences: increased pulse rate, faster breathing, higher blood pressure, a weakening of the immune system, a decrease in the production of endorphins (a neurochemical that makes us feel happy), ulcers, heart attacks, strokes, and clinical depression.

- Excessive stress may turn into anxiety. Test anxiety, which hinders performance and results in physical, emotional, cognitive, and behavioral consequences, is one of several kinds of anxiety that results from excessive stress.

Stressors

To create a goal to manage stress more effectively, begin by identifying your stressors. **Stressors** are situations or actions that cause stress. How you *perceive* and *handle* external situations or stressors—rather than the situations themselves—is the cause of stress. Taking some form of action to reduce or eliminate stressors empowers you to have greater control over your stress and to alter your perception of external situations. For example, if an upcoming test is a stressor, you can create a plan of action and use specific techniques to take control of the situation. Other stressors, such as the terminal illness of a loved one, are out of

> **Stressors** are situations or actions that cause stress.

Stress Test

DIRECTIONS: Go to Exercise 4.6 in Appendix C, page C10, to complete the Social Readjustment Rating Scale (Stress Test). You will be asked to circle all the events (stressors) you have experienced in the past 12 months. Each event has a point value. After totaling all the point values for events, you will be able to identify your stress level score.

CONCEPT CHECK   4.14

Is stress always bad? Explain. What might happen if you experience stress but do not create goals to manage your stress?

your immediate control; the only control you have is how you handle your reaction to the stressor.

Stressors may be positive or negative. Divorce, personal injury, loss of a job, or family problems are negative stressors. Events such as marriage or a vacation may be positive stressors. The number of stressors you face at one time, both positive and negative, affect your overall stress level. In 1967, Dr. Thomas H. Holmes and Dr. Richard H. Rahe developed a "stress test," the Social Readjustment Rating Scale (SRRS), to help individuals identify their stress levels. The stressors and the stress scores on SRRS remain applicable today. (See **Exercise 4.6**.)

Essential Strategies for Managing Stress

Managing stress involves active participation on your part to change habits, behaviors, and emotional attitudes. After identifying your stress levels and stressors, create a plan of action to implement the effective stress-management strategies that appear in **Figure 4.9**.

FIGURE 4.9   Essential Strategies for Managing Stress

- Use coping strategies. (See Figure 4.10.)
- Use positive self-talk, affirmations, and visualizations.
- Seek social support from family and friends.
- Use time management and goal setting to organize yourself.
- Avoid chaos, clutter, and confusion by setting priorities.
- Engage in physical activity.
- Choose a healthy lifestyle. (See Excerpt 3 in Appendix D.)
- Use relaxation strategies.
- Calm yourself with meditation, guided imagery, Visualizing Success, yoga, or soothing environments.
- Keep a journal; sort your feelings out by writing and expressing ideas.

© Cengage Learning 2015

FIGURE 4.10 Methods for Coping with Stress

Type of Coping Method	Examples
Cognitive	Thinking of stressors as challenges rather than as threats; avoiding perfectionism
Emotional	Seeking social support; getting advice
Behavioral	Implementing a time-management plan; when possible, making life changes to eliminate stress
Physical	Using progressive relaxation; meditation; exercise

Source: Bernstein/Nash, *Essentials of Psychology*, 4e, Houghton Mifflin Company, © 2008, p. 414. Reprinted with permission.

Coping Strategies

Coping strategies are cognitive, emotional, behavioral, and physical strategies used to manage and overcome stressors and difficult situations. **Figure 4.10** shows examples of the four main coping methods.

- *Cognitive coping strategies* involve changing the way a person thinks and perceives stressors. Instead of perceiving a situation as hopeless, frightening, or insurmountable, use motivational strategies, such as positive self-talk, affirmations, and Visualizing Success, to alter your perception of the situation. Look at the situation as an opportunity to use your problem-solving skills to create a plan of action to overcome the situation.

- *Emotional coping strategies* involve identifying and expressing emotions to other people. Having a strong, positive social support network of friends, family, and coworkers provides you with an outlet to share your emotions, analyze the reality of situations, brainstorm solutions, and receive support and encouragement. Many research studies show that social interaction can reduce stress, improve overall health and the immune system, stimulate cognitive processes, and stave off depression. Not sharing your stress and frustrations may result in *catastrophic thinking*, a state of mind in which your perception of the problem and its severity becomes distorted and greatly exaggerated. Left unchecked, your stress level increases and your ability to manage stress decreases.

- *Behavioral coping strategies* involve changing patterns or behaviors to address the source of stress. For example, you can use a time-management schedule as well as goal-setting and test-preparation strategies to reduce stress about an upcoming test. If the source of your stress includes procrastinating about doing a specific task, such as finalizing financial aid papers, applying for a scholarship, or filing your taxes, using goal-setting strategies helps you deal with the source of the stress. Changing your behavior by using strategies to increase motivation, set goals, and stop procrastination will eliminate the stressor.

- *Physical coping strategies* involve the use of physical activity to reduce or eliminate a person's response to specific stressors. Engaging in activities that create positive emotions reduces the intensity of your emotional reaction to stress and the tendency to dwell on negative situations. Redirecting your

Coping strategies are cognitive, emotional, behavioral, and physical strategies used to manage and overcome stressors and difficult situations.

Cognitive coping strategies involve changing the way a person thinks and perceives stressors.

Emotional coping strategies involve identifying and expressing emotions to other people.

Behavioral coping strategies involve changing patterns or behaviors to address the source of stress.

CONCEPT CHECK 4.15
Describe the four categories of coping strategies and one specific technique or strategy for each category.

Physical coping strategies involve the use of physical activity to reduce or eliminate a person's response to specific stressors.

emotions by spending time on a favorite hobby, exercising, or using relaxation techniques reduces the physiological effects of stress.

Relaxation Techniques

Relaxation techniques can help reduce stress levels, improve emotional health, and create a state of mind and body that perhaps can best be described as "Ahhhhhhh." In a relaxed state, the body is not tense and the mind is not wandering; you are alert and ready to learn. Relaxation techniques help you manage emotional situations, such as anxiety, nervousness, tension, stress, apprehension, hyperactivity, restlessness, and feelings of defeat, frustration, or being overwhelmed. The following six easy-to-use relaxation techniques require only a few minutes of your time. Try each technique, select ones that work well for you, and use them on a regular basis.

- The *perfect place technique* involves taking a mental vacation and visualizing a perfect, stress-free place to relax. Use the following steps for this technique:

  1. Close your eyes, breathe in slowly, and visualize a perfect place where you feel relaxed, confident, safe, comfortable, and content.

  2. Continue breathing in and out slowly as you create this mental picture of a perfect place. Make your image more vivid by adding sounds, smells, sights, tastes, and tactile sensations.

  3. Use the power of association to recall the mental picture and the soothing sensations of this perfect place whenever you need to separate yourself in a healthy way from stress and stressful situations.

- The *soothing mask technique* involves using imagination to create and pull a mask over your face to block out reactions to stress. Use the following steps for this technique:

  1. Close your eyes and place your hands on the top of your head.

  2. Slowly move your hands down your forehead, down your face, and to your neck. As you do this, picture your hands gently pulling a *soothing mask* over your face, removing worries, fears, or stresses from your mind.

  3. Keep your eyes closed for another minute. Feel the soothing mask resting on your face, blocking out stressful thoughts or feelings. As you practice this technique, you will be able to visualize the soothing mask without using your hands.

- The *relaxation blanket technique* involves visualizing pulling a soft, warm blanket up to your neck to release tension. Use the following steps for this technique:

  1. Sit comfortably in your chair, close your eyes, and focus your attention on your feet.

  2. Imagine pulling a soft, warm blanket up over your feet, up over your legs, lap, and chest until the blanket is snuggled around your shoulders and against your neck. Focus on the way your body feels warm and relaxed.

  3. Keep your eyes closed for another minute as you enjoy the warmth and comfort of the blanket. Recall this feeling during times of stress.

CONCEPT CHECK   4.16

What is the value of using relaxation techniques? Which of the specific relaxation strategies work most effectively for you to reduce your stressors?

The **perfect place technique** involves taking a mental vacation and visualizing a perfect, stress-free place to relax.

The **soothing mask technique** involves using imagination to create and pull a mask over your face to block out reactions to stress.

The **relaxation blanket technique** involves visualizing pulling a soft, warm blanket up to your neck to release tension.

- The *breathing by threes technique* involves inhaling and exhaling slowly as a way to reduce stress. Use the following steps for this technique:

  1. Count to three as you inhale slowly through your nose. Count to three as you hold your breath. Finally, count to three as you exhale slowly.

  2. Repeat this several times. You will feel your body begin to slow down and relax. Use this any time you feel an onset of stress.

- The *deep breathing technique* involves taking deep breaths and exhaling slowly as a way to reduce stress. Use the following steps for this technique:

  1. Take a deep breath to fill your lungs. You may think your lungs are full, but there is room for one more breath of air. Inhale once again.

  2. Now slowly exhale and feel your body relax.

  3. Repeat this deep breathing several times. If you feel lightheaded or dizzy after trying this exercise, discontinue and use an alternative relaxation technique.

- The *deep muscle relaxation technique* involves tensing and releasing different groups of muscles as a way to reduce stress. Use the following steps for this technique:

  1. Identify the areas of your body where you feel tension.

  2. Make a clenched fist tight enough so that you can feel your fingers pulsating. Breathe several times, feel the tension in your fingers and your hands, and then breathe slowly as you uncurl your fists until they are totally relaxed. Pay close attention to the different sensations as you go from tense to relaxed.

  3. Continue this with other muscle groups that tend to hold tension: shoulders, arms, lower back, legs, chest, fingers, or face. As you work to release tension from your different muscle groups, your total body moves into a state of greater relaxation.

Intrapersonal Strategies

Intrapersonal intelligence involves developing skills related to personal growth, self-understanding, self-motivation, intuition, and spirituality. Using intrapersonal skills shifts your focus from the outside world to your inner world—your thoughts, feelings, inspirations, and goals. Following are three ways to use your intrapersonal skills to reduce or eliminate stress.

1. **Take time to center yourself.** Engage in a mind-calming activity such as meditation, yoga, prayer, or biofeedback to center yourself and return to a state of calmness and serenity. Sitting in a sauna, soaking in a hot tub or warm bath, or sitting near a fountain of water can also be a mind-calming experience. Centering activities provide a way to block out and temporarily shield yourself from the rest of the world.

2. **Keep a journal.** In a journal, describe your feelings or concerns privately and tap into some of your innermost thoughts in a nonthreatening way. Putting your emotions on paper often reduces the intensity of the emotions, disperses some of the negative energy, and helps you discover solutions or new directions to take with the situation.

The **breathing by threes technique** involves inhaling and exhaling slowly as a way to reduce stress.

The **deep breathing technique** involves taking deep breaths and exhaling slowly as a way to reduce stress.

The **deep muscle relaxation technique** involves tensing and releasing different groups of muscles as a way to reduce stress.

3. **Strive to strengthen self-esteem.** As you recall from Figure 2.3, positive self-talk, high achievement, positive perception of self and others, rewarding relationships, and improved self-confidence are characteristics of high self-esteem, which often reflect fewer stressors than the characteristics associated with low self-esteem. Using strategies to boost your confidence, your self-perception, and your self-esteem provides you with additional coping strategies to reduce the effects of stressors.

CHECK POINT 4.3

Answers appear in B3.

Multiple Choice See Test-Taking Strategies 10–15 in Appendix A.

_____ 1. Which statement is *not* true about stress?

a. Excessive stress hinders performance and cognitive abilities.

b. With effective stress-management skills, a person can avoid experiencing stress.

c. In some situations, stress can be beneficial.

d. Stress is caused by the ways you perceive and handle stressors.

_____ 2. You can learn to handle or manage stress by

a. using relaxation strategies and shifting your focus from a negative stressor to a more positive activity.

b. creating a strong support network.

c. using cognitive or behavioral coping strategies.

d. doing all of the above.

_____ 3. Which of the following statements is inaccurate?

a. Stressors are often created by external situations.

b. Ignoring stress is often an effective strategy to help it go away.

c. Excessive stress may become anxiety and may cause physical illnesses.

d. Both positive and negative stressors can disrupt a person's normal daily pattern or routine.

 Access Chapter 4 Practice Quiz 3 in your College Success CourseMate, accessed through *CengageBrain.com*.

Goal: Become a Procrastination Manager

④ *Explain how to become a procrastination manager by using effective strategies to identify and reduce procrastination.*

Procrastination is a learned behavior that involves putting off or postponing something until a later time. Chronic procrastinators have ingrained certain behavioral and cognitive patterns into their way of "doing life." They consistently choose low-priority tasks over high-priority tasks. Fortunately, because procrastination is a learned behavior, it can be unlearned, reduced, or eliminated.

> **Procrastination** is a learned behavior that involves putting off or postponing something until a later time.

Do you know any procrastinators? Procrastinators often exhibit the following characteristics:

● Accept and even boast about being procrastinators

● Pride themselves on being able to do things quickly, at the last minute, and under pressure

- Often wait for a "push," a threat of a specific consequence, a crisis, or some outside force to get the momentum to do what needs to be done
- Focus on proving they can complete a task in a short time frame, but may show little concern about the quality of the final product
- Use their procrastination as a legitimate excuse for not performing on high levels or not completing projects

Habitual or chronic procrastinators can create new behavioral and cognitive patterns that place a higher value on working first on high-priority tasks—even when they may not be as exciting or enjoyable as the low-priority tasks. Managing and reducing procrastination begins by understanding when and why procrastination occurs.

When You Procrastinate

Any time you find yourself avoiding a specific task or making statements such as "I'll do it when I am in the mood," "I have plenty of time to do it later," "I can let it slide a few more days," or "I will wait because I work better under pressure," recognize that you most likely are procrastinating. Become aware of your procrastination patterns and *when* you procrastinate. **Place a check next to the statements that describe you.**

_____**I tend to procrastinate when faced with specific kinds of tasks.** Any time you procrastinate, examine the task that you are postponing or avoiding. You may find yourself procrastinating about doing tasks that are uninteresting, too challenging or confusing, or difficult. For example, do you plan and follow through with studying for your computer class but procrastinate about studying for your writing or your math class? Do you empty the dishwasher but procrastinate when faced with doing the laundry? Examine the tasks involved when you procrastinate to look for patterns or kinds of tasks that trigger your procrastination. Formulate a plan of action to change your attitude and reaction to the task.

_____**I tend to procrastinate about beginning a specific task.** If you drag your feet and make excuses to avoid beginning a task, the source of your procrastination may be due to lack of motivation, lack of confidence in your ability to do the work, confusion about what steps are involved, or uncertainty about how to begin to tackle the task. Breaking the task down, setting goals, using the GPS Strategy, identifying incentives, and placing the task higher on your priority list can help you break through your procrastination pattern.

_____**I tend to start tasks but then procrastinate during the middle of the process.** When procrastination sets in during the middle of a process, you may have lost interest, motivation, or a sense of purpose in persevering to completion. Other times you may find procrastination in the middle of a process occurs due to time-related issues: you underestimate the length of time needed, you have other demands on your time that seem more urgent, or you fail to use your time-management skills and schedules. As soon as your momentum starts to shift, create a plan of action that utilizes strategies to boost your time-management, goal-setting, and motivation skills.

Procrastinators put off or postpone tasks for a variety of reasons and tend to choose low-priority tasks. Often they attempt to rationalize or justify their behavior. When and why do you procrastinate?

CONCEPT CHECK   4.17
What are common learned behaviors of procrastinators that would be beneficial to "unlearn"?

_____ **I procrastinate close to the end of the completion of a task.** Procrastinating close to the completion of a task or project is a way to quit and to avoid the final results. The underlying cause may be related to fear: fear of being evaluated or judged on your work, fear of failure, or fear of success. People who fear success become concerned that excellence on performance will put pressure on them to repeat that level of excellence on future tasks as well. Use strategies such as visualizing success, positive self-talk, incentives, and a goal organizer to motivate yourself to finish the task.

_____ **I tend to start multiple tasks, jumping from one to another, and making less important tasks seem more important or urgent.** This behavior is a common sign of the onset of procrastination. Procrastinators can get so caught up in this whirlwind behavior that they do not realize all the busy work is a mask for avoiding specific tasks. When you find yourself scurrying around, sometimes aimlessly keeping busy, take time to identify the task you are avoiding. Use the ABC Method for prioritizing the tasks you need to accomplish. Focus your attention on the tasks with highest importance and refrain from dedicating time to the less urgent or low-priority tasks.

CONCEPT CHECK **4.18**

Why is it important to analyze behavior patterns to identify when and why you procrastinate? Give examples of when and why you sometimes procrastinate.

Why You Procrastinate

Reasons for procrastinating vary for different tasks, situations, and individuals. In some cases, procrastinating will not have any serious consequences. For example, procrastinating about moving a stack of magazines to the garage or putting your CDs back in their cases has no dire consequences. In other cases, procrastinating leads to increased stress and additional problems. Procrastinating about paying your bills, studying for a test, or filling your tires with air will have more serious consequences, some of which could alter your goals or course for the future.

We all procrastinate at one time or another. When you are aware of _why_ you procrastinate, dig deep to discover your reason for putting off something important that needs to be done. **Check all of the following behaviors or underlying beliefs that tend to trigger your procrastination:**

_____ Lack of interest, motivation, or purpose

_____ Lack of confidence or low self-confidence

_____ Lack of strategies or skills for the assignment

_____ Difficulty, complexity, or length of an assignment

_____ Confusion or lack of know-how

_____ Weak time-management skills

_____ Poor judgment of time needed (overestimate or underestimate)

_____ Fear of failure or fear of success

As you conduct an honest search for the reasons you procrastinate, you may discover additional behaviors or beliefs that trigger this self-defeating pattern of behavior. Understanding both _when_ and _why_ you procrastinate is the first step to overcome the learned behavior of postponing or avoiding productive activity. **Figure 4.11** summarizes common causes of procrastination.

FIGURE 4.11   Causes of Procrastination

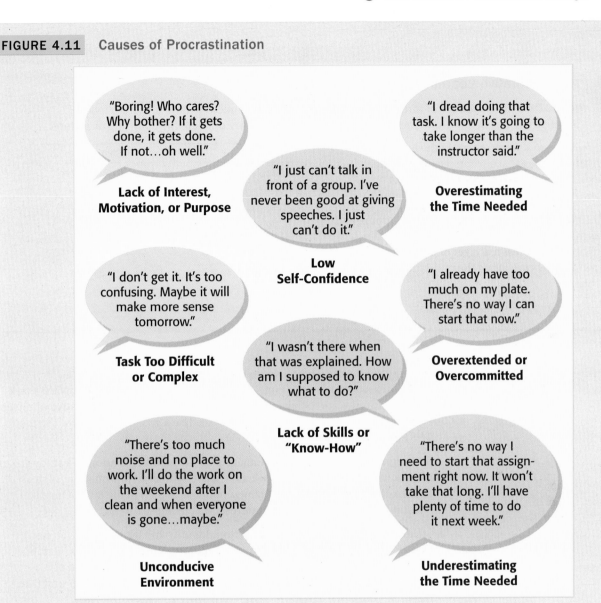

Essential Strategies to Combat Procrastination

Learning to reduce or eliminate procrastination can empower you, enhance your self-esteem, strengthen your self-discipline, and put you in greater control of your life. In addition to the time-management, goal-setting, motivation, and other self-management strategies that you have already learned, you can use the following ten recommended strategies to combat procrastination.

- **Strategy 1: Use your intrapersonal intelligence.** Explore *when* and *why* you procrastinate about a specific task. Use those insights to identify appropriate strategies to deal directly with the underlying issues.

GROUP PROCESSING

A Collaborative Learning Activity

DIRECTIONS: Form groups of three or four students. Each group needs to have a chart to record information. Select one group member to be the group recorder. Complete the following directions.

1. Create a two-column chart. In the left column, brainstorm and list any ten reasons people experience stress or procrastinate about assignments or tasks.

2. In the second column, brainstorm as a group. List as many different strategies a person could use to become a stress manager or a procrastination manager by combating the problems in the left column.

Reason	Strategies
Lack of motivation	• *Use goal organizer to identify importance* • *Break task into steps; use rewards for completing each step*

© Cengage Learning

Strategy 2: Identify a purpose and meaning. Avoid labeling a task as "meaningless, stupid, or boring" or expressing a negative attitude toward a task, as these attitudes and behaviors lower motivation and create a negative mindset. Find a purpose or a valid reason for the task. Use a goal organizer and use the GPS Strategy; identify the benefits.

Strategy 3: Create an interest. Engage a family member, a tutor, or a study group to work with you on the task. Seek alternative sources of information, such as a video, Internet searches, magazines, or books related to the topic. Once you become familiar with the topic, interest often increases.

Strategy 4: Take charge of the situation. Identify and list the steps you need to perform to break the cycle of procrastination about a specific task. Gather up all the supplies or materials you need to get started. Create a goal or a plan of action. Select an appropriate work environment. *Take charge* and take responsibility of the situation.

CONCEPT CHECK 4.19

Explain which strategies to combat procrastination you can use to manage your procrastination. What additional strategies can you suggest to combat procrastination?

Strategy 5: Prioritize and stick to the order. When you feel overwhelmed or overextended, make a list of tasks that must be done. Use the ABC Method to prioritize them by their importance or prioritize them by completion date requirements. Tackle the high-priority tasks first. Schedule time on your weekly schedule to work on these tasks.

Strategy 6: Use the GPS Strategy to set goals. Set goals with due dates and timelines. Identify the goal, the purpose or importance, and the steps to use to get you started and keep you going.

Strategy 7: Relax your personal standards. If you tend to be a perfectionist, lower your unrealistically high standards or expectations. You can continue to produce quality work without always having to be the "best." Avoid spending excessive time redoing parts of a task or the final outcome, such as a paper, when your work already shows quality.

- **Strategy 8: Be flexible and willing to change.** Be willing to give up the attitude that "I have always done things this way" or the false belief that "I work best under pressure or stress." Be willing to try new strategies and to create new behavior patterns that have the potential to produce higher quality work and reduce stress.

- **Strategy 9: Face your fear of failure.** Focus on your positive traits, your accomplishments, and the skills you have acquired. Use positive self-talk to negate self-doubts, silence self-criticism, and combat the fear of failure. Build your self-confidence by mentally rehearsing the steps of the task several times before you begin.

- **Strategy 10: Visualize success.** Create a mental picture of yourself working through a task, feeling positive about your work, and completing the task on time.

- **Strategy 11: Make a contract with yourself.** Make a contract with yourself to stop using excuses for not getting things done. Begin by creating a plan of action (a goal). Push yourself to "just do it." Finish your contract with an incentive, such as an extrinsic or an intrinsic reward.

- **Strategy 12: Use your interpersonal skills.** Seek the help, advice, and support of friends, family, and other students in class. If you feel you lack the skills or the know-how to do an assignment, meet and discuss the assignment with other students. If your work environment is not conducive to getting tasks done, discuss the situation with family or friends and make the necessary adjustments.

CHECK POINT 4.4

Answers appear on page B3.

True or False? See Test-Taking Strategies 1–9 in Appendix A.

_____ 1. Procrastination is a learned behavior that can be reduced or eliminated.

_____ 2. Students with a Perceiving personality preference always have problems with procrastination because of their preferred way to structure assignments.

_____ 3. If a person starts a task and later procrastinates, he or she may fear failure or find the task to be too complex or difficult.

_____ 4. Procrastination often involves selecting high-priority tasks over low-priority tasks.

_____ 5. For a chronic procrastinator, procrastination always begins right before he or she is close to completing the task.

_____ 6. Low levels of interest, self-confidence, and motivation may all be triggers that cause procrastination.

Access Chapter 4 Practice Quiz 4 in your College Success CourseMate, accessed through *CengageBrain.com*.

CHAPTER 4
REFLECTIVE WRITING 2

On separate paper, in a journal, or online in this textbook's College Success CourseMate, respond to the following questions:

1. Which strategies or techniques in Chapter 4 will you use to become a more skillful goal setter, stress manager, and procrastination manager? Be specific.

2. How will implementing these strategies or techniques benefit you? What differences do you expect to see because of your use of these strategies?

Access Chapter 4 Reflective Writing 2 in your College Success CourseMate, accessed through *CengageBrain.com*.

ACTIVITY

Chapter 4 Critical Thinking

PURPOSE: Goal setting is a process that has lifelong applications. At the beginning of each new year, many people make New Year's resolutions to change their lifestyle to become healthier, lose weight, or exercise more. Read Excerpt 3: Adopting a Healthy Lifestyle in Appendix D. Then complete the following activity.

DIRECTIONS:

1. Based on Excerpt 3, write a **long-term goal** that is meaningful and sincere for you.

2. Then write two or more **intermediary goals** that will help you move toward achieving your long-term goal.

3. Select any section in Excerpt 3. Write a **short-term goal**. Include the steps in the GPS Strategy.

4. Select any section in Excerpt 3. Use the GPS Strategy to write an **immediate goal** that you can achieve within the next few days. Follow your plan of action to complete the goal. Write a brief summary describing the process and the outcome.

Terms to Know

By yourself or with a partner, practice reciting or writing definitions for the following terms. You may also practice defining these terms by using the online flashcards or comparing your answers to the online glossary.

goals p. 102

long-term goal p. 103

intermediary goal p. 103

Learning Objectives Review

① *Explain how to use the GPS Strategy, visualization, extrinsic and intrinsic rewards, and other strategies to create a plan of action for term-long projects and for immediate, short-term, intermediary, and long-term goals.*

- Goals are well-defined plans of action aimed at achieving specific outcomes or results. Goals are roadmaps to guide you to your desired outcomes.

- Immediate, short-term, intermediary, and long-term are four kinds of goals based on the length of time required to achieve the goal.

- The GPS Strategy involves using a three-step approach for creating or planning goals: Goal, Purpose, and Steps.
- A goal organizer is a chart that consists of six questions to help you plan a course of action to achieve a specific goal.
- A five-step approach guides you through the process of planning and achieving a term-long goal. This approach involves doubling estimated time needed for steps and assigning dates for completion of the steps.
- A variety of strategies help you monitor your progress and help you become a skillful goal setter.

2 *Discuss ways to achieve goals by using intrinsic and extrinsic motivation, the Incentive Theory, the Expectancy Theory, and Maslow's Hierarchy of Needs.*

- Motivation is the driving force that moves a person to take action, create plans of action, and persevere to achieve goals.
- Intrinsic (inner) and extrinsic (outer) motivation drive people to achieve their goals. Intrinsic motivation in many cases tends to be more effective and fulfilling.
- The Incentive Theory of Motivation, the Expectancy Theory of Motivation, and Maslow's Hierarchy of Needs are three theories that explain motivators that drive people to take action to achieve goals or perform in specific ways.

3 *Explain how to become a stress manager by using coping, relaxation, and intrapersonal strategies to combat stressors.*

- Stress is a reaction or response to events or situations that threaten or disrupt a person's normal patterns or routines. Some stress is normal. Excessive stress is harmful, hinders performance, and results in physical consequences.
- Stressors are situations or actions that cause stress. Stressors may be positive or negative.
- Using coping strategies (cognitive, emotional, behavioral, and physical), relaxation techniques, and other stress-reducing strategies reduces stress and reactions to stressors.

4 *Explain how to become a procrastination manager by using effective strategies to identify and reduce procrastination.*

- Procrastination is a learned behavior that involves putting off or postponing something until a later time. It also involves choosing low-priority tasks over high-priority tasks.
- Understanding *when* and *why* you procrastinate is important to the process of becoming an effective procrastination manager.
- Twelve strategies can be used to combat procrastination. The goal is to reduce or eliminate the self-destructive habit of procrastinating.

Terms to Know
continued

short-term goal p. 105

immediate goal p. 105

GPS Strategy p. 106

goal organizer p. 107

Visualizing Success p. 110

extrinsic rewards p. 111

intrinsic rewards p. 111

motivation p. 113

intrinsic motivation p. 113

extrinsic motivation p. 113

Incentive Theory of Motivation p. 115

Expectancy Theory of Motivation p. 116

self-fulfilling prophecy p. 116

Maslow's Hierarchy of Needs p. 117

stress p. 119

stressors p. 119

coping strategies p. 121

cognitive coping strategies p. 121

emotional coping strategies p. 121

behavioral coping strategies p. 121

physical coping strategies p. 121

perfect place technique p. 122

soothing mask technique p. 122

relaxation blanket technique p. 122

breathing by threes technique p. 123

deep breathing technique p. 123

deep muscle relaxation technique p. 123

procrastination p. 124

 Access Chapter 4 Flashcards and Online Glossary in your College Success CourseMate, accessed through *CengageBrain.com.*

Chapter 4   Review Questions

Answers appear on page B3.

Fill-in-the-Blanks See Test-Taking Strategies 21–24 in Appendix A.

1. Visualizing _____ is the name of a strategy that involves visualizing your performance or completion of a goal.

2. _____ rewards are not physical incentives but instead are internal feelings, emotions, and responses that motivate a person to perform and achieve goals.

3. The driving force that moves a person to take action, create plans, and persevere to achieve goals is called _____ .

4. To reduce stress, people can learn to use cognitive _____ strategies to change the way they think about and perceive situations or stressors.

5. The deep _____ technique to reduce stress involves inhaling and exhaling slowly and with control.

Multiple Choice See Test-Taking Strategies 10–15 in Appendix A.

_____ 1. A(n) _____ goal is a plan of action to achieve specific results within one or two years and possibly be a subgoal for a long-term goal.
   a. short-term
   b. immediate
   c. intermediary
   d. long-term

_____ 2. Identifying a _____ is the second step in the GPS Strategy for goal setting.
   a. goal
   b. part of a goal
   c. purpose
   d. priority

_____ 3. The _____ Theory of motivation involves extrinsic or intrinsic rewards.
   a. Rewards
   b. Hierarchy
   c. Expectancy
   d. Incentive

_____ 4. A _____ organizer helps you plan and think about goals.
   a. short-term
   b. goal
   c. time-manager
   d. priority

_____ 5. Setting goals for a term-long project
   a. begins by listing all the tasks or steps required to finish the project.
   b. includes doubling the amount of time you estimate you need for each task.
   c. involves writing target dates on your term calendar and your weekly schedule.
   d. involves all of the above.

_____ 6. Which of the following names the levels of needs, from basic to complex, in Maslow's Hierarchy of Needs?
   a. physiological, belonging, esteem, safety, self-actualization
   b. self-actualization, esteem, love and belonging, physiological, safety
   c. physiological, safety, love and belonging, esteem, self-actualization
   d. physiological, love and belonging, safety, esteem, self-actualization

_____ 7. Which of the following is *not* a recommended goal-setting strategy to keep yourself motivated?

   a. Visualize yourself achieving your goal.

   b. Use a checklist or a journal to track your progress.

   c. Select meaningful intrinsic or extrinsic rewards that motivate you.

   d. Write your goals in a safe place so other people cannot see them and possibly discourage you from achieving your goals.

_____ 8. Procrastination

   a. may stem from lack of interest, fear of failure, or faulty beliefs.

   b. occurs when low-priority tasks take the place of high-priority tasks.

   c. is a learned behavior that can be altered by using effective strategies.

   d. involves all of the above.

Short-Answer Questions See Test-Taking Strategies 32–36 in Appendix A.

On separate paper, answer the following questions. Use complete sentences and terminology from this chapter in your answers.

1. Define any one theory of motivation. Explain how it works to motivate people to move forward and work to achieve goals.

2. In your opinion, what are the five most important strategies to use to become an effective goal setter? Briefly explain why each is important.

 Access Chapter 4 Enhanced Quiz and Chapter 4 Study Guide in your College Success CourseMate, accessed through *CengageBrain.com*.

Access all Chapter 4 Online Materials in your College Success CourseMate accessed through *CengageBrain.com*.

5 Processing Information into Your Memory

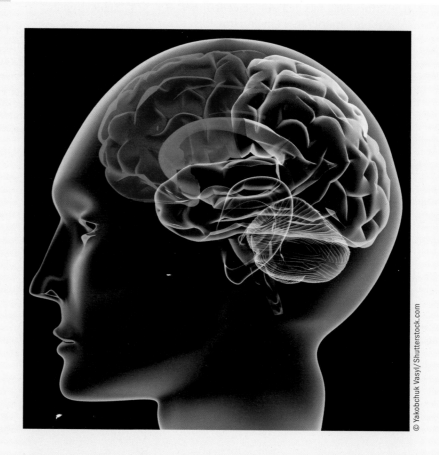

© Yakobchuk Vasyl/Shutterstock.com

For centuries, people have been fascinated by the workings of the human mind. Researchers and cognitive psychologists are now able to use sophisticated technology to study the human brain, its processing functions, and its complex structure. In this chapter, you will learn about memory models that depict ways information is processed into your memory. Twelve essential memory processes will provide you with the tools to strengthen your processing and memory skills.

1 MEMORY PROCESSES AND STORAGE CENTERS

Three Key Memory Processes

Three Memory Storage Centers

Three Storage Center Memory Processes

2 THE INFORMATION PROCESSING MODEL WITH WORKING MEMORY

Working Memory

Output

3 PROCESSES IN WORKING MEMORY

Attitude, Interest, Intention

Elaborative Rehearsal

Multisensory Strategies

Selectivity

Self-Quizzing and Feedback

Associations and Retrieval Cues

Rehearsal Time and Pace

Access Chapter 5 Expanded Outline in your College Success CourseMate, accessed through *CengageBrain.com.*

YOUR CHAPTER MAPPING

After reading information under each heading, return to the chapter visual mapping below. Add key words to show subheadings and important details related to each heading.

Access Chapter 5 Visual Mapping in your College Success CourseMate, accessed through *CengageBrain.com.*

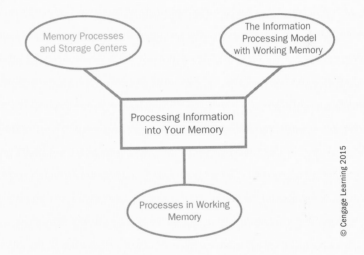

© Cengage Learning 2015

LEARNING OBJECTIVES

1 *Discuss the relationships between three key memory processes (encoding, storage, and retrieval) and three main memory storage centers (sensory, short-term, and long-term).*

2 *Sketch the Information Processing Model with working memory and summarize the processes that occur in each part of the model.*

3 *Identify and explain seven different learning processes used frequently in working memory.*

Processing Information into Your Memory

ANSWER, SCORE, and **RECORD** your profile before you read this chapter. If you need to review the process, refer to the complete directions given in the profile for Chapter 1 on page 4.

Access Chapter 5 Profile in your College Success CourseMate, accessed through *CengageBrain.com.*

ONLINE: You can complete the profile and get your score online in this textbook's College Success CourseMate.

	YES	NO
1. I have a general understanding of the ways I work with information to prepare it for my long-term memory.	_____	_____
2. I am aware of and pay attention to the different kinds of information I receive from my senses: sight, sound, smell, taste, and touch.	_____	_____
3. I try to take information in rapidly so I have more time to study or do other things.	_____	_____
4. I am aware of ways to use my conscious mind (working memory) to process information to store in my long-term memory system.	_____	_____
5. After studying a chapter carefully, I am able to perform or demonstrate that learning has taken place.	_____	_____
6. I use the processes of visualizing, reciting, multisensory strategies, and self-quizzing to learn new information.	_____	_____
7. I take time to relate or associate new information to information that I already know.	_____	_____
8. I study factual information the same way I study steps to perform a process.	_____	_____
9. Instead of working with information in new ways or examining it on deeper levels, I use rote memory to memorize more quickly.	_____	_____
10. I am confident in my ability to use effective strategies to boost my ability to process information without overloading working memory.	_____	_____

QUESTIONS LINKED TO THE CHAPTER LEARNING OBJECTIVES:

Questions 1–3: objective 1   Questions 6–9: objective 3

Questions 4–5: objective 2   Question 10: all objectives

Memory Processes and Storage Centers

1 *Discuss the relationships between three key memory processes (encoding, storage, and retrieval) and three main memory storage centers (sensory, short-term, and long-term).*

Understanding memory processes lays a strong foundation for many study skills strategies that you will learn in this textbook. Brain research, learning theories, and models of memory are more complex and more detailed than we will cover in this textbook, but understanding basic processes will equip you with essential information to help you increase your learning potential and personalize your approach to learning different kinds of information.

Metacognition is the process of understanding *how* you learn, *what* you need to learn, and finally, *which* strategies or techniques would be the most effective or best matched to the learning task. Understanding key memory processes is the first step to using the powerful process of metacognition.

Three Key Memory Processes

Understanding how your memory works and how to make your memory work more efficiently is of interest to most people, especially college students. Imagine the empowered feelings and unlimited success you would experience if you could develop memory skills to convert, store, and retrieve as needed all the important information you read or hear in class. Strengthening your memory involves a myriad of complex processes and interactions, but you can begin the process by understanding and applying what researchers have learned about memory. On a fundamental level, memory involves three basic memory processes: *encoding, storage, and retrieval.*

- *Encoding* is the process of attaching special memory codes to information so that long-term memory can process, categorize, and store it for later use and retrieval. Four kinds of encoding—visual, linguistic, kinesthetic, and semantic—will be explained later in this chapter.
- *Memory storage* is the process of holding or maintaining coded information for a given period of time. Coded information that is processed and stored in long-term memory is maintained for extended periods of time or stored permanently. In addition to remaining in storage, this information changes as it integrates with new, related information to expand or broaden in breadth and depth.
- *Memory retrieval* is the process of recalling, pulling back into use, or recovering coded information from memory. When you engage in a discussion or a debate and wish to use specific facts or concepts, you retrieve the details from memory. The same is true when you take a test; you need to be able to access your memory storage to locate and use the information that answers test questions.

Encoding, storage, and retrieval are the most basic processes involved in the complex process of developing memory. **Figure 5.1** shows these three basic processes. As you examine Figure 5.1, carefully read the text that accompanies the figure.

CONCEPT CHECK 5.1

Metacognition is the process of understanding what three things about the learning process?

Metacognition is the process of understanding *how* you learn, *what* you need to learn, and finally, *which* strategies or techniques would be the most effective or best matched to the learning task.

CONCEPT CHECK 5.2

What are the four ways you encode information for further processing? What does long-term memory do with coded information?

Encoding is the process of attaching special memory codes to information so that long-term memory can process, categorize, and store it for later use and retrieval.

Memory storage is the process of holding or maintaining coded information for a given period of time.

Memory retrieval is the process of recalling, pulling back into use, or recovering coded information from memory.

FIGURE 5.1   Three Key Processes in Memory

Human memory depends on three sequential processes: encoding, storage, and retrieval. Some theorists have drawn an analogy between these processes and elements of information processing by computers, as depicted here. The analogies for encoding and retrieval work pretty well, but the storage analogy is somewhat misleading. When information is stored on a hard drive, it remains unchanged indefinitely and you can retrieve an exact copy. Human memory storage is a much more dynamic process. People's memories change over time and are rough reconstructions rather than exact copies of past events.

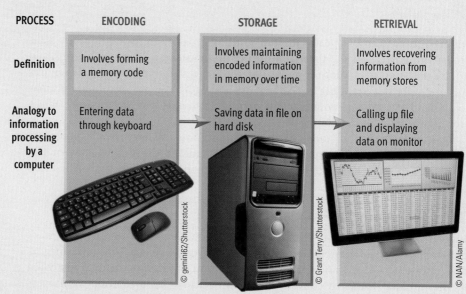

PROCESS	ENCODING	STORAGE	RETRIEVAL
Definition	Involves forming a memory code	Involves maintaining encoded information in memory over time	Involves recovering information from memory stores
Analogy to information processing by a computer	Entering data through keyboard	Saving data in file on hard disk	Calling up file and displaying data on monitor

From Weiten, *Psychology*, 9E. © 2013 Cengage Learning

CHAPTER 5 REFLECTIVE WRITING 1

On separate paper, in a journal, or online in this textbook's College Success CourseMate, respond to the following questions.

1. What kinds of problems do you encounter when you try to learn *new* information in your college courses?

2. Figure 5.1 shows an analogy between computer processing and memory processing. However, our memories are not computers, and they tend to encounter more "software problems" and glitches than machines. What variables do you believe result in your processing system working less efficiently than a computer?

    Access Chapter 5 Reflective Writing 1 in your College Success CourseMate, accessed through *CengageBrain.com.*

Three Memory Storage Centers

Sensory memory, short-term memory, and long-term memory are three memory storage centers that hold information for further processing or storage. However, there is no guarantee that the information that enters the first two memory storage

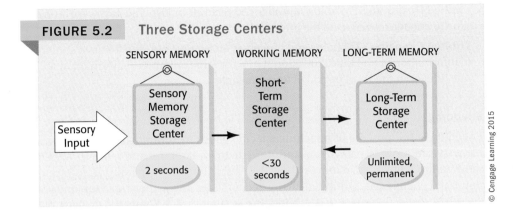

FIGURE 5.2   Three Storage Centers

SENSORY MEMORY   WORKING MEMORY   LONG-TERM MEMORY

Sensory Input → Sensory Memory Storage Center (2 seconds) → Short-Term Storage Center (<30 seconds) ⇄ Long-Term Storage Center (Unlimited, permanent)

© Cengage Learning 2015

centers will be processed further into long-term memory. Instead of being processed further, information may be dumped or discarded from memory. **Figure 5.2** shows these three storage centers. The following sections explain the sequence of processing or discarding information that enters into memory centers. (Working memory is discussed later.)

Sensory Input and Sensory Memory

Sensory input refers to all the sensory stimuli from the physical world that we receive through our five senses—sight, sound, touch, taste, and smell. Sensory input may be in the form of letters, numbers, words, visual images, sounds, smells, or tactile sensations, such as textures or the hardness or softness of objects. Sensory input enters the sensory memory center.

  Sensory memory is a temporary storage center that receives and holds sensory input for 1 or 2 seconds. *Selective attention* is the process of focusing on or attending to specific stimuli that are important to process further. If you use selective attention to attend to the information, the information moves forward into short-term memory. If you do not give attention to the information, it is dumped or discarded; in other words, it is not processed further—it is gone. This effortless process of discarding information is actually a valuable process, for without it our memory would bottleneck or get overloaded if we automatically processed everything that our senses take in from our environment. It is important to realize that you must make a concerted effort to identify or mark the information that you do not want discarded. Selective attention determines the fate of sensory input after it enters the sensory memory center.

Short-Term Memory

Short-term memory (STM) is a temporary storage center in working memory that receives information from the sensory center and briefly holds that information for further processing or encoding. Again, if you do not use selective attention to hold the information active so you can code it for long-term memory, the information will be dumped or discarded; in other words, it will not be processed further—it will be gone. A well-focused mind with the intent to learn is essential because short-term memory has two significant limitations:

Sensory input refers to all the sensory stimuli from the physical world that we receive through our five senses—sight, sound, touch, taste, and smell.

Sensory memory is a temporary storage center that receives and holds sensory input for 1 or 2 seconds.

Selective attention is the process of focusing on or attending to specific stimuli that are important to process further.

CONCEPT CHECK   **5.3**
Which holds stimuli longer, sensory memory or short-term memory? What is the value of the limited duration of these two memory centers?

Short-term memory (STM) is a temporary storage center in working memory that receives information from the sensory center and briefly holds that information for further processing or encoding.

- **Limited Duration:** STM holds stimuli for 30 seconds or less. You have very little time to encode and process the information.
- **Limited Capacity:** STM holds and processes an average of seven items or chunks of information at one time. You cannot process large amounts of information at one time or in the short period of time available.

Encoding

Encoding is the process of attaching specific codes to stimuli so that long-term memory can process, categorize, and store them for later use and retrieval. When information is encoded, it moves along the path to long-term memory. If information is not encoded, it is dumped, discarded, or fades away. There are four kinds of encoding: visual, linguistic, kinesthetic, and semantic. (See **Figure 5.4** on page 144 for the four kinds of encoding.)

Long-Term Memory

Long-term memory (LTM) is a permanent storage center that holds chunks of information received from working memory. Long-term memory is your personalized mental filing cabinet, data center, or memory warehouse that permanently "files away" and stores coded information received from short-term memory. The coded information is not shoved into long-term memory randomly or in an unorganized manner; that would make accessing the information difficult or impossible. Following are important points about long-term memory and its storage capacity:

- LTM has unlimited capacity; it never runs out of storage space.
- Encoded information is imprinted in LTM so it becomes permanent, but not necessarily always accessible. Variables, such as injury, medications, stress, anxiety, or partial encoding can block access to the imprinted information.
- Information is categorized and organized, not randomly scattered throughout long-term memory.
- *Schemas* are sets of memories or clusters of related information that form large concepts or frameworks to which other related ideas, facts, and details can be attached.
- As new information enters long-term memory and connects with existing schemas, the schemas expand and strengthen. Because schemas include personal experiences or understanding of concepts, schemas among people will vary.
- The number of schemas in a person's memory system is unlimited.

Three Storage Center Memory Processes

Selective attention, encoding, and building schemas are important memory processes that occur in the first two storage centers to prepare information for the third storage center, long-term memory. **Figure 5.3** summarizes the processes included in the sensory memory storage center, the short-term storage center, and the long-term storage center. This section introduces you to five memory processes to boost

---

CONCEPT CHECK   5.4

How does long-term memory storage differ in terms of duration and capacity from short-term memory? How are memories organized or structured in long-term memory?

Long-term memory (LTM) is a permanent storage center that holds chunks of information received from working memory.

Schemas are sets of memories or clusters of related information that form large concepts or frameworks to which other related ideas, facts, and details can be attached.

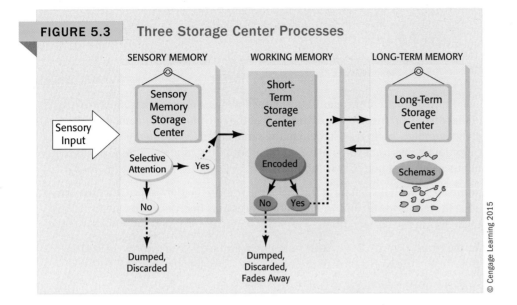

FIGURE 5.3   Three Storage Center Processes

your memory. After reading and understanding the following sections that expand on the key processes in Figure 5.3, you will explore your dynamic working memory system and the memory processes activated in working memory.

Selective Attention Processes

Selective attention is the process of focusing on or attending to specific sensory stimuli that are important to process further. Failure to use selective attention to "grab hold" of stimuli to move them forward into short-term memory results in stimuli simply disappearing—dropping out, getting dumped, or being discarded. For example, if you are in a room filled with people talking, you cannot take in and process all the conversations, all the visual stimuli, or all the other sensory stimuli in the room. If you did, you would experience sensory overload and would be unable to process anything clearly. Instead, you focus your selective attention on a specific conversation or on a smaller group of people, and you ignore the other stimuli. The ignored stimuli follow the automatic route—they drop out or get dumped. Following are additional important points about selective attention:

- Selective attention works when you study. As you read your textbook, the letters and words in a sentence enter your sensory memory. When you are using selective attention, you recognize that a sentence is important, select it for further cognitive processing and encoding, and immediately begin attaching meaning to the words. However, if you shift your focus from your book to a television screen or another distraction, the sensory input of the printed sentence fades and the television image or other distraction quickly replaces the textbook information. In other words, the distraction disrupts the encoding process you had started with the printed material.

- Consciously using selective attention will help you control and limit the sensory stimuli that you allow to enter into your memory systems.

- Your environment is filled with all kinds of stimuli that can easily distract you and throw you off course. You strengthen your ability to use selective attention by using the concentration strategies in Chapter 3 during all stages of the learning process.

© Cengage Learning 2015

CONCEPT CHECK   5.5

What is selective attention and what is its function? What kinds of activities can disrupt your selective attention?

EXERCISE 5.1

Capacity of Short-Term Memory

DIRECTIONS:

1. How big is your short-term or immediate memory span? Look at the following chart. Ask someone to read to you the numbers in the top row on the left side of the chart at the rate of about one number per second. Without looking at the numbers, try to repeat them in the same order. Continue this test on the next row and continue on additional rows until you make a mistake. Your immediate memory span is the maximum number of items you can repeat perfectly without error.

2. Do this test again, but this time begin with the letters at the top of the row on the right side. Continue row by row, with someone reading the letters to you and you repeating the letters in order. Stop when you make a mistake restating the letters in the correct order.

3. Repeat the same process for the rows of words. Begin with someone reading the three words on the top line. Do not look at the words. Repeat the words back in the same order. Stop when you make a mistake.

4. Answer the following questions:
   a. Was the immediate memory span the same for all three tests?
   b. Was your immediate memory span largest for numbers, letters, or words?
   c. Was your immediate memory span smallest for numbers, letters, or words?
   d. Try any one test again. Did you increase your memory span or not?

```
9 2 5                           G M N
8 6 4 2                         S L R R
3 7 6 5 4                       V O E P G
6 2 7 4 1 8                     X W D X Q O
0 4 0 1 4 7 3                   E P H H J A E
1 9 2 2 3 5 3 0                 Z D O F W D S V
4 8 6 8 5 4 3 3 2               D T Y N R H E H Q
2 5 3 1 9 7 1 7 6 8             K H W D A G R O F Z
8 5 1 2 9 6 1 9 4 5 0           U D F F W H D Q D G E
9 1 8 5 4 6 9 4 2 9 3 7         Q M R H X Z D P R R E H
```

```
CAT   BOAT   RUG
RUN   BEACH   PLANT   LIGHT
SUIT   WATCH   CUT   STAIRS   CAR
JUNK   LONE   GAME   CALL   WOOD   HEART
FRAME   PATCH   CROSS   DRUG   DESK   HORSE   LAW
CLOTHES   CHOOSE   GIFT   DRIVE   BOOK   TREE   HAIR   THIS
DRESS   CLERK   FILM   BASE   SPEND   SERVE   BOOK   LOW   TIME
STONE   ALL   NAIL   DOOR   HOPE   EARL   FEEL   BUY   COPE   GRAPE
AGE   SOFT   FALL   STORE   PUT   TRUE   SMALL   FREE   CHECK   MAIL   LEAF
LOG   DAY   TIME   CHESS   LAKE   CUT   BIRD   SHEET   YOUR   SEE   STREET   WHEEL
```

From Bernstein/Penner/Clarke-Stewart/Roy, *Psychology*, 9E. © 2012 Cengage Learning

- Selective attention works more smoothly without having to deal with intrusive thoughts, such as daydreaming, stress, general anxiety, self-talk, or distractions (television, radio, stereo, or iPods). Intrusive thoughts take up memory space that memory processing needs. The result is divided attention and a disruption in the process of focusing attention on incoming stimuli or information you intend to process.

MEMORY PROCESS 1: Intentionally use selective attention.

Use selective attention to narrow your focus to only the stimuli that you wish to process further. See your focus of attention as a filter that screens out sights, sounds, people, or other stimuli that may interfere with working on the important information to process.

EXERCISE 5.2

Sensory Memory and Selective Attention

DIRECTIONS: Complete each of the following activities to increase awareness of the function of sensory memory and selective attention.

1. To see how quickly sensory memory receives sensory input and how briefly it holds on to this input, look briefly across the room you are in. Shut your eyes and move your head to the right. Open your eyes for a second and shut them again. Notice how the images remained for only a second or two and then faded. Imagine how overloaded your memory would become if your mind held onto the steady stream of sights, sounds, smells, tastes, and tactile sensations that you experience.

   Questions: **What happened when you did this activity?**

   What other situations have you experienced where images stayed for only a few seconds?

2. "Sensory memory allows the sensation of a visual pattern, sound, or touch to linger for a brief moment after the sensory stimulation is over. In the case of vision, people really perceive an *afterimage* rather than the actual stimulus. You can demonstrate the existence of afterimages for yourself by rapidly moving a lighted sparkler or flashlight in circles in the dark. If you move a sparkler fast enough, you should see a complete circle even though the light source is only a single point. Sensory memory preserves the sensory image long enough for you to perceive a continuous circle rather than a separate point of light." (Weiten, p. 279)

   Question: **In what other situations have you experienced this afterimage?**

3. It is clear that people have difficulty if they attempt to focus their attention on two or more inputs simultaneously. "Although people tend to think they can multitask with no deterioration in performance, research suggests that the human brain can effectively handle only one attention-consuming task at a time. (Lien, Ruthruff, & Johnston, 2006). When people multitask, they really are switching their attention back and forth among tasks, rather than processing them simultaneously." (Weiten, p. 276)

   Questions: **What examples can you give that show your attempt to multitask while reading or studying?**

   How do these research results apply to texting while driving?

Sources: Adapted from Weiten, *Psychology* 9e (Wadsworth, Cengage Learning, © 2013), p. 275–276.

Encoding Processes

Four common kinds of encoding, shown in **Figure 5.4**, are visual, linguistic, kinesthetic, and semantic. Encoding, which begins during the brief time that stimuli are in short-term memory, translates the stimuli into meaningful forms for long-term memory. Even though initial stimuli are encoded in their original form (visual, linguistic, kinesthetic, or semantic), you can consciously or intentionally encode information in new ways so you can process it more effectively and thoroughly. For example, you may hear interesting information, but you intentionally encode the information into a visual form by taking notes or creating a picture of what you just heard.

When you study and practice (rehearse) information, you engage in the process of encoding on a deeper level. For example, if you see a diagram, a passage, or watch a demonstration, you can quickly consider new ways to think about or encode the information. As soon as your mind turns toward other ways to encode, for example, recalling the sounds you heard during the demonstration, creating a movie in your mind of the information, or moving hands to simulate a process, you encode on a deeper level. Your intentional actions also hold the information in short-term memory for a few more seconds so you can work with and process it more completely.

The detailed characteristics and strategies you learned in Chapter 1 for visual, auditory, and kinesthetic learning style preferences apply directly to encoding processes and strategies in this chapter. (Review pages 7-12 in Chapter 1.) Following is information about the fourth form of encoding, semantic encoding:

CONCEPT CHECK 5.6

Define the four basic ways to encode information for further processing. What relationship do you see between these four kinds of encoding and the cognitive learning styles in Chapter 1?

FIGURE 5.4   Four Common Kinds of Encoding

1. **Visual encoding**, also called *imaginal coding,* processes visual information:
   - Colors, brightness, shapes, locations of objects in space
   - Pictures, diagrams, images of objects and people, written symbols

2. **Linguistic encoding,** also called *acoustical* or *auditory coding,* processes sounds and language information:
   - Letters, words, phrases, sentences, syntax, meanings
   - Sounds, volume, pitch, rhythms

3. **Kinesthetic encoding,** also called *physical* or *motor coding,* processes large-muscle and small-muscle movement:
   - Actions performed by full-body movement
   - Actions performed by hand or foot movements

4. **Semantic encoding**, also called *conceptual* or *abstract coding,* processes general meanings of basic knowledge, objects, events, or personal experiences:
   - Categories, big pictures, units, or generalized concepts
   - Episodic memories
   - Emotional reaction or significance

- *Semantic encoding*, also called *conceptual coding* or *abstract coding*, processes the general meaning of basic knowledge, objects, events, or personal experiences.

- Semantic memories form a mental encyclopedia or resource of general knowledge you have learned over the years.

- Semantic encoding involves processing categories, concepts, or abstract generalizations of information and storing that information as one chunk or unit of memory. A variety of details are linked together to form a concept or unit of memory. For example, the concept you have about riding a bus, road trips, rodeos, soccer games, lab experiments, or graduation will differ from the concept or semantic memories others may have for the same topics. Your semantic memory is a generalization you have created based on your experiences.

An *episodic memory* is a memory of a specific experience (an episode) that includes specific details and emotions. Sometimes many of the details are clear, but the memory may not include specific details about the time or place. For example, you may have an episodic memory of your first time riding a bike without training wheels. You recall many details of the experience, but you may not be able to remember exactly when or where the experience occurred.

- You can semantically encode information by intentionally forming big pictures of concepts, generalizations, or experiences that include not only images but also senses, emotions, or feelings of significance. This process expands concepts already in your memory system by adding more details.

> **Semantic encoding**, also called *conceptual coding* or *abstract coding*, processes the general meaning of basic knowledge, objects, events, or personal experiences.

> **Episodic memory** is a memory of a specific experience (an episode) that includes specific details and emotions.

MEMORY PROCESS 2: Encode information on deeper levels.

Intentionally use visual, auditory, kinesthetic, and semantic encoding strategies. Be creative and use a variety of strategies to hold the information in your memory for a longer time by working with it in new ways. Review the multisensory strategies in Chapter 1.

Encoding Information

PURPOSE: You can translate sensory information that you receive into four different codes: visual, linguistic (auditory), kinesthetic (motor), and semantic (general meanings or concepts). Your instructors use a variety of approaches to present information in ways that promote the use of different kinds of encoding.

DIRECTIONS: Work by yourself, with a partner, or in a small group to answer the following questions:

1. What was a main topic discussed in the previous class? _____

2. Complete the following chart to show different ways you could encode the new information on the topic.

Visual Codes	
Linguistic Codes	
Motor Codes	
Semantic Codes	

© Cengage Learning

Short-Term Memory Processes

Encoding is not the only process or activity that occurs in short-term memory. As you recall, you need to attend to or act upon information quickly when it first enters your short-term memory. You have up to 30 seconds to respond to the incoming information and do something with it. If there is no attempt to work with the information when it enters short-term memory, it quickly fades and drops out of memory. For example, if you ask someone for a phone number or directions, unless you rehearse (practice) the information, encode it in a new way, or work with it, within 30 seconds you most likely will not recall the information accurately.

> **MEMORY PROCESS 3: Work immediately with incoming stimuli.**
>
> To keep the new information active and move it further along into memory, you need to consciously work with the information to prevent it from getting dumped or discarded. *Waste no time getting busy* by choosing some form of action to work with the incoming stimuli.

In addition to having limited duration, short-term memory (STM) has a limited capacity. On the average, STM holds fewer than nine items or chunks of information at one time. A chunk of information may be as small as new words or phrases, or it may involve larger images or steps, such as in a process. Following are additional points about the capacity of short-term memory.

CONCEPT CHECK   5.7

How many chunks of information can STM hold at one time? Why does the number of chunks it can process at one time vary?

- The size of chunks of information will vary depending on your familiarity with the material. For example, a student with limited background in chemistry may need to break some sentences in a chemistry book into word-sized chunks; however, a student with a strong chemistry background may be able to process larger chunks of information.

- Studies show that the average memory span for *new* information is three to five items or chunks of information. The average memory span for *familiar* information is five to nine chunks of information at one time.

- If too much information enters short-term memory at one time, or enters too fast, short-term memory becomes overloaded and some or all of the information is discarded or shoved out of the way for lack of space.

- Pay attention to the number of items you are trying to learn as a chunk. If there are too many items, chunking down or breaking the list of items into small groups or units will be more effective. For example, a list of twelve items is too long of a list for short-term memory. STM will become overloaded, and all twelve items will be difficult to process and learn. However, breaking the list into three sets of four items each accommodates STM's capacity.

- Understanding sizes of chunks of information can help you read and process textbook information more effectively. Read a small section of information, pause to make associations and to work with the information, and check your comprehension before moving to the next section of information to learn.

- STM's limited capacity influences the effectiveness of study strategies. Cramming for tests or attempting to read complex textbooks quickly results in limited information getting processed efficiently. In fact, stimuli may be dumped and not processed at all.

- You can use the Magic 7 ± 2 Theory discussed in Memory Process 4 as a guideline for the number of chunks of information to use without exceeding the capacity of short-term memory.

MEMORY PROCESS 4: Use the Magic 7 ± 2 Theory.

The *Magic 7 ± 2 Theory* states that immediate memory span is 7 items, plus 2 items or minus 2 items. Thus the range of immediate memory span is between five and nine items or chunks of information. For new and unfamiliar information, you may want to reduce the number of items to work with at one time to 3 to 5 items. On average, strive to work with 5 to 9 items or chunks of information at one time. For more than 9 items, chunk down to create smaller units to work with at one time.

The **Magic 7 ± 2 Theory** states that immediate memory span is 7 items plus 2 items or minus 2 items.

Processes to Work with Schemas

Schemas are sets of memories (clusters of related information) that form large concepts or frameworks to which other related ideas, facts, and details can be attached. The number of schemas in a person's memory system is unlimited. For example, you already have schemas for concepts such as shelter, fast food, pets, multiplication, cancer, global warming, taxes, loyalty, and football. **Figure 5.5** shows three graphic ways to diagram schemas with related details: hierarchy, visual mapping (or concept map), and category list.

Understanding the concept of schemas provides one explanation as to why learning new information sometimes is difficult, while other times it is relatively easy. The information in your schemas affects how you understand and process new information. For example, any new information you take in about biology gets interpreted or understood based on the information about and experiences you already have that are related to biology. The same would be true if you and a friend enrolled in a French class. If you have never studied a foreign language, you may feel confused and struggle with the course until you begin to form a schema for French. If your friend already speaks Spanish, he or she already has foreign language schemas in long-term memory and learning French would be less difficult for your friend.

CONCEPT CHECK   5.8

How many schemas do you have in your long-term memory? Name five schemas in your memory that are broad and well-developed, and five that are very weak or possibly even nonexistent.

FIGURE 5.5   Schemas: Big Pictures

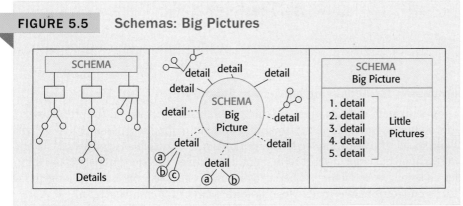

© Cengage Learning 2015

MEMORY PROCESS 5: Connect to and expand existing schemas.

Make a concerted effort to think about schemas and background information that you already have in your LTM. To increase the likelihood that you will be able to locate information in long-term memory when you need to activate and use it, make connections or associations to existing schemas.

- Ask yourself: *How are these things related or connected? What larger category of information does this belong to or get attached to in memory? How can I link these things together in the learning process?*

- Create visual notes, such as visual mappings, hierarchies, or categories with listed details to show relationships among kinds and levels of information.

EXERCISE 5.4

Transfer These Skills: Semantic Networks and Schemas

DIRECTIONS:

1. **Semantic Networks:** Go to Excerpt 4: Semantic Networks in Appendix D. Read and study the diagram and the caption that goes with the diagram.

2. **Course Concept:** The diagram in Excerpt 4 begins with the concept "fire engine." Select any concept you wish to use from one of your current courses. Create a semantic network for your concept. Pattern your semantic network after the diagram and the information that appears in the caption in Excerpt 4.

3. **Schema:** Expand the visual mapping at the beginning of this chapter. The schema expands the topic of this chapter: Processing Information into Your Memory.

4. **Contrasting:** Write a short paragraph to explain key differences between semantic networks and visual mappings.

Processes for Accessing Long-Term Memory

Long-term memory is a permanent storage center for information. The processes that move information back and forth and in and out of long-term memory occur with rapid speed. The following section on working memory explains in greater detail how information encoded in short-term memory is further encoded, prepared, and transferred to long-term memory. Chapter 6 discusses effective processes and strategies to locate and retrieve information in long-term memory for immediate use.

CHECK POINT 5.1

Answers appear on page B3.

Fill-in-the-Blanks See Test-Taking Strategies 21–24 in Appendix A.

1. _____ involves understanding how you learn, what you need to learn, and which strategies would be most effective or best matched to the learning task.

2. The process of attaching special memory codes to information so stimuli can be further processed into memory is called _____.

3. Information you code, process, and store permanently is stored in _____-_____ memory.

4. _____ is the process of pulling information out of long-term memory to use in a specific way.

 Access Chapter 5 Practice Quiz 1 in your College Success CourseMate, accessed through *CengageBrain.com*.

True or False? See Test-Taking Strategies 1–9 in Appendix A.

_____ 1. All sensory memory is first encoded linguistically.

_____ 2. Stimuli remain in sensory memory longer than they remain in short-term memory.

_____ 3. Short-term memory is limited in duration but not in capacity.

_____ 4. Using selective attention is one way to hold information longer in your sensory memory and in your working memory.

_____ 5. Schemas are clusters of related information in long-term memory.

_____ 6. Encoding results in deeper level learning.

_____ 7. Linguistic encoding processes auditory information; kinesthetic encoding processes images of experiences or events as one unit of memory.

_____ 8. You must identify and work with information in sensory and short-term memory to keep it from getting dumped or discarded.

The Information Processing Model with Working Memory

2 *Sketch the Information Processing Model with working memory and summarize the processes that occur in each part of the model.*

The *Information Processing Model* is a cognitive model that consists of three memory centers: sensory memory, working memory (which includes short-term memory), and long-term memory. The Information Processing Model provides a foundation for understanding the kinds of thinking activities, connections, and processes that are necessary for learning to take place. This model, which includes working memory, provides a more comprehensive and contemporary model to use to discuss thinking, learning, and memory. **Figure 5.6** shows the previously discussed memory processes and storage centers, with the following new details:

● A large area called *working memory* includes short-term memory.

The **Information Processing Model** is a cognitive model that consists of three memory centers: sensory memory, working memory (which includes short-term memory), and long-term memory.

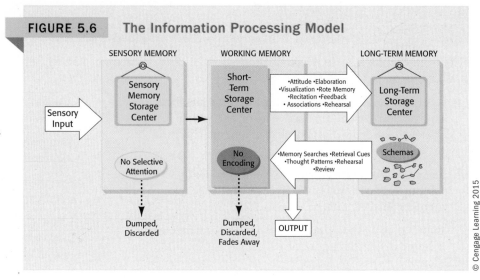

FIGURE 5.6   The Information Processing Model

The large arrow pointing to the right shows these actions or processes: attitude, elaboration, visualization, rote memory, recitation, feedback, associations, and rehearsal. The large arrow pointing to the left shows these actions or processes: memory searches, retrieval cues, thought patterns, rehearsal, and review.

© Cengage Learning 2015

- A variety of processes move information into long-term memory.

- A variety of processes pull information out of long-term memory and place it back into working memory where it can be used, integrated, and applied to new situations.

- Output demonstrates that learning has taken place; output may be the ability to provide an answer to a test question, problem solve, or perform a specific task.

Working Memory

The Information Processing Model consists of previously discussed memory processes and storage centers, but it includes a large area labeled "*working memory.*" ***Working memory (WM)*** refers to all cognitive processes or activities that occur in our conscious mind. Following are important points about working memory:

Working memory (WM) refers to all cognitive processes or activities that occur in our conscious mind.

- Anything that you are aware of doing or thinking occurs in working memory.

- Each time you pay attention to new information, rehearse, practice, make connections, link information, recall concepts or details, get feedback, problem solve, and achieve some form of output, you go beyond the limitations of short-term memory and begin using the larger, more encompassing working memory.

CONCEPT CHECK   5.9
Define the term "working memory" and discuss the kinds of cognitive work or processes that occur in this memory center.

- To understand new information, working memory searches for related information in long-term memory, activates it, and brings that information back into your working memory—your conscious mind.

- Working memory integrates the retrieved information with new information to form a larger, stronger, or more comprehensive unit of meaning or schema. Working memory then returns this expanded unit of meaning to long-term memory until it is needed and retrieved at a later time.

- As you work in new ways with new information, you encode the information on deeper levels using the same four kinds of coding as shown in Figure 5.4. The effectiveness of your strategies to encode information on deeper levels directly affects your ability to retrieve or recall information from long-term memory at a later time.

- As you work with information, your working memory rapidly moves encoded information both into and out of long-term memory. All in-depth learning and processing take place in working memory as you think about the material.

- When you work with *familiar* information (not new information), working memory holds a large "cloud" of activated information. For example, if you are skilled at troubleshooting and correcting computer problems, as you work with computers, your working memory activates large amounts of information you already know about computers.

- Working memory manages all cognitive functions, including the encoding processes that initially take place in short-term memory.

Output

When you successfully move information through your information processing system, you will be able to show output. *Output* is some form of action, demonstration, or performance that shows learning has taken place. Output may include recognition tasks or recall tasks. *Recognition tasks* are a form of output that demonstrates your ability to retrieve specific information or details when some kind of prompt or clue is provided. *Recall tasks* are a form of output that demonstrates your ability to retrieve specific information or details imprinted in your LTM when no prompt or clue is provided. In general, recall tasks are more difficult to perform than are recognition tasks. The following are examples of these two forms of output:

Recognition Tasks

- Recognize the correct answer from a list of options, such as in a multiple-choice question or a quiz-show format

- Recognize parts of an object when the labels for the parts are provided

- Recognize familiar faces, pictures, sounds, or tunes

Recall Tasks

- Respond with a correct answer when no clues or prompts are provided

- Use specific steps from memory to solve a math problem, to perform a process or a procedure, or to create or construct a product

- Recall and explain information from memory with accurate details

- Use critical thinking skills to evaluate, draw a conclusion, or debate a point

- Write an effective essay or report without referring to printed sources of information

Output is some form of action, demonstration, or performance that shows that learning has taken place.

Recognition tasks are a form of output that demonstrates your ability to retrieve specific information or details when some kind of prompt or clue is provided.

Recall tasks are a form of output that demonstrates your ability to retrieve specific information or details imprinted in your LTM when no prompt or clue is provided.

CONCEPT CHECK 5.10

What are the differences between the recognition and recall forms of output? Give two examples of each type of output that would appear on tests and two examples of each type of output that would be used in a class discussion.

EXERCISE 5.5

Labeling the Information Processing Model

DIRECTIONS:

1. Without referring to Figure 5.6, label the following chart to show *Sensory Input, Sensory Memory, Working Memory, Short-Term Memory, Dumped, Long-Term Memory, Schemas,* and *Output.*

2. Add the arrows to the chart to show the direction of the flow of stimuli and information.

3. Check the accuracy of your work by comparing it to Figure 5.6.

4. Then, put your notes and a picture of the model out of sight. On a blank piece of paper, draw and label all the parts of the model totally from memory. Finally, check your accuracy.

Information Processing Model

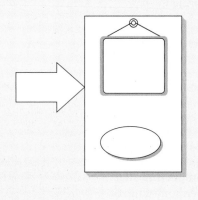
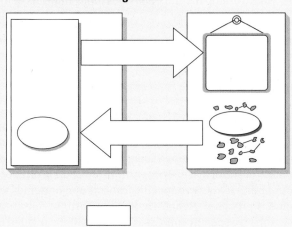

© Cengage Learning 2015

CHECK POINT 5.2

Answers appear on page B3.

Multiple Choice See Test-Taking Strategies 10–15 in Appendix A.

_____ 1. You can make a strong impression of new information by
  a. thinking or pondering the new information.
  b. focusing your attention on details.
  c. rereading the information several times over several different days.
  d. doing all of the above.

_____ 2. The Information Processing Model
  a. consists of three memory centers.
  b. includes sensory memory.
  c. includes working memory with short-term memory.
  d. includes long-term memory for permanent storage.

_____ 3. Which of the following is not accurate about working memory?
  a. Working memory includes anything you are aware of doing or thinking.
  b. Working memory works with encoded information moving in and out of long-term memory.
  c. Information is held in working memory as long as you are working with the information using processes such as rehearsal, deeper encoding, or associations.
  d. Working memory is another name for short-term memory with limited capacity and duration.

_____ 4. In the Information Processing Model, output

    a. refers to some form of demonstration that learning has taken place.

    b. may be in the form of recognition tasks.

    c. may be in the form of recall tasks.

    d. involves all of the above.

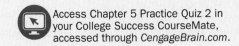 Access Chapter 5 Practice Quiz 2 in your College Success CourseMate, accessed through *CengageBrain.com*.

Processes in Working Memory

3 *Identify and explain seven different learning processes used frequently in working memory.*

Open almost any psychology textbook and you will find extensive information on memory, learning theories, and research. As research continues, information about memory and brain functions evolves and expands upon—and sometimes disputes—current understanding. In this textbook, the focus is on effective memory and learning strategies that are applicable to you as a college student.

Learning college material involves a variety of processes in working memory that you *initiate, activate, maintain*, and *control*. Knowing how to apply the processes in **Figure 5.7** and use working memory to imprint information in long-term memory empowers you to take charge of your academic performance and learning experiences.

> **CONCEPT CHECK** 5.11
>
> *Which of the processes in Figure 5.7 do you already understand and use well? Which ones do you need to learn more about to use effectively?*

Attitude, Interest, and Intention

In Chapter 2, you learned about the power of creating a strong, confident mindset and ways your attitude and level of interest affect your motivation, performance, and outcomes. In Chapter 4, you learned about setting and achieving goals and creating a drive or a motivation to achieve your plans of action. All of those self-initiated skills activate working memory and play a key role in boosting your memory. Each time you select strategies to practice or rehearse information, the process begins by

---

FIGURE 5.7   Learning Processes in Working Memory

1. Attitude, Interest, Intention

2. Elaborative Rehearsal

3. Multisensory Processing

4. Selectivity

5. Self-Quizzing and Feedback

6. Associations and Retrieval Cues

7. Rehearsal Time and Pace

© Cengage Learning 2015

your intention, or desire to process information and learn. The strategies you select may vary depending on the two main kinds of information you are learning: declarative (factual) or procedural (process) knowledge.

Declarative Knowledge

Declarative knowledge (factual knowledge) is information that includes facts, sets of details, definitions, concepts, events, or experiences. Learning a specific fact (1 meter = 100 centimeters), a set of details (three kinds of cognitive learning styles), a definition (working memory refers to all cognitive processes that occur in our conscious mind), a concept (the Theory of Multiple Intelligences), about an event (Boston Marathon bombing), or recalling an experience (a first job interview) all involve declarative knowledge in your working memory.

Procedural Knowledge

The second kind of information you may be working with is procedural knowledge. *Procedural knowledge* (process knowledge) is information that involves steps or processes used to solve problems or create specific products with accuracy and speed. Every time you perform a series of steps (balance your checkbook), apply a sequence of rules (subtract a double-digit number from a triple-digit number), unconsciously perform a procedure (ride a bike or rollerblade), or repeat a habit without having to think consciously about the individual steps (conduct Internet searches), you are working with procedural knowledge in working memory.

MEMORY PROCESS 6: Select appropriate strategies to work with declarative and procedural knowledge.

For declarative knowledge, select rehearsal strategies that involve working with factual information in new ways. Rearrange the information, create associations, use mnemonics or memory tools, recite the information, or practice quizzing yourself or a partner. For procedural knowledge, select rehearsal strategies that emphasize repetition of the original process *multiple times* over a period of several days and often over several months until it becomes automatic. Your intention is to perform the steps repeatedly, with the goal to increase speed and accuracy. To avoid using rote memory, explain each step in your own words to verify your understanding.

Declarative knowledge (factual knowledge) is information that includes facts, sets of details, definitions, concepts, events, or experiences.

CONCEPT CHECK 5.12

How does studying declarative knowledge differ from studying procedural knowledge? Why are different processes used for these two kinds of information?

Procedural knowledge (process knowledge) is information that involves steps or processes used to solve problems or create specific products with accuracy and speed.

© Andresr/Shutterstock.com

The amount of information you are required to learn each term can feel daunting. What memory processes do you use to help imprint information into your memory and manage the process of learning different kinds of information?

Elaborative Rehearsal

Elaborative rehearsal, also called *elaboration*, is the process of thinking about, pondering, or working with and encoding information in new ways. Elaborative rehearsal involves working with the information to achieve higher levels of comprehension and to activate critical thinking skills. When information from short-term memory moves into more active working memory, using elaborative rehearsal helps you do the following:

- Personalize information during the encoding and rehearsal processes of learning by "digging deeper" to clarify the meaning of new, unfamiliar information
- Generalize information; identify patterns, trends, and relationships, such as cause and effect or comparisons and contrasts
- Make stronger connections and associations to other long-term memory schemas
- Chunk down or break concepts into smaller units of meaning to understand how and why to use specific steps or processes
- Recognize applications of processes or other ways to use information

Elaborative rehearsal forces you to move beyond rote memory. ***Rote memory*** is the process of using repetition to learn information *in the exact form* in which it was presented. Rote memory works for tasks such as memorizing a telephone number, the spelling of a word, or memorizing a direct quotation, but it is ineffective for learning factual information from textbooks because you give insufficient attention to comprehending the information or learning ways to manipulate or use the information. When you use rote memory to memorize information from a textbook or to cram for a test, you may find yourself unable to respond to questions that present the information in a form other than the exact form you memorized.

Rote memory has limited value for learning, comprehending, and applying college course information. To avoid using rote memory, make a concerted effort to go beyond rote memory by attaching meaning and explanations to the information. Ask questions. Explain steps and processes, such as with math problems, and try other activities with the material, such as mentally summarizing the steps or parts or contemplating other applications for a process.

> **MEMORY PROCESS 7: Use elaborative rehearsal to process information.**
>
> Working with information in creative, personalized ways helps strengthen your understanding and your ability to recall the information at a later time.
>
> - Copy and rearrange information, group items together in new ways, convert information to pictures, or create visual mappings, timelines, or other graphic formats to show relationships, patterns, trends, and different levels of information.
> - Take time to question the information you are studying: *Why does this work this way? Why is this important? How can I use this? How can this apply to other situations?*

Multisensory Strategies

In Chapter 1, you learned about the significance of using multisensory strategies to encode information visually, linguistically (auditorily), and kinesthetically. Each type of encoding provides you with different paths into long-term memory that you can use to recall or retrieve information when you need it. Multisensory strategies frequently use the two processes of visualizing and reciting.

Elaborative rehearsal, also called *elaboration*, is the process of thinking about, pondering, or working with and encoding information in new ways.

CONCEPT CHECK 5.13
How does using elaborative rehearsal reduce or eliminate using rote memory? What kinds of problems might you encounter if you rely on rote memory?

Rote memory is the process of using repetition to learn information *in the exact form* in which it was presented.

Visualization

Visualization is the process of using visual encoding to make pictures or movies in your mind. For many students, information presented in a visual or graphic form, such as a picture or a diagram, is often easier to process and recall than information presented in print text such as paragraphs. Visualizing activates your working memory to encode information visually, creates memory cues to imprint in long-term memory, and strengthens your visual memory skills. The process of visualization involves "seeing" the pictures in your mind, without looking at the visual form itself, and rehearsing the mental images accurately. Following are important points and strategies for using visualization.

- To visualize, close your eyes and strive to see the picture, the graphic, or the movie "on the inside of your eyelids" or look up and to the left, toward the ceiling, to retrieve the visual image.
- Create movies in your mind as you read to increase comprehension. Visualize the characters, the setting, important details, and the unfolding action or sequence of events as soon as you begin reading.
- Visualize the sequence of steps required to complete a specific process.
- Rehearse frequently to strengthen the mental image. Visualizing occurs in your mind, so practice "seeing" objects or movies in your mind.
- Check the accuracy of the image by referring back to the original visual form.
- Read **Excerpt 2: Practice Visualization** in Appendix D for applications of visualization.
- Visualizing may involve the process of reading and then drawing a picture to represent the key elements. This picture is used to visualize an image to store or imprint in long-term memory. For example, after reading a textbook passage about the penetration of different kinds of radiation, a student drew the picture in the margin to clarify the concepts. Practice visualizing your drawing.

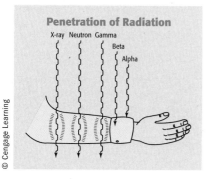

Recitation

Recitation is the process of explaining information clearly, out loud in your own words, and in complete sentences without referring to printed materials. Verbalizing or reading information out loud encodes the information linguistically but reciting information out loud goes further: it requires you to pull the information, out of your long-term memory, and it becomes a form of self-quizzing with feedback. Many reading and note-taking strategies include the process of recitation because of its powerful effects on the learning process and memory. Using recitation in working memory is a powerful way to boost your memory. Reciting helps you do the following:

- Encode information linguistically and use your auditory channel to send information to your long-term memory
- Practice using your own words to explain ideas in a coherent manner
- Assess and critique your ability to explain information clearly

The *Look-Away Technique* is another effective strategy that includes recitation. The *Look-Away Technique* involves looking at printed information and then looking away to recall and recite the details without any visual prompts. For example, after reading a passage or practicing your notes or textbook highlighting, look away from the printed materials and recite. Look back at the printed information to check the accuracy of the information you recited. When using this technique for graphs, charts, or other visual materials, you can include a step to create a visual image in memory before looking away and reciting.

MEMORY PROCESS 8: Use multisensory strategies to create strong impressions.

Multisensory strategies activate two or more sensory channels to memory. You can use multisensory strategies with combinations of visual, auditory, and kinesthetic encoding in a variety of ways.

- Ask questions, verbalize, recite frequently, and create rhymes, jingles, or songs to work with information and create new auditory codes for memory.

- Visualize information, such as objects, charts, printed materials, and steps to processes. Make movies in your mind. Rehearse the mental images to create a strong imprint or impression in your long-term memory.

- Use the Look-Away Technique and the See-Say-Do Strategy to activate your three main sensory channels.

- Use flashcards to rehearse definitions and factual information. Visualize, recite, and sort flashcards into categories. (See Chapter 9, page 286, to learn more about the use of flashcards.)

GROUP PROCESSING

A Collaborative Learning Activity

1. Form groups of three or four students. Select one student to record your group's responses to the questions that follow the excerpt You may be asked to share your response with the class.

2. Read the excerpt "The Greenhouse Effect." Then study the picture a student drew to help clarify the information.

The Greenhouse Effect

A window pane transmits sunlight. It is nearly transparent, and much of the shortwave energy passes through. Only a little energy is absorbed to heat up the glass. However, the walls and furniture inside a room absorb a large part of the solar radiation coming through the window. The energy radiated from the furniture, unlike the original solar energy, is all long-wave radiation. Much of it is unable to pass out through the window pane. This is why the car seats get so hot on a hot, sunny day when all the windows are closed. Try putting a piece of glass in front of a hot object to see how the heat waves are cut off. A greenhouse traps energy in this way when the sun shines, and so does the atmosphere. From *Investigating the Earth,* American Geological Institute.

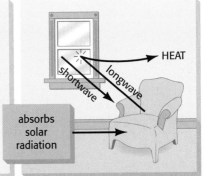

3. Discuss how the student who converted the text to a picture used the processes of intention, interest, attitude, and elaborative rehearsal.

4. Use visualization to create a clear image of the student's drawing. Stare at the picture, then look away, and mentally rehearse the picture. Then draw it without looking.

Selectivity is the process of identifying and separating main ideas and important details from a larger body of information.

CONCEPT CHECK   5.16
Define the process of selectivity and explain how you can use it when you read, study, or take notes.

Selectivity

Selectivity is the process of identifying and separating main ideas and important details from a larger body of information. As you recall, short-term memory has a limited capacity. Working memory has its limitations as well and can become overloaded when too much information enters it too quickly, reducing the ability to process effectively. Trying to learn everything—every detail, every example, every word you read or hear—is not possible, certainly not reasonable, and would result in overloading your working memory. Selectivity helps you do the following:

- Identify and select which concepts, main ideas, and significant supporting details are important to attend to and learn
- Decide what to survey in a chapter, highlight in a textbook, write in your notes, and what to study for a test
- Identify what information you can ignore or do not need to process
- Avoid cluttering long-term memory schemas with insignificant, disorganized, and nonessential information
- Avoid overloading working memory

MEMORY PROCESS 9: Use selectivity when you study.

Focus your attention on the information that is meaningful and relevant. When you read, highlight your textbook, or take notes, select the main ideas or the most important details to learn. Do not try to remember or memorize every single detail.

CONCEPT CHECK   5.17
Name the steps in the Feedback Model. Give an example of a specific kind of information moving through the steps of this model.

Self-quizzing is the process of testing yourself so you can receive feedback about the accuracy and completeness of your understanding.

Feedback is the process of verifying how accurately and thoroughly you have or have not learned specific information.

Self-Quizzing and Feedback

You have learned that information encoded in short-term memory is moved forward into working memory for further processing. You have many options for working with information in working memory. How do you know if the learning strategies you are using are effective? Self-quizzing and feedback provide you with confirmation that your working memory is active; in addition, they slow down the learning process so you do not attempt to push too much information too quickly through working memory.

Self-quizzing is the process of testing yourself so you can receive feedback about the accuracy and completeness of your understanding. Self-quizzing occurs each time you do any of the following:

- Visualize, recite, or use the Look-Away Technique
- Rework math problems without looking at the original problems
- Mentally rehearse or mentally summarize details

Feedback is the process of verifying how accurately and thoroughly you have or have not learned specific information. Feedback provides you with strategies to monitor your learning progress and assess the effectiveness of the learning strategies you chose to use.

FIGURE 5.8   The Feedback Model

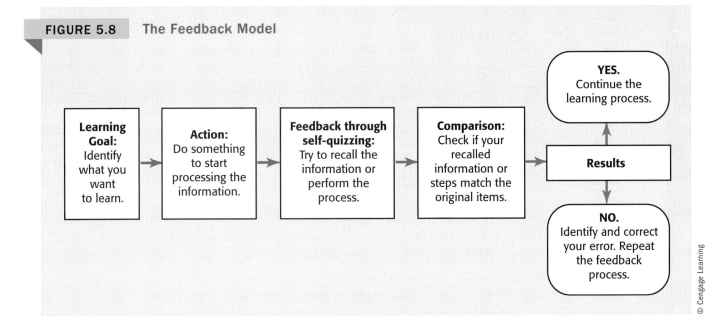

© Cengage Learning

Positive feedback is a response that shows you accurately understand specific information. Receiving positive feedback increases confidence, interest, concentration, and motivation. It also reinforces or strengthens the mental impression of the information.

Negative feedback is a response that shows you have limited or inaccurate understanding of specific information. It makes you aware of faulty or incomplete memory of information. If you receive negative feedback, you have the opportunity to adjust your strategies to achieve higher levels of performance and positive feedback.

The *Feedback Model* is a five-step process that demonstrates whether learning has or has not taken place. **Figure 5.8** shows the five steps of the Feedback Model: a learning goal→an action→feedback through self-quizzing→comparison to check accuracy→a positive or negative result.

Positive feedback is a response that shows you accurately understand specific information.

Negative feedback is a response that shows you have limited or inaccurate understanding of specific information.

The **Feedback Model** is a five-step process that demonstrates whether learning has or has not taken place.

MEMORY PROCESS 10: Include feedback in learning processes.

Get feedback about the accuracy of your learning during all stages of learning: at the beginning stages of taking in information, during rehearsal stages, and during review stages.

- Use self-quizzing, partner quizzing, and feedback to monitor and assess the effectiveness of your effort to learn.
- Create practice tests to complete by yourself or with a partner without access to textbooks or notes.
- Use positive or negative feedback to adjust your review materials and study methods.

CONCEPT CHECK 5.18

What might happen if you avoid getting feedback throughout the learning process? How can negative feedback have a positive effect?

EXERCISE 5.6

Textbook Case Studies

DIRECTIONS:

1. Read each case study carefully. Respond to the question at the end of each case study by using strategies from Chapter 5 to answer each question. Answer in complete sentences.

2. Write your responses on paper or online in this textbook's College Success CourseMate, Textbook Case Studies. You will be able to print your online response or e-mail it to your instructor.

CASE STUDY 1: Ayo attends college on an athletic scholarship. As a result of the demands of training, practices, and games, he has insufficient time to study. He crams as much reading and homework as possible into a few blocks of time each day. However, his methods are not working. The information just does not seem to be "sticking," and he is unable to recall what he read or what homework he completed. What memory processes is Ayo not using effectively to get better results from his study hours?

CASE STUDY 2: Eduardo spends far more time studying than do any of his other friends or classmates. His learning goal when he studies is to highlight almost every sentence in his textbook and then memorize the highlighted details. He rereads the highlighted information frequently because he believes this overlearning will trigger his memory. Eduardo does not understand why all his time and effort are not paying off. He does poorly on most tests because few of the questions use the exact wording that he memorized. Which memory strategies would help Eduardo achieve better results on his tests?

 Access Chapter 5 Textbook Case Studies in your College Success CourseMate, accessed through *CengageBrain.com*.

Associations and Retrieval Cues

Association is the process of linking together two or more items or chunks of information to process into long-term memory. Associations are an essential component of cognitive processing as long-term memory is organized around schemas and associations. *Paired associations* are two items linked together in working memory and sent to long-term memory to be imprinted. Recall of one item triggers recall of the second item. Terms and definitions and pictures to words are examples of paired associations.

Associations are powerful retrieval cues to help locate information in long-term memory. *Retrieval cues* are forms of information used to conduct memory searches to locate information stored in long-term memory. Words, phrases, pictures, graphics, familiar objects, numbers, tunes, personal experiences, familiar situations, or mnemonics (memory tools) are common kinds of retrieval cues. Following are additional ways to create and use associations.

- Connect and integrate new information with previously learned or familiar information. Ask yourself: *What do I already know about this? How is this similar to something I already know? Where have I experienced or seen something like this before? What schema does this belong in? What is familiar and what is new?*

> **Association** is the process of linking together two or more items or chunks of information to process into long-term memory.

> **Paired associations** are two items linked together in working memory and sent to long-term memory to be imprinted.

> **Retrieval cues** are forms of information used to conduct memory searches to locate information stored in long-term memory.

- Identify key parts of the information that you need to learn. Use these details, such as colors, sounds, or movement, to create clearer, more detailed images linked together in memory.

- Create and practice paired associations so recalling one part of the association triggers recall of the other part.

- Create an association between information and where you learned the information. Ask yourself: *Did I learn this from the textbook? Was this a part of a lab project or homework assignment? Did we discuss this in class? Do I have this in my notes or handouts?*

- Create chains of associations to use in memory searches to recall information.

- Use associations to create mnemonics (memory tools). (See Chapter 6.)

CONCEPT CHECK   5.19

What specific paired associations have you recently created? How do associations help improve memory?

MEMORY PROCESS 11: Create and practice associations and retrieval cues.

Creating associations and retrieval cues holds new information longer in your working memory to provide time to begin encoding the information in new ways. Keep information in long-term memory active and accessible by rehearsing and using retrieval cues on an ongoing basis. With ongoing practice, you will be able to increase the speed and accuracy of locating and recalling information from long-term memory to demonstrate output.

Rehearsal Time and Pace

The ability to comprehend and remember what you have studied diminishes when you overload your memory system by trying to study too much information at one time (cramming) or by studying for too long a period of time (marathon studying). Learning to monitor your intake speed and use spaced practice or distributed practice gives your mind time to absorb, integrate, process, and comprehend the information you are studying.

CONCEPT CHECK   5.20

Why does it not work to rush the learning process? Why are cramming and marathon studying not recommended working memory processes?

As you process and rehearse information, work slowly enough to allow sufficient time to retrieve meanings and related information from long-term memory and return them to working memory. For example, read a short section of information, pause to think and make connections and associations, then read a little more, and pause to make new connections or associations. Continue to practice or rehearse (a process referred to as overlearning) even after you feel you have learned the information. Overlearning enhances the ability to recall information quickly and with less effort.

MEMORY PROCESS 12: Do not rush the learning process.

The learning process and its many cognitive functions take time. As you learn more rehearsal strategies, the importance of giving yourself ample time to use the strategies effectively increases. Creating associations, linking information, reading and identifying key ideas at a comfortable pace, visualizing, reciting, self-quizzing, and using elaborative rehearsal processes and strategies require time and multiple contacts with the information. Learning is not a fast process, so it is important to be patient, attentive, and move forward at a steady pace.

EXERCISE 5.7

Working Memory Inventory

DIRECTIONS: Go to Exercise 5.7: Working Memory Inventory in Appendix C, page C11, to complete the Working Memory Inventory to assess the effectiveness of the study skills and working memory strategies you currently use. You can retake the inventory at different times during the term.

CHAPTER 5 REFLECTIVE WRITING 2

 On separate paper, in a journal, or online in this textbook's College Success CourseMate, respond to the following questions.

1. What did you learn about your memory processes when you took the Working Memory Inventory in Exercise 5.7? Be specific. If your instructor did not assign the inventory, go to Appendix C to complete it before answering this question.

2. What processes or strategies in Chapter 5 are most beneficial for you to learn to master? Explain their significance to your process of building a stronger memory.

 Access Chapter 5 Reflective Writing 2 in your College Success CourseMate, accessed through *CengageBrain.com*.

CHECK POINT 5.3

Answers appear on page B3.

True or False? See Test-Taking Strategies 1–9 in Appendix A.

_____ 1. Trying to process large amounts of information quickly may overload your working memory.

_____ 2. Your interest level and attitude have little effect on the functions of working memory.

_____ 3. Working memory strategies differ for factual and procedural information.

_____ 4. Repetition or rehearsal multiple times of information in its exact original form is the most effective approach to work with declarative knowledge.

_____ 5. Elaborative rehearsal always involves fancy, elaborate strategies that require extensive time to use correctly.

_____ 6. The best questions to use for elaborative rehearsal are *who, what* and *when* questions that emphasize rote memory.

_____ 7. Visualizing and reciting are effective strategies to use in working memory to create a stronger impression or imprint of information in long-term memory.

_____ 8. Using selectivity is one way to avoid overloading working memory with insignificant or less important information.

Access Chapter 5 Practice Quiz 3 in your College Success CourseMate, accessed through *CengageBrain.com*.

Chapter 5 Critical Thinking

PURPOSE: This chapter discusses twelve memory processes to boost your learning potential. As you know, critical thinking involves working with information in new ways, problem solving, applications, and creativity. Use your critical thinking skills to complete any *one* of the following options.

DIRECTIONS:

1. Create a chart, a visual mapping, a brochure, or a PowerPoint presentation that organizes the twelve processes in a clear, meaningful way. For each process, attach significant details or explanations as to how you can use the process when studying.

2. Personalize and apply the processes. For each process, write a paragraph explaining specific ways you can apply the process to studying for one of your courses.

3. Select any *three* concepts from the Terms to Know list for this chapter. Conduct an Internet search for all three concepts to locate new information that you can use to expand your schema for each term. Print the information with the URL source. Summarize your findings.

Learning Objectives Review

Terms to Know

1. *Discuss the relationships between three key memory processes (encoding, storage, and retrieval) and three main memory storage centers (sensory, short-term, and long-term).*

- Metacognition is a process designed to help you understand how you think, process, learn, and apply memory strategies to improve your performance.

- Encoding, memory storage, and mental retrieval are three key memory processes.

- Sensory input moves through the sensory memory storage center and the short-term memory storage center for visual, auditory, kinesthetic, or semantic encoding before entering the permanent, long-term memory storage center.

- Short-term memory is limited in duration and capacity.

- Encoding is the process of attaching codes to stimuli so that long-term memory can accept, understand, use, and store the information.

- Long-term memory is a permanent storage center that holds chunks of information indefinitely in schemas.

- Five memory processes help you develop or strengthen selective attention, encode information, and create or connect to schemas in long-term memory.

2. *Sketch the Information Processing Model with working memory and summarize the processes that occur in each part of the model.*

- The Information Processing Model consists of three main memory centers: sensory memory, working memory, and long-term memory. Short-term memory is a part of the working memory center.

By yourself or with a partner, practice reciting or writing definitions for the following terms. You may also practice defining these terms by using the online flashcards or comparing your answers to the online glossary.

metacognition p. 137

encoding p. 137

memory storage p. 137

memory retrieval p. 137

sensory input p. 139

sensory memory p. 139

selective attention p. 139

short-term memory (STM) p. 139

long-term memory (LTM) p. 140

schemas p. 140

semantic encoding p. 145

episodic memory p. 145

Magic 7 ± 2 Theory p. 147

Information Processing Model p. 149

working memory (WM) p. 150

output p. 151

recognition tasks p. 151

Terms to Know (continued)

recall tasks p. 151

declarative knowledge p. 154

procedural knowledge p. 154

elaborative rehearsal p. 155

rote memory p. 155

visualization p. 156

recitation p. 156

Look-Away Technique p. 156

selectivity p. 158

self-quizzing p. 158

feedback p. 158

positive feedback p. 159

negative feedback p. 159

Feedback Model p. 159

association p. 160

paired associations p. 160

retrieval cues p. 160

 Access Chapter 5 Flashcards and Online Glossary in your College Success CourseMate, accessed through *CengageBrain.com.*

- The Information Processing Model includes other important parts and processes: sensory input, selective attention, dumping or discarding, encoding, rehearsal and retrieval paths, and output.

- Working memory refers to all cognitive processes or activities that occur in your conscious mind. Therefore, anything that you are aware of thinking or doing occurs in working memory.

- Output involves demonstrating or performing to show that learning has taken place. Output may involve recognition tasks or recall tasks.

3 *Identify and explain seven different learning processes used frequently in working memory.*

- You can initiate, activate, maintain, and control processes in working memory by using working memory strategies.

- Working memory processes declarative (factual) and procedural (process) knowledge. Strategies to process both kinds of information vary.

- Elaborative rehearsal involves using a variety of strategies to process information on deeper levels.

- Seven processes help move information through working memory more effectively. These include going beyond rote memory, visualizing, reciting, selectivity, self-quizzing and feedback, and creating associations.

- The Feedback Model is a five-step process that shows whether learning has or has not taken place. It may result in positive or negative feedback.

- Associations, including paired associations, link two or more items together in memory and create retrieval cues to locate and recall information from long-term memory.

- Learning involves dedicating sufficient time to processing and rehearsing information.

Chapter 5   Review Questions

Answers appear on page B3.

True or False? See Test-Taking Strategies 1–9 in Appendix A.

_____ 1. Short-term memory and working memory hold all sensory stimuli until all of the information is thoroughly learned.

_____ 2. Long-term memory can recognize and process linguistic, kinesthetic, visual, and semantic codes.

_____ 3. Most sensory input that you ignore in sensory memory fades or is discarded from memory.

_____ 4. When you use self-quizzing, the information you are using moves through the steps of the Feedback Model.

_____ 5. Using selective attention can delay or prevent stimuli from fading or being discarded.

_____ 6. People can control and direct what goes into long-term memory, but they cannot control or direct what goes into and out of the other memory systems.

_____ 7. Rote memory is more effective for procedural knowledge than it is for declarative knowledge.

_____ 8. Creating an interest, setting learning goals, creating and using associations, and self-quizzing are processes to strengthen working memory.

_____ 9. The Magic 7 ± 2 Theory refers to the range of items in the immediate memory span.

_____ 10. Multisensory learning strategies involve using multiple forms of encoding.

Matching See Test-Taking Strategies 16–20 in Appendix A.

Match the terms below with the descriptions at the right. On the line, write the letter from the list at the right to show your answer.

_____ 1. Schemas

_____ 2. Long-term memory

_____ 3. Output

_____ 4. Selective attention

_____ 5. Sensory input

_____ 6. Semantic memory

_____ 7. Working memory

_____ 8. Sensory memory

_____ 9. Short-term memory

_____ 10. Rote memory

a. Stimuli received by our five senses from the physical world

b. A memory with generalized meaning of basic knowledge or concepts

c. A temporary storage center that holds stimuli for only a few seconds

d. Conscious memory that includes all mental activities that you are aware of performing

e. Memorizing information in its exact form without using elaborative rehearsal

f. Includes recognition tasks and recall tasks

g. Clusters of related information in long-term memory

h. Permanent memory with unlimited capacity

i. The process of focusing on specific input or stimuli

j. A temporary storage center in working memory

Recall Question In the space below, draw and label the parts of the Information Processing Model.

Access Chapter 5 Enhanced Quiz and Chapter 5 Study Guide in your College Success CourseMate, accessed through *CengageBrain.com.*

Access all Chapter 5 Online Materials in your College Success CourseMate accessed through *CengageBrain.com.*

6 Rehearsing and Retrieving Information from Memory

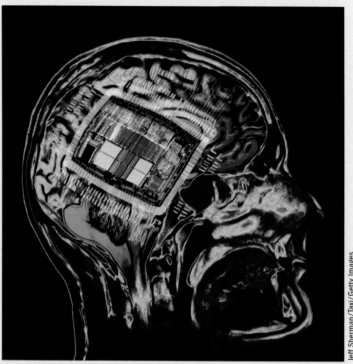

Jeff Sherman/Taxi/Getty Images

Now that you have learned strategies to process information into your long-term memory, this chapter shifts the focus to the processes to use to retrieve or recall information stored in memory. The Twelve Principles of Memory in this chapter are the foundation for many study skills strategies presented throughout this textbook. The mnemonic (memory tool) SAVE CRIB FOTO provides you with a retrieval cue to trigger your memory and to recall quickly these twelve principles. Finally, you will learn about mnemonic systems to use to boost your memory and your ability to recall information that otherwise is difficult to recall efficiently or completely. By using the strategies and skills in this chapter, you will strengthen your ability to access the information you have imprinted and stored in long-term memory.

CHAPTER OUTLINE

 Access Chapter 6 Expanded Outline in your College Success CourseMate, accessed through *CengageBrain.com*.

YOUR CHAPTER MAPPING

After reading information under each heading, return to the chapter visual mapping below. Add key words to show subheadings and important details related to each heading.

 Access Chapter 6 Visual Mapping in your College Success CourseMate, accessed through *CengageBrain.com*.

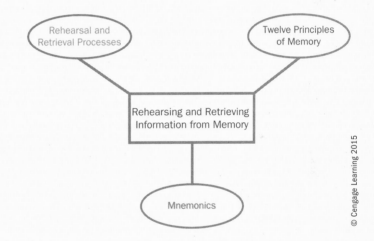

© Cengage Learning 2015

LEARNING OBJECTIVES

1 Explain four processes that work in your conscious mind (memory searches, retrieval cues, thought patterns, and rehearsal/review) and six forgetting theories that explain why forgetting sometimes occurs.

2 Explain the Twelve Principles of Memory represented by the mnemonic SAVE CRIB FOTO.

3 Explain how to create and use mnemonics to learn academic information.

167

Rehearsing and Retrieving Information from Memory

ANSWER, SCORE, and **RECORD** your profile before you read this chapter. If you need to review the process, refer to the complete directions given in the profile for Chapter 1 on page 4.

Access Chapter 6 Profile in your College Success CourseMate, accessed through *CengageBrain.com*.

ONLINE: You can complete the profile and get your score online in this textbook's College Success CourseMate.

	YES	NO
1. When I attempt to recall information, I take the time to use associations and retrieval cues to search my memory for the information.	_____	_____
2. Information I study is fixed in memory so I do not spend time with additional practice.	_____	_____
3. I focus attention on recalling the items in the middle of lists as they are often the most difficult to recall.	_____	_____
4. I understand why forgetting might occur, so I use strategies to combat forgetting.	_____	_____
5. I know how to use the memory principles of Selectivity, Association, Intention, Big and Little Pictures, and Time on Task.	_____	_____
6. I know how to use the memory principles of Visualization, Elaboration, Concentration, Recitation, Feedback, and Ongoing Review.	_____	_____
7. I avoid cluttering my mind with mnemonics or memory tricks because they are too hard to remember.	_____	_____
8. I use picture and word associations to trigger recall of information stored in long-term memory.	_____	_____
9. I tend to have problems remembering the items I wish to include in speeches, essays, or discussions.	_____	_____
10. I am confident in my ability to use effective strategies to rehearse and retrieve information from long-term memory.	_____	_____

QUESTIONS LINKED TO THE CHAPTER LEARNING OBJECTIVES:

Questions 1–4: objective 1   Questions 7–9: objective 3

Questions 5–6: objective 2   Question 10: all objectives

Rehearsal and Retrieval Processes

1 *Explain four processes that work in your conscious mind (memory searches, retrieval cues, thought patterns, and rehearsal/review) and six forgetting theories that explain why forgetting sometimes occurs.*

In Chapter 5, you learned twelve memory processes used in the Information Processing Model to take in and learn new information. **Figure 5.6** in Chapter 5 shows effective strategies to imprint information in schemas in long-term memory where it is permanently stored. Figure 5.6 also shows the commonly used processes to move information *from* your long-term memory back into working memory with output as the final demonstration that learning has taken place.

The majority of cognitive activities that are a part of learning occur in working memory. *What* you do in working memory and *how* you encode information in working memory have a major impact on how well you are able to locate information in long-term memory and show some form of *output.* Conducting memory searches, using retrieval cues, tracking your thought patterns, and rehearsing learned information are processes that you can use to increase the efficiency of accessing your long-term memory. There are times, however, that a variety of processes hinder recall and result in forgetting. Understanding the reasons that forgetting occurs leads to solutions to avoid recall failure.

> **CONCEPT CHECK** 6.1
>
> *How are retrieval cues important in the process of conducting memory searches? How would a lack of clear retrieval cues affect your output?*

CHAPTER 6
REFLECTIVE WRITING 1

On separate paper, in a journal, or online in this textbook's College Success CourseMate, respond to the following questions.

1. Discuss the processes you use to try to retrieve or recall information that you know you have learned. For example, when you are taking a test, how do you find the answers in your memory? If someone asks you about something you did several months ago, how do you retrieve or recall the details from memory? If your instructor calls on you in class to respond to a question, how do you locate the answer in memory?

2. What are your review practices or habits? How and when do you review classwork, textbook information, or lecture notes? Does the amount of time you use to review seem sufficient?

Access Chapter 6 Reflective Writing 1 in your College Success CourseMate, accessed through *CengageBrain.com.*

Conducting Memory Searches

Working memory involves rapid and complex interactions with information you have stored in your long-term memory schemas. Working memory frequently uses memory searches to locate, activate, and bring learned information back into your conscious mind (working memory). A **memory search** involves using associations or information linked together to locate information stored in long-term memory.

Sometimes a memory search is quick, and the answer to a question immediately comes to mind; other times, your working memory requires more extensive

> A **memory search** involves using associations or information linked together to locate information stored in long-term memory.

searches to retrieve information. As an example, if someone asks you where you were born, for most people the answer is immediate. However, answering the question "Where was your maternal grandmother born?" may require a more in-depth memory search and "chatting your way" to the answer by using associations:

> My mother was born in Detroit, Michigan, but her family had moved there right before she was born. I remember when we drove up to the northern peninsula of Michigan and passed the house in Copper Harbor where she grew up. I can still picture the little brown house at the end of the rocky road. I remember Grandma saying that she was born in that house.

If you are pressed for the exact address, perhaps no amount of memory searching will produce the answer, for it is likely that you never learned or imprinted the address into your memory. Sometimes after extensive memory searches, you will conclude that the information you are searching for was never clearly recorded in your long-term memory.

EXERCISE 6.1

Memory Searches

PURPOSE: When you try to recall answers to questions, often you need to "chat to yourself" about the information and conduct memory searches for the answer. Sometimes you cannot find answers; perhaps the information was never learned, or if learned, it was not practiced on a regular enough basis to be accessible.

DIRECTIONS: In the following chart, read the questions and write the answer to as many of the questions as possible. Pay attention to your memory search process. Check one of the last three columns to show how you responded to the question.

Question	Answer	Immediately Knew the Answer	Needed to Do a Memory Search	I Do Not Know
1. How many states are in the United States?				
2. Which state was the 49th state to join the Union?				
3. What is the capital city of New Mexico?				
4. What is the value of the Roman numeral XL?				
5. There are two cups in one pint. How many cups are in one gallon?				
6. Which fraction is smaller: 6/7 or 2/3?				
7. What is the name of your third grade teacher?				
8. What is photosynthesis?				

Creating and Using Retrieval Cues

Retrieval cues are forms of information used to conduct memory searches to locate information stored in long-term memory. Retrieval cues, which are an essential element of the learning process, link one piece of information to another. Retrieval cues trigger memory of the information and its meaning. The following points about retrieval cues are important to review:

CONCEPT CHECK   6.2
What kinds of information can work as retrieval cues?

- Words, phrases, pictures, graphics, familiar objects, numbers, tunes, personal experience, familiar situations, or mnemonics (memory tricks) associated with units of information are forms of retrieval cues.

- To attach or associate new information to your existing schemas, your working memory first uses retrieval cues to seek and locate related information in long-term memory.

- Associations are powerful retrieval cues to link together chunks of information. *Paired associations,* questions that activate associations, and chains of associations (semantic schemas) give you access to your long-term memory.

- Multisensory learning strategies create multiple retrieval cues and sensory paths into long-term memory.

Tracking Your Thought Patterns

Paying attention to the way you think and tracking your thought patterns increase your awareness of the complexity of thinking and learning and help you realize the importance of creating strong retrieval cues and strong associations to link chunks of information. Jackson, a student like you, read this test question: *What are three of Gardner's intelligences that rely heavily on physical movement and activity? Explain your answer.* The following reflects Jackson's thought patterns and processes:

Stockbyte/Getty Images

Tracking your thought patterns as you conduct memory searches, use retrieval cues, and recall associations increases your awareness of the ways you organize and store information. When you attempt to recall learned information, do you give yourself sufficient time to activate these processes?

Gardner ... eight intelligences .... What are the eight intelligences? The first .... language .... oh yeah, we talked about the word "lingua" .... Right, linguistic. The visual one is called .... What the heck is that word? Architects have it. They work with space .... oh right .... spatial. The two people ones .... I remember seeing the group of people I drew in my notes .... interpersonal. The other is about me .... intrapersonal. What was that chart I copied in my notes? Come on, think! I remember trees. The last one is about nature .... the naturalist. Okay, only three more to go. Oh yeah, the two M's .... musical and mathematical .... What's the last one? What did we talk about in the group when we listed people for each intelligence? Oh yeah, the other was Lance Armstrong and Michael Jordan .... athletes. That's right, bodily-kinesthetic. Now I can use this to answer the question. *(His thoughts continued.)*

CONCEPT CHECK 6.3

What does "track your thought patterns" mean? What are positive effects of using this process?

Thought processes, schemas created, and memory searches vary from person to person. Heather approached the question from a different angle by recalling a memory tool (a mnemonic) that she created for the eight intelligences. She wrote the eight intelligences on a piece of paper and selected an initial letter for each intelligence: L, L, M, K, S, I, I, and N. She rearranged the letters to form two words: *SLIM LINK*. She had to practice converting the letters to the original words to keep the information fresh and active. The following reflects Heather's thought patterns and processes:

Easy SLIM LINK! S = spatial; L = linguistic; I = interpersonal; M = musical; L = logical-mathematical; I = intrapersonal; N = naturalist; and K = kinesthetic .... I mean bodily-kinesthetic. Okay .... Now which three deal with physical movement and activity? Bodily-kinesthetic is one for sure. Interpersonal involves interacting with people, so that has movement and activity. Musical .... that will be my third choice. Okay, now I just need to explain my reasoning .... *(Her thoughts continued.)*

Tracking your thought patterns emphasizes the importance of having a variety of retrieval cues and associations to use. It reveals weaknesses in your processing approaches when you did not consciously create strong retrieval cues. Finally, it activates your working memory and focuses your attention on specific details imprinted in your schemas.

Tracking Thought Patterns

DIRECTIONS: In the large box, write a question about a topic, experience, or concept that you cannot immediately answer without conducting a memory search. Begin conducting a memory search to locate the answer. In the oval shapes, write the retrieval cues you used to "skip along" from one thought to another to finally arrive at the answer.

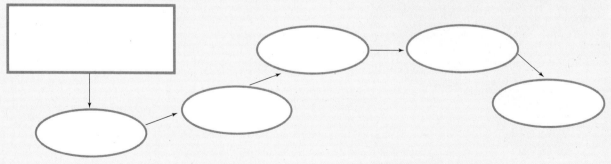

EXERCISE 6.2

© Cengage Learning 2015

Rehearsal and Review

Rehearsal means practice. Rehearsal is important for imprinting, locating, and retrieving information from long-term memory. Even when you have effectively learned and imprinted information in long-term memory, failure to practice retrieving the information through a process called Ongoing Review may hinder your ability to access and use the information at a given time. Ongoing Review not only increases your ability to locate and recall chunks of information from memory schemas, but it also increases the speed and accuracy of locating and pulling needed information back into working memory.

CONCEPT CHECK 6.4
What are the benefits of rehearsing and reviewing frequently? What are the consequences if these processes are not used?

Activating Memory

Information you have imprinted but have not used for a length of time may need to be reactivated. You know that the information was learned, but it has become "rusty" or covered with "cobwebs." For example, you need to practice speaking a foreign language to keep it active. If you learned to speak a foreign language as a child, but you have not practiced it for many years, you can still understand a few basic words and perhaps general sentence structures, but you "lost access" to the vocabulary and can no longer speak fluently. However, the information is still in your memory; it needs to be reactivated by reviewing language materials or socializing with speakers of that language.

Primacy-Recency Effect

You can overload working memory by attempting to process information too quickly or in units too large for working memory to handle effectively. When striving to learn or memorize a list of items, chunking down the list of items into manageable units, using the Magic 7 ± 2 Theory, and reorganizing the list into meaningful groups of items can improve memory. Effectively remembering information in the list, or in any learning activity, is also affected by the order of the information. This is called the primacy-recency effect. The *primacy-recency effect* states that items at the beginning and the end of lists are easier to recall than are items in the middle of lists. As a result, rehearsing and reviewing items in the middle of lists multiple times is essential for the recall of entire lists. Following are applications of the primacy-recency effect:

The **primacy-recency effect** states that items at the beginning and the end of lists are easier to recall than are items in the middle of lists.

- The *primacy effect* states that better recall of the first few items studied or memorized occurs because such items receive more attention. For example, if you are learning a list of fifteen items, breaking the list into three groups of five items each is effective. After you learn the items in Group 1, add the items from Group 2 to the original list and study the ten items. Thus, you have practiced the Group 1 items twice. Finally, when you are able to recall items in Group 1 and Group 2, you then add Group 3. By this time, you have studied Group 1 three separate times; in other words, Group 1 receives more of your attention. This same recency effect works when you study any materials in stages or steps and rehearse the first stage or step throughout the rehearsal process.

- The *recency effect* occurs because the last items studied are the freshest in your memory. You can use this to your benefit when studying or preparing for a test, a class discussion, or a performance task. Do a final review close to the time of the task without placing other distractors or activities between the last review. This keeps the information close in memory for retrieval.

CONCEPT CHECK 6.5
Why are items at the beginning of a list and at the end of a list easier to remember? Why are items in the middle of a list the most difficult to recall?

EXERCISE 6.3

Lists to Memorize and Recall

DIRECTIONS:

1. Study the memory processes in List 1. On separate paper, write the list of processes without looking at the list.

2. Look at List 2. In the space next to List 2, reorganize the list of items into logical groups. After studying your reorganized list, look away and write the items in order.

List 1
• Elaboration
• Selectivity
• Association
• Time on Task
• Visualization
• Recitation
• Concentration
• Ongoing Review
• Interest
• Feedback
• Big and Little Pictures
• Organization

List 2
• toothbrush
• pots and pans
• sofa
• coffee table
• silverware
• razor
• soap
• lamps
• spices
• bath towels
• television
• plates

ANSWER THE FOLLOWING QUESTIONS:

1. How many items in List 1 did you recall accurately? Did you try to memorize the items in the order they were presented, or did you rearrange the list? Explain your results.

2. How many items in List 2 did you recall accurately? Was reorganizing the list helpful? Why or why not?

 Access Chapter 6 Topics In-Depth: Forgetting Theories, in your College Success CourseMate, accessed through *CengageBrain.com*.

The **Decay Theory** states that stimuli decay or fade from memory because they are too weak to be processed.

Six Forgetting Theories

Even when you use selective attention, encoding strategies, working memory processes, and retrieval strategies, you will encounter times when you are not able to locate, retrieve, or recall information. Following are reasons that forgetting or failure to locate and retrieve information may occur throughout the learning process:

• **Decay Theory:** The *Decay Theory* states that stimuli decay or fade from memory because they are too weak to be processed. Unattended or ignored stimuli that enter sensory memory or short-term memory are dumped or discarded. In this case, information is not actually forgotten because it never was encoded or learned.

- **Displacement Theory:** The *Displacement Theory* states that too much information entering the memory system too quickly forces some stimuli to be shoved aside or displaced. Too much information coming into short-term memory too rapidly overloads working memory. Some of the stimuli that are not yet encoded are shoved aside or displaced to make room for new stimuli.

The **Displacement Theory** states that too much information entering the memory system too quickly forces some stimuli to be shoved aside or displaced.

- **Interference Theory:** The *Interference Theory* states that new information and old, previously learned information can interfere with clear and accurate recall of information. Confusion occurs between the old and the new information. Failure to retrieve the information may be due to unclear imprinting or lack of distinguishing differences between the similar items.

The **Interference Theory** states that new information and old, previously learned information can interfere with clear and accurate recall of information.

  - *Retroactive interference* occurs when new information interferes with retrieval of "old," previously learned information. The new information is fresher in working memory and overrides the ability to recall the older, previously learned information.

  - *Proactive interference* is the opposite of retroactive interference. Proactive interference occurs when previously learned information was imprinted so strongly that it gets retrieved instead of the new information. This sometimes occurs when the new information contradicts or does not integrate logically with the old information.

The **Incomplete Encoding Theory** states that incomplete encoding during the rehearsal process in working memory causes an inability to recall information accurately.

- **Incomplete Encoding Theory:** The *Incomplete Encoding Theory* states that incomplete encoding during the rehearsal process in working memory causes an inability to recall information accurately. If the learning process is interrupted or attention is diverted from the process, information is only partially encoded and thus only partially learned.

The **Retrieval Failure Theory** states that several variables may result in failure to locate information in memory: lack of effort, isolated details, or weak organization.

- **Retrieval Failure Theory:** The *Retrieval Failure Theory* states that several variables may result in failure to locate information in memory: lack of effort, isolated details, or weak organization. Memorizing isolated details without organizing them logically, associating them to other concepts, creating retrieval cues, or connecting them to existing schemas makes location of information in long-term memory difficult.

The **Emotional Blocks Theory** states that stress, intrusive thoughts, emotions, or anxiety can hinder the ability to access information stored in long-term memory.

- **Emotional Blocks Theory:** The *Emotional Blocks Theory* states that stress, intrusive thoughts, emotions, or anxiety can hinder the ability to access information stored in long-term memory. In addition, sleep deprivation, pain, as well as some medications may prevent you from accessing and retrieving information that you "know you know."

CONCEPT CHECK 6.6

Which forgetting theories occur during the process of taking in and attempting to learn new information? Which occur during the process of trying to retrieve information?

GROUP PROCESSING

 A Collaborative Learning Activity

Form groups of three or four students. Select a recorder to record all of the responses of members in the group.

DIRECTIONS:

1. In the Solutions column below, brainstorm and list strategies students could use to combat each kind of forgetting. Select from the array of strategies and processes you have learned from Chapters 1–6. You may refer back to pages 174–175 to review the description of the theory and reasons that forgetting occurs.

2. You may be asked to share your results with the class.

Solutions for Forgetting Theories	
Theory	Solutions
• Decay Theory	
• Displacement Theory	
• Interference Theory	
• Incomplete Encoding Theory	
• Retrieval Failure Theory	
• Emotional Blocks Theory	

© Cengage Learning 2015

CHECK POINT 6.1

Answers appear on page B3.

Multiple Choice See Test-Taking Strategies 10–15 in Appendix A.

_____ 1. The majority of cognitive activities that are a part of learning
   a. reflect *what* you encode and *how* you encode it.
   b. occur in working memory.
   c. occur in our conscious mind.
   d. do all of the above.

_____ 2. Which of the following is *not* true about memory searches?
   a. They produce immediate results.
   b. They involve using associations to connect related items.
   c. They scan schemas for relevant information.
   d. They activate previously learned information.

(continued)

_____ 3. The primacy-recency effect states that a person remembers

a. the items in the middle of a list better than the items at the end of a list.

b. the items in the middle of a list better than the items at the beginning of a list.

c. items at the beginning and the end of the list better than items in the middle of the list.

d. all items as a unit if there are less than eighteen items in the list.

_____ 4. Which of the following is *not* true about retrieval cues?

a. They may involve words, pictures, or mnemonics.

b. They are created in sensory memory and reinforced in short-term memory.

c. They link together chunks of information.

d. They may include semantic encoding.

_____ 5. Which of the following statements about forgetting theories is accurate?

a. New information can interfere with recall of old information, or the reverse may also occur.

b. Emotional blocks only occur when a person experiences negative emotions such as anger, fear, sadness, or ineptness.

c. The Displacement Theory refers to stimuli in long-term memory schemas that get shoved out or displaced to make room for new items.

d. The Retrieval Failure Theory states that forgetting occurs early in the learning process in the sensory memory center.

 Access Chapter 6 Practice Quiz 1 in your College Success CourseMate, accessed through *CengageBrain.com*.

Twelve Principles of Memory

 2 *Explain the Twelve Principles of Memory represented by the mnemonic SAVE CRIB FOTO.*

You have learned about a wide variety of memory strategies and processes. How can you consolidate the information and see it as an organized unit of meaningful information? The answer is to explore how the Twelve Principles of Memory in this section consolidate the memory processes. The *Twelve Principles of Memory* are a compiled set of memory principles that encompass memory strategies and processes that promote powerful learning. **Figure 6.1** summarizes these Twelve Principles of Memory. Understanding these memory principles will help you in the following ways:

- Integrate or consolidate memory strategies and processes you have already learned
- Provide you with rationale for using the various steps in learning strategies
- Alert and activate your working memory (conscious mind) and hold stimuli in working memory longer to provide time for further, deeper processing
- Increase your awareness of the cognitive processes necessary for successfully learning, utilizing, and retrieving information
- Empower you with guidelines to analyze, modify, personalize, and strengthen your approach to learning

Mnemonics are memory techniques or memory tools that serve as bridges to help you recall information from long-term memory. In this chapter, the keyword mnemonic SAVE CRIB FOTO will help you recall quickly the Twelve Principles of

The **Twelve Principles of Memory** are a compiled set of memory principles that encompass memory strategies and processes that promote powerful learning.

CONCEPT CHECK 6.7
How are the Twelve Principles of Memory grouped and presented to help you learn and recall all twelve principles? Were you able to recall all twelve principles in Exercise 6.3?

Mnemonics are memory techniques or memory tools that serve as bridges to help you recall information from long-term memory.

> **FIGURE 6.1**   Twelve Principles of Memory (SAVE CRIB FOTO)
>
> 1. **S**electivity: Select what is important to learn and what can be ignored.
> 2. **A**ssociation: Associate or link together chunks of information.
> 3. **V**isualization: Picture in your mind the information you are learning.
> 4. **E**laboration: Encode information in new ways and on deeper levels.
> 5. **C**oncentration: Stay focused and use selective attention.
> 6. **R**ecitation: Repeat information verbally in your own words.
> 7. **I**ntention: Create a learning goal with clearly defined desired outcomes.
> 8. **B**ig and Little Pictures: Recognize different levels of information.
> 9. **F**eedback: Check the accuracy of your learning, and use forms of self-quizzing.
> 10. **O**rganization: Reorganize or structure information in meaningful ways.
> 11. **T**ime on Task: Dedicate and schedule ample time to process.
> 12. **O**ngoing Review: Practice retrieving information from long-term memory.

© Cengage Learning 2015

SAVE CRIB FOTO is a mnemonic, with each letter in these three words representing one of the Twelve Principles of Memory.

Memory. **SAVE CRIB FOTO** is a mnemonic, with each letter in these three words representing one of the Twelve Principles of Memory. For mnemonics to work effectively, however, you must practice translating the mnemonic back into the original items it represents. Figure 6.1 summarizes the Twelve Principles of Memory. Carefully examine the cognitive process represented by each of the letters.

EXERCISE 6.4

Memory Principles Inventory

PURPOSE: The Memory Principles Inventory helps you to identify which of the Twelve Principles of Memory you currently use effectively and which you need to strengthen. Understanding how you process information is the first step in the powerful process of using metacognition.

DIRECTIONS: Go to Exercise 6.4 in Appendix C, page C12–C14, to complete the Memory Principles Inventory.

Selectivity

Principles
SAVE
CRIB
FOTO

© Cengage Learning

Selectivity is the process of identifying and separating main ideas and important details from a larger body of information. You learned about Selectivity in Chapter 5, with Memory Process 9. Each time you use Selectivity, you hone your skills in identifying important concepts, main ideas, and supporting details, and in discarding the insignificant information that is not necessary to process into memory. Following are additional ways to utilize Selectivity:

- **Main ideas, concepts, or themes:** Use your course syllabus, the introduction in your textbook, and your lecture notes to help you identify the main ideas, concepts, or themes that receive frequent or repeated emphasis.

- **Important details:** Use chapter features, such as lists of terminology, definitions, marginal notes, boxed features, steps or formulas to solve problems, chapter summaries, and chapter review questions to help you identify and select important details.

- **Examples:** Use examples to grasp concepts, but do not focus on them as details to memorize. Examples in textbooks and lectures provide you with background information, capture your attention, and clarify concepts, but often these are not details you need to memorize or learn thoroughly.

- **Study tools:** Create study tools, such as visual mappings, index card notes, lectures and textbook notes, and other kinds of study tools that clearly identify main ideas and important details.

- **Textbook skills:** Use Selectivity to decide what to survey in a new textbook chapter, highlight, write in notes, or study for tests.

CONCEPT CHECK **6.8**

What is Selectivity and how can you use it when you read textbooks, study for tests, and take textbook and lecture notes?

Association

Association is the process of linking together two or more items or chunks of information to process into long-term memory. You learned about Association in Chapter 5, with Memory Process 11. Creating associations is an essential process because the schemas in long-term memory are organized around associations and linked information. Following are additional ways to utilize Association:

- **Vivid and detailed:** Identify key parts of the information you are learning. Then create clear, vivid associations that include sufficient details so the associations will not be confused with other similar information.

- **Link images:** Instead of separating two items into two different images, form one picture that contains both images. To strengthen the image, add colors, sounds, or action.

- **Rehearse:** Practice repeating and working with paired associations and association chains, which are multiple items linked together in memory. Track your thought patterns and be aware of the relationship of associations.

- **Mnemonics:** Create and personalize mnemonics to help recall associations for information that otherwise may be difficult to use. The next section in this chapter discusses mnemonics.

Principles

s**A**VE

CRIB

FOTO

© Cengage Learning

Visualization

Visualization is the process of using visual encoding to make pictures or "movies" in your mind. You learned about visualizing in Chapter 1 and then again in Chapter 5, with Memory Process 8. Visualization is an integral process in many study skills strategies because of its power to imprint information in long-term memory and to strengthen your ability to locate information during the process of retrieval. Following are additional ways to utilize Visualization:

- **Details:** To create a strong image or impression of information, include details such as size, shape, color, brightness, texture, and movement.

- **Meaning:** Personalize the association by thinking about the purpose, uses, functions, and personal experiences related to the item.

Principles

sA**V**E

CRIB

FOTO

© Cengage Learning

- **Comparisons:** Identify how items are similar. Visualizing similarities creates a stronger image and helps avoid confusing similar items in memory. Then focus also on how the items differ.

- **Accuracy:** After visualizing an object, list, passage, steps of a process, or action sequence, refer back to the original source (object, printed passage, or paper) to check the accuracy of your visual image. Correct any errors or practice again with details that you initially omitted.

- **Mental rehearsal:** Practice frequently so the image stays fresh in memory and you can retrieve it quickly and accurately.

Principles
SAV**E**
CRIB
FOTO

© Cengage Learning

Elaboration

Elaboration, also called *elaborative rehearsal*, is the process of thinking about, pondering, or working with and encoding information in new ways. Elaboration promotes learning on a deeper level with increased understanding. You learned about Elaboration in Chapter 5, with Memory Process 7. Following are additional ways to utilize Elaboration:

- **Creativity:** Use your creativity to devise new ways to learn information. Using your creativity reduces the tendency to use rote memory.

- **Similarities and differences:** Pay close attention to how details are similar and how they are different. Doing so creates a more vivid impression.

- **Integrate:** Weave big ideas and details together in meaningful ways. Show levels of information and relationships.

EXERCISE 6.5

Working with the Twelve Principles of Memory

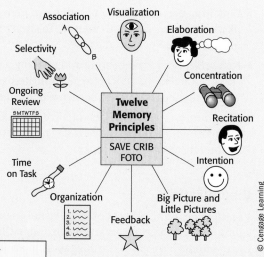

© Cengage Learning

DIRECTIONS:

1. On your own paper, copy the visual mapping on the right, or go to this textbook's College Success CourseMate for a full-page worksheet for this visual mapping with graphics. The visual mapping will appear under the Topics In-Depth section of Chapter 6.

2. Add the following retrieval cue words to the visual mapping. Connect each cue word to the principle of memory it represents.

picking and choosing	focusing	self-quizzing
linking ideas	explaining out loud	structuring logically
seeing in your mind	having a purpose or goal	using minutes/hours
working with and expanding	larger ideas and details	repeated practice

3. After reading about all Twelve Principles of Memory, attach additional cue words to each of the principles.

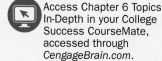

Access Chapter 6 Topics In-Depth in your College Success CourseMate, accessed through *CengageBrain.com*.

Concentration

Concentration is the ability to block out external and internal distractions in order to stay focused on one specific item or task. You learned about Concentration in Chapter 3 and again in Chapter 5, with Memory Process 1 (selective attention). Following are additional ways to utilize Concentration:

- **Environment:** Select a conducive learning environment that has limited distractions.

- **Selective attention:** Intentionally control your mind and your attention. Push yourself to stay focused and refrain from getting sidetracked by distractions.

- **Multitasking:** Avoid multitasking. As you recall, multitasking disrupts thought patterns and concentration.

Principles

SAVE

CRIB

FOTO

© Cengage Learning

Recitation

Recitation is the process of explaining information clearly, out loud in your own words, and in complete sentences without referring to printed materials. You learned about Recitation in Chapter 1 and again in Chapter 5, with Memory Process 8. Following are additional ways to utilize Recitation:

- **Teach:** Recite by explaining or teaching information to someone else. Explaining and teaching verifies your understanding of the information.

- **Pairing:** Pair reciting with visual information. After examining graphs, pictures, diagrams, or other printed items, talk, recite, and explain what you recall from the visual materials.

- **Techniques:** Use the See-Say-Do Strategy, the Look-Away Technique, and other recitation strategies that are steps in almost all textbook reading, notetaking, and studying strategies.

Principles

SAVE

c**R**IB

FOTO

© Cengage Learning

CONCEPT CHECK   6.11

How does Recitation differ from verbalizing? What strategies do you use that involve reciting?

Intention

Intention is the process of creating a purpose or a goal to act or perform in a specific way. Intention involves setting a *learning goal* that clearly states what you plan to accomplish and a *plan of action* that shows how you intend to achieve your goal. You learned about Intention in Chapter 3, with the discussion of goal-setting strategies. Following are ways to utilize Intention:

- **Metacognition:** One component of metacognition is to identify and focus on what you need to learn, and another component is to identify strategies to use to complete tasks. Intention involves the *what* and the *how* associated with metacognition.

- **Kind of knowledge:** Differentiate between declarative and procedural knowledge, and then use Intention to select learning goals and appropriate strategies to work with the information.

- **GPS System:** Identify your intention by utilizing the steps in the GPS System: *goal*, *purpose*, and *steps*.

Principles

SAVE

CR**I**B

FOTO

© Cengage Learning

Intention is the process of creating a purpose or a goal to act or perform in a specific way.

CONCEPT CHECK   6.12

What is the GPS System? How is it related to the memory principle of Intention?

Principles
SAVE
CRI**B**
FOTO

© Cengage Learning

Big and Little Pictures is a process of identifying different levels of information.

CONCEPT CHECK 6.13
What problems might you encounter if you do not identify different levels of information as you study, create study tools, and take notes?

Big and Little Pictures

Big and Little Pictures is a process of identifying different levels of information. In Chapter 5, with Memory Process 5, you learned about connecting to and expanding schemas with related details. Memory Process 5 refers to the memory principle of Big and Little Pictures. The "big pictures" are the schemas, themes, concepts, and main ideas. The "little pictures" are the supporting details, such as facts, definitions, examples, parts, or components of a larger concept. Both higher and lower levels of information are important in the learning process. Using the principle of Big and Little Pictures helps you identify levels of information, organize details under larger concepts, such as headings, categories, or main ideas, and organize information logically to improve memory searches and recall.

The memory principle of Big and Little Pictures is sometimes referred to as seeing "the forest and the trees." If you focus only on the forest, you miss the meaning and beauty of individual trees. If you focus only on a few individual trees, you miss seeing how all the trees together make the forest. Following are additional ways to utilize Big and Little Pictures:

- **Questions:** Ask yourself questions that focus your attention on the levels of information: *Is this a recurring theme? Was this a chapter heading? Is this a main idea or a schema? Is this an important supporting detail? Under what category or big picture does this belong? What big picture do these details support?*

- **Highlighting:** Highlight textbooks and notes carefully to clearly show which information represents the "big picture" and which represents the important supporting details. (See Chapter 9.)

- **Outlines:** Create outlines of lectures and textbook chapters. Outlines clearly identify and organize levels of information.

- **Study tools:** Create study tools, such as diagrams, lists divided into categories, visual mappings, and hierarchies to show levels of information. Rehearse by reciting the big pictures first, followed by the supporting small pictures or details. This rehearsal or review pattern begins with the big picture and ends with the small pictures.

Principles
SAVE
CRIB
FOTO

© Cengage Learning

Feedback

Feedback is the process of verifying how accurately and thoroughly you have or have not learned specific information. You learned about Feedback in Chapter 5, with Memory Process 10. Self-quizzing is a feedback strategy used frequently in many study skills strategies. Following are additional ways to utilize Feedback:

- **Processes:** Reciting, the Look-Away Technique, self-quizzing, and partner quizzing put you in control of monitoring your progress and understanding. Take the time to use Feedback throughout the learning process.

- **Write:** Write summaries, create lists of information, and write steps of processes without referring to printed materials. Check your accuracy.

- **Rework:** Rework math problems multiple times as you rehearse math problem-solving processes. Rework the steps of any processes that work with procedural knowledge. Use Feedback to check your accuracy.

- **Test questions:** Create and complete practice test questions so you get feedback on your understanding before you face test-taking situations.

Organization

Organization is the process of creating a meaningful, logical structure or arrangement of ideas and information. It does not refer to organizing your workspace or your materials. Using the principle of Organization helps you do the following:

- Reorganize, regroup, or rearrange information in ways that are easier for you to memorize or learn
- Discover new ways to connect important details to "big ideas" or schemas
- Use your creativity to personalize the information
- Clarify or simplify information by creating meaningful study tools
- Increase comprehension, concentration, interest, and motivation

Following are additional ways to utilize Organization:

- **Organizational patterns:** Imitate the way authors and instructors organize information. Identifying their patterns of organization can help you follow their logic and understand the material more quickly.
- **Draw:** Interpret printed information by converting it to diagrams, charts, or pictures to show relationships, such as comparisons, contrasts, cause and effect, examples, definitions, processes, or whole-and-parts. (See Chapter 10.)
- **Rearrange:** Rearrange lecture and textbook information in ways that make sense to you. This may include developing index card notes, flashcards, visual notes, drawings, or rewriting notes for clarity.
- **Headings:** When taking notes, organize notes under headings to break information into meaningful units that you can process one unit at a time.
- **Reorganize:** Reorganize information by making lists of details placed under categories or by creating timelines to organize events or steps chronologically (by a time sequence).

Principles

SAVE

CRIB

F**O**TO

© Cengage Learning

Organization is the process of creating a meaningful, logical structure or arrangement of ideas and information.

CONCEPT CHECK   6.14

Define the memory principle of Organization. How does the way you organize information affect the imprinting and retrieval processes in long-term memory?

Textbook Case Studies

DIRECTIONS:

1. Read each case study carefully. Respond to the question at the end of each case study by using strategies from Chapter 6 to answer each question. Answer in complete sentences.

2. Write your responses on paper or online in this textbook's College Success CourseMate, Textbook Case Studies. You will be able to print your online response or e-mail it to your instructor.

CASE STUDY 1: By the end of the week, Curtis needs to read a thirty-page chapter and be prepared to discuss it in class. The night before class he spends one hour reading quickly through the chapter. He jots down a few words, phrases, and main ideas and shoves the list in his book so that he will be prepared for the class discussion the next day. Instead of a class discussion, however, the instructor gives a short quiz. Curtis unsuccessfully tries to recall information from his brief notes, but he is only able to answer two of the ten questions. What strategies should Curtis have used to achieve better results?

(continued)

Exercise 6.6 (continued)

CASE STUDY 2: Cerina spends a lot of time learning and feels she is ready for tests. On the day of the test, she tends to rush through test questions without taking time to think about and search for answers in memory. If she knows the answer, she quickly writes it on the test. If she does not know the answer, she gets frustrated and moves on to the next question. Needless to say, she does not perform well on tests. She constantly complains that she forgets more than she remembers. What memory processes or strategies can Cerina use to combat the forgetting and retrieve more information from long-term memory?

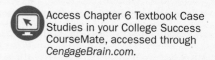

Access Chapter 6 Textbook Case Studies in your College Success CourseMate, accessed through *CengageBrain.com.*

Principles
SAVE
CRIB
FO**T**O

© Cengage Learning

Time on Task is the process of allocating sufficient time and using spaced or distributed practice effectively to learn, rehearse, and retrieve information in memory.

Time on Task

Time on Task is the process of allocating sufficient time and using spaced or distributed practice effectively to learn, rehearse, and retrieve information in memory. Researchers also have found a high correlation between the amount of time spent studying and the grades earned in courses. You learned about Time on Task in Chapter 3, with time-management skills, and in Chapter 5, with Memory Process 12. Following are additional ways to utilize Time on Task:

- **Study habits:** Eliminate ineffective study habits, such as cramming, spending insufficient quality time studying, spending the minimal amount of time studying with hopes to simply "get by," or using time-wasting strategies instead of direct, step-by-step strategies proven to be effective.

- **Time management:** Use time-management strategies, such as the 2:1 ratio or the 3:1 ratio, 50-minute study blocks for one subject, spaced practice, and weekly and daily schedules.

Principles
SAVE
CRIB
FOT**O**

© Cengage Learning

Ongoing Review is the process of practicing previously learned information days and even weeks after the initial learning occurred.

Ongoing Review

Ongoing Review is the process of practicing previously learned information days and even weeks after the initial learning occurred. Even though information in long-term memory is considered to be permanent, without practicing retrieval or using Ongoing Review, information can fade, become confused with other memories, or be difficult to locate and retrieve. Ongoing Review is such a crucial step in the learning process that you will find it as the final step of most reading, notetaking, and study skills strategies. Following are ways to utilize Ongoing Review:

- **Retrieval practice:** Reactivate paths to schemas in long-term memory by practicing retrieval cues, associations, and visualizations. Mentally rehearse and conduct memory searches over several sessions and periods of time.

- **Final review:** Conduct a final review right before you know you will need to use the information. Use the recency effect to your advantage.

CONCEPT CHECK   6.15

How does the principle of Ongoing Review affect working memory? What causes of forgetting does use of Ongoing Review decrease or eliminate?

- **Overlearn:** *Overlearning* is the process of continuing to rehearse and review even with feedback or proof that learning has taken place. By overlearning the information, you can access it in your long-term memory more quickly, efficiently, and accurately.

> **Overlearning** is the process of continuing to rehearse and review even with feedback or proof that learning has taken place.

Answers appear on page B3.

CHECK POINT 6.2

True or False? See Test-Taking Strategies 1–9 in Appendix A.

_____ 1. Memorizing large sections of information word-by-word shows effective use of the memory principles of Selectivity, Rote Memory, and Elaboration.

_____ 2. When you identify main ideas and important supporting details, you are using the memory principle of Selectivity.

_____ 3. The goal of the memory principles of Visualization, Recitation, and Association is to create strong retrieval cues for long-term memory.

_____ 4. The purpose of the memory principle of Intention provides goal-oriented behavior that triggers working memory and adds motivation to learn.

_____ 5. The memory principle of Organization focuses your attention on working in a quiet, well-organized study environment with all required materials arranged to avoid wasting time trying to get organized.

 Access Chapter 6 Practice Quiz 2 in your College Success CourseMate, accessed through *CengageBrain.com*.

CHAPTER 6
REFLECTIVE WRITING 2

 On separate paper, in a journal, or online in this textbook's College Success CourseMate, respond to the following questions.

1. Based on the results of the Memory Principles Inventory in Exercise 6.4, which of the Twelve Principles of Memory do you already use consistently and effectively? Do you agree with the results? Why or why not?

2. According to the results of the same inventory, which Principles of Memory do you need to learn to use

more consistently and efficiently? What are your goals or plans of action to increase your use of these principles?

 Access Chapter 6 Reflective Writing 2 in your College Success CourseMate, accessed through *CengageBrain.com*.

 ## Mnemonics

3 *Explain how to create and use mnemonics to learn academic information.*

Mnemonics are memory tools that serve as bridges to help you recall information from long-term memory. Mnemonics always involve creating some form of an association. You may want to use mnemonics to create associations and retrieval cues for information that is otherwise difficult to recall. However, use mnemonics

Access Chapter 6 Topics In-Depth: Peg Systems in your College Success CourseMate, accessed through *CengageBrain.com*.

> **FIGURE 6.2**   **Mnemonic Systems**
>
> **1.** Acronyms
>
> **2.** Acrostics
>
> **3.** Word associations
>
> **4.** Picture associations
>
> **5.** Loci Method
>
> To learn about the mnemonic peg systems *Human Body Pegs*, *Rhyming Pegs*, and *Number Pegs*, go to Chapter 6 Topics In-Depth in your College Success CourseMate.

© Cengage Learning 2015

CONCEPT CHECK   6.16

What mnemonics have you created and used? How can overuse of mnemonics cause problems retrieving information?

Acronyms are words or phrases made by using the first letter of key words in a list of items to remember.

sparingly; if you use mnemonics too extensively, they increase the amount of information you need to remember. If you do not memorize the mnemonic in its exact form, or if you do not practice translating the mnemonic back into its original meaning, it can hinder and confuse you rather than help you recall information accurately. **Figure 6.2** shows the kinds of mnemonics you can learn to use to retrieve important information from memory.

Acronyms

Acronyms are words or phrases made by using the first letter of key words in a list of items to remember. An acronym forms an association and works as a retrieval cue to recall the original items in the list. The mnemonic SAVE CRIB FOTO is an acronym for the Twelve Principles of Memory.

A classic acronym is the word HOMES for the five Great Lakes in the northern United States: Huron, Ontario, Michigan, Erie, and Superior. For any acronym to work, you must practice translating the letters of the acronym back into the original words that the letters represent. For example, if you are asked to name the Great Lakes or name the Twelve Principles of Memory, giving the answer "HOMES" or "SAVE CRIB FOTO" would not suffice. Use the following steps to create an acronym:

1. **List items:** Write the list of items you need to remember.

2. **Write letters:** On paper, write the *first letter* of each item in the list. If an item in the list consists of more than one word, select only one key word to use for that item.

3. **Rearrange letters:** Unless the items in the list must be learned in the original order, rearrange the letters to form a word or a phrase. If you do not have at least one vowel (*a, e, i, o, u,* and sometimes *y*), you will not be able to create an acronym that is a real word in English. A real word is easier to recall than a nonsense word, so strive to rearrange the letters to create a real word or phrase.

4. **Practice:** Practice translating your acronym. For your acronym to be useful to you, memorize the acronym, repeat it several times, and practice translating it back to the original words in the list of items.

Acrostics

If you are not able to create an acronym, you can always use the first letter of each key word to create an acrostic. **Acrostics** are *sentences* made by using the first letter of key words in a list of items to remember. You can use the letters in their original order, or you can rearrange the letters to create the sentence.

A classic example of an acrostic is the sentence, *Please excuse my dear Aunt Sally*. The first letters of each word in this sentence represent the order of operations in math problems: parentheses, exponents, multiplication, division, addition, and subtraction. Note that you cannot add additional words to the sentence. Use acrostics sparingly as they tend to be more difficult to use effectively and result in one more piece of information you need to remember. As with acronyms, you must practice translating the acrostic into the original words for items in your list.

> **Acrostics** are sentences made by using the first letter of key words in a list of items to remember.

EXERCISE 6.7

Creating Acronyms and Acrostics

PURPOSE: Acronyms are a common type of mnemonic used to remember items in a list. When you cannot create an acronym, you can create an acrostic.

DIRECTIONS: Create an acronym or an acrostic as indicated for the following items.

1. A pediatrician's advice for food a child should eat when he or she has a stomach flu: bananas, applesauce, toast, rice. (Letters to use: b a t r) Acronym: _____

2. Ten body systems in humans: skeletal, digestive, muscular, endocrine, circulatory, nervous, reproductive, urinary, respiratory, and integumentary. (Letters to use: s d m e c n r u r i) Acronym: _____

3. The seven coordinating conjunctions used to form compound sentences: for, and, nor, yet, but, so, or. (Letters to use: f a n y b s o) Acronym: _____

4. Vertical structures of the atmosphere, beginning with the closest to the Earth: troposphere, stratosphere, mesosphere, and thermosphere. (Letters to use: t s m t) Acrostic: _____

   _____

5. Skeletal (bone) structure of the arm: humerus, ulna, radius, carpals, phalanges. (Letters to use: h u r c p) Acrostic: _____

   _____

Word Associations

If you have strong language or musical skills, you can use those skills to create word associations that use rhymes, jingles, short songs, and raps that work as memory tools to recall information. The following examples of word associations demonstrate the use of linguistic and musical skills to create mnemonics:

- Use *i* before *e* except after *c* or when sounded like *a* as in *neighbor* and *weigh*.
- In fourteen hundred and ninety-two, Columbus sailed the ocean blue.
- Spring forward; fall back (for daylight saving time).
- Who invented dynamite? *Alfred Nobel had quite a fright when he discovered dynamite.*

- Which way should you turn a jar lid to open or a bolt to tighten? *Righty tighty, lefty loosy.*

- What is the difference between *stalagmites* and *stalactites*? (Stalagmites are deposits of minerals that project upward from the floor of a cavern; stalactites project downward from the ceiling of a cavern.) You can use this jingle to differentiate between the two: *When the mites go up, the tights come down.*

- Use a familiar tune. Create lyrics with information you need to learn and sing them to a favorite tune or melody such as "Happy Birthday" or "Rudolph the Red-Nosed Reindeer."

Picture Associations

To use picture associations effectively, you need to actively look for and think about ways to create simple associations that will be easy to remember and use to recall information. Actively search for a familiar object or picture to use in your association.

The picture in the margin shows picture associations for the three cognitive learning styles. **Figure 1.3** on page 17 shows a picture association for Multiple Intelligences. The graphic in **Exercise 6.5** shows picture associations for the Twelve Principles of Memory. Following are tips for creating effective picture associations:

- Visualize the shape and colors of the objects. Add sounds and smells to the association when appropriate.

- Exaggerate parts of an object by making them larger than their real size or turning them into whimsical cartoon figures to make recall easier.

- Use large, bold capital letters when adding letters, words, or labels to your pictures.

Following are suggestions for using picture associations to remember different kinds of information:

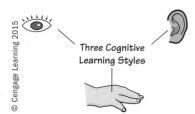

Picture Associations

Three Cognitive Learning Styles

© Cengage Learning 2015

1. **To remember a person's name:** Associate the name with an object or another person you know with that name. For example, to remember a classmate's name, Annie Carpenter, picture Annie as a carpenter wearing a carpenter's apron with ANNIE printed across the apron. Associate a person's name, such as William Herschel, an English astronomer who discovered the planet Uranus in 1781, to your uncle who is also named William. Link your Uncle William, who was an avid football fan, to Herschel Walker, a great NFL running back. Then create an image of your Uncle William with arms draped over William Herschel's shoulder as they both gaze at an evening sky.

2. **To remember a definition:** Associate the meaning with an object that has a similar characteristic. For example, assume you have problems remembering the difference between a waxing moon and a waning moon. Begin by thinking about waxing your car. The more you wax, the shinier it gets. A waxing moon also increases its shine and size as the portion of moon illuminated increases. Waning means the opposite; the size of the illuminated part of the moon decreases.

3. **To remember a specific number:** Find and visualize a number pattern within the number.

4. **To remember a cause-and-effect relationship:** Picture the items as an action movie. The cause begins the action until it reaches the effect.

Picture Associations—Forgetting Theories

DIRECTIONS: A student used picture associations to help remember the different forgetting theories. Choose from the list of theories, and under each of the following pictures, identify the forgetting theory represented.

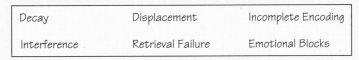

Decay	Displacement	Incomplete Encoding
Interference	Retrieval Failure	Emotional Blocks

_____   _____   _____   _____   _____   _____

© Cengage Learning 2015

The Loci Method

The *Loci Method* is a mnemonic technique that involves associating items or topics with specific rooms in a familiar building. *Loci* (pronounced *lo-sigh*) means *locations*. This method dates back to the early times of Greek orators, who could deliver lengthy speeches without any written notes by making instead mental notes that associated parts or topics of their speeches with familiar rooms or locations in a building. They mentally walked through each room visualizing an item in each room that was associated to the topic to be discussed. They then used this structure to deliver organized, fluent speeches. You can also use the Loci Method to memorize points you want to make in a speech, in an essay, or in a discussion. Use the following steps for the Loci Method:

1. **Items:** Make a list of the items you need to remember.

2. **Floor plan:** Draw a floor plan of a familiar location.

3. **Pictures:** On paper or mentally, attach pictures. Attach a picture of the first item you need to remember inside the first location or room on your floor plan. Walk through the floor plan, attaching one item to each room. You can exaggerate the size or shape of the picture or hang it in an unusual position to make it stand out in your memory.

4. **Practice:** Visually practice (visualize) walking through all the rooms and reciting the important information associated with the items in the rooms.

> The **Loci Method** is a mnemonic technique that involves associating items or topics with specific rooms in a familiar building.

> **CONCEPT CHECK**   **6.18**
> *Explain the steps for using the Loci Method. What familiar floor plan would you use for this method?*

In the following example, Charles uses the Loci Method for a speech about the effects of earthquakes. He sketches a floor plan of his apartment and numbers six locations on the floor plan. At each of the first six locations, he mentally attaches a picture that represents the topic he wants to address in his speech. In the following list, the bold faced items show the topics he plans to discuss in chronological order. After memorizing the floor plan and the objects, he practices *visualizing* and *reciting* his speech. (Note: This same method could be used to write an essay response when the test question is provided prior to the test, or to prepare for an important discussion.)

1. At the front door, picture a poster that says "Enter at your own risk." A picture shows the parking lot and landscaping all shifted out of place to represent the first effect: **ground displacement**.

2. In the living room, picture sliding piles of magazines and newspapers to represent the second effect: **landslides**.

3. In the kitchen, picture a sink filled with muddy water to represent the process where pressure turns solid soils into mud to represent the third effect: **liquefaction**.

4. In the bathroom, picture the tub filled with water and the water sloshing back and forth from one end of the tub to the other to represent the fourth effect: **seiche**.

5. In the bedroom, picture a large surfing poster on the wall with an enormous wave that is going to consume the surfers to represent the fifth effect: **tsunami**.

6. In the closet, picture the electric panel with flames and smoke to represent the sixth effect: **fires**.

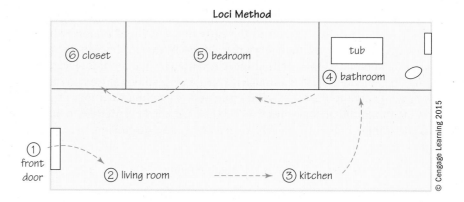

Loci Method

© Cengage Learning 2015

EXERCISE 6.9

Transfer These Skills: The Loci Method

DIRECTIONS:

1. Identify a series of steps, a sequence of events, or a list of points that you want to include in a speech, an essay, or a discussion for one of your current classes.

2. Draw a floor plan of a familiar place. Number the rooms to show the order that you will mentally walk. In each room, attach a picture that represents the item you need to remember.

3. Practice mentally walking through the floor plan and reciting the information represented by the pictures in each room. Your instructor may ask you to recite your information in class.

CHECK POINT 6.3

Answers appear on page B3.

Definitions See Test-Taking Strategies 29–31 in Appendix A.

On separate paper, write a definition for each of the following terms:

1. mnemonics:

2. acrostics:

3. acronyms:

4. Loci Method:

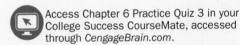
Access Chapter 6 Practice Quiz 3 in your College Success CourseMate, accessed through *CengageBrain.com*.

ACTIVITY

Chapter 6 Critical Thinking

PURPOSE: Strategies and skills that you learned in previous chapters integrate well with information in this chapter. Use your critical thinking skills to identify relationships and associations between previously learned information and new information. Connecting and integrating information strengthen understanding and schemas in long-term memory.

DIRECTIONS: Work with a partner, in a small group, or by yourself to explore answers to the following questions. Be prepared to share your answers with the class.

1. We have three memory centers: sensory, working, and long-term. In which memory center are the Memory Principles most actively used? Explain your answer.

2. Using a principle of memory triggers or activates one or more other principles of memory. For example, to use Selectivity, you need to know how to use Big and Little Pictures. On paper, list all Twelve Principles of Memory. Across from each principle, list other principles that you activate when you use that specific principle effectively.

Terms to Know

By yourself or with a partner, practice reciting or writing definitions for the following terms. You may also practice defining these terms by using the online flashcards or comparing your answers to the online glossary.

memory search p. 169

primacy-recency effect p. 173

Decay Theory p. 174

Displacement Theory p. 175

Interference Theory p. 175

Incomplete Encoding Theory p. 175

Retrieval Failure Theory p. 175

Emotional Blocks Theory p. 175

Twelve Principles of Memory p. 177

mnemonics p. 177

SAVE CRIB FOTO p. 178

Intention p. 181

Big and Little Pictures p. 182

Organization p. 183

Time on Task p. 184

Ongoing Review p. 184

overlearning p. 185

acronyms p. 186

acrostics p. 187

Loci Method p. 189

 Access Chapter 6 Flashcards and Online Glossary in your College Success CourseMate, accessed through *CengageBrain.com*.

Learning Objectives Review

1 *Explain four processes that work in your conscious mind (memory searches, retrieval cues, thought patterns, and rehearsal/review) and six forgetting theories that explain why forgetting sometimes occurs.*

- Conducting memory searches involves using associations and information linked together to "chat your way" to locate information stored in long-term memory. Some memory searches are short; others require lengthier searching.

- Retrieval cues are essential to the learning process, for they trigger recall of memory.

- Tracking thought patterns involves an awareness of how you think and process information.

- Rehearsing retrieval and reviewing keeps information in long-term memory active and accessible; frequent rehearsal and review increase speed and accuracy of recall.

- The primacy-recency effect identifies which information in lists is easier to recall and which is more difficult to recall accurately.

- Six forgetting theories explain why recalling information is not always successful: Decay, Displacement, Interference, Incomplete Encoding, Retrieval Failure, and Emotional Blocks.

2 *Explain the Twelve Principles of Memory represented by the mnemonic SAVE CRIB FOTO.*

- SAVE CRIB FOTO is a mnemonic that represents the Twelve Principles of Memory that encompass memory strategies and processes that promote powerful learning.

- The Twelve Principles of Memory appear throughout this textbook and as integral parts of many study skills strategies: Selectivity, Association, Visualization, Elaboration, Concentration, Recitation, Intention, Big and Little Pictures, Feedback, Organization, Time on Task, and Ongoing Review.

3 *Explain how to create and use mnemonics to learn academic information.*

- Mnemonics are memory tools that serve as bridges to help recall difficult-to-remember information from long-term memory.

- Acronyms and acrostics use letters from words to create key words or sentences to translate back into the words of the original items to help remember them.

- Word and picture associations are mnemonics that link two or more items together to trigger recall.

- The Loci Method is a mnemonic based on linking pictures to various rooms that appear in a floor plan.

Chapter 6   Review Questions

Answers appear on page B3.

True or False? See Test-Taking Strategies 1–9 in Appendix A.

_____ 1. The memory principle of Selectivity relies on the use of the principles of Time on Task and Ongoing Review to work effectively.

_____ 2. You are using the memory principle of Visualization effectively when you glance at pictures, photographs, or charts.

_____ 3. "CRIB" in the mnemonic SAVE CRIB FOTO represents the following memory processes: Concentration, Rehearsal, Interest, and Big and Little Pictures.

_____ 4. Self-quizzing, reciting, and the Look-Away Technique are ways to get feedback on how well you understand information.

_____ 5. When you conduct memory searches, retrieval cues often are associations.

_____ 6. Mnemonics function as effective retrieval cues as soon as you create them.

_____ 7. The primacy-recency effect refers to limiting the size of units of information to attempt to retrieve from memory at a given time.

_____ 8. The forgetting theories that describe an inability to recall information imprinted in memory are the Decay Theory and the Displacement Theory.

Listing Questions See Test-Taking Strategies 25–28 in Appendix A.

1. List five principles of memory to use to break the habit of using rote memory to learn and practice information. After each principle, write one or two sentences briefly explaining why the principle would discourage rote memory.

2. List the six theories of forgetting that explain why recall of information from long-term memory sometimes cannot be achieved.

Access Chapter 6 Enhanced Quiz and Chapter 6 Study Guide in your College Success CourseMate, accessed through *CengageBrain.com*.

Access all Chapter 6 Online Materials in your College Success CourseMate, accessed through *CengageBrain.com*.

7

Preparing for Upcoming Tests

ImageSource/Getty Images

Tests in college are a standard method to assess your understanding of course material. As you approach the middle of a term and midterm exams, laying a strong foundation to perform well on tests involves exploring test-preparation strategies, kinds of test questions, and test-taking strategies. When faced with apprehension or test anxiety, using the skills you learned and becoming familiar with additional strategies can reduce or eliminate test anxiety. This chapter also refers to the removable Essential Test-Taking Skills guide in Appendix A, which provides you with specific strategies and skills for objective, recall, math, and essay tests.

YOUR CHAPTER MAPPING

After reading information under each heading, return to the chapter visual mapping below.

Add key words to show subheadings and important details related to each heading.

 Access Chapter 7 Visual Mapping in your College Success CourseMate, accessed through *CengageBrain.com*.

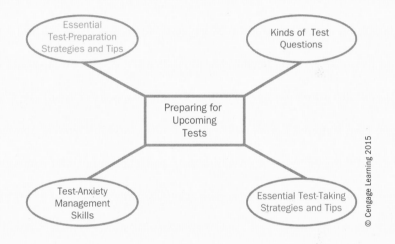

© Cengage Learning 2015

 Access Chapter 7 Expanded Chapter Outline in your College Success CourseMate, accessed through *CengageBrain.com*.

LEARNING OBJECTIVES

1 *Discuss effective strategies to organize materials and time, create a five-day study plan and summary notes, and use memory strategies to review for upcoming tests.*

2 *Identify the different kinds of objective, recall, math, and essay questions that appear on tests, and explain at least two strategies for answering each type of question.*

3 *Describe effective test-taking strategies to increase your performance on classroom, online, and computerized tests.*

4 *Identify the four main sources of test anxiety, and summarize strategies to reduce or eliminate test anxiety before and during the taking of tests.*

Preparing for Upcoming Tests

ANSWER, SCORE, and **RECORD** your profile before you read this chapter. If you need to review the process, refer to the complete directions given in the profile for Chapter 1 on page 4.

ONLINE: You can complete the profile and get your score online in this textbook's College Success CourseMate.

Access Chapter 7 Profile in your College Success CourseMate, accessed through *CengageBrain.com*.

	YES	NO
1. When I start studying for tests, I organize my materials, use special time-management schedules, and predict possible test questions.	_____	_____
2. I reread chapters multiple times and rewrite all my notes as a way to prepare for upcoming tests.	_____	_____
3. I make a five-day study plan and summary notes to prepare for major tests.	_____	_____
4. On multiple-choice questions, I select the first answer or option that seems to answer the question.	_____	_____
5. I create an outline or plan for an essay before I begin developing the individual paragraphs.	_____	_____
6. On tests, I answer or guess at an answer, and then move systematically to the next question.	_____	_____
7. I learn from my graded tests by looking for patterns of errors, correcting errors, and adjusting my study and test-taking strategies.	_____	_____
8. My grades are lower than they should be because I struggle with test anxiety.	_____	_____
9. I deal with test-anxiety issues by being prepared for tests and controlling attitudes and beliefs that otherwise could hinder my test-taking skills.	_____	_____
10. I am confident in my test-preparation and test-taking skills and abilities.	_____	_____

QUESTIONS LINKED TO THE CHAPTER LEARNING OBJECTIVES:

Questions 1–3: objective 1   Questions 8–9: objective 4

Questions 4–5: objective 2   Question 10: all objectives

Questions 6–7: objective 3

Essential Test-Preparation Strategies and Tips

1 *Discuss effective strategies to organize materials and time, create a five-day study plan and summary notes, and use memory strategies to review for upcoming tests.*

Tests are inevitable in the college setting as well as in many workplace settings. No one wants to be caught off guard, unprepared, or lack the necessary skills to perform well on tests. Test-preparation skills involve organizing materials, organizing time, creating a positive mindset to perform well, and using effective test-preparation strategies that bring good results. Following are important points to keep in mind before beginning the review process to prepare for an upcoming test:

- Complete all reading or homework assignments so you do not need to mix review time with new learning time.

- If you have used ongoing review prior to the announcement of a test, you will find that preparing for a test will involve *reviewing* and not *studying to learn* information for a test.

- Preparing for tests should be a matter of "brushing up" or refreshing your memory. If you did not dedicate adequate time for ongoing review each week, you now will need to dedicate more time to prepare for a test.

EXERCISE 7.1

Academic Preparation Inventory

Your grades on tests often reflect the effectiveness of your study and review strategies. Identifying your strengths and weaknesses *before* a test and *after* you receive test results provides you with an opportunity to identify which strategies work and which you need to modify or replace. Go to Exercise 7.1 in Appendix C, page C15, to complete this inventory.

Using Appendix A: Essential Test-Taking Skills

Throughout this chapter you will be accessing important information and strategies in **Appendix A: Essential Test-Taking Skills.** For quick reference to Appendix A, consider removing Appendix A from your textbook, punching three holes in the pages, and creating a section in your notebook for this valuable resource. Appendix A provides detailed directions for performing well on all kinds of tests, so it is a resource that you will want to use not only this term, but also for future terms. Take a few minutes to survey Appendix A.

Organizing Your Materials

Preparing for a test requires additional time and organization, both of which can be demanding in a schedule that already is filled with other demands from your courses and in your personal life. The following suggestions can help you organize your materials in an efficient and effective manner.

Pay Attention to Test Details

Your goal is to be prepared and avoid, if possible, surprises or unexpected content on an upcoming test. Use the following tips to find out as much as you can about an upcoming test. Listen carefully to your instructor's description of the test and the topics or chapters that the test will cover. Take notes on materials or topics your instructor emphasizes that you should review or need to know.

1. If your instructor indicates the kinds of test questions that will appear on the test, jot these down as you may use different strategies to prepare for different kinds of test questions.

2. Talk to other students who have already completed the course and tutors who are familiar with the course. Ask them for study suggestions and about the kinds of test questions to expect. Remember, however, that instructors do change test questions and formats, so do not feel overly confident about an upcoming test based on information you obtained from previous students or from tutors.

3. If previous tests are available to examine, take the time to look at and practice with the tests.

Gather Your Course Materials

Review your course syllabus and class assignment sheets so you know specifically which chapters and topics will be included on the test. Gather together and organize your notes and assignments, chapter by chapter. Identify topics that received special attention in class or through assignments as the test may place greater emphasis on these topics. Pulling together and organizing your materials before you begin the serious review process promotes effective and efficient use of time.

Predict Test Questions

Predicting test questions is an excellent method for preparing for tests and reducing test anxiety. Predicting test questions becomes easier when you become familiar with the kinds of tests your instructor uses.

   Figure 7.1 shows the kind of information to study and the type of practice to use when you predict specific kinds of question formats will appear on a test.

CONCEPT CHECK   **7.1**

Does knowing the type of questions that will be used on an upcoming test affect the way you study for the test? Explain.

Organizing Your Time

Preparing for upcoming tests, especially major tests such as midterm or final exams, is time-consuming and time-intensive. Using time-management skills throughout the term places you in a better position to prepare for tests, helps you avoid the need to cram, or removes the feeling of being underprepared, which is one source of test anxiety.

Use Ongoing Time-Management Strategies

In Chapter 3, you learned to use effective time-management strategies. Use the following time-management and test-preparation strategies consistently

FIGURE 7.1   Predicting and Studying for Different Kinds of Tests

If You Predict…	Study This Kind of Information:	Practice May Include:
Objective Questions	• Definitions of key terms • Categories or lists of information • Details: names, dates, theories, rules, events	• Writing and later answering true-false, multiple-choice, and matching questions • Working with a study partner to exchange practice questions
Recall Questions	• Information presented in lists • Definitions of terminology • Cornell recall columns (Chapter 9) • Questions formulated before, during, and after reading • Chapter summaries • Details on visual notes (Chapter 11)	• Reciting and using the Look-Away Technique • Writing summaries and answers to questions to practice expressing ideas • Writing and answering fill-in-the-blanks, listing, and definition questions • Working with a study partner to exchange practice questions
Math Questions	• Problem-solving examples and prototypes	• Reworking math problems • Writing the problem-solving steps
Essay Questions	• Themes • Relationships • Major concepts	• Outlining chapters to see headings and relationships • Reviewing notes for recurring themes • Using Essential Test-Taking Skills in Appendix A for all kinds of questions

© Cengage Learning 2015

throughout the term to build confidence about your ability to perform well on tests:

1. **Fixed study blocks:** Schedule sufficient fixed study blocks to complete regular assignments and review course content on an ongoing basis.

2. **Spaced practice:** Use spaced practice, not marathon studying, to learn and review information.

3. **Schedules:** Create and follow a weekly time-management schedule.

4. **Review schedules:** Add specific blocks of time on your weekly schedule specifically for review. Spread your review time out over several different time blocks and several different days.

5. **Five-day plan:** Use the *five-day study plan* in the following section to prepare for major tests.

6. **Summary notes:** Create a special set of review notes called *summary notes* during this test-preparation, review process.

Use the Recency Effect

The *recency effect* states that the items you will remember more easily are items that you most recently practiced. When using a five-day study plan, you utilize this recency effect when the fifth day of this plan is the day before a test. You can also

> The **recency effect** states that the items you will remember more easily are items that you most recently practiced.

utilize this recency effect by reviewing summary notes one final time right before you go to bed the night before a test. For the greatest impact, avoid placing any other kinds of stimuli, such as television or a movie, between your review time and your sleep. As you sleep, your mind may continue thinking about and integrating the information you reviewed. You can also gain the benefits of the recency effect by reviewing summary notes one final time the day of the test or the hour before the test.

Creating a Five-Day Study Plan

> A **five-day study plan** is a plan of action that helps you organize your materials and schedule time to review for a major test, such as a midterm or a final exam.

A *five-day study plan* is a plan of action that helps you organize your materials and schedule time to review for a major test, such as a midterm or a final exam. This plan promotes spaced practice and ongoing review; it reduces tendencies to procrastinate, cram, or experience test anxiety. Use the following steps to create a five-day study plan:

Step 1: Identify Specific Topics to Review

Begin by making a list of all the topics and materials that you need to review for the upcoming test. Following is an example for a sociology course.

Terminology	Lecture notes	Textbook notes
Study guides	Chapter reviews	Homework assignments
Guest speaker notes	Notes from video	Two discussion papers

Step 2: Schedule Specific Days and Times to Review

Organize specific blocks of time on days 1, 2, 3, and 4 for review sessions. On day 5, dedicate all of your study time to reviewing your *summary notes*. Mark the study/review days and times on your calendar or your weekly schedule. Coordinate these times with other students if you are going to review with a study partner or study group.

Day 1	Day 2	Day 3	Day 4	Day 5
Monday Review Times:	Wednesday Review Times:	Friday Review Times:	Saturday Review Times:	Sunday Final Review Times:
8–9:00 AM	8–9:00 AM	8–9:00 AM	10:00 AM–12:00 PM	2–4:00 PM
3–5:00 PM	3–5:00 PM	3–5:00 PM	4–6:00 PM	7–9:00 PM

Step 3: Create a Plan of Action

Identify which chapters and which materials you will review on day 1, day 2, day 3, and finally on day 4. To avoid wasting review time, create a pattern or plan for reviewing each time you sit down. For example, your plan may be to use this sequence of review activities: review study guide, review chapter summary, review textbook notes, review terminology, review homework, review class handouts, and review lecture notes. Throughout this review process, plan to make *summary notes* for the information you feel you need to review further on day 5 and right before the test. Following is an example of a plan of action.

Example of a Plan of Action

Monday	Wednesday	Friday	Saturday	Sunday
8-9:00 AM (Ch. 1) class study guide homework Q handouts	8-9:00 AM (Ch. 2) study guide homework Q video notes	8-9:00 AM (Ch. 3) class study guide handouts homework Q	10-12:00 PM (Ch. 4) study guide (no handouts) homework Q 2 short papers	2-4:00 PM Review summary notes; self-quiz on Ch. 1 & 2
3-5:00 PM (Ch. 1) lecture notes textbook notes Notes-Guest speaker	3-5:00 PM (Ch. 2) lecture notes textbook notes	3-5:00 PM (Ch. 3) lecture notes textbook notes	4-6:00 PM (Ch. 4) lecture notes textbook notes	7-9:00 PM Review summary notes; self-quiz on Ch. 3 & 4

© Cengage Learning

Creating Summary Notes

Summary notes are specific notes that include concepts, definitions, details, steps, or other information that you need to review further before the day of the test. If you have used effective learning strategies and ongoing review, as you review your text-book and lecture notes, you will recognize concepts, facts, and terms that you already know well. These do not need to appear on your summary notes. Your summary notes are special sets of notes for information that you know you need to give more attention to and study further. **Figure 7.2** shows a variety of formats that are commonly used for summary notes that you create as you prepare for an upcoming test.

> **Summary notes** are specific notes that include information that you need to review further before the day of the test.

> CONCEPT CHECK 7.2
>
> *How are the summary notes you create to prepare for an upcoming test different from your regular textbook and lecture notes?*

Transfer These Skills: Summary Notes and Five-Day Study Plan

PURPOSE: Creating summary notes and organizing a five-day study plan are two important processes you can use to organize your materials and your time for an upcoming test. Both take time but each has the potential to increase your test-taking performance.

DIRECTIONS: Unless your instructor provides you with alternative directions, choose to do one of the following assignments to demonstrate your ability to transfer skills from this chapter to other courses. On your paper, identify the course, the instructor, and the assignment option you selected.

1. For any one of your classes, create summary notes for an upcoming test. Use a variety of summary note formats. Remember, your summary notes reflect only the information that you know you need to study further to prepare for the test.

2. For any one of your classes, create a five-day study plan that shows the specific topics you need to review, the target dates and times for reviewing, the steps, and your plan of action. Use the format shown above for each step of the five-day study plan.

FIGURE 7.2 Formats Commonly Used for Summary Notes

Lists/categories of
information to remember

Comparison charts to
compare or contrast
different subjects studied

Notes based on topics
that include textbook
and lecture information

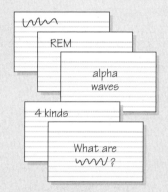

Flashcards of categories,
terminology, and study
questions

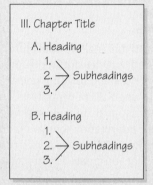

Chapter outlines made
by using headings and
subheadings

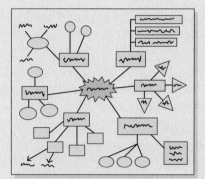

Visual mappings for individual
chapters or topics that appear in
several different chapters

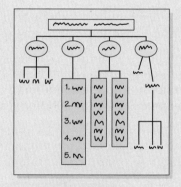

Large hierarchies made on
poster paper to include several
topics or chapters

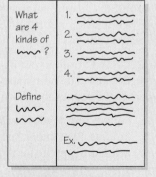

Cornell notes with study
questions on the left for
self-quizzing

Using Effective Memory Strategies to Review

Preparing for tests by reviewing course content activates the array of memory strategies you learned to use in Chapters 5 and 6. Preparing for tests involves revisiting concepts, main ideas, and important details through the use of the following learning and memory strategies. Use the index of this textbook to locate reference pages for each of the following topics. Review the strategies in Chapters 5 and 6 if necessary.

Twelve memory processes	**Twelve Principles of Memory**	**Positive and negative feedback**
Memory searches	**Retrieval cues**	**Mental rehearsal**
Look-Away Technique	**Mnemonics**	**Paired associations**

CONCEPT CHECK   7.3

How can the processes of visualization and recitation be used together to review material for an upcoming test? How can the memory principles of Selectivity and Big and Little Pictures be used together?

CHECK POINT 7.1

Answers appear on page B3.

True or False? See Test-Taking Strategies 1–9 in Appendix A.

_____ 1. Students who do not use a five-day study plan may need to resort to last-minute cramming.

_____ 2. The recency effect states that you will remember the first items you study at the beginning of a review session.

_____ 3. Studying throughout the day before a test and then enjoying a movie or some type of recreational activity the night before a test are effective test-preparation strategies that also reduce stress.

_____ 4. The feedback you receive from the Look-Away Technique can help you decide what information to put into summary notes.

_____ 5. It is best not to rely on learning course materials a day or two before a test.

_____ 6. In a five-day study plan, a plan of action involves identifying the topics to review, times to review, and planning a course of action with specific steps to prepare for upcoming tests.

_____ 7. It is dishonest and a form of cheating if you talk to students who previously took tests for the class you are in or if you look at tests previously used in the class.

_____ 8. Summary notes are always brief and limited to topics that you need to mentally rehearse.

 Access Chapter 7 Practice Quiz 1 in your College Success CourseMate, accessed through *CengageBrain.com*.

Kinds of Test Questions

2 *Identify the different kinds of objective, recall, math, and essay questions that appear on tests, and explain at least two strategies for answering each type of question.*

Understanding types of test questions is an important step in the process of strengthening your test-preparation and test-taking skills. **Figure 7.3** provides you with information about the different formats for test questions that you may encounter on your tests. To learn more about each kind of test question, and to familiarize yourself with fifty-two easy-to-use strategies for all test question formats, refer to the Essential Test-Taking Skills guide in Appendix A. When you know an upcoming test will focus on a specific type of test question, you may refer to that specific section in

FIGURE 7.3   Test Question Formats

Kind of Question	Level of Difficulty	Includes	Requires
Recognition: Objective Questions	Easiest	True-False Multiple-Choice Matching	Read and recognize whether information is correct; apply a skill and then recognize the correct answer.
Recall Questions	More demanding	Fill-in-the-Blanks Listings Definitions Short Answers	Retrieve the information from your memory and then respond.
Math Questions	Demanding	Problem-Solving	Use procedural knowledge to complete steps of processes.
Essay Questions	Most difficult	Essays	Retrieve the information from memory, organize it, and use effective writing skills to respond.

Appendix A to prepare for the test. You can remove the Essential Test-Taking Skills guide and place it in your notebook for quick reference in any of your classes. For now, the following common test-question formats will help you begin to anticipate what to expect on upcoming tests.

Important Terminology for Objective Questions

As you work with true-false, multiple-choice, and matching questions, you will encounter important terminology. Refer to Appendix A, page A3–A4, to familiarize yourself with the following important test-question terminology for objective questions:

Modifiers	Definition clues	Relationship clues
Negatives	Stems	Options
Distractors	Levels of response	Immediate response
Delayed response	Assisted response	Educated selection

True-False Questions

True-false questions are objective questions that require you to recognize if a statement is true or false.

True-false questions are objective questions that require you to recognize if a statement is true or false. Mark a question *true* only when the complete statement is true and accurate. If any part of the statement is false or inaccurate, you must mark the statement as *false*. **See Appendix A, Test-Taking Strategies 1–9, pages A5--A12, for more details.** Following is an example of a true-false question:

_____   1. A five-day study plan must always be scheduled for five consecutive days prior to the test day. *Answer: False*

Multiple-Choice Questions

Multiple-choice questions are objective questions that require you to select the best answer from a group of options to complete an opening statement.

Multiple-choice questions are objective questions that require you to select the best answer from a group of options to complete an opening statement. At times, more than one option may complete the statement accurately, but only one option is the best, most inclusive, or most complete answer. Multiple-choice questions may show three, four, or five options. Sometimes the last option includes "all of the above," which means every option is accurate. **See Appendix A, Test-Taking Strategies 10–15, pages A12–A19, for more details.** Following is an example of a multiple-choice question:

_____ 1. Kinds of encoding to prepare stimuli for long-term memory include:

    a. linguistic and visual coding

    b. kinesthetic coding

    c. semantic coding

    d. all of the above   *Answer: d*

> **CONCEPT CHECK**   **7.4**
>
> *What are the three kinds of objective test question formats? What do they have in common?*

Matching Questions

Matching questions are objective questions that require you to match items in the left column with items in the right column. Matching questions often test your ability to match terminology with definitions; people, places, or dates with descriptions, characteristics, or events; or match causes and effects. **See Appendix A, Test-Taking Strategies 16–20, pages A19–A22, for more details.** Following is a partial example of the matching question format:

> **Matching questions** are objective questions that require you to match items in the left column with items in the right column.

_____ 1. reciting

_____ 2. See-Say-Do Strategy

_____ 3. learning modalities

    a. learning styles

    b. multisensory learning strategy

    c. explaining out loud, in your own words without referring to printed information   *Answers: 1. c 2. b 3. a*

Important Terminology for Recall Questions

As you work with listing and short-answer recall questions, you will encounter important terminology. Refer to Appendix A, page A22, to familiarize yourself with the following important test-question terminology:

- *Closed questions*: Questions that require specific answers
- *Open-ended questions*: Questions that have a variety of possible answers
- *Direction words*: Words in test questions that indicate what is expected in the answers

> **Closed questions** are questions that require specific answers.

> **Open-ended questions** are questions that have a variety of possible answers.

> **Direction words** are words in test questions that indicate what is expected in the answers.

Fill-in-the-Blanks Questions

Fill-in-the-blanks questions are recall questions that require you to write a term or a word on each blank line to complete the statement. Words that complete these statements are often vocabulary or terminology words. Correct answers often require that you spell the words in the blanks correctly. **See Appendix A, Test-Taking Strategies 21–24, pages A22–A24, for more details.** Following is an example of a fill-in-the-blanks question:

> **Fill-in-the-blanks questions** are recall questions that require you to write a term or a word on each blank line to complete the statement.

1. _____ is the process of postponing a task for a later time.
Answer: Procrastination

Objective Test Questions

DIRECTIONS: Read and review Test-Taking Strategies 1–20 in Appendix A, pages A5–A22. Then answer the following questions.

TRUE OR FALSE?

_____ **1.** To answer true-false questions correctly, you cannot personalize the question by responding with your opinion.

_____ **2.** To be true, every part of a true-false question must be true.

_____ **3.** When you have reservations about an answer on a true-false question, you should explain your answer next to the question.

_____ **4.** Negatives are words in a sentence that make the sentence false.

_____ **5.** *Always, never, best,* and *everyone* are word definition clues.

_____ **6.** The left column in matching questions often contains course-specific vocabulary terms.

_____ **7.** In a matching test, each item in the right column must be matched up with an item in the left column.

MULTIPLE CHOICE

_____ **1.** Which of the following statements is not true?

a. Before you convert each option into a true-false statement, you should finish the stem in your mind and check if one of the options matches your preliminary answer.

b. On a multiple-choice question, when you combine the stem with each option, only one statement can be true, so all the remaining statements must be false.

c. The *best* answer will form a completely true statement.

d. To be sure you write the correct answer, you can circle the correct answer before you write the answer on the line.

_____ **2.** If a multiple-choice question has four options, how many distractors are there?

a. one

b. two

c. three

d. four

_____ **3.** Multiple-choice questions are similar to true-false questions in that both types of questions

a. may have 100 percent and in-between modifiers.

b. have only one correct answer.

c. may include a definition clue or a relationship clue.

d. show all of the above.

Listing Questions

Listing questions are recall questions that require you to generate a list of items from memory to answer a question. *Closed questions* require specific items in the answer. *Open-ended questions* have a variety of possible answers. Listing questions often begin with one of these direction words: *list, name,* or *what are.* Unless the directions ask you to add details about each item, your answer simply lists the items. **See Appendix A, Test-Taking Strategies 25–28, pages A24–A26, for more details.** Following is an example of a listing question that is a closed question that requires a specific answer.

1. List the three memory systems in the Information Processing Model.
   Answer: *1. sensory memory*
   2. working memory
   3. long-term memory

> **Listing questions** are recall questions that require you to generate a list of items from memory to answer a question.

Definition Questions

Definition questions are recall questions that require you to define and expand upon a vocabulary term. Simply writing a word-for-word textbook definition is not sufficient. Instead, you can use a three-part definition: (1) identify the category to which the term belongs, (2) define the term, and (3) give one more detail about the term. **See Appendix A, Test-Taking Strategies 29–31, pages A26–A28, for more details.** Following is an example of a definition question.

1. What is the definition of the Take Charge Technique?
   Answer: *The Take Charge Technique is a concentration technique. It involves taking responsibility for your environment by seeking alternative places to study or by modifying your existing place of study so you have few or no distractions. When you use this technique, you find solutions rather than blame others for your inability to concentrate.*

> **Definition questions** are recall questions that require you to define and expand upon a vocabulary term.

> **CONCEPT CHECK** 7.5
> *What are the four kinds of recall question formats? Why are recall questions considered more demanding than recognition (objective) questions?*

Short-Answer Questions

Short-answer questions are recall questions that require you to pull information from memory to write a short answer to a question. Often times you can answer the question in five to seven sentences. Direction words for short-answer questions include *discuss, tell, identify, describe, explain why, explain how,* and *when.* Short-answer questions may be closed or open-ended questions. **See Appendix A, Test-Taking Strategies 32–36, pages A28–A31, for more details.** Following is an example of a short-answer question.

1. Explain what the Retrieval Failure Theory states about forgetting.
   Answer: *The Retrieval Failure Theory states that failure to locate information in long-term memory may be the result of lack of effort, memorizing details in isolation, or using a weak system to organize information. Lack of effort shows lack of intention to imprint information clearly in long-term memory. Information that is memorized in isolation rather than associating it to related schemas becomes difficult to locate. Information that is not organized in a logical way also makes locating and retrieving the information from long-term memory difficult to do.*

> **Short-answer questions** are recall questions that require you to pull information from memory to write a short answer to a question.

Recall Questions

DIRECTIONS: Read and review Test-Taking Strategies 21–36 in Appendix A, pages A22–A31. Then answer the following questions.

TRUE OR FALSE?

_____ **1.** The second sentence in an answer for a definition question should state important details that show you understand the term.

_____ **2.** Well-developed answers to definition questions should consist of one or two sentences.

_____ **3.** Short-answer questions should consist of sentences written in paragraph form and not as a list of points.

_____ **4.** A closed question for a listing question allows many different answers as long as the information is course specific.

_____ **5.** In a well-written fill-in-the-blanks question, the number of blanks indicates the number of words required to complete the sentence.

FILL-IN-THE-BLANKS

1. Answers for an _____ - _____ question may vary from one student to another.

2. When writing an answer for a short-answer question, your _____ sentence should be direct and to the point so your instructor knows you understand the question.

3. _____ words in short-answer questions indicate the type of answer that is expected.

4. A well-developed answer to a definition question shows _____ levels of information.

Important Terminology for Math Questions

When students think about math courses and math tests, they often focus on using numbers and processes to solve problems; they pay less attention to math terminology. However, understanding and knowing how to define math terminology lays the foundation for discussing math principles, understanding concepts, and working steps of problem-solving processes. Spend ample time learning definitions of math terminology you encounter in your math textbooks. Refer to Appendix A, page A31, to familiarize yourself with the following important test-question terminology for math:

Algebraic expressions	Algebraic symbols	Algorithms
Equations	Prototypes	Word or story problems

Problem-Solving Questions

Problem-solving questions are questions that require you to use procedural knowledge to apply a series of steps to solve a problem. Problem-solving questions may involve story problems or solving a mathematical equation. Usually your answer must show all the steps used to solve the problem. **See Appendix A, Test-Taking**

Problem-solving questions are questions that require you to use procedural knowledge to apply a series of steps to solve a problem.

Strategies 37–44, pages A31–A37, for more details. Following is an example of a problem-solving question:

1. Use the power rule to solve the following equation: $(2^3)^4 = ?$

   Answer: $(2^3)^4 = 2^{3 \times 4} = 2^{12} = 4,096$

Important Terminology and Test Formats for Essay Questions

As you work with essay questions, you will encounter important terminology. Refer to Appendix A, page A37, to familiarize yourself with the following important test-question terminology:

Thesis statement	Direction words	Organizational plan
Five-paragraph format	Main idea	Supporting details

Essay Questions

Essay questions require you to retrieve information from memory and organize it into several paragraphs with main ideas that are related to a thesis statement. Essay questions involve higher-level thinking, organizational skills, and writing skills. **See Appendix A, Test-Taking Strategies 45–51, pages A37–A43, for more details.** Following are examples of essay questions that require multiple paragraphs in the response.

> **Essay questions** require you to retrieve information from memory and organize it into several paragraphs with main ideas that are related to a thesis statement.

1. Explain the meaning of the following statement: *The Myers-Briggs Personality Indicator is based on opposite poles of preferences and characteristics.*

2. How do self-talk, locus of control, and self-efficacy affect a person's academic performance?

Strengthen Your Essay Writing Skills

Do you find essay questions to be the most challenging kind of question on tests? Some students prefer objective test questions while others prefer essay questions. Students who do well on essay tests often have developed the following skills:

- Ability to answer questions directly and with the kind of information expected by the question
  - *Review Figure 13: Direction Words for Essay Questions* (Appendix A)
  - *Review Figure 14: Thesis Sentences* (Appendix A)
- Ability to organize information clearly so the reader can follow the reasoning or explanations, and ability to include main ideas (big pictures) and sufficient supporting details (little pictures)
  - *Review Figure 15: Organizational Plans for Essay Questions* (Appendix A)
  - *Review Key Elements in a Five-Paragraph Essay* (Appendix A)
  - *Review Pre-Writing Guide for Essay Question* (Appendix A)
- Ability to show the relationships between the different levels of information and use transition words to connect sentences and paragraphs together smoothly
- Ability to express ideas clearly by using effective choice of words, vocabulary, and course terminology
- Ability to use correct spelling, grammar, and sentence structures in paragraphs

Essay Test Questions

DIRECTIONS: Read and review Test-Taking Strategies 45–51 in Appendix A, pages A37–A43. Then answer the following questions.

TRUE OR FALSE?

_____ **1.** A well-developed essay answer must include the "big pictures" (concepts) and the "little pictures" (supporting details).

_____ **2.** Once you have written an answer for an essay question, you should not attempt to add additional information because the results will be a difficult-to-read answer.

_____ **3.** The last paragraph of an essay answer should always emphasize your personal opinion.

_____ **4.** More in-depth details always would be required for an essay question that begins with the word *summarize* than would be required for a question that begins with the word *explain*.

_____ **5.** The thesis statement directly states the main point of the entire essay.

_____ **6.** If you make an organization plan for an essay answer, you should turn it in with your test if you run out of time and are not able to finish your essay answer.

FILL-IN-THE-BLANKS

1. The _____ sentence in an essay states the main point the writer intends to develop throughout the entire essay.

2. Details used to develop the thesis appear in the _____ of the essay.

3. The direction word _____ requires you to identify different parts of something and discuss each part with details.

Kinds of Essay Tests

Unlike other test-taking formats, instructors may use a variety of formats for essay tests, some of which provide you with greater opportunities to prepare your essay answer in advance. Following are essay formats and situations you may encounter in your courses.

- **Topics are announced in advance.** Gather pertinent information on the announced topics. Use the index of your textbook to locate information on the topic and prepare a set of detailed notes. Predict possible questions, organize your information, and practice writing answers to the questions you predicted.

- **Questions are announced in advance.** Use the index in your textbook to locate and organize pertinent information. Create and memorize an outline or organizational plan for your answers. Practice writing essay answers for each question.

- **Essays will be completed in class.** For in-class essay tests, you may be assigned specific questions to answer or you may be given a choice of questions from which you select the questions to answer. In all cases, you will be challenged to retrieve and organize information from memory. Use the following suggestions to prepare for in-class essay tests.

  - *Predict test questions.* Use your course syllabus to identify concepts, trends, themes, or categories of information that you are expected to learn. Write practice test questions based on these materials.

  - *Create summary notes.* Essay questions often require you to compare, contrast, summarize, explain, discuss, or apply information about major topics, themes, theories, or models. Create summary notes with important supporting details for topics that you predict may be in essay test questions.

- *Practice writing essay answers.* Work with a partner or in a study group to create practice essay questions and answers. When you practice organizing information and presenting your ideas *before* an actual essay test, you become more comfortable with the essay-writing process.

- **Books may be used for the essay test.** Open-book essay tests require less retrieval of information from memory and more organizational skills to locate information in the textbook. Become familiar with the index of your book so you can look up topics quickly. Use a special highlighter to mark important facts (dates, names, events, statistics, and terminology) and quotations you may wish to use in your answer. Use tabs to mark significant pages such as those with important summary charts, tables, lists, steps, or visual materials.

- **Essay test is done at home.** Take-home essay tests provide you with more time to organize and develop your essay answer. Create a plan of action that provides you with sufficient time to develop a polished essay answer. Set your completed essay aside for a day; then, reread it; proofread for spelling, grammar, and mechanics; revise if you see ways to strengthen it; and type the final version.

CONCEPT CHECK **7.6**
Which is a more difficult essay question test format: an in-class essay question when the topic is given in advance or a take-home essay question? Explain your answer.

CHECK POINT 7.2

Answers appear on page B3.

Fill-in-the-Blanks See Test-Taking Strategies 21–24 in Appendix A.

1. _____ questions, which are more demanding than recognition questions and less difficult than essay questions, require a person to retrieve information from memory in order to answer the question.

2. Both _____ questions and open-ended questions appear in listing, short-answer, and essay questions.

3. Well-developed answers to _____ questions often explain a vocabulary term by using three levels or kinds of information.

Listing Questions See Test-Taking Strategies 25–28 in Appendix A.

1. List the four kinds of questions that are categorized as *recall questions.*

2. What kinds of test questions are categorized as *objective questions?*

 Access Chapter 7 Practice Quiz 2 in your College Success CourseMate, accessed through *CengageBrain.com.*

CHAPTER 7
REFLECTIVE WRITING 1

 Before starting this writing assignment, complete Exercise 7.6: Test-Taking Skills Inventory, on page 212. On separate paper, in a journal, or online in this textbook's College Success CourseMate, respond to the following questions:

1. According to the inventory results in Exercise 7.6, what was your score? What strategies can you learn to use more effectively to improve your test-taking skills?

2. Based on test grades this term for your various classes, how do your grades reflect your overall progress in your courses? Explain with specific details.

 Access Chapter 7 Reflective Writing 1 in your College Success CourseMate, accessed through *CengageBrain.com.*

Test-Taking Skills Inventory

PURPOSE: Use the following self-assessment inventory to evaluate your general test-taking skills and identify areas you can strengthen. The perfect score is 60.

DIRECTIONS: Read each statement about test-taking skills. Circle the degree to which you use these test-taking skills.

1 = seldom or never   2 = sometimes   3 = always or almost always

1. I complete all of my assignments and reading prior to a test.   1 2 ③

2. I set ample time aside to study specifically for a test.   ① 2 3

3. I use self-quizzing and feedback methods when I study.   1 ② 3

4. I know definitions for all course-specific terminology.   1 ② 3

5. I feel confident that I studied sufficiently to do well on a test.   1 ② 3

6. I use the four levels of response for answering test questions.   1 ② 3

7. I rehearse factual information using a variety of strategies, and I rehearse procedural information by using ample repetition.   ① 2 3

8. I read directions carefully and understand direction words.   ① 2 3

9. I read carefully and pay attention to modifiers, clue words, negatives, and other details in test questions.   1 ② 3

10. I use the essential strategies for answering objective questions: true-false, multiple-choice, and matching test questions.   1 ② 3

11. I use educated selection (guessing) only as a last resort.   1 2 ③

12. I use the essential strategies for answering recall questions: fill-in-the-blanks, definition, and listing questions.   1 ② 3

13. I include sufficient details to answer short-answer questions.   1 ② 3

14. I respond with the correct kind of information for closed questions and open-ended questions.   1 2 ③

15. I memorize prototypes for different kinds of math problems.   ① 2 3

16. I create an organizational plan for essay test answers.   ① 2 3

17. I develop a strong thesis statement for essay test answers.   ① 2 3

18. I include ample details in essays to support the thesis.   1 ② 3

19. I use available test-taking time to check my answers and work.   1 ② 3

20. I analyze error patterns and learn from my tests.   ① 2 3

Your Total Score: __36__

Essential Test-Taking Strategies and Tips

3 *Describe effective test-taking strategies to increase your performance on classroom, online, and computerized tests.*

Feeling slightly nervous or apprehensive when you first enter the classroom or when the instructor distributes the test is a normal reaction to testing situations. Strive to use strategies to calm your nerves, establish a positive state of mind, and mentally prepare to do well on the test. Following are strategies to establish a positive mindset for tests:

- Arrive to class early. Rushing in at the last minute or arriving late adds stress and does not allow you time to mentally prepare.

- Use positive self-talk, a quick relaxation or visualization technique, or a concentration technique to focus your mind.

- Focus only on yourself; ignore other students and their nervous reactions to the test.

- If you have a few minutes before the test is distributed, mentally rehearse information from your summary notes. Or, if allowed, review your summary notes one final time.

- Listen carefully to the directions. Your instructor may announce corrections on the test, suggestions for completing the test, the amount of time available for the test, and other important directions.

Creating a Plan of Action to Begin a Test

Begin strengthening your test-taking skills by using the Essential Classroom Test-Taking Strategies in **Figure 7.4**. You can use these strategies from the beginning to the end of a test-taking situation. Details for each strategy appear in the following sections.

Jot Down Important Information

As soon as you receive the test, jot down important information on the back of the test, in the margins of the test, or on separate scratch paper. For example, you may

---

FIGURE 7.4   Essential Classroom Test-Taking Strategies

- Jot down important information.
- Survey the test and budget your time.
- Decide on a starting point.
- Use your test time wisely.
- Read directions and questions carefully.
- Answer all questions.
- Change answers carefully.
- Use the four levels of response to answer questions.

© Cengage Learning 2015

Performing well on tests involves developing effective test-preparation and test-taking skills. What strategies do you use to prepare for upcoming tests? What strategies do you use to move through tests with confidence and efficiency?

want to quickly write down formulas, mnemonics, lists, or facts that you may need to refer to quickly during the test. You may also want to add specific items that you reviewed immediately prior to the test so they will be fresh in your memory.

Survey the Test and Budget Your Time

Glance through the test to become familiar with the types of questions on the test, the point value of different questions or sections on the test, and the overall length of the test. Be sure to check to see if questions appear on the backs of the test pages.

Then, quickly estimate the amount of time you can spend on each section of the test. This is especially important if the test has short-answer or essay questions because those questions tend to take more time to write answers. If you wish, jot down estimated times to begin each section of the test.

Decide on a Starting Point

Many students prefer to work through the pages of the test in the order in which the questions are presented, but you do *not* have to work in this order. You can begin with the part of the test that feels the most comfortable, has the highest point value, or with which you feel most confident.

Use Your Test Time Wisely

Avoid the urge to bolt out of the classroom as soon as you finish a test. After answering all of the questions, use the remaining time to check your answers. Use all available test time to proofread, revise, or refine answers for short-answer or essay questions. Use available time to check math calculations and the steps used to show your work.

Answering Questions

When you first receive a test, you may feel somewhat overwhelmed by the number of questions and the different kinds of questions. The way you approach each question and select an answer affects your grade, so work carefully and thoughtfully by doing the following.

Read Directions and Questions Carefully

The number one cause of students making unnecessary errors on tests has to do with hastily reading directions and questions. Read directions slowly. Be sure you understand the directions before proceeding. Ask for clarification if the directions are not clear. Read questions carefully, paying close attention to key words and direction words. To help yourself stay focused on the question, *circle direction words and key words* in the questions as well as in the directions.

CONCEPT CHECK   **7.7**

What strategies can you use within the first five minutes of receiving a test? How will these strategies affect your attitude toward the test?

Answer All Questions

Do not leave answer spaces blank if you start to run out of time. In most cases, you will automatically lose points if you leave an answer space blank. When you are running out of time, pick up your pace, read faster, spend less time pondering answers, and make a quick choice or use an *educated selection* strategy for an answer if necessary. For essay questions, if you do not have time to write a complete answer, provide an outline or a list of points you would have developed further had you had sufficient time.

Change Answers Carefully

Do *not* change answers if you are panicking or feeling that time is running out. If you work carefully before answering questions, rely on your self-confidence that the answer you already selected is the best. However, sometimes other questions on the test give you clues or help you recall information that may have you questioning your original answer. In such cases, when you can clearly justify a reason to change an answer, *do* change answers.

Use the Four Levels of Response

Some students who have not yet learned effective test-taking strategies move through a test by reading a question, answering it with certainty or hesitancy, and then moving on to the next question. This approach works if students immediately know the correct answer for each question. When students are not able to answer all the questions immediately, using the four levels of response is a more effective approach that brings better results. The *four levels of response* are sequential steps students can use to answer test questions: *immediate*, *delayed*, *assisted*, and *educated selection*. **Figure 7.5** summarizes the four levels of response. Additional details about the four levels of response appear in Appendix A, page A4.

> The **four levels of response** are sequential steps students can use to answer test questions: immediate, delayed, assisted, and educated selection.

As an effective test-taker and critical thinker, you can use a variety of questions to "jump-start" your memory as you conduct memory searches for correct answers.

FIGURE 7.5 Four Levels of Response to Answer Test Questions

1. **Immediate Response,** the first level of response to a test question, involves immediately knowing the answer.

2. **Delayed Response,** the second level of response to a test question, involves carefully rereading a question and seeking retrieval cues, associations, visualizations, or auditory cues to help you retrieve an answer from memory.

3. **Assisted Response,** the third level of response to a test question, involves using other questions in the test to assist you with answering a question.

4. **Educated Selection,** also called *educated guessing,* is the fourth level of response to a test question that involves using a variety of strategies to increase your odds in selecting the correct answer.

© Cengage Learning

Following are definitions of each level of response followed by examples of questions you can use for each level.

Immediate response involves immediately knowing the answer.

Immediate response, the first level of response to a test question, involves immediately knowing the answer. When you read the question, you know the answer with certainty.

Am I sure this is correct?

Delayed response involves conducting a memory search to retrieve the answer from long-term memory.

Delayed response, the second level of response to a test question, involves conducting a memory search to retrieve the answer from long-term memory. This may involve rereading the question carefully, using retrieval cues and associations, visualizations, or auditory cues to recall learned information.

What do I know that is related to this question?
If I go into "retrieval mode," can I recall an association, visualization, or mnemonic to help me remember?
When did we discuss this? What chapter is this from?
What other things belong in a category with this term?
Is this a vocabulary term? Will recalling a definition help me answer the question?

Assisted response involves using other questions in the test to assist you with answering the question.

Assisted response, the third level of response to a test question, involves using other questions in the test to assist you with answering the question. Select key words in the question; scan other test questions to look for this word or concepts related to the word as these may trigger recall of the correct answer.

After carefully rereading the question, is the answer now more apparent?
What is a key word in the question? Can I find that word in another question somewhere in the test?
Is there another question that I can use to help me recall this answer?

Educated selection involves using a variety of strategies to increase your odds in selecting the correct answer.

Educated selection, the fourth level of response to a test question, involves using a variety of strategies to increase your odds in selecting the correct answer. Educated selection sometimes is referred to as *educated guessing*; however, logical analysis goes beyond random guessing.

How can I use some logic to think this through?
Which answer is not feasible? Why?
What words in the question can help me use educated selection strategies?

CONCEPT CHECK   7.8

If you read a question and do not know the answer, what strategies are more effective than just guessing an answer?

See strategies 9, 14, 15, 23 and 27 in **Appendix A: Essential Test-Taking Skills** for educated selection strategies for objective test questions.

Learning from Your Tests

Do you sometimes receive your graded tests, look at the grade, and then stick the test into your notebook or backpack? A more effective approach involves using the tests for valuable feedback and then analyzing the effectiveness of your learning strategies. With the information you learn from analyzing your test, create a plan of action to adjust your study and learning strategies to bring even better results on your next test.

Examine the Questions You Answered Correctly

Understanding what processes you used to answer questions correctly helps you recognize what is working for you. Answer the following questions:

What strategies did I use to learn this information?

What was the original source of the information? Did I learn the information in class, through a homework assignment, from the textbook, or from a combination of sources?

Was the information new to me or did I already know this information at the time it was presented?

Look for Patterns of Errors

Repeat the process you used to examine the questions you correctly answered, but this time examine the processes, strategies, and sources of the information for the questions that you answered incorrectly. For example, perhaps the information that you missed the most frequently appeared mainly in the textbook or as information presented in class during lectures. Perhaps you skipped reciting or using review strategies for the topics in the questions you answered incorrectly. This feedback makes you more aware of the need to focus greater attention on your strategies for textbook reading or on your notetaking skills for class lectures.

Correct Your Errors

You want to override or erase incorrect information and replace it with accurate information. Create and practice new associations so the next time you need to retrieve that information from your schemas, you will recall accurate information. Frequently during the course of a term, previously learned information appears again on future tests or as knowledge upon which new information is built. Therefore, taking time to learn the correct information strengthens the memory schema with accurate details.

> **CONCEPT CHECK 7.9**
>
> *How can you use graded tests to improve performance? How can graded tests affect your attitude and mindset about tests?*

Textbook Case Studies

EXERCISE 7.7

DIRECTIONS:

1. Read each case study carefully. Respond to the question at the end of each case study by using *specific* strategies discussed in this chapter. Answer in complete sentences.

2. Write your responses on paper or online in the College Success CourseMate, Textbook Case Studies. You will be able to print your online response or e-mail it to your instructor.

CASE STUDY 1: Adolpho has not been in school for fifteen years. He never learned how to study or take tests. He works hard, and he is able to respond in class and in study groups to questions that are related to the current assignment. However, when it is time to take tests that cover several chapters of information, he freezes and goes blank. What test-preparation and test-taking strategies would you recommend Adolpho start using?

CASE STUDY 2: Jenny does not study much for her communications class because she is taking the class for pass/no pass rather than a letter grade. As the end of the term approaches, she realizes that she may not have enough points to pass the class. She intends to deal with the situation the way she usually deals with tests—cramming in the day or two before the final exam. What test-preparation strategies would you suggest that Jenny use during the final two weeks of the term?

 Access Chapter 7 Textbook Case Studies in your College Success CourseMate, accessed through CengageBrain.com.

Computerized Tests

Students who take online courses encounter online or computerized testing on a fairly regular basis. However, many students who attend classes on campus also encounter the use of computerized tests. In many cases, students must check into a computer lab to complete the assigned tests.

Computerized tests usually consist of multiple-choice questions. These tests may be written by the instructor, but more often they consist of questions from a test bank generated by the textbook author or publisher. Some of the test banks randomly assign test questions of varying levels of difficulty; other test banks allow the instructor to tag which questions to use on a test.

One advantage of taking computerized tests is that students usually receive immediate feedback and a test score. If the response is immediately recorded as *correct*, the positive feedback increases students' confidence level. Another advantage is that the time limit to complete the test is less rigid than when students take the test in class. Students control the pace for answering questions, so they may feel less stress.

There are some disadvantages of taking computerized tests. Students may be anxious or uncomfortable taking computerized tests if they have limited experience or skills using computers. Students may also have increased stress or frustration if they receive any negative feedback that an answer is incorrect. Another disadvantage is that many computer tests do not allow students to go back to previous questions to change answers or use the test-taking strategy of assisted response. Finally, students do not have access to a printed copy of the test to view, correct answers, or use to study for a final exam.

If you have not already experienced computerized testing, chances are good that you will at some time during your college career. For practice taking computerized tests, go to the College Success CourseMate for this textbook to complete Practice Quizzes and Enhanced Quizzes for each chapter. **Figure 7.6** summarizes seven essential strategies for taking computerized tests. Following are details about these strategies.

Know the Rules for Computerized Testing

Prior to taking a computerized test, gather as much information as possible about the rules for computerized testing. Ask questions such as the following:

> *Is there a tutorial or practice test?*
> *May I take the test more than once?*

CONCEPT CHECK   **7.10**

Do you prefer computerized tests over paper-pencil tests? Why or why not?

FIGURE 7.6   **Essential Strategies for Taking Computerized Tests**

- Know the rules for computerized testing.
- Allow yourself ample time to complete the test.
- Understand the computer and the testing software commands.
- Read and choose answers carefully.
- Learn from incorrect answers.
- Use relaxation techniques.
- Discuss your test-taking experience.

© Cengage Learning

Is there a time limit for completing the test?

May I have blank scratch paper and pen to work out problems or to organize my thoughts?

Will I be able to get a printed version of the test to use for studying after the test is scored?

Allow Yourself Ample Time to Complete the Test

For many students, taking computerized tests requires more time than taking tests in the classroom. Select a time of day when you feel mentally sharp and are not rushed or pressed for time. When you enter the lab, choose a computer that is not in the line of a steady flow of traffic so you will experience fewer distractions. Finally, do not postpone taking the test or wait until close to the deadline to complete the test.

Understand the Computer and the Testing Software Commands

Ask for help if you are unfamiliar with the computer, need help logging on, or do not understand how to select or change answers. Ask for help if you do not know how to save your test results. Read all the directions carefully. Notice whether or not the software program allows you to return to previous questions or change previous answers.

Read and Choose Answers Carefully

The strategies for multiple-choice questions used for paper-pencil tests are the same as those used for computerized tests. See **Appendix A, Essential Test-Taking Strategies 10–15, pages A12–A19** for more test-taking strategies applicable to computerized tests.

Do not answer too quickly. Once you have decided on your answer, reread the opening part of the question with the option you believe completes the statement correctly. You can often avoid careless mistakes by double-checking an answer before selecting it as your final answer.

Learn from Incorrect Answers

Do *not* immediately move to the next question if you receive feedback that your answer is incorrect. Instead, use this feedback as a learning opportunity. Reread the question and if the correct answer is provided, study the correct answer. Similar information may appear in another question, so the feedback may help you answer later questions correctly. This strategy also keeps your mind focused on the materials and reduces the tendency to move too hastily to the next question.

Use Relaxation Techniques

Pause and use a short relaxation technique if you find yourself tensing up, feeling discouraged, or getting irritated. Working memory needs to remain free of mental clutter; stress or anxiety affects thinking processes. The breathing by threes technique, using positive self-talk, or stretching your arms, rolling your shoulders, or shaking out your hands help reduce stress.

Discuss Your Test-Taking Experience

Before you leave the test, jot down any questions that concerned or confused you. Discuss these questions with your instructor. Make a brief list of topics you need to review or study further. After taking several tests, if you remain uncomfortable with computerized tests, ask lab assistants or your instructor for additional test-taking strategies. Talk to other students to learn their strategies. Ask your instructor if there is an option to take a paper-pencil or written test.

Practice Test-Taking Skills

DIRECTIONS: Go to Exercise 7.8: Practice Test-Taking Skills in Chapter 7 Topics In-Depth in your College Success CourseMate to practice answering objective and recall questions. After printing the exercise, you may work by yourself, with a partner, or in a small group to complete this exercise. If your instructor does not assign this exercise, you may complete the practice questions and use the exercise as a review tool for a midterm exam for this course.

Access Chapter 7 Topics In-Depth: Exercise 7.8 Practice Test-Taking Skills in your College Success CourseMate, accessed through *CengageBrain.com*.

CHECK POINT 7.3

Answers appear on page B3.

True or False? See Test-Taking Strategies 1–9 in Appendix A.

_____ 1. Looking for patterns of errors, using assisted response, and correcting errors are processes that students cannot do while taking computerized tests.

_____ 2. Once you mark an answer, you should never go back and change that answer.

_____ 3. The third level of response to answer test questions involves using other parts of the test to search for clues to answer a question.

_____ 4. When taking computerized tests, it is important to move through the test as quickly as possible to avoid forgetting information that appeared in earlier questions.

_____ 5. Educated selection is also referred to as educated guessing.

Access Chapter 7 Practice Quiz 3 in your College Success CourseMate, accessed through *CengageBrain.com*.

 ## Test Anxiety Management Skills

4 *Identify the four main sources of test anxiety, and summarize strategies to reduce or eliminate test anxiety before and during the taking of tests.*

Stress is a reaction or response to events or situations that threaten to disrupt a person's normal patterns or routines.

Test anxiety is excessive stress that hinders a person's ability to perform well before or during a test.

Stress is defined as a reaction or response to events or situations that threaten to disrupt a person's normal patterns or routines. Stress specifically related to an upcoming test can be beneficial and motivate people to perform on higher levels; however, excessive stress that becomes *test anxiety* creates negative responses and consequences. *Test anxiety* is excessive stress that hinders a person's ability to perform well *before* or *during* a test. The following points are also important to understand:

• Students who experience bouts with test anxiety can learn strategies to reduce the effects, duration, and intensity of this form of anxiety.

FIGURE 7.7   Symptoms Related to Test Anxiety

Kinds of Symptoms	Examples of Symptoms of Test Anxiety		
Physical	Rapid heartbeat Upset stomach, nausea Abnormal nervousness Tight muscles, tension	Blurred vision Increased blood pressure Shakiness	Headaches Clammy palms More than normal sweating
Emotional	Fear, anger, frustration Irritable, short-tempered Fatigue	Feelings of hopelessness or lack of control of a situation	"Fight or flight" feelings Anxious, nervous, panicky Depressed

Cognitive	Mind filled with intrusive
	   thoughts
	Poor concentration
	Inaccurate or limited recall
	Confusion, disorientation
		Impulsive responses
		Negative self-talk
		Lack of clear thinking
		Misdirected attention "Going
		   blank"
			Fixating on one item too long
			Careless mistakes
			Overemphasis on negative
			   thoughts

Behavioral	Crying, sobbing Strained facial expressions	Slumped posture Procrastination	Shaky voice Aggressive behavior

© Cengage Learning 2015

- Test anxiety before and during a test can exhibit its presence in physical, emotional, cognitive, and behavioral forms. **Figure 7.7** shows common symptoms related to test anxiety.

- Common signs of test anxiety include becoming ill or emotionally distraught, experiencing confused or disorganized thinking, or using avoidance strategies to procrastinate studying for a test.

- During a test, test anxiety affects cognitive processing and can immobilize thinking skills. A student may "go blank," make excessive careless mistakes, mark answers in the wrong place, or quit due to frustration.

Test Anxiety Inventory

PURPOSE: Some students may experience test anxiety, which impacts their test performance; other students may experience test-related stress that actually motivates them to perform well. This inventory provides you with information about test anxiety indicators you may experience.

DIRECTIONS: Go to Exercise 7.9 in Appendix C, page C16, to complete the Test Anxiety Inventory.

EXERCISE 7.9

Sources of Test Anxiety

Test anxiety is a *learned behavior*. As such, it can be unlearned. If you experience test anxiety, begin by analyzing the source of your anxiety. What triggers your test anxiety? Sometimes listening to the kinds of comments you make about tests will help you identify the source of your test anxiety. *Under-preparedness, past experiences, fear of failure,* and *poor test-taking skills* are four common sources of test anxiety.

Under-Preparedness

Students who do not apply study skills on a regular basis often need to resort to *cramming,* which is an attempt to learn large amounts of information in a short period of time. Cramming is a survival technique that often backfires. Frequently, students who cram become even more aware of how much *they do not know.* Feeling under-prepared can create test anxiety and lead to poor test performance. Following are student comments that indicate under-preparedness:

> *I am nervous about this test because I did not have enough time to study or review.*
> *When I started reviewing, I realized how much I still needed to learn.*
> *Everyone else seems to know more than I do. I should have studied more.*
> *I can't keep up; there's too much information to learn in this class.*

Return to pages 197–203 in this chapter to review strategies students can use to prepare for upcoming tests and not trigger test anxiety caused by under-preparedness.

CONCEPT CHECK **7.11**

For students who face a bout with test anxiety due to under-preparedness, what test-preparation strategies could they have used to avoid this excessive stress?

Past Experiences

Low self-esteem is often the result of past experiences that left a person with a negative self-image or perception of his or her limited ability to perform well. Having experienced frustration, disappointment, or a sense of failure in past testing situations can create a cycle of negative self-talk, self-doubt, low self-esteem, and low self-confidence. Sometimes students who have experienced negative past experiences lay the blame for poor performance on other people instead of taking responsibility for their test results. Following are student comments that reflect test anxiety due to past experiences:

> *I never get decent grades on tests. I simply am not a good test taker.*
> *I did not do well on the last test, so this test probably won't be any different.*
> *Instructors write tricky tests that are not fair and are designed to flunk most students.*
> *Tests make me feel stupid and embarrassed.*

Students who encounter test anxiety due to beliefs, emotions, and attitudes based on previous experiences can try the following strategies to decrease or eliminate test anxiety:

- Use affirmations and positive self-talk to develop a stronger, positive self-image.
- Develop an internal locus of control.
- Focus on the present and not on the past.

Fear of Failure

CONCEPT CHECK **7.12**

What strategies can students use to reduce or eliminate test anxiety based on fear of failure?

Another source of test anxiety is the fear of failure. Students with a fear of failure worry about the negative consequences of poor grades, which in turn increases stress levels which may trigger test anxiety. As discussed in Chapter 2, they also worry about disappointing other people.

Poor Test-Taking Skills

For many students, the source of test anxiety is linked directly to the lack of test-preparation skills and the lack of test-taking skills. Taking tests requires understanding various kinds of test questions as well as how to read and interpret questions accurately, conduct memory searches for answers, select answers carefully, and write appropriate answers. Following are student comments that reflect that poor test-taking skills are the source of test-anxiety:

I have never learned how to be a good test-taker. No one ever taught me.
I never know what to study or how to organize enough time to review.
I get nervous taking tests because I do not really know how to answer different kinds of questions.
I make a lot of mistakes because I have problems understanding the directions or the kind of answers that the instructor expects.
I never have enough time on tests to really show how much I know.

The majority of this chapter and all of **Appendix A: Essential Test-Taking Skills** focus on powerful and effective strategies for performing well on tests. Spend ample time understanding and applying the strategies to avoid test anxiety due to poor test-taking skills. Use the Practice Quizzes and Enhanced Quizzes in this textbook's College Success CourseMate to practice your test-taking skills. Practicing test-taking skills in a non-testing situation builds confidence and improves test-taking performance.

GROUP PROCESSING

A Collaborative Learning Activity

1. Form groups of three or four students. Your group will need to have a chart to record responses. Select one member of your group to be the group recorder.

2. Create the following chart. In the Strategies column, brainstorm and list strategies students could use to "unlearn" the behaviors and beliefs that cause test anxiety. Use your knowledge of memory strategies, self-regulation or self-management strategies, and strategies from this chapter to compile ways students can combat test anxiety.

Source	Strategies
Under-preparedness	
Past Experiences	
Fear of Failure	
Poor Test-Taking Skills	

© Cengage Learning

Access Chapter 7 Topics In-Depth: Strategies to Reduce Test Anxiety in your College Success CourseMate, accessed through *CengageBrain.com*.

Strategies to Reduce Test Anxiety *Before* a Test

In the Group Processing Activity, you and members of your group listed an array of strategies from previous chapters to deal with test anxiety. Using strategies related to time management, goal setting, motivation, the twelve memory processes, and the Twelve Principles of Memory help you prepare for tests and create a positive mindset to perform well.

Systematic desensitization is an anxiety-reducing strategy that involves a series of activities designed to reduce strong negative emotional reactions to an upcoming situation.

A final strategy you can learn to use *before* a test to create a positive mindset and reduce or eliminate test anxiety is called *systematic desensitization.* **Systematic desensitization** is an anxiety-reducing strategy that involves a series of activities designed to reduce strong negative emotional reactions to an upcoming situation. You can use this strategy before the day of a test by replacing your fear-based thoughts with positive thoughts that emphasize the successes you have already experienced. Systematic desensitization stops the fear from accelerating and getting blown out of proportion You can use systematic desensitization in the following ways:

1. **Reduce your emotional response to trigger words.** Make a list of specific situations or words that trigger your test anxiety. For example, "There will be a test next Monday" may trigger early test anxiety. After you have your list of *trigger situations or words,* visualize yourself reacting differently to those situations or words. See yourself responding in a more positive and constructive way. "Good. I have time to make a five-day plan, or I have stayed current with my work, so I can be ready for this test."

2. **Create a mock test situation to imitate the real test situation.** Predict and write practice test questions. Decide on an appropriate amount of time to answer the test questions. Create a test environment as close as possible to the real thing. If the classroom in which you will take a test is empty, be in that room when you take your practice test.

3. **Capture the feelings of the mock situation with less stress and anxiety.** Create an image of yourself in the mock situation taking the test in a relaxed, alert manner. Remind yourself that there is no need to be overly nervous about one test.

CONCEPT CHECK   7.13

Fears often become overexaggerated. How could you use systematic desensitization to deflate an overexaggerated fear? Give specific details.

Strategies to Reduce Test Anxiety *During* a Test

You can reduce or eliminate most test anxiety that occurs during a test by using the essential strategies for taking tests shown in **Figure 7.4**, page 213. The following strategies address specific symptoms that you might experience during a bout with anxiety during a test.

- **When you "go blank" and are unable to recall the needed information, do the following:**

  1. Use a quick relaxation technique to calm yourself down.

  2. Use positive self-talk. Become your own cheerleader.

  3. Reread the question in a whisper voice. Go into retrieval mode by conducting a new memory search. If necessary, place a check mark to return to the question later. Do not stay stuck on the question.

- **When your eyes start jumping from the printed line or skip over words when you read, do the following:**

  1. Use your arm, a blank index card, or a blank piece of paper to block off the rest of the test. Restricting your vision so you only see the question that you are contemplating helps your eyes stay focused on a line of information.

  2. Use your pencil to point to each word as you read silently. Doing this keeps your eyes from skipping words or jumping to other lines of print.

- **When you notice yourself making excessive careless mistakes in selecting or marking the correct answer, do the following:**

  1. Slow down the reading and answering process. Rush less and think more.

2. Activate your auditory channel by mouthing or quietly whispering the words as you read the directions, questions, and options for answers.

3. Highlight key words in the questions. Check to ensure that your answer relates to the key words.

4. Before moving to the next question, ask yourself: *Does this answer make sense?*

- **When your mind shifts away from the test and your concentration begins fading quickly, do the following:**

1. Become more active and interactive with the test. Circle direction words and highlight key words in directions and questions.

2. Use positive self-talk and force yourself to keep your eyes on the test. "*I can do this. My eyes and my mind stay focused on the paper. I can figure this out.*"

CHAPTER 7
REFLECTIVE WRITING 2

 On separate paper, in a journal, or online in this textbook's College Success CourseMate, respond to the following questions.

1. For the majority of test-taking situations you encounter, what strategies do you use that help you enter the classroom feeling confident and well-prepared for the test?

2. Which specific skills in this chapter will help you the most in terms of preparing for tests, performing well on tests, and managing test anxiety? Discuss at least four skills and include specific strategies you intend to use.

 Access Chapter 7 Reflective Writing 2 in your College Success CourseMate, accessed through *CengageBrain.com*.

CHECK POINT 7.4

Answers appear on page B3.

Definitions See Test-Taking Strategies 29–31 in Appendix A.

1. Define the term *test anxiety*.

2. Define the term *open-ended question.*

Essay Question See Test-Taking Strategies 45–51 in Appendix A.

DIRECTIONS: Choose one of the following essay questions to answer. Create an organizational plan for your answer. Use the five-paragraph format to write an essay answer. Proofread, revise, and print your answer.

Essay Question 1: Discuss ways students can avoid test-anxiety caused by under-preparedness. Include test-preparation strategies for any three of these areas: organizing materials, organizing time, creating review study tools, or using effective memory-boosting strategies.

Essay Question 2: Discuss how past experiences and fear of failure may trigger test anxiety. Then summarize strategies students could use to reduce or eliminate test anxiety caused by past experiences or fear of failure.

 Access Chapter 7 Practice Quiz 4 in your College Success CourseMate, accessed through *CengageBrain.com*.

ACTIVITY

Chapter 7 Critical Thinking

DIRECTIONS:

1. To help prepare for a major upcoming test, predict and practice writing six review questions that cover the chapters and topics that will be included in the test. Write one question for each level of questions in Bloom's Taxonomy: remembering, understanding, applying, analyzing, evaluating, and creating.

2. Submit your questions to your instructor. Questions may be discussed in class, presented to the class for review activities, or used on the upcoming test.

Terms to Know

By yourself or with a partner, practice reciting or writing definitions for the following terms. You may also practice defining these terms by using the online flashcards or comparing your answers to the online glossary.

recency effect p. 199

five-day study plan p. 200

summary notes p. 201

true-false questions p. 204

multiple-choice questions p. 204

matching questions p. 205

closed questions p. 205

open-ended questions p. 205

direction words p. 205

fill-in-the-blanks questions p. 205

listing questions p. 207

definition questions p. 207

short-answer questions p. 207

problem-solving questions p. 208

essay questions p. 209

four levels of response p. 215

immediate response p. 216

delayed response p. 216

assisted response p. 216

educated selection p. 216

Learning Objectives Review

❶ *Discuss effective strategies to organize materials and time, create a five-day study plan and summary notes, and use memory strategies to review for upcoming tests.*

- Appendix A: Essential Test-Taking Skills is a valuable resource with fifty-two detailed strategies for responding to all kinds of test questions.

- Organizing materials to prepare for a test involves jotting down tips from the instructor, gathering materials to review, and predicting test questions.

- Time-management strategies, a five-day study plan, and using the recency effect are strategies to organize time effectively to prepare for tests.

- Summary notes, special notes designed specifically for final reviews, help students be better prepared for upcoming tests.

- Memory strategies used to learn information and imprint information into memory are also used to review for upcoming tests.

❷ *Identify the different kinds of objective, recall, math, and essay questions that appear on tests, and explain at least two strategies for answering each type of question.*

- Four kinds of questions that you will encounter on college tests include: objective questions, recall questions, math questions, and essay questions.

- Appendix A provides detailed strategies for responding to objective questions, which include true-false, multiple choice, and matching questions.

- Appendix A provides detailed strategies for recall questions, which include fill-in-the-blanks, listing, definition, and short-answer questions.

- Appendix A provides detailed strategies for responding to math questions, which often include problem-solving and word problems.

- Appendix A provides detailed strategies for organizing and writing answers for essay test questions.
- Different test-preparation strategies are used for essay tests which provide students with topics or questions in advance, in-class essays, open-book essays, and take-home essays.

3 *Describe effective test-taking strategies to increase your performance on classroom, online, and computerized tests.*

- Jotting down information, surveying and budgeting time, deciding on a starting point, and using test time wisely are four strategies to use to create a plan of action to begin a test.
- Carefully reading directions and questions, answering all questions, changing answers carefully, and using four levels of response to answer questions are effective test-taking strategies.
- Using the following four levels of response for answering questions can improve your test results: immediate response, delayed response, assisted response, and educated selection (educated guessing).
- You can learn from your tests by examining correct answers, looking for patterns of errors in incorrect answers, and correcting errors.
- Computerized tests differ from paper-pencil tests. Seven essential strategies can boost your computerized test performance.

4 *Identify the four main sources of test anxiety, and summarize strategies to reduce or eliminate test anxiety before and during the taking of tests.*

- Test anxiety is excessive stress that affects performance. Symptoms of test anxiety may be physical, emotional, cognitive, or behavioral.
- Four common sources of test anxiety include under-preparedness, past experiences, fear of failure, and poor test-taking skills.
- Test anxiety is a learned behavior that can be "unlearned" by using effective test-anxiety management strategies before and during a test.

Terms to Know
continued

stress p. 220

test anxiety p. 220

systematic desensitization p. 224

 Access Chapter 7 Flashcards and Online Glossary in your College Success CourseMate, accessed through *CengageBrain.com*.

Chapter 7   Review Questions

Answers appear on page B3–B4.

True or False? See Test-Taking Strategies 1–9 in Appendix A.

_____ 1. A five-day study plan promotes spaced practice for test-preparation.

_____ 2. You can use the recency effect by doing a final review one or two hours before the time of a test.

_____ 3. Instructors usually announce or remind students about upcoming tests, but they never provide suggestions about what to study or what kinds of test questions to expect.

_____ 4. Recall questions include listing, multiple-choice, definition, and short-answer questions.

_____ 5. Summary notes are a detailed compilation of all of your textbook and lecture notes organized day by day and chapter by chapter.

_____ 6. Memory strategies to prepare for upcoming tests include using visualizations, associations, recitation, procrastination, stress, and test-anxiety.

Multiple Choice See Test-Taking Strategies 10–15 in Appendix A.

_____ 1. Effective test-preparation skills
  a. reduce the necessity to cram for tests and use rote memory techniques.
  b. include time-management and goal-setting techniques.
  c. involve making summary notes and predicting, writing, and answering practice test questions.
  d. include all of the above.

_____ 2. In a five-day study plan, you
  a. begin by listing the topics and materials you need to review.
  b. schedule review times on a calendar.
  c. may set aside more than one study block for each day in the plan.
  d. do all of the above.

_____ 3. Which of the following statements is _not_ true about test anxiety?
  a. A person's self-esteem and locus of control may contribute to test anxiety.
  b. Test anxiety is productive and beneficial for many students.
  c. A person's lack of test-preparation and test-taking skills may trigger test anxiety.
  d. Test anxiety is a learned behavior that can be altered, eliminated, or "unlearned."

_____ 4. Cramming
  a. is a survival technique used for under-preparedness.
  b. is highly effective when used the day before a test.
  c. processes large amounts of information efficiently.
  d. involves all of the above.

_____ 5. Which of the following is _not_ an effective test-taking strategy?
  a. Leave some questions temporarily unanswered when taking a test.
  b. Read directions and questions carefully to avoid unnecessary mistakes.
  c. Do not feel that you must work through the test questions in the order that they appear on the test.
  d. Your original answer is always the correct one, so avoid returning to questions to change the original answer.

Definitions See Test-Taking Strategies 29–31 in Appendix A.

Write a definition for the following terms. Each answer should include a three-part definition.

1. Systematic desensitization

2. Summary notes

3. Test anxiety

4. Closed questions

Short-Answer Questions See Test-Taking Strategies 32–36 in Appendix A.

On separate paper, answer any two of the following questions. Include details and chapter terminology in your answers.

1. True-false questions sometimes are considered by students to be "easy," yet students can answer incorrectly if they do not read questions carefully. Identify any three true-false strategies students can use to perform well on true-false tests.

2. Your instructor indicates that a section of matching questions will appear on the test. What kinds of information should you review to prepare for an upcoming test with matching questions?

3. Identify which one of the four levels of response cannot be used on computerized tests and explain why it cannot be used.

4. What strategies are effective for students who have difficulty organizing ideas to answer essay questions?

Take-Home Essay Question See Test-Taking Strategies 45–51 in Appendix A.

Question: Discuss strategies that you can use to prepare for tests, take tests, and learn from tests to improve your performance in your courses this term. Use the space below to draw your organizational plan for your essay.

Access Chapter 7 Enhanced Quiz and Chapter 7 Study Guide in your College Success CourseMate, accessed through *CengageBrain.com*.

Access all Chapter 7 Online Materials in your College Success CourseMate, accessed through *CengageBrain.com*.

8 Selecting a Reading System

© Stockbyte/Getty Images

Many college students have reading habits and use techniques that they have established over many years of reading, yet those habits and techniques may be inadequate to handle the demands of college-level reading and comprehension. In this chapter, you will begin the process of replacing old reading habits and techniques with more effective ones designed to strengthen your reading skills and improve comprehension of textbook materials.

1 FIRST STEPS OF THE READING PROCESS

Developing Positive Attitudes and Behaviors

Identifying Purposes for Reading

Adjusting the Reading Rate

Surveying a Textbook

Surveying an Article or an Essay

2 ESSENTIAL TEXTBOOK READING PROCESSES

Using a Reading System

Surveying a Chapter

Writing Focus Questions

Reading Carefully

Reviewing

3 THREE SPECIFIC READING SYSTEMS

SQ4R

The Outline Reading System

A Customized Reading System

4 READING PROCESSES FOR ONLINE E-BOOKS

Advantages of E-Textbooks

E-Textbook Challenges

Navigating the Essential Study Skills E-Textbook

Effective Reading Strategies for E-Textbooks

 Access Chapter 8 Expanded Chapter Outline in your College Success CourseMate, accessed through *CengageBrain.com*.

YOUR CHAPTER MAPPING

After reading information under each heading, return to the chapter visual mapping below. Add key words to show subheadings and important details related to each heading.

 Access Chapter 8 Visual Mapping in your College Success CourseMate, accessed through *CengageBrain.com*.

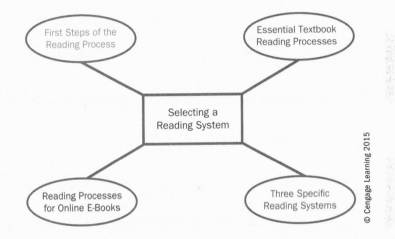

© Cengage Learning 2015

LEARNING OBJECTIVES

1 *Discuss the importance of attitude, purpose for reading, reading rate, and the process of surveying as first steps in the reading process.*

2 *Identify and explain the essential processes used in an effective textbook reading system.*

3 *Compare and contrast the steps used in three reading systems: SQ4R, the Outline Reading System, and a Customized Reading System.*

4 *Explain effective reading strategies to use for online e-textbooks.*

© Cengage Learning 2015

Selecting a Reading System

ANSWER, SCORE, and **RECORD** your profile before you read this chapter. If you need to review the process, refer to the complete directions given in the profile for Chapter 1 on page 4.

ONLINE: You can complete the profile and get your score online in this textbook's College Success CourseMate.

Access Chapter 8 Profile in your College Success CourseMate, accessed through *CengageBrain.com.*

	YES	NO
1. I find that reading textbooks is difficult and confusing for me to do, so I read only enough to get by or to get a general understanding of the content.	_____	_____
2. I verbalize, visualize, and ask myself questions about content when I read textbook chapters.	_____	_____
3. I survey new textbooks and know how to use the sections in the front and the sections in the back of the textbook.	_____	_____
4. I use a textbook reading system that begins with surveying new chapters, involves some form of notetaking and reciting, and ends with a review of the chapter content.	_____	_____
5. I take notes and recite only when a textbook chapter is difficult for me to understand.	_____	_____
6. I take the time to create questions when I am reading and studying information from a textbook.	_____	_____
7. I have one textbook reading system and use that system to read all of my textbooks.	_____	_____
8. I read online e-textbook chapters more quickly and with fewer pauses than when I read traditional printed textbooks.	_____	_____
9. I use the read-record-recite cycle when I read online e-textbooks and printed textbooks.	_____	_____
10. I am confident in my ability to select effective processes and an effective reading system for my textbooks.	_____	_____

QUESTIONS LINKED TO THE CHAPTER LEARNING OBJECTIVES:

Questions 1–3: objective 1

Questions 4–6: objective 2

Question 7: objective 3

Questions 8–9: objective 4

Question 10: all objectives

First Steps of the Reading Process

1 *Discuss the importance of attitude, purpose for reading, reading rate, and the process of surveying as first steps in the reading process.*

As a college student, you will spend thousands of hours reading thousands of textbook pages filled with information you will be required to learn. You will also be required to comprehend information from other sources, such as Internet and online articles, excerpts, journal reviews, library books, and reference materials. You can save yourself time and increase your academic performance by developing and strengthening your college-level reading skills from basic skills to more advanced, critical reading skills.

Developing Positive Attitudes and Behaviors

The reading process begins as soon as you sit down with a textbook in front of you. *Do you look forward to reading and learning from your textbook, or does a negative attitude kick in? Do you value the reading process enough to set aside adequate time to read and work with textbook information without interruptions, or do you try to read quickly to get it done, or do you multitask during the reading process?* The attitude and choice of behaviors you bring to the reading process affect the quality of the reading experience.

Figure 8.1 shows important attitudes and behaviors that lay a strong foundation for the first steps of the reading process for college-level readers.

FIGURE 8.1   Attitudes and Behaviors for College-Level Readers

- **Begin with an attitude to learn.** A positive, inquisitive, receptive attitude signals to your working memory that the information is important to grasp and learn.

- **Create reading goals.** Know your intention or purpose for reading. Is it to get an overview, comprehend in-depth details, compare sources of information, or review?

- **Be patient and do not rush the reading process.** Thorough reading requires time for your mind to mull over, absorb, process, and integrate new information.

- **Be persistent.** You may need to reread difficult sections of material more slowly and multiple times. To comprehend, you may need to break paragraphs into smaller units, chunk information in new ways, and analyze details more carefully. Persistent readers do not skip a paragraph because it is difficult to understand, nor do they quit or give up when the content is more difficult than anticipated.

- **Use all available resources.** Take the time and show the effort to learn by being a resourceful reader. Use textbook resources, online supplementary materials, computer and lab resources, study guides, tutors, and study groups.

- **Adjust your reading rate.** Do not expect or attempt to use the same reading rate for all materials. Some materials can be read one page at a time, while other materials will require reading one paragraph, or even smaller sections of a paragraph, slowly and repeatedly in order to understand the information.

- **Take responsibility for your learning.** Attending class and listening to lectures is not sufficient to master course content. Creating a strong habit of scheduling adequate time to read and learn from textbooks reflects genuine goals to be an effective and successful college student.

| FIGURE 8.2 | Purposes for Reading |

Purposes	Description
Recreational Reading	• Use to read newspapers, magazines, short stories, poetry, or fiction. • Read to be entertained, read for pleasure, or read to stay updated on current events.
Overview Reading	• Use for new material or difficult material. • Survey or skim to create a *big picture* or framework before reading thoroughly. • Read through difficult material uninterrupted and without stalling to become familiar with the topic before beginning thorough reading.
Thorough Reading	• Use for textbook or course-related materials. • Use reading flexibility to adjust to levels of difficulty. • Read slowly and systematically to allow your brain time to acquire and process new information and skills. • Read to understand paragraph structures, organizational patterns, and to identify important information to record in notes. • Use elaborative rehearsal strategies to practice new information.
Comparative Reading	• Use for two or more articles, excerpts, or books on the same subject. • Compare or contrast, organize, and analyze for similarities and differences in points of view, rationale, implications, interpretations, models, or approaches.

© Cengage Learning

Identifying Purposes for Reading

Making sense of what you read does not occur automatically. With some reading materials, you are able to read and quickly grasp the meaning of new information without much effort or struggle, yet with other reading materials, you need to work to understand, process, store, retrieve, and use the information. **Figure 8.2** shows four different purposes for reading. *Purposes for reading*—which include recreational, overview, thorough, and comparative—represent different reading skills and reading goals for different kinds of reading material.

Recreational Reading

Recreational reading is the process of reading for the main purpose of being entertained or keeping up to date on current events. Television, the Internet, smartphones, digital tablets, laptops, and DVDs offer extensive access to news, current events, sports, games, movies, and other forms of entertainment. For many recreational readers, downloading newspapers, magazines, and books onto e-readers— such as a Kindle, a Nook, or an iPad tablet—has increased recreational reading. Despite the temptation to rely on digital media for information, traditional newspapers, books, and magazines remain important as sources for all types of reading material. Whether using traditional or digital e-reader materials, creating and strengthening the habit of reading has many benefits:

- Reading for enjoyment does not require analysis or memory work.
- Recreational reading exposes the reader to new concepts and vocabulary.
- Reading for enjoyment lays a foundation for thorough reading, which focuses on comprehension, higher-level thinking skills, and memory work.
- Recreational reading reduces a dislike or negative attitude toward books.

Purposes for reading, which include recreational, overview, thorough, and comparative, represent different reading skills and reading goals for different kinds of reading material.

Recreational reading is the process of reading for the main purpose of being entertained or keeping up to date on current events.

CONCEPT CHECK   8.1

What kinds of recreational reading do you do on a regular basis? Do you read printed materials or electronic materials on an e-reader or tablet?

Overview Reading

Overview reading is the process of skimming or reading materials without interruption. Overview reading helps the reader form a big picture or a schema for the topic before engaging in more in-depth, thorough reading. You can use overview reading to:

- **Survey:** Scan the content of a new textbook, chapter, or a test.
- **Tune-in to the flow of action:** Get a sense of the flavor of a short story, essay, play, or excerpt by reading without stopping or pausing to analyze. This type of overview reading often stirs your imagination, creates an emotional connection with the words, immerses you in the material, and keeps the unity of the plot and the characters' actions moving steadily forward.
- **Gain background basics:** Get a sense of the material in a difficult or complex section or chapter of a textbook without focusing on immediately understanding the details. Reading *carefully but continuously* all the way through can provide you with basic background information, lay a foundation for more thorough reading, and alert you to sections that seem confusing or complicated.

Thorough Reading

Thorough reading is the process of reading slowly and systematically in order to comprehend and process printed or digital information. Reading is more than simply reading a string of words silently or out loud. Instead, reading is a complex process that involves many cognitive functions and processes designed to help the reader understand and use different levels of information. Following is a brief description of the process of reading to comprehend:

- As you read a chunk of information, your working memory retrieves related information from long-term memory to help you understand new information.
- Working memory then integrates the new information with retrieved information and returns the unit of information back into long-term memory and the appropriate schemas.
- The interaction and exchange of information between memory systems happens quickly and continually throughout the reading process.
- Integrated information is used on higher, critical reading levels to compare, contrast, question, challenge, prove, solve problems, or show other kinds of relationships.

Learning college-level reading strategies saves you time and improves college-level comprehension. You cannot afford to spend your valuable time reading page after page in the *automatic pilot mode*. The **automatic pilot mode** is a state of mind in which you mechanically go through specific motions without registering information into your memory. As you work through this chapter and Chapter 9, you will strengthen your thorough reading and comprehension skills. **Figure 8.3** shows essential thorough reading skills that lay a strong foundation for comprehension.

Comparative Reading

Comparative reading is the process of using higher-level critical thinking and reading skills to compare and contrast two or more sources of printed or digital information.

Overview reading is the process of skimming or reading materials without interruption.

CONCEPT CHECK 8.2
What are effective uses for overview reading? How does overview reading affect comprehension?

Thorough reading is the process of reading slowly and systematically in order to comprehend and process printed or digital information.

CONCEPT CHECK 8.3
Why does thorough reading require a time commitment to do effectively? What reading actions are involved in thorough reading?

Automatic pilot mode is a state of mind in which you mechanically go through specific motions without registering information into your memory.

Comparative reading is the process of using higher-level critical thinking and reading skills to compare and contrast two or more sources of printed or digital information.

| FIGURE 8.3 | Essential Strategies for Thorough Reading |

- **Create a plan of action**. Use a systematic reading system to move you through the reading assignment and processes.

- **Use a warm-up activity**. Begin a study block by surveying or reviewing to create a mindset for careful, thorough reading.

- **Verbalize and visualize**. Reading out loud (verbalizing) activates auditory channels to memory. Visualizing activates visual memory.

- **Adjust your reading rate**. Slow down the intake process to give your mind sufficient time to attach meaning to words, process and integrate information, and create associations.

- **Relate new information to existing schemas in your long-term memory**. Thinking about associations and linking different chunks of information lead to greater comprehension. Ask questions such as *What do I already know about this topic? How is it similar and how is it different from previous learning or past experiences? What are the important points and details?*

- **Recognize different levels of information as you read**. Strive to become an analytical reader who can recognize major themes, large concepts (schemas), main ideas, and important supporting details.

- **Learn terminology and definitions**. Knowing definitions of key terms lays the foundation for more complex learning and provides you with tools to communicate subject matter effectively to others.

- **Use spaced practice or spaced studying**. Spreading the reading process and activities over several different time periods actually cuts down total learning time. Avoid *marathon studying*, or in this case, *marathon reading*, which can overload your working memory.

- **Use elaborative rehearsal and active learning techniques as you read**. Actions that engage you in the reading and learning process help you maintain attention and concentration, encode information in new ways, and make stronger impressions of the information for memory.

- **Include some form of feedback as you study**. Use self-quizzing, reciting, and Look-Away Techniques to check the thoroughness and accuracy of your comprehension and memory.

© Cengage Learning 2015

Assignments that involve comparative reading may involve contrasting two or more articles, essays, or reports about the same topic, model, or approach but with different points of views or different authors. After surveying the two different sources of information, use the following suggestions to compare or contrast the sources:

- What do the two sources have in common?

- What are the major differences in approaches, points of views, or outcomes?

- Do the authors or sources of each article carry the same level of authority or credibility?

- Does one provide more supporting details or prove the thesis statement better?

- Based on the assignment, what elements of the readings should be compared or contrasted?

Adjusting the Reading Rate

Thorough reading requires flexibility to adjust your reading approach to various levels of difficulty. Some textbooks are easy to read and understand; others require a considerable amount of attention and effort. In any given textbook, you may be able to read some sections more quickly, but then you may need to slow the reading process for more difficult sections. Following are important points about using flexibility during thorough reading:

- Selecting an appropriate amount of material to read before pausing to think about or work with information prevents overloading your working memory.

  - **Textbooks with relatively easy levels of difficulty:** Stop at the end of each *page* to think about the information, create visual images of the material, and associate it to other information in long-term memory.

  - **Textbooks with average levels of difficulty:** Use a *read-pause approach* after each paragraph for most textbooks. Stop at the end of *each paragraph* to think about and process the information. Identify main ideas, important details, and meanings of terminology.

  - **Textbooks with difficult reading levels and complex content:** Stop at the end of *each sentence* or *group of sentences* to check understanding and think about and process the information.

- *Chunking* information is a process of grouping information into meaningfully sized units of information to comprehend and process. Chunking gives working memory sufficient time to grasp, associate, and integrate information for understanding. It also helps you avoid going into automatic pilot mode, which results in little or no information registering in your memory.

  - When you *chunk up,* you look beyond the paragraph to determine how the paragraph fits into the bigger picture and in the context of surrounding material. Reread the previous paragraphs and read ahead to the following paragraph or paragraphs to find the natural flow or progression of information.

  - When you *chunk down,* you break the information into smaller units, perhaps as small as individual sentences or phrases, to identify the meanings of details.

> **Chunking** information is a process of grouping information into meaningfully sized units of information to comprehend and process.

Surveying a Textbook

Surveying is the process of previewing or skimming information to get an overview. Surveying is one form of overview reading designed to help the reader get the big picture and set up schemas for all kinds of reading materials or for tests. Surveying a new textbook before you begin reading specific chapters acquaints you with the book's philosophy, organization, and special features; it also provides you with suggestions for using the book more effectively. Surveying a textbook is a process that usually requires less than 30 minutes of your time at the beginning of the term. Following are the sections of a textbook you should survey to familiarize yourself with the textbook and its features.

> **Surveying** is the process of previewing or skimming information to get an overview.

1. The **table of contents** is the "roadmap" for the textbook. It provides you with an overview of the organization of the topics (chronological or thematic), chapter headings and subheadings, page numbers, and other textbook features.

2. The **introductory materials** include the *Preface, Introduction, To the Teacher,* and *To the Student.* The *Preface* or the *Introduction* provides insight into the philosophy, objectives, and structure of the book. The *To the Teacher* and *To the Student* sections feature valuable suggestions, study strategies, explanations, and ways to use textbook features.

> **CONCEPT CHECK** 8.4
>
> *What is the value of surveying a textbook? Which sections of a textbook do you think you will use most frequently? Explain why.*

The **appendix** is a section in the back of a book that contains supplementary materials that were not included within the chapters.

3. An *appendix* is a section in the back of a book that contains supplementary materials that were not included within the chapters. Answer keys, additional exercises, practice tests, supplementary readings, or important tables, graphs, charts, or maps are kinds of materials that may appear in an appendix.

The **glossary** is a minidictionary in the back of a book that contains definitions of course-specific terminology.

4. The *glossary* is a minidictionary in the back of a book that contains definitions of course-specific terminology. Definitions in a glossary are limited to the meanings of terms as used in the textbook. Bold, italic, or colored print within textbook chapters often indicate *key terms* that appear in the glossary. Use the following strategies with textbooks that do have a glossary.

- Each time you see words in special print in a chapter, locate the terms in the glossary to see if the glossary provides more details or clarifies the definition.
- As you encounter terminology while reading each chapter, place a star next to or highlight those terms in the glossary. Use the glossary as a review tool to prepare for tests.
- Make separate definition cards or vocabulary sheets with the definitions of key terms to review to prepare for tests.

The **index** is an alphabetical listing of significant topics that appear in the book.

5. The *index* is an alphabetical listing of significant topics that appear in the book. The index is a valuable textbook section used to quickly locate pages for specific topics. Textbooks may have a *subject index,* an *author index,* or an *index of illustrations*. Topics are frequently cross-referenced so they appear in more than one place in the index. The following strategies will help you use the index effectively:

- After a lecture or class discussion, locate an unfamiliar term in the index of your book to find the page number in your textbook that further explains the term or concept.
- When you are assigned a specific topic for a research paper, an essay, a writing assignment, a project, or a test, use the index to locate pages in the textbook that discuss the topic. Turn to the page numbers provided to read or review the information.

EXERCISE 8.1

Surveying This Textbook

PURPOSE: Surveying a textbook, designed to familiarize you with the textbook structure and features, takes fifteen to thirty minutes. Surveying a chapter, designed to help you create a mindset for a new topic and get an overview or a big picture of upcoming information, usually takes less than twenty minutes.

DIRECTIONS:

Part I: Survey the front and the back section of this textbook. Then answer the following questions on separate paper.

1. What did you learn from reading the introductory information? How did it help familiarize you with this textbook?

Exercise 8.1 (continued)

2. What kind of information appears in the appendixes?

3. The glossary for this textbook is online. Explain how to access the online glossary.

4. Explain how you have already used the index this term.

Part II: After reading "Surveying a Chapter," survey a chapter in this textbook that you have not yet read. Then answer the following questions on separate paper.

1. Which features helped you begin to formulate a big picture of the chapter?

2. What benefits did you gain by examining visual materials?

3. What kinds of information in the margins helped you understand the new content?

4. What end-of-the-chapter features did you survey? What benefits did you gain by surveying these features?

Surveying an Article or an Essay

Surveying an article, an excerpt, an essay, or any other short reading requires a minimal amount of time but can provide you with valuable information. Following are six basic steps to use to survey an article or an essay:

1. **Think about the title**. Without reading the article or essay, what does the title mean to you? What do you predict that article will be about? What understanding or opinions do you already have about the subject?

2. **Identify the author**. Look in the byline or footnote for the author's name, affiliation with specific groups or organizations, additional publications, or other personal information. Think of ways the available information may relate to the subject matter and the author's point of view.

3. **Read and think about any introductory material**. Introductory material for short articles often provides necessary background information about the topic and the author.

4. **Read the first paragraph carefully**. The thesis statement, the main point or purpose of the entire article, often appears in this paragraph.

5. **Skim through the rest of the article**. Read the headings, subheadings, and side notes.

6. **Read the concluding paragraph**. The concluding paragraph often restates the thesis statement and summarizes the main ideas in the article.

To practice surveying articles, go to any of the excerpts in **Appendix D**. Use the above steps to survey and you will soon realize how much information you can obtain through the process of surveying before beginning thorough reading.

CHAPTER 8
REFLECTIVE WRITING 1

On separate paper, in a journal, or online in this textbook's College Success CourseMate, respond to the following questions.

1. What are your reading habits and interests? How often do you engage in recreational reading? What kinds of materials do you enjoy reading?

2. What type of reading is difficult or challenging for you? What specific difficulties do you encounter frequently?

 Access Chapter 8 Reflective Writing 1 in your College Success CourseMate, accessed through *CengageBrain.com.*

CHECK POINT 8.1

Answers appear on page B4.

Multiple Choice See Test-Taking Strategies 10–15 in Appendix A.

_____ 1. Which of the following is *not* true about the reading process?
  a. Reading is a complex process of recalling and creating associations.
  b. You can use overview reading to become familiar with new material before reading and studying the details more thoroughly.
  c. Chunking information into appropriate sizes gives your working memory time to process and integrate information.
  d. When you have strong reading skills, your reading goal may be to use your *automatic pilot* to read many of your college textbooks.

_____ 2. Effective textbook reading strategies include
  a. selecting meaningful and manageable sizes of information to process at one time.
  b. identifying a purpose and a process to use for reading a textbook.
  c. using spaced practice and including rehearsal techniques to reinforce concepts.
  d. all of the above.

_____ 3. Surveying a textbook
  a. does not require several hours to do correctly.
  b. provides an opportunity to examine the index and glossary.
  c. familiarizes the reader with the content of appendixes.
  d. does all of the above.

_____ 4. Students with effective college-level reading skills
  a. move into the reading process without feeling the need to create reading goals.
  b. exhibit a positive attitude toward reading and a willingness to persist with difficult materials.
  c. use their skills to read at a faster reading rate than they use for recreational reading.
  d. exhibit all of the above characteristics.

 Access Chapter 8 Practice Quiz 1 in your College Success CourseMate, accessed through *CengageBrain.com.*

Essential Textbook Reading Processes

2 *Identify and explain the essential processes used in an effective textbook reading system.*

Using a systematic approach for reading textbook chapters may take more time than you are used to spending for reading a chapter, but you will process and comprehend the information more thoroughly, eliminate the need to reread chapters multiple times to learn the content, and in the long run, save valuable study time.

Numerous reading systems are available for college students to use with college textbooks. No single textbook reading system is the most effective to use with all textbooks. As critical readers, a worthy reading goal is to familiarize yourself with individual textbooks, examine the kinds of information you will need to learn, pay attention to the level of complexity or difficulty of the content, and then select or create a textbook reading system that works most effectively for you and for each of your individual textbooks.

Using a Reading System

There are no shortcuts for reading and learning from college textbooks. Opening a chapter and surveying instead of reading or reading quickly from beginning to end does take less time than using a reading system, but it results in lower comprehension and ineffective use of your time. **Figure 8.4** shows you options and textbook reading processes to use to create a powerful reading system that strengthens your textbook reading skills. Note that *surveying* and *reviewing* are standard, essential steps to use in all reading systems. The following sections explain how to use the options in Figure 8.4.

Surveying a Chapter

Surveying is the process of previewing or skimming information to get an overview. Surveying a chapter is so important that most textbook reading systems begin with the process of surveying the chapter. You can survey a new chapter as a *warm-up* activity at the beginning of a study block before you begin thorough reading. Surveying a chapter is an effective part of the reading process because it does the following:

- Focuses your mind on the upcoming reading assignment
- Creates interest, enhances your motivation, and boosts confidence in mastering new material
- Reduces the tendency to procrastinate about starting to read a new chapter
- Forms a big picture or schema of the chapter and helps you connect new information to information you already know
- Familiarizes you with graphic and marginal materials used to explain concepts
- Provides you with a general idea about the length and difficulty level of the material
- Helps you set realistic reading and studying goals, manage your time, and select an appropriate reading process to use to work your way through the chapter

Surveying a chapter requires fewer than 20 minutes. For longer chapters, you can modify the process by surveying as many pages of the chapter as you think that you realistically can cover in one or two study blocks; survey the remaining pages at

> **CONCEPT CHECK** **8.5**
> *What may be some consequences of not taking the time to survey a new chapter?*

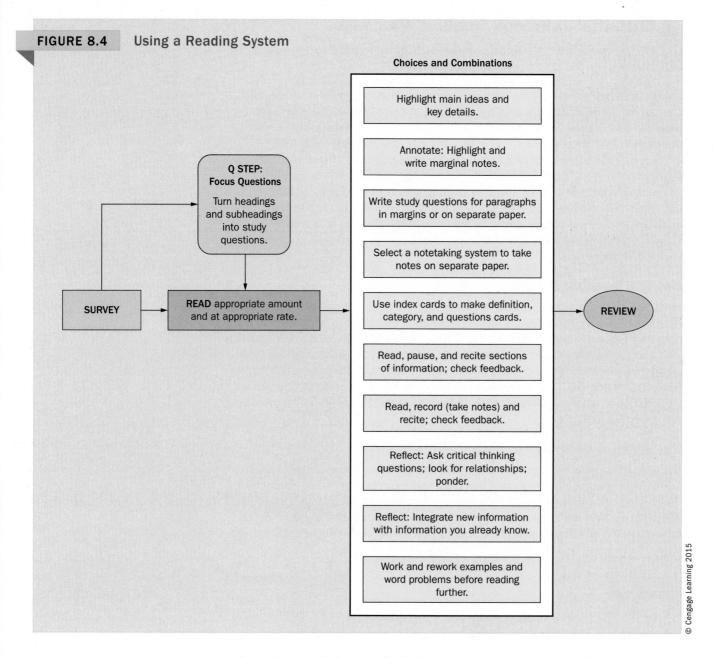

FIGURE 8.4   Using a Reading System

© Cengage Learning 2015

the beginning of a later study block. Following are the parts of a chapter to include in surveying:

- **Introductory materials:** Read the title of the chapter carefully; take a moment to think about the topic and relate the topic to information you already know. Read any lists, paragraphs, or visual materials that state the objectives for the chapter or introduce the chapter's content.

- **Headings and subheadings:** Different font colors and different formats or designs in a chapter differentiate headings from subheadings. Move through the chapter by glancing over the headings and subheadings to see the skeletal structure of the chapter. Later, if you wish, you can use the headings and the subheadings to create a chapter outline.

- **Visual materials:** Examine visual materials, such as charts, graphs, diagrams, pictures, and photographs. Read the information and the captions that appear with the visual materials.

- **Marginal notes:** Marginal notes may be brief explanations, short definitions, lists of key points or objectives, or study questions that appear in the margins of the textbook pages. Marginal notes provide you with background details and emphasize important points to learn.

- **Terminology:** Skim over the terminology to get a general idea of terms you will need to learn. During surveying, do not spend time reading definitions for all the terminology.

- **End-of-the-chapter materials:** Read the chapter summary, list of key concepts, chapter review questions, or any other end-of-the-chapter materials. These materials highlight or summarize the important concepts and information you should learn in the chapter.

EXERCISE 8.2

Transfer These Skills: Surveying a Chapter

DIRECTIONS: Surveying before beginning the process of careful, thorough reading works effectively as a *warm-up activity* at the beginning of a study block. Select any textbook you are currently using. At the beginning of a study block, survey a new chapter. Then answer the following questions on your own paper.

1. Write the name of your textbook as well as the chapter number and title.

2. How did the introductory materials in the chapter help you focus your attention on the new chapter?

3. What was the value of reading all headings and subheadings in the chapter?

4. What other special features in the chapter did you examine during surveying?

5. What end-of-the-chapter materials appeared in this chapter? How did they help you obtain a big picture of the chapter?

Writing Focus Questions

The *focus question step* in the reading process involves turning the chapter title, each heading, and each subheading into questions. In Figure 8.4, notice that the *Q Step* or *focus questions step* is one step to use after surveying a chapter. Write the questions directly in your textbook next to the title, headings, or subheadings, or write them on notebook paper or index cards, leaving space to write the answers later. The 10 to 20 minutes it takes to write these focus questions is time well spent. You get one additional overview of the chapter, and you create a purpose for reading,

The **focus question step** in the reading process involves turning the chapter title, each heading, and each subheading into questions.

focus your attention on upcoming information, and activate working memory. Use the following suggestions when you write your questions:

- **Strive to use a variety of questions**. The wording of each question elicits a different kind of response. For example, answers to questions that begin with the following words elicit specific kinds of responses:

  What ... (Answer gives specific facts.)
  How ... (Answer gives steps/processes.)
  Which ... (Answer gives specific items.)
  Where ... (Answer gives specific locations.)

  Why ... (Answer gives reasons.)
  When ... (Answer gives time periods.)
  Who ... (Answer identifies specific people.)

- **Modify or delete some words in headings and subheadings** if necessary. Following are examples of questions for the beginning of this chapter. The italic print shows words added to the title, heading, and subheadings to create questions.

  Title: *How should I* Selecting a Reading System?

  Heading: *What are the* First Steps of the Reading Process?

  Subheading: *How do* ~~Developing a~~ Positive Attitude and Behaviors *affect reading?*

CONCEPT CHECK 8.6

Explain how to use headings and subheadings to create focus questions. Why do you think these questions are referred to as "focus" questions?

If you are reading an e-textbook, you may not be able to write questions directly across from the title, headings, or subheadings, but you can use the "notes" feature to create a list of questions or create a Word file for your questions. If you are using the printed textbook, you can write your questions in the book.

If you choose to use the Q Step in your reading process, you will have a set of questions to use to review after reading the chapter, as a warm-up activity at the beginning of a study block, or during a later review session to prepare for a test. After creating your focus questions, move to the next step: READ.

Reading Carefully

Some students feel that they should be able to "read fast" to get through chapters. Others read chapters without speeding through them—only to find at the end of the chapters that they must reread the chapter because they do not remember much of what they read the first time. The *read step* in the reading process involves reading *carefully and thoroughly*. The following suggestions promote effective, careful, thorough reading:

The **read step** in the reading process involves reading *carefully and thoroughly*.

- **Decide if overview reading of chapter contents would be beneficial**. Because overview reading involves reading straight through without pausing, use it sparingly. Do not take notes or highlight when your intention is to do overview reading. Overview reading is beneficial for difficult or unfamiliar content to help you begin to form schemas or to give you a "flavor" for the materials before beginning the process of thorough reading. Overview reading is not effective unless you commit to moving through the chapter a second time to examine, analyze, interpret, memorize, integrate, and comprehend what you are reading by using thorough reading strategies.

- **Begin thorough reading**. For most textbooks, you should read *one paragraph at a time* and then stop to dissect, analyze, and comprehend the content of the paragraph. Skilled readers of college textbooks are aware of the importance of selecting the appropriate amount of information to read (*chunking*) before pausing and the appropriate *reading rate* to use that give their mind sufficient time to grasp the information.

- **Take the time to use effective reading strategies**. Figure 8.3 and other sections of this chapter, as well as Chapters 9 and 10, will provide you with a variety of strategies to use to unlock the meaning of difficult paragraphs, integrate concepts, and strengthen comprehension. Create the mindset of being open to trying new strategies and replacing some of your former strategies for reading textbooks which may not be as powerful or effective.

Choices and Combinations for Your Reading Process

As shown in Figure 8.4, after reading and pausing, you then have a variety of options to use to work with the information to increase comprehension and process the information into memory. For textbooks that are not very challenging, selecting one or two of the choices will suffice. For example, after reading, you may want to highlight and recite. For more complex or difficult textbooks, you may wish to use several of the choices to boost your comprehension and memory of the content: annotate, write study questions in margins, and reflect to integrate information.

Skillful readers do not use the same strategies for every textbook. Instead, they know how to use a variety of strategies and then select the strategies that work most effectively for the textbook and the content. **Figure 8.5** summarizes options to record (takes notes) and reflect. Regardless of which combination you choose, the steps should be clear in your mind and easy for you to recall and apply.

FIGURE 8.5   Combinations for a Reading System

SURVEY	READ SLOWLY	RECORD OPTIONS	RECITE	REFLECT OPTIONS	REVIEW CHAPTER
		Highlight textbook.		Look for relationships.	
		Annotate: Highlight and make marginal notes.		Integrate new and old information.	
		Make Cornell Notes.		Rearrange information in new meaningful ways.	
		Make 2- or 3-column notes.		Think critically about the topics.	
		Make outline.		Use critical thinking questions to think more deeply.	
		Make index cards.		Compare different sources of information.	
		Make visual mappings, hierarchies, or charts.		Formulate questions to pose in class.	

© Cengage Learning 2015

The **record step** in the reading process involves taking notes to capture important information encountered in textbooks.

The **recite step** in the reading process involves restating and explaining textbook information out loud and in your own words and without looking at the printed materials.

The **Read-Record-Recite Cycle** is a thorough reading strategy that involves reading a short section, taking notes, and then reciting without looking at the printed materials.

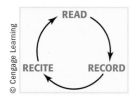

© Cengage Learning

CONCEPT CHECK 8.7

Explain how to use the Read-Record-Recite Cycle throughout a chapter. How does this differ from the way you usually read a textbook chapter?

The **reflect step** in the reading process involves comprehending, elaborating, and using critical thinking skills to think seriously and deeply about the information you read.

CONCEPT CHECK 8.8

How could you use Bloom's Taxonomy in a reflect step of a reading system you create for a government or social science course?

The **review step** in the reading process involves using immediate and ongoing review to practice rehearsing and recalling information from long-term memory.

Record or Take Notes

The *record step* in the reading process involves taking notes to capture important information encountered in textbooks. After reading a paragraph or section of information, pause, and then identify the information you wish to record in notes. Taking time to record information (take notes) helps you stay actively involved in the learning process, which reduces the tendency of slipping into automatic pilot mode, or reading without clearly understanding or recalling. Taking notes holds information in working memory and provides more time for you to encode it clearly and accurately for your long-term memory. Comprehension improves when you actively strive to identify key concepts, important details, and relationships. Your notes become a valuable, time-saving, reduced or a condensed form of the information you need to study and learn.

After learning how to use all of the notetaking systems that appear in Figure 8.5, you will have the tools to personalize or tailor your approach to learning. You will possess the skills required for the third component of metacognition: strategies to use that are best matched to the task you are learning.

Recite Main Ideas and Details

The *recite step* in the reading process involves restating and explaining textbook information out loud and in your own words and without looking at the printed materials. If you are recording information or taking notes, you can recite after you take your notes. After reciting, look back at the textbook or your notes to check your accuracy.

The *Read-Record-Recite Cycle* is a thorough reading strategy that involves reading a short section, taking notes, and then reciting without looking at the printed materials. This three-part cycle works effectively for both traditional and e-textbooks. Using the Read-Record-Recite Cycle automatically slows down the reading process, promotes taking notes on key points, and provides feedback on the effectiveness of your strategies and your comprehension. You can use the Read-Record-Recite Cycle to move through any chapter efficiently and thoroughly.

Reflect and Think Critically

The *reflect step* in the reading process involves comprehending, elaborating, and using critical thinking skills to think seriously and deeply about information you read. Reflecting requires a willingness to set time aside to contemplate points of view, identify relationships, and integrate information from multiple sources. Adding a reflect step to your reading process promotes personalizing and internalizing the information you are studying.

Reviewing

The *review step* in the reading process involves using immediate and ongoing review to practice rehearsing and recalling information from long-term memory. Reviewing provides an opportunity to work with information before the process of inputting new information begins. Following are activities you can use to review the content in the chapter:

- Answer the chapter review questions that appear at the end of the chapter.
- Answer the questions you formulated during the *focus question step.*
- Study and recite from the notes that you took in the *record step.*

- Write a summary. In paragraph form, summarize the important concepts and details.
- Create additional study tools, such as flashcards, study tapes, or visual notes.
- Create a chapter outline. Use the outline to recite details for each section of the outline.
- Rework math problems from class or from your textbook. Compare the steps you used and your answers with those in the textbook. Check your answers for accuracy.
- For language courses, copy sentences or grammar exercises from the textbook. Rework the assignment, diagram the sentences, or identify parts of speech within sentences.

CONCEPT CHECK   8.9

The review step for different textbooks may vary. What different review activities would you use for your various textbooks this term?

EXERCISE 8.3

Reading Process Inventory

Go to Exercise 8.3 Appendix C, page C17, to complete the Reading Process Inventory to self-assess your awareness and skills of textbook reading processes.

CHECK POINT 8.2

Answers appear on page B4.

True or False? See Test-Taking Strategies 1–9 in Appendix A.

_____ 1. Not taking the time to survey reading materials may reduce motivation, reduce your ability to relate information quickly to a schema, and increase procrastination.

_____ 2. Surveying is a process that is used only to become familiar with the front and back sections of a new textbook.

_____ 3. Surveying a chapter involves overview reading.

_____ 4. Surveying a chapter involves reading headings, subheadings, visual materials, all the marginal notes, all the definitions, and all the review questions.

Listing Questions See Test-Taking Strategies 25–28 in Appendix A.

On separate paper, answer the following questions.

1. List six parts or features of a chapter that students should look at during the process of surveying the chapter.

2. List reasons that recording notes is an effective process to use during the reading process.

 Access Chapter 8 Practice Quiz 2 in your College Success CourseMate, accessed through *CengageBrain.com*.

GROUP PROCESSING

A Collaborative Learning Activity

Form groups of three or four students. Then complete the following directions.

DIRECTIONS:

1. Each student brings two different textbooks to the group. These may be textbooks the students are using this term or textbooks used in previous terms.

2. Each student takes a few minutes to show how he or she would survey a chapter of one of the books and how surveying that chapter helps the student prepare to read the chapter.

3. Together, discuss what reading processes and system the group recommends for the individual textbooks.

Three Specific Reading Systems

③ *Compare and contrast the steps used in three reading systems: SQ4R, the Outline Reading System, and a Customized Reading System.*

You already know that you can create a reading system specifically designed by you for your textbooks. An effective reading system involves powerful processes proven to be effective: surveying, reading carefully and thoroughly, taking notes, reciting, thinking and reflecting, and reviewing. In the following sections, you will learn specific reading systems to use.

SQ4R

One of the first textbook reading systems, SQ3R, was developed by Francis E. Robinson in 1941. The letters represent a five-step process: *survey, question, read, recite,* and *review.* In other courses and textbooks, you may encounter different reading systems, but upon close examination, you will notice that other reading systems often use different labels for steps very similar to those in SQ3R. The reason is that the steps and activities used in the SQ3R are powerful and proven to increase comprehension and enhance learning.

SQ4R is a six-step system for reading and comprehending textbook chapters: **s**urvey, **q**uestion, **r**ead, **r**ecord, **r**ecite, and **r**eview. SQ4R adds a fourth "R" to remind students to record important information (take notes). To gain the most benefit from this system, use all six steps shown in **Figure 8.6** each time you use the SQ4R system to read a textbook chapter.

> **CONCEPT CHECK   8.10**
>
> *What are the benefits of using all six steps of the SQ4R reading system? What would happen if you skip one or more of the steps?*

> **SQ4R** is a six-step system for reading and comprehending textbook chapters: survey, question, read, record, recite, and review.

Transfer These Skills: SQ4R

EXERCISE 8.4

PURPOSE: Learning to use a reading system, such as SQ4R, requires practice. With practice, the system becomes more comfortable and automatic.

DIRECTIONS: Use any textbook from one of your courses. Use all six steps of SQ4R for a new chapter. On separate paper, briefly summarize the activities you performed during each step.

FIGURE 8.6   The Six Steps of SQ4R

1. **Survey** the chapter to get an overview.

2. Write **Questions** for each heading and subheading.

3. **Read** the information, one paragraph at a time.

4. **Record** by selecting a form of notetaking to record information.

5. **Recite** the important information from the paragraph.

6. **Review** the information learned in the chapter.

© Cengage Learning

 Access Chapter 8 Topics
In-Depth: Expanded
SQ4R Visual Mapping
in your College Success
CourseMate, accessed through
CengageBrain.com.

The Outline Reading System

The *Outline Reading System* is an active reading system that involves creating outline notes during the reading process and using the outline notes to review. After *surveying* the chapter, you can begin the process of reading and developing your chapter outline notes. The outline reading system is effective for the following reasons:

> The **Outline Reading System** is an active reading system that involves creating outline notes during the reading process and using the outline notes to review.

- Automatically triggers a reading goal that involves reading to understand, identify, and capture key concepts and phrases into notes

- Involves active learning as you use the cycle of read, pause, and take notes

- Requires slower, careful reading to identify information to write in the outline

- Promotes using Selectivity to identify what is important and what is not

- Results in chunking information into meaningful units that show different levels of information

- Promotes critical reading skills to think about, comprehend, and organize information

- Results in a set of notes that works as a study tool for immediate and ongoing review

Outlines provide a *skeleton* or an overview of the basic structure of printed materials or, in this case, of a complete chapter. Some textbooks provide basic chapter outlines in the chapter introductory materials; however, chapter outlines often include only the chapter's headings and subheadings. You can use the textbook's chapter outline as a starting point, but the Outline Reading System requires the reader to add more details and to expand and personalize the outline during the reading process.

Formal Outlines

Formal outlines are highly structured, logically organized, detailed notes that show levels of information and relationships among larger concepts and smaller supporting details. You may already be familiar with formal outlines because

FIGURE 8.7   Formal and Informal Outlines

Formal Outline Format	Informal Outline Format
Chapter Title:	**Chapter Title:**
I. First Main Heading (use Roman numeral)	I. First Main Heading (use Roman numeral)
A. Subheading (use capital letter)	A. Subheading (use capital letter)
1. Supporting Detail (use Arabic numeral)	1. Supporting Detail (use Arabic numeral)
2. Supporting Detail	2. Supporting Detail
B. Subheading	B. Subheading
1. Supporting Detail	1. Supporting Detail
a. Minor detail (use lowercase letter)	— Minor detail – Can add subideas
b. Minor detail	— Minor detail – Can add subideas
(1) Subidea of minor detail (use Arabic numeral in parentheses)	2. Supporting Detail
(2) Subidea of minor detail	II. Second Main Heading
2. Supporting Detail	A.
II. Second Main Heading	1.
A.	2.
1.	3. *See graph, page XX.*
2.	B.
3. *See graph, page XX.*	
B.	

many composition instructors require formal outlines with your essays or papers. **Figure 8.7** shows the use of Roman numerals, capital letters, Arabic numerals, lowercase letters, and Arabic numerals inside parentheses. Following are the standard requirements or rules that you must follow when you develop a formal outline:

- **Roman numerals:** Use Roman numerals for main headings or main topics. Roman numerals from one to fifteen are written as I, II, III, IV, V, VI, VII, VIII, IX, X, XI, XII, XIII, XIV, and XV.

- **Alignment:** When you indent to show a lower level of information, place the new letter or the new number directly below the first letter of the first word that appears in the line above. For example, in Figure 8.7, notice how the "A" for the subheading appears directly below the "F" for the first main heading.

- **Two or more subheadings:** Each level in the formal outline must have *at least two subheading or subtopics* under each category. If you do not have two items [A, B; 1, 2; a, b; or (1), (2)], try renaming the larger category so you do not end up with only one item under that category.

- **Wording:** Most outlines consist of key words and short phrases; full sentences are seldom used.

Informal Outlines

For many students, the Outline Reading System works more effectively by using the *informal outline format*. Examine Figure 8.7 to note the differences between the formal and the informal outline format. Following are the benefits of using the informal outline format:

- Easier to organize by using the following format:
  - Use Roman numerals for headings; capital letters for subheadings; and Arabic numerals (1, 2, 3) for details.
  - Use dashes for all other levels of minor details.
- Less confusing and frustrating by simply using dashes for minor details
- Less cumbersome and more flexible as you can relax or modify the outline rules required by the formal outline format
- Can "mix and match" by using key words, phrases, or short sentences for any level of your outline

Using a reading system that involves systematic steps helps you move through the chapter in an organized, meaningful way. When you use this system, you will engage yourself in the reading process and be less likely to slip into *automatic pilot mode*. Use the following steps and suggestions for using the Outline Reading System.

CONCEPT CHECK   **8.11**

Why would a student prefer to use the informal outline format when using the Outline Reading System?

The Outline Reading System

1. Survey the chapter to get an overview. Pay special attention to headings and subheadings.

2. At the top of your notes, write the name of the chapter. Then create a heading that says *Introduction*. Read the introduction. Number important points.

3. Start your outline with the main heading. Use Roman numeral "I" for the first main heading in the chapter.

4. Use a capital "A" for the first subheading. Read the information, paragraph by paragraph. Use numbers 1, 2, 3, or more to list the important points under the subheading. If there are minor details you want to include, simply use dashes to jot down the details.

5. Make a note to return to the textbook to review any important charts or graphic materials.

6. Capture information in meaningful ways. You need to be able to understand your notes later, so do not be too brief or use only words or short phrases that lose meaning over time. Because this is an informal outline, you can regroup information, create new lists inside boxes, or add any other details that will help you capture the important points.

EXERCISE 8.5

Using the Outline Reading System

DIRECTIONS:

1. Unless your instructor assigns a different chapter in this textbook or in another textbook, use the Outline Reading System for this chapter.

2. Below is the beginning of the outline. As you read through the chapter, continue the outline on your own paper or on a computer.

Chapter 8

Introduction

   1. Old reading habits may be inadequate for college texts

   2. Replace old habits/techniques to strengthen reading skills & comprehension

I. **First Steps of the Reading Process**

   A. Developing Positive Attitudes and Behaviors

      1. Attitude & behaviors — affect reading experience

      2. Review Figure 8.1, page 233

   B. Identifying Purposes for Reading

      1. 4 purposes: recreational, overview, thorough, comparative (Figure 8.2, page 234)

      — Recreational: entertained, updated, current events

Studying from Outline Notes

Outlines provide an excellent study tool to practice reciting and to give you immediate feedback about your level of understanding and recall of textbook information. Use the following tips to study from your outlines.

- **Read and explain line by line**. Read what appears on the first line with the Roman numeral. Recite what you know about the topic. Speak in complete sentences. Move to the next line of information. Recite what you know; strive to integrate and link ideas together and explain relationships. Recite as though you are teaching another person.

- **Check your accuracy and completeness of information**. As you recite, you will quickly become aware of your familiarity with the topic. Refer to your outline notes or your textbook to check your accuracy or to see what kinds of information you did not include in your reciting.

- **Branch off your outline to expand it by adding more clue words**. You can break away from the general structure of the outline at this point by jotting down key words or details that you did not initially include in your reciting. These clue words can guide you through the reciting process the next time you use your outline to review the contents of the chapter. Notice the clue words in the following example of an outline about stress responses.

B. Stress Responses

    1. Physical Stress Responses: The GAS *general adaptation syndrome* — alarm / resistance / exhaustion

    2. Emotional Stress Responses — fear, anger / diminish, persist, severe

    3. Cognitive Stress Responses — ruminative thinking; catastrophizing

    4. Behavioral Stress Responses

© Cengage Learning

- **Use the outline to write a summary.** Many students learn and remember information more readily when they use their own words to explain and connect information in a logically sequenced manner and when they express themselves in writing. You can use the levels of information in your outline to organize and to write a summary. Include main ideas and briefly mention important supporting details.

A Customized Reading System

A *Customized Reading System* is an active reading system you design for a specific textbook based on the author's suggestions and the chapter features. Your goal with this system is to establish a consistent routine to use to read and study each chapter. Following are the steps to use.

Step 1: Use the Author's Suggestions

Carefully read the *To the Student* or the *Preface* information in the front of the textbook. List the author's suggestions for reading and using the textbook.

Step 2: Use the Chapter Features

Examine the chapter features in the first few chapters. In some textbooks, such as composition and math textbooks, the chapter format and the chapter features "dictate" a reading process for you to use—work through each section and each feature in the order presented. For example, the textbook structure may begin with definitions of terminology, then move to an example or a prototype with explanations, and then provide problem sets to solve by applying the steps shown in the prototype or example.

Step 3: Create Your Customized System

Using the information learned by surveying, create a list of steps that you will use consistently and habitually to read and comprehend the information in each chapter. (See **Figure 8.8**.) To work successfully, your customized approach to reading the textbook should do the following:

- Utilize effective study skills strategies and memory processes
- Incorporate at least one form of notetaking to organize and record information
- Include reworking problem sets or portions of homework assignments
- End with review activities

A **Customized Reading System** is an active reading system you design for a specific textbook based on the author's suggestions and the chapter features.

CONCEPT CHECK   8.12
Which of your textbooks is well suited for you to use a Customized Reading System? What steps would you use for reading the chapters?

FIGURE 8.8   A Customized Reading System for a Math Textbook

Step 1:   **Read the introduction, goals, and objectives.**

Step 2:   **Read the definitions.** Create a vocabulary sheet or definition flashcards each time you encounter new terminology, formulas, equations, and symbols.

Step 3:   **Study examples until you understand the problem type and steps involved.** Choose one example to memorize as a *prototype*. Create meaningful notes.

Step 4:   **Practice new skills.** Rework the example problems. Check your accuracy.

Step 5:   **Do new problem sets.** These usually mirror the problem types shown by the examples. Pay attention to underlying patterns. Apply the steps; check work.

Step 6:   **Do mixed problem sets.** Look for underlying patterns. Match problem types to prototypes you have memorized. Apply the steps; check answers.

Step 7:   **Do the real-world story problems.** Look for familiar underlying patterns. Apply RSTUV steps (Appendix A, Strategy 41, page A34). Check work. Be sure to label units in the solution.

Step 8:   **Review the chapter.** Read the chapter summary. Do review problems. Rework several examples and problems from the chapter. Recite and study the terminology, formulas, equations, and problem-solving steps.

© Cengage Learning

CHAPTER 8
REFLECTIVE WRITING 2

On separate paper, in a journal, or online in this textbook's College Success CourseMate, respond to the following questions:

1. Which skills in this chapter provided you with valuable textbook reading skills or processes that you had not previously used? How will these skills or processes improve your textbook reading and learning performance? Explain with specific details.

2. Discuss your results from the Reading Process Inventory (Exercise 8.3). What did you learn about your current textbook reading habits and skills? What adjustments do you wish to make to modify your approach to textbook reading?

 Access Chapter 8 Reflective Writing 2 in your College Success CourseMate, accessed through *CengageBrain.com*.

Answers appear on page B4.

CHECK POINT 8.3

Fill-in-the-Blanks See Test-Taking Strategies 21–24 in Appendix A.

1. In the SQ4R reading system, the "Rs" represent the following processes in sequential order: _____, _____, _____, and _____.

2. The process of _____ a new chapter before beginning thorough reading is recommended for all reading systems.

3. In the Outline Reading System, Roman numerals, such as I, II, and III, are often used to show main _____ used in the chapter.

Short Answers See Test-Taking Strategies 32–36 in Appendix A.

Question: What textbook reading system works most effectively for this textbook? Explain the specific steps or processes you use. Write your answers on separate paper.

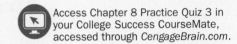 Access Chapter 8 Practice Quiz 3 in your College Success CourseMate, accessed through *CengageBrain.com*.

Reading Processes for Online E-Books

4 *Explain effective reading strategies to use for online e-textbooks.*

Digital e-books (electronic books) use technology to offer an alternative way to read textbooks and other materials. Digital reading can be at your fingertips by using various devices: a computer, a digital tablet, an electronic reader, or even a smartphone. Textbooks that have an e-book option provide you with alternative access to textbook information.

Advantages of E-Textbooks

As a student, you may have several options for using e-textbooks. If you enroll in an online course, an e-textbook may be a required part of the course and one of the main sources of course information; however, you may also have the option of using a printed version of the textbook to use side-by-side with the e-textbook. Some students find that certain reading and studying strategies work more effectively with printed materials, so having both printed and digital formats is advantageous. If you enroll in a course on campus that uses a printed version of the textbook, you may choose to access the e-textbook to take advantage of the digital format, features, and supplementary materials. Following are advantages for using e-textbooks with or without pairing with a printed version of a textbook.

- The digital format for many students is motivational. Some studies show that it is the digital format rather than the content that students favor. Many students use technology on a regular basis, so e-textbooks are simply another type of information to access via electronic devices.

- Digital books are readily accessible on electronic devices. Electronic devices, such as iPads, Kindle Fire, Nook, and other tablets are lightweight, hold multiple books, and are easier to carry around than multiple textbooks.

- Many digital textbooks are interactive. Students can click on links to complete online exercises and self-correcting quizzes that provide immediate feedback.

They can also view and enlarge colorful graphics, utilize online dictionaries and glossaries as they read, and download extensive apps (applications) related to course content. Students can also access high-resolution educational video and audio materials linked from the textbook website to other specific websites, or they can visit sites such as KhanAcademy.com for hundreds of videos demonstrating math problem-solving skills, or YouTube.com for videos demonstrating course-related processes or background information.

● Working with digital textbooks involves active learning as students use visual and kinesthetic skills to interact with the materials. With a few clicks, readers can highlight important text, type notes next to text, and print notes and sections of information.

E-Textbook Challenges

For many students, reading, comprehending, and remembering what they read occurs more consistently and smoothly when they read printed materials versus digital materials. As a result, for content that requires more thorough reading and studying, students may choose to download and print sections of the e-textbook pages or have a printed version available. To increase success using e-textbooks as the main source of course information, consider the following challenges and strive to adjust your reading habits to address the problems.

● **Distractions:** E-mails and social networking disrupt the reading process. If you find it difficult to refrain from responding to your e-mail, Facebook, or Twitter messages, use a program or app such as *Self-Control* to block access to your social media sites while you are reading.

● **More rereading required:** Digital text is processed differently by the brain. Until the brain is "trained" to process digital information more efficiently, reading digital information multiple times may be necessary to understand content more fully. Consider using active reading strategies and notetaking strategies to reduce the need to reread multiple times.

● **Shallow reading:** Students using digital devices may tend to do more "surface reading," or skimming. The result is less retention of online material compared to reading printed materials. Students may want to make a more concerted effort to force their eyes to use the traditional pattern for reading: left to right instead of roaming more quickly to the bottom of the screen.

● **Getting lost in a string of details:** As students read screen-by-screen, attention focuses on the details on the screen. Students may lose sight of the "big picture," the overall headings, and structure of the chapter. To connect details to the bigger pictures, use chapter outlines and notetaking systems to focus on the relationship between headings and details.

● **Losing sense of location:** Sometimes our brain recalls words or pictures based on the location in a chapter where the information was learned. For example, you might "see" or visually remember that specific information appeared in the upper corner of a textbook page. Digital books often lack such spatial landmarks or make visual images more difficult for the reader to form. In some digital books, readers see what percentage of a book or chapter they have read, but they are not given actual page numbers, so putting the screen information in context or in a specific location in the chapter is difficult. Comparing the digital format to a printed version increases the sense of location of information in chapters.

- **Automatic pilot mode:** When reading e-textbooks, students may experience reading mechanically without grasping, comprehending, or registering information in memory. As soon as you feel yourself reading screen-by-screen without comprehending the content, change your strategy. Start highlighting, taking notes, or using active reading strategies.

- **Eye strain:** Eye strain reduces the ability to concentrate, create visual images of digital material, and comprehend the digital content. With many digital devices, you can change the font, the font size, and the brightness or the contrast on the screen. Change your position or location when there is a glare on your monitor or screen. Place the monitor or device at least 20 inches from your eyes. Take breaks by looking *away from the screen every 20–30 minutes.*

CONCEPT CHECK 8.13

What experiences have you had with using e-books for recreational and academic reading? What were the advantages and the challenges of digital reading?

Navigating the *Essential Study Skills* E-Textbook and CourseMate

To access this textbook's interactive e-textbook, you must purchase an access code that gives you permission to log on to this textbook's College Success Course-Mate, accessible from *CengageBrain.com.* Once you have redeemed your code on CengageBrain and accessed the CourseMate, you have the following options:

- Click on "Chapter e-Book" in the left-hand navigation menu to access the entire student textbook online. You will be able to select specific chapters and sections of chapters to read and study.

- Use the same left-hand site navigation menu to access chapter features mentioned in the e-textbook such as the Expanded Chapter Outline, Visual Mapping, Profile, a list of Concept Checks, Case Studies, Topics In-Depth, Reflective Writing Assignments, Glossary, Flashcards, Enhanced and Practice Quizzes, and Chapter Study Guides.

- On the menu for Chapter 8, click on Topics-in-Depth: Navigating the Essential Study Skills E-Textbook for explanations and processes to use e-textbook features.

 Access Chapter 8 Topics In-Depth in your College Success CourseMate, accessed through *CengageBrain.com.*

Effective Reading Strategies for E-Textbooks

Reading e-books or digital materials may require adjusting the reading strategies traditionally used for printed textbooks. However, many of the essential strategies that appear in Figure 8.1 and Figure 8.3 apply to both printed textbooks and digital e-textbooks. You can use the following strategies with any of your online textbooks.

CONCEPT CHECK 8.14

Explain how textbook reading processes for e-textbooks differ from reading processes for printed versions of the textbook. Be specific.

- **Survey a chapter:** Surveying printed textbooks involves moving page by page through a chapter. If your e-textbook has a PDF file, you can use traditional surveying strategies with the PDF file that reflects exact textbook pages with visual materials and other textbook features. If your e-textbook does not have a PDF file, you will need to change your strategy. E-textbooks organize information in levels and menus, so survey headings and topics by clicking on sections of the menu. You can also survey by using any available chapter outlines.

- **Write focus questions:** You can write focus questions by using the e-textbook's "Add Notes" feature, by opening a word processing program to write questions, or by writing questions on separate paper. If you are pairing a printed version

Olaf Speier/Alamy Limited

What are the advantages and disadvantages of digital and printed textbooks? Which do you prefer and why?

with an e-book version, you can write your focus questions in the printed version of the textbook.

- **Take notes:** Use the e-textbook's feature to highlight important information as a form of notetaking. For more detailed notes, open a word processing file to take separate notes or create notes on separate paper as you would with a printed version of the textbook.

- **Use the Read-Record-Recite Cycle:** For some students, the tendency may be to read digital textbooks screen after screen without pausing to think about information, take notes, recite, or reflect the content. With e-textbooks, make a concerted effort to pause after each paragraph or after the end of a page. Identify key points, and highlight or take some form of notes. Recite the information before continuing the reading process. Reciting slows down the reading intake process and provides valuable feedback.

- **Learn definitions:** Use terminology features included in your e-textbook. With some digital e-books, you can click on a word within the text to see the definition. For the greatest benefit of e-textbooks, use other online exercises or flashcards to practice defining course-specific terminology.

Learning from college textbooks involves tailoring or customizing the learning process to best understand the level and content of materials, as well as your learning style preferences. Reading and learning from e-books involves a willingness to explore strategies that produce positive results for you, build and strengthen comprehension, and boost memory. It also involves developing critical reading and critical thinking skills. The reading process for e-books differs from reading printed textbooks, so being flexible and willing to adjust your approach for each individual e-textbook is essential. It is important to remember that reading is a process that involves intentional effort and strategies to learn the information—whether the information is delivered in a digital format or a printed format.

Textbook Case Studies

DIRECTIONS:

1. Read each case study carefully. Respond to the question at the end of each case study by using *specific* strategies discussed in this chapter. Answer in complete sentences.

2. Write your responses on paper or online in this textbook's College Success CourseMate, Textbook Case Studies. You will be able to print your online response or e-mail it to your instructor.

CASE STUDY 1: Justine reads all her textbooks the way that she reads paperback books. She starts at the beginning of the chapter and does not stop until she reaches the end of the chapter. She often finds that she needs to reread chapters two or three times before she can retain the information. What reading processes and strategies can Justine use to comprehend a textbook chapter better and spend less time rereading?

EXERCISE 8.6

Exercise 8.6 (continued)

CASE STUDY 2: The instructor spent half the class time talking about a concept that was unfamiliar to Simon. Simon had not had a chance to read the last three chapters, so he thought perhaps the concept appeared in those chapters. When he sat down to work with a study partner, Simon started flipping through the chapters page by page and eventually located the section of information. What strategies would help Simon be a more efficient reader and student?

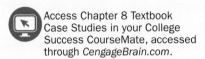

Access Chapter 8 Textbook Case Studies in your College Success CourseMate, accessed through *CengageBrain.com*.

CHECK POINT 8.4

Answers appear on page B4.

Short Answers See Test-Taking Strategies 32–36 in Appendix A.

Go online to this textbook's e-book. Experiment and explore how to use *any four* of the following features. On separate paper, briefly explain the process you used to access the feature and the kind of information you discovered for each feature.

Table of contents	Glossary	Notes and highlights
Print	Appendixes	Topics In-Depth
Bookmarks	Add highlights	Practice quizzes
Index	Add notes	End-of-chapter materials

Access Chapter 8 Practice Quiz 4 in your College Success CourseMate, accessed through *CengageBrain.com*.

Chapter 8 Critical Thinking

ACTIVITY

PURPOSE: In this age of technology, for many people the computer is an integral part of daily personal and professional life. We use the Internet for e-mail, banking, travel plans, shopping, information searches, online courses, and reading e-books. Needless to say, many additional uses of computers occur in the work environment as most businesses and professions now rely heavily on computers for the majority of their operations and transactions. The more we integrate technology into our lives, the greater is the need to learn new skills to use the online sources of information cautiously and effectively. Critical thinking is an essential skill to use when accessing the Internet for information, some of which is reliable and some of which is not.

(continued)

Critical Thinking (continued)

DIRECTIONS:

1. Unless your instructor assigns you a specific website or topic, follow the directions below.

2. Go to a website to locate an online news article. Review the article for the following criterion related to reliability, quality, and usefulness.

3. Print a copy of the article. Be sure that the source of the article is provided.

4. Summarize your evaluation of the article in terms of reliability, quality, and usefulness.

Reliability	Quality	Usefulness
Contact information included	Avoids broad generalizations	Relates to your goals
Satisfactory author credentials	Up-to-date resources and references	Relates to your writing or research outline
Publication has a respectable reputation	Consistency of facts	Appropriate or similar audience
Sponsoring organization(s) of the author and/or publication are identified	Appropriate grammar and spelling	Appropriate level of detail for your goals
Blind peer-review process	From an online database	
Contacted author provided additional information	Avoids bias or one-sided perspectives	
	Comprehensive review	
	Citations and references are accurate and complete	
	Resource is original source	
	Support or corroboration of facts	

From Watkins/Corry, *E-Learning Companion*, 4e © 2014 Cengage Learning

---

Terms to Know

Learning Objectives Review

By yourself or with a partner, practice reciting or writing definitions for the following terms. You may also practice defining these terms by using the online flashcards or comparing your answers to the online glossary.

purposes for reading p. 234

recreational reading p. 234

overview reading p. 235

thorough reading p. 235

automatic pilot mode p. 235

comparative reading p. 235

① *Discuss the importance of attitude, purpose for reading, reading rate, and the process of surveying as first steps in the reading process.*

- Creating reading goals, not rushing the reading process, being persistent, using resources, and taking responsibility for learning are several important attitudes and behaviors that affect the quality of the reading experience.

- Recreational, overview, thorough, and comparative are four purposes for reading; each has different reading goals and uses different reading strategies.

- Thorough reading, which is the type of reading used for textbooks, includes essential strategies of creating a plan of action, using a warm-up activity, verbalizing, visualizing, adjusting the reading rate, and relating information and concepts. Learning terminology, using spaced reading, elaborative rehearsal, and feedback are additional essential strategies to use during thorough reading.

- Adjusting the reading rate for different textbooks, levels of difficulty, and degree of complexity is important for reading textbooks. Adjusting the reading rate involves chunking information into meaningful, manageable units to read and comprehend.
- Surveying a textbook provides the reader with an overview of the important features in a textbook: table of contents, introductory materials, the appendixes, the glossary, and the index.
- Surveying an article or an essay provides the reader with valuable background information prior to reading carefully and thoroughly.

2 *Identify and explain the essential processes used in an effective textbook reading system.*

- Even though a systematic reading approach takes more time than reading a chapter quickly, comprehension is better and rereading chapters multiple times is not necessary.
- A reader has several options for textbook reading systems to use, but surveying a chapter and reviewing are two processes that are a part of most effective systems.
- Surveying a chapter is an example of overview reading that involves looking at introductory materials, headings, subheadings, visual materials, marginal notes, terminology, and end-of-chapter materials.
- Writing focus questions, reading carefully, recording or taking notes, reciting, reflecting, and reviewing are essential processes to use in textbook reading systems.

3 *Compare and contrast the steps used in three reading systems: SQ4R, the Outline Reading System, and a Customized Reading System.*

- SQ4R is a six-step reading system that involves surveying, questioning, reading, recording, reciting, and reviewing.
- The Outline Reading System involves creating formal or informal outline notes during the reading process. The outline notes created during the reading process work effectively as a study and review tool after the chapter has been read.
- A Customized Reading System is a system that includes essential processes tailored for a specific textbook. This system uses the author's suggestions and chapter features based on effective reading and memory processes.

4 *Explain effective reading strategies to use for online e-textbooks.*

- Electronic books (e-books) are also referred to as digital books. E-books are portable, lightweight, and interactive.
- To get the full benefits of an e-textbook requires taking the time to learn to navigate the online textbook, its features, and its interactive resources. Instead of presenting information in a linear manner, digital textbooks are organized around levels of information presented as menus.
- Some reading strategies for printed textbooks are also effective for digital textbooks. Other strategies, such as surveying a chapter, may need to be modified or may be better suited for a printed version of the textbook.
- Writing focus questions, taking notes, using the Read-Record-Recite Cycle, and working with terminology are important skills to use with digital textbooks.

Terms to Know
continued

chunking p. 237
surveying p. 237
appendix p. 238
glossary p. 238
index p. 238
focus question step p. 243
read step p. 244
record step p. 246
recite step p. 246
Read-Record-Recite Cycle p. 246
reflect step p. 246
review step p. 246
SQ4R p. 249
Outline Reading System p. 249
Customized Reading System p. 253

 Access Chapter 8 Flashcards and Online Glossary in your College Success CourseMate, accessed through *CengageBrain.com.*

Chapter 8   Review Questions

Answers appear on page B4.

True or False? See Test-Taking Strategies 1–9 in Appendix A.

_____ 1. For thorough reading of textbook chapters, the reading rate may vary for different sections in a chapter.

_____ 2. Formulating questions should only be done before you begin to survey a chapter.

_____ 3. Surveying a chapter or doing overview reading before you begin the process of thorough reading helps create a mindset and schemas for new information.

_____ 4. A positive attitude about reading and about a specific textbook affects the quality and effectiveness of the reading experience.

_____ 5. The final step in SQ4R is the same final step used in most reading systems.

_____ 6. In the Outline Reading System, outline notes are created after the student has read thoroughly the chapter at least one time.

_____ 7. A Customized Reading System allows students to create shortcuts to move through chapters quickly and focus only on the sections that are difficult for them.

_____ 8. Everyone finds that digital readers work most effectively for recreational reading but do not work well for academic or textbook reading.

Multiple Choice See Test-Taking Strategies 10–15 in Appendix A.

_____ 1. Which of the following statements is inaccurate?

a. All e-textbooks have links to the textbook table of contents, glossary, index, and companion audio and video materials.

b. Students have a variety of textbook reading systems to consider using to read, analyze, and comprehend textbook chapters.

c. Students can survey, write questions, and take notes using special features that are available for many digital textbooks.

d. Many textbook reading strategies work effectively for printed and digital formats.

_____ 2. Which of the following is *not* true about using an e-textbook?

a. If an e-book is interactive, you may be able to access online activities by clicking on a specific icon or link.

b. You can use the SQ4R reading system, or a modified version of it.

c. The e-book pages may look the same as the traditional textbook pages.

d. E-textbooks include only text and never graphic materials.

_____ 3. Which of the following processes appear in a variety of textbook reading systems?

a. Reciting

b. Reciting and taking notes

c. Surveying and reviewing

d. All of the above

_____ 4. Which of the following statements is *not* true or accurate?

a. Chunking up refers to working with a larger section of material to understand a concept or clarify the meaning of information.

b. Overview reading can be used to survey a chapter or read without pausing in order to get a big picture, develop a sense of the flow of action, or gain basic background information before conducting thorough reading.

c. Recreational reading tends to use a slower reading rate than thorough and comparative reading.

d. The process of reflecting involves taking time to think about relationships, ponder details, or make connections between concepts.

_____ 5. The process of surveying a new chapter
    a. may be easier to do with printed textbooks than with digital textbooks.
    b. may be easier to do with materials that are organized in a linear, sequential way rather than in a menu format that shows levels of information.
    c. involves looking at headings, subheadings, marginal notes, graphics, bold print, and end-of-chapter materials.
    d. involves all of the above.

Short-Answer Questions See Test-Taking Strategies 32–36 in Appendix A.

Write your answers on separate paper or in the space provided.

1. What are the benefits of surveying before reading?

2. How does the structure of a textbook chapter show the "skeleton" of the chapter and assist a student using the Outline Reading System?

Essay See Test-Taking Strategies 45–51 in Appendix A.

Question: Reading college-level textbooks involves using a variety of strategies to comprehend the material and boost memory. Summarize essential reading strategies college students should use to read and understand their textbooks.

 Access Chapter 8 Enhanced Quiz and Chapter 8 Study Guide in your College Success CourseMate, accessed through *CengageBrain.com*.

Access all Chapter 8 Online Materials in your College Success CourseMate, accessed through *CengageBrain.com*.

9 Strengthening Reading and Notetaking Skills

Digital Vision/Getty Images

Textbooks are a focal point for learning and mastering course content. Sometimes students are fooled by the sense that they seem to understand and remember what they read, so they feel there is no need to analyze information as a critical reader or to capture key concepts and details in notes to study and review. Over time, however, information can fade, become inaccessible, or become confused with new information. Using active reading strategies to comprehend and record notes provides you with study tools to use to keep information active in your memory. In addition, research shows a high correlation between notetaking skills and test performance. The better students' comprehension skills, the better are their notes; better notes are linked to better grades.

Access Chapter 9 Expanded Chapter Outline in your College Success CourseMate, accessed through *CengageBrain.com*.

YOUR CHAPTER MAPPING

After reading information under each heading, return to the chapter visual mapping below. Add key words to show subheadings and important details related to each heading.

Access Chapter 9 Visual Mapping in your College Success CourseMate, accessed through *CengageBrain.com*.

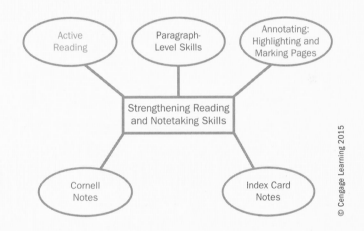

© Cengage Learning 2015

LEARNING OBJECTIVES

1 *Define active reading and describe its relationship to active learning and critical reading.*

2 *Summarize paragraph-level strategies to identify paragraph elements, learn terminology and definitions, and create definition cards and vocabulary sheets.*

3 *Explain the value of annotating textbooks and how to highlight, annotate, and study from annotations.*

4 *Describe the three kinds of cards used in a comprehensive set of index card notes; explain ways to study from index card notes.*

5 *Identify the Five R's of Cornell and describe the processes used for each of the five steps in the Cornell Notetaking System.*

Strengthening Reading and Notetaking Skills

ANSWER, SCORE, and **RECORD** your profile before you read this chapter. If you need to review the process, refer to the complete directions given in the profile for Chapter 1 on page 4.

Access Chapter 9 Profile in your College Success CourseMate, accessed through *CengageBrain.com*.

ONLINE: You can complete the profile and get your score online in this textbook's College Success CourseMate.

	YES	NO
1. I tend to be more of a passive reader than an active reader.	_____	_____
2. I know how to identify, highlight, and mark main ideas and supporting details that are important to learn.	_____	_____
3. I use different kinds of clues in sentences to identify the definition or meaning of course terminology.	_____	_____
4. I make flashcards or vocabulary study sheets only for words that are new or difficult to remember.	_____	_____
5. When I highlight a textbook, I often over-mark or highlight too much information.	_____	_____
6. I work with chapter information by writing inside paragraphs or making brief notes in the textbook margins.	_____	_____
7. I create definition, category, and question flashcards to use as study tools.	_____	_____
8. I condense information by writing organized notes and recall columns with brief questions to answer and terms to define.	_____	_____
9. I recite my textbook notes, reflect and work with them in new ways, and review on a regular basis.	_____	_____
10. I am confident in my ability to read college textbooks and use different notetaking systems to take notes on textbook chapters.	_____	_____

QUESTIONS LINKED TO THE CHAPTER LEARNING OBJECTIVES:

Question 1: objective 1   Question 7: objective 4

Questions 2–4: objective 2   Questions 8–9: objective 5

Questions 5–6: objective 3   Question 10: all objectives

Active Reading

1 *Define active reading and describe its relationship to active learning and critical reading.*

Comprehending what you read is a complex process that involves active learning and active reading. *Active reading* is the process of using effective strategies to engage working memory to achieve specific reading goals. Active reading places heavy demands on your working memory, requires your undivided attention, and cannot be done quickly or effortlessly. Your working memory requires time to accomplish the following:

- Attach meaning to printed words
- Associate chunks of new information with previously learned information
- Move information rapidly back and forth through the different memory systems
- Analyze information by identifying its individual parts, characteristics, patterns, and relationships
- Integrate information to form generalizations

Active readers are active learners. Active readers commit themselves to the reading process by creating a mindset that reflects their intention to engage actively in the reading process, comprehend content, process the information, and achieve reading goals. **Check the active reading strategies you use when you read textbooks**.

_____Read with a pen in your hand so you are ready to work with the information, write notes in the margins of your textbooks, and use a variety of notetaking systems to record information on paper.

_____Make flashcards for definitions, lists of key points, and study questions.

_____Interact with the materials by copying diagrams, making study tools, writing practice test questions, and converting printed text into pictures.

_____Identify and label organizational patterns used in paragraphs.

_____Examine graphic materials and add notes to the materials.

Active readers are critical readers. College-level readers move beyond basic reading skills by acquiring and strengthening higher-level critical reading skills. **Check the critical reading skills you are aware of doing when you read college textbooks.**

_____Evaluate the logic, accuracy, and structure of information.

_____Question the content, accuracy, completeness, and relevance of information.

_____Identify the author's purpose and point of view.

_____Follow the author's development of ideas and details by understanding organizational patterns and the logical flow of ideas.

_____Understand and interpret graphic or visual materials.

_____Make inferences and assumptions; draw conclusions.

_____Apply the information to new situations or to solve problems.

_____Implement levels of Bloom's Taxonomy: *remembering, understanding, applying, analyzing, evaluating,* and *creating.*

> **Active reading** is the process of using effective strategies to engage working memory to achieve specific reading goals.

CONCEPT CHECK **9.1**
What is active reading? What kinds of learning activities do active readers use to engage in the reading process?

Active Reading Inventory

Acknowledging the complexity of reading and understanding textbook material supports the fact that reading is an active process that requires effort, attention, commitment, and effective reading skills. Go to Exercise 9.1 in Appendix C, page C18, to complete the Active Reading Inventory as a way to assess your familiarity and use of active reading strategies.

CHAPTER 9 REFLECTIVE WRITING 1

On separate paper, in a journal, or online in this textbook's College Success CourseMate, respond to the following questions:

1. Which of your textbooks is the most challenging for you this term? Explain the kinds of challenges that textbook presents and what you find to be difficult about the textbook.

2. After completing **Exercise 9.1 Active Reading Inventory**, discuss your total score. Do you agree with the results? Why or why not? Which active reading skills do you need to strengthen?

 Access Chapter 9 Reflective Writing 1 in your College Success CourseMate, accessed through *CengageBrain.com*.

CHECK POINT 9.1

Answers appear on page B4.

True or False? See Test-Taking Strategies 1–9 in Appendix A.

_____ 1. Active reading strategies should be used only for complex, difficult textbooks.

_____ 2. Active reading engages your working memory to grasp concepts and process new information.

_____ 3. Active reading is defined as reading out loud.

_____ 4. Writing, which may include highlighting, taking notes, drawing diagrams, and writing questions, is a key process in active reading.

_____ 5. Active reading is not passive reading and does not use automatic pilot mode when reading.

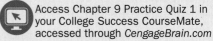 Access Chapter 9 Practice Quiz 1 in your College Success CourseMate, accessed through *CengageBrain.com*

Paragraph-Level Skills

2 *Summarize paragraph-level strategies to identify paragraph elements, learn terminology and definitions, and create definition cards and vocabulary sheets.*

Active reading engages the reader in the thorough reading process. For most textbooks, *thorough reading* involves reading one paragraph at a time, and then stopping to understand, analyze, and digest the important information in each paragraph before moving on to the next paragraph. Working with paragraph elements and course terminology helps you understand the content of paragraphs more easily and improves overall comprehension.

Paragraph Elements

Each time you read and analyze a paragraph, focus your attention on the three basic paragraph elements in **Figure 9.1**. The topic, the main idea, and the supporting details represent three levels of information.

The Topic of a Paragraph

The *topic* of a paragraph is a word or a phrase that states the subject of a paragraph. Every paragraph has a topic that tells what the author is writing about in the paragraph. You can often identify the topic by asking yourself the following questions: *In one word or one phrase, what is this paragraph about? What word is repeated several times in the paragraph? Does that word work as the topic? What word or phrase do the details tell more about or explain?*

> The **topic** of a paragraph is a word or a phrase that states the subject of a paragraph.

The Main Idea and the Topic Sentence

The *main idea* of a paragraph states the author's most important point about the topic of the paragraph. The *topic sentence*, also called the *main idea sentence*, is the sentence in a paragraph that includes the topic and states the author's main idea for the paragraph. Actively search for the topic sentence as it is an essential key for understanding the information in a paragraph. Use the following tips to help you locate and work with the topic sentence:

> The **main idea** of a paragraph states the author's most important point about the topic of the paragraph.

> The **topic sentence**, also called the *main idea sentence*, is the sentence in a paragraph that includes the topic and states the author's main point or main idea for the paragraph.

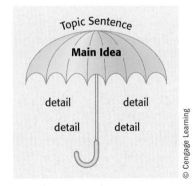

- **The topic sentence is like an umbrella**. It needs to be broad enough for all of the other sentences and supporting details in the paragraph to "fit under it." In a well-written

© Cengage Learning

FIGURE 9.1 Three Paragraph Elements

1. **The topic of the paragraph:** the subject
2. **The main idea of the paragraph:** the author's main point
3. **The important details of the paragraph:** details that support the main idea

© Cengage Learning

CONCEPT CHECK   **9.2**

What techniques can you use to identify the topic sentence of a paragraph? How will understanding the topic sentence help you comprehend the paragraph?

paragraph, each sentence relates to or supports the topic sentence. Ask yourself the following questions to help you identify the topic sentence:

- What is the topic (subject) of this paragraph?
- Is there a big picture or an "umbrella sentence" that contains this topic word?
- What is the main idea that the author wants to make about the topic? Which sentence states the main idea?
- Which sentence is broad enough to encompass the content of the paragraph?
- Do all the important details in the paragraph fit under this sentence?

- **Examine the first, the last, and then the sentences in the middle of the paragraph**.

  - *First Sentence*: Topic sentences appear most frequently as the first sentence of paragraphs. This is particularly true in textbooks.
  - *Last Sentence*: If the first sentence is not the "umbrella sentence," check the last sentence. Sometimes the last sentence summarizes the main point of the paragraph and thus states the main idea.
  - *Other Sentences*: If the first and the last sentences do not state the main idea, carefully examine each sentence in the body of the paragraph.

- **Highlight or underline the complete topic sentence.** Highlighting the topic sentence in each paragraph makes the author's most important point stand out in your mind and forms a clear impression of the significance of the paragraph. Strategies for effective highlighting appear in Figure 9.8.

- **Write implied main ideas in the margin.** On occasion, you will encounter a paragraph that has no stated main idea, which means you will not find a topic sentence in the paragraph. Instead, the main idea is *implied.* Use the details in the paragraph to draw your own conclusion about the main idea. Write the main idea in the margin.

Important Supporting Details

Supporting details in a paragraph are facts, explanations, causes and effects, examples, and definitions that develop, support, or prove the main idea. In a well-developed paragraph, the details in each sentence must relate to the topic and the topic sentence, which states the main idea. Use the following tips to identify and work with important supporting details:

- Be selective. Decide which details are important to learn and which details provide understanding but are not essential to learn. You can ask yourself: *What details would I want to include in my explanation of the main idea to someone else?* Highlight only those details.
- Highlight or underline the key words or phrases that can serve as retrieval cues or associations to trigger recall of information later from your long-term memory. Strategies for effective highlighting appear in Figure 9.8.
- Carefully examine bulleted lists of information and marginal notes in your textbook. Highlight key supporting details that appear in these lists or notes.

Supporting details in a paragraph are facts, explanations, causes and effects, examples, and definitions that develop, support, or prove the main idea.

CONCEPT CHECK   **9.3**

What kinds of information in a paragraph can function as supporting details? How do you know which details are important and which details you can ignore?

Identifying Main Ideas

DIRECTIONS: Carefully read each paragraph from the textbook, *The Internet*. Identify the topic sentence with the main idea. Completely highlight the topic sentence.

1. "One of the most important tools you can use to assess the quality of information on the Web is the author's identity. On Wikipedia, contributors may post and edit articles anonymously, in which case the author is identified only by the IP address of his or her connection to the Internet. Even when the author or editor of an article chooses to be identified, it is through the Wikipedia account name, and the biographical information included on the user page is entered by the account holder. That information can be limited or incorrect if the account holder so chooses." (p. 177)

2. "Many people consult a weather forecast daily because they want to know the weather conditions before dressing and venturing out for the day. When planning a vacation, they can review weather patterns for their intended destination. Before packing for a trip, they can obtain detailed weather information to guide their clothing choices. Some people enjoy seeing the weather conditions for family and friends who live elsewhere. Many also want to follow current weather conditions when there is a major storm—whether snow, wind, rain, hurricane, etc. These weather forecasts, conditions, and other information are available on the Web." (p. 193)

3. "Periodicals—magazines, journals, and other articles—related to almost any industry, field, or topic abound. Originally periodicals were available only in printed format at libraries, but now thousands of periodicals are available on the Web. If you know what periodical you want to search, you could go directly to its Web site. If you are more interested in articles related to a particular topic, then you can use a periodical database to locate them." (p. 221)

From Schneider, Evans. *The Internet*, 9e. © 2013 Course Technology, Cengage Learning

For additional practice, go to any of the excerpts in Appendix D.

Terminology and Definitions

Course-specific vocabulary and definitions are other paragraph-level details you will encounter as you read college textbooks. Developing effective vocabulary skills lays a strong foundation for understanding the textbook concepts, participating in class discussions, writing effective essays, and using higher-level critical reading and thinking skills. Look for a list of course-specific terms to learn and words in bold or special print that often identify terminology. The definition for a term in bold or special print usually appears within the same sentence or in the following sentence. Following are basic strategies to use to work with terminology:

- **Circle terminology and highlight key words.** See the annotation strategies on page 279–283.

- **Use word clues, punctuation clues, word structure clues, and context clues** to find the definitions for terminology or unfamiliar words.

- **Use the textbook glossary** to verify and learn more about the terminology words.

- **Use the textbook's online glossary, flashcard drills, or vocabulary exercises.**

- **Make definition flashcards or vocabulary sheets** to recite, rehearse, and review definitions.

CONCEPT CHECK 9.4
Why is learning definitions of terminology important? What strategies help you find definitions in paragraphs?

As you read with an alert mind, you will notice many ways terminology and definitions appear in paragraphs. In Example 1, the entire paragraph defines one specific term (*galaxy*) by expanding the paragraph with details that further explain the term. However, another word that may be unfamiliar, *stellar nebulae*, appears in the paragraph and should be marked as a term to know.

Example 1

Galaxies

Portions of these clouds begin to collapse to form the millions of stars that together make up galaxies. A **galaxy** is a grouping of millions or billions of individual stars. Each one of these stars sprang up from the giant molecular clouds known as stellar nebulae. Galaxies appear as faint clouds of light when viewed through a telescope, unlike the bright points of light given off by stars. When viewed with powerful telescopes, galaxies are revealed to be amazing objects that contain billions of stars.

From Butz, *Science of Earth Systems*, 2e. © 2004 Cengage Learning

In Example 2, the paragraph introduces three terms (*meteoroids*, *meteors*, and *meteorites*), but you need to look further in the paragraph for definitions of each term.

Example 2

Meteoroids

Main Idea | Smaller chunks of rock that are located in the solar system are called **meteoroids, meteors,** and **meteorites.** Meteoroids are fast-moving chunks of rock that travel through space at high velocities. These rocks are the remains of the early solar system, comets, and fragments of our own Moon and nearby planets. These objects range in size from tiny grains of sand to large boulders. When a meteoroid's orbit crosses that of Earth, it may burn up in the atmosphere, creating a meteor, also known as shooting star. It is estimated that more than 1000 tons of meteoroid material rains down on the Earth every day! Meteors that make it all the way to the Earth's surface are called meteorites. Meteorites are grouped into three categories based on their composition. ①Stony meteorites are composed of silicate rock material. ②Iron meteorites are composed of an iron-nickel alloy and are very dense. ③Stony-iron meteorites are composed of a mixture of silicate rock and iron.

From Butz, *Science of Earth Systems*, 2e. © 2004 Cengage Learning

Word Clues to Identify Definitions

Word clues are words that link the vocabulary word to its definition that appears in another part of the same sentence.

Word clues are words that link the vocabulary word to its definition that appears in another part of the same sentence. Familiarity with word clues—such as *defined as*, *is* or *are*, or *known as*—will help you locate definitions in paragraphs more quickly. **Figure 9.2** shows word clues that are used frequently in sentences to define terminology. Following are tips to use when you work with vocabulary terms and definitions:

FIGURE 9.2   Common Word Clues in Definition Sentences

also	defined as	referred to as	known as	is/are called
is/are	to describe	mean/means	which is	or
involves	shows	presents	defines	consists of

1. *Subintelligences* **are** core abilities that are a part of a larger individual intelligence.

2. The *question step of SQ4R* **involves** turning the chapter title, each heading, and each subheading into a question.

3. The *process pattern* **presents** a specific procedure or order of steps to use to do, create, repair, or solve problems.

4. A *legend* **defines** values for the symbols used in the graphic.

5. *Line graphs*, **also called** linear graphs, plot points on a coordinate grid or graph to form one continuous line to show trends and compare data.

© Cengage Learning 2015

- **Locate the definition.** The definition may appear before or after the terminology word that appears in special print. However, the terminology word may be inserted within parts of the definition. Reading and thinking carefully are essential for using information within a sentence to define a word.

- **Be selective.** Do not automatically highlight all the words that surround the word in bold or special print. Read and think carefully about which words are essential words for the definition.

- **Compare to the glossary.** If your textbook has a glossary, compare the definition you highlight to the definition in the glossary in the appendix.

CONCEPT CHECK 9.5
What are common word clues and common punctuation clues? How do these two kinds of clues help you identify definitions?

Punctuation Clues to Identify Definitions

Punctuation clues signal the definition of terminology within the sentence. The punctuation clues—such as commas, dashes, parentheses, and colons—separate the definition from the other words in the sentence. Use the punctuation clues to help identify the words to highlight that are important parts of the definition. Be aware, however, that each of these punctuation marks may serve other functions in sentences, so their appearance does not automatically mean they are functioning as definition clues. **Figure 9.3** shows the four kinds of punctuation clues with example sentences.

Punctuation clues signal the definition of terminology within the sentence.

Word Structure Clues to Understand Meanings

Word structure clues involve using the meanings of prefixes, suffixes, base words, and roots to determine the general meaning of unfamiliar words. You can use word structure clues to break apart or analyze course terminology or any other words you might encounter that are unfamiliar to you. If using word structure clues results in only a vague understanding of the word, refer to a dictionary or glossary for a more complete definition. **Figure 9.4** shows the four word parts and a diagram that explains word structure clues.

Word structure clues involve using the meanings of prefixes, suffixes, base words, and roots to determine the general meaning of unfamiliar words.

FIGURE 9.3   Four Kinds of Punctuation Clues for Definitions

Punctuation Clue		Example Sentence with Example Highlighting
Commas	**, ,**	The **Myers-Briggs Type indicator (MBTI),** a personality inventory, does not evaluate your modalities, skill levels, or abilities.
Dashes	**— —**	A **personality preference**—the more natural, more comfortable, and more automatic personality style— produces better results with less effort or struggle.
Parentheses	**( )**	The four pairs of **opposites** (poles) in the **core building blocks** (or scales) represent how you focus your attention, take in information, make decisions, and manage your life.
Colon	**:**	Unlike the Sensing personality preference that represents traditional ways to take in information, the **Intuition personality preference** represents the opposite: new, experimental, and novel ways of taking in information.

© Cengage Learning 2015

FIGURE 9.4   Word Structure Clues

WORD PARTS

Prefixes	Units of meaning attached to the beginning of words
Suffixes	Units of meaning attached to the end of words to indicate a specific part of speech (noun, verb, adjective, or adverb)
Bases	English words that have meaning and can stand by themselves
Roots	Units of meaning (often Greek or Latin) that do not form English words until other word parts are attached to them

prefix + base word or root + suffix

re- + -ject + -ed

"back"   "throw"   past-tense verb ending

© Cengage Learning

CONCEPT CHECK   9.6
What are word structure clues? Why is understanding word structure clues important for students in health careers?

Using word structure clues to understand and recall terminology is an extremely valuable skill in science and health science courses, for much of the terminology used in those courses derives from Greek or Latin roots and word parts. (See **Excerpt 5: Building Blocks of Medical Terminology** in **Appendix D.**) Learning the meanings of structural word parts can save you time, increase your comprehension, and expand your vocabulary. Can you use your knowledge of word parts to define the meaning of the terms to the left and to the right of the drawing in **Figure 9.5**? Do you know the meaning of these prefixes: post-, tachy-, epi-, and intra-? Do you know the meaning of these roots: cardio and derma? Do you know the meaning of these suffixes: -logy, -ist, -gram, -pathy, -itis, -plasty, and -al?

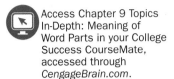

Access Chapter 9 Topics In-Depth: Meaning of Word Parts in your College Success CourseMate, accessed through *CengageBrain.com*.

FIGURE 9.5   Using Prefixes, Roots, and Suffixes for Meaning

cardi/o

cardiac
cardiology
cardiologist
cardiogram
cardiopathy
postcardiopathy
tachycardia

**derm/o
dermat/o**

dermatology
dermatologist
dermatitis
dermatoplasty
epidermis
intradermal

The combining form for each body part is the basis for many terms.

From Mitchell, Haroun. *Introduction to Health Care*, 2e, p. 96. © 2007 Cengage Learning

FIGURE 9.6   Kinds of Context Clues

Context Clue	Definition	Strategy	Example Sentence
Synonyms	Words with exact or similar meanings	Try substituting a familiar word (a synonym) for the unfamiliar word.	*probity:* The judge has a keen sense of recognizing a person's honesty and integrity. For that reason, the probity of the witness was not questioned.
Antonyms	Words with opposite meanings	An unfamiliar word is understood because you understand its opposite.	*impenitent:* Instead of showing shame, regret, or remorse, the con artist was impenitent.
Contrasts	Words that show an opposite or a difference	Look for words such as *differ, different, unlike,* or *opposite of* to understand the differences.	*thallophyte:* Because the fungi is a *thallophyte,* it differs from the other plants in the garden that have embedded roots and the rich foliage of shiny leaves and hardy stems.
Comparisons or Analogies	Words or images that indicate a likeness or a similarity	Look for the commonality between two or more items.	*cajole:* I sensed he was trying to *cajole* me. He reminded me of a salesman trying to sell me a bridge.
Examples	Examples that show function, characteristics, or use of the term	Look for ways that the examples signal the meaning of the term.	*implosion: Implosions* are not rare in Las Vegas. The most recent one collapsed an old, outdated casino to make room for a new megaresort. Dust and debris filled the air, but the nearby buildings suffered no damage.

© Cengage Learning

Context Clues to Understand Meanings

Context clues are words in a sentence or in surrounding sentences that provide hints about the general meanings of unfamiliar words. By carefully reading the sentence with the unfamiliar word and then rereading the surrounding sentences, you can often pick up hints or context clues about the *general* meaning of the word. **Figure 9.6** shows five categories of words that often function as context clues to provide you with general meanings of unfamiliar words.

> **Context clues** are words in a sentence or in surrounding sentences that provide hints about the general meanings of unfamiliar words.

As you read, strive to pay attention to unfamiliar words; skipping over them and not attempting to figure out their meaning can affect comprehension. After using context clues, if you cannot draw a conclusion about the general meaning of unfamiliar words, refer to a dictionary or a glossary for clearer definitions.

Using Word and Punctuation Clues

DIRECTIONS: The words in bold print are terminology words. Circle the words in bold print. Highlight only key words that define the word or show the formal definition of the word.

1. More than 600 muscles make up the system known as the **muscular system**.

2. **Muscles** are bundles of muscle fibers held together by connective tissue.

3. **Visceral**, or smooth, **muscle** is found in the internal organs of the body, such as those of the digestive and respiratory systems, and the blood vessels and eyes.

4. Cardiac muscle and visceral muscle are **involuntary**, meaning they function without conscious thought or control.

5. **Skeletal muscle** is attached to bones and causes body movement.

6. Skeletal muscle is **voluntary** because a person has control over its action.

7. Skeletal muscles attach to bones in different ways. Some attach by **tendons**, which are the strong, tough, fibrous connective-tissue cords.

8. Other muscles attach by **fascia**, a tough, sheet-like membrane that covers and protects the tissue.

From Simmers et al., *Introduction to Health Science Technology*, 2e © Cengage Learning

---

CONCEPT CHECK   9.7

Compare and contrast the format and content used on definition flashcards and vocabulary sheets. How are they similar and how are the different?

Definition cards are flashcards with the term on the front and a three-part definition on the back: the category, the formal definition, and then one more detail.

Definition Cards and Vocabulary Sheets

Understanding and being able to define course-specific terminology lays a strong foundation for understanding textbook information and being prepared for tests. Many test questions are based directly on knowing and understanding the course terminology. Creating definition cards or creating vocabulary sheets provides you with study tools to use to practice and review terminology and to expand your vocabulary by learning unfamiliar words you encounter as you read.

Create Definition Cards

Definition cards are flashcards with the term on the front and a three-part definition on the back: the category, the formal definition, and then one more detail. If you wish, include the chapter and the page number. **Figure 9.7** shows an example of a definition card and a vocabulary sheet. Following are important tips to use for creating and using definition cards.

- **Three kinds of information:** To prepare for questions that test your understanding of terminology, write three kinds of information on the backs of your cards:

  - The **category** to which the word belongs
  - The **formal definition**
  - One or more **additional details** to expand the definition

- **Self-quizzing and feedback:** Use your definition cards frequently for self-quizzing and immediate feedback. Look at the front and then recite the information on the back. Turn the card over to check your accuracy.

- **Reflection:** You can sort the cards into two piles: ones you know and ones you need to review further. You can also sort the cards into different categories of information. Try writing a summary by using all of the cards placed in the same category.

- **Test-preparation:** If you anticipate fill-in-the-blank questions, read the back and then *name and spell* the word on the front. Check your accuracy.

Create Vocabulary Sheets

Vocabulary sheets are a form of *two-column notes* that show the term in the left column and a three-part definition in the right column. By creating vocabulary sheets, you create your own glossary of terms. **Figure 9.7** shows the beginning of a vocabulary sheet. To study from a vocabulary sheet, cover the right column with a piece of paper. Say the word and recite the definition. Remove the paper and check your accuracy. Reverse the order: cover the left column, read the right column, and then *say and spell* the term.

> **Vocabulary sheets** are a form of *two-column notes* that show the term in the left column and a three-part definition in the right column.

FIGURE 9.7   Notetaking Options for Terminology and Definitions

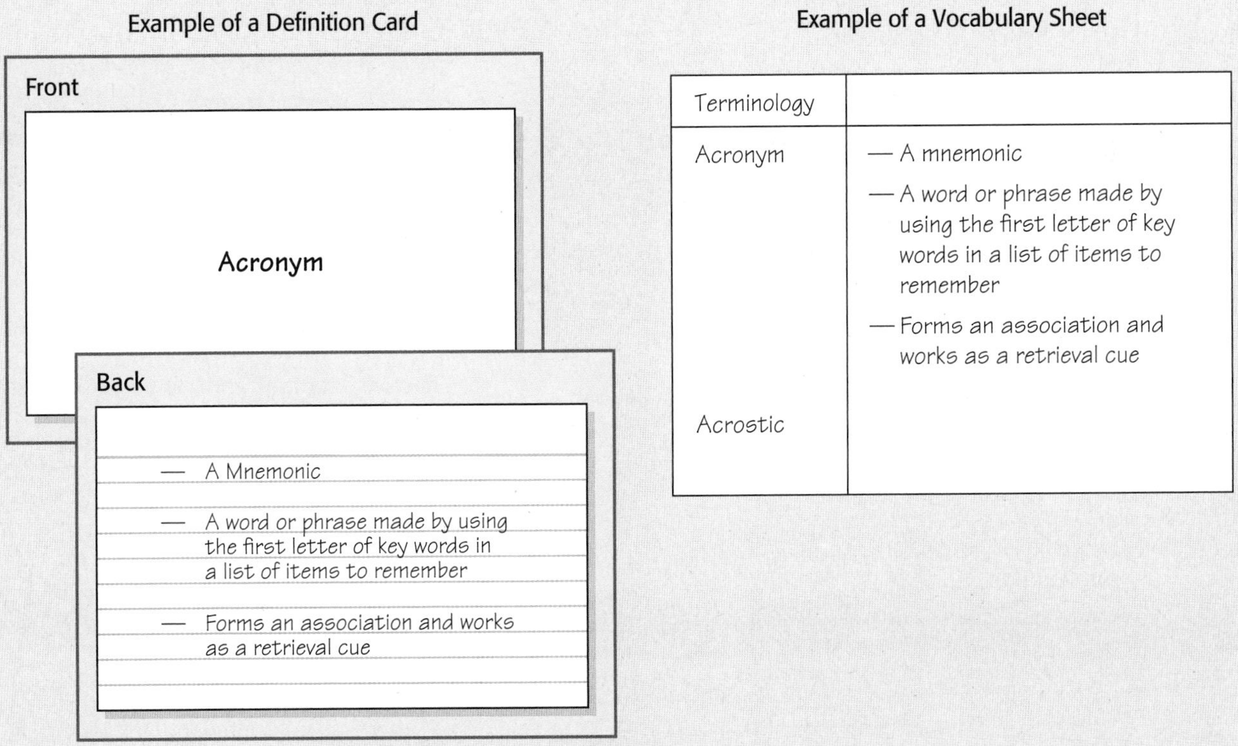

Example of a Definition Card

Front

Acronym

Back

— A Mnemonic

— A word or phrase made by using the first letter of key words in a list of items to remember

— Forms an association and works as a retrieval cue

Example of a Vocabulary Sheet

Terminology	
Acronym	— A mnemonic — A word or phrase made by using the first letter of key words in a list of items to remember — Forms an association and works as a retrieval cue
Acrostic	

Transfer These Skills: Vocabulary

DIRECTIONS: Create one of the following vocabulary study tools: a set of definition cards or two-column vocabulary sheets.

1. Your instructor will assign one of the following, or will offer you a choice of options to use.

   a. Create vocabulary study tools for any chapter of this textbook. Include all the terminology used in the Terms to Know for the chapter.

   b. Create vocabulary study tools for any chapter of a textbook used in another course. Copy the list of terminology in the chapter and then use each term in your definition cards or your vocabulary sheets.

   c. Create definition cards for a specific excerpt in Appendix D.

2. Practice reciting the terminology and the definitions. You may be asked to demonstrate use of your definition cards or vocabulary sheets in class or in a small group.

CHECK POINT 9.2

Answers appear on page B4.

Multiple Choice See Test-Taking Strategies 10–15 in Appendix A.

_____ 1. Which of the following statements is inaccurate?

   a. The topic often is a word that appears several times within a paragraph.

   b. Details in a paragraph support or develop the main idea of the paragraph.

   c. Details in a paragraph support or develop multiple main ideas within the paragraph.

   d. The most common location of the topic sentence is the first sentence of a paragraph.

_____ 2. The topic sentence of a paragraph

   a. should be completely underlined so it stands out from the other sentences.

   b. expresses the author's main idea for the paragraph.

   c. may appear in any location of a paragraph.

   d. is characterized by all of the above.

_____ 3. Definition clues within sentences may involve using

   a. word clues, word structure clues, or punctuation clues.

   b. word clues, such as the words _defined as, are called,_ or _means._

   c. punctuation signals, such as the use of commas, dashes, and parentheses.

   d. the meaning of prefixes, suffixes, and roots.

_____ 4. Which statement about supporting details in a paragraph is not true?

   a. Supporting details may be facts, explanations, and examples.

   b. All supporting details in a paragraph are important and need to be memorized.

   c. Marginal notes sometimes organize or emphasize important supporting details in a paragraph.

   d. Course-specific terminology and definitions are important supporting details in paragraphs.

_____ 5. Which of the following is true about learning definitions for course terminology?

   a. Effective definition cards show three levels of information: the category, the formal definition, and an additional detail.

   b. Self-quizzing and feedback often involve reciting definitions.

   c. Vocabulary sheets and definition cards are effective study tools.

   d. All of the above statements are true.

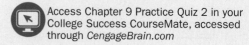 Access Chapter 9 Practice Quiz 2 in your College Success CourseMate, accessed through _CengageBrain.com_

Annotating: Highlighting and Marking Pages

3 *Explain the value of annotating textbooks and how to highlight, annotate, and study from annotations.*

Annotating is the process of highlighting, underlining, making marginal notes, or marking specific information in printed materials. The term *marking* is a general term that includes *highlighting, underlining, circling,* or *writing* within the paragraph. Highlighting (using different colors of highlighter pens) is preferred by most students because it tends to make information stand out more than underlining. Annotating is an active learning process that holds information longer in working memory and reduces the risk of information fading or being displaced before it is processed into memory. **Figure 9.8** summarizes essential strategies for annotation.

> **Annotating** is the process of highlighting, underlining, making marginal notes, or marking specific information in printed materials.

Marking Paragraph Elements

After you carefully read a paragraph, go back through the paragraph to search for the main idea, important supporting details, terminology, and definitions. Following are additional guidelines for marking paragraph elements effectively:

- **Highlight the topic sentence completely.** Completely highlight the topic sentence with the main idea. This is the only sentence in a paragraph that should be completely highlighted.

- **Mark only important supporting details.** Be selective. Only highlight key words or important short phrases to avoid over-marking.

- **Circle terminology and definitions.** Circle terminology that appears in special or bold print. Highlight key words that define the term.

FIGURE 9.8   Essential Strategies for Annotations

To Create Annotations:

- Highlight the **complete topic sentence**.
- Selectively highlight **key words or phrases** that support the topic sentence.
- **Circle terminology** and **highlight key words** in definitions.
- **Enumerate steps** or lists of information.
- Make **marginal notes** to emphasize important ideas and integrate information.

To Study Annotations:

- **Reread** out loud only the marked annotations.
- **Verbally string the ideas** together by adding your own words.
- **Recite** without looking. Check your accuracy.
- Decide if you want **additional study tools**: write a summary or create a set of notes using a different notetaking system
- Use **spaced practice, immediate review**, and **ongoing review**.

© Cengage Learning 2015

Highlighting and annotating textbooks helps identify important information and reduce the amount of information to study and review further. What effective strategies do you use to avoid over-marking and defeating the purpose of highlighting and annotating?

VisualField/iStockphoto.com

CONCEPT CHECK   9.8
How should you highlight and mark text? How can you avoid over-marking?

- **Avoid over-highlighting.** Over-highlighting defeats the purpose of highlighting, which is to reduce or condense the amount of information in paragraphs and chapters to study and review. Strive to be selective by limiting highlighting in paragraphs to no more than one-third of the paragraph.

- **Highlight examples sparingly.** You do not need to highlight every example, just a few specific examples that would work as memory cues.

- **Be selective.** Do not mark words such as *to, and, with, also,* and *in addition* because they are not key memory trigger words. Also, you do not need to mark a key word or a topic that appears multiple times.

Enumerating Steps or Lists of Information

Enumerating means "numbering."

Ordinals are words that signal a numbered sequence of items.

Enumerating means "numbering." A paragraph with a topic sentence that uses words such as *kinds of, reasons, advantages, causes, effects, ways,* or *steps* often has a list of supporting details that you should be able to identify. For example, if a topic sentence states there are "five reasons" for something, you should be able find those five reasons in the paragraph. The following points about enumerating are important:

- **Use ordinals and placeholders to signal steps or lists.** *Ordinals* are words that signal a numbered sequence of items. Ordinals, or "number words" such as *first, second,* or *third,* help you identify individual items. *Placeholders* are words such as *next, another,* and *finally* that substitute for ordinals and signal that additional items belong in the list of items you are enumerating.

- **Create easy-to-remember lists.** Enumerating or numbering serves as a memory device because it is easier to remember a fixed quantity of items than it is to recall an unknown quantity of items.

- **Write numerals.** To enumerate, simply write the numerals (1, 2, 3) above the individual items in the paragraph that appear by an ordinal or a placeholder word.
- **Make lists as marginal notes.** Often times, you will find that writing a brief list of the items in the margin, as a marginal note, is also helpful.
- **Use enumeration to clarify.** Notice how enumeration clearly identifies the six uses of podcasting in the following excerpt.

Podcasting's original use was to make it easy for people to create and broadcast their own radio shows, but many other uses soon followed. Podcasts are used by the media to store and disseminate interviews with politicians and professors on specific subjects; by colleges and universities to record lectures for distance learning classes; and by movie studios to promote new movie releases. Some podcasts have different names that further identify the type of content they contain, such as a Godcast to denote a religious broadcast, a vidcast to identify a video feed, or a learncast to identify content that is educational in nature, such as a podcast produced by a university or other educational institution.

From Schneider, Evans. *The Internet*, 9e. © 2013 Course Technology, Cengage Learning

How can enumeration in textbook paragraphs help your memory? What kind of information is appropriate for marginal notes?

Writing Marginal Notes

Marginal notes are brief notes written in the margins of textbook pages. Marginal notes give you a glimpse of the important points in a paragraph. To avoid cluttered or difficult-to-read marginal notes, be selective and brief. The following tips help you to create meaningful marginal notes:

Marginal notes are brief notes written in the margins of textbook pages.

- **Select meaningful information:** The following kinds of information work effectively as marginal notes:

numbered lists of key ideas	study questions
diagrams or pictures	definitions of unfamiliar terms
short comments or reactions	key words to define
definitions of terms	? for unclear information

- **Use brackets for large sections of information:** Rather than over-mark or clutter the margins with too many details, draw a bracket next to large sections of information or entire paragraphs that are densely written. You can add a note or abbreviation next to the bracket.
- **Use abbreviations to call attention to specific kinds of information:** You can use abbreviations next to brackets to draw your attention to sections you want to return to for further studying. The following are abbreviations you may want to use:

EX. = example or examples	Q. = question
DIFF. = differences	CE. = cause-effect
SUM. = summary	RE. = reasons why...?
F. = important fact	REL. = important relationship
IMP. = important to reread	FORM. = formula
DEF. = lengthy definition	H. = hypotheses

- **Use marginal notes to clarify information.** Notice how the marginal notes in the following excerpt organize and clarify the details in the paragraph.

Ecology

biotic
- plants
- animals
- bacteria
- fungi

INTERACT

abiotic
- air
- water
- rocks
- minerals
- light
- soil etc.

Two words that are important to the study of ecology are *biotic* and *abiotic*. The term biotic refers to any living organism, including plants, animals, bacteria, and fungi. Abiotic refers to the nonliving factors of the environment that interact with the biotic world. These include air, water, rocks, minerals, temperature, altitude, light, and soil. Scientists who study ecology are called ecologists. Ecologists study the interaction of the biotic and abiotic world in different levels of relationships on the Earth.

From Butz, *Science of Earth Systems*, 2e. © 2004 Cengage Learning

Annotating Text

EXERCISE 9.5

DIRECTIONS:

1. Your instructor will assign one of the following for you to use to practice annotating text:
   a. A specific excerpt located in Appendix D of this textbook
   b. A section from one of the chapters in your textbook
   c. A section or chapter from one of your textbooks for another course

2. Use the annotation strategies shown in Figure 9.8 and pages 279–283 to annotate the assigned material.

3. Go to Exercise 9.5 in Appendix C, page C19, to complete the Annotation Checklist. Use the checklist to assess the annotations created for this assignment. Note: You may use this checklist throughout the term to self-assess your annotating skills.

Studying from Annotations

To be truly effective, you need to practice using your annotations by personalizing, reciting, and working with the information in new ways. Simply rereading your highlighted notes tends to give a false sense that you "know" the information and have processed it into your long-term memory. Review Figure 9.8, Essential Strategies for Annotations, and use these strategies after you finish reading a paragraph, a group of paragraphs, or the end of a section in your textbook.

Reread Out Loud

CONCEPT CHECK   9.10

What strategies for studying annotations are more effective than just rereading highlighted areas?

When you reread or verbalize only the marked information, it will sound broken or fragmented; however, you will hear yourself stating only main ideas and important supporting details. Read slowly so that your working memory has time to absorb the key points and to make associations.

Verbally String Ideas Together

Stringing ideas together is the process of adding your own words to convert annotated text into full sentences and explanations. Use the following tips to string ideas together:

- After reading fragmented annotated text, use the annotations as guides to help you string ideas together more coherently. Use your own words to form full sentences that use the highlighted words and phrases. Verbalizing in this manner personalizes information as you state it in less formal language.

- Use transition words, such as *therefore*, *however*, or *also*, and ordinals, such as *first*, *second*, or *next* to list details or items.

- If you wish to create an auditory study tool, tape yourself stringing ideas together.

> **Stringing ideas together** is the process of adding your own words to convert annotated text into full sentences and explanations.

Recite Without Looking

Take your eyes off the textbook and begin paraphrasing. Use complete sentences to recite and explain what you learned. Glance down at the annotated information and marginal notes to check your accuracy. If you omitted important points or stated some information incorrectly, redo the reciting process and correct your errors.

Write Summaries or Take Notes on Paper

By writing a summary or recording notes on paper, you may not need to return to the textbook to study the information further. Your summary or notes pull out the important information and organize it in a more concise format for studying. Your summary and your notes should include the same information that you stated when you verbally strung ideas together.

Use Spaced Practice and Review

Once you have annotated your textbook, taking time to rehearse (practice) the information is essential. To review annotations of the entire chapter, use *spaced practice*. Review sections of the chapter at one time, not the entire chapter without breaks. When you finish the chapter, do an *immediate review* and plan time to return to the information within the next week or two for *ongoing review*. You will find that the more frequently you return to review the information, the more thoroughly you will learn what is important to know.

Practicing Annotating and Stringing Ideas Together

EXERCISE 9.6

DIRECTIONS:

1. Go to Excerpt 5: Building Blocks of Medical Terminology in Appendix D.

2. Annotate this excerpt. Be selective. Use the strategies shown in Figure 9.8.

3. Return to your annotated excerpt. Use the strategies in Figure 9.8 to study your annotations. You may be asked to string ideas out loud in class, with a partner, or in small groups.

CHECK POINT 9.3

Answers appear on B4.

Listing and Short-Answer Questions See Test-Taking Strategies 25–28 and 32–36 in Appendix A.

Answer the following questions on separate paper.

_____ 1. List four different ways to "mark" textbook paragraphs.

_____ 2. List four strategies to use to avoid over-marking a paragraph.

_____ 3. Describe steps to use to study from chapter annotations.

 Access Chapter 9 Practice Quiz 3 in your College Success CourseMate, accessed through *CengageBrain.com*.

Index Card Notes

④ *Describe the three kinds of cards used in a comprehensive set of index card notes; explain ways to study from index card notes.*

Index card notes involve creating three types of flashcards to use as study tools: *definition cards, category cards,* and *question cards.* Index card notes are effective study tools for learning definitions for terminology, lists of items under a specific category, steps in a process, or answers to questions that you predict will appear in one form or another on an upcoming test. Index card notes work effectively to study facts, dates, formulas, rules, and steps to perform a process.

> **Index card notes** involve creating three types of flashcards to use as study tools: definition cards, category cards, and question cards.

A Comprehensive Set of Index Card Notes

Select a size of index card notes to use for notetaking. If you wish to use colored index cards, one color could be for definition cards, one for category cards, and one for question cards. On the top of the front side of the cards, write the chapter number, if you wish. To create stronger visual impressions of information on your index cards, use highlighters to emphasize key points and add pictures that you can use as retrieval cues. With practice, you can look up and to the left to picture the information on your cards. As you create each of the following kinds of cards, be selective. Limit each card to one topic to avoid cluttered, difficult-to-use cards. **Figure 9.9** shows examples of question, definition, and category index card notes. Following are the kinds of cards in a comprehensive set of index card notes:

> **Category cards** are flashcards with a category or topic on the front and a list of items that belong to the category on the back.

- *Definition cards* are flashcards with the term on the front and a three-part definition on the back: the category, the formal definition, and then one more detail.

> **Question cards** are flashcards with a study question on the front and answers to the question on the back.

- *Category cards* are flashcards with a category or topic on the front and a list of items that belong to the category on the back. Do not clutter the back of the card with any additional details; you want to be able to visually memorize the list of items.

> **CONCEPT CHECK** 9.11
> *Describe the different kinds of information that appear on each of the three kinds of index card notes.*

- *Question cards* are flashcards with a study question on the front and answers to the question on the back. Predicting and writing practice test questions on your index cards provides you with effective study tools to use by yourself, with a study partner, or in a study group for ongoing review or to prepare for an upcoming test.

FIGURE 9.9 Kinds of Index Card Notes

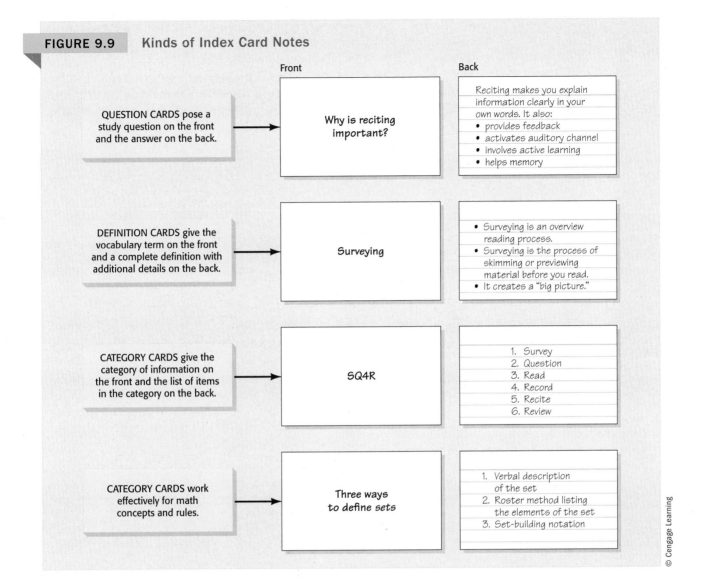

Studying from Index Card Notes

Index card notes are portable and convenient to use. You can carry them in a small plastic pouch or bag, hold them together with a rubber band, and punch a hole in the top of the cards and attach them to a large metal ring. Use the following suggestions to study your index card notes:

- **Use the cards for self-quizzing.** Look at one side of the card and recite the information on the reverse side. Check the reverse sides of the cards for immediate feedback on the accuracy and completeness of the information you recited.

- **Ask others to quiz you.** You can practice explaining information clearly by asking study partners, friends, or family members to use your cards to quiz you. Because all the information appears on the card, the person quizzing you does not necessarily need to know the information.

CONCEPT CHECK 9.12

What is a warm-up activity? Briefly discuss three or more ways you can use index card notes to study and review course content.

- **Sort the cards into two piles.** One pile contains the cards you know and can explain accurately. The other pile contains cards you need to study further. Continue rehearsing the pile of cards you need to study further.

- **Use your cards as a warm-up activity at the beginning of a study block.** Working with your cards before you begin a new assignment puts you in the mindset for the subject, activates previously learned information, and promotes ongoing review.

GROUP PROCESSING

 A Collaborative Learning Activity

Form groups with three or four students. Then complete the following directions.

DIRECTIONS:

1. Have each student in your group choose a different chapter to review and to use for creating index card notes.

2. Each student creates a set of index card notes that includes three definition cards, three category cards, and three question cards for a total of nine cards.

3. Shuffle together all the cards created by members of your group. Take turns drawing a card and using the card to quiz another person in your group. Continue taking turns until all of the cards have been used for review.

CHECK POINT 9.4

Answers appear on B4.

Fill-in-the-Blanks See Test-Taking Strategies 21–24 in Appendix A.

1. _____ card notes are effective study tools to use to learn facts, definitions, rules, and steps.

2. _____ cards are flashcards that include the category, formal definition, and details about the vocabulary term.

3. _____ cards show a topic on the front of the card and a list of details or items that belong under the topic on the back of the card.

4. _____ cards, which work effectively to review for tests, pose a question on the front and answers on the back.

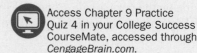 Access Chapter 9 Practice Quiz 4 in your College Success CourseMate, accessed through *CengageBrain.com*.

Cornell Notes

5 *Identify the Five R's of Cornell and describe the processes used for each of the five steps in the Cornell Notetaking System.*

The Cornell Notetaking System is one option to use to take textbook notes. In Chapter 8, you learned about *outline notes*. In this chapter you learned about *annotating* and *index card notes*. In Chapter 11, you will learn about other notetaking systems. The Essential Strategies for Textbook Notetaking in **Figure 9.10** apply to all notetaking systems.

Creating a goal to learn how to use a variety of notetaking systems provides you with the tools to select the most appropriate system or systems to use for your various textbooks. Textbook notes are important for the following reasons:

- Notetaking involves **condensing or reducing** large amounts of information into more manageable units that are easier to study and review.

- Notetaking requires you to **think carefully** about information, break it down, analyze it, and select what is important to learn. If you have difficulty understanding what you are reading, you will have difficulty taking notes.

- Notetaking processes involve **multisensory strategies.** Writing notes encodes visual images such as words, phrases, lists, or charts. Reciting encodes information linguistically. Writing encodes information kinesthetically.

- Studying from well-developed notes is **more time efficient** than reading and rereading chapters of information. Effective textbook notes save you time in the long run.

CONCEPT CHECK 9.13

What are the benefits of taking notes? What different notetaking systems have you learned to use?

FIGURE 9.10   **Essential Strategies for Textbook Notetaking**

- **Understand what you read before taking notes.** Read a paragraph or chunk of information, pause, think about the information, be sure that you understand it, and then take notes.

- **Be selective.** Your notes should be a *condensed* version of the textbook, not a word-for-word copy of the textbook pages. Capture only the important concepts, main ideas, and supporting details in your notes.

- **Paraphrase or reword.** Shorten textbook explanations or information by using your own words to state main ideas and important details as long as your wording presents the information accurately.

- **Include textbook reminders in your notes.** Instead of copying large charts or lengthy sections of important text, write a reminder in your notes to see page XX in the textbook.

- **Label your notes.** As you progress through the term, you will have many pages of notes. To avoid confusion, include textbook chapter numbers and number each page of your notes.

- **Use spaced practice.** Make several contacts with your notes over different periods of time. You can use them as a warm-up activity to put you in the mindset of the subject the next time you sit down to study, or you can schedule time each week to review your notes for the week.

- **Use feedback strategies.** Use the Look-Away Technique with reciting and visualizing to check the completeness and accuracy of your learning.

- **Review your notes.** Use immediate review to create a strong impression in memory. Use ongoing review to keep information active and accessible in working memory.

© Cengage Learning 2015

Textbook Case Studies

DIRECTIONS:

1. Read each case study carefully. Respond to the question at the end of each case study by using *specific* strategies discussed in this chapter. Answer in complete sentences.

2. Write your responses on paper or online in this textbook's College Success CourseMate, Textbook Case Studies. You will be able to print your online response or e-mail it to your instructor.

CASE STUDY 1: Shauna learns by writing information and studying from handwritten information. However, when she creates outline notes or Cornell notes, she notices that her notes are longer than the textbook chapters. She copies everything and her notes become a steady stream of unorganized information. What notetaking strategies could Shauna use to produce more effective and useful notes?

CASE STUDY 2: With Cornell notes, Erick has learned to condense information effectively into the right column. However, in his recall column, Erick makes lists of important information, writes definitions for key terms, and writes study questions with their answers. He reads all the information out loud. What adjustments does Erick need to make in the way he uses his Cornell notes so he tests his memory more effectively?

 Access Chapter 9 Textbook Case Studies in your College Success CourseMate, accessed through *CengageBrain.com.*

The Five R's of Cornell Notetaking

> The **Cornell Notetaking System** is a five-step notetaking process used to take notes from textbooks and from lectures.

The *Cornell Notetaking System* is a five-step notetaking process used to take notes from textbooks and from lectures. This powerful notetaking system was designed by Dr. Walter Pauk at Cornell University more than forty-five years ago when he recognized students' need to learn how to take more effective notes. Many college and university instructors consider this the most effective notetaking system for college students.

> The **Five R's of Cornell** are record, reduce, recite, reflect, and review.

The *Five R's of Cornell* are record, reduce, recite, reflect, and review. The goal of the Cornell Notetaking System is to take notes that are so accurate and detailed that you *may not need to go back to the book to study*. To avoid weakening this powerful system, use all five R's shown in **Figure 9.11** to record and study your notes.

Preparing to Take Notes

To prepare your notebook paper for Cornell notes, draw a two-and-one-half-inch margin down the left side of your notebook paper. (Check if your campus bookstore carries Cornell or "law notebook" paper with the wider left margin.) The following tips are important for the Cornell system:

- Only make columns on the front side of your notebook paper as you will *not* be taking notes on the back of these pages.

- Use the back of each page to list or summarize points when you do the fourth R: *reflect*.

- Label pages. On the top of the first page, write the course name, chapter number, and date. For all the following pages, just write the chapter number and the page number of your notes.

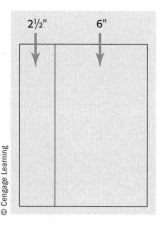

2½"   6"

© Cengage Learning

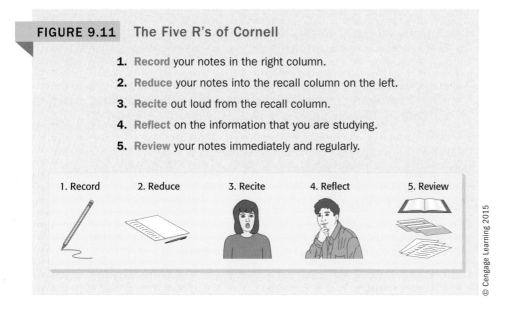

FIGURE 9.11   The Five R's of Cornell

1. **Record** your notes in the right column.

2. **Reduce** your notes into the recall column on the left.

3. **Recite** out loud from the recall column.

4. **Reflect** on the information that you are studying.

5. **Review** your notes immediately and regularly.

1. Record   2. Reduce   3. Recite   4. Reflect   5. Review

© Cengage Learning 2015

Step One: Record Notes

The *record step* in the Cornell system involves taking notes in the right column. Read each paragraph carefully, decide what information is important, and then record that information on your paper. Your notes should be a *reduced version* of the textbook. Be selective. Use the following suggestions for recording notes in the right column:

- **Skeleton of notes:** The headings and subheadings in the textbook are the *skeleton* or outline of the chapter. They serve as guides for identifying main categories of information.

- **Textbook headings and new headings:** Write a textbook heading on your paper. Underline it so it stands out and gives your notes structure. You do *not* need to number the headings. Reserve the use of numbers for details. If you wish to regroup or reorganize information into new headings or subheadings that are more helpful for understanding topics, you can add new headings or subheadings in your notes.

- **Details:** To separate details and avoid what appears to be an endless stream of random details, number the details. Numbering helps you create a stronger impression about the number of important points under each heading, and it breaks the information into smaller, more manageable units.

- **Minor supporting details:** Indent or use dashes to show minor supporting details under the main details that are numbered.

- **Sufficient information:** Your notes need to show the big picture and the little pictures (details), so be sure to record sufficient information to be meaningful later.

- **Meaningful phrases or short sentences:** Shorten or paraphrase information. Avoid using only individual words or short phrases that may lose their meaning when you return to them later. If phrases by themselves are not meaningful units of thought, convert them into short sentences.

The **record step** in the Cornell system involves taking notes in the right column.

- **Double-spacing between headings:** Leave a space after the end of one section before you begin a new heading. This double spacing visually separates sections or "chunks" of information and helps avoid crowded or cluttered notes that are difficult to study.

- **Charts and diagrams:** When you encounter important visual materials, sketch them or *summarize* the conclusions you make after studying the visual materials. In your notes, write a reminder to return to a specific page to review the graph or chart.

- **Marginal notes:** Carefully read marginal notes (or sidebars) that may appear in your textbooks. If this information does not appear within the regular text, include important points from the marginal notes in your notes.

- **Annotations:** If you have already highlighted or annotated the information, move the same information into your notes. Notice the annotations in **Figure 9.12**. Then examine **Figure 9.13** to see how a student created a set of the Cornell notes on a computer to reflect the annotations.

> **CONCEPT CHECK**   9.14
> *Summarize strategies to use for each of the Five R's of Cornell notetaking.*

Step Two: Reduce

After you have finished taking notes for the chapter, you are ready to close the book and reduce your notes one step further. The *reduce step* in the Cornell system involves condensing notes into the recall column. The *recall column* is the left column in the Cornell notes that shows headings, key words, and study questions. Figure 9.13 shows the right notetaking column and the left recall column with the reduced notes. Use the following suggestions to create an effective recall column:

> The **reduce step** in the Cornell system involves condensing notes into the recall column.

> The **recall column** is the left column in the Cornell notes that shows headings, key words, and study questions.

- **Copy headings.** To structure and organize your recall column, copy the headings from the right column into the left column and underline them. The headings should appear directly across from the headings in your notes.

- **Reread your notes.** Reread a section of your notes. If your notes seem vague or incomplete, go back to the book, reread, and add more details to your notes.

- **Create study questions.** Under the headings in your recall column, write brief study questions about the information in the right column. Your study questions can be in an abbreviated form such as *Why? Name the 6 ... Related to X how?*

- **Define key words.** In your recall column, across from your notes that define a key term, write "def." and the *key word* to cue you later to recite the definition for the word.

- **Do not write too much.** Do not clutter the recall column with too much information. Do *not write answers* to your study questions, definitions, or completed lists of information. You want to challenge yourself in the next step to see if you can recall the information from memory.

Step Three: Recite

> The **recite step** in the Cornell system involves using information in the recall column to explain information out loud in your own words without referring to detailed notes.

The *recite step* in the Cornell system involves using information in the recall column to explain information out loud in your own words without referring to detailed notes. Use the following suggestions to recite from your recall column:

- **Cover up the right column.** To avoid the tendency to look at your notes as you recite, use a blank piece of paper to cover your notes on the right side of your paper. All you will see are the headings, your study questions, and key words in the left column.

FIGURE 9.12 Forgetting—Why We, Uh, Let's See; Why We, Uh … Forget!

Why do we forget?

We don't expect sensory memories and short-term memories to remain with us for long. But when you deliberately encode and store information in long-term memory, you want it to stay there (after all, it's supposed to be *long*-term). For EX. example, when you study for an exam, you count on your long-term memory to retain the information at least until you take your exam.

Why do we forget long-term memories? The more you know about how we "lose" memories, the better you will be able to hang on to them. Most forgetting tends to occur immediately after memorization. Herman Ebbinghaus (1885) famously tested his own memory at various intervals after learning. To be sure he would not be swayed by prior learning, he memorized *nonsense syllables*. These are meaningless three-letter words such as "cef," "wol," and "gex." The importance of using meaningless words is shown by the fact that "Vel," "Fab," and "Duz" are no longer used on memory tests. People who recognize these words as detergent names find them very easy to remember. This is another reminder that relating new information to what you IMP. already know can improve memory.

By waiting various lengths of time before testing himself, Ebbinghaus plotted a curve of forgetting. This graph shows the amount of information remembered after varying lengths of time (● Figure 7.8). Notice that forgetting is rapid at first

and is then followed by a slow decline (Hintzman, 2005). The same applies to meaningful information, but the forgetting curve is stretched over a longer time. As you might expect, recent events are recalled more accurately than those from the remote past. Thus, you are more likely to remember that *The* EX. *King's Speech* won the "Best Picture" Academy Award for 2010 than you are to remember that *Million Dollar Baby* was the 2004 winner.

As a student, you should note that a short delay between studying and taking a test minimizes forgetting. However, this is no reason for cramming. Most students make the error of *only* cramming. If you cram, you don't have to remember for very long, but you may not learn enough in the first place. If you use short, daily study sessions *and* review intensely before a test, you will get the benefit of good preparation and a minimum time lapse.

The Ebbinghaus curve shows less than 30 percent remembered after only 2 days have passed. Is forgetting really that rapid? No, not always. Meaningful information is not lost nearly as quickly as nonsense syllables. After 3 years, students who took a university psychology course had forgotten about 30 percent of the facts they learned. After that, little more forgetting occurred (Conway, Cohen, & Stanhope,1992.). Actually, as learning grows stronger, some knowledge may become nearly permanent (Berntsen & Thomsen, 2005).

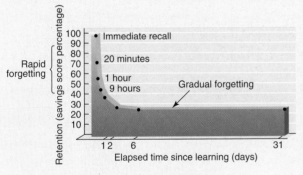

●Figure 7.8 **The curve of forgetting. This graph shows the amount remembered (measured by relearning) after varying lengths of time. Notice how rapidly forgetting occurs. The material learned was nonsense syllables. Forgetting curves for meaningful information also show early losses followed by a long gradual decline, but overall, forgetting occurs much more slowly. (After Ebbinghaus, 1885.)**

From Coon, Mitterer. *Introduction to Psychology*, © 2013 Cengage Learning

- **Begin reciting.** Begin reciting by looking at and then telling about the information in the recall column. Answer the questions, define terms, and tell what you remember about the key words. Talk out loud in complete, coherent sentences.

- **Use feedback.** After reciting a section of information, pull down the paper that covered the right column. Check your accuracy and the completeness of your recited information. If you have difficulty reciting, or if you "go blank," pull down the paper, reread your notes, cover them, and try reciting again.

FIGURE 9.13   Forgetting—Cornell Notes

The following set of Cornell notes is based on the information in Figure 9.12, Since the excerpt did not have headings and subheadings, notice how headings were added to organize the information. This is an option you always can use to personalize and organize your notes.

<u>Forgetting – Why We...Forget</u>

<u>Intro</u>	<u>Intro</u>
Expect which memory to remain when study?	1. We don't expect sensory or short-term memories to remain for long
	2. We do expect info we encode or study to be in LTM when needed for exam
<u>Forgetting</u>	<u>Forgetting – Why do we forget long-term memories?</u>
Most forgetting occurs when?	1. Most forgetting – immediately after memorization
	2. Herman Ebbinghaus –
Ebbinghaus – Did what?	• tested own memory – different intervals – memorized nonsense syllables
	• nonsense – not swayed by prior learning
	3. Reminder: relate new info to what already know con improve memory

<u>Curve of Forgetting</u> | <u>Ebbinghaus Curve of Forgetting</u>

Def. curve

1. Curve of forgetting: graph that shows amount of info remembered after varying lengths of time

2. Curve shows:

Curve shows what?

   • Forgetting most rapid at first

   • Forgetting followed by slower, gradual decline

   • applies same way to meaningful info over longer time

   • remember recent events more accurately than those from past

     Ex. Academy Award winners this year vs. 2010

Studying – reduce forgetting
How?

3. For studying:

   • Short delay between studying and taking test minimizes forgetting

   • Cramming – don't have to remember long but may not learn enough

   • Better: short, daily study and review before a test

<30% explain

4. Curve shows: <30% remembered after 2 days (Nonsense syllables) = 70% forgotten!

   –Meaningful info not lost as quickly.

   –Ex. After 3 yrs, psych students forgot about 30% facts. Not much more forgetting then

Any knowledge permanent?

5. Imp.– Learning grows stronger ⟶ some knowledge almost permanent

   See Ebbinghaus Curve Figure in book.

Draw curve

● **Adjust the recall column.** If the recall column lacks sufficient cues to direct your reciting or to focus you on the important points, add more key words or study questions to the recall column. If you find that the recall column provides you with too much information that results in simply reading with little information left to recite from memory, cross out (or whiteout) some of the details before you recite again.

● **Track your progress:** If you wish, star items in the recall column that you recited with accuracy. Check or place an arrow next to information that you need to practice further.

Practice Cornell Notetaking

DIRECTIONS:

1. Your instructor will provide directions for you to create a set of Cornell notes with recall columns for one of the following:

   a. A specific excerpt in Appendix D

   b. An excerpt from a new source that is provided by the instructor

   c. A specific section of information your textbook for this course or for another course

2. Read the assigned materials carefully. If you wish or if assigned, highlight main ideas and important supporting details and terminology. Make useful marginal notes.

3. Create Cornell notes that show a notetaking column and a developed recall column.

4. Go to Exercise 9.8: Cornell Notetaking Self-Assessment Checklist in Appendix C, page C20. Use the checklist to assess the quality of your Cornell notes. Note: The back of the checklist (page C21) shows an instructor assessment form that your instructor may use to evaluate your notes.

Step Four: Reflect

The *reflect step* in the Cornell system involves thinking seriously, comprehending, and using elaborative rehearsal strategies to work with information in new ways. The reflect step is a creative and highly individualized step, so no two students will create identical study tools or use the same rehearsal activities. Decide *what works best for you* and the materials you are studying. Use the following tips for reflecting on your notes:

● **Think and ponder.** Take time to think about the topic, relationships among details, and the importance of the information you are studying.

● **Line up your recall columns.** To see an informal outline and an overview of all the information in your set of notes, arrange the pages of your notes so you can see a lineup of all the recall columns.

● **Write a summary.** Look only at the information in the recall columns. Write a summary using full sentences and paragraphs to summarize the main ideas and important details.

● **Write on the back of your notes.** Use the back of your note paper to make lists of information, write study questions, add diagrams or charts, or jot down questions you want to ask in class.

> The **reflect step** in the Cornell system involves thinking seriously, comprehending, and using elaborative rehearsal strategies to work with information in new ways.

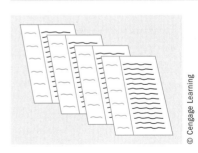

© Cengage Learning

Access Chapter 9 Topics In-Depth: Cornell with SQ4R in your College Success CourseMate, accessed through *CengageBrain.com*.

CONCEPT CHECK **9.16**

What are effective reflect, immediate review, and ongoing review strategies to use by yourself? With a partner? In a study group?

The **review step** in the Cornell system involves using immediate and ongoing review.

Immediate review is the process of rehearsing information before you end a learning task.

Ongoing review is the process of practicing previously learned information days and even weeks after the initial learning occurred.

• **Make study tools.** Reinforce your learning by creating study tools that you can use throughout the term: index card notes, visual mappings, charts, or mnemonics.

Step Five: Review

The **review step** in the Cornell system involves using immediate and ongoing review. **Immediate review** is the process of rehearsing information before you end a learning task. Use immediate review with your notes after you finish the reflect step. This review helps create a stronger impression of the information before you set it aside and move on to something new.

Ongoing review is the process of practicing previously learned information days and even weeks after the initial learning occurred. Ongoing review keeps information active and accessible in your memory system. Ongoing review saves you time in the long run; when you prepare for tests or exams, you will not need to cram or spend excessive time "relearning" information.

CHAPTER 9 REFLECTIVE WRITING 2

 On separate paper, in a journal, or online in this textbook's College Success CourseMate, respond to the following questions:

1. Which notetaking system or systems do you prefer to use to take notes from your textbooks? Explain your preference or preferences.

2. What is the value of taking textbook notes? How does notetaking help improve your academic performance?

 Access Chapter 9 Reflective Writing 2 in your College Success CourseMate, accessed through *CengageBrain.com*.

CHECK POINT 9.5

Answers appear on B4.

True or False? See Test-Taking Strategies 1–9 in Appendix A.

_____ 1. You should always read the entire chapter before taking Cornell notes.

_____ 2. If you take Cornell notes, you never need to return to the textbook to reread sections.

_____ 3. The Five R's of Cornell are not *read, record, recite, reflect,* and *review.*

_____ 4. Headings are used to help organize information in both columns of Cornell notes.

_____ 5. An effective recall column includes questions without answers and terminology without the written definitions.

Matching See Test-Taking Strategies 16–20 in Appendix A.

_____ 1. Five R's of Cornell

_____ 2. the record step

_____ 3. reciting

_____ 4. reflecting

_____ 5. recall column

_____ 6. headings

_____ 7. content of recall column

a. questions, key words, headings

b. involves explaining in your own words

c. thinking, pondering, summarizing, questioning

d. record, reduce, recite, reflect, review

e. read, record, recite, reflect, review

f. involves taking notes

g. main topic or category of information

h. the left column of Cornell notes

 Access Chapter 9 Practice Quiz 5 in your College Success CourseMate, accessed through *CengageBrain.com.*

ACTIVITY

Chapter 9 Critical Thinking

PURPOSE: Vocabulary study sheets are one form of "two-column notes." In some ways, this two-column notetaking format is a simplified version of Cornell notes. As you recall from Bloom's Taxonomy, critical thinking involves *applying* and *creating,* so this activity provides you with the opportunity to create new uses for two-column notes.

DIRECTIONS:

1. Use the format of two-column notes. Brainstorm a variety of ways you could use this two-column note format to take other kinds of notes. Jot down or list your ideas. What would the columns show? Which of your textbooks could you use for your two-column notetaking system?

2. Put your ideas to work! Create a set of two-column notes for some type of textbook content that does not involve terminology and definitions. You may be asked to share your system with the class or students in a small group.

Learning Objectives Review

Terms to Know

1. *Define active reading and describe its relationship to active learning and critical reading.*

- Active reading is a process of using effective strategies to engage working memory to achieve specific reading goals.

- Active readers use active learning strategies; active readers are also critical readers who move beyond basic reading skills to use higher-level reading skills.

By yourself or with a partner, practice reciting or writing definitions for the following terms. You may also practice defining these terms by using the online flashcards or comparing your answers to the online glossary.

active reading p. 267

topic p. 269

Terms to Know

 Access Chapter 9 Flashcards and Online Glossary in your College Success CourseMate, accessed through *CengageBrain.com*.

Learning Objectives Review

2 *Summarize paragraph-level strategies to use to identify paragraph elements, learn terminology and definitions, and create definition cards and vocabulary sheets.*

- Thorough reading involves reading, usually one paragraph at a time, to understand, analyze, and digest the information in the paragraph.

- The topic, the main idea, and the supporting details are the three paragraph elements active readers learn to identify.

- The main idea states the author's most important point about the topic. The main idea sentence is also called the topic sentence.

- Terminology and definitions are important supporting details in paragraphs. Circling terminology and highlighting key words in definitions separate the information from other kinds of supporting details.

- Word clues, punctuation clues, word structure clues, and context clues help identify definitions for course-specific terminology and unfamiliar words.

- Definition flashcards and vocabulary sheets are study tools to practice reciting definitions.

3 *Explain the value of annotating textbooks and how to highlight, annotate, and study from annotations.*

- The process of annotating, which includes highlighting, underlining, marking, enumerating, and making marginal notes, holds information longer in working memory so it can be processed.

- Specific strategies guide students through the process of annotating textbooks selectively and in useful ways.

- Annotating is effective only when students take time to study the annotations. A process of stringing ideas together and reciting are review processes to use.

4 *Describe the three kinds of cards used in a comprehensive set of index card notes; explain ways to study from index card notes.*

- A comprehensive set of index card notes includes definition cards, category cards, and question cards. Each type of card has a different purpose and kind of information.

- Studying from index card notes includes reciting, self-quizzing, and using the cards as review tools.

5 *Identify the Five R's of Cornell and describe the processes used for each of the five steps in the Cornell Notetaking System.*

- Record, reduce (in the recall column), recite, reflect, and review are the five R's of the Cornell Notetaking System.

- Recording occurs in the right column; reciting from condensed notes occurs by using the left column, the recall column.

- Using a variety of strategies for recording and reducing notes results in organized, easy-to-use notes to practice and learn textbook content.

Chapter 9   Review Questions

Answers appear on page B4.

True or False? See Test-Taking Strategies 1–9 in Appendix A.

_____ 1. Active reading occurs naturally and automatically for all college students.

_____ 2. It is always best to read the whole chapter first and then go back to take notes.

_____ 3. All notetaking systems should result in a reduced version of textbook information.

_____ 4. The Cornell Notetaking System consists of six steps: read, reduce, record, recite, reflect, and review.

_____ 5. The main idea always appears as the first sentence in textbook paragraphs.

_____ 6. Annotating involves a variety of processes: marking main ideas, circling terminology, writing marginal notes, and possibly using abbreviations next to brackets.

_____ 7. Too much information in the Cornell recall column causes you to read and not do much reciting.

_____ 8. Word clues, which are also called word structure clues, are words that help you define terminology or unfamiliar words.

_____ 9. Definition cards usually provide more detailed definitions of terminology than appear on vocabulary sheets.

_____ 10. Index card notes include cards that provide definitions, cards that list items under categories, and cards that pose study questions with the answers on the back.

Multiple Choice See Test-Taking Strategies 10–15 in Appendix A.

_____ 1. Which of the following is _not_ true about stringing ideas together from your annotated notes? Stringing ideas together

    a. should occur after you have created written summaries.

    b. involves connecting ideas by using transition words and informal language.

    c. involves activating the auditory channel by verbalizing.

    d. may occur after each paragraph or after sections of information.

_____ 2. Annotating a textbook includes

    a. writing notes in the margins.

    b. highlighting topic sentences and key words.

    c. circling terminology and enumerating items in a list.

    d. doing all of the above.

_____ 3. The five R's of the Cornell Notetaking System

    a. involve developing and using two columns of information.

    b. do not represent the processes of reading reciting, recalling, reviewing, and revising.

    c. involve using active learning strategies of writing, reciting, and working with information in new ways.

    d. are described by all of the above statements.

Access Chapter 9 Enhanced Quiz and Chapter 9 Study Guide in your College Success CourseMate, accessed through _CengageBrain.com_.

Access all Chapter 9 Online Materials in your College Success CourseMate, accessed through _CengageBrain.com_.

10 Analyzing and Organizing Chapter Content

kali9/iStockphoto.com

Learning from textbooks requires a wealth of knowledge about textbooks in various content areas, the relationships formed among concepts and different kinds of details, and strategies to analyze and organize vast amounts of information. After learning about the differences among textbooks from varied disciplines and content areas, your attention will shift to identifying organizational patterns and interpreting graphic materials. In this chapter, you will learn ways to create visual notes (visual mappings, hierarchies, and comparison charts) to record information in new, creative ways.

Access Chapter 10 Expanded Chapter Outline in your College Success CourseMate, accessed through *CengageBrain.com*.

YOUR CHAPTER MAPPING

After reading information under each heading, return to the chapter visual mapping below. Add key words to show subheadings and important details related to each heading.

 Access Chapter 10 Visual Mapping in your College Success CourseMate, accessed through *CengageBrain.com*.

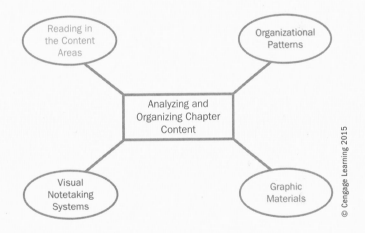

© Cengage Learning 2015

LEARNING OBJECTIVES

1. *Discuss strategies to use when reading college textbooks for different disciplines and content areas.*

2. *Define and discuss the seven organizational patterns used to organize details in paragraphs.*

3. *Explain and use strategies to read and interpret six kinds of graphic materials.*

4. *Explain and demonstrate how to create and study from three kinds of visual notes: visual mappings, hierarchies, and comparison charts.*

Analyzing and Organizing Chapter Content

ANSWER, SCORE, and **RECORD** your profile before you read this chapter. If you need to review the process, refer to the complete directions given in the profile for Chapter 1 on page 4.

ONLINE: You can complete the profile and get your score online in this textbook's College Success CourseMate.

Access Chapter 10 Profile in your College Success CourseMate, accessed through *CengageBrain.com.*

	YES	NO
1. I always use the same study strategies for both factual and process information.	____	____
2. I understand how textbooks for different disciplines differ in content and structure.	____	____
3. I can identify clue words used to signal examples, definition, process, and chronological paragraph patterns.	____	____
4. I have difficulty creating diagrams to show the flow of ideas and important details in a comparison-contrast or a cause-effect paragraph.	____	____
5. I use titles, captions, and legends to better understand charts and graphs.	____	____
6. I know how to analyze and interpret the data that appears on bar and line graphs.	____	____
7. I use the Look-Away Technique to study visual notes, such as visual mappings, hierarchies, and comparison charts.	____	____
8. I use sentences in visual notes to write level-three details.	____	____
9. I study visual notes by memorizing the skeleton of the notes and reciting details.	____	____
10. I am confident in my ability to read different kinds of textbooks and create visual notes for my courses.	____	____

QUESTIONS LINKED TO THE CHAPTER LEARNING OBJECTIVES:

Questions 1–2: objective 1   Questions 7–9: objective 4

Questions 3–4: objective 2   Question 10: all objectives

Questions 5–6: objective 3

Reading in the Content Areas

 Discuss strategies to use when reading college textbooks for different disciplines and content areas.

Understanding the differences among textbooks from various content areas or disciplines helps you select the most appropriate reading and study skills strategies to

| FIGURE 10.1 | Common Reading Skills in Content Areas |

Subjects	Declarative Knowledge	Procedural Knowledge	Organizational Patterns	Graphic Materials	Survey Chapter	Learn Terminology	SQ4R Reading System	Outline Reading System	Customized Reading System
Composition	X	X	X		X	X			X
Literature	X	X	X		X	X			X
Social Sciences	X	X	X	X	X	X	X	X	
Science	X	X	X	X	X	X	X	X	
Mathematics	X	X	X	X	X	X			X

use for each textbook. **Figure 10.1** summarizes common reading skills and strategies for different content areas and kinds of textbooks. Notice in Figure 10.1 that each of the content areas and subject matters involves working with two kinds of knowledge: declarative (factual) knowledge and procedural (process) knowledge.

You learned about *declarative knowledge* and *procedural knowledge* in Chapter 5. Declarative knowledge involves using elaborative rehearsal strategies to work with factual information in new and creative ways. Strategies may involve rearranging information in more meaningful ways; creating associations, mnemonics, and notes; and using recitation, visualization, and other working memory strategies to rehearse the information. Procedural knowledge involves using repetition of steps and processes in their original form. When working with procedural knowledge, your goals are to internalize the process so you can perform it more automatically, increase problem-solving speed and accuracy, and generalize the steps so you can apply them to solve new problems.

CONCEPT CHECK 10.1

Based on Figure 10.1, what reading skills are common to most textbooks in the various content areas? How do composition and literature textbooks differ from social science and science textbooks?

CHAPTER 10
REFLECTIVE WRITING 1

On separate paper, in a journal, or online in this textbook's College Success CourseMate, respond to the following questions.

1. What are the major differences you have noticed about the textbooks you are using this term for different courses? Which of your textbooks have the most difficult content for you to master? Explain why the content is difficult.

2. After completing Exercise 10.1 on page 308, the Reading in the Content Areas Inventory, what did you learn about the reading strategies you use for textbooks in different content areas? Discuss the results of the inventory.

Access Chapter 10 Reflective Writing 1 in your College Success CourseMate, accessed through *CengageBrain.com.*

Composition Textbooks

CONCEPT CHECK   10.2
What are examples of factual information and process information that you will need to learn in a composition course?

Composition courses encompass a wide range of writing skills. Becoming an accomplished writer requires foundation skills of proper grammar, punctuation, usage, sentence structures, and well-developed, expressive vocabulary. On a higher level, writers need to know how to write for specific audiences, specific purposes, and within specific contexts; organize information and use transitions effectively; use analytical reading and critical thinking skills; and, finally, be skilled in using effective library and online research skills.

As you examine your composition textbooks, reflect on responses for the following questions:

1. Why is a *customized reading system* often effective for composition textbooks?

2. What "student-friendly features" appear in your composition textbooks to help you have a positive experience and guide you through the process of developing your writing skills?

3. Does your composition textbook provide step-by-step explanations, clear examples, and ample exercises to use to practice developing your skills?

4. Which notetaking systems work most effectively for your composition textbook?

Literature Textbooks

Most colleges offer a variety of literature courses with different purposes, content, and *genres* (categories of literature). The writing in literature textbooks is designed to convey images, evoke emotions, develop themes and characters, and engage readers in the action of the plots. For many courses, online summaries and synopses, or *Cliff Notes* (a special series of handbooks to help you interpret literary works), are resource tools that you can use. Following are characteristics of the content in literature courses:

- *Survey courses* involve the study of major writers and literary works from a specific period of time, nationality, or culture. Other literature courses may focus on specific genres, such as short stories, poetry, drama and plays, mythology, essays, or novels.

- "Rhetorical modes" you may encounter in literature courses refer to different organizational patterns: description, narration, definition, examples, classification, comparison, contrast, cause, effect, analysis, and argumentation.

- Readers need to learn to identify, understand, and interpret imagery, symbolism, multiple meanings, and figurative speech. For example, *metaphors* compare one object to another *without* using the words *like* or *as. Similes* compare one object to another by *using* words such as *like* or *as. Personification* gives human qualities or capabilities to objects, ideas, or animals. *Alliteration* is the repetitive use of one letter sound at the beginning of a series of words. Finally, *hyperbole* is the use of exaggeration to create a specific effect.

Read Two or More Times

Grasping the plot, connecting with the action, understanding the unfolding of the plot, and responding emotionally to literature often involves reading the selection at least two times. For the *first reading*, read through the complete selection, unin-terrupted, to get an overview; do not stop to analyze or take notes. For the *second reading*, and possibly the *third reading*, use thorough reading strategies to analyze and interpret the key literary elements. Write comments next to important passages, take notes on paper, or create visual mappings or charts to show important details.

Create Literary Concept Maps

Different concept maps (visual mappings) or schemas for literature identify specific sets of conventions or standards, characteristics, and literary terminology used to think about and analyze the structure, content, and purpose of different kinds of literature. As you study different literary forms, you can create concept maps that show key elements to use in analyzing or discussing specific literary forms. For example, **Figure 10.2** shows a schema or concept map to memorize and use any time you need to analyze a short story. Concept maps to analyze poetry, drama, and novels will differ.

As you examine your literature textbooks, reflect on responses for the following questions:

1. Why is a *customized reading system* often effective for literature textbooks?

2. What genres or types of literary work appear in your textbook?

3. How does your textbook provide you with guidelines or skills to analyze the literature?

4. What special features that are unique to your textbook appear in the chapters?

5. What notetaking system would work most effectively for your literature textbook?

FIGURE 10.2   Key Elements in a Short Story

Theme: The main point, the subject, the meaning, or the purpose

Setting: The location and the time of the story

Characters: The main character and the minor characters

- **Physical characteristics:** age, gender, body type, facial features, race or ethnic group
- **Social characteristics:** family, occupation, economic status, religion, political point of view, cultural background
- **Psychological characteristics:** beliefs, motives, attitudes, personality, likes/dislikes, mental state of mind
- **Moral characteristics:** values, conflicts, beliefs, ethics

Plot: Sequence of events from beginning to a turning point, and finally to a climax or conclusion

Point of View: Who tells the story, first, second, or third person

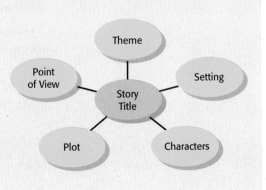

Social Science Textbooks

CONCEPT CHECK   10.3

What kinds of courses are categorized as "social science" courses? What are common characteristics or standard features found in many social science textbooks?

The term *social science* refers to a large category of academic disciplines that study societies and humanity from different perspectives. Social scientists pose theories, create models, and examine trends based on research, scientific methods, and observational studies. Following are common fields of social science:

Common Fields of Social Science		
Anthropology	Ethnic Studies	Library Science
Archaeology	Finance	Linguistics
Business	Foreign Policy	Marketing
Communications	Geography	Philosophy
Counseling	History	Political Science
Criminal Justice	Information Science	Psychology
Economics	International Relations	Public Administration
Education	Journalism	Sociology
Environmental Studies	Law	Women's Studies

Many topics in social science textbooks may be familiar to you because they often relate to personal experiences you have encountered. However, reading and studying social science textbooks involve moving beyond personal experiences and into an academic look at aspects of human relationships in society. The following characteristics reflect the content of social science textbooks:

- Each social science textbook has its own "style or personality." Take time to familiarize yourself with the chapter layout and common features.

- Social science textbooks are rich with graphic materials designed to create interest and curiosity, explain concepts and theories, and condense statistics and data into visual forms. Take time to examine, analyze, and interpret all graphic materials that appear in the chapters.

- Some textbooks use case studies to show how social scientists research topics, gather data, and form theories or create models. Read the case studies carefully and note the processes used and the outcomes or conclusions drawn.

- Some textbooks, such as history textbooks, use a narrative, storytelling approach to explain the unfolding of events influenced by specific individuals, groups, governments and cultural factors, such as economics, religion art, and social structures.

As you examine your social science textbooks, reflect on responses for the following questions:

1. Why is surveying an important process to use for a social science textbook chapter?

2. What special features appear throughout each chapter to help you learn the content?

3. Which reading systems and notetaking systems work effectively for your social science textbooks?

4. Why are reading, analyzing, and interpreting graphic materials important skills to use when reading social science textbooks?

Science Textbooks

The "hard sciences" or natural sciences include biology, chemistry, computer science, engineering, environmental science, geology, and physics. Science textbooks are densely written and often include complex scientific processes and reasoning, theories, predictions, explanations, evidence, patterns, numbers, symbols, formulas, graphic materials, and definitions. Because of the complexity of information in science textbooks and the critical thinking skills associated with the study of science, your reading goal for science textbooks is to read slowly, sometimes sentence by sentence, to comprehend, process, and integrate information. The study of the sciences also includes:

- **Inductive arguments:** observing experiments and analyzing evidence or proof to arrive at a conclusion
- **Hands-on content:** personally participating in laboratory demonstrations, experiments, or observations
- **Parts-to-whole concepts:** understanding how parts relate to whole concepts or frameworks
- **Conceptual understanding:** understanding scientific concepts in order to solve problems in the appropriate context
- **Problem-solving skills, analysis, and application:** knowing how to approach a problem, following steps to solve a problem, using problem analysis to explain the thinking processes used to reach a solution, and using steps for everyday applications
- **Use of the Scientific Method:** experimenting, hypothesizing, collecting and analying data, and drawing conclusions. See **Excerpt 7: The Scientific Method** in **Appendix D**.

As you examine your science textbooks, reflect on responses for the following questions:

1. Why will you often find yourself reading more slowly when reading to comprehend your science textbook?

2. How do the content and textbook difficulty level affect your time-management plans for reading and learning the content of your science textbook? Will you need to use the 3:1 ratio for studying your science textbook?

3. What special features in the chapters are unique to this textbook? How do they help you or guide you through the chapter?

4. What strategies are effective to use when you begin a new chapter that contains unfamiliar information and for which you lack background knowledge or experience?

5. What textbook reading and notetaking systems work most effectively for your science textbook?

Mathematics Textbooks

Studying mathematics is similar to studying a foreign language: it involves learning a language of symbols and formulas. Studying mathematics is also similar to studying fields of science: it involves learning and using formulas, equations, proofs, and problem-solving steps to reach solutions. The following points about studying math and using your math textbooks are important to remember:

- Studying mathematics involves learning a progression of concepts and skills, each building on previously learned information and setting a foundation for higher-level skills. Failure to learn lower-level skills often leads to partial and inaccurate learning and "skill gaps" that cause problems when you attempt to work with higher-level skills.

- Studying math involves using repetition of steps in their original form. To avoid using rote memory with limited understanding of concepts or steps, strive to explain concepts and steps in your own words to strengthen comprehension.

- When learning math concepts, you often need to direct your mind to switch back and forth between new information and information stored in long-term memory. The process is complex and involves many cognitive processes, so strive to maintain undivided attention as you work with your math textbooks and notes.

- Plan ample time to practice the essential repetition of problem-solving steps, recall prototypes (models), rework previous problems, increase problem-solving speed, and increase accuracy.

- Use effective time-management and study strategies: study math every day of the week; use the 3:1 ratio; survey chapters or topics before lectures so you are familiar with the chapter contents; schedule a study block shortly after class to begin working problem sets and refining or revising your notes; and utilize all available resources, such as math lab videos, online videos, tutors, tutorials, or other supplemental materials.

Study Examples and Memorize Prototypes

A *prototype* is a model of a specific type of math problem. By memorizing and understanding a prototype, you can then use it as a reminder of the steps to use to solve a new problem that is similar or of the same problem type. Prototypes often appear in chapters when a new type of math problem or equation with explanations and examples are introduced. Use the following steps when you encounter an important prototype:

A **prototype** is a model of a specific type of math problem.

1. Study the example carefully, step by step, until you can follow the steps and understand the logic behind the process.

2. Practice verbally explaining each step of the process to solve that type of problem; then express the same information using mathematical symbols and equations. Read the equation out loud.

3. Without referring to the text, rework the example problem and check your accuracy. Correct any mistakes immediately.

4. Memorize and use the prototype (model) on the problem sets that involve the same pattern or type of math problems.

5. Compare a new problem to the example problem (the prototype) to verify that both belong in the same category or type of problem. Then apply the problem-solving steps.

FIGURE 10.3 **Prototype: Dividing Fractions**

How to Calculate

To divide fractions, invert the second fraction and multiply.

$$\frac{a}{b} \div \frac{c}{d} = \frac{a}{b} \times \frac{d}{c} = \frac{a \times d}{b \times c}$$

For example,

$$\frac{2}{15} \div \frac{4}{9} = \frac{2}{15} \times \frac{9}{4} = \frac{\cancel{2}^{1}}{\cancel{15}_{5}} \times \frac{\cancel{9}^{3}}{\cancel{4}_{2}} = \frac{1 \times 3}{5 \times 2} = \frac{3}{10}$$

↑
invert second fraction and multiply

Example 1: Simplify and express the answer in reduced form.

1) $\frac{3}{7} \div \frac{9}{14}$

   a) Invert and multiply. $\frac{3}{7} \times \frac{14}{9}$

   b) Reduce. $\frac{\cancel{3}^{1}}{\cancel{7}_{1}} \times \frac{\cancel{14}^{2}}{\cancel{9}_{3}} = \frac{2}{3}$

From Helms *Mathematics for the Health Sciences* © 2013 Cengage Learning

Figure 10.3 shows a prototype to memorize and example problems for dividing fractions. Remember to rework these problems multiple times until the steps are automatic, accurate, and can be performed quickly.

Use a Customized Reading System

A *customized reading system* is a system you design for a specific textbook based on the author's suggestions and the chapter features. Your goal with this system is to establish a consistent routine to use to read and study each chapter. **Figure 8.8** on page 254 provides you with an example of a customized reading system for a mathematics textbook. As you examine your math textbook and consider creating a customized reading system, reflect on responses for the following questions:

1. In sequential order, what are the key features that appear in each chapter? How can you use these features to customize your reading approach?

2. When will you plan review times and which prototypes, problems, or examples will you rework to improve your speed and accuracy?

3. How is terminology defined in the chapters? What kind of notetaking system will you use for terminology and definitions?

4. Look ahead to Chapter 11 to learn about two-column and three-column notetaking systems (pages 355–360). What would be the benefits of adding one of these notetaking systems to the steps in your customized reading system?

EXERCISE 10.1

Reading in the Content Areas Inventory

Go to Chapter 10 Topics In-Depth, Exercise 10.1: Reading in the Content Areas Inventory in your College Success CourseMate. Complete the inventory to evaluate the effectiveness of the reading strategies you use for composition, literature, social science, science, and mathematics textbooks.

 Access Chapter 10 Topics In-Depth: Exercise 10.1 Reading in the Content Areas Inventory in your College Success CourseMate, accessed through *CengageBrain.com*.

CHECK POINT 10.1   Answers appear on page B4.

True or False? See Test-Taking Strategies 1–9 in Appendix A.

_____ 1. You can identify and use prototypes to recall steps of a process in composition, math, and science textbooks.

_____ 2. Factual knowledge is also called declarative knowledge; elaborative rehearsal strategies are recommended for learning factual knowledge.

_____ 3. Literature textbooks are the only type of textbook that use figurative language.

_____ 4. You can strengthen your comprehension skills by acquiring background knowledge about an unfamiliar topic before you begin reading the textbook.

 Access Chapter 10 Practice Quiz 1 in your College Success CourseMate, accessed through *CengageBrain.com*.

Organizational Patterns

2 *Define and discuss the seven organizational patterns used to organize details in paragraphs.*

> **Organizational patterns** are paragraph patterns that writers use to present details in a logical, meaningful order.

Organizational patterns are paragraph patterns that writers use to present details in a logical, meaningful order. Understanding organizational patterns helps you unlock the meaning of what you read, identify relationships among the details within a paragraph, and follow the internal logic and natural progression of information. Paragraphs may exhibit characteristics of more than one organizational pattern, but one dominant pattern will reflect the purpose of the paragraph. In the following sections, you will learn more about paragraph patterns, clue words that signal each type of paragraph pattern, diagram formats to use to convert information into visual forms, and an example paragraph for each of the following organizational patterns:

chronological pattern	definition pattern
process pattern	examples pattern
comparison-contrast pattern	cause-effect (causal) pattern
whole-and-parts pattern	

The Chronological Pattern

The *chronological pattern* presents details in a logical time sequence. When working with the chronological order of events, the sequence of events from first, to second, to third, etc., is clear. The clue words help identify the progression of events sequentially. **Study the chronological pattern chart, read and annotate the chronological paragraph, and create a diagram that shows the important details in the paragraph.**

> The **chronological pattern** presents details in a logical time sequence.

Chronological Pattern	Clue Words	Diagram for This Pattern
• Details are presented in a logical time sequence: *chronological order*. • Details happen in a specific, fixed order to reach a conclusion or an ending. • This pattern is often used to tell a story (a narrative) or explain a sequence of events.	when then before next after first second finally	1. → 2. → 3. → 4. → **Conclusion or Ending**

© Cengage Learning

A Chronological Paragraph Pattern: The Great Tsunami of 2004

"As many as 2 million people were made homeless by the disaster. An unprecedented international relief effort, designed to feed and house these refugees and to contain the spread of epidemic diseases, began within hours. In many cases, it was clear that recovery efforts were profoundly successful, sometimes in unexpected ways. In India's Tamil Nadu State, for example, there were new roads, housing and utilities, and jobs training.... In the tsunami's wake, the social fabric was transformed."

Source: Hobbs. *Fundamentals of World Regional Geography,* 3e, p. 254–255.

> **CONCEPT CHECK** **10.6**
>
> *How are details organized in a chronological pattern? What words signal a chronological pattern in a paragraph?*

The Process Pattern

The *process pattern* presents a specific procedure or order of steps to use to do, create, repair, or solve problems. The steps are sequential, but the final box in the diagram shows how this pattern differs from the chronological pattern: the final box is an end product or solution, not a conclusion or an ending. **Study the process pattern chart, read and annotate the process paragraph, and create a diagram that shows the important details in the paragraph.**

> The **process pattern** presents a specific procedure or order of steps to use to do, create, repair, or solve problems.

Process Pattern	Clue Words	Diagram for This Pattern
• Details explain a procedure or how something works. • Details may provide directions to complete a specific series of steps to do, create, repair, or solve something. • Steps must be done in chronological order. • Outcome is a finished product or a solution. • Science, social science, and mathematics textbooks use this pattern frequently.	steps process procedure first second before after when as soon as next finally outcome result	1. → 2. → 3. → 4. → **End Product or Solution**

© Cengage Learning

Process Paragraph Pattern: Life of a Star

"The life of a star begins when a diffused area of a spinning nebula begins to shrink and heat up under the influence of its own weak gravity. Gradually, the cloudlike sphere flattens and condenses at the center into a knot of gases called a **protostar** (*protos, "first"*). The original diameter of the protostar may be many times the diameter of our solar system, but gravitational energy causes it to contract, and the compression increases its internal temperature. When the protostar reaches a temperature of about 10 million degrees Celsius (18 million degrees Fahrenheit), nuclear fusion begins. That is, hydrogen atoms begin to fuse to form helium, the process that liberates even more energy. This rapid release of energy, which marks the transition from *protostar* to *star*, stops the young star's shrinkage."

Source: Garrison. *Oceanography: An Invitation to Marine Science,* 8e, p. 11.

The Comparison-Contrast Pattern

The *comparison-contrast pattern* shows similarities and differences between two or more subjects. To work with this pattern, begin by identifying two or more different topics or subjects. Then identify categories of information used to show likenesses or differences between the subjects. Categories may be *characteristics, traits, purpose, function, duration, location,* or specific labels such as *language, religion, education, economy, imports, exports,* etc. **Study the comparison-contrast pattern chart, read and annotate the details in the paragraph, and create a diagram that shows the important details.**

The **comparison-contrast pattern** shows similarities and differences between two or more subjects.

CONCEPT CHECK **10.7**

How do process patterns differ from comparison-contrast patterns? What are common clue words that signal these paragraph patterns?

Comparison or Contrast Pattern	Clue Words	Diagram for This Pattern		
• Comparison shows likenesses and/or differences between two or more objects or events (the subjects). • Contrast shows only differences between two or more objects or events. • Categories label the columns.	also similarly likewise but in contrast on the other hand however although while		**Characteristic**	**Purpose**	**Duration**
		Subject A			
		Subject B			

© Cengage Learning 2015

Comparison-Contrast Paragraph Pattern: New Media

"The timeliness of feedback depends on whether we use synchronous or asynchronous media. **Synchronous media** allow for an instantaneous reply from another communicator. For instance, when two people are online using instant messaging at the same time, the communication is synchronous. Each communicator can ask questions, get instant feedback, and immediately confirm that his messages are received and understood. Conversely, **asynchronous media** enable communication and collaboration outside the constraints of time and place. For example, email is asynchronous when you send a message and have to wait for a response because, say, the receiver is not at her desk or is not responding to email at that time. When you rely on asynchronous media, feedback may not be as timely as it would be if you used face-to-face communication."

Source: Waldeck, Kearney, Plax. *Business & Professional Communication in a Digital Age,* p. 127.

The Whole-and-Parts Pattern

The *whole-and-parts pattern* shows the individual parts, components, or entities that together create a whole object, concept, or theory. Information in a paragraph that can be represented in a pie chart or a diagram with labeled parts frequently uses the whole-and-parts pattern. **Study the whole-and-parts pattern chart, read and annotate the details in the paragraph, and create a diagram that shows the important details.**

> The **whole-and-parts pattern** shows the individual parts, components, or entities that together create a whole object, concept, or theory.

Whole-and-Parts Pattern	Clue Words	Various Diagrams for This Pattern
• The individual parts, components, or entities create the whole object, concept, or theory. • The details identify, define, and explain each individual part of the whole item. • Diagrams may include any *whole item* with its *parts* clearly identified and labeled. • Science and social science textbooks use this pattern frequently.	parts X number of parts categories subsystems sections left right front back consists of is composed of together make	

Whole-and-Parts Paragraph Pattern: United Kingdom

"The islands of Great Britain and Ireland, off the northwestern coast of Europe, are known as the British Isles. They are home to the Republic of Ireland, with its capital at Dublin, and the much larger United Kingdom of Great Britain and Northern Ireland (often referred to simply as "Britain"), with its capital at London. The United Kingdom is made up of the entire island of Great Britain, with its political units of England, Scotland, and Wales; the northeastern corner of Ireland, known as Northern Ireland; and most of the smaller outlying islands."

Source: Hobbs. *Fundamentals of World Regional Geography,* 3e, p. 92.

The Definition Pattern

The **definition pattern** uses explanations, characteristics, examples, analogies, and negations to define a term.

The *definition pattern* uses explanations, characteristics, examples, analogies, and negations to define a term. In some paragraphs, one word is the key term that the entire paragraph defines, but additional words may also appear in special print and be defined. **Study the definition pattern chart, read and annotate the details in the paragraph, and create a diagram that shows the important details.**

Definition Pattern	Clue Words	Diagram for This Pattern
• Information throughout the paragraph defines a specific term. • Explanations, characteristics, analogies, examples, and negations may be used to define a term. • The term the paragraph defines often appears in bold print in the first sentence.	means is/are is defined as can be considered referred to as	

© Cengage Learning

Definition Paragraph Pattern: Nonverbal Messages

"When we attempt to communicate with another person, we use both verbal and nonverbal communication. **Nonverbal messages** are "messages without words" or "silent messages." These are the messages (other than spoken or written words) we communicate through facial expression, voice tone, gestures, appearance, posture, and other nonverbal means. Research indicates that our nonverbal messages have much more impact than verbal messages. In fact, some researchers suggest that as much as 75 percent of our communication is nonverbal. . . ."

Source: Reece, Brandt, Howie. *Effective Human Relations,* 11e, p. 31.

The Examples Pattern

The **examples pattern** uses examples to expand a reader's understanding of a term, a concept, or a theory.

The *examples pattern* uses examples to expand a reader's understanding of a term, a concept, or a theory. In some paragraphs, the clue words *for example* or *another example* are used when multiple examples develop the topic or concept. In other paragraphs, the entire paragraph is one extended example designed to strengthen your understanding of the concept. **Study the examples pattern chart, read and annotate the details in the paragraph, and create a diagram that shows the important details.**

CONCEPT CHECK   **10.8**

What kind of details can you use in a definition paragraph? What kind of details can you use in an examples paragraph?

Examples Pattern	Clue Words	Diagram for This Pattern
• An idea, term, or theory is expanded through the use of examples. • One extended example may be used throughout the paragraph, or multiple examples may be used.	for example another example an illustration of this	

© Cengage Learning

Examples Paragraph Pattern: Diversity in Today's Work Force

"Diversity has become a prominent characteristic of today's work force. A number of trends have contributed to greater work force diversity. Throughout the past two decades, participation in the labor force by Asian Americans, African Americans, and Hispanics has increased; labor force participation by adult women has risen to a record 60 percent; the employment door for people with physical or mental impairments has opened wider; and larger numbers of young workers are working with members of the expanding 50-plus age group. Within this heterogeneous work force, we will find a multitude of values, expectations, and work habits."

Source: Reece, Brandt, Howie. *Effective Human Relations,* 11e, p. 7.

The Cause-Effect (Causal) Pattern

The *cause-effect pattern*, also known as the *causal pattern*, shows the relationship between two or more items by indicating which items or actions cause specific effects. One cause may produce several effects, or several causes may result in one effect. Notice the two different diagrams you can use based on the number of causes or the number of effects. **Study the cause-effect pattern chart, read and annotate the details in the paragraph, and create a diagram that shows the important details.**

The **cause-effect pattern**, also known as the *causal pattern*, shows the relationship between two or more items by indicating which items or actions cause specific effects.

Cause-Effect Pattern	Clue Words	Diagram for This Pattern
• Show the relationship between two items in which one item causes the other item to happen. • One cause may have more than one effect or outcome. • Several causes may produce one effect or outcome.	because since so therefore caused by result in	CAUSE → Effect, Effect, Effect Cause, Cause, Cause → EFFECT

© Cengage Learning

Cause-Effect Paragraph Pattern: Fight or Flight Syndrome

"Our natural response to stress is as old as life itself—adapted by almost all species as a means of coping with threats to survival. When faced with an unexpected or possibly threatening situation, human beings—like animals—instinctively react with a **fight or flight syndrome**: Adrenaline pours into the bloodstream, heart rate and blood pressure increase, breathing accelerates, and muscles tighten. The body is poised to fight or run. Ironically, the same instincts that helped our ancestors survive are the ones causing us physical and mental health problems today."

Source: Reece, Brandt, Howie. *Effective Human Relations,* 11e, p. 305.

Organizational Patterns

Understanding organizational patterns helps you unlock the meaning of paragraphs and strengthen comprehension. Go to Exercise 10.2 in Appendix C, page C22, for paragraphs to use to continue to develop your ability to analyze, annotate, and diagram different organizational patterns. Your instructor will provide you with specific directions for working with these paragraphs and indicate if this is an exercise to complete on your own, in a group, or in a class discussion.

CHECK POINT 10.2

Answers appear on page B4.

True or False? See Test-Taking Strategies 1–9 in Appendix A.

_____ 1. The comparison-contrast pattern, the cause-effect pattern, and the whole-and-parts pattern show relationships between two or more items or subjects.

_____ 2. All paragraphs exhibit characteristics of each of the organizational patterns, but only one pattern is dominant.

_____ 3. Writers use organizational patterns to show an internal logic for the order of details.

_____ 4. *When, before, steps, in contrast, means, for example, because,* and *subsystems* are clue words that help identify the kind of organizational pattern used in paragraphs.

 Access Chapter 10 Practice Quiz 2 in your College Success CourseMate, accessed through *CengageBrain.com.*

Textbook Case Studies

DIRECTIONS:

1. Read each case study carefully. Respond to the question at the end of each case study by using *specific* strategies discussed in this chapter. Answer in complete sentences.

2. Write your responses on paper or online in this textbook's College Success CourseMate, Textbook Case Studies. You will be able to print your online response or e-mail it to your instructor.

CASE STUDY 1: Cecilia does not have problems reading the words in her textbook, but she often has problems figuring out what details are important and understanding how the details are organized. She usually just rereads the chapter one or two times more.

What strategies will help Cecilia become a more active reader with improved comprehension?

CASE STUDY 2: Several of Jeremy's "get-by" reading strategies that he acquired in high school are proving to be ineffective for his college textbooks. His current strategies involve looking through a chapter, reading the notes in the margins, examining graphs and charts, and reading the summary. He then reads only the sections of information that appear to have new or unfamiliar information. Jeremy visited the tutoring center to learn more effective strategies for his geology textbook. If you were the tutor Jeremy visited, what strategies would you recommend he begin using for his geology textbook?

 Access Chapter 10 Textbook Case Studies in your College Success CourseMate, accessed through *CengageBrain.com.*

Graphic Materials

(3) *Explain and use strategies to read and interpret six kinds of graphic materials.*

Graphic materials are printed representations that convert printed or verbal information into a visual format, such as drawings, charts, or pictures. Graphic materials include pictures, illustrations, diagrams, pie charts, flow charts, tables, bar graphs, and line graphs. Many textbooks, especially science, social science, and mathematics textbooks, use graphic materials to convey important information about data, statistics, trends, and relationships. A picture is worth a thousand words, so learning how to read and interpret graphic materials is essential.

Many graphic materials include captions and legends to help you interpret the information. A *caption* is a short explanation or description that accompanies a graphic. A *legend* defines values for the symbols used in the graphic. Captions and legends provide you with essential information for understanding and interpreting graphic materials, so read them carefully.

To gain the greatest benefits from graphic materials, use the eight Essential Strategies for Working with Graphic Materials in **Figure 10.4**.

Andresr/Shutterstock.com

Why are bar graphs, diagrams, flow charts, and other kinds of graphic materials important to analyze and understand? How should you study and review graphic materials?

Graphic materials are printed representations that convert printed or verbal information into a visual format, such as drawings, charts, or pictures.

A **caption** is a short explanation or description that accompanies a graphic.

A **legend** defines values for the symbols used in the graphic.

CONCEPT CHECK 10.9
In addition to visual appeal, what other purposes do graphic materials serve? What essential strategies can you use to learn from graphic materials?

FIGURE 10.4   Essential Strategies for Graphic Materials

- **Carefully read the features in the graphic.** Read the titles, captions, legends, and labels that appear with graphic materials.
- **Examine the details carefully.** Look at sizes, colors, spatial positions, likenesses and differences, relationships, patterns, and trends.
- **Verbalize or "string ideas together."** Talk to yourself about the information. Use some of your own words to explain the information and the relationships you see.
- **Visualize the graphic.** Create a strong visual image or impression of the basic features of the graphic. Practice using this as a retrieval cue to recall and rehearse information.
- **Ask yourself questions about the content.** Create questions about specific parts of the graphic materials, questions that compare two or more items, and questions that focus on the cause-effect relationships, trends, and patterns.
- **Copy important graphic materials into your notes.** Unless the graphic materials are too complex, include them in your notes. Color-code the parts of the graphics and add labels and captions. For more complex graphics, list important points you learned from the graphic and list textbook page references for later review.
- **Expand the graphic materials in your notes.** Add your own reminders, details, or explanations to the graphics you copied into your notes.
- **Write a short summary under the graphics in your textbook or in your notes.**

© Cengage Learning

The circle of thought begins as our sensory systems take in information from the world. Our perceptual system describes and elaborates this information, which is represented in the brain in ways that allow us to make decisions, formulate plans, and guide our actions. As those actions change our world, we receive new information—and the circle of thought begins again.

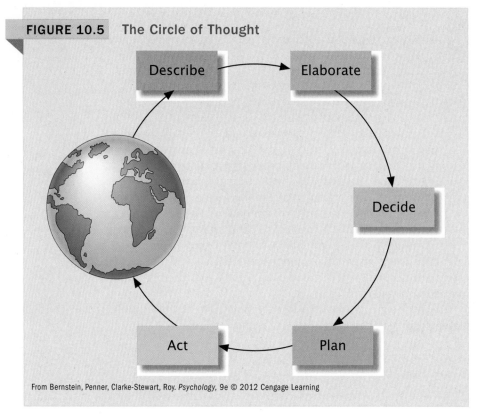

FIGURE 10.5   The Circle of Thought

From Bernstein, Penner, Clarke-Stewart, Roy. *Psychology*, 9e © 2012 Cengage Learning

Photographs, Illustrations, and Diagrams

Photographs, illustrations, and *diagrams,* which include cartoons, sketches, and drawings, provide background information and clarify concepts. In addition to adding visual appeal, graphic materials are informative and provide visual images to memorize and use as retrieval cues to recall information from long-term memory. **After carefully examining the diagram in Figure 10.5, answer the following questions or complete the following directions:**

1. What did you learn from the title and the labeled boxes in the diagram? How did the labeled boxes and the arrows help clarify the diagram?

2. Verbalize. Read the labeled boxes out loud while looking at the diagram.

3. Stare at the diagram to create a visual impression in memory. Use the Look-Away Technique. Were you able to visualize the diagram and recall important details?

4. Do the essential strategies in Figure 10.4 work to understand and remember this diagram? Explain.

Pie Charts

Pie charts, also called *circle graphs*, show a whole unit (100 percent) divided into individually labeled parts or sectors. Pie charts are based on a whole-to-parts

Pie charts, also called *circle graphs*, show a whole unit (100 percent) divided into individually labeled parts or sectors.

organizational pattern. Some pie charts show the size of each sector, usually presented as percentages of the whole (100 percent), making comparison of sectors easier and more accurate. With other pie charts, you may need to estimate the percentage represented by each sector of the chart if the size differences are important. After examining the basic parts of a pie chart, compare and contrast sectors, make generalizations about the categories of information, ponder relationships between segments, and pose questions about the information. Refer to the paragraphs in the textbook that explain the pie chart. Jot down or attach key words to the pie chart to clarify or summarize details learned in the paragraphs. **After carefully examining the pie chart in Figure 10.6, answer the following questions or complete the following directions:**

1. Which sector is the largest and which is the smallest? Does this surprise you? Why or why not?

2. Is the combined percentage of religious affiliations in the four smallest sectors larger or smaller than the sector for those who claim no religious affiliation?

3. What religious affiliations are grouped in the category of "Other" affiliations?

4. Create two questions based on the content of this pie chart.

5. What generalizations can you make based on this pie chart and its sectors?

CONCEPT CHECK   10.10
Discuss the way pie charts and flow charts organize information. What reading strategies work effectively to understand both kinds of visual graphics?

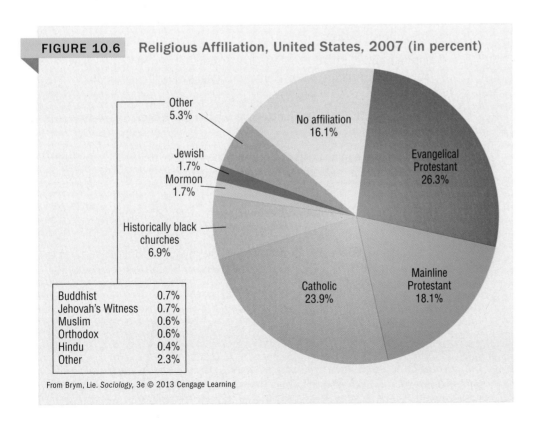

FIGURE 10.6   **Religious Affiliation, United States, 2007 (in percent)**

From Brym, Lie. *Sociology*, 3e © 2013 Cengage Learning

The antecedents are the stressful features of the work environment that cause burnout. The three components of the burnout syndrome appear in the center of the diagram. The results of burnout are listed on the right.

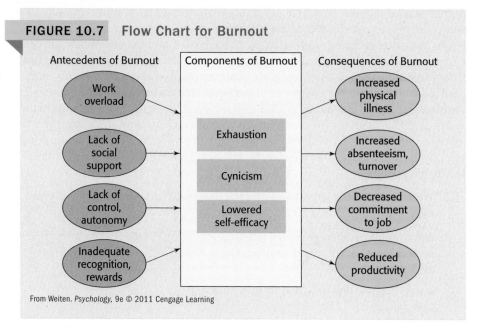

FIGURE 10.7   Flow Chart for Burnout

From Weiten. *Psychology*, 9e © 2011 Cengage Learning

Flow charts, also called *organizational charts*, show levels of organization or a directional flow of information from one topic or level to another.

Flow Charts

Flow charts, also called *organizational charts*, show levels of organization or a directional flow of information from one topic or level to another. To remember information in flow charts, use the essential strategies in Figure 10.4. **Examine the details and flow of information in Figure 10.7. Answer the following questions or complete the following directions:**

1. What important information did you learn from the caption for the chart, the labels on the sections of the chart, and by following the arrows in the flow chart?

2. While looking at the chart, verbalize or string ideas together to explain the chart.

3. Visualize the three main parts of the chart: the heading for the items on the left, the heading for the items in the middle, and the heading for the items on the right.

4. Using the direction shown by the arrows, recite information about each part of the chart.

5. Personalize and reflect on this information. Do you agree with the concepts in the flow chart? Have you or any of your family or friends experienced this sequence of events?

6. Write a short summary about the important information to remember.

Tables

Tables, also called *comparison charts*, *grids*, or *matrixes*, use *columns* and *rows* to organize information on various topics or to show data to use to solve problems.

Tables, also called *comparison charts*, *grids*, or *matrixes*, use *columns* and *rows* to organize information on various topics or to show data to use to solve problems. Tables require careful reading as they often contain a considerable amount of data

FIGURE 10.8 The 10 Leading States in U.S. Nonfuel Mineral Production for 2009

State	$	Most Important Commodities in Order of Value
1. Nevada	5,510,000,000	Gold, copper, sand and gravel, lime, stone
2. Arizona	5,420,000,000	Copper, molybdenum, sand and gravel, cement, stone
3. Utah	4,000,000,000	Copper, molybdenum, gold, magnesium metal, potash
4. California	3,600,000,000	Sand and gravel, cement, boron minerals, stone, gold
5. Texas	2,900,000,000	Cement, stone, sand and gravel, salt
6. Alaska	2,480,000,000	Zinc, gold, lead, silver, sand and gravel
7. Florida	2,170,000,000	Phosphate rock, stone, cement, sand and gravel
8. Colorado	1,960,000,000	Molybdenum, sand and gravel, gold, cement, stone
9. Wyoming	1,940,000,000	Soda ash, clays, helium, sand and gravel, cement
10. Missouri	1,800,000,000	Stone, cement, lead, lime, sand and gravel
All States	57,100,000,000*	

*The total nonfuel mineral production for 2009 was 22% less than it was for 2008.

From Monroe, Wicander. *The Changing Earth: Exploring Geology and Evolution*, 6e © 2011 Cengage Learning

in the boxes (cells) of the chart. When tables appear without lines that divide columns and rows, you can add those lines to the table if doing so will help you see the information more clearly. **After examining the table in Figure 10.8, answer the following questions or complete the following directions:**

1. The *skeleton* of a table consists of the title, the labels at the top of the columns, and the subjects that label the rows. While looking at the table, verbalize the skeleton of Figure 10.8.

2. What nonfuel minerals are important commodities in Nevada, but not in Alaska? Which commodity in Nevada is the most important in terms of value?

3. In dollar value, what was the difference between the highest and the lowest of nonfuel mineral production income in 2009?

4. Was nonfuel mineral production higher or lower in 2008? How do you know this?

Bar Graphs

Bar graphs use vertical or horizontal bars to show frequency of occurrence for different subjects or data being graphed and to show trends. Bar graphs frequently appear in many textbooks, so knowing how to read and interpret the graphs is important. Begin by reading the title and the caption. Then read the label that appears on the *horizontal line*, called the *x axis*, and on the *vertical line*, called the *y axis*. Notice that one axis identifies the data that is being graphed while the other axis shows the frequency of an occurrence or event, which may be shown in percentages, quantities, or a unit of measurement. Finally, use the height (or the length) of the bars to obtain information about each bar and to compare information. As you encounter bar graphs in your textbooks, spend ample time analyzing the chart as a variety of

CONCEPT CHECK 10.11
Where would you find each of the following on a table graphic: skeleton, columns, rows, and cells? What kind of information appears in each?

Bar graphs use vertical or horizontal bars to show frequency of occurrence for different subjects or data being graphed and to show trends.

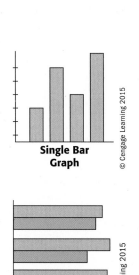

Single Bar Graph

© Cengage Learning 2015

Double Bar Graph: Horizontal

© Cengage Learning 2015

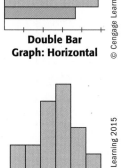

60 65 70 75 80 85 90

Histogram

© Cengage Learning 2015

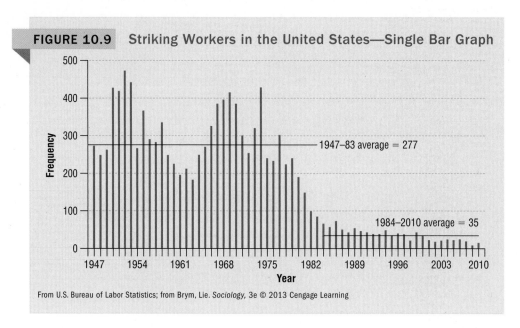

FIGURE 10.9   Striking Workers in the United States—Single Bar Graph

1947–83 average = 277

1984–2010 average = 35

From U.S. Bureau of Labor Statistics; from Brym, Lie. *Sociology*, 3e © 2013 Cengage Learning

A **histogram** is a bar graph that shows a *range of values* for each bar on the *x* axis, or the base of the chart.

formats are used to present information. Following are several kinds of bar graphs you will encounter:

- **Single bar graph:** One set of bars shows the data being graphed and the frequency or occurrence of an event.
- **Double bar graph:** Two sets of bars show related data to compare or contrast. The *legend* for a double bar graph defines the colors or distinguishing patterns of each of the bars.
- **Vertical** and **horizontal bar graphs:** The bars may be displayed as vertical bars (rising from the bottom of the chart) or horizontal bars extending from the left side of the graph.
- **Histograms:** A *histogram* is a bar graph that shows a *range of values* for each bar on the *x* axis, or the base of the chart.

After carefully examining the bar graph in Figure 10.9, answer the following questions or complete the following directions:

1. What is the title or topic of this bar graph? What does the *x* axis show? What frequency does the *y* axis show?

2. Which year had the most strikes with more than 1,000 workers in the United States? Which year had the fewest strikes? What might be the reason for the difference between the numbers of strikes during those two years?

3. From 1947 to 2010, how many years had more than 300 strikes involving 1,000 workers or more?

4. What trends do you see in this graph? Summarize or make generalizations based on the information in this graph.

CONCEPT CHECK   **10.12**

How do bar graphs differ from line graphs? What do bar graphs and line graphs have in common? Which type of graph may show trends and relationships?

Line Graphs

Line graphs, also called *linear graphs*, plot points on a coordinate grid or graph to form one continuous line to show trends and compare data. When you encounter line graphs, carefully read the *horizontal axis* and the *vertical axis*, and then look for trends as well as increases, decreases, and changes in the occurrence of a particular action or event. Following are common kinds of line graphs you will encounter in your textbooks:

- **Single line graphs:** One line plots data and shows trends. After examining the vertical and horizontal axes, look for patterns and trends. Ask yourself questions that compare and contrast different points on the line graph.

- **Double line graphs:** Double line graphs show two line graphs within one chart. Double line graphs are used to compare trends and patterns between the two subjects. As with double bar graphs, legends may be used to define line colors or line patterns used in the graph. Carefully examine the information, ask questions about the different subjects at different points on the graph, and conclude or summarize the information.

  After examining the double line graph in Figure 10.10, answer the following questions or complete the following directions:

  1. What important features appear in this double line graph? How do the title and the caption help you understand this chart?

  2. When does the largest gap in retention occur between massed practice and spaced practice? What is the percentage difference? What implications does this have for learning?

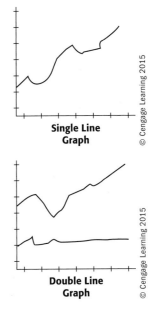

> **Line graphs**, also called *linear graphs*, plot points on a coordinate grid or graph to form one continuous line to show trends and compare data.

Single Line Graph

© Cengage Learning 2015

Double Line Graph

© Cengage Learning 2015

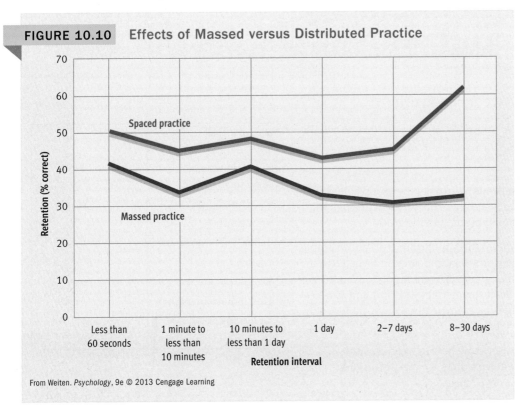

FIGURE 10.10   Effects of Massed versus Distributed Practice

Retention (% correct) (vertical axis, 0 to 70)

Spaced practice

Massed practice

Retention interval (horizontal axis): Less than 60 seconds · 1 minute to less than 10 minutes · 10 minutes to less than 1 day · 1 day · 2–7 days · 8–30 days

From Weiten. *Psychology*, 9e © 2013 Cengage Learning

3. After one day from the learning experience, how much original information does a person *remember* if spaced practice was used? How much information is *lost* after one day from the learning experience if massed practice was used?

4. Verbalize this chart. Explain out loud what this chart depicts.

5. Are all of the essential strategies in Figure 10.4 applicable to this line graph? Explain why or why not.

CHECK POINT 10.3

Answers appear on page B4.

True or False? See Test-Taking Strategies 1–9 in Appendix A.

_____ 1. In most cases, you can interpret and understand graphic materials by reading the caption and briefly glancing at the details.

_____ 2. "Stringing ideas together" is a strategy that involves using your own words to explain the information and the relationships between data in graphic materials.

_____ 3. Bar graphs and line graphs, but not histograms, show data and trends.

_____ 4. Because graphic materials effectively condense printed information into visual forms, students should always copy the illustrations, graphs, or charts into their notes.

Access Chapter 10 Practice Quiz 3 in your College Success CourseMate, accessed through *CengageBrain.com*.

GROUP PROCESSING

A Collaborative Learning Activity

Form groups of three or four students. Then complete the following directions.

DIRECTIONS:

1. Each student needs to bring to the group at least one textbook used in another course. Skim through the various textbooks brought to the group.

2. From the textbooks in your group, find one example of each of the kinds of graphic materials listed in the chart, or find as many different kinds of examples as possible in the designated time period. Indicate on the chart the name of the textbook that shows each type of example.

3. Spend time discussing how to interpret and understand each graphic. You may be asked to share your examples with the class.

Kind of Graphic	Textbooks
Photographs, illustrations, and diagrams:	
Pie chart:	
Flow chart:	
Table:	
Histogram:	
Double bar graph:	
Horizontal bar graph:	
Single line graph:	
Double line graph:	

© Cengage Learning

Visual Notetaking Systems

4 *Explain and demonstrate how to create and study from three kinds of visual notes: visual mappings, hierarchies, and comparison charts.*

Visual notes are a form of notetaking that organizes information into diagrams or charts that use colors, pictures, and shapes to help imprint information into visual memory. Visual notes, also called *graphic organizers*, include visual mappings (also called *concept maps*), hierarchies, and comparison charts. Visual notes are effective because they do the following:

- Utilize memory strategies, involve multisensory skills, and personalize information
- Utilize creative use of colors, pictures, symbols, and graphic formats to create strong visual images, impressions, associations, and retrieval cues, all of which improve recall
- Organize and rearrange information in meaningful ways to be used as reflect activities, study tools, and lecture and textbook notes
- Promote effective recitation, lead to elaborative rehearsal, and increase concentration

As you begin experimenting with the use of visual notes, you will find that there are basic guidelines to use, but there are few fixed rules because visual notetaking is a creative process, and you may wish to display or arrange information in ways that are unique to you. Realize, however, that you cannot create effective visual notes if you do not understand the information you are reading. Visual notes are based on identifying the three basic levels of information and the relationship each has to the other: topics or subjects; main ideas, headings, or categories; and important, significant supporting details.

To receive the greatest benefit from your visual notes, you need to spend time studying, visually memorizing, and reciting from your notes. **Figure 10.11** summarizes the five Essential Strategies for Studying Visual Notes.

> **Visual notes** are a form of notetaking that organizes information into diagrams or charts that use colors, pictures, and shapes to help imprint information into visual memory.

CONCEPT CHECK 10.13

What is the value of knowing how to create and use visual notes? What are different kinds of visual notes you can use that show topics, main ideas, and important supporting details?

FIGURE 10.11 Essential Strategies for Studying Visual Notes

- **Imprint the skeleton:** Imprint the basic structure (the skeleton) in your visual memory. Look intently (stare) at the first two levels of information. Carve a mental image of the skeleton into your memory. Do *not* focus your attention on the lower-level details.

- **Visualize:** Visualize the skeleton of your notes. Close your eyes, look away, or *look up and to the left* to recall the image. Practice visualizing or "seeing" the words, the shapes, and the colors in your visual notes. Look back at your notes to check your accuracy.

- **Recite:** Recite and explain the topic and the main headings. Without looking at your visual notes, name the first two levels of information. Then begin reciting, explaining in complete sentences, all that you remember about each heading. Look back at your notes to check your accuracy.

- **Reflect:** Use reflect activities for elaborative rehearsal. Following are three suggestions:

  1. Without referring to your notes, redraw the skeleton. Label each part.

  2. Record yourself reciting information about each part of your visual notes.

  3. Convert the information into a written summary, developing one paragraph for each heading and its details.

- **Review:** Use immediate and ongoing review. Mentally rehearse, visualize, and recite your visual notes frequently to keep the image sharp and the content fresh in your memory and readily accessible.

Visual Mappings

Visual mappings are diagrams that place the topic in the center of a diagram with main ideas branching off the center, followed by details branching off the main ideas. Visual mappings are also called *cognitive maps, mind maps,* and *clusters.* You can use visual mappings to show the headings, subheadings, and important details in a chapter or to show levels of information in a paragraph. You can also use visual mappings to show details for a topic that appeared in several different chapters and lectures. As you recall, you can also use visual mappings to create summary notes to review for a test or to brainstorm ideas to include in an essay, a paper, or a speech.

Level-One Information: The Topic

Level-one information refers to the subject or the topic of visual notes. The topic may be the title of a chapter, the name of a lecture, or a specific subject. Once you have identified your topic, place it inside a geometric shape or inside a picture shape in the center of the page.

Level-Two Information: Main Ideas or Headings

Level-two information refers to the main ideas associated with or linked to the specific topic. If you are creating a visual mapping for a textbook chapter, use the headings in the chapter for level-two information. The examples of visual mappings for SQ4R and Cornell Notes in **Figure 10.12** show steps of the SQ4R process and steps of the Cornell Notetaking System as the level-two information. Level-one and level-two information show the *skeleton* of the visual mapping; take time to visually memorize this skeleton. The following guidelines help you develop level-two information on your visual mapping:

- **Create your own headings.** In addition to the headings indicated in the printed materials, you can add headings, such as "Introduction" or "Summary," or any other special heading to show a specific chart, diagram, or items that you want to include on the visual mapping.

FIGURE 10.12　**Visual Mappings**

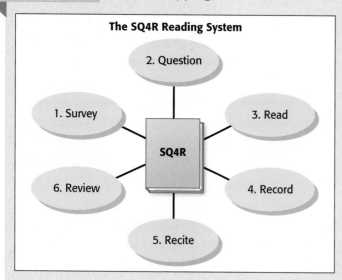

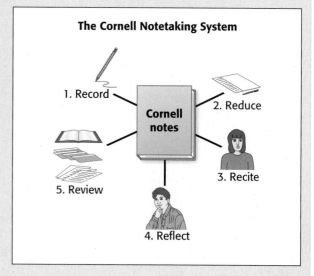

© Cengage Learning 2015

- **Use effective spacing.** Visually appealing and uncluttered mappings are easier to visualize and memorize. Before you begin adding the level-two information, count the number of main ideas to decide how to space them evenly around the page. Place them relatively close to the topic so you will have room to add level-three details later.

- **Use clockwise organization.** The most common organization for level-two information is clockwise, beginning at the eleven o'clock position. If there is a definite sequence to the information, such as steps that you must learn in order, you may add numbers to the lines that extend from the topic or add numbers inside the borders of level-two information.

- **Use connectors.** Draw a line from the topic in the center to each main idea to connect the level-two subtopics to the main topic.

- **Add borders, shapes, or pictures.** To make the main ideas or categories stand out, you can place a border or shape around each item or add a picture next to each main idea.

- **Use colors.** Colors strengthen visual memory and create a stronger visual impression. Experiment with the use of colors: shade in the main ideas, use different colors for different levels of information, or add colors to pictures used as retrieval cues.

Level-Three Information: Supporting Details

Level-three information refers to the major supporting details that explain, support, or prove the main idea. These details are key words that work as retrieval cues to trigger recall of information. Later, when you study your visual mapping and recite, you will convert these key words into full sentences to explain the information in greater detail. Notice how level-three details (the eight personality preferences) appear in **Figure 10.13**. Use the following guidelines for adding level-three information to your visual mapping:

- **Add key words.** Use only key words on level three. Strive to avoid long phrases or full sentences as they will clutter your visual mapping.

- **Decide how to organize details.** You can arrange the details in any order; they do not need to be organized in a clockwise direction.

- **Space details evenly.** Space details somewhat evenly around the main idea so each detail is clear and easy to read. Cluttered or crowded level-three details become distractions and are difficult to use to check your accuracy after reciting.

- **Select details carefully.** Be selective. Include only as many major details as you need to help you remember key information about each main idea.

- **Write on a horizontal plane.** To make your mapping easy to read, keep all your writing horizontal. Avoid writing at a slant or sideways or turning the paper as you write, resulting in words written upside down. Our visual memories are trained to recall writing that appears on horizontal lines.

- **Add optional borders.** You do not need to add borders around level-three information if the details stand out clearly; however, including borders is an option.

- **Personalize with pictures or with other designs.** Pictures and designs help imprint information in your visual memory and are often easier to recall than words, so include pictures when appropriate.

- **Add other variations.** Visual mappings are creative study tools, so use any other variations that help with the process of visually imprinting the information.

Notice that Figure 10.13 includes a *legend* that defines the levels of information.

Level-three information refers to the major supporting details that explain, support, or prove the main idea.

CONCEPT CHECK 10.14
What kinds of information do the first three levels of a visual mapping show? What are basic guidelines to use so the visual mapping is organized logically, is easy and interesting to read, and is uncluttered?

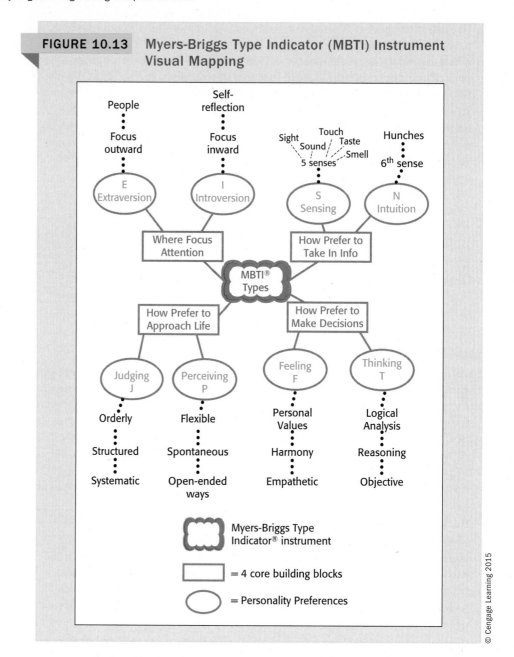

FIGURE 10.13 Myers-Briggs Type Indicator (MBTI) Instrument Visual Mapping

© Cengage Learning 2015

Level-Four Information: Minor Details

Level-four information refers to minor details that directly explain or support level-three information. Notice the words and short phrases used for level-four information in Figure 10.13. Use the following guidelines for level-four information:

- **Be extremely selective and brief.** Too many minor details or long phrases or sentences will clutter your mapping and make it difficult to use as a study tool.

- **Branch minor details off major details.** You can branch in any direction or order.

- **Cluster minor details.** To avoid cluttering your visual mapping or branching information too widely across your paper, you can group or cluster minor details together, show them as lists, or place them inside a box to save space.

- **Use larger paper.** To create extensive visual mappings with a variety of details and levels of information, work on unlined legal paper, drawing paper, or poster-sized paper. Crowded, cluttered visual mappings lose their purpose and their power if they are difficult to visualize.

- **Create separate visual mappings.** If a visual mapping, such as for a chapter, becomes too large, consider reorganizing the information into several different visual mappings; narrow the scope of each mapping by chunking the information into more meaningful units.

Studying from Visual Mappings

Studying from visual mappings strengthens your visual memory skills and provides you with visual images you can use to retrieve important information from memory. Even though you will learn details about a topic during the process of creating the visual mapping, you will gain the most benefit by using the essential strategies in Figure 10.11. Following is a brief summary of the steps to use:

1. **Imprint the skeleton:** Create a mental image of the skeleton of your mapping. Memorize it.

2. **Visualize:** Without looking at the visual mapping, pull the image from memory.

3. **Recite:** Recite the skeleton and then recite details about each heading. Look at the details on the visual mapping to check your accuracy.

4. **Reflect:** Use a reflect activity for elaborative rehearsal.

5. **Review:** Use ongoing review to mentally rehearse and recite the visual mapping multiple times.

Transfer These Skills: Visual Mappings

EXERCISE 10.4

DIRECTIONS: Your instructor will assign one of the following topics for you to use in this exercise. Remember that you will use the *skeleton* of your visual mapping (level-one and level-two information) to create a strong visual image, so it should be well-organized and uncluttered.

1. Create a visual mapping for one of these topics:

   a. A specific section or chapter of information from this textbook

   b. A specific excerpt in Appendix D

   c. A specific section or chapter from a textbook you use in another course

2. Create a visual mapping with *three* or *four* levels of information. Give attention to how you organize and present the details to avoid a cluttered visual mapping.

3. Evaluate the effectiveness of your visual mapping by completing the Exercise 10.5: Visual Notes Checklist in Appendix C, page C23.

4. Practice studying from your visual mapping. You may be asked to demonstrate the Look-Away Technique to visually recall your work and recite its details.

FIGURE 10.14   Levels of Information in Hierarchies

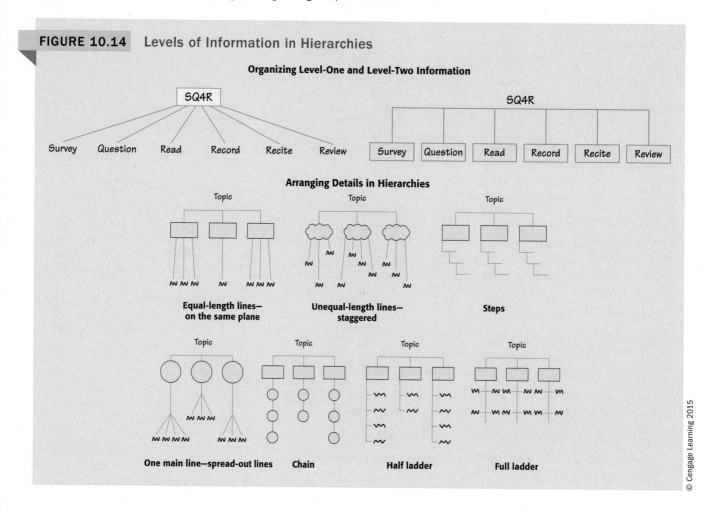

© Cengage Learning 2015

Hierarchies

Hierarchies are diagrams that place the topic on the top line of a diagram with main ideas branching down from the topic, followed by details branching down from the main ideas. Hierarchies arrange information in levels of size and importance from the top down. If visual mappings with lines extending in all directions are difficult for you to visualize, you may prefer the more linear structure of hierarchies. **Figure 10.14** shows two different ways to organize level-one and level-two information and multiple ways to organize the details for level-three information.

Level-One and Level-Two Information: The Hierarchy Skeleton

Level-one and level-two information in hierarchies is identical to level-one and level-two information used in visual mappings. The skeleton of a hierarchy that you will visually memorize includes the topic and the level-two headings or main ideas. To make a hierarchy, begin by placing the topic or the subject on the top line. Then determine the number of main ideas or headings to be placed under the topic. Branch *downward* to level two to write the main ideas. Use the following guidelines for writing level-two information on your hierarchy:

- **Use legal-size paper.** To have adequate room for the level-two and later the level-three information, consider using legal paper (8 1/2" × 14").

- **Space the main ideas evenly.** Spacing level-two information evenly helps avoid a cluttered or crowded look.
- **Use connectors.** Clearly connect levels of information by using lines.
- **Always write horizontally.** Your visual memory is not set up to visualize slanted writing, so imagine horizontal lines on your paper so you print on a horizontal plane.
- **Add colors, shapes, or pictures.** These visual features strengthen the visual image.
- **Add other level-two headings if necessary.** You can add headings, such as "Intro" for introductory information, or you may want a heading to show a specific graph or chart. If the printed material has a summary, you may want to add a final heading, "Summary."

Level-Three and Level-Four Information: Supporting Details

Be very selective. Use only key words or short phrases for level-three and level-four details. Because the lower levels on your hierarchy tend to have numerous supporting details, consider different ways to place the details on the paper to avoid a cluttered or crowded look. (See Figure 10.14.)

Studying from Hierarchies

Use the essential strategies in Figure 10.11 on page 323 to study your hierarchy: imprint the skeleton; visualize; recite; reflect; and review. With frequent practice, you should be able to recall quickly and accurately the skeleton with the first two levels of information in your hierarchy. By reciting as you practice, you activate your auditory channel and strengthen your auditory memory and ability to recall the details. Glancing at the hierarchy after reciting provides you with important feedback to check your accuracy of information about details. Select a meaningful reflect activity, and then use ongoing review.

Hierarchy for Professional Leadership

EXERCISE 10.5

Unless your instructor gives you directions to create a hierarchy from other materials, go to Excerpt 6: Professional Leadership in Appendix D. Complete the following directions.

DIRECTIONS:

1. Carefully read the excerpt. You may wish to highlight or annotate this excerpt to help you identify important details for your hierarchy.

2. On the top line of your hierarchy, write the topic "Professional Leadership."

3. Decide how many ideas or concepts you will use as headings on level two. Remember, you can create additional headings on level two, such as, "Definition," "Categories of Leaders," or whatever other headings you would find helpful. Because hierarchies involve creativity, your hierarchy most likely will differ from the hierarchies of others.

4. Develop your hierarchy by adding level-three information.

5. Practice studying from your hierarchy. You may be asked to visualize and recite from your visual image.

NOTE: You can use the **Exercise 10.5: Visual Notes Checklist** in **Appendix C** to evaluate the effectiveness of your hierarchy.

Comparison Charts

Comparison charts are diagrams that organize information for two or more subjects into a chart or a grid with columns and rows. Comparison charts, also known as *matrixes*, *grids*, or *tables*, organize a large amount of information into a format that clearly compares and contrasts information for two or more subjects. You can easily create comparison charts on a computer by using the *Tables* feature.

Labeling a Comparison Chart

Place the title of the comparison chart above the chart. On a comparison chart, the *columns* run up and down, and *rows* run across the page. (See **Figure 10.15**.) The columns are labeled with categories or the characteristics to be compared or contrasted. The rows are labeled with the different subjects to be compared or contrasted. The details appear in the intersecting boxes (cells) on the chart.

Identifying the subjects usually does not tend to cause problems for students. However, identifying categories to label the top of columns can be more difficult as it requires you to think carefully about and analyze the information you have read. Ask yourself: *What categories of information were discussed for all or most of the subjects?* You can use the general category "Characteristics," but more specific categories tend to be more useful. **Figure 10.16** shows a variety of categories you can use to label the columns in your comparison chart.

Completing a Comparison Chart

To complete a comparison chart, identify individual words or short phrases (the details) to place inside the cells. Use a logical system for filling in the cells. For example, begin by writing details in the cells one row at a time. Another option is to

FIGURE 10.15 **The Structure of a Comparison Chart**

categories→ subjects ↓	column 1 *Characteristics*	column 2 *Uses*	column 3 *Advantages*
Subject 1			
Subject 2			
Subject 3			

© Cengage Learning

FIGURE 10.16 **Common Categories for Subject Disciplines**

Literature	author	tone	theme	setting	main plot	characters/traits	actions
Sociology and Anthropology	culture family	location economy	government transportation	religion foods	beliefs tools	education imports/exports	tribe
History	events	time period	location	leaders/rulers	wars/conflicts	influences	
Psychology	kinds/types	traits	problems	frequency	duration	applications	
Science	terminology equations	kinds/types theorems	causes problems	effects solution	relationships applications	proofs examples	

© Cengage Learning 2015

focus on one column at a time; after writing details in the cells for the first column, continue to add details in cells for the remaining columns. Use the following suggestions for filling in the details:

- **Be selective.** Include only significant words or phrases. Avoid using full sentences.
- **Use dashes or bullets** to separate the individual details in the cells.
- **Leave cells blank** when there are no details for a specific cell. If information is not available for numerous cells under one category, the category is ineffective and needs to be renamed or eliminated.

EXERCISE 10.6

Visual Notes for Excerpts

DIRECTIONS: Create a visual mapping, hierarchy, or comparison chart for one of the following excerpts from this chapter. Include at least three levels of information.

- Process Paragraph Pattern: Life of a Star (page 310)
- Comparison-Contrast Paragraph Pattern: New Media (page 311)
- Whole-and-Parts Paragraph Pattern: United Kingdom (page 311)
- Definition Paragraph Pattern: Nonverbal Messages (page 312)
- Examples Paragraph Pattern: Diversity in Today's Work Force (page 313)
- Cause-Effect Paragraph Pattern: Fight or Flight Syndrome (page 313)

Attaching Other Forms of Notes

On occasion, a printed section of material will contain important information that does not fit within the categories of your chart. When you encounter such information, you may write a paragraph, create a list of the important points, or redraw a diagram next to or following your comparison chart. Information from an introductory paragraph, definitions, important diagrams or charts, or important points from the chapter conclusion or even from other chapters are the kind of information you may want to attach to your comparison chart.

Studying from Comparison Charts

The steps to study hierarchies appear in Figure 10.11. As with all forms of visual notes, begin by memorizing and creating a strong mental impression of the *skeleton*. In this case, the skeleton consists of the categories across the top of the chart and the subjects down the left side of the chart. After you visualize the skeleton, begin reciting the information that appears in the cells. You can recite by moving across the hierarchy rows, or you can recite by moving down the hierarchy columns. Proceed then to think critically about the information, the relationships among details, and among the subjects. Ask yourself questions such as the following:

How is the first subject similar to the second subject? How is it different?

How is the first category of information different for each subject?

Why does this occur for the first subject but not for the second subject?

Why does this subject not have information in a specific cell of the chart?

Did some event in a cell for one subject cause something to occur for a different subject?

After reciting, select reflect activities that encourage further work with the chart. For example, you could redraw the comparison chart, and without referring to printed information, complete the chart with details. You could also refer to the chart to write a summary about each subject, or write a summary about each category of information as it applies to the individual subjects. To keep the information active in your memory, use immediate and ongoing review strategies.

CHAPTER 10
REFLECTIVE WRITING 2

 On separate paper, in a journal, or online in this textbook's College Success CourseMate website, respond to the following questions.

1. This chapter focuses on analyzing and organizing details in textbook content. Which section was the most informative and helpful in terms of understanding textbook materials: paragraph organizational patterns, interpreting graphic materials, or creating visual notes? Explain how you will benefit from this information.

2. Explain how creating visual notes and study tools affects your level of motivation and confidence in learning subject matter.

 Access Chapter 10 Reflective Writing 2 in your College Success CourseMate, accessed through *CengageBrain.com*.

CHECK POINT 10.4

Answers appear on page B4.

Multiple Choice See Test-Taking Strategies 10–15 in Appendix A.

_____ 1. Which statement is *not* true about visual mappings?
   a. To avoid clutter, visual mappings should include only two levels of information.
   b. In a well-developed mapping, different levels of information are easy to identify.
   c. For consistency in "reading" a visual mapping, a standard format for ordering level-two information is recommended.
   d. Pictures, shapes, and colors strengthen visual memory and recall of information.

_____ 2. In studying hierarchies, you should
   a. place larger concepts on higher levels.
   b. begin by visually memorizing the skeleton.
   c. recite details on levels three and four.
   d. do all of the above.

_____ 3. In visual mappings, level-one information and level-two information
   a. should be visually memorized as the skeleton of the visual mapping.
   b. show the topic and its main headings.
   c. are the only levels of information that you should visually memorize.
   d. do all of the above.

_____ 4. Comparison charts do not
   a. always have details in every cell.
   b. show likenesses or differences.
   c. ever show more than two subjects.
   d. do any of the above.

 Access Chapter 10 Practice Quiz 4 in your College Success CourseMate, accessed through *CengageBrain.com*.

Chapter 10 Critical Thinking

DIRECTIONS: Read the following paragraph carefully. Complete the questions that follow.

"The process of investigating nature is known as the **scientific method**, which holds that no concept or model of nature is valid unless the predictions are in agreement with experimental results. That is, all hypotheses—tentative answers—should be based on as much relevant data as possible and then should be tested and verified. If a hypothesis does not withstand rigorous testing, it must be modified and retested, or rejected and replaced by a new hypothesis. An attitude of curiosity, objectivity, rationality, and willingness to go where the evidence leads is associated with use of the scientific method. Note carefully that the scientific method not only is used in scientific work but also is applicable in many areas of our daily lives."

Source: Shipman et al. *An Introduction to Physical Science, 10e,* p. 3.

QUESTIONS:

1. What organizational pattern is used for this paragraph?_____

2. Use highlighting and annotation strategies to mark the paragraph.

3. On separate paper, diagram the important details in this paragraph.

Learning Objectives Review

1 *Discuss strategies to use when reading college textbooks for different disciplines and content areas.*

- Declarative (factual) knowledge and procedural (process) knowledge appear in textbooks for all content areas. Elaborative rehearsal strategies work effectively for declarative knowledge; repetition works effectively for procedural knowledge.

- Some reading skills, such as using organizational patterns in paragraphs, learning terminology, and surveying chapters, work effectively for all content area textbooks.

- Some reading skills and strategies vary for composition, literature, social science, science, and mathematics textbooks. For example, interpreting graphic materials occurs most frequently in social science, science, and mathematics textbooks.

- A Customized Reading System works most effectively for composition, literature, and mathematics textbooks.

2 *Define and discuss the seven organizational patterns used to organize details in paragraphs.*

- Seven organizational patterns in paragraphs show a logical, meaningful order of details: chronological, process, comparison-contrast, whole-and-parts, definition, examples, and cause-effect.

Terms to Know

By yourself or with a partner, practice reciting or writing definitions for the following terms. You may also practice defining these terms by using the online flashcards or comparing your answers to the online glossary.

prototype p. 306

organizational patterns p. 308

chronological pattern p. 309

process pattern p. 309

comparison-contrast pattern p. 310

whole-and-parts pattern p. 311

definition pattern p. 312

examples pattern p. 312

cause-effect pattern p. 313

graphic materials p. 315

caption p. 315

legend p. 315

pie charts p. 316

flow charts p. 318

Terms to Know

 Access Chapter 10 Flashcards and Online Glossary in your College Success CourseMate, accessed through *CengageBrain.com.*

Learning Objectives Review

- Knowing how to identify clue words in paragraphs strengthens comprehension. Clue words include the following: *when, first, next, steps, process, outcome, in contrast, however, means, is defined as, for example, because, since, caused by, parts, section, and consists of.*
- Diagram formats for each of the organizational patterns may be used to visually depict the details in paragraphs.

❸ *Explain and use strategies to read and interpret six kinds of graphic materials.*

- Graphic materials are visual representations that convert verbal or printed information into visual formats, such as photographs, illustrations, diagrams, pie charts, flow charts, tables, bar graphs, or line graphs.
- In addition to learning how to interpret graphic materials, using essential strategies to study and work with graphic materials improves comprehension.
- *Pie charts* show a whole unit and its individual parts or labels. *Flow charts* are organizational charts that show the directional flow of information. *Tables*— also called comparison charts, grids, or matrixes—present information in columns and rows.
- *Bar graphs* use single or double bars, arranged vertically or horizontally, to graph data and show trends. Bar graphs have an *x* axis and a *y* axis. Histograms, a form of bar graph, show a range of values for each bar on the base of the chart.
- *Line graphs* plot points on a coordinate or grid to compare data and show trends. Legends may be used to explain the lines in single line or double line graphs.

❹ *Explain and demonstrate how to create and study from three kinds of visual notes: visual mappings, hierarchies, and comparison charts.*

- Visual notes (*visual mappings, hierarchies,* and *comparison* charts) organize information into diagrams or charts that use colors, pictures, and shapes to help imprint information into visual memory.
- Visual notes use levels of information to organize topics, main ideas, and supporting details.
- Visual mappings begin with a topic in the center, followed by details spiking out in all directions.
- Hierarchies begin with the topic on the top line, followed by details dropped down to lower levels.
- Comparison charts use rows, columns, and cells to organize information.
- Studying visual notes involves imprinting the *skeleton* of the notes into your memory, visualizing, reciting, reflecting on the details, and reviewing.

Chapter 10   Review Questions

Multiple Choice See Test-Taking Strategies 10–15 in Appendix A.

_____ 1. Which of the following is *not* true about elaborative rehearsal? Elaborative rehearsal works effectively to

   a. use rote memory to recite special terminology in literature courses.

   b. identify and diagram organizational patterns.

   c. learn factual information in science and social science textbooks.

   d. reorganize and practice information in new ways.

_____ 2. Understanding ways to learn procedural knowledge will help you with coursework in

   a. math classes.

   b. science classes.

   c. composition classes.

   d. all classes that include steps and processes to learn.

_____ 3. Which of the following graphics are the least likely to show comparisons of data?

   a. Pie charts or circle graphs

   b. Photographs or illustrations

   c. Double bar graphs or double line graphs

   d. Tables

_____ 4. Which of the following organizational patterns frequently appears in science textbooks?

   a. Process pattern

   b. Definition pattern

   c. Cause-effect pattern

   d. All of the above patterns

_____ 5. Which of the following statements is *not* true or accurate?

   a. Pie charts are based on a parts-and-whole organizational pattern for information.

   b. Tables condense large amounts of data into columns and rows.

   c. A histogram is a bar graph that shows a range of values for each bar.

   d. Captions that accompany graphs define symbols, colors, or line patterns in the graphs.

_____ 6. Which of the following clue words are not used for the organizational pattern that is shown?

   a. Chronological pattern: when, next, after, first, finally

   b. Definition pattern: because, since, so, therefore, resulted in

   c. Comparison-contrast pattern: similarly, likewise, but, however, also

   d. Whole-and parts pattern: categories, sections, subsystems, front, back

_____ 7. You can use visual mappings, hierarchies, and comparison charts to

   a. take lecture or textbook notes.

   b. create summary notes before a test.

   c. create study tools for elaborative rehearsal.

   d. do all of the above.

_____ 8. When you visualize your notes, you should

   a. first create a visual image of level 1 and level 2 information.

   b. be creative and make changes each time you visualize.

   c. stare at the paper for at least fifteen minutes.

   d. keep your eyes focused on the notes when you recite.

_____ 9. Which statement is *not* true?

   a. Procedural knowledge is also called process knowledge.

   b. A chronological pattern is a time-order or time-sequenced pattern.

   c. Flow charts are also referred to as organizational charts.

   d. Line graphs are also known as vertical axis graphs.

 Access Chapter 10 Enhanced Quiz and Chapter 10 Study Guide in your College Success CourseMate, accessed through *CengageBrain.com*.

Access all Chapter 10 Online Material in your College Success CourseMate, accessed through *CengageBrain.com*.

11 Strengthening Listening and Lecture Notetaking Skills

© Stockbyte/Getty Images

U nderstanding factors that impact your listening skills and using effective listening strategies help improve your listening performance in all four kinds of listening: active, critical, empathic, and appreciative. Developing strong listening skills directly affects your ability to take quality lecture notes. In this chapter, you will learn notetaking systems that are ideal for lectures, plus a variety of strategies to help you keep up with the speaker, deal with common lecture notetaking problems, identify important points for your notes, and organize your notes in meaningful ways. The result will be effective sets of notes that you can use to recite, rehearse, reflect, and review lecture information.

Access Chapter 11 Expanded Chapter Outline in your College Success CourseMate, accessed through CengageBrain.com.

YOUR CHAPTER MAPPING

After reading information under each heading, return to the chapter visual mapping below. Add key words to show subheadings and important details related to each heading.

 Access Chapter 11 Visual Mapping in your College Success CourseMate, accessed through CengageBrain.com.

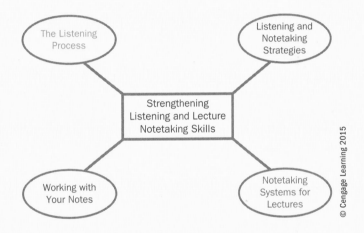

© Cengage Learning 2015

LEARNING OBJECTIVES

1 *Discuss listening and memory processes, factors that influence the quality of listening, the four kinds of listening, and steps to create an effective listening plan.*

2 *Discuss strategies to use to capture important lecture information; manage thinking, speaking, and writing discrepancies; and strengthen notetaking skills.*

3 *Explain how to use two-column and three-column notes, book notes, partial outline notes, and PowerPoint notes for classroom lectures.*

4 *Discuss strategies to study and learn from lecture notes.*

Strengthening Listening and Lecture Notetaking Skills

ANSWER, SCORE, and **RECORD** your profile before you read this chapter. If you need to review the process, refer to the complete directions given in the profile for Chapter 1 on page 4.

Access Chapter 11 Profile in your College Success CourseMate, accessed through *CengageBrain.com.*

ONLINE: You can complete the profile and get your score online in this textbook's College Success CourseMate.

	YES	NO
1. I adjust my listening goals to different kinds of listening situations.	_____	_____
2. I am easily distracted in lectures by thoughts, actions, and things around me that disrupt my concentration.	_____	_____
3. I have an effective listening plan that I use to increase the quality of my listening experiences.	_____	_____
4. I frequently paraphrase, abbreviate, and use shortened sentences in my lecture notes.	_____	_____
5. I often feel unprepared for lectures and unfamiliar with lecture topics or content.	_____	_____
6. I stop taking notes when the speaker sidetracks from the topic.	_____	_____
7. I know how to use several different kinds of notetaking systems, so I select the one that is best suited for each class, the instructor, and the content.	_____	_____
8. When instructors give copies of PowerPoint slides, I stop writing as I do not need to take additional notes.	_____	_____
9. I spend time going over my notes and filling in missing information as soon after the lecture as possible.	_____	_____
10. I am confident in my ability to use effective listening and lecture notetaking skills in my classes.	_____	_____

QUESTIONS LINKED TO THE CHAPTER LEARNING OBJECTIVES:

Questions 1–3: objective 1

Question 9: objective 4

Questions 4–6: objective 2

Question 10: all objectives

Questions 7–8: objective 3

The Listening Process

1 *Discuss listening and memory processes, factors that influence the quality of listening, the four kinds of listening, and steps to create an effective listening plan.*

Listening is an active process that involves taking in auditory stimuli, attaching meaning to words, and understanding the message presented by the words you hear. Hearing, which involves receiving auditory stimuli and sound waves, does not automatically mean that you are listening. Hearing is only the starting point of listening; listening is an active process that engages the listener in a variety of cognitive processes.

We use four kinds of verbal communication skills to communicate with others: listening, speaking, reading, and writing. Listening is the most frequently used of the four verbal communication skills, yet listening skills are often the weakest. Despite all of the time we spend listening, most of us aren't very good at it. In fact, listening efficiency is low for most people, and what we do remember from listening situations often is distorted or inaccurate. Poor listening habits may be the result of the lack of training, lack of instruction, or lack of courses that teach listening skills.

> **Listening** is an active process that involves taking in auditory stimuli, attaching meaning to words, and understanding the message presented by the words you hear.

Listening and Memory Processes

We need to use effort and undivided attention to activate our listening processes. Within a matter of seconds from receiving auditory stimuli, we need to respond to the stimuli in some way to avoid losing it completely. Stimuli (words) that we identify as important to process further then enter our short-term memory, the memory system that has a limited capacity and duration. Again, we must make a conscious effort to keep the information active for further processing into working memory. Without attention, the stimuli will drop out of our memory system and will not be processed.

The entire process of listening effectively involves complex processes. As we listen, we have to attach meaning to words we hear by continuously tapping into long-term memory to associate the new information with information we already know or understand. In a rapid-fire manner, information moves back and forth between working memory and long-term memory, building in strength as we integrate old and new information.

Unfortunately, the movement of information back and forth between memory systems often is not an uninterrupted process. *Fluctuating attention* is a natural process; we listen, tune out briefly, refocus on listening, and continue with this fluctuation. We may briefly tune out from listening for a variety of reasons. Too much new information coming into memory at one time may overload working memory, so we listen less intently or tune out. Too much complex, technical, or unfamiliar information is difficult to understand, so instead of persevering and trying harder to follow the speaker and the message, we tune out and shift our thoughts elsewhere. Listening may also fluctuate when internal or external distractions disrupt the listening process as we shift our attention away from the speaker and the message.

Our attitude may also cause listening to fluctuate. If the speaker provides us with too little new or challenging information, we get bored and let our minds wander. Our positive or negative self-talk can also take over and disrupt the listening process. Instead of listening to the speaker, we listen to our inner voice telling us things such as, *I already know this. This is boring. I am really not interested in this. I already know what the speaker is going to say. This isn't important. I don't agree with this. He doesn't know what he is talking about. She's outdated. I can read this in the textbook.*

Our memory system is challenged even further during the listening process because in addition to processing auditory stimuli, we must also process visual stimuli from PowerPoint slides, overhead transparencies, or the instructor writing on whiteboards or blackboards. Effective listening requires rapid-fire shifting of attention to multiple stimuli and tasks. To be an effective listener, one must commit to the process of developing effective listening skills, maintaining undivided attention, and eliminating ineffective listening habits or patterns.

CONCEPT CHECK   **11.1**

Why is listening not a process that happens automatically and without effort?

Influencing Factors

Good listening is similar to concentration: it is here one second and then it is gone. Effective listening involves a willingness to eliminate poor listening habits, which are learned behaviors and are influenced by internal and external distractions. You may begin listening to a speaker with the full intention of "staying tuned in," listening attentively, following the ideas, and making every effort to understand the information, but then your thoughts suddenly shift and you find yourself doodling, daydreaming, or attempting to multitask by engaging in tasks unrelated to listening to the speaker. **Figure 11.1** summarizes personal factors that either enhance or hinder the listening process.

FIGURE 11.1   **Personal Factors that Enhance or Hinder the Listening Process**

Your Attitude *Positive attitude enhances listening ability; negative attitude hinders it.*	Your interest level in the topic Your attitude toward the subject Your attitude toward the speaker
The Topic *Familiarity enhances listening; lack of background hinders it.*	Your familiarity with the words, terminology, or topic Your personal background and cultural experiences Difficulty level of the course or presentation Quantity of information presented
External Distractors *Ability to block out distractors enhances listening; attending to distractors hinders it.*	Noise and movement in the listening environment Room temperature or lighting Interruptions or disruptions by others in the room
Physical Factors *Comfort, proximity to speaker, and positive physical and emotional state enhance listening; opposites of these factors hinder it.*	Length of time required to remain seated Sitting posture during the lecture Seating location in relation to the speaker Personal physical and emotional state at the time

Listening interferences are thoughts, actions, or things that disrupt or shut down the listening process. **In the following list, check the listening interferences that you have experienced during lectures.**

___X___ I could not get interested in the topic of the lecture.

_____ I lacked motivation to focus my attention on the lecture and the details.

___X___ Things around me distracted me, and I couldn't get back on track listening.

_____ I pretended I was listening, but I really wasn't.

___X___ The information was too complicated or technical, so I couldn't stay focused.

___X___ The speaker's voice distracted and annoyed me (high- or low-pitched, soft or quiet tone, booming or assertive tone).

___X___ The speaker's speech pattern of overusing certain phrases, such as "You know" or "Uhhh," interfered with my ability to listen closely to the speaker.

___X___ The speaker's rapid pace of speaking made it difficult to listen closely or follow the speaker's ideas.

_____ The speaker's slow pace of speaking made staying focused difficult to do, so my mind frequently wandered.

___X___ The disorganized, loosely structured, or difficult-to-follow method of presenting information was too distracting.

EXERCISE 11.1

Classroom Listening Factors Inventory

DIRECTIONS: Go to Exercise 11.1 in Appendix C, page C24–C25, for a listening inventory to increase your awareness of behaviors and attitudes that influence your ability to listen during classroom lectures. Your responses will provide you with insights on ways to strengthen your classroom listening skills.

Kinds of Listening

As you begin a listening activity, identify your listening goal. Is your purpose for listening to acquire or learn new information, or is it to understand, interpret, or evaluate the speaker's message? Is your purpose to understand and relate to another person, or is it to enjoy or be entertained by the speaker? Understanding your listening goal each time you approach a listening situation can help you select appropriate strategies to strengthen your listening skills. **Figure 11.2** shows four kinds of listening and the listening goals for each.

FIGURE 11.2   Kinds of Listening and Listening Goals

Kinds of Listening	The Listening Goal is to...
Active	Understand and learn new information
Critical	Understand, interpret, examine, and analyze a speaker's message
Empathic	Understand and relate to another person's feelings and emotions
Appreciative	Enjoy, appreciate, and acknowledge a speaker and his or her message

© Cengage Learning 2015

Active Listening

Active listening is the process of giving undivided attention to a speaker with the goal of understanding and learning new information. Many of your college active-listening experiences will occur in classroom settings: in lectures, in labs, in small groups, or in partner activities. Following are important characteristics of active listeners:

- Demonstrate a positive attitude toward the speaker and the topic by showing an interest and an intention to learn.

- Use a positive physical stance or posture; instead of turning away, crossing arms, or looking way, sit attentively and make direct eye contact with the speaker.

- Give the speaker your full attention. Refrain from responding to interferences, distractions, or self-talk.

- Be prepared and ready to learn. Read ahead in your textbook to gain familiarity with a topic. Have necessary materials, such as notebook, pen, and textbook, with you before the listening process begins.

- Engage with the speaker at appropriate times. Ask questions to clarify or check your understanding.

Active listening is the process of giving undivided attention to a speaker with the goal of understanding and learning new information.

Critical Listening

Critical listening is the process of giving undivided attention to a speaker with the goal of understanding, interpreting, analyzing, and evaluating the content of the message. Critical listening is a higher, more complex form of listening that goes beyond active listening and involves critical thinking skills. Following are important points about critical listening:

- Critical listening is difficult, if not impossible, to do without pre-existing background knowledge and familiarity with the topic.

- Critical listening requires separating your emotions and opinions from those of the speaker so you can understand and evaluate the speaker's message and point of view.

- Critical listening involves determining validity or logic of the information, examining the speaker's evidence, and determining if the evidence supports the speaker's point of view.

- For more information about critical listening, read **Excerpt 8: How to Listen Critically** in **Appendix D.**

Critical listening is the process of giving undivided attention to a speaker with the goal of understanding, interpreting, analyzing, and evaluating the content of the message.

Empathic Listening

Empathic listening is the process of giving undivided attention to another person with the goal of understanding that person's feelings, emotions, and thoughts related to a specific topic or situation. Your listening goal is to *empathize* or relate to the other person. Following are important points about empathic listening:

- Empathic listeners pay attention to people's verbal and nonverbal cues to identify the emotion being exhibited (anger, frustration, disappointment, resentment, excitement, enthusiasm, self-pride, and so on) and to relate to the speaker's situation, feelings, or point of view.

- In many empathic listening situations, the person talking wants someone to listen and understand; he or she does not necessarily want to be consoled or given advice or guidance.

- Empathic listeners avoid being judgmental and avoid criticizing, making negative comments, or telling the other person that he or she is "wrong." Instead, they use positive words or gestures to communicate that they *understand* the feeling or the situation—even if they do not agree with the other person.

- Empathic listening involves patience to give the person talking sufficient time to express emotions and process feelings with you. Try not to interrupt or insert your own ideas into the process.

- Empathic listening skills are valuable in college courses that use group activities that encourage or require students to interact on more personal levels. Listen to and observe what the person wants to communicate to you.

Appreciative Listening

Appreciative listening is the process of listening to a speaker for the purpose of enjoying, appreciating, and acknowledging the speaker and the message in positive ways. Being drawn into a story by a captivating storyteller, laughing at an instructor's humorous anecdotes or examples in a lecture, marveling at the ease with which a student gives a class presentation, listening to an actor practice a scene from an upcoming play, or listening to someone describe a vacation to an exotic location are examples of appreciative listening. The following points are important about appreciative listening:

- Appreciative listening is not a passive, laid-back process. To feel the richness of the words, to be moved emotionally by a message, the listener must take an active role by paying close attention to details, connecting with the speaker, and allowing emotional responses to occur.

- An appreciative listener can demonstrate appreciation and enjoyment through nods of agreement, eye contact, facial expressions, compliments or expressions of gratitude, and, when appropriate, applause.

An Effective Listening Plan

An effective listening plan is a series of eight steps you can follow to increase the quality of your listening experience. These steps work effectively for listening to lectures, engaging in group discussions, or participating in listening situations at home or at work.

1. **Attitude:** Begin by setting the stage for positive listening. The attitude you bring to the listening situation affects the quality of your listening. Be mentally

Empathic listening is the process of giving undivided attention to another person with the goal of understanding that person's feelings, emotions, and thoughts related to a specific topic or situation.

CONCEPT CHECK 11.2
What are different listening goals for four kinds of listening that skilled listeners know how to use?

Appreciative listening is the process of listening to a speaker for the purpose of enjoying, appreciating, and acknowledging the speaker and the message in positive ways.

CHAPTER 11
REFLECTIVE WRITING 1

On separate paper, in a journal, or online in this textbook's College Success CourseMate, respond to the following questions:

1. On a scale of one to ten, with ten representing "highly effective," how do you rate your effectiveness as an active listener during lectures? Explain.

2. After completing Exercise 11.1: Classroom Listening Factors Inventory, comment on your inventory scores for A, B, and C, which show your effective listening behaviors and attitudes. Do you agree with the results? Why or why not? Which behaviors or attitudes do you wish to change?

 Access Chapter 11 Reflective Writing 1 in your College Success CourseMate, accessed through *CengageBrain.com*.

---

prepared and motivated to set distractions aside and give your undivided attention to the speaker. Self-talk about the speaker and the topic should be positive and supportive.

2. **Purpose:** Take time to create a clear listening goal and identify your purpose. What do you intend to learn from this listening experience? Why is it important, valuable, or beneficial to you?

3. **Image:** Pay attention to the image you present of yourself to the speaker. Use overt behaviors that show you are a good listener, attentive, and interested. Instead of hiding in the back of the room, sit closer to the front where you can interact with the speaker. Make direct eye contact and use body language, such as nods or sitting upright instead of slouching, to send signals of interest or approval to the speaker. Show you are prepared, organized, and ready to listen by having your notebook, pen, and other materials ready to use. Have all your "busyness" of settling in done before the speaker begins talking.

4. **Depth:** Intend to listen intently to actively search for and identify meaning, structure, and relationships. Strive to follow the speaker's line of thinking, understand details as they unfold, and grasp both the details and the overall big picture of the topic.

5. **Notes:** Auditory memory often is not sufficiently reliable or accurate to use to recall information at a later time, so taking notes to capture key points provides you with information that you can later use to study, memorize, or learn. Include the speaker's key points, important details, and notes that appear on blackboards, whiteboards, slides, or transparency masters.

6. **Refocus:** If at any time during the listening experience you become aware of your mind wandering or your listening fluctuating, act quickly to activate concentration strategies to get your mind refocused and back on track. Use concentration strategies discussed in Chapter 3 as well as the concentration strategies that appear in this chapter.

7. **Feedback:** Providing the speaker with positive feedback shows your interest, appreciation, and understanding of the speaker's topic and presentation.

CONCEPT CHECK   **11.3**

Explain key behaviors demonstrated by an effective listener who uses the eight steps in an effective listening plan.

Positive feedback may be in the form of verbal communication, such as *Thank you* or *That was very interesting*, follow-up clarification questions about the topic, or paraphrased statements to confirm that you understood the information correctly. Nonverbal communication, such as nods, smiles, or applause, can also provide positive feedback.

8. **Questions:** The final step of the listening process is to ask questions. You can ask yourself questions about what you just learned, its significance, and its relationship to previously learned information, or you can write study questions based on your notes. This final step also includes asking the speaker questions about the presentation. There are four kinds of questions you can use for this stage of the listening process:

- **Open-ended questions:** Ask questions that have a variety of possible answers or explanations.

- **Closed questions:** Ask questions that require specific details for answers.

- **Probing questions:** Ask for more details or greater depth by using question words, such as *Why? Where? When? What? How?*

- **Leading questions:** Ask questions that include the details you hope to hear in the answer. Leading questions sometimes use paraphrasing of information; for example, you could ask, *Would you say then that all monetary incentives work to motivate employees?*

CHECK POINT 11.1

Answers appear on page B4.

True or False? See Test-Taking Strategies 1–9 in Appendix A.

_____ 1. Speaking is the most frequently used communication activity in college courses.

_____ 2. Listening is a challenging process partly due to the limited capacity and duration of working memory and partly due to listener and speaker interferences.

_____ 3. Your attitude, familiarity with the topic, internal and external distractors, and a speaker's speech patterns affect your ability to listen effectively.

_____ 4. Leading questions are the best kind of questions to ask speakers as a part of an effective listening plan.

_____ 5. The beginning of an effective listening plan focuses on the kinds of questions to ask the speaker and the kinds of notes to take.

Matching See Test-Taking Strategies 16–20 in Appendix A.

Match the primary kind of listening used in each listening situation. Answers may be used more than once.

_____ 1. A debate about storing nuclear waste

_____ 2. Student project that involves a skit

_____ 3. Instructor explanation of steps for a lab assignment

_____ 4. Student expressing frustration about a tutoring session

_____ 5. Class discussion about thesis of a short story

_____ 6. A lecture reviewing a psychology chapter

a. active listening

b. critical listening

c. appreciative listening

d. empathic listening

Access Chapter 11 Practice Quiz 1 in your College Success CourseMate, accessed through *CengageBrain.com*.

Listening and Notetaking Strategies

Discuss strategies to use to capture important lecture information; manage thinking, speaking, and writing discrepancies; and strengthen notetaking skills.

In your classes, you will use your listening skills for partner or small group activities, during discussions, and during question-and-answer or review sessions. However, classroom lectures and presentations will place the greatest demands on your listening skills because not only do you need to use effective listening skills, but you also need to process what you hear and convert the information into meaningful lecture notes. Effective notetaking for lectures involves the following:

- Identifying and capturing main ideas and supporting details in your notes
- Showing the structure or outline of the lecture in an organized way
- Showing clearly the different levels of information
- Providing sufficient details to develop topics or support main points; if your notes are too brief and lack sufficient details, they will not be very helpful when you need to study the information or prepare for tests.

CONCEPT CHECK   11.4
Why is the process of taking lecture notes difficult for many students to do well?

Listen for Six Kinds of Information

You can hone your listening skills for lectures by understanding the kinds of information that are important to understand and then capture in your notes. Following are the kinds of information to listen for carefully, as they provide the foundation and the content of your lecture notes:

- **Headings** or categories of information signaled by key words
- **Main ideas** or topic sentences that state the most important points about a topic
- **Terminology** and definitions
- **Supporting details** that explain or develop the main ideas
- **Verbal clues** the speaker gives indicating what is important to know
- **Conclusion**, which summarizes the important points

Listen for Key Words Signaling Headings

Many instructors introduce a new topic or category of information by using signal words. You can use signal words, such as the signal words in the following list, to help you organize lecture information and create headings for your notes. When the words are repeated, they signal supporting details. For example, if the instructor says, "Let's look at the major *causes* of global warming," the word *causes* signals a new heading. As the lecture progresses, the instructor will use the word *causes* several more times to identify and explain each individual cause, which you can then number as details. Following are key words to listen for as they may help you identify major headings or topics.

CONCEPT CHECK   11.5
What different kinds of information are important to listen for or identify when taking notes? What are examples of signal words that can help you identify important topics and main ideas for your notes?

advantages	effects	parts	steps
benefits	factors	principles	solutions
causes	findings	purposes	techniques
characteristics	functions	reasons	types of
conclusions	kinds of	rules	uses
disadvantages	methods	stages	ways

Listen for Main Ideas

Main ideas are the main points the instructor makes about a specific topic or heading. Your instructor often will use transition words to connect or move from one main idea to another. Signal words—such as those in the following box—may be ordinals, placeholder words, or repeated key words. Recognizing these signal words in a lecture helps you number individual points or main ideas in your notes.

| First… | Second… | Third… |
| The next… | Another… | The final… |

Listen for Terminology and Definitions

Listen carefully for terminology and definitions provided in lectures as they are important details to include in your notes. Word clues—such as those in the following box—often signal definitions and help you identify key words to include in your notes.

| X means… | X is defined as… | The definition of X is… |
| X is also called… | X, also referred to as… | X, also known as… |

When you hear these words, use the abbreviation *DEF* to signal that you are writing a definition. Or you may want to use the equals symbol (=) to connect a word to a definition. For example, you could write *paraphrasing = rephrasing or saying in your own words*.

CONCEPT CHECK   11.6

In addition to definitions, what other kinds of supporting details should appear in your notes? How do you know what is important to include or exclude?

Listen for Supporting Details

Listen carefully for dates, names, facts, statistics, and examples because they are additional kinds of supporting details that are important to include in your notes. These details develop, support, or "prove" the main idea and help you understand concepts more thoroughly. Following are important points to know about details in lectures:

- **Ordinals** (number words) provide you with verbal clues for organizing the details in your notes. When you hear "first," make that point number 1 in your notes. Continue to use ordinals and *placeholder words* that represent a number: *first, second, next, also, in addition, another,* and *last* or *finally*.
- **Examples or anecdotes** provide vivid examples that serve as memory triggers, retrieval cues, or associations for a specific main idea or concept. Listen carefully to the examples or anecdotes. Decide which examples or anecdotes would work best to trigger your memory about the topic and briefly include those in your notes. Your notes do not need to "retell the whole story" with all its details.

Listen for Verbal Clues

As you become accustomed to your different instructors and their lecture styles, you will be able to use their verbal, visual, and nonverbal clues to help identify important information. There are several kinds of verbal clues that can help you identify important information.

- **Key words** such as *kinds of, steps, advantages of,* and so forth, are verbal clues that signal that the information is important.

- **Direct statements** are stronger, more direct signals of information that you should include in your notes. Following are examples of direct statements: *This is important. You need to know this. This will be on the next test. As I have already said... (ideas are repeated). Be sure you copy this information (from the overhead screen or chalkboard). If you haven't already done so, be sure you read carefully the information on pages.... I can't emphasize enough the importance of....*

- **Voice qualities**, such as a person's intonation (pitch of his or her voice), volume of voice, and rate of speech, are also verbal clues. Listen to the speaker's patterns carefully. Does he or she speak louder, more enthusiastically, faster, slower, or at a different pitch when giving important information? Many speakers may not even be aware of the verbal patterns they use to emphasize important points, but skilled listeners can identify the patterns and use the information to help select the important ideas for their notes.

CONCEPT CHECK **11.7**

What is your own definition for verbal and nonverbal clues? What important information can you learn from both of these kinds of clues?

Listen for the Conclusion

Listen carefully when the instructor summarizes the main points at the end of a lecture. The summary or conclusion reinforces the main points made in the lecture. As soon as you hear a summary or conclusion begin, add a heading in your notes that says "Conclusion." List the main points included in the conclusion as they indicate the points the instructor deemed as most important.

Speaking, Thinking, and Writing Rates

The processes of listening and taking lecture notes occur rapidly and require undivided attention. It is a complex set of processes that involves thinking and listening skills—transferring the information into notes while simultaneously taking in new information presented by the speaker. The process of taking lecture notes is overwhelming for many students. Understanding the different rates of speaking, thinking, and writing explains some of the difficulty of keeping up with the speaker to take lecture notes.

The Rate of Speaking

Rate of speaking (or rate of speech) indicates the average number of words a speaker says per minute.

The *rate of speaking* (or rate of speech) indicates the average number of words a speaker says per minute. In personal conversations, for example when you want to discuss serious issues or want to be sure the listener understands your points, you may speak slower than 100 words per minute. Other times in casual conversations, for example when you have exciting news to share, you may speak much faster than the normal rate of 125–150 words per minute for conversations. Following are key points about the rate of speaking in lectures:

- The average rate of speaking during a lecture is 100–125 words per minute—a rate that provides a little more time to create basic understanding and to take notes.

- You will likely encounter three general speaking rates instructors use during lectures: too slow, comfortable, or too fast.

- When the speaking rate is fast, you will have to increase your level of concentration and increase your rate of writing.

- When an instructor speaks too slowly, you may have difficulty staying focused, or you may find your attention fluctuating. As soon as you become aware of your inattentiveness, make a concerted effort to use strategies to increase concentration and eliminate distractions.

The Rate of Thinking

The *rate of thinking* indicates the average number of words or small units of information a person thinks per minute. The average is 400 words per minute. When an instructor speaks slowly, your *rate of thinking* far outpaces the instructor's rate of speech, so your mind tends to wander off the subject.

> **Rate of thinking** indicates the average number of words or small units of information a person thinks per minute.

The Rate of Writing

The *rate of writing* indicates the average number of words a person writes per minute. An average rate of writing is 30 words per minute. When an instructor speaks too fast, your *rate of writing* is too slow to capture the instructor's ideas on paper. When an instructor speaks at a comfortable pace, taking notes may still be demanding, but the discrepancies among speaking, writing, and thinking rates will not create as many notetaking difficulties.

> **Rate of writing** indicates the average number of words a person writes per minute.

Strategies to Manage Rate Discrepancies

Dealing with the discrepancies among the rate of speaking in lectures, rate of writing, and rate of thinking requires flexibility and familiarity with a variety of strategies you can use to adjust to specific lecture situations. **Figure 11.3** shows nine essential strategies for dealing with rate discrepancies.

Maintain Undivided Attention

When your mind wanders, you start daydreaming, doodling, or tending to other tasks because of the large discrepancy between the speaker's slow rate of speech and your much faster rate of thinking—as a result, you may miss important information and find switching back into the listening mode more difficult to do. Your

> **CONCEPT CHECK 11.8**
> *How do you respond to the differences among speaking, thinking, and writing rates? What strategies do you use to deal with the discrepancies that cause you the most difficulties?*

FIGURE 11.3 Essential Strategies for Dealing with Rate Discrepancies

1. Keep writing.
2. Mentally summarize.
3. Predict the next point or an answer to a question.
4. Paraphrase the speaker.
5. Use abbreviations and symbols.
6. Use modified printing.
7. Leave a gap and start writing again.
8. Shift to paragraph form.
9. Tape the lecture.

© Cengage Learning 2015

listening goal is to use strategies to keep your mind focused on the speaker and to maintain undivided attention, even though the presentation of information is not demanding. Use the following three strategies to deal with the discrepancy between a slow rate of speech and a fast rate of thinking:

- **Strategy 1: Keep writing.** Even if the details do not seem vital to your notes, write them down, as this keeps your working memory active and focused on the content of the lecture. You can always cross out or eliminate unnecessary information later.

- **Strategy 2: Mentally summarize.** While you wait for new information to be introduced, in your mind, mentally summarize, list, or question the main ideas and details that have been presented. You can ask yourself basic questions, such as *What are the three points the speaker just made? Is this the way the textbook presented this information?*

- **Strategy 3: Predict the next point or an answer to a question.** With active listening, you can often "mentally tune in" to the speaker's outline or organizational plan for the lecture. Predict the next point that would naturally follow the sequential development of information. Then listen carefully to determine if your prediction was correct.

Increase Your Writing Rate

Notetaking problems frequently occur because the rate of speech during a lecture is faster than your rate of writing. Your notetaking goal is *not* to write fast enough to write word for word; that is not feasible, practical, nor useful as notes should be *condensed* versions of information. Your goal is to develop a writing fluency or speed that is fast enough to write important information in your notes. Research studies show that writing fluency has the greatest impact on the quality of your notes. The following three time-saving strategies can improve your writing rate and fluency:

- **Strategy 4: Paraphrase the speaker.** *Paraphrasing* is the process of using your own words to rephrase or restate another person's words without losing the original meaning. Paraphrasing begins as a mental process that must be done quickly. As soon as you capture the speaker's words, interpret the information quickly, condense it using your own words, and write the shortened form in your notes. Your "sentences" do not need to be grammatically correct. You may omit words such as *the, an, and, there, here,* and other words that do not add to the overall meaning. Paraphrasing is perhaps one of the most difficult parts of notetaking, but with practice and familiarity with different instructors' lecture styles, your skills at paraphrasing will improve, and so will your writing fluency.

- **Strategy 5: Use abbreviations and symbols.** Using abbreviations and symbols increases your writing speed. When you find content-related words that you use frequently, create your own abbreviations for the terms or use common abbreviations, such as the following:

BC for *because*	**PRES** for *president*
EX for *example*	**SOC** for *social or sociology*
IMP for *important*	**SOL** for *solutions*
POL for *politics*	**W/Out** for *without*

CONCEPT CHECK **11.9**

Why is it important to maintain a focus and concentrate during a lecture, even when the information is not challenging? What strategies work for you to increase your concentration level during lectures?

Paraphrasing is the process of using your own words to rephrase or restate another person's words without losing the original meaning.

Symbols are another form of abbreviations to use to increase your writing speed. Symbols frequently appear in math notes, but you can use symbols for other words as well. Following are common symbols you can use in your notes:

&	and	$\rightarrow$	leads to; causes
@	at	<	less than
$\downarrow$	decreases	>	more than; greater than
$\neq$	doesn't equal	#	number
=	equals	+/−	positive/negative
$\uparrow$	increases	$\therefore$	therefore
+	add; also	−	subtract
×	times	/	divide; per
( )	quantity	p∧q	conjunction *and*
~p	negation (not *p*)	p∨q	disjunction *or*

- **Strategy 6: Use modified printing.** Modified printing is a style of handwriting that is functional and increases writing speed by using a mixture of cursive writing and printing. While taking notes, you can relax your handwriting standards and experiment with switching back and forth from printing and cursive writing to increase your writing speed.

CONCEPT CHECK 11.10

How can you increase your writing speed to capture more details from a lecture? Which strategies work well for you to increase your writing fluency?

Do Not Stop When You Fall Behind

Most students at one time or another experience frustration when they are not able to keep up with the speaker—even when using strategies to increase their writing speed. A normal tendency is to simply give up—stop taking notes and just listen. Sometimes that may not be a bad option, but later you may regret not having a written record of the information. Try using the following three strategies when you fall behind.

- **Strategy 7: Leave a gap and start writing again.** Instead of giving up, leave a gap in your notes and start taking notes again for as long as you can keep up with the instructor. After class, ask another student or the instructor to help fill in the gaps.

- **Strategy 8: Shift to paragraph form.** Sometimes becoming overly concerned with the notetaking format slows you down. If you find yourself spending too much time trying to decide how to number, label, or indent a detail, stop using your notetaking format and shift instead to writing paragraphs. Continue to paraphrase and use abbreviations or symbols in your paragraphs when possible. See **Figure 11.4** for an example of shifting to paragraph form.

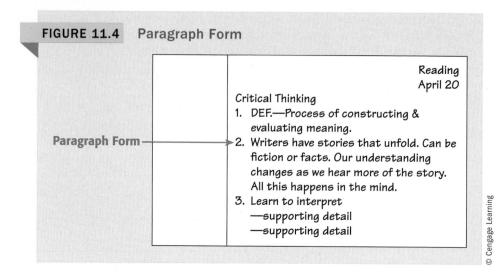

FIGURE 11.4 Paragraph Form

Paragraph Form

> Reading
> April 20
>
> Critical Thinking
> 1. DEF.—Process of constructing & evaluating meaning.
> 2. Writers have stories that unfold. Can be fiction or facts. Our understanding changes as we hear more of the story. All this happens in the mind.
> 3. Learn to interpret
>   —supporting detail
>   —supporting detail

© Cengage Learning

- **Strategy 9: Tape the lecture.** If you consistently have difficulties keeping up with one instructor's style and rate of speech in lectures, ask your instructor for permission to tape the lectures. If permission is granted, sit near the front of the room to tape the lecture. The tape recorder is used to supplement, not replace your lecture notes, so you must continue to take notes as you record the lecture. After class, return to specific sections of the tape so you can listen to the information one more time and add missing details in your notes.

Strategies to Strengthen Notetaking Skills

Taking meaningful, comprehensive lecture notes is a challenge because of the multiple processes that are involved. Combining the strategies already discussed and the following strategies will strengthen your notetaking skills and help you achieve your lecture notetaking goals of capturing and organizing important information from lectures.

- **Familiarize yourself with the topic *before* class.** Become familiar with the terminology, main concepts, and key details by previewing the chapter that will be discussed in class; read the chapter if time permits.

- **Activate your visual skills.** Try to visualize information as it is presented. Turn on the "movie in your mind" to create a visual association with the verbal information.

- **Deal with sidetracking.** If the instructor *sidetracks* by discussing information that does not seem to fit within the order or the outline of the topics, continue to take notes on the *sidetracked information* as it may be important. Write sidetracked information on the *back side* of the previous page of notes, or include sidetracked information in your regular notes but place these notes inside a box to separate them from your regular notes. (See **Figure 11.5.**)

FIGURE 11.5   Ways to Take Notes on Sidetracking

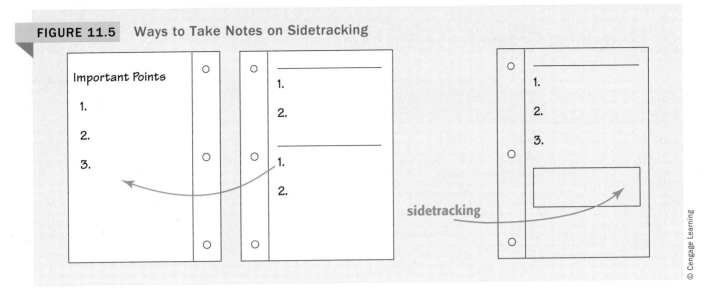

- **Watch for visual clues**. Information that instructors write on the chalkboard or visual graphics that instructors display on a screen are visual clues that information is important. Include visual information as much as possible in your notes. Following are additional suggestions to use:

  - If you recall seeing the same chart or visual information in your textbook, jot down a quick reminder to yourself to refer to the textbook chapter.

  - If the visual information does not appear in your textbook, sketch the visual graphic and jot down as many details as possible.

  - Ask questions about the visual materials. This provides you with the opportunity to get more information from the instructor as to what information from the visual graphic is important to place in your notes.

- **Watch for nonverbal clues**. Watch your instructor's *nonverbal clues* or patterns as well. Body stance, hand gestures, and facial expressions (forehead wrinkles, eyebrows rise) are nonverbal clues that communicate to observant listeners. Following are other points about nonverbal clues.

  - If the instructor pauses to look at his or her notes or simply pauses to allow you time to write, the pauses are nonverbal clues that suggest the information is important to include in your notes.

  - Nonverbal clues, such as pauses or glances toward the wall or ceiling, may signal that the instructor is shifting to another heading or main idea, or that he or she wants to verify that all the important details have been mentioned.

  - Writing information on the board, pointing to parts of it over and over, and circling words on the board are also nonverbal clues indicating that information is important.

EXERCISE 11.2

Matching Problems to Solutions

DIRECTIONS: Read each problem in the list on the left. Then find the solution to the problem from the list on the right. Write the letter of the solution on the line. You may use each answer only once.

_____ 1. I often tune the speaker out because I don't like the person or the topic.

_____ 2. I often pretend I am listening, but I am really thinking about other things.

_____ 3. I fall behind during a lecture because I try to write everything the speaker says.

_____ 4. I get bored and start daydreaming when the speaker talks slowly.

_____ 5. I end up with confused notes because the speaker sidetracks so often.

_____ 6. I am often told that I look bored, disinterested, and rude because of the way I sit.

_____ 7. Friends ask me to listen to their problems and then get annoyed when I give my opinion.

_____ 8. I get frustrated taking lecture notes because the terminology is unfamiliar.

_____ 9. When lectures follow the sections in the book, there is too much to capture in Cornell notes.

_____ 10. I can't write fast enough to record all of a speaker's anecdotes and examples.

_____ 11. My notes are a jumbled mess—the information all runs together.

_____ 12. Controversial subjects trigger my emotions, and I stop listening so I can form my argument.

a. Stop pretending; use strategies to focus.

b. Paraphrase instead of trying to capture every word.

c. Adjust your attitude toward the speaker so you can hear the content of the message.

d. Use good posture with an open-body position, and use eye contact.

e. Summarize or jot just a key point instead of trying to write the whole story.

f. Use the Book Notes System; take notes in the book.

g. Use critical thinking skills and separate your emotions from the listening process.

h. Be an empathic listener without giving advice or opinion.

i. Take separate notes on the back side of your note paper.

j. Use the format of a notetaking system for more structure.

k. Keep writing, anticipate new points, or mentally summarize.

l. Familiarize yourself with the chapter before the lecture.

GROUP PROCESSING

A Collaborative Learning Activity

Form groups of three or four students. Then complete the following directions.

1. On a large chart, make two columns. In the left column, brainstorm problems that students encounter when they take lecture notes. List as many problems as you can think of within a ten-minute period.

2. In the right column, brainstorm possible solutions for each of the problems. Include solutions you know from personal experience and solutions that appear in this chapter.

CHECK POINT 11.2

True or False? See Test-Taking Strategies 1–9 in Appendix A.

_____ 1. The most common cause of notetaking problems is the discrepancy between thinking and speaking rates.

_____ 2. If you think at 400 words per minute and your instructor speaks at 80 words per minute, you may need to use strategies, such as mentally summarizing, to stay attentive to the lecture.

_____ 3. Paraphrasing, using abbreviations, and modified printing are strategies to help you increase your writing fluency.

_____ 4. Following a lecture, you should always schedule time on the weekend to refine, complete, and review your notes.

_____ 5. Verbal clues and nonverbal clues provide you with information about what is important to capture in your notes.

_____ 6. The rate of writing is faster than the rate of thinking but not faster than the rate of speaking.

Access Chapter 11 Practice Quiz 2 in your College Success CourseMate, accessed through *CengageBrain.com*.

Notetaking Systems for Lectures

 Explain how to use two-column and three-column notes, book notes, partial outline notes, and PowerPoint notes for classroom lectures.

Being familiar and comfortable with a variety of notetaking systems allows you to select the most appropriate and effective notetaking system to use for specific lecture styles and course content. **Figure 11.6** shows notetaking systems that are recommended for specific kinds of lectures; however, you can select from the other options if they seem better suited to your notetaking needs.

Two-Column Notetaking System

The *Two-Column Notetaking System* is a method of notetaking that shows topics, vocabulary terms, or study questions in the left column and details or explanations in the right column. Two-column notes are a simplified version of Cornell notes. In this notetaking system, you can vary the width of each column to suit the content and your preferences. Use the following two steps to create two-column notes:

> The **Two-Column Notetaking System** is a method of notetaking that shows topics, vocabulary terms, or study questions in the left column and details or explanations in the right column.

- **Step 1: Write the topic in the left column.** Use the *left column* to write the subject, topic, main idea, vocabulary term, or a question.

- **Step 2: Write notes in the right column.** Directly across from the item in the left column, write details or explanations. As with Cornell notes, be brief, but not so brief that the information loses meaning over time. You can number details, use bullets for items in a list, or simply write the information in meaningful phrases or short sentences.

Two-column notes are easy to create and use when you take lecture or textbook notes. They are informal and reflect your preferences for the kinds of information you want to appear in each column. Use the following tips to create your two-column notes:

- **Be selective.** Do not clutter your notes with unnecessary information. Capture only the important information presented by the speaker.

FIGURE 11.6   Lecture Notetaking Options

	Cornell Notes	Two-Column Notes	Three-Column Notes	Outline Notes
Lectures *Mostly declarative knowledge: facts, definitions, examples, explanations*	Show headings. Number details. Create recall column.	Write topics, terminology, and questions in the left column. Number details in the right column.		Use I, II, III for topics. Use A,B,C for main ideas. Use 1, 2, 3 for details. Add a recall column if you wish.
Discussions		Write questions or topics in the left column. Write comments and explanations in the right column.		
Math or Procedural Knowledge Content *Steps, processes, equations*		Write the topic, process, or equation in the left column. Write the steps and the solution in the right column.	Write the process or equation in the left column; write the steps in the middle column; write explanations in the right column. **OR** Leave the middle column empty for reworking the problem later.	
PowerPoint Presentations		Write slide number in the left column. Write and number details in the right column.	Write the slide number in the left column. Sketch the slide in the middle column. Add notes or comments in the right column.	

© Cengage Learning

- **Space your notes.** To create stronger impressions of "chunks" of related information, leave a space between each new item or group of related items in your notes. The notes in the right-hand column should not look like a nonstop, steady stream of endless information.
- **Sketch diagrams or charts.** When the speaker presents diagrams or charts, you can sketch them in the left column and summarize them in the right column, or you may write a question about the chart in the left column and sketch the chart in the right column.

    In the following two-column notes from a lecture about forgetting theories, the left column includes a main heading (Five Theories), a term to define, and a

EXAMPLE: Forgetting Theories

Five Theories	5 theories explain why info may be forgotten or inaccessible in memory
Def.—Decay Theory	1. A forgetting theory that occurs in STM; stimuli too weak or unattended to 2. Stimuli decays or fades away
What happens to stimuli in STM?	Ignored stimuli decay from STM within 28 seconds

© Cengage Learning 2015

EXAMPLE: Practice Visualization (Lecture notes from Excerpt 2 in Appendix D)

Worst-case scenario	1. Imagine worst-case scenario — —tremble & signs of nervousness — neg. images in mind — increases anxiety — leads to self-fulfilling prophecy
Self-fulfilling prophecy ⟶	2. Images you hold set you up to perform in the way imagined

© Cengage Learning 2015

question that was posed during the lecture. The right column shows the details. In the second example, two terms, *worst-case scenario* and *self-fulfilling prophecy* appear in the left column; the right column shows details about each term.

Two-Column Notes for Math Lectures

Two-column notes are ideal for math lectures that often involve explanation and demonstration of steps to use to solve equations. During the lecture, write the math topic or principle in the left column with an explanation in the right column. You can also write the equation in the left column and the steps and solution in the right column. For some math classes, you may want to make two columns on graph paper to facilitate lining up columns of numbers in equations or graphing problems. Following are examples of two-column notes for math lectures.

Lisa F. Young/Shutterstock.com

How do taking lecture notes for math courses differ from taking lecture notes for other kinds of courses? What kinds of information should you capture in your notes from a math lecture?

EXAMPLE: Multiplying Negative and Positive Numbers

When both numbers are positive	Answer is positive. Example: $4 \times 9 = 36$
When both numbers are negative	Answer is positive. Example: $-5 \times -4 = 20$
When one number is positive and the other is negative	Answer is negative. Example: $(-3) \times 4 = -12$

© Cengage Learning 2015

EXAMPLE: Percentages to Fractions

Write 120% as fraction	$120\% = 120 \times \dfrac{1}{100} = \dfrac{120}{100} = 1\dfrac{1}{5}$
Write $16\dfrac{2}{3}\%$ as a fraction	$16\dfrac{2}{3}\% = 16\dfrac{2}{3} \times \dfrac{1}{100} = \dfrac{50}{3} \times \dfrac{1}{100} = \dfrac{50}{300} = \dfrac{1}{6}$

© Cengage Learning 2015

Your notetaking goal for math lectures is to copy the *exact* steps for solving a problem in your notes and to include brief explanations or paraphrase the instructor's explanation of each step. The following are five tips to increase your math notetaking skills.

1. **Copy signs and symbols accurately.** Omitting a sign or symbol or copying it incorrectly will affect not only the quality of your notes but also the accuracy of applying the steps to solve similar problems.

2. **Listen and watch for patterns.** Problems solved in class consist of underlying patterns used to solve similar problems at a later time. Look for similarities in problem patterns.

3. **Listen and watch for prototypes.** A specific problem discussed and solved in class may be the prototype (model) to memorize as an example for solving similar problems with similar characteristics. Your instructor may state that the steps used in a specific problem will be the same steps you need to use in a set of additional problems in your textbook, so listen carefully for the verbal clues from your instructor.

4. **Record explanations for steps.** Often the explanations remind you *when* to use a specific process and when *not* to use a specific process. They also tell you *why* a specific step is important.

5. **Write reminders to see the textbook.** If you are already familiar with the chapter, some of the problems presented in class may also be explained in your textbook. If your instructor indicates the problem is from the textbook, use an abbreviation such as *TXBK* next to the problem.

CONCEPT CHECK **11.11**

How is the Two-Column Notetaking System different from the Cornell Notetaking System? In what ways are they similar?

Two-Column Notes for Discussions

Two-column notes work effectively to capture different answers to questions posed during a lecture or questions used in a discussion group. Write the question, or a simplified version of the question, in the left column. Jot down different responses in the right column. Identify different responses by numbering or using dashes.

EXAMPLE: Discussion Topic

What was Jacob's motive?	1. wanted revenge or retaliation 2. wanted to impress Sarah 3. wanted to regain sense of pride and honor
What point of view was used?	1. first person — Jacob 2. 1st-person narrative — Jacob told his own version of story

© Cengage Learning 2015

EXERCISE 11.3

Transfer These Skills: Two-Column Notes

DIRECTIONS:

1. Create a set of two-column notes for any lecture class you attend this term. Place the topics or main points in the left column. Write the corresponding details across from each topic or main point in the right column. Organize the details by using numbering or dashes to separate individual details.

2. If your instructor requests feedback from the instructor of your other class, use the *Instructor Questionnaire* for Exercise 11.3 in the College Success CourseMate Topics In-Depth. Schedule an office appointment with the instructor to get feedback on your set of two-column notes.

Access Chapter 11 Topics In-Depth: Exercise 11.3 Transfer These Skills: Two-Column Notes in your College Success CourseMate, accessed through *CengageBrain.com*.

3. Turn your notes and the questionnaire in for grading or feedback.

Three-Column Notetaking System

The *Three-Column Notetaking System* is a method of notetaking that shows topics, vocabulary terms, or study questions in the left column, followed by two categories of details in the remaining two columns. The labels you use for the two categories of information will vary depending on the lecture content. It will be up to you to decide how to label each column in your notes and how wide to make each column.

> The **Three-Column Notetaking System** is a method of notetaking that shows topics, vocabulary terms, or study questions in the left column, followed by two categories of details in the remaining two columns.

Use Three-Column Notes to Define Terms

In the following example, the instructor wanted to help students prepare for an upcoming test. The instructor chose to discuss and review important terminology for the chapter. As the instructor identified a term, the student wrote the term in the first column. The student used the second column to write the definition and the third column to add any additional details or applications presented by the instructor. This three-column format is ideal for working with terminology because it follows the pattern you learned in Chapter 9 for studying terminology. For math terminology presented in lectures, write the term in the first column. As the instructor defines or explains the term, write the information in the middle column. In the third column, add any related details, rules, or explanations. You can also use this three-column notes format to create other kinds of study and review tools.

Example: Definitions and Applications

Topic/Concept	Definition or Explanation	Details
continental shelf	shallow, sloping area located around the margins of continents	• Average depth 400 feet • On average stretch out from land 45 mi • About 90% of all fish and shellfish harvested from continental shelves

Source: Adapted from Butz, *Science of Earth Systems,* p. 419.

Use Three-Column Notes for Math

CONCEPT CHECK 11.12

Why are three-column notes more useful at times than two-column notes? What different categories of information can you use to label the three columns in this notetaking system?

When you know you will need to review and rework math problems presented in lectures, consider using the three-column notetaking system. Begin by copying the original math problem in the first column. Then, skip the middle column. In the third column, write the steps discussed in the lecture to solve the problem. After the lecture when you are ready to review, fold the third column back so you cannot see the problem-solving steps. Rework the problem in the middle column. Unfold the third column to check your accuracy.

Example: Math Problems

Fold this column back until you rework the problem.

Original Math Problem	Space to Rework the Problem	Original Solution from Textbook or Class
Leave the answer in exponential form: $4^5 \times 4^7$		$4^5 \times 4^7 = 4^{5+7} = 4^{12}$

© Cengage Learning 2015

Study Your Two-Column and Three-Column Notes

CONCEPT CHECK 11.13

Explain how reciting and feedback are used when you study from two-column and three-column notes.

Use recitation to study from your two-column and three-column notes. For both kinds of notes, look only at the left column. Cover up the right column(s). Recite the information on the right, and then uncover the column(s) to check your accuracy. Continue to study by reversing the process; cover up other columns, recite, and check your accuracy. Notice how recitation and feedback are the same processes used to study Cornell notes. For math notes taken with a three-column system, rework the problems or equations, and then compare your results with the original problem and solution.

The Book Notes System

The *Book Notes System* is a method of notetaking that involves marking a textbook as the instructor moves systematically through a chapter. Lecturing straight from the textbook is not very common, but does occur on occasion, such as in technical, reading, composition, and some math courses. When an instructor moves systematically through the textbook chapter, discussing various headings, emphasizing certain details, demonstrating how to solve problems, or working textbook exercises with you in class, you can take notes directly in your textbook. Use the following strategies to take book notes:

- Use a specific colored marker to highlight the information the instructor discusses.
- Write notes in the margins to reflect any additional information or explanations.
- Use symbols, such as arrows or stars, to draw your attention to sections discussed.
- After class, use the textbook markings and marginal notes to develop a separate set of follow-up or summary notes on notebook paper if you wish.

> The **Book Notes System** is a method of notetaking that involves marking a textbook as the instructor moves systematically through a chapter.

CONCEPT CHECK 11.14

When can you use the Book Notes System effectively? Why is it not possible to use this system for many of your lecture classes?

Textbook Case Studies

DIRECTIONS:

1. Read each case study carefully. Respond to the question at the end of each case study by using *specific* strategies discussed in this chapter. Answer in complete sentences.

2. Write your responses on paper or online in this textbook's College Success CourseMate, Textbook Case Studies. You will be able to print your online response or e-mail it to your instructor.

CASE STUDY 1: Aisha is very uncomfortable sitting in a classroom. She often feels like other students are watching her, so she sits in the back corner. She has a lot of problems taking notes. Her notes are too brief and ineffective for studying. She does not include information written on the board because she cannot see it clearly. At other times, she simply loses her concentration. When she does try taking notes, she cannot write fast enough to get all of the instructor's words on her paper. What would you recommend Aisha do to improve her notetaking skills?

CASE STUDY 2: Alex prefers to listen to a lecture on a topic before reading his textbook. He believes the lecture will highlight for him the important points he should learn when he reads the chapter. During a lecture, he frequently annoys his classmates and instructors by interrupting the instructor to ask irrelevant questions or to ask the instructor to repeat information or to slow down. He always seems confused. Consequently, he spends more time talking than listening and taking notes. What techniques does Alex need to learn in order to be a more effective listener and leave lectures with more effective lecture notes?

 Access Chapter 11 Textbook Case Studies in your College Success CourseMate, accessed through *CengageBrain.com*.

Partial Outline Notes

In some lectures, the instructor may provide you with a partial outline of the lecture at the beginning of the class. With the partial outline as the skeleton of the main topics in the lecture, your goal then is to complete the outline by filling in the missing details. **Figure 11.7** shows an example of an instructor's outline presented before the lecture begins. Following are important points about completing lecture outline notes:

- Partial outlines organize the different levels of information for you. Usually, the instructor's lecture will follow the outline without sidetracking to other topics. Knowing that you need to listen carefully for the appropriate details to complete the outline increases concentration and active listening skills.

- If sufficient space is not provided on the partial outline for you to add all the details you want in your notes, you can branch out on the page to add details. Later, if you wish, you could rewrite or type the outline with your expanded notes.

- If you tend to take detailed notes and notice that the partial outline may lack sufficient space, you can begin to take outline notes on your own paper. Use the handout as a guide for structuring your own outline notes.

FIGURE 11.7   Example of an Instructor's Lecture Outline

Outline for Feb. 5 Lecture

Practice Effective Listening

I. Direct and Indirect Listening

   A. Direct Listening Cultures

      1. Def-

      2. Countries

         a.

         b.

         c.

   B. Indirect Listening Cultures

      1. Def-

      2. Countries

         a.

         b.

   C. Culturally Sensitive Words

      1.

      2.

      3.

   D. Gender-Sensitive Words

      1.

      2.

New Lecture Notes

EXERCISE 11.5

DIRECTIONS:

1. For this assignment, your instructor will provide you with a new lecture situation. This may involve taking notes for a lecture presented by a guest speaker, taking notes on a specific video, taking notes from one of your lecture classes, or taking notes on a lecture your instructor presents on a new topic.

2. Select the most appropriate notetaking system to use to take a complete set of notes:
    a. Cornell notes
    b. Informal outline notes
    c. Two-column notes
    d. Three-column notes
    e. PowerPoint notes

3. Go to Exercise 11.5 in Appendix C, page C26–C27, for the Lecture Notetaking Checklist. Complete the checklist and refer to "Scoring Your Responses" to evaluate the effectiveness of your notes.

PowerPoint Notes

PowerPoint Notes are lecture notes based on a series of slides that include visual graphics and key points or topics. PowerPoint slides are a form of visual graphics that has become popular and widely used for classroom lectures and presentations. A special projector hooked to a computer projects individual slides created by using the Power-Point program. Instructors click through a series of slides. As a slide with words, graphics, and possibly other special effects, such as animations, appears on the wall or screen, the instructor refers to the slide in his or her lecture. Sometimes the instructor reads what is on the slide and then clarifies or expands with details; other times the instructor discusses the slide but does not read word-for-word what appears on the slide.

> **PowerPoint Notes** are lecture notes based on a series of slides that include visual graphics and key points or topics.

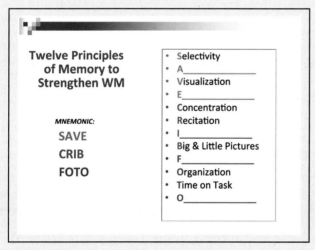

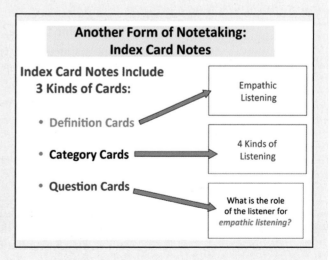

Slides created with Microsoft PowerPoint® © Cengage Learning 2015

Instructors use PowerPoint slides in a variety of ways, which means you will need to be familiar with a variety of methods for taking notes on PowerPoint slides. Even though you may have access to the entire PowerPoint presentation, your instructor will provide additional details or explanations about the content in the slides. Do not sit back and rely solely on the slides; take notes to capture additional key points.

Multiple Slides on a Page

When your instructor provides you with a printed copy of multiple PowerPoint slides on a page, usually four to six slides per page, listen carefully for explanations or details not included on the slides. Use lines to branch off each slide; place key words at the end of each line or branch. If sufficient space is not available to connect key ideas to each slide, use the two-column notetaking system; write the slide number in the left column and the details about each slide in the right column.

PowerPoint Slides with a Notes Column

CONCEPT CHECK   11.15

What do you see as advantages or disadvantages of instructors using PowerPoint slides in their lectures or discussions? Why is it necessary to take notes on PowerPoint slides?

Your instructor may provide you with a printed copy of the PowerPoint slides, usually two or three slides per page, with a "notes" column on the right. In the notes column, take notes on explanations and details not included in the original slide. Using bullets for separate details helps you group information into meaningful parts.

Partial PowerPoint Slides

When your instructor provides you with a printed copy of partially completed PowerPoint slides, listen carefully for and watch for the missing details. Write the details on the lines provided on the partial PowerPoint slides. When information is presented that is not on the slide, jot down the key points in the space next to the picture of the PowerPoint slide.

PowerPoint Outline

Some instructors may provide you with a printed outline of the PowerPoint slides, but not the slides themselves. As with lecture outline notes, add details to the end of the lines of the outline. If there is sufficient space and if you have sufficient time, sketch the PowerPoint slide to show any additional details that do not appear in the outline.

PowerPoint Slides to Download

If your instructor announces that the PowerPoint slides used in class will be available to download online after class, select a notetaking system to take notes on each PowerPoint slide. Again, the two-column notetaking system is efficient to use for taking notes on PowerPoint presentations. After class, when you download the slides, attach your notes to the printed slides or attach details to the pictures of each slide. You can use these same techniques if you are taking an online course and the "lecture" involves the use of PowerPoint slides.

Transfer These Skills: PowerPoint Notes

DIRECTIONS: Do one of the following activities for taking notes on PowerPoint slides. Attach a short paragraph explaining the process you used for taking notes.

1. Demonstrate how to take notes on PowerPoint slides used in any one of your classes this term. Write the name of the course and instructor on your PowerPoint notes. You may be asked to share your notes in class or to turn them in for instructor comments.

2. Your instructor may use PowerPoint slides for a chapter in this textbook. Demonstrate ways to take notes on the slides presented in class. You may be asked to share your notes in class or to turn them in for instructor comments.

CHAPTER 11
REFLECTIVE WRITING 2

On separate paper, in a journal, or online in this textbook's College Success CourseMate, respond to the following questions.

1. Which strategies in this chapter were the most beneficial for helping you become a more effective listener? Be specific.

2. Which strategies in this chapter were the most beneficial for helping you take more effective lecture notes? Be specific.

Access Chapter 11 Reflective Writing 2 in your College Success CourseMate, accessed through *CengageBrain.com*.

CHECK POINT 11.3

Answers appear on Appendix B4.

True or False? See Test-Taking Strategies 1–9 in Appendix A.

_____ 1. Effective notetakers use Cornell notes for lectures, outline notes for math courses, and two- or three-column notes only for discussions.

_____ 2. The content of the lecture and the instructor's lecture style often determine which notetaking system would be the most effective to use.

_____ 3. Every student should master one specific notetaking system and then always use that system consistently for taking notes in every class.

_____ 4. The Book Notes System is designed to be used when you read a textbook before the instructor discusses the information in class.

_____ 5. The Two-Column Notetaking System is a simplified version of the Cornell System.

_____ 6. Partial outline notes are ineffective because they limit the kind of information you can include in your notes.

Access Chapter 11 Practice Quiz 3 in your College Success CourseMate, accessed through *CengageBrain.com*.

Working with Your Notes

(4) *Discuss strategies to study and learn from lecture notes.*

Taking lecture notes helps you stay focused on the lecture and keeps your mind from wandering. The most significant purpose of taking notes, however, is to create study tools to use *after* the class has ended. As you learned in Chapter 3, scheduling a study block as soon after a lecture as possible gives you the opportunity to work with your notes while the information is still fresh in your mind. The following five strategies are effective for any of the notetaking systems you choose to use for lecture notes. Use these effective strategies as soon after class as possible:

1. **Complete your notes.** Add missing details, fill in gaps, and correct any misspelled key terms that appear in your notes. Confer with other students or your instructor, or refer to your textbook for missing information or correct spellings. If you chose to use the Cornell Notetaking System, complete the reduce step by creating the recall column.

2. **Add more structure to your notes.** If your notes lack a clear structure or appear disorganized, insert headings, number the individual details, or separate details with bullets. Highlight specific concepts or key words, or use a colored pen to circle terminology to create more structure for your notes.

3. **Supplement your notes.** As you work with your notes, you may want to make lists of information, brief outlines of main ideas, or clarifying questions that you would like to ask in class. Each type of notetaking system recommends that you write only on the front side of your notebook paper. Use the back sides for adding supplementary notes or questions.

4. **Rewrite your notes when justified.** Do not spend valuable time rewriting lecture (or textbook) notes simply for the sake of producing a neater set of notes. However, if the physical process of rewriting notes by hand or on a computer boosts memory and encodes information in a form that is easier to recall, take the time to rewrite and possibly even reorganize your notes.

5. **Recite, reflect, and review your notes.** The true value of your notes involves using them *after* the lecture. Spend time digesting the information, reciting the information, reworking problems, rehearsing, and reflecting. At the beginning of your next study block for the class, you can use your notes as a *warm-up activity*. Schedule time each week to use your notes for *ongoing review*.

CONCEPT CHECK   **11.16**

To get the most value from your notes, what strategies do you use to work with and study your notes?

CHECK POINT 11.4

Answers appear on Appendix B4.

Short Answer See Test-Taking Strategies 32–36 in Appendix A.

Answer the following short-answer questions on separate paper.

1. Describe ways you can improve your notes after a lecture.

2. What are the advantages and disadvantages of copying, rewriting, or typing your notes after a lecture?

 Access Chapter 11 Practice Quiz 4 in your College Success CourseMate, accessed through *CengageBrain.com*.

Chapter 11 Critical Thinking

BACKGROUND: Critical reading, critical listening, and critical thinking all involve working with information on deeper levels, analyzing the development of information for logic, consistency, accuracy, and sufficient details to support an argument or develop an idea.

DIRECTIONS:

1. Read Excerpt 8: How to Listen Critically and Guidelines for Critical Listening in Appendix D.

2. What do critical reading of online materials, critical thinking, and critical listening have in common? Create a list of key words or key actions that are shared by critical readers, critical thinkers, and critical listeners.

Learning Objectives Review

Terms to Know

1 Discuss listening and memory processes, factors that influence the quality of listening, the four kinds of listening, and steps to create an effective listening plan.

- Of the four verbal communication skills, listening is the most frequently used and often the weakest. Weak listening skills may be due to lack of training as well as the way our memory system processes information.

- Due to the limitations of short-term memory, using effort and undivided attention is essential to prevent stimuli from dropping out of our memory.

- Listening fluctuation, or the process of tuning in and tuning out, is a natural process that occurs for a variety of reasons. Listening interferences and influencing personal factors affect the quality of our listening experiences.

- Four kinds of listening, each with different listening goals, include active listening, critical listening, empathic listening, and appreciative listening.

- An eight-step listening plan improves the quality of listening and ability to use this verbal communication skill more effectively.

2 Discuss strategies to use to capture important lecture information; manage thinking, speaking, and writing discrepancies; and strengthen notetaking skills.

- Effective notetaking involves learning how to capture six kinds of information from lectures: headings, main ideas, terminology, supporting details, verbal cues, and the conclusion.

- The rates of speaking, thinking, and writing cause difficulties during the process of taking lecture notes. An average rate of speaking in a lecture is 125 words per minute; the average rate of thinking is 400 words per minute, and the average rate of writing is 30 words per minute.

- Three strategies are available to maintain undivided attention; three strategies are available to increase writing rate; and three strategies are available to use when you cannot keep up with the speaker.

By yourself or with a partner, practice reciting or writing definitions for the following terms. You may also practice defining these terms by using the online flashcards or comparing your answers to the online glossary.

listening p. 339

listening interferences p. 341

active listening p. 342

critical listening p. 342

empathic listening p. 343

appreciative listening p. 343

rate of speaking p. 348

rate of thinking p. 349

rate of writing p. 349

paraphrasing p. 350

Two-Column Notetaking System p. 355

Three-Column Notetaking System p. 359

Book Notes System p. 361

PowerPoint Notes p. 363

 Access Chapter 11 Flashcards and Online Glossary in your College Success CourseMate, accessed through *CengageBrain.com*.

- Familiarizing yourself with the topic, visualizing, dealing with sidetracking, watching for visual clues, and watching for nonverbal clues are additional strategies to use to strengthen your notetaking skills.

③ *Explain how to use two-column and three-column notes, book notes, partial outline notes, and PowerPoint notes for classroom lectures.*

- The Two-Column Notetaking System uses modified Cornell notes. During a lecture, begin by recording notes in the left column and then add details in the right column. Two-column notes work effectively for a variety of notetaking settings.

- The Three-Column Notetaking System begins with the topics, questions, or math problems on the left and then different categories of information in the remaining two columns to the right. Effective uses include taking notes to define terms and to capture math lecture information and explanations.

- The Book Notes System is an effective system for lectures in which the instructor moves systematically through the chapter, highlighting important points or expanding on sections with additional details.

- Partial outline notes are used in some lectures when instructors provide students with an outline that needs to be completed with details during the lecture.

- PowerPoint notes are based on the instructor using a series of PowerPoint slides to present information. Effective notetakers know a variety of ways to take notes when instructors use PowerPoint slides.

④ *Discuss strategies to study and learn from lecture notes.*

- Taking lecture notes by itself is of little value; the true value comes from working with your notes and using your notes to learn and review information.

- Five strategies are effective for working with all kinds of notes as soon after class as possible. These include completing notes, adding structure, supplementing notes, rewriting notes, and using the processes of reciting, reflecting, and reviewing.

Chapter 11   Review Questions

Answers appear on page B4.

Multiple Choice See Test-Taking Strategies 10–15 in Appendix A.

_____ 1. Which of the following is the most frequently used form of communication?
   a. Writing
   b. Listening
   c. Reading
   d. Speaking

_____ 2. Your listening efficiency or ability may be influenced by
   a. your attitude toward the subject and familiarity with the subject.
   b. the limitations of your short-term memory processes.
   c. the speaker's style of delivery, tone of voice, and rate of speech.
   d. all of the above.

_____ 3. Which of the following is *not* true about writing fluency?

    a. Your writing fluency has minimal effect on the quality of your notes.

    b. Writing fluency refers to a person's rate of writing.

    c. A person with high writing fluency most likely knows how to paraphrase.

    d. A person with low writing fluency may fall behind while taking notes during a lecture.

_____ 4. Listening goals

    a. vary for each of the four kinds of listening.

    b. involve understanding different kinds of information for different purposes.

    c. for critical listening involve higher-level thinking skills, such as analysis.

    d. involve all of the above.

_____ 5. Which of the following is *not* true?

    a. An effective listening plan involves steps related to attitude, purpose, image, and depth of details.

    b. Empathic listeners focus on a person's feelings in order to give advice and guidance.

    c. An effective listening plan involves steps related to taking notes, refocusing, giving feedback, and asking questions.

    d. Familiarizing yourself with the topic before class promotes active listening.

_____ 6. When taking lecture notes, strive to

    a. capture main ideas and important details.

    b. increase writing speed by using abbreviations and modified printing.

    c. listen for word clues that help you organize levels of information.

    d. do all of the above.

_____ 7. The best notetaking system to use in lecture classes is

    a. always the Cornell system.

    b. a notetaking system that works well with the lecturer's style and content.

    c. two-column notes with the topic or question on the right.

    d. a formal outline that shows specific levels of information.

_____ 8. Paraphrasing

    a. involves rephrasing and shortening a speaker's words.

    b. is an effective strategy to use to keep up with the speaker when taking notes.

    c. can be used to pose questions to the speaker.

    d. involves all of the above.

_____ 9. Notes for PowerPoint presentations

    a. must have a sketch of the slide to be effective and meaningful.

    b. are always written on a handout that provides a place next to graphics to take notes.

    c. vary depending on how the instructor uses the slides and the handouts provided.

    d. are less detailed than Cornell notes used for many kinds of lectures.

Short-Answer Questions See Test-Taking Strategies 32–36 in Appendix A.

Write your answers on separate paper.

1. What strategies can you use to combat the effects of a discrepancy between the rate of speech and the rate of writing?

2. Explain the different notetaking systems that you would select to take lecture notes for a sociology class, lecture notes for a math class, and lecture notes for a PowerPoint presentation.

Access Chapter 11 Enhanced Quiz and Chapter 11 Study Guide in your College Success CourseMate, accessed through *CengageBrain.com*.

Access all Chapter 11 Online Materials in your College Success CourseMate, accessed through *CengageBrain.com*.

12 Using Technology

Tetra Images/Erik Isakson/Alamy

The computer and digital technology revolution has changed the way we perform many daily tasks, the way we communicate, read books, complete coursework, conduct business and finances, shop, take and store photographs, listen to music, and watch videos or movies. Changes in technology, software, hardware, and electronic devices occur at a rapid pace, leaving many people feeling outdated or out of touch with existing or new technology. This chapter is designed to examine basic computer concepts, common elements in online courses, use of the Internet and websites, and, finally, useful resources and applications for students to use.

Access Chapter 12 Expanded Chapter Outline in your College Success CourseMate, accessed through *CengageBrain.com*.

YOUR CHAPTER MAPPING

After reading information under each heading, return to the chapter visual mapping below. Add key words to show subheadings and important details related to each heading.

Access Chapter 12 Visual Mapping in your College Success CourseMate, accessed through *CengageBrain.com*.

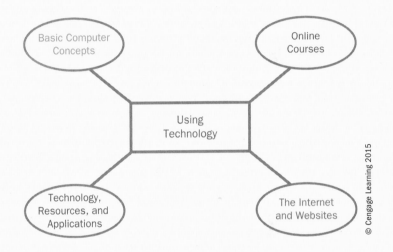

© Cengage Learning 2015

LEARNING OBJECTIVES

1 *Discuss basic computer concepts, including your level of computer literacy and essential computer skills for online courses.*

2 *Discuss key concepts of online courses, including advantages, disadvantages, online math courses, use of discussion boards, and online conduct and etiquette.*

3 *Explain strategies for conducting Internet searches, evaluating online materials, and avoiding plagiarism.*

4 *Demonstrate a willingness to explore new technology, resources, and applications.*

© Cengage Learning 2015

Using Technology

ANSWER, **SCORE**, and **RECORD** your profile before you read this chapter. If you need to review the process, refer to the complete directions given in the profile for Chapter 1 on page 4.

ONLINE: You can complete the profile and get your score online in this textbook's College Success CourseMate.

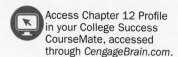 Access Chapter 12 Profile in your College Success CourseMate, accessed through *CengageBrain.com*.

	YES	NO
1. I know how to perform simple tasks on a computer, such as writing, saving, and printing a document.	___	___
2. I know how to access, write, receive, save, and print e-mail messages.	___	___
3. I have adequate computer skills that I could take an online class with confidence.	___	___
4. I manage time well and have good self-discipline, so I am confident that I can complete online coursework on time.	___	___
5. I often send e-mails or bulletin board messages without proofreading or checking them for inappropriate wording or comments.	___	___
6. I get frustrated or confused when I have to use search engines to find websites or databases online.	___	___
7. I know that all information on the Internet is reliable and accurate or it would not be allowed to be posted online.	___	___
8. I understand how to write and cite information to avoid being guilty of plagiarism.	___	___
9. I am familiar with a variety of apps (applications) to use on a smartphone or tablet.	___	___
10. I am confident in my ability to use existing technology and to learn new technology when there is a need to update my skills, my hardware, my software, or my digital devices.	___	___

QUESTIONS LINKED TO THE CHAPTER LEARNING OBJECTIVES:

Questions 1–2: objective 1   Question 9: objective 4

Questions 3–5: objective 2   Question 10: all objectives

Questions 6–8: objective 3

Basic Computer Concepts

1 Discuss basic computer concepts, including your level of computer literacy and essential computer skills for online courses.

In this age of technology, for many people the computer is an integral part of daily personal, academic, and professional life. We use computers and the Internet for e-mail, banking, travel plans, shopping, information searches, online courses, reading e-books, creating and saving documents, creating or accessing databases, organizing and storing photographs, playing games, locating maps and driving directions, and performing more advanced tasks such as managing inventories, investing, drafting blueprints, analyzing data, and creating and editing movies.

Computers and the ability to use technology to perform a variety of tasks and access information are creating an enormous gap between two groups of people: those who have computer skills and competencies and those who have limited or no computer skills or familiarity with technology. Some adults may not have had access, interest, or opportunities to learn basic skills to use computers or other electronic devices.

Understanding basic computer concepts, such as those in **Figure 12.1**, is a starting point to open the door to the world of digital technology. Learning *about computers* is a starting point, but you must also learn how to *use computers*. Fortunately, college campuses offer a variety of computer and technology courses for beginners as well as for advanced users who need to learn new software, upgrade skills, and delve into the world of creating new software, programs, applications, and digital devices.

CONCEPT CHECK   12.1
How do you use computer technology in your daily life?

Computer Literacy

Computer literacy means having knowledge and competency to use computers, computer programs, and computer applications efficiently. On a very basic level, being computer literate refers to having skills to perform simple tasks and use basic programs such as Microsoft Word, Internet Explorer, PowerPoint, e-mail, and social networking programs, such as Facebook, Twitter, or LinkedIn. On a more advanced level, being computer literate includes understanding the following:

- How computer hardware and software work
- How to create folders, subdirectories, file names, and file extensions
- How to troubleshoot computer problems
- How to update systems
- How to assess, install, and update security software systems
- How to figure out (or self-teach) how to use new programs or applications
- How to integrate and utilize features of a wide range of programs and applications

Computer literacy means having knowledge and competency to use computers, computer programs, and computer applications efficiently.

CONCEPT CHECK   12.2
How are the computer skills of a person with basic computer literacy skills different from the computer skills of a person with advanced computer literacy skills?

With the rapid development of new hardware and software, staying current with technology is challenging. For beginners, new programs or changes with familiar programs can be frustrating and confusing. However, as you become more familiar and more comfortable using a computer, the learning curve to use new technology becomes an exciting process to learn a new program or learn a more efficient way of performing a task. Assess your basic computer skills by completing **Exercise 12.1**.

FIGURE 12.1   Answers to Basic Questions about Computers

Perhaps one of the best ways to learn to use computers is to enroll in introductory computer classes to begin the process of learning to use technology. Textbooks for introductory courses often are easy to read, understand, and use to learn computer processes. The following questions and answers appear in the introductory section of the textbook *Computer Concepts 2013.*

What do I need to know about my computer? Computers come in many packages, including small handheld smartphones, sleek tablets, portable notebooks, and stationary desktop models. A computer runs software applications (also called programs) that help you accomplish a variety of tasks. (p. 0-4)

PC or Mac? Microcomputers are sometimes divided into two camps: PCs and Macs. PCs are manufactured by companies such as Dell, Lenova, Acer, and Hewlett-Packard. Macs are manufactured by Apple. Most PCs and some Macs use an operating system called Microsoft Windows. (p. 0-4)

What is the Windows desktop? Microsoft Windows is an example of a type of software called an operating system. The operating system controls all the basic tasks your computer performs, such as running applications software, manipulating files on storage devices, and transferring data to and from printers, digital cameras, and other devices. The operating system also controls the user interface—the way software appears on the screen and the way you control what it does. (p. 0-6)

What is a mouse? A mouse is a device used to manipulate items on the screen, such as the buttons and icons displayed on the Windows desktop. The mouse controls an on-screen pointer. The pointer is usually shaped like an arrow, but it can change to a different shape, depending on the task you're doing. For example, when the computer is busy, the arrow shape turns into an hourglass or circle signifying that you should wait for the computer to finish its current task before attempting to start a new task. (p. 0-8)

How do I tell the software what I want to do? Word processing, photo editing, and other software designed for use on computers running the Windows operating system is referred to as Windows software. Most Windows software works in a fairly uniform way and uses a similar set of controls. Each software application appears within a rectangular area called a window, which can include a title bar, a menu bar, a ribbon, a workspace, and the various (other) controls. (p. 0-11)

How do I create and save a document? To create a document, simply type text in the workspace provided by word processing software, such as Microsoft Word, OpenOffice Writer, LibreOffice Writer, or Apple iWork Pages . . . . It is a good idea to save your document every few minutes, even if it is not finished. When you save a document, use the Save icon at the top of the screen. Your computer is probably configured to save documents on the hard disk in a library called Documents or a folder called My Documents. There is no need to change that until you gain more experience. (p. 0-14)

How do I print a document? To print a document, simply click the File tab, File menu, or Office button, and then select Print. Your computer displays a window containing a series of print options. If you want to print a single copy of your document, these options should be correct, so you can click the Print or OK button to send your document to the printer. (p. 0-15)

What is the Internet? The Internet is the largest computer network in the world, carrying information from one continent to another in the blink of an eye. The computers connected to this network offer many types of resources, such as e-mail, instant messaging, social networking, popular music downloads, and online shopping. (p. 0-16)

What is the Web? Although some people use the terms *Internet* and *Web* interchangeably, the two are not the same. The Web—short for World Wide Web—is just one of the many resources available over this communications network. (p. 0-16)

How do I access the Internet? Most digital devices can be configured to connect to the Internet over the telephone, cell phone, satellite, or cable television systems. Internet access can also be obtained from school computer labs, local service providers such as your cable television company, and the national internet service providers such as AOL, AT&T, Comcast, Verizon, and EarthLink. (p. 0-16)

How do I use a browser? A browser lets you enter a unique Web page address called a URL, such as www.google.com. You can also jump from one Web page to another by using links. Links are usually underlined; and when you position the arrow-shaped mouse pointer over a link, it changes to a hand shape. (p. 0-16)

From Parsons, Oja. *Computer Concepts* © 2013 Course Technology, Cengage Learning

EXERCISE 12.1

Assessing Your Basic Computer Skills

DIRECTIONS: Use the following inventory to assess your basic computer skills. Check the tasks or processes that you know how to do. The items you do not check are items you can learn to perform by asking someone to teach you, finding instructions online, or enrolling in a computer course.

COMPUTER BASICS

I know how to:

_____ 1. Turn the computer on and off.

_____ 2. Use the mouse, the touchpad, or trackpad to interact with the items on the screen.

_____ 3. Print the information that appears on the screen.

_____ 4. Print an entire document.

_____ 5. Use the following on the keyboard: *tab, caps lock, shift, control (ctrl), backspace, delete,* and *spacebar.*

E-MAIL

I know how to:

_____ 1. Open an e-mail program, create an e-mail address, and use a password.

_____ 2. Compose and change or revise an e-mail before sending it.

_____ 3. Send and save an e-mail.

_____ 4. Open, respond, save, or delete e-mails received from others.

_____ 5. Print an e-mail message sent or received.

_____ 6. Use *instant messaging* within the e-mail program.

_____ 7. Create a *contacts list* or an address book.

_____ 8. Identify, block, or delete spam.

_____ 9. Log off or sign out before closing the browser.

WORD PROCESSING

I know how to:

_____ 1. Create or write a document.

_____ 2. Save a document (letter, report, notes) into a folder.

_____ 3. Save or back up a document on a flash drive (external device).

_____ 4. Print a document or print selected pages of a document.

_____ 5. Print multiple copies of a page or a document.

_____ 6. Delete sections of a document or an entire document.

_____ 7. Edit or change parts of a document.

_____ 8. Locate, retrieve, and open a specific document.

_____ 9. Move a file from one location to another in the directory.

_____ 10. Select and highlight text.

_____ 11. Add page numbers.

_____ 12. Cut and paste (move) highlighted text.

_____ 13. Insert or add text or an object into a file.

_____ 14. Use the spell check to correct misspellings.

_____ 15. Select and change fonts, font style, font size, and font color.

_____ 16. Use bold, italics, and underlining features.

_____ 17. Change line spacing (single spacing, double spacing).

_____ 18. Use basic icons on the toolbar or menu bar.

(continued)

Exercise 12.1 (continued)

INTERNET SEARCHES

I know how to:

_____ 1. Use a browser to access the Internet.

_____ 2. Use search engines to locate specific information.

_____ 3. Use links or URL addresses to get to specific websites.

_____ 4. Download and print items from websites.

_____ 5. Identify the source of website information.

_____ 6. Assess the authenticity, accuracy, and currency of information.

_____ 7. Save specific URLs as *favorites* or *bookmark* specific sites.

_____ 8. Search library or subject databases.

Computer Skills for Online Courses

At some point during your academic life, you will likely consider enrolling in one or more online courses. Many schools that offer online courses provide orientation courses or workshops to introduce students to the skills and format of the online courses. These orientations often include clear explanations of the following:

- Accessing the course online

- Creating and using a user name, a password, and signing in with an access code

- Understanding course requirements, expectations, and grading systems

- Using the e-mail system to send and receive e-mail messages

- Downloading and uploading e-mail attachments and documents

- Submitting different types of assignments

- Reading discussion boards; posting responses to discussions

- Navigating the management system

- Viewing videos and using links

- Surfing the Internet, using a browser, and locating specific information

CONCEPT CHECK 12.3

What computer skills are necessary to take an online course?

In addition to having basic computer skills for online courses, you will also need to have a computer with Internet access and the proper technology requirements for the course. Your online course or university will provide you with these requirements. For example, for certain courses, your computer may need to have these programs: Java, Adobe, and Microsoft Office with PowerPoint. Dial-up Internet is too slow for online courses, so you will need to have a high-speed Internet service or plan to do your online course work in a computer lab or a library with Internet access. Some online courses may also require that you have a cell phone for texting, as well as a social media account, such as Facebook, Twitter, LinkedIn, or Google Plus. Again, you will be informed of these requirements in advance as they may influence your decision about taking a specific online course.

Answers appear on page B4.

CHECK POINT 12.1

True or False? See Test-Taking Strategies 1–9 in Appendix A.

_____ 1. Software applications are also called programs.

_____ 2. The Internet is not the same as the web.

_____ 3. Knowing how to use an e-mail system to send and receive e-mail is one requirement of most online courses.

_____ 4. To be considered computer literate, a person must know how to install, evaluate, and integrate a variety of programs on a desktop computer, troubleshoot, and repair hardware.

_____ 5. Computer literacy includes knowing how to perform basic computer tasks and use common programs and applications.

CHAPTER 12
REFLECTIVE WRITING 1

On separate paper, in a journal, or online in this textbook's College Success CourseMate, respond to the following questions:

1. Do you consider yourself computer literate? Do you have basic computer literacy skills or advanced skills? Explain your answer.

2. What electronic or digital devices do you use on a regular basis? In general, what is your attitude about the use of technology in your personal, academic, and employment world?

Access Chapter 12 Reflective Writing 1 in your College Success CourseMate, accessed through *CengageBrain.com*.

Online Courses

Discuss key concepts of online courses, including advantages, disadvantages, online math courses, use of discussion boards, and online conduct and etiquette.

Online courses offer an alternative to courses that require classroom attendance and participation. Some students prefer classroom courses with an instructor and students present for interactions, discussions, and questions. They like the consistency of a specific time and place for class, the predictability of the daily topic based on the syllabus, and the instructor-created pace for the class. Other students prefer online courses for some or all of the following reasons:

- **Convenience and flexibility:** Students can work on assignments and learn course content anytime and anywhere that they have access to a computer. They are not locked into a specific time period to "be in class."

- **Self-paced learning:** Students can move through familiar materials faster and spend more time with difficult materials. They can review PowerPoint slides or instructional videos as many times as needed to grasp the concepts or understand difficult materials. As long as the course content and assignments are posted and available online, students are in control of the pace of learning and completion of the course.

- **Time to think before responding:** Students have time to formulate answers to discussion questions. Many discussions are asynchronous, meaning they do not require students to all be online at a given time to participate in a discussion. Students read the discussion questions and respond when they are ready and have reflected on the answers.

- **Motivation:** Many students are proficient and motivated by technology. They are familiar with programs and applications and enjoy using the computer to complete tasks independently.

- **Monitor grades:** Checking grades and monitoring progress are easier because many online courses have a virtual grade book that shows points or grades earned on assignments, missing assignments, and the current grades.

- **Multisensory:** Many students benefit from the multisensory materials that are often a part of online courses. They can watch and listen to videos that demonstrate processes or teach specific topics. They use kinesthetic, hands-on skills with each keystroke and as they maneuver around the screen and websites. They feel more engaged when working on a computer and online.

- **Participation:** Many students are more willing to participate in online discussions than in face-to-face discussions or classroom activities. They feel more relaxed and open to sharing ideas.

CONCEPT CHECK   12.4

What are the advantages of taking online courses? What rigors of online courses should students consider before enrolling in an online course?

Rigors of Online Courses

Students who have completed online courses are the first to tell you that many times online courses are more difficult, not easier, than in-person classroom courses. Students have to be self-directed learners in order to manage online courses. They need to have strong time-management skills, which involve planning sufficient time for online course work, following the schedule to complete assignments in a timely manner, and committing to study times on a regular basis. Students often learn by trial and error that they cannot earn a good grade in an online course by procrastinating and then trying to fulfill all the course requirements in a short period of time at the end of the term. Unfortunately, each term there will be students who realize this too late and end up dropping out of the courses instead of finishing the requirements and earning credits and a grade.

Success in online courses requires students to use self-discipline and demonstrate strong self-motivation to set an effective pace for working through the course assignments. Effective online students are also aware of the following:

- Online courses are demanding and often involve more reading than in-class courses.

- Online courses are more time-consuming than in-class courses. Online students often need to use the 3:1 ratio to have sufficient time to listen to online lectures, complete assignments, and engage in required discussions.

- Even though students can work on the course at any time, many students find they are able to stay more current with the course work if they treat the class as one that meets at a specific time. In other words, they log onto the course about the same time and the same days each week. A pattern for online course time can help students stay current and on track.

- Creating a calendar of assignment dates, quizzes and tests, scheduled lectures, scheduled chats, discussions, or online group meetings is essential to manage the time effectively. Self-imposed structure for course management and self-discipline to follow plans of action (goals) increase the success rate for completing online courses.

- Instead of asking questions in class and getting immediate responses from other students or the instructor, students need to post questions on a discussion board, e-mail other students, or contact their instructor via e-mail and then wait to get answers to questions.

- Grading of online courses often involves writing more papers, completing more discussions on discussion boards, and submitting more assignments to the instructor.

- The final grade may be based on assignments submitted to the instructor, journal summaries, papers or reports, creating web or PowerPoint presentations, and participating in assigned discussions or chat sessions.

- Online courses require more self-discipline. When studying "offline," there are always distractions that break concentration. However, when students are working online, there are greater distractions and tendencies to divide attention by checking and responding to e-mail, using social media to connect with friends, or diverting attention to videos and websites that are not related to the course or the content being studied.

- Sometimes problems with the computer or the software occur. Students need to know how to get technical support to resolve computer problems. When students are given directions for correcting the computer problems, they need to have sufficient computer skills to get their computers back online or they need to take extra time to find someone to help them resolve their computer problems. Computer problems may cause delays in listening to lectures, receiving and completing assignments, engaging in discussions, taking tests, or communicating with the instructor.

CONCEPT CHECK 12.5
What difficulties or problems might students encounter when enrolled in online courses? How can they deal with these difficulties or problems?

- Students need to make a regular habit of backing up or saving their work on an internal and external program. Saving on an internal program involves saving work on the computer. However, if the computer runs into problems or stops working, students want to have all their work saved on an external drive, which can be a CD, or a thumb drive or flash drive. For students with more advanced computer skills, they can save their work in a "cloud" program.

- Students need to use effective reading and notetaking strategies for online courses. Chapter 8 discussed a variety of reading and notetaking strategies that work effectively for online e-books used for online courses.

Online Math Courses

Online math courses frequently utilize instructional videos to demonstrate the steps to solve specific types of problems. Students taking online math courses rely heavily on learning from the short videos, which often remain online so students can review the videos multiple times to understand math processes. In addition to videos, online math courses also use PowerPoint presentations, which provide visual tools without the audio to present problem-solving skills and solutions for working problem sets. Students taking online math courses can also expect the following to occur:

- A special course orientation explains course management tools and special pop-up boxes or features of the program that provide students with access to math symbols that will be required when showing their work.

- Many online math courses have a "math lab" feature. The math lab can provide more detailed explanations, a help section, tutorials, a place to submit assignments, and specific directions for completing and submitting assignments.

- Some online courses analyze students' work and then adjust the assignments to provide greater focus, additional practice, and explanations for trouble areas.

- Some form of online discussions or discussion forums are often included to promote interaction, questions, and connecting to other students and the instructor.

- Online math courses may have e-textbooks and the option to purchase a printed version of the textbook. Students may have the option of printing e-book pages to use to review steps and processes or to rework math problem sets.

- Watching videos, moving through PowerPoint slides, engaging in discussion forums, and completing problem-solving assignments require time. The 3:1 ratio for studying is essential for math courses that meet in classrooms as well as courses that are online. In fact, online courses may require even more than the 3:1 ratio for students to watch videos or review PowerPoint slides multiple times.

Discussion Boards

Many online courses require students to respond to prompts or questions on discussion boards. *Discussion boards* are places on a website where one question or a series of questions appear for students to read, respond to, and post responses online. *Discussion threads* are categories or groups of questions that appear online in discussion boards. Each discussion thread usually has a narrowed or specific focus. Sometimes the discussion board begins with an introduction, a reference to a previous lesson or set of skills, or specific directions for the current discussion. Following are additional important points about discussion boards:

- Participating in discussions is an assignment that often affects your final grade. Your responses may be graded, or "participation points" may be calculated into your grade.

- Responses to discussion questions should be reflective, insightful, thoughtful, and complete. You have time to formulate effective and detailed responses, so do not make the mistake of responding quickly as though you are responding to a basic e-mail question.

- Many discussion questions are open-ended, meaning that varied responses may all be correct as long as they are logical, relate to the question, reflect course content, and are supported by specific details.

- Before posting your response, check for spelling, punctuation, and grammatical errors. Correct these errors before sending your response.

- Responses to discussion questions may include personal examples or applications. For the best results, use relevant examples or applications that relate directly to the question posed on the discussion board. Do not sidetrack to unrelated topics.

Discussion boards are places on a website where one question or a series of questions appear for students to read, respond to, and post responses online.

Discussion threads are categories or groups of questions that appear online in discussion boards.

CONCEPT CHECK **12.6**

What strategies should you use so your responses posted on a discussion board are appropriate and meaningful?

Why is computer literacy and familiarity with different forms of technology essential in today's world? What kinds of technology do you use in your daily life? What technology skills do you need to strengthen?

- Some discussion questions may require that you locate, read, and review a specific article or online resource. In such cases, the best responses will include direct reference to the assigned article or online resource. Do not try to bluff your way through the assignment without reading the article or going to the online resource.

- Be an active, respectful participant. Do not dominate the discussion, respond in negative ways to other students' responses, or criticize other students' work.

Online Conduct and Etiquette

As you enroll in online courses, you very likely will encounter an online code of conduct developed by your institution. The code of conduct clearly states expectations, guidelines, and rules for your online conduct or behavior. Take time to read this document carefully as violations of this code of conduct could have severe consequences. Codes of conduct restrict any behaviors that harass or threaten the safety of other students or instructors; they restrict any form of disruptive behavior that interferes with the learning process or other students' progress. The code of conduct also may require you to attach a form with each assignment that states the work you submit is original, is not copied illegally from other sources, and has appropriate citations attached to information that is not original.

As you work online, understanding online etiquette is also important. Because most of your communication with your instructor and with other students occurs in writing, using the following etiquette, often referred to as *netiquette* (net etiquette), creates a positive impression of you as a person:

- Communicate with your instructor and other students using a formal, respectful level of conversation. Avoid abbreviations, slang terms, or incomplete sentences, such as those that you might use when you e-mail or Twitter (tweet) to your friends.

- Avoid using profanity and politically incorrect, rude, insensitive, and abusive language.

- Do not use all capital letters in your communications. All capital letters is a printed way of screaming at other people.

- Reread or proofread all your messages or e-mails before sending them. Correct errors or "auto corrections" that may have changed your original words to words you had not intended to use.

Listing Questions Use Test-Taking Strategies 25–28 in Appendix A.

1. List four advantages of taking courses online.

2. List four reasons online courses for some students are more difficult than courses in a classroom.

3. List three online etiquette guidelines to use when writing e-mails or responding on a discussion board.

The Internet and Websites

③ *Explain strategies for conducting Internet searches, evaluating online materials, and avoiding plagiarism.*

The **Internet** is a massive interconnected network system that allows people and computers all over the world to communicate in multiple ways.

The **Internet** is a massive interconnected network system that allows people and computers all over the world to communicate in multiple ways. In Figure 12.1, you learned that a service provider is required to get Internet access. Once you are "online," there is a multitude of activities and sources of information to use to be informed of current events, connect with family, friends, and experts, access forms of entertainment, communicate with other students, participate in online courses, and conduct searches or research topics for personal, academic, or professional use. Many of these Internet resources are user friendly, not too difficult to learn, and usually include some form of step-by-step instructions, tutorials, or prompts on the screen that guide you through the process. To learn more about any type of program or product, or about almost anything at all, you can go to YouTube.com, type in the topic, and locate a variety of short video clips that explain how to use different programs, products, or types of technology.

Internet Search Strategies

Knowing how to navigate the Internet is an essential skill for conducting research online. Following are common places online to locate information for specific topics of interest:

● **Reference resources:** Encyclopedias and almanacs are helpful for a broad overview of a specific topic and for gathering facts and statistics. Online encyclopedias are easy to use and provide a large amount of general information in a relatively short time. Dictionaries and thesauruses are useful to find definitions, multiple meanings, etymology, and synonyms.

- **Public access catalogs and library catalogs:** Online catalogs assist you in locating library facilities that house printed versions of books you wish to find. They also assist you in searching for books on a specific topic. Once you identify titles, you can use the web to locate information, such as summaries or articles, about specific books or authors. Becoming familiar with your college's online catalog provides you with immediate information as to the availability of a specific book. If your library participates in an inter-library lending program, you may be able to request a copy of the book from another library and have it delivered to your campus.

- **Periodical databases:** Online database searches help you locate full-text newspaper and journal articles on very specific subjects. You can focus your search on narrowed topics or subjects as well as narrow the search to specific dates. Your search will provide you with links or a URL to locate the article online. The *URL*, short for the Uniform Resource Locator, is an online address for a specific website.

> The **URL**, short for the Uniform Resource Locator, is an online address for a specific website.

- **World Wide Web search:** The *World Wide Web*, also called the *web*, is a part of the Internet that has a massive collection of files or websites. You can use the web (www.) for general or specific information. If you know the specific URL address, you can type the URL in your browser's location box at the top of the computer screen. When you click on *Enter* or *Search*, you will be taken to the specific URL address or web page. A web page is a document that looks similar to a page in a book; however, a web page can be more interactive than a page of a book, with sound, animation, videos, or links to other web pages. If you do not know the URL, you can type key words or phrases to do a general search for websites with information related to your topic. Following are important points to understand about conducting web searches:

> The **World Wide Web**, also called the *web*, is a part of the Internet that has a massive collection of files or websites.

  - A search begins by typing in key words or phrases for a category, topic, subject, person, or product. If you use too few key words or your key words are too broad, your options of websites to explore may be too extensive to be helpful. Experiment using different key words or narrowing key words to describe more specifically the kind of information you seek.

  - There are many different search engines to get you to these websites. You may want to try several different search engines, such as the following popular search engines, as they often return different results: Google, Yahoo, AOL, Bing, WebCrawler, Dogpile, and Ask.

  - The URL address begins with *http* and ends with a domain suffix that shows the origination (domain) of the website. There are hundreds of domain suffixes, many related to names of countries. Following are common domain suffixes you will encounter online:

    - **.edu** indicates an educational institution site
    - **.com** indicates a commercial site
    - **.gov** indicates a government site
    - **.org** indicates an organization
    - **.net** indicates an administrative site

> **CONCEPT CHECK   12.7**
> *What online sources can you use to research a specific topic for a paper or a speech? What is the value of using different kinds of resources?*

Forums, Wikis, Blogs, and Tweets

DIRECTIONS: Throughout this textbook, you have learned a variety of study strategies to help you comprehend information and capture important information in your notes. After carefully reading the following excerpt, select one of the following activities to work with the information in the excerpt.

1. Take a complete set of notes on separate paper. Use either the Cornell Notetaking System or the two-column system.

2. Make a comprehensive set of index card notes for the information in this excerpt. Remember to include three kinds of index card notes: definition, category, and question cards.

3. Highlight and annotate this excerpt. Finish by writing a short summary using your own words.

FORUMS, WIKIS, BLOGS, AND TWEETS

- **What about asynchronous communications?** Instant messaging, chat, and VoIP are forms of **synchronous communications**; the people communicating have to be online at the same time and the conversation happens in real time. The Internet also supports several types of asynchronous communications, including Internet forums, wikis, blogs, and tweets.

  The basic idea behind **asynchronous communications** is that one person posts a message using the Internet. That message can later be read by designated recipients or by the public, depending on the limitations set by the poster.

- **How do forums work?** An **Internet forum** is a Web-based online discussion site where participants post comments to discussion threads. Those comments can be read at a later time by other participants. Most forums have a moderator who monitors discussion threads, weeds out disruptive participants, and handles membership requests.

- **Are forums the same as wikis?** No. Forums allow participants to comment on the material posted by other participants, but those comments are separate posts and the original post is not modified. A **wiki** allows participants to modify posted material.

  Wikipedia is the best known wiki. Participants can post material pertaining to a topic, and other participants can modify it. Wikis can also include discussion pages where participants comment on topic material. For example, in a wiki topic about climate change, the discussion page might contain comments pointing out statements in the orignial post that cannot be verified.

- **How do blogs work?** A **blog** (short for Web log) is similar to an online diary; it is maintained by a person, a company, or an organization, and contains a series of entries on one or more topics. Blog entries are text-based, but can also include graphics and video. They are typically displayed in reverse chronological order on one long Web page.

  Most blogs are open to the public, so blogging has become a form of personal journalism; a way to make your views public. They have been used extensively for political commentary. Some bloggers have been tapped as commentators on headline news shows on CNN and FOX. To set up your own blog, you can use a blog hosting service such as Blogger or WordPress. For a list of popular blogs, check out Technorati.

- **What's a tweet?** A **tweet** is a short message of 140 characters or less, posted to the Twitter Web site. Twitter is sometimes referred to as a microblogging service because tweets are similar to blog entries, except for their length. Your tweets are displayed in reverse chronological order on your profile page. By default, your tweets are open to the public, but you can restrict access to a list of approved viewers. Viewer comments on your tweets are also posted on your profile page.

  Twitter participants can subscribe to other people's tweets, a process referred to as "following." When you are a follower, you can quickly access tweets from the people you are following to find out what they are doing and thinking.

From Parsons, Oja *Computer Concepts* © 2013 Course Technology, Cengage Learning

FIGURE 12.2   Evaluating Online Information

Cindy Griffin, author of *Invitation to Public Speaking*, offers the following suggestions for gathering and selecting Internet information for research reports, essays, presentations, or speeches.

Is the information reliable? Check the domain in the URL. Is it .com (a commercial enterprise that might be trying to sell something), .org (a non-profit organization, more interested in services and issues than in commerce), .edu (an educational institution), or .gov (a government agency)? What bias might those operating the site have about your topic? Do they make any disclaimers about the information they post on the site? What makes this information reliable or not?

Is the information authoritative? URLs that include a tilde (~) often indicate that a single individual is responsible for the information on a website. Can you find the person's credentials posted on the site? Can you contact the person and ask for credentials? Can you find the person's credentials in any printed sources, such as a *Who's Who* reference? Regardless of whether the material was authored by a single person, an organization, an institution, or a company, is the author an expert on the subject of the site?

How current is the information? Many web pages include a date that tells you when it was posted or last updated. If you don't see such a date, you may be able to find it in your browser's View or Documents menu. If you determine that the website is current, is the time frame relevant to your subject or arguments? You may find great information, but if it doesn't relate to the time frame of your speech, it's not relevant or ethical to use.

How complete is the information? Much of the text posted on the Internet consists of excerpts from printed materials, and what is left out may be of more use than what is included. For example, a site may contain one paragraph from a newspaper article, but that paragraph may not reflect the overall message of the article. If you want to use an excerpted portion of a printed work, you must locate the complete work to ensure that you are using that material accurately.

Is the information relevant? Many interesting facts and stories appear on the web, but be sure those you use as supporting material do more than just tell a great story. Your information must help you develop your thesis . . . . Ask yourself whether the information fits your needs. Does it help develop your main ideas, or does it take you in a different direction?

Is the information consistent and unbiased? Is the information you find consistent with information you find on other sites, from printed sources, or from interviews? Can you find other sources to support the statements, claims, and facts provided by the website? If the information is inconsistent with other sources, it may reflect new findings about a topic, but it also may reflect an unfounded or unsubstantiated claim. Many sites only present one side of an issue. To guarantee a less biased presentation and more comprehensive picture of your topic, search at a number of different sites and be sure to cross-check what you find against information you obtain from more established sources such as books and other printed documents. Be wary of outrageous or controversial claims that can't be checked for accuracy or aren't grounded in reasonable arguments or sources.

From Griffin, *Invitation to Public Speaking* 3e, © 2009 Cengage Learning

Evaluating Online Materials

Information on any given topic is at your fingertips within a few keystrokes. Access is easy, and search results often produce abundant sites to access for information. However, not all information found online is accurate, reliable, valid, or authentic. Because anyone can post almost anything on website pages without having the information evaluated, authenticated, or scrutinized for accuracy, you need to read online materials carefully. When you are using the Internet to search for information for academic purposes, such as writing a report or preparing for a speech, accept the information as accurate only after careful examination. **Figure 12.2** provides suggestions for selecting and evaluating online information to use for academic purposes, such as to write a report or to give a presentation or a speech.

In addition to the evaluation strategies that appear in Figure 12.2 and the checklist in the Chapter 8 Critical Thinking activity for evaluating reliability, quality, and usefulness of online information, you can use the following questions to evaluate website information before using its contents for academic purposes or referring to it in other forms of communication:

1. **Are there spelling or grammatical errors?** Question the quality and credibility of information when you see spelling errors and grammatical errors, as these "red flags" indicate the website is an informal personal posting.

2. **Can information presented as facts be proven or verified by data, research, or objective evidence?** Factual data can be cross-checked with other websites and sources. However, if the same information appears in multiple places, search to find and verify the original source of the information. It is possible that multiple websites reprinted the same information, even if the information from the original source is not accurate or proven. If information cannot be verified or is not consistent with research or tested data, the information may be subjective but camouflaged to look objective.

3. **Is the point of view or information presented objective or subjective?** Even though statements may sound objective or authoritative, are they really expressing an opinion in an attempt to convince the reader to accept a specific point of view? Words such as *should*, *would*, and *must* often signal a subjective point of view and an opinion. Does the content serve a specific purpose, such as to sell, convince, or promote, or do existing links send you to other websites designed to sell, convince, or promote a specific belief, product, or agenda?

4. **What are the author's credentials?** Is the author affiliated with a reputable institution, organization, or association directly related to the topic of the website? You should be able to verify the author's qualifications and affiliations. Check the URL to see if the information comes from an educational institution, government, organization, or commercial domain and if it relates to the topic presented by the author.

5. **Is the information reliable and complete?** The reliability of information is strengthened when authors list their sources or refer to other research studies or databases. Check whether the site gives bibliographic information or links to other sites with information consistent with information you are evaluating. Can the information on the website "stand alone" or make sense in its entirety, or do you sense that it may be only a portion of a larger piece of information? If the information was pulled out and placed by itself, the information may be taken out of context or conflict with other sections of the original document, report, or article.

6. **Is the information current?** Check the footer for dates when the information was first created or posted. Check to see if the authors have updated, revised, or edited the information. Because information such as research studies, results of polls or surveys, and test results can be posted relatively quickly on the Internet, information online may be more current than information in printed form in publications or books.

CONCEPT CHECK   **12.8**

How can you spot or identify online information that you should not use in academic work because it is not credible, accurate, or reliable?

7. **Is the information relevant for your purpose?** If you are conducting Internet searches for a specific purpose, such as information for an essay, paper, report, or presentation, you may find hundreds or even thousands of documents related to your topic. Narrowing your search will help you locate information that is relevant to your purpose. However, if you are looking for facts to support a specific point of view or to support a specific thesis, you will want to discard some information that you locate because it does not serve your specific purpose or is simply not relevant for your assignment.

8. **Is the information from a "wiki" collaborative website or a personal blog?** Even though information may be accurate or informative, it has a greater potential to be incomplete, biased, inaccurate, and lack reference to the writer's credentials. In the case of a wiki website, multiple users, either identified by their user names or anonymous, may add or change the information; as a result, verifying the accuracy of the information is difficult or impossible to do.

Transfer These Skills: Internet Searches

EXERCISE 12.3

DIRECTIONS: The Internet provides us with a wealth of information to examine, critique, and explore. Complete the following directions to show your ability to conduct Internet searches.

1. Select a topic that relates to this class, one of your other classes, or select from one of the following topics: Howard Gardner's Multiple Intelligences, Maslow's Hierarchy of Needs, or Bloom's Taxonomy.

2. Use your college library's online catalog to identify resources that are available for your topic. Briefly list or summarize the resources that are available.

3. Conduct an Internet search for your topic on the web. Select one website to explore. Read and use strategies you learned in this chapter to evaluate the information. Write the URL address and a brief summary of the information. Include indicators you used to evaluate the quality and accuracy of the information.

4. Go to the Wikipedia encyclopedia online. Search for the topic you selected for this exercise. Read the information and compare it to the information you located during your Internet search.

5. Summarize similarities and differences between the two sources of information.

Plagiarism

You have likely heard the term *plagiarism* before, but do you know what plagiarism means and the many ways plagiarism can occur? *Plagiarism* is the act of using someone else's words, work, or ideas without acknowledging the author or without citing the source of the information. The choice of words and the way in which the

> **Plagiarism** is the act of using someone else's words, work, or ideas without acknowledging the author or without citing the source of the information.

ideas are presented give the reader the impression that the words or ideas are your original words or ideas. Following are important points about plagiarism:

- Plagiarism in college courses often has serious consequences, which may range from receiving a failing grade for the course, being required to appear before an ethics board or committee, being placed on academic probation, or even being expelled from the college or university.

- Most colleges and universities have clear policies about plagiarism. Read your college's academic standards. Many classes post warnings about plagiarism with each writing assignment in class or online.

- Citing sources properly can be complicated. Ask if workshops, study guides, or tutorials are available to help you understand and avoid plagiarism in your course work. Check to see if your writing lab provides assistance with explanations and examples of plagiarism and strategies to use to avoid plagiarism.

- Many syllabi alert students to the fact that instructors take measures to identify students who plagiarize. Many institutions have academic plagiarism detectors to catch students who plagiarize. For example, Turnitin.com is a website instructors can use to analyze students' papers for plagiarism. As a student, you can search the Internet to locate programs that will analyze your work for plagiarism. (Google or search for the word *plagiarism* or *check for plagiarism*.)

- Some instructors, especially instructors for online courses, require students to sign a document that states the work is original and to submit the document with each written assignment.

- Plagiarism involves trying to pass someone else's work off as your own. This includes using materials prepared by another person or agency that engages in selling or sharing term papers, other academic materials, or information from the Internet that is not properly identified or cited. Buying term papers is risky, and such term papers often are readily identified as plagiarized and illegal.

- There is no need to cite facts or ideas that are commonly understood, are not attributed to or cannot be connected to a specific author, are used frequently by reputable sources without being cited, and are considered to be common knowledge.

- There are two kinds of plagiarism: *intentional plagiarism* and *unintentional plagiarism*.

Intentional Plagiarism

Intentional plagiarism occurs when students buy term papers or written assignments from other students and try to pass them off as their own work. Cutting and pasting words, phrases, sentences, paragraphs, or full articles without citing the sources is also intentional plagiarism. The student doing the cutting and pasting is fully aware that he or she is attempting to take a shortcut in writing a paper by lifting other people's words and ideas and placing them into a document. Some students attempt to create a paper by cutting and pasting from multiple sources; they fail to understand that most instructors can quickly identify when writing styles within a paper are not consistent—an instant indicator of plagiarism. In addition, a plagiarism detector program would quickly identify the work as coming from multiple authors. Another form of plagiarism involves copying the exact words of sentences and then simply substituting a few of the words in the sentences by using synonyms that have the same or similar meaning—without citing the source.

CONCEPT CHECK **12.9**
What is intentional plagiarism? How can instructors identify plagiarism?

Unintentional Plagiarism

Unintentional plagiarism occurs when students do not cite the sources properly or do not place quotation marks correctly around direct quotations. Understanding how to cite sources, indicating where you found the information and acknowledging the person whose words or ideas you are using, is the basic way to avoid plagiarism. The following points are important about unintentional plagiarism:

- Guidelines for citing sources are usually included in your composition and research courses. Learn the required way to cite sources. Because citing methods can vary for different kinds of sources as well as different kinds of courses, consider creating your own guide or manual for citing information properly.

- Properly citing sources makes it possible for readers to identify the source of the information and understand that the information is not your original work. Proper citations also provide necessary information for readers to locate, retrieve, read, and review your source of information.

- Citing sources from information taken from the World Wide Web differs from the way to cite sources from printed materials. Rules for citing electronic information are fluid; therefore, follow the guidelines provided by your instructor or presented in course materials.

- In general, citations from the web include the name of the author, the title of the article, the copyright and publisher information, and then the date you accessed the article online. Sometimes the URL (the address of the article on the web) will be required. In the following list of online resources, note the inclusion of the word "web" in the citation.

CONCEPT CHECK 12.10
How can you avoid unintentional plagiarism? What are MLA and APA styles?

- There are two principal academic citation styles: the MLA style (Modern Language Association) and the APA style (American Psychological Association). The following websites provide you with specific guidelines:

  - Cornell University Library. MLA Citation Style. "Citing Materials from Online Sources." Web. 18 December 2012.

    http://www.library.cornell.edu/resrch/citmanage/mla

  - B. Davis Schwartz Memorial Library. "MLA Handbook for Writers of Research Papers, 7th edition." Web. 18 December 2012.

    http://www2.liu.edu/cwis/cwp/library/workshop/citmla.htm

  - Purdue University. APA Formatting and Style Guide. "Reference List: Electronic Sources: Web Publications." Web. 18 December 2012.

    http://owl.english.purdue.edu/owl/resources/560/10

  - Purdue University. Purdue OWL. "MLA Formatting and Style Guide." Web. 18 December 2012.

    http://owl.english.purdue.edu/owl/owlprint/747/

  - Purdue University. Welcome to Purdue OWL. "Overview and Contradictions." Web. 18 December 2012.

    http://owl.english.purdue.edu/owl/owlprint/589

  - Plagiarism.org. Plagiarism 101. "What Is Plagiarism?" Web. 20 December 2012.

    http://plagiarism.org/plagiarism-101/what-is-plagiarism

CHECK POINT 12.3

Answers appear on page B4.

Multiple Choice See Multiple Choice Strategies 10–15 in Appendix A.

_____ 1. Which statement is inaccurate?

     a. The Internet is a network system that makes global communication possible.

     b. Internet research strategies include locating reference materials, library catalogs, databases, and files on the web.

     c. All web pages are required to have one of the following domain suffixes: .edu, .com, .gov, .org, or .net.

     d. Different search engines are available to use to search for specific information.

_____ 2. Because anyone can post almost anything on the web,

     a. not all information found online is accurate or reliable.

     b. you need to use strategies to evaluate, authenticate, and scrutinize information for accuracy, completeness, and reliability.

     c. collaborative websites, such as a wiki encyclopedia, may be unreliable and may be posted by anonymous writers.

     d. all of the above are true.

_____ 3. Unintentional plagiarism

     a. sometimes occurs when students do not properly cite or acknowledge that words, ideas, or graphics they use in coursework belong to someone else.

     b. occurs when a student pays someone else to write a paper instead of writing the paper himself or herself.

     c. occurs when a student cuts and pastes sections of someone else's work and claims the work is original and not from another source.

     d. is a more serious offense or conduct violation than is intentional plagiarism.

End-of-the-Term Profile

EXERCISE 12.4

PURPOSE: Throughout this term, you have completed the chapter profiles and have recorded your results in Appendix B on the Master Profile Chart. As you acquired more skills throughout the term, very likely your habits and attitudes changed. Completing the End-of-the-Term Profile will demonstrate the progress you have made this term.

DIRECTIONS:

1. If you have not already done so, use one color of pen to connect the responses that show your original profile scores. Your Master Profile chart will then appear as a line graph that connects the twelve points on the chart.

2. Complete the directions for the End-of-the-Term Profile located in Appendix B, page B2

3. Compare your pre- and post-profile scores. Discuss your results in the Reflective Writing 2 assignment.

CHAPTER 12
REFLECTIVE WRITING 2

On separate paper, in a journal, or online in this textbook's College Success CourseMate, respond to the following questions.

1. After completing Exercise 12.4, examine your pre- and post-profile scores on your Master Profile Chart in Appendix B. In which areas did you show the most progress or gain? What strategies did you learn to use to produce the change? Be specific.

2. Which areas on your Master Profile Chart show the least gain? Why do you think this is so? What strategies do you still need to use more effectively for those categories?

Access Chapter 12 Reflective Writing 2 in your College Success CourseMate website, accessed through *CengageBrain.com*.

Technology, Resources, and Applications

4 *Demonstrate a willingness to explore new technology, resources, and applications.*

The computer technology evolution started in the 1930s with the invention of the first computer. We have seen this technological evolution take us from massive computers that required the space of entire rooms, to desktop computers, to laptop (notebook) computers, to netbooks, to tablets, and now to smartphones that have many of the capabilities of mini-computers with Internet access. This evolution moved forward rapidly with the invention of new operating and networking systems, new hardware and software programs, and new electronic devices with increased capabilities and applications.

In the early 1960s, researchers found ways for people using the same kind of computers to communicate with each other. In 1972, this ability for computers to communicate from different locations evolved into the creation of the Internet and multiple networks that made global communication via e-mail possible. With each new phase of the technological evolution, advances are made through new inventions and the creation of technology with greater capabilities. Internet providers, such as Yahoo, Hotmail, Google Mail, and America Online (AOL) emerged. The Internet revolutionized the computer and forms of communication. In addition to e-mail, websites have evolved as a major marketing and communication tool for businesses, organizations, and institutions. Developing websites and web pages initially required sophisticated technical skills, but software now makes it possible for individuals to develop and post their own web pages on the Internet. Technology and the Internet have evolved to include social networking sites, such as Facebook and LinkedIn, video sites, such as YouTube, and music sites, such as Pandora. Computers, smartphones, and printers can link to each other wirelessly; *cloud computing* makes it possible to create a document on one computer and retrieve it on another computer, without the use of a disk or a thumb drive to transfer data.

Computers and the ongoing use of technology are here to stay. There is no slowing down the development of new electronic devices, new software, or new hardware, so becoming comfortable with new technology and being willing to learn new pro-grams, applications, and devices is advantageous and, in many cases, essential as more and more forms of employment and academic programs require the use of technology to perform essential functions or responsibilities. As an example of the explosion of new technology and applications, the terms *netbooks*, *smartphones*, and *tablets*, as well as the terms in Exercise 12.2, did not exist in the early stages of computer or Internet development but are prevalent phrases today: s*ynchronous communications*, *asynchoronous communications*, *Internet forum*, *wiki*, *blog*, *tweet*, and *Twitter*. If you feel that new terminology surfaces so rapidly that it is difficult to stay current, you are not alone. Do you remember when the following terms were first introduced but now are understood by many users of technology? What is the meaning of *Twitter hashtags* and *handles*, *cloud computing*, *getting hacked*, *spam*, *firewalls*, *spyware*, *viruses*, *widgets*, *Bluetooth*, and *cybersecurity suites?*

New Technology and Digital Devices

Does technology sometimes cause frustration? Yes. Can new digital products be intimidating and cause a person to doubt his or her ability to learn the new technol-ogy? Yes. Are some of the new electronic devices too expensive to afford? Yes. How-ever, none of these obstacles should be a reason not to experiment with using new technology. Often the fear of new technology is overcome by hands-on experiences where you can see the value of a product or a process, realize that you can learn to use new technology, and discover that the technology is exciting, valuable, and enjoy-able to use. After identifying the programs and electronic devices that you know how to use in Exercise 12.5, you are encouraged to find one or two other students to intro-duce you to two programs or devices in the exercise that you do not know how to use.

GROUP PROCESSING

 ### A Collaborative Learning Activity

Form groups of three or four students. Each group needs to have a chart to record information. Select a group recorder. Complete the following directions.

DIRECTIONS:

1. Divide your chart into two columns: Personal Use and Academic Use.

2. Students in the group who have smartphones or tablets need to share their knowledge and experience with the students who do not use smartphones. Compile lists of favorite mobile apps (applications) that are useful and valuable for smartphones or tablets. Under each column, give the name or title of the app and a brief description of its function or use if needed to understand the app; indicate if it is free or give the purchase price. You may also go to the Apps Store or Android Marketplace on your phone or tablet to search for additional apps that interest members of your group. Your instructor may collect your results, compile them, and print or post them online for you to explore and use.

Personal Use	Academic Use
No Glasses Lite (magnify pages to read) – free	Merriam-Webster's Dictionary – free

Familiarity with Technology

DIRECTIONS: In the following checklist, check the items that you do *not* know how to use or access. Then, ask other classmates, friends, family members, or assistants in computer labs on campus to show you how to use any two of the items in the list that you checked. Ask them to sign their name next to the item to indicate that they showed you how the program or device works.

____iPad	____YouTube video
____iPod	____Video game on Wii
____iPod Touch	____Podcast
____Smartphone	____Online Merriam-Webster's Dictionary
____Kindle or Nook	____3-D Blue Ray
____E-textbook online	____Spreadsheet
____FaceTime on a phone	____Skype
____Facebook	____E-mail
____Blog	____Online forum
____iTunes	____Google search
____Pandora	____Twitter
____Flash drive (also called thumb drive)	____Cloud computing
____Memory card	____Online bill paying
____WiFi	____PowerPoint presentation software

Applications

An **app** is a common term used for mobile *applications*, which are programs that run on smartphones and tablets, such as iPads. Users have thousands of applications to choose from in the Apple Apps Store or Android Marketplace and then download to their phones or tablets. Some are free, and some sell for a small fee. Each app is represented by an icon, or a small picture associated with the app. When the mobile device (smartphone or tablet) is turned on, the user sees a screen with the apps and simply touches the app he or she wishes to activate or turn on. Apps include Internet programs, such as YouTube, Facebook, Skype, and e-mail, as well as thousands of apps for organizations, weather and maps, specific stores, games, videos, music, and businesses. **Figure 12.3** shows twenty top technology picks. Identify one or more of the technology picks in the figure that are new to you, and to use a mobile device to access the websites or apps.

> An **app** is a common term used for mobile *applications*, which are programs that run on smartphones and tablets, such as iPads.

FIGURE 12.3 Top Twenty Technology Picks

Lucy MacDonald, M.A.

Online Faculty and Faculty Development Trainer and Consultant

College professor Lucy MacDonald retired from teaching in 2002 and relocated to Sarasota, Florida. Her students begged her not to give up her teaching website for College Success, so she registered her free website (howtostudy.org), opened it to students throughout the world, and continued to expand and update the content. In 2012, half a million students from 90 percent of the world's countries visited her website. Professor MacDonald reads and edits all the reviews that appear on the website.

From apps to videos to websites, here are twenty useful study strategies to jump-start your college success. Explore, learn, and enjoy!

USEFUL STUDY APPS

1. Electronic Planners

Electronic planners allow you to bring your schedule wherever you go. The *iStudiez Pro* app lets you list your classes, labs, and due dates. It even lets you attach your assignments. You can also track your grades with this app and calculate your grade point average (GPA). Color-coding makes your schedule visually easy to read and categorize.

Strategy: Use this app to set up alerts for when assignments are coming due.

Available: iStudiezPro app is available for iPhone, iPad, or Mac.

See it here: *http://istudentpro.com/*

2. Task Manager

Task managers help you set up a to-do list that works for you. The *iProcrastinate* app allows you to break up term-long projects step-by-step so you can work in manageable chunks and check off the pieces as you complete them. You can choose to look at your to-do list with the calendar, weekly, or daily view, so you can see exactly what is due for each day.

Strategy: Create categories for your tasks—classes and gym workouts—so you can see what is due for each category you have and begin to prioritize tasks.

Available: The iProcrastinate app is available for iPhone, iPad, or Mac.

See it here: *http://www.iprocrastinateapp.com/*

3. Notetaking

Taking notes is a study habit that will help you succeed in college. The *Evernote* app allows you to make your notetaking strategy personal to the way you learn by letting you upload pictures, videos, and audio comments into your notes. *Evernote* even backs up your notes for you, so there are no worries about misplacing or losing them.

Strategy: If you can't remember where information is in your notes, use the search feature in *Evernote* to look it up to make studying quick and easy.

Available: The Evernote app is available for a smartphone, tablet, laptop, and desktop.

See it here: *http://evernote.com/download/*

4. Flashcards

Flashcards allow you to remember facts quickly. The *Study Blue* app lets you create personal flashcards to help you study on the go. Create flashcards by typing them out, taking pictures, or adding audio notes.

Strategy: While waiting for the bus, study for a test by using the Study Blue flashcards on your mobile device and have the app score your results!

Available: The Study Blue app is available for iPad, iPhone, iPod, and Android.

See it here: *http://www.studyblue.com/mobile-flashcards-app/*

5. Dictionary with Voice Search

Knowing the spelling of words is crucial to writing college assignments. The Merriam-Webster's Collegiate Dictionary app lets you look up words with voice search. Just say the word and let the app find the spelling of the word for you. You can also use this app to look up definitions, word origins, synonyms, and to hear the words pronounced.

Strategy: Use this app to look up hard to spell words like *turquoise* when you don't have access to spell check. Also use this app to see definitions.

Available: The Merriam-Webster's Dictionary app is available for iPad, iPhone, and Android.

See it here: *http://www.merriam-webster.com/ dictionary-apps/android-ipad-iphone-windows.htm*

6. **Web Page Reader**

College often requires you to read web pages and online articles, and these online readings often have distracting ads that can prevent you from being focused. The *Readability* app allows you to customize your reading experience by removing the clutter from the web page and presenting just the article you want to read. You can also share your reading list with your classmates.

Strategy: Sync the articles you find so you can keep your research in one place and have the same reading experience each time.

Available: The Readability app is available for iPad, iPhone, Android, laptop, and desktop.

See it here: *www.readability.com/apps*

7. **Annotate Pages**

Annotating your pages is an excellent way to think critically about the material you are studying. The *Neu.Annotate* app lets you write on and mark up portable document format (pdf) pages. You can highlight text, add notes or photos, or add stamps to indicate you want to review the material for an exam.

Strategy: Use this feature to annotate online homework readings for class and upload your work into an online server like DropBox for collaborative study groups.

Available: The Neu.Annotate app is available for iPhone, iPad, iTunes, or Mac.

See it here: *http://www.neupen.com/*

8. **Group Studying**

Group studying in college allows you to share ideas and get help from your peers. The *Screen Chomp* app allows you to create short videos with audio comments of writing notes, ideas, questions, on an online whiteboard. You can then send them as mp4 files to your classmates for help or extra ideas. They can then write their own comments

on the same screen in a different color and record their own audio comments to send back to you.

Strategy: Use this app when working on team projects so all members of the project can participate no matter where they are.

Available: The Screen Chomp app is available for iPad.

See it here: *http://www.techsmith.com/ screenchomp.html*

VIDEOS ON THE WEB

9. **Learning Strategies Videos**

Trying different learning strategies allows you to pinpoint the way you learn in order to help you study more effectively. Dartmouth College's Academic Skills Center lets you look at seven separate learning strategy videos so you can explore new learning strategies and find out which ones work best for you. These videos include the following:

- Classes: Notetaking, Listening, Participation
- Studying in Math and the Sciences
- Managing Your Time
- Active Reading: Comprehension and Rate
- Improving Concentration, Memory, and Motivation
- Preparing and Taking Tests and Exams
- Getting Adequate Sleep

Strategy: Set aside some time and watch these videos with your classmates to discuss how to make these strategies work best for you.

See it here: *http://www.dartmouth.edu/~acskills/ videos/*

10. **Library Research**

Locating information is an essential part of your college education. While many students may immediately think of Google to find information, academic research often requires different tools. "Why can't I just Google?" is a short YouTube video that explains why you need to explore options beyond Google and what works best for academic research.

Strategy: Watch this video before the start of a college research project.

See it here: *http://youtu.be/N39mnu1Pkgw*

11. Video Study Groups

Video study groups allow students with vastly different schedules to study and work together on projects. *Eyejot* lets you record videos of yourself and send them to your study group. You can also store these videos so you can view them later.

Strategy: Use *Eyejot* to show illustrations from your textbook to your study partners so you all know what is being discussed.

See it here: *http://corp.eyejot.com/*

COMPREHENSIVE WEBSITES

12. How to Study

How to Study is a comprehensive website dedicated to helping students learn better study habits. The website has two parts: the first has resources in eighteen different study strategies from time management to test taking; the second is arranged by subject areas from accounting to theater. This website allows you to find study strategies specific for the subject you are studying, as well as strategies on how to write specifically for that discipline.

Strategy: Review the seven steps of the How to Study Model to discover how you can be successful in your exams (*http://www.howtostudy. org/overview.php*). Select other topics to learn new study strategies for your courses.

See it here: *http://www.howtostudy.org*

13. Study Guides and Strategies

The Study Guides and Strategies website offers 250 study guides in 39 languages to help students of all backgrounds succeed in college. Set up like a filing system, the site offers ten "folders" for specific topics as well as study guides and interactive activities for the following areas: Learning and Studying, Internet, Project and Time Management, Writing and Vocabulary, Thinking and Evaluation, Reading and Research, and Math and Science.

Strategy: Use the "Writing" folder and the "Writing and Vocabulary" study guide to walk you through your first college writing assignment. Use the other folders and study guides to explore strategies related to your courses and topics of interest.

See it here: *http://www.studygs.net*

14. Online Writing Lab

The Online Writing Lab (OWL) at Purdue University includes general writing resources, research and citation help, and subject-specific writing advice to help you become a better writer. Writing sections, such as "Avoiding Plagiarism," will allow you to understand how to develop your writing with academic integrity to get the best grade you can.

Strategy: Use this site to find answers to your writing questions and needs. You can also contact OWL Mail Tutors for extra help on specific writing questions.

See it here: *http://owl.english.purdue.edu/owl/*

TOPIC-SPECIFIC WEBSITES

15. Learning Styles in the World of Work

The Kingdomality website presents a fun, eight-question survey to find out what your job would have been in the Middle Ages in order to help you pinpoint what your job style is today. Similar job preferences appear in today's employment market.

Strategy: Use this website to help you choose a college major that fits your job style.

See it here: *http://www.Kingdomality.com*

16. Priority Management

Learning how to prioritize will help you managing multiple assignments with non-negotiable deadlines. The What's Important website presents a matrix of *important/not important* and *urgent/ not urgent* to see where you are not spending your time wisely enough, which may lead to not being able to get the important and urgent tasks done.

Strategy: Use this website if you are getting behind in your work to find out if you are prioritizing less important tasks over the important tasks.

See it here: *http://www.jcu.edu.au/tldinfo/ learningskills/git/whatsimportant.html*

17. Discipline-Specific Reading Skills for Biology

Textbook reading skills may differ discipline to discipline. Learning how to customize your textbook reading strategies to specific subjects will allow you to develop the skills necessary to retain the type of information you need to excel in your courses. The Biology Reading Skills website presents advice on how to read specifically for your biology course.

Strategy: Use this website at the beginning of your biology course so you know the best way to read your textbook for maximum retention.

See it here: *http://cc.pima.edu/~carem/BIOREAD.html*

18. **Strategies for Studying Math**

Studying strategies may vary from discipline to discipline. Learning how to identify the best strategies for your discipline ensures that you will succeed in your major and general education courses. In addition to content help, the How to Study Math website lists thirty-six possible situations you may find yourself in when studying for math and offers techniques to help you study.

Strategy: Review this website when you are preparing for a math test for some tips on what to study when you are studying the day before or the day of the test.

See it here: *http://www.lanecc.edu/testing/how-study-math*

19. **Bloom's Taxonomy**

Bloom's Taxonomy is a classification system for levels of complexity of thinking or cognitive skills. The six levels of Bloom's Taxonomy are Remembering, Understanding, Applying, Analyzing, Evaluating, and Creating. Three levels are lower-order thinking skills; three levels are higher-order critical thinking skills. This website provides you with a list of common verbs used in questions for each level in Bloom's Taxonomy.

Strategy: Use the drop down menu for each level of the taxonomy to familiarize yourself with a list of question prompts that shows the kinds of questions associated with that level.

See it here: *http://ctl.mesacc.edu/blooms/*

20. **GPA Calculator**

Grade point average (GPA) is based on your grades and your college's credit system. The GPA Calculator will help you figure out your current GPA. Knowing your GPA may be important for maintaining scholarships or for completing job applications.

Strategy: Use the GPA Calculator throughout the semester to make sure your GPA is where it needs to be.

See it here: *http://www.back2college.com/gpa.htm*

 Access Chapter 12 Topics In-Depth: Top Twenty Technology Picks in your College Success CourseMate, accessed through *CengageBrain.com.*

CHECK POINT 12.4

Answers for this question do not appear in Appendix B.

Application

1. Conduct an Internet search for the history of any one of the following topics:

    desktop computers   the Internet   tablets   Facebook   YouTube

2. On separate paper, draw a timeline to show the years of key inventions or developments for the topic you selected for the Internet search.

ACTIVITY

Chapter 12 Critical Thinking

In Bloom's Taxonomy, critical thinking includes applying and creating processes. There are extensive ways you can apply technology to daily activities, use for academic endeavors, and use to create new products or outcomes. If your instructor chooses to assign a Chapter 12 Critical Thinking activity, you will be asked to apply technology to a specific assignment or task. Your assignment may include any of the following:

Perform an Internet search

Respond to a discussion board

Create or respond to a blog

Activate a specific app

Examine a wiki site

Locate and evaluate a specific URL

Participate in an online forum

Examine a plagiarism detection program

View an online video

Explore one of the Top Twenty Technology Picks

Terms to Know

By yourself or with a partner, practice reciting or writing definitions for the following terms. You may also practice defining these terms by using the online flashcards or comparing your answers to the online glossary.

computer literacy p. 373

discussion boards p. 380

discussion threads p. 380

Internet p. 382

URL p. 383

World Wide Web p. 383

plagiarism p. 387

app p. 393

 Access Chapter 12 Flashcards and Online Glossary in your College Success CourseMate, accessed through *CengageBrain.com*.

Learning Objectives Review

1 *Discuss basic computer concepts, including your level of computer literacy and essential computer skills for online courses.*

- Computers are an integral part of daily personal, academic, and professional life. The ability to use basic technology for a variety of tasks is essential.

- Computer literacy means having knowledge and competency to use computers, computer programs, and computer applications efficiently. Basic computer literacy involves the ability to perform specific tasks; advanced computer literacy refers to more in-depth and sophisticated competencies.

- Students enrolled in online courses benefit greatly by taking online orientations or workshops to learn how to access the course, locate and submit assignments, navigate the management system, and use various forms of communication. They also need to be sure their computer and Internet program meet the requirements for the online course.

2 *Discuss key concepts of online courses, including advantages, disadvantages, online math courses, use of discussion boards, and online conduct and etiquette.*

- Students should be aware of the advantages and disadvantages of taking online courses.

- To succeed in online courses, students need to have strong time-management skills, be self-directed, and have strong self-motivation.

- Online math courses frequently rely on numerous videos for instruction and to demonstrate application of problem-solving tests. Ample time is required to complete online math courses.
- Many online courses require students to use discussion boards to discuss work and assignments. Students should follow online conduct and etiquette guidelines when writing or responding to online questions.

3 *Explain strategies for conducting Internet searches, evaluating online materials, and avoiding plagiarism.*

- Conducting Internet searches may include accessing reference materials, library catalogs, databases, and the World Wide Web. Students should know how to access all kinds of materials to search for desired information.
- Not all online materials are accurate, reliable, current, or complete. Students can use a variety of strategies to evaluate the quality of online materials.
- Plagiarism, which involves trying to pass someone else's work off as your own, is a serious offense. Instructors have access to plagiarism detection software programs to identify plagiarized work.
- There are two kinds of plagiarism: intentional plagiarism and unintentional plagiarism; unintentional plagiarism can be avoided by learning how to properly cite sources.

4 *Demonstrate a willingness to explore new technology, resources, and applications.*

- The computer technology evolution began in the 1930s; computer technology rapidly moved forward through the invention of new hardware and software.
- In 1972, the Internet was created when researchers found ways to communicate electronically between connected computers. Use of the Internet has drastically changed the way we communicate and perform daily functions.
- Computer technology continues to advance. Instead of being intimidated or frustrated by technology, students can become interested and excited about the new hardware, software, electronic devices, and mobile applications available for them to use in many aspects of their lives.

Chapter 12   Review Questions

Definitions See Test-Taking Strategies 29–31 in Appendix A.

On separate paper, write a three-part definition for each of the following terms:

1. discussion threads
2. World Wide Web
3. domain suffixes on a URL
4. plagiarism
5. computer literacy

Short-Answer Questions Use Test-Taking Strategies 32–36 in Appendix A.

On separate paper, answer any *three* of the following six questions.

1. What are some reasons some students may consider online courses to be more difficult or more demanding than in-person classroom courses?
2. Why are online videos an important component of online math courses?
3. Describe netiquette guidelines that students should use when responding to discussion boards.
4. Summarize strategies to use to evaluate online Internet information.
5. How can you avoid intentional plagiarism?
6. How can you avoid unintentional plagiarism?

 Access Chapter 12 Study Guide in your College Success CourseMate, accessed through *CengageBrain.com*.

Access all Chapter 12 Online Material in your College Success CourseMate, accessed through *CengageBrain.com*.

Linda Wong

Essential
Test-Taking Skills

Appendix A
Contents for Essential Test-Taking Skills

Introduction

Throughout your college years, you will encounter many different kinds of tests and a variety of test-taking situations. This *Essential Test-Taking Skills* guide will help you recognize and understand different types of test questions and key elements in different test-question formats. Understanding how to read and respond to a variety of test questions will increase your test-taking performance and your grades.

Essential Test-Taking Skills provides you with **fifty-two** specific, easy-to-use strategies for understanding, interpreting, and answering the following kinds of test questions:

- **Objective test questions**, which include true-false, multiple-choice, and matching questions

- **Recall test questions**, which include fill-in-the-blanks, listing, definition, and short-answer questions

- **Math test questions**, which involve solving problems, applying equations, and answering word- or story-problem questions

- **Essay test questions**, which involve using a series of paragraphs to develop a thesis statement for an answer

For *Essential Study Skills, 8th edition*, you can use the following resources to strengthen your test-preparation and test-taking skills:

- Chapter 7: Preparing for Upcoming Tests

- Exercise 7.5: Practice Test-Taking Skills in Chapter 7 Topics In-Depth in your College Success CourseMate.

- Practice Quizzes and Enhanced Quizzes in each chapter: Go to Quizzes in your College Success CourseMate, accessed through *CengageBrain.com*.

- Check Points throughout each chapter to practice answering test questions

- Chapter Review Questions in each chapter with self-correcting answer keys

- Online Chapter Study Guides

Remove this handy test-taking guide and place it in your notebook for quick reference.

Objective Test Questions

Objective test questions, also called recognition questions, require that you recognize whether information is correct or incorrect and then apply skills to identify the correct answer. The following easy-to-use strategies discuss each type of objective test question: true-false, multiple-choice, and matching. Applying these strategies will build your confidence for taking objective tests and improve your test performance.

Familiarize Yourself with Terminology for Objective Tests

To lay a foundation of understanding for objective test questions, read through the following glossary of terms. These terms are used throughout the sections for true-false, multiple-choice, and matching questions.

- **Modifiers:** Modifiers are words that tell to what degree or frequency something occurs. Absolute (100 percent) and in-between modifiers appear in objective test questions.

- **Definition clues:** Definition clues are words that signal that the question is testing your understanding of the meaning or the definition of terminology.

- **Relationship clues:** Relationship clues are words that signal that the question is testing your understanding of the relationship between two subjects.

- **Negatives:** Negatives are words or prefixes in words that carry the meaning of "no" or "not."

- **Stems:** Stems are the beginning part of a multiple-choice question that appears before the options for answers.

- **Options:** Options are the choices of answers to use to complete a multiple-choice question.

- **Distractors:** Distractors in multiple-choice questions are the incorrect answers or incorrect options.

- **Four levels of response:** The four levels of response are systematic steps to use to identify the best answer for an objective test question.

Four Levels of Response to Answer Test Questions

Do you move through tests by reading questions, answering them with certainty or hesitancy, and then moving on to the next question? Many students use this approach of plowing through tests—question after question—feeling confident about some answers and doubtful about others. Using the following four levels of response to answer test questions provides you with a structured, step-by-step process that leads to more correct answers and more self-confidence in your ability to perform well on tests.

- **Immediate response:** Read the question carefully. If you immediately know the answer, write the answer with confidence and move to the next question.

- **Delayed response:** If you do not immediately know the answer, reread the question carefully, and then conduct a memory search. Recall what you do know about the topic; strive to trigger an association that will link you to the answer. If you cannot answer with certainty, *leave the answer space empty.* Place a check mark next to the question and return to it after you have answered as many questions as possible on the remainder of the test.

- **Assisted response:** Return to the unanswered questions, the ones with the check mark reminder next to them. Identify one or two key words in the question. Scan through the other parts of the test for these key words and for other clues or associations that may help trigger recall of information to help you select an answer.

- **Educated selection:** Use an educated-selection strategy (educated guessing) to select an objective test-question answer if all else fails. Educated selection involves more than just guessing; it involves using logic and thinking skills to decide on the most reasonable answer. However, realize that educated selection is a last-resort strategy that may increase your odds for selecting the correct answer, but it does not guarantee that all answers will be correct. The following sections provide you with educated selection strategies to use with true-false, multiple-choice, and matching questions.

True-False Questions

True-false questions are the most basic kind of objective test question. Because they are usually one-sentence statements, students tend to read and respond too quickly without paying sufficient attention to key words in the true-false statement. Therefore, pay close attention to the following key elements or words in true-false questions:

- Items in a series

- Smaller words known as modifiers

- Definition and relationship clues

- Negative words that affect overall meaning

Nine Easy-to-Use Strategies for True-False Questions

Are you sometimes confused or unsure of how to read or interpret true-false questions? Do you later understand your incorrect answers when you review a graded test? Following are easy-to-use strategies that will help you understand and interpret true-false questions and select correct answers with more confidence and accuracy.

Understand How to Read and Respond to True-False Questions   STRATEGY 1

- **Read each statement carefully.** Pay attention to every word in the statement. If you tend to misread questions, point to each word as you read and circle the key words.

- **Be sure you completely understand the statement.** Read it a second time if necessary. For clarity, translate difficult words into more informal words. Create a visual picture of the information.

- **Be objective when you answer.** Do not personalize the question by interpreting it according to what you do or how you feel. Instead, answer according to the information presented by the textbook author or your instructor in class.

- **Do not add your reasoning or argument to the side of a question.** Frequently, the only information that the instructor will look at is the T or the F answer, so other notes, comments, or clarifications will be ignored during grading.

- **Make a strong distinction between the way you write a T and an F.** Trying to camouflage your answer so it can be interpreted as a T or an F will backfire. Unclear letters usually are marked as incorrect.

- **Mark a statement as TRUE only when the statement is completely true.** If any part of a statement is inaccurate or false, you must mark the entire statement as FALSE.

Carefully Check Each Item in a Series of Items   STRATEGY 2

- A true-false question is TRUE only when the entire statement is true.

- If one item in a series of items is false, the entire statement becomes a FALSE statement.

- Items in a series are separated by commas, so use the commas as signals to check each item carefully.

- The words in bold print in the following examples turn the statements into false statements.

    F 1. Effective lecture notes show ***details of all examples***, *main ideas, important details,* and *sketches of visual materials* used by the instructor.

    F 2. *Active listening, critical listening,* ***informal listening***, and *appreciative listening* are the four kinds of listening, each with different purposes.

STRATEGY 3   Understand and Identify Modifiers

- **Modifiers** are words that tell to what degree or frequency something occurs. There is a huge difference between saying that something *always* happens and saying that something *sometimes, often,* or *seldom* happens.

- **Figure 1** shows two kinds of modifiers to watch for in true-false statements: 100 percent modifiers and in-between modifiers.

- Pay close attention to modifiers, for a single modifier alters the meaning and the accuracy of the statement.

- As you read questions, actively look for and circle 100 percent and in-between modifiers in statements.

FIGURE 1   Learn to Recognize These Modifiers

100 percent	In-Between	100 percent
all, every, only	some, most, a few	none
always, absolutely	sometimes, often, usually	never
everyone	may, seldom, frequently	no one
everybody	some, few, most	nobody
best	average, better	worst
		least, fewest

Any adjective that ends in *est*, which means "the most," such as largest, smallest ...	Any adjective that ends in *er*, which means "more," such as larger, smaller ...
Absolute phrases: is/are, definitely, with certainty, beyond a doubt, without exceptions	Non-absolute words: perhaps, possibly, maybe, tend to

© Cengage Learning

STRATEGY 4   Pay Close Attention to 100 Percent Modifiers

- **100 percent modifiers**, also called *absolute modifiers,* are words that indicate absolutes or a total degree without any exceptions. In Figure 1, the 100 percent modifiers appear in the first and the third columns. Words such as *best* or *worst* show the extremes and indicate that there is *nothing* that is better or worse; they are absolutes.

- When you identify a 100 percent modifier, ask yourself: *Is this accurate? Does this happen or occur all the time without any exceptions?* If you answer "yes," then the statement is TRUE. If you answer "no," then the statement is FALSE.

- In the following examples, the 100 percent modifiers appear in boldface print. Notice how statements with 100 percent modifiers may be true, or they may be false.

  F   1. Sentences with absolute modifiers are **always** false.

  F   2. Sentences with absolute modifiers are **never** false.

  T   3. Well-written true-false statements have **only** one correct answer.

Pay Close Attention to In-Between Modifiers

STRATEGY 5

- **In-between modifiers** are words that indicate something occurs in varying degrees or frequency. The in-between modifiers appear in the middle column of Figure 1.

- In-between modifiers allow for more flexibility, variance, or exceptions because they indicate that a middle ground exists where situations or conditions do not occur as absolutes (100 percent of the time).

- When you identify an in-between modifier, ask yourself: *Is this accurate? Does this happen or occur this frequently or to this degree?*

- In the following examples, the in-between modifiers appear in boldface print. Notice how statements with in-between modifiers may be true, or they may be false.

  T   1. Spaced practice is **usually more** effective than massed practice for studying textbook information.

  T   2. **Sometimes** students can reduce stress by changing their sleeping or their eating habits.

  F   3. The Look-Away Technique **seldom** provides students with effective feedback.

Watch for Definition Clues

STRATEGY 6

- **Definition clues** are words that signal that the question is testing your understanding of the meaning or the definition of terminology.

- Word phrases such as *defined as, states that,* or *also known as* may be working as clues for definitions.

- **Figure 2** shows common definition clues and the sentence pattern often used in statements that test your understanding of definitions.

- Circle definition clues when you see them in true-false statements.

- Then underline the terminology word and ask yourself: *What is the definition I learned for this word?*

- Compare your definition to the definition that appears in the statement. If your definition matches the test question definition, answer TRUE.

FIGURE 2	Learn to Recognize These Definition Clues

Clues That Signal Definitions		Sentence Pattern Used
defined as	also known as	
are/is	means	
states that	which is/are	
referred to as	involves	
is/are called	measures	
is an example of	suggests that	

© Cengage Learning 2015

- If there is a discrepancy, analyze the test question definition carefully because it may be saying the same thing but simply using different words. If your definition and the definition in the statement are not the same, answer FALSE.

- In the following sample test questions, the definition clue appears in boldface print. Notice that the definition clue appears between the terminology word and the definition.

  __T__ 1. Annotating **is** the active learning process of marking textbooks to show main ideas and supporting details.

  __F__ 2. Marathon studying **is also known as** distributed practice.

  __T__ 3. A traditional IQ test **measures** intellectual abilities in the areas of verbal, visual-spatial, and logical mathematics.

STRATEGY 7   Look for Relationship Clues

- **Relationship clues** are words that signal that the question is testing your understanding of the relationship between two subjects.

- Relationships often show cause and effect—one item causes another item to occur.

- Relationships may also show other organizational patterns: chronological, process, comparison-contrast, and whole-and-parts.

- **Figure 3** shows common relationship clue words and a sentence pattern often used in statements that show relationships.

- Circle relationship clues when you see them in true-false statements.

- Then underline the key words for the two subjects involved in the relationship.

- Ask yourself: *What do I know about how these two subjects are related to each other?*

- Compare your relationship idea with the relationship presented in the question.

- If the relationship in the statement is logical, answer TRUE.

- If the relationship statement varies considerably from your thoughts about the relationship, analyze the accuracy and logic of the statement more carefully. If the statement shows a faulty relationship, answer FALSE.

FIGURE 3   Learn to Recognize These Relationship Clues

Clues That Signal Relationships		Sentence Pattern Used
increases	result	
produces	since	
reason	so, so that	Subject A ⟵ relationship clue ⟶ Subject B
affects	creates	
because	decreases	check carefully
causes	effects	
before/after	differs	
consists of	leads to	

© Cengage Learning

- In the following examples, the relationship clue appears in boldface print. Notice that the relationship clue appears between the two subjects in all but the last example, which shows a second sentence pattern that places the relationship clue in the front of the sentence.

    T 1. Linking a picture to a word **creates** an association that you can use as a retrieval cue.

    F 2. Rote memory is effective for learning textbook information **because** it promotes deep comprehension and memorization of important facts.

    F 3. **Because** rote memory promotes deep comprehension and memorization of important facts, it is effective for learning textbook information.

Watch for the Use of Negatives

STRATEGY 8

- **Negatives** are words or prefixes in words that carry the meaning of "no" or "not."

- Negatives affect the meaning of the sentence; if you ignore or miss them, the meaning of the sentence is the opposite of the correct meaning.

- For example, if you skip over and ignore the negative in the following statement, *The ABC Method is **not** a goal-setting technique*, then your mind reads the statement as *The ABC Method is a goal-setting technique*.

- **Figure 4** shows words and common prefixes often used as negatives in true-false statements.

- Negatives can cause some confusion in understanding or interpreting a statement accurately. If a question with a negative word or prefix confuses you, use the *Negative Cover-Up Technique*:

    - *Cover up the negative* and reread the statement without the negative.

    - If the sentence has two negatives, cover up *only one* negative.

    - If the statement without the negative makes a *true* statement, the answer to the original question will be the opposite: FALSE.

FIGURE 4	Learn to Recognize These Common Negatives

Negative Words	Negative Prefixes
no	dis (disorganized)
not	im (imbalanced)
but	non (nonproductive)
except	il (illogical)
	in (incomplete)
	ir (irresponsible)
	un (unimportant)

© Cengage Learning

- If the statement with the negative removed is a false statement, the answer to the original question will be the opposite: TRUE.

- In the following examples, the negatives appear in boldface print. If the negatives confuse you, use the Negative Cover-Up Technique to better understand the question before answering.

  __F__ 1. A **dis**organized desk is **not** an external distractor.

  __F__ 2. The principle of Selectivity is **not** used during the fourth step of SQ4R.

  __T__ 3. Using chained associations is **not im**practical during a test when you need to conduct a memory search to find an answer to a question.

STRATEGY 9   Use Educated Selection as a Last Resort

- **Educated selection**, sometimes referred to as *educated guessing*, is the fourth level of response for answering objective test questions.

- Educated selection is more than random guessing because it often involves using common sense, basic logic, critical thinking skills, and specific test-taking strategies to improve your odds for supplying the correct answers for objective test questions.

- Even though educated-selection strategies may help you gain a few additional points on a test, the strategies do not always result in correct answers, so do not become overly confident about taking tests simply because you know how to use educated-selection strategies.

- **Figure 5** summarizes five educated-selection strategies that apply to true-false questions.

Select True: In-Between Modifiers

- **In-between modifiers** allow for exceptions or for the statement sometimes to apply and sometimes not to apply.

- If you are using educated selection, and you see an in-between modifier in a true-false question, or in an option in a multiple-choice question, select TRUE.

| FIGURE 5 | Educated-Selection Strategies for True-False Questions |

1. Select *true* if there is an in-between modifier.

2. Select *true*, the "wild-shot guess," if there are no other clues in the true-false statement.

3. Select *false* if there is a 100 percent modifier.

4. Select *false* if there is a relationship clue.

5. Select *false* if the statement is obviously incorrect, silly, or ridiculous.

© Cengage Learning

- Notice how the in-between modifiers work in the following true-false questions. Also notice how you use a variety of thinking skills other than random guessing to select answers.

__T__ 1. **Sometimes** reviewing notes from a previous paragraph can help you understand a difficult paragraph.

__T__ 2. People **often** use empathic listening to try to understand another person's feelings.

Select True: The "Wild-Shot Guess"

- For true-false questions, if there are no modifiers to use, and no relationship is shown, you may need to use TRUE, the "wild-shot guess."

- If you run out of time on a test and simply must guess, select TRUE. There is a logical reason for this. When instructors write tests, they often prefer to leave the correct, accurate information in your mind. Therefore, they tend to write more true statements than false statements.

Select False: 100 Percent Modifiers

- The **100 percent modifiers** are the *absolutes*, meaning that they are the extremes; no exceptions are allowed.

- Few things happen or exist without exceptions, so the odds are in your favor that true-false questions, or options in multiple-choice questions, with 100 percent modifiers will be false. Select FALSE.

- Notice how the 100 percent modifiers work in the following true-false questions.

__F__ 1. Classroom attendance in college is required for **every** class.

__F__ 2. **Always** begin by studying your favorite subject first.

Select False: Relationship Clues

- If you cannot determine the correct answer for a cause-effect or relationship question, select FALSE. Why? Relationship questions often involve higher-level thinking skills, and test writers can easily write questions that show false relationships.

- Notice how the following true-false questions do not show a true or accurate relationship.

> __F__ 1. Lack of motivation is the **reason** unsuccessful students avoid using time management.
>
> __F__ 2. Cramming is ineffective **because** it uses only ten of the Twelve Principles of Memory.

Select False: Obviously Incorrect Answers

- If you read statements that are ridiculous, foolish, or insulting, mark them FALSE in true-false statements or eliminate them as answers (options) for multiple-choice questions.

- If you read statements that have unfamiliar terms, mark them FALSE. If you have attended class regularly and have done all the reading assignments, odds are in your favor that statements with unfamiliar terms are false.

- Notice how this works in the following examples.

> __F__ 1. Howard Gardner's Multiple Intelligences Theory applies only to people with IQs over 175.   *Ridiculous*
>
> __F__ 2. Howard Gardner added an eighth intelligence called psychic/intuitive to his Multiple Intelligence Theory.   *Unfamiliar term*

Multiple-Choice Questions

Multiple-choice questions may be the most frequently used type of question that appears on both paper-pencil and computerized tests. As a form of objective test questions, unless directions indicate otherwise, only one answer is correct. Students must carefully read and analyze answer options before selecting the best one for each question. When answering multiple-choice questions, pay attention to the following parts or elements of the question:

- The **stem**, which is the beginning of the question
- The **options**, which are the choices of answers
- The **distractors**, which are the options that are *not* the correct answer

Six Easy-to-Use Strategies for Multiple-Choice Questions

Do you sometimes answer multiple-choice questions incorrectly because you select the first possible answer without reading the other options? Do you have difficulty selecting the best answer from the list of options? The following six easy-to-use strategies provide you with step-by-step processes to use to analyze multiple-choice questions and select the best option to answer the questions.

> STRATEGY 10   **Understand How to Read and Respond to Multiple-Choice Questions**

- **Read the directions carefully.** Unless indicated otherwise, select only one answer. Realize, however, that some directions may state that you should mark all the correct answers.

- **Use the three-step approach** for answering multiple-choice questions. Identify which options form true statements when used with the stem and which options form false statements when used with the stem. (See Strategy 11.)

- **Read all of the options** before you select your answer. Do not stop reading and analyzing as soon as you find an acceptable answer. A later option may be more comprehensive or a better answer.

- **Pay attention to modifiers, definition clues, relationship clues, and negatives.** After you combine the stem with each option to create true-false statements, use the same strategies you use for answering true-false questions.

- **Choose the *best* answer.** One or more of the answers may be correct, but only the most inclusive (with the broadest information), most accurate, or most complete is the best answer.

- **Select "All of the Above"** only when every option is accurate and forms a true statement when combined with the stem. If any one option forms a false statement, you cannot select "All of the above" as your answer.

- **Expect different formats.** Some tests may have a blank line within the stem. Your task is to select an answer from a list of answers that fits on the blank line to form an accurate statement. On some computerized tests, you may find a drop-down box on the blank line within the stem. The options appear in the drop-down box. You simply click on the option that best completes the statement.

- **Avoid careless mistakes.** To avoid writing the wrong letter on the line, circle the letter of the best answer and then write the letter on the line. You may not need to use this strategy all the time, but it is effective when you get nervous, tend to respond too quickly, or your eyes skip around because of test anxiety.

- **Use the four levels of response.** If you do not immediately know the answer, conduct a memory search. Cross off options you know are distractors. If you cannot confidently select an answer, use assisted response later to look through the test for assistance. As a last resort, use educated selection to write an answer to a multiple-choice question.

Use the Three-Step Approach for Answering Multiple-Choice Questions

STRATEGY 11

Step One: Finish the Stem in Your Mind

- Read the stem carefully and, without looking at the options, quickly finish the stem in your mind. This step puts you in retrieval mode and into a long-term memory schema related to the statement.

- Then glance down to see if any of the options are similar to what you had in mind.

- For practice, how would you complete each of the following stems in your mind?

1. A mnemonic is _____.

2. When you _____ time on your weekly schedule, you exchange time blocks of a social activity and a study block.

3. Metacognition is _____.

Step Two: Create True-False Statements

- Create a true-false statement by reading the stem of a multiple-choice question with the "a" option in the list of options.

- Continue by creating true-false statements by reading the stem with each of the remaining options. If you have four options, you will have four true-false questions to examine.

- Following is an example of creating three true-false statements for a question with three options:

> _____ 1. Schemas in long-term memory are
>   a. small details attached to larger impressions.
>   b. clusters of related information or concepts.
>   c. visually encoded impulses.

By combining the stem and the options, you create three true-false statements:

1. Schemas in long-term memory are small details attached to larger impressions.

2. Schemas in long-term memory are clusters of related information or concepts.

3. Schemas in long-term memory are visually encoded impulses.

Step Three: Identify the Distractors and Select the Answers

- Examine each of the true-false statements you create by combining the stem with each option. Use the true-false test-taking strategies you have learned.

- Cross off the *distractors*, the options that you know are false.

- Examine the remaining statements and select the *best* answer from those options. The following example shows how to use *step three* of this process.

> ~~1.~~ Schemas in long-term memory are small details attached to larger impressions.   *This is false, so cross off this option.*
>
> 2. Schemas in long-term memory are clusters of related information or concepts.   *This forms a true statement.*
>
> ~~3.~~ Schemas in long-term memory are visually encoded impulses. *This is false, so cross off this option.*

| STRATEGY 12 | Choose the Most Inclusive or Comprehensive TRUE Statement |

- When you combine a stem with the options, the result may be some *true* and some *false* statements.

- In such situations, you must then carefully examine the *true statements* to decide which statement is the *most inclusive, most comprehensive,* or *most accurate* and thus is the correct answer.

- The following example shows how two of the true-false statements created by adding the options to the stem form true statements (*b* and *d*), and two form false statements (*a* and *c*). However, *b* is the *best* option because it is more comprehensive and includes the information stated in option *d*.

> **b** 1. The Incentive Theory of Motivation suggests that
> a. a person must receive monetary rewards in order to be motivated.
>   *False*
> b. both positive rewards and negative consequences may activate specific behaviors and increase motivation.   *True*
> c. unobtainable rewards are the greatest motivators to push for higher goals.   *False*
> d. positive rewards activate specific behaviors and kinds of motivation.
>   *True*

Carefully Examine "Not" or Exclusion Questions

STRATEGY 13

- One type of multiple-choice question you may encounter is a "*not*" or an exclusion question. This kind of question asks you which of the options is *not true* or does *not belong* in the same category as the other options.

- When the options are complete sentences, read each option as a true-false statement by itself. Then carefully examine the statement or statements marked *false* because these statements will reflect what is *not true* or what *does not belong* in a given category. One of these statements will be the correct answer.

- In the following example, you are looking for the *false* statement, the "not true" statement. Systematic desensitization *is* a strategy to decrease test anxiety; it *does* replace negative emotional responses with positive ones, and it *does* involve visualizing different responses to words that trigger anxiety. The statement that is *not true*, and thus is the correct answer, is option *c*.

> **c** 1. Which of the following statements is **not** true about systematic desensitization?
> a. It is a strategy to use to decrease test anxiety.   *True*
> b. It replaces negative emotional responses with positive ones.   *True*
> c. It involves a four-step process to use during a test to reduce procrastination.   *False*
> d. It may involve visualizing a different response to words that trigger anxiety.   *True*

Use True-False Educated-Selection Strategies

STRATEGY 14

- The educated-selection strategies you use for true-false questions (Figure 5) also work for multiple-choice questions when you combine the stem with the options to form your own true-false statements.

- Select TRUE for options with in-between modifiers and FALSE for statements that have 100 percent modifiers, relationship clues, or options that obviously are incorrect answers.

- Remember to cross off and then ignore all the distractors.

- In the first example that follows, both *b* and *c* have in-between modifiers. However, before randomly guessing between these two options, think carefully. Option *c* does not show accurate information; option *b* makes sense and is the correct answer.

- In the second example, notice the key words that you can use to analyze the question and select the best answer.

___**b**___ 1. Intrapersonal intelligence is an intelligence that
a. **always** shows leadership and group charisma.   *False*
b. **often** involves a special interest in personal growth and insights.
True?
c. **seldom** is combined with linguistic or interpersonal intelligence.
True?
d. is **never** taught in schools.   *False*

___**d**___ 2. Systematic desensitization
a. **causes** a person to react more mildly to criticism from authorities.
False
b. works **because** the immune system is strengthened.   *False*
c. should **never** be used to avoid undesirable situations.   *False*
d. **helps** a person change his or her negative reaction to specific events.
True

STRATEGY 15	**Use Educated-Selection Strategies for Multiple-Choice Questions**

In addition to the educated-selection strategies in Figure 5 that also apply to multiple-choice questions, **Figure 6** shows five additional educated-selection strategies for multiple-choice questions. Even though these strategies help you analyze questions more carefully and guide you to selecting an answer, do not feel overly confident or rely on these strategies, except as a last resort, because they will not always produce a correct answer.

Select a Middle Number

- When the options in a multiple-choice question are numbers, chances are better that the correct answer is one of the numbers in the middle range.

FIGURE 6	Educated-Selection Strategies for Multiple-Choice Questions

1. Select one of the **middle numbers** when numbers are the options.
2. Select one of the "**look-alikes**" when two options are almost identical.
3. Select the **longest** or the **most inclusive** option.
4. Select c, the **wild-shot guess** if there are no other clues.
5. Select "**All of the above**" in specific situations.

- Therefore, treat the highest and the lowest numbers as distractors; eliminate them.

- That leaves you with two options. Try to reason through to make the better choice from the remaining two options.

- If any one of the other educated-selection strategies applies (such as choose *c*), consider that strategy as well to choose your answer.

> __c__ 1. An average rate of thinking speed is
>   a. 800 words per minute. *Eliminate the highest.*
>   b. 600 words per minute. *Choose between these*
>   c. 400 words per minute. *two options.*
>   d. 200 words per minute. *Eliminate the lowest.*

Select One of the "Look-Alikes"

- Some questions have two options that look almost identical except for one or two words. Chances are good that the correct answer is one of these two options.

- Eliminate the other options and focus on these two "look-alikes."

- Carefully think through and associate the information with what you have learned. If you cannot decide, choose either one. You have a fifty-fifty chance of being correct.

- In the following example, focus on *c* and *d* because they are "look-alikes." Now try to reason your way through this. You have already eliminated *a*, which deals with language. Because *c* also relates to language, it, too, must be incorrect. This leaves you with *d* as the correct answer, which it is. (Notice in this case how the guessing strategy to use *c* does not work—there are no guarantees!)

> __d__ 1. Compared to the left hemisphere of the brain, the right hemisphere of the brain
>   a. understands spoken language better.
>   b. has better logical abilities.
>   c. perceives words better.
>   d. perceives emotions better.

Select the Longest or Most Inclusive Option

- Look at the *length* of the options. If one option is much longer than the others, choose it. Sometimes more words are needed to give complete information, so selecting the longest option may result in a correct answer.

- Also look at the *content* of the options. An option that covers a wider range of possibilities is more likely to be correct.

- Sometimes two or three options may be correct to some degree, but one option contains more information or is a broader idea. This answer is the most inclusive, so choose it.

- Notice in the following example how all of the options are correct to some degree. However, *d* is the longest and includes a wider range of information.

The answers *a*, *b*, and *c* fit under the information given in *d*. Therefore, *d* is the best option.

> **d** 1. You can reduce test anxiety by focusing on
>   a. the test and not on other students. *True*
>   b. conducting careful memory searches. *True*
>   c. positive statements and affirmations. *True*
>   d. effective test-taking skills related to both your actions and your
>   thoughts. *True*

Select C: The "Wild-Shot Guess"

- For multiple-choice questions, many instructors favor the *c* answer for the correct answer. If you try writing some of your own multiple-choice questions, you may find that you, too, tend to put more correct answers in the *c* position than in any other position.

- The position of *c* seems to hide the answer best and force the reader to read through more of the options.

Select "All of the Above" in Specific Situations

- If you know for certain that two options are correct, but you are not sure about the third option, and the fourth option is "All of the above," choose "All of the above."

- If you do not know for certain that two are correct, and you have found no other clues to help you, you can choose "All of the above." However, be aware that this strategy is not very reliable, especially if the option "All of the above" is used throughout the test.

- Apply this strategy to options that are variations of "All of the above." Examples of these variations are *doing all of the above, involves all options,* and *includes all of the strategies.*

Matching Questions

Matching questions consist of two columns of information. The left column often consists of key words or terminology. The right column contains definitions, descriptions, events, examples, or other factual information that matches with the items in the left column. Matching questions are created through the use of *paired associations.* The following are examples of paired associations you may encounter on matching tests:

- Words and their definitions

- Dates and events

- Problems and their solutions

- People and what they did

- Terms and their function or purpose

- Causes and effects

Five Easy-to-Use Strategies for Matching Questions

Do you tend to get confused and frustrated with the process of matching items from two columns? Do you sometimes use answers more than once or almost finish the matching tests only to find that the remaining items do not belong together or match? If so, the following five strategies will provide you with a systematic method to use to avoid confusion, frustration, and incorrect matches.

Examine the Matching Format Carefully

STRATEGY 16

- Read the directions carefully. Usually you can use each item on the right only once. If you can use an item on the right more than once, the directions usually indicate this.

- Count the number of items in each column. If both columns show an equal number of items, each item will be used once. If the right column contains *more* items than the column on the left, some items on the right will be extra and will not be used.

Work Systematically

STRATEGY 17

- Use a systematic approach for matching items on the two lists. If you *incorrectly* match an item on the right with an item on the left, the result will be two or more incorrect answers rather than one.

- Read through the list with the shortest entries to familiarize yourself with the topics and the kinds of paired associations in the matching test. If the items in each column are about equal length, read the left column.

- Start with *a*, the first item at the top of the right column. Scan the items in the left column to find a match.

- Once you see a definite match, write the letter on the line and *cross off the letter you used so you do not reuse it.* Crossing off used letters also helps avoid confusion.

- Do *not* make a match unless you are confident that the item on the right matches the item on the left. When in doubt, leave the item unmatched and move to the next letter in the column to look for its match.

- After you have matched as many items as possible by using immediate and delayed response, return to the unmatched items. Use assisted response by looking through other parts of the test for related information that may help you match up the remaining items.

- **Figure 7** shows the systematic approach to matching items on a matching test.

Look for Word Clues and Grammar Clues

STRATEGY 18

- Word clues (helper words) can help you find correct matches. For example, if you see a word such as *system, technique, process,* or *rule* in the right column, narrow your focus by searching for choices in the left column that deal specifically with a *system, technique, process,* or *rule.*

- Grammar clues can help you find correct matches. If an item in the right column is a *plural*, the match in the left column will also refer to a *plural*. Similarly, *singular* items in the right column are matched with *singular* items in the left column.

- In the following example, notice how the word clues in bold print in the right column help you match to the items in the left column. The words in italics in the left column match up to the boldface words in the right column.

__c__	1. core *abilities* (plural)	a. **two kinds** of locus of control (2)
__e__	2. assisted *response*	b. a cognitive learning **style** (singular)
__e__	3. relaxation *technique*	c. **subintelligences** (plural)
__a__	4. *internal* and *external* (2)	d. soothing mask **technique** (1 technique)
__b__	5. visual *learner* (singular)	e. third level of **response** for test questions (response)

FIGURE 7   Steps for Answering Matching Questions

Matching

① Directions say to use each answer once.

② Two answers are extra and won't be used.

⑤ Use delayed response. Use helper words to try to connect the items that you do not know well.

⑥ Use assisted response. Use the rest of the test for assistance in finding more answers.

⑦ Use educated guessing. Fill in any remaining blanks with letters you did not already use.

Match the items on the left to the items on the right. Write the letter of each answer on the line. Each item on the right may be used only one time.

③ Read the shorter list.

④ Start with "a." Do only the ones you know.

__h__ 1. working memory	a. permanent storage center
____ 2. motivation	b. associating items together
__a__ 3. long-term memory	c. short-term memory and feedback loop
__j__ 4. affirmations	d. feeling, emotion, or desire that elicits an action
__f__ 5. chunking	e. feedback
____ 6. sensory stimuli	f. group into bigger units or break into smaller units
__b__ 7. linking	
__i__ 8. primacy-recency effect	g. procedural memory
____ 9. self-efficacy	h. conscious mind
____ 10. result of self-quizzing	i. items easiest to recall in a list
	j. positive statements written in present tense
	k. belief in one's own abilities
	l. words, sounds, pictures

Connect Items in Each Column by Making Logical Sentences

STRATEGY 19

- As you look at an item in the right column, ask yourself questions to find logical matches. For example, in Figure 7, item *k*, ask yourself, "What item on the left has something to do with belief in one's abilities?"

- When you think you have found a match, connect the two items by forming a sentence. For example, for *k* in Figure 7, you could say, "Self-efficacy is the belief in one's own abilities."

- When the items in the matching example in Strategy 18 are matched up, you can check the logic of your answers by forming sentences that make sense:

  Core abilities are subintelligences.

  Assisted response is the third level of response for test questions.

  A relaxation technique is the soothing mask technique.

  Internal and external are two kinds of locus of control.

  Visual learner is a cognitive learning style.

- If you cannot form a logical sentence by connecting an item on the right with an item on the left, chances are that the two items are not a match.

Write an Answer in Every Space

STRATEGY 20

- If you have not been able to match all the items after using the above strategies, fill in the missing blanks with the remaining letters. Refrain from the urge to start changing answers that you previously marked with certainty.

- An empty answer line obviously will be wrong, so filling in the remaining answers with "leftover" letters may result in one or more correct answers, but this strategy is risky and should only be used as a last resort.

Recall Test Questions

Recall questions are questions that require you to conduct memory searches to retrieve (recall) information from your memory to respond with an answer. Unlike objective test questions, recall questions do not provide you with direct clues or answers to recognize as accurate or not. Recall questions require higher levels of thinking and processing information.

By using effective study strategies that include creating associations that link two or more items in memory, you will be able to recall correct answers for the following kinds of questions:

- Fill-in-the-blanks to complete sentences

- List items or steps in a process

- Define specific terminology

- Write a short paragraph or short answer

- Solve a word problem or an equation (See math tests.)

Familiarize Yourself with Terminology for Recall Tests

In strategies for recall questions, you will encounter terms that are specific to recall questions. Read through the following glossary of terms before proceeding to the strategies for recall tests.

- **Closed questions:** Closed questions are questions that require specific answers. Sometimes the answers must appear in a specific order, such as giving the steps of a process. Other times the answers are limited to course-specific concepts, topics, or details that may appear in any order.

- **Open-ended questions:** Open-ended questions are questions that have many possible answers. A variety of answers may be correct if they reflect course content, show logical connections to course material, or reflect understanding of concepts, topics, or details.

- **Direction words:** Direction words are words in test questions that signal a specific kind of answer that is required. *List, define, discuss, tell, describe, explain why*, and *when* are a few examples of direction words.

Fill-in-the-Blanks Questions

Fill-in-the-blanks questions are recall questions in the form of sentences that have one or more missing words. The words used to "fill in the blanks," or to complete the statement, usually are key terms that appear in your textbook, course materials, or lectures.

- In most cases, fill-in-the-blanks questions are *closed questions*, which means you must use specific words rather than a variety of possible words for a correct answer.

- Spelling is important. Usually your instructors require you to spell words correctly to receive full points. On computerized tests, misspelled words will be marked as incorrect answers.

Four Easy-to-Use Strategies for Fill-in-the-Blanks Questions

Do you sometimes go blank and have difficulty thinking of the exact word needed to complete fill-in-the blanks questions? When you receive your graded test and see the correct answer, do you recognize the word? Using the following three strategies will help you recall the words needed to complete this type of question.

STRATEGY 21   **Understand How to Read and Respond to Fill-in-the-Blanks Questions**

- **Identify the number of words required to complete the statement.** You can write only one word per blank space. (See Strategy 22.)

- **Identify the kind of word needed for each blank space.** Based on the position of the word in the sentence, you often can recognize that the missing word is a noun (naming an object, concept, step, process, or person) or a verb stating some type of action.

- **Conduct memory searches for answers.** Use key words in the statement to trigger associations. Ask yourself the following kinds of questions: *What do we call … . Who … . Where did I learn this? What is this related to?* This type of memory search and questioning works well during the delayed response to answering a question.

- **Form complete sentences.** When you read the completed sentence with the filled-in words, the sentence must make sense and be grammatically correct.

Determine the Number of Words Required in the Sentence

- You can write only one word on each blank line. If there is only one blank line, you will write only one word. Trying to write a two-word phrase on a single line will result in an incorrect answer.

- In the following examples, only one word completes each statement. Remember, you must spell answers correctly.

  1. An _____ personality preference describes a person who tends to focus attention on the inner world of ideas, thoughts, and reflection.
  Introversion

  2. _____ motivation is the driving force that comes from within you to take action. *Intrinsic*

- When you see two or more blank lines, a comma between each blank line signals that your response will require a series of separate items.

- If no commas separate the blank lines, your response is a two- or a three-word term, expression, or phrase.

- The following examples show both types of statements that require more than one-word answers:

  1. _____ _____ is also known as your conscious mind.
  Two-word answer: Working memory

  2. You can use the Increase-Decrease Method to adjust the time you plan to spend in the three main areas of your Pie of Life: _____, _____, and _____. *Answers in any order: school, work, leisure*

  3. The five R's of Cornell in order are _____, _____, _____, _____, and _____. *Answers in order: record, reduce, recite, reflect, review*

Modify the Four Levels of Response to Provide Answers

- **Write the correct word for a blank if you immediately know the answer.**

- **Use delayed response.** Conduct a memory search. Try to recall an association to help you recall the term. If you cannot recall the correct word to fill in the blank, leave the question unanswered. Place a check mark next to the question. Return to it later.

- **Use assisted response to fill in the blanks.** If you cannot recall the necessary word, identify other key words in the statement, skim through the rest of the test to look for those key words. Try inserting a possible word into the statement, then read the statement, remembering that the completed sentence must be grammatically correct, make sense, and be logical.

- **Write a substitute word, a synonym, or even a phrase to complete the sentence.** A *synonym* is a word with a similar meaning. Even though a substitute word, a synonym, or a short phrase is not the exact answer for the fill-in-the-blanks statement, you may receive partial points for your effort.

Study Course Terminology to Prepare for a Test

- Many key words used to answer fill-in-the-blanks questions will be course vocabulary.

- Use flashcards to study. Read the definition side of your flashcards. *Recite* the key term and *spell* it. Turn the card over to check your answer and the spelling of the key word.

- If your textbook provides a list of terms, use the terms to write your own practice fill-in-the-blanks test questions. Practice completing your own questions. Check your spelling.

- Use any textbook or online exercises that include practice filling in missing words and spelling key terms correctly.

Listing Questions

Listing questions are recall questions that ask for a specific list of ideas, items, or steps that belong together in a specific category. Unless the directions say otherwise, answers on listing questions are words or phrases, not complete sentences.

Four Easy-to-Use Strategies for Listing Questions

Do you have problems providing the number of items required to complete a listing question? Do you tend to include items in your list that do not answer the question? The following four easy-to-use strategies will help you complete listing questions with appropriate answers.

Understand How to Read and Respond to Listing Questions

- **Underline the key words in the question.** This helps you focus on what kind of information you need to include in your answer.

- **Pay attention to the number of items required in your answer.** If the question asks you to "List five kinds of ...," number your answer one to five. Begin listing the five different answers. If the question does not indicate how many items to include in your list, list as many items as possible. Avoid duplicating or restating items.

- **Identify the question as a closed or an open-ended question.** (See Strategy 26.)

- **Use words or phrases for your answers.** Unless the directions say differently, you do not need to answer by using complete sentences.

Identify Questions as Closed or Open-Ended Questions

- **Closed questions** are questions that require specific answers. Some closed questions, such as questions about the steps used in a specific process, require that you list the items in their proper order.

- The following are examples of *closed* listing questions:

  1. What are the Four Levels of Response to use for answering objective questions? *Specific order required: immediate, delayed, assisted, educated selection*

  2. List the four most common ways to encode information to process into memory. *Nonspecific order: linguistic, visual, kinesthetic, semantic*

- **Open-ended questions** are questions that have a variety of possible answers.

- To answer open-ended questions, you can list a variety of answers as long as the items in your answers relate to or belong in the category of the question. Items in your list may come from different chapters and different parts of the course.

- Often answers to open-ended questions were not studied as a specific list of information. Therefore, you must pull together information that relates to the question. For this reason, students who rely on rote memory often find open-ended questions challenging.

- The following are examples of open-ended questions that have a variety of possible correct answers:

  1. List any four subintelligences of Gardner's musical intelligence.

  2. List five *reflect activities* a student could use during the fourth step of the Cornell Notetaking System.

  3. List three statements a student with an external locus of control might make after performing poorly on a test.

Modify the Four Levels of Response to Provide Answers

STRATEGY 27

- **Write immediate responses to develop your list.** List as many items as possible to answer the question.

- **Use delayed response.** Conduct memory searches for answers. Use the key words you underlined in the question to trigger associations and answers to expand your list. Ask yourself questions: *What else belongs here? What other things are related to the answers I already listed?* Place a check mark next to the list if you were not able to complete it.

- **Use assisted response.** Return to the listing questions that are not complete. Use other parts of the test to locate items to complete your list.

- **Write a substitute word, synonym, or phrase to complete the list.** An empty space brings only one result: no points for your answer—so attempt to complete the list. Avoid restating an item already listed as duplicate answers will not receive points.

Predict Listing Questions When You Study

STRATEGY 28

- As you read and take notes, watch for items that appear in lists or steps in a process.

- Create study tools, such as flashcards, for these lists. Practice reciting these lists from memory.

- Predict listing questions when you use self-quizzing strategies to prepare for an upcoming test. Write your own test questions that require you to list specific items or steps in a process.

- Use chapter objectives and chapter summaries as additional sources for lists of information to learn.

Definition Questions

Definition questions are recall questions that ask you to define and expand upon a word or terminology. For definition questions, a one-sentence answer that simply provides a formal definition of a term often is insufficient and does not earn you the maximum points for the question.

Three Easy-to-Use Strategies for Definition Questions

Do you tend to have problems recalling definitions for course-specific terminology? Do you tend to receive only partial points for short answers to definition questions? The following three easy-to-use strategies provide you with a step-by-step process to write strong answers that define terminology.

| STRATEGY 29 | Understand How to Read and Respond to Definition Questions |

- **Read the question carefully; underline the word you need to define.**

- **Use paired associations.** When you studied the term, you paired it with the definition. Say the word to yourself; conduct a memory search for the definition. Try to recall hearing yourself reciting or reading the definition on your flashcard or vocabulary sheet. Try to visualize the information in your notes.

- **Include three or more sentences in your answer.** Simply defining the term is usually insufficient and results in an underdeveloped answer. By using the category-definition-expanded detail format, you demonstrate greater understanding of the meaning of the term. (See Strategy 30.)

- **Use assisted response.** If you are not able to define the word after conducting a memory search, place a check mark next to the question, and move to another question. Later, use other parts of the test for clues you can use to complete your answer.

| STRATEGY 30 | Practice Writing Definitions with Three Levels of Information |

1. **Name the category associated with the term.** To identify the category, ask yourself: *In what group or category of information does this belong? In what chapter (topic) did this appear? What is the "big picture" word or schema for this word?*

2. **Give the formal definition.** Give the course-specific definition you learned from your textbook or from class lectures.

3. **Expand the definition with one more detail**. **Figure 8** shows seven methods and examples for expanding an answer for a definition question.

| FIGURE 8 | Methods to Expand a Definition Answer |

Method	Example
Add one more fact.	Distributed practice often occurs when the 2:1 ratio is used.
Give a synonym.	Distributed practice is the same as spaced practice.
Give an antonym, a contrast, or a negation.	Distributed practice is the opposite of marathon studying or massed practice.
Give a comparison or an analogy.	Distributed practice is like working on a goal a little every day instead of trying to complete all the steps in one block of time.
Define the structure of the word.	The root of neuron is neuro, which means nervous system.
Give the etymology.	The term locus comes from the Latin loci, which means place, so locus of control refers to a place that is the source of the control.
Give an application.	Surveying can be used to become familiar with a new textbook, chapter, article, or test.

© Cengage Learning

Predict and Study for Definition Questions

STRATEGY 31

- Use key words in boldface print or lists of important terms in each chapter to predict definition questions.

- Spend ample time reciting definitions and explaining what terms mean and how they are used. With a strong understanding of course-specific terminology, you will have a solid foundation for other concepts and skills in the course.

- Create flashcards or vocabulary study sheets for vocabulary terms you need to know. Use your textbook and glossary to clarify definitions.

- Work with a partner or in a study group to practice reciting and explaining terminology out loud. Use the three levels of information in your response.

- Use self-quizzing and practice writing definitions as you prepare for tests. Use feedback throughout the process to evaluate your understanding.

- Examine and study other students' answers for definition questions. Notice the category, definition, and the expanded detail other students use in their answers. Following is an example of weak and strong answers.

Question: Define the term *distributed practice*.
Weak Answer: It means you practice at different times.
Strong Answer: Distributed practice is a time-management strategy. Distributed practice means that a task or study blocks are spread or distributed over time. Distributed practice, also known as spaced practice, is the opposite of marathon studying or massed practice.

Short-Answer Questions

Short-answer questions are recall questions that require a short paragraph for an answer. After carefully reading the question, you must conduct memory searches to locate or recall relevant information in long-term memory to answer the question. Unlike listing questions, your answer will consist of five or more sentences written in paragraph form. Writing information in lists instead of full sentences usually does not suffice or earn you full points.

Five Easy-to-Use Strategies for Short-Answer Questions

Do you tend to have difficulty expressing your ideas in a clear, well-organized way? Do you sometimes write answers that do not directly answer the short-answer question? The following five strategies show how to organize and develop answers for short-answer questions.

STRATEGY 32 · Understand How to Read and Respond to Short-Answer Questions

- **Read the question carefully to determine if the question is closed or open-ended.** Doing this directs your memory searches for the kind of information needed to answer the question. Are you looking for specific details that perhaps were a part of a list or set of steps, or are you searching for a variety of possible answers related to the topic?

- **Underline key words in the question.** Key words focus your attention on the subject or topics that must appear in your answer. As you work on developing your answer, check back to the underlined key words to check that you are focusing on the topic and including important details. This also helps you avoid wandering off course with nonessential information.

- **In your response, include key words that appear in the question.**

- **Answer in complete sentences.** Answers to short-answer questions often are graded not only on the content, but also on your writing skills. Use correct grammar, punctuation, and spelling. If time permits, proofread to correct grammar, punctuation, and spelling errors.

- **Answer in paragraph form.** (See Strategies 35 and 36.)

- **Write legibly.**

- **Use assisted response if necessary.** Scan through other parts of the test to identify additional details to include or to strengthen your answer.

STRATEGY 33 · Pay Attention to and Circle Direction Words

- **Direction words** are words in test questions that signal a specific kind of answer is required.

- To get full points for your answer, your response must reflect the expectation associated with the question word.

- As soon as you identify a direction word in a question, *circle it*. Review in your mind what is required by this direction word.

FIGURE 9	Direction Words for Short-Answer Questions

Direction Word	What Is Required
Discuss/Tell	Tell about a particular topic.
Identify/What are?	Identify specific points. (This is similar to a listing except that you are required to answer in full sentences.)
Describe	Give more specific details or descriptions than are required by "discuss."
Explain/Why?	Give reasons. Answer the question "Why?"
Explain how/How?	Describe a process or a set of steps. Give the steps in chronological (time sequence) order.
When?	Describe a time or a specific condition needed for something to happen, occur, or be used.

© Cengage Learning

- **Figure 9** shows common direction words used for short-answer questions.

- Notice in the following examples how each of the test questions has the same subject: *visual mappings.* However, think how answers will vary slightly because of the different direction words used.

Why is recitation important to use while studying a visual mapping?

Explain how to create a visual mapping.

How should you study from a visual mapping?

When should you use visual mappings?

© Cengage Learning

Make a Mental Plan or a Short List of Key Ideas

STRATEGY 34

- **Conduct a memory search.** Use your memory search to identify appropriate details related to the key words and the direction word in the question.

- **Create a mental plan or a short list of ideas to use as a guide to write your answer.** This helps you save valuable test time as your answer stays focused and you avoid wandering off the topic. If for some reason you run out of time to write a paragraph answer, turn in your list of ideas for possibly partial points for your answer.

- **Refer to your mental plan or list of ideas to write your answer.** Develop the list into full sentences and a well-planned paragraph.

Start Your Paragraph with a Strong, Focused Opening Sentence

STRATEGY 35

- Begin your answer with a sentence that is direct and to the point. Do not beat around the bush or save your best information for last. The first sentence of your answer should clearly state the main idea of your answer and include the key words from the question.

FIGURE 10	Examples of Opening Sentences
Question:	(Why) is <u>recitation</u> important in the <u>learning process</u>?
Weak:	Recitation is important because it helps a person learn better.
Strong:	Recitation, one of the Twelve Principles of Memory, is important in the learning process for three reasons.
Strong:	Recitation is important in the learning process because it involves the auditory channel, feedback, and practice expressing ideas.

© Cengage Learning

- The first sentence, when well written, lets your instructor know right away that you are familiar with the subject, your answer is "on target," and you are responding appropriately to the direction word and providing the required kind of information.

- Your opening sentence may indicate the number of items that you will discuss or even possibly list the series of items you will explain further.

- **Figure 10** shows differences in quality in three opening sentences. The first one does not get to the point. The second and third examples are direct, focused, and show confidence.

STRATEGY 36   Expand Your Answer with Details

- Support your opening sentence by expanding into a paragraph with details.

- For a strong answer, use course-related terminology or examples used in class or in your textbook.

- Stick to the point. Do not pad the answer with unrelated information or attempt to write too much or to write an essay.

- **Figure 11** shows a weak answer and a strong answer to the question, "Why is recitation important in the learning process?"

FIGURE 11	Weak and Strong Answers
Weak:	Recitation is important because it helps a person learn. Everyone wants to do the very best possible, and recitation helps make that happen. When you recite, you talk out loud. You practice information out loud before a test.
Strong:	Recitation is important in the learning process because it involves the auditory channel, gives feedback, and provides practice expressing ideas. When a person states information out loud and in complete sentences, he/she encodes information linguistically and keeps information active in working memory. Reciting also gives feedback so that a person knows immediately whether or not the information is understood accurately and on the level that can be explained to someone else. Taking time to recite also provides the opportunity to practice organizing and expressing ideas clearly.

© Cengage Learning

Math Test Questions

Performing well on math tests requires an alert mind ready to manage a variety of thinking processes and tasks that result in an exact, correct answer. Because math tests require you to apply a sequential set of skills and concepts to solve new problems, memorizing specific answers is not possible. To prepare for math tests, spend ample time using repetition to rework problems multiple times, checking your understanding of each step of the process, and checking your answers for accuracy. Your learning goal during studying and test preparation is to increase your accuracy and your problem-solving speed so you can work new problems and move through the test without wasting time or running out of time to complete the test.

Familiarize Yourself with Math Terminology

Your math textbooks include a wide range of special terminology required to understand, explain, and use mathematical operations and formulas. Study the meanings of all key terms in your textbook that appear in boldface print. Practice reciting definitions, giving examples of concepts, rules, formulas, or equations. Creating and using a glossary of terms helps you understand and communicate mathematical concepts. Following are examples of key terms and their definitions.

- **Algebraic expressions:** statements that show values by using letters, symbols, and numerals. Examples include: $x - 5$ (means a number decreased by 5) and $x + 8$ (means eight more than x).

- **Algebraic symbols:** marks or signs used in mathematical expressions and equations to represent specific processes or functions. For example, the symbol "/" may mean: divide, quotient, or per.

- **Algorithms:** sequences of steps and operations used to solve problems.

- **Equations:** mathematical sentences or linear arrangements of mathematical symbols used to show equalities on each side of an equal sign.

- **Prototypes:** original formulas or examples of problems that serve as models to use to solve new problems with similar characteristics.

- **Word problems or story problems:** a series of sentences that presents a variety of facts that are needed to solve a problem.

Eight Easy-to-Use Strategies for Math Tests

Do you tend to make specific kinds of errors on math tests? Do you forget to show all your work, omit mathematical signs, use incorrect steps to solve problems, or make careless errors? Do you use specific strategies to answer word problems or to check your work before you turn in a test for grading? Do you run out of time to complete math tests? The following eight strategies will help you increase your performance on math tests.

Understand How to Read and Respond to Math Test Questions   STRATEGY 37

- **Jot down important information to refer to during the test.** Before you survey or begin the test, jot down information you do not want to forget and believe you will need to have ready to use. This may include specific formulas, equations, problem-solving steps (algorithms), or prototypes.

- **Survey the test.** Skim through the test to familiarize yourself with the types of questions, different test question point values, and the length of the test.

- **Create a quick plan for budgeting your time.** Ideally, you will have time to complete the easier problems, adequate time to tackle more difficult problems, and time available at the end of the test to check your answers.

- **Circle direction words and underline key words.** These two actions help you maintain a focus on what is required and what is essential for a complete answer. Pay special attention to directions or questions that ask you to provide two-part answers.

- **Begin with familiar or the easiest problems.** You do *not* need to work problems in the order that they appear in the test. By starting with familiar problems or the easiest problems, you create a mindset for the material, and you build self-confidence.

- **Show all the steps to solve a problem.** Skipping steps or not showing all your work may reduce the points you earn for the test question. Showing all the steps that lead to the solution also helps you or your instructor identify errors if answers are incorrect.

- **Do not spend too much time on one problem.** If you struggle completing a specific problem, work as many steps as possible and then move on to another problem. (See Strategy 42.)

- **Do not change answers without a valid reason.** During bouts of test anxiety, students sometimes start changing answers quickly at the last minute. If you carefully worked through a problem and felt confident about your answer, do not change the answer unless you find an error during the process of carefully checking your work.

STRATEGY 38   Use Prototypes to Solve New Problems

- A **prototype** is a model of a specific type of math problem that can be used to solve new problems with similar characteristics. By memorizing and understanding a prototype, you can use this model to solve new problems more quickly and more confidently.

- Prototypes often appear in textbooks when you are introduced to a new type of math problem or equation. Explanations and examples accompany the prototype.

- Study prototypes carefully. Memorize them. Practice explaining the steps in the prototype. Your goal is to be able to recognize when to use or apply the prototype and its steps to new problems on tests.

- **Figure 12** shows examples of prototypes.

STRATEGY 39   Identify and Think about the Pattern of the Problem

- Read the problem carefully. Ask yourself:

  What do I already know about this kind of problem?

  What problems did I study that are similar?

FIGURE 12   Examples of Prototypes

Prototype: Convert Centigrade to Fahrenheit

Fraction Formula   Decimal Formula

$(°C \times \frac{9}{5}) + 32 = °F$ $(°C \times 1.8) + 32 = °F$

Prototype: Exponential Notation

6^4 "Six to the fourth power" means $6 \times 6 \times 6 \times 6$

Prototype: Add Fractions with Different Denominators

Find the total of $\frac{1}{2} + \frac{1}{3}$

1. Find the common denominator: $\frac{1}{2} = \frac{3}{6}$ $\frac{1}{3} = \frac{2}{6}$

2. Add the fractions: $\frac{3}{6} + \frac{2}{6} = \frac{5}{6}$

© Cengage Learning 2015

What steps did I use to solve similar problems?

What prototypes did I memorize that I can use to solve this problem?

- Conduct a memory search or use associations to recall the prototype (model) problem you memorized for this pattern and the steps or formula you used to solve that problem.

- Focus your attention on the specific steps used in the prototype and then apply those steps to the new math test problem.

Use Basic Strategies to Solve Word Problems

STRATEGY 40

- **Read carefully.** Carefully examine all the details, including any tables or charts related to the word problem. Reread until you understand what the question requires you to do.

- **Focus first on the problem-solving details and not on the operations you will need to use.** Understanding the relationship between relevant facts and identifying the unknown details should occur before shifting your focus to the mathematical operations needed to solve the problem.

- **Restate the problem in your own words.** If you have problems understanding the question after rereading it several times, try restating the same problem in your own words. Sometimes using your own words without distorting the question adds clarity.

- **Underline key words.** This includes information that is needed to solve the problem. Making a list of the facts given to solve the problem may be helpful.

- **Cross out nonessential details.** Some details in word problems are not needed to solve the problems. Ignore these details, which are distractors.

- **Draw a simple picture of the problem.** Putting the information into a picture form may provide a clearer understanding of the information and help you see what you will need to do to solve the problem.

- **Visualize the story.** Visualizing the story and its details is a "mental drawing." Visualizing the details may help you identify the processes needed to solve the problem. Visualizing may also help you estimate reasonable answers before performing the precise calculations. Try visualizing the following word problem.

> **Word Problem:** After playing tennis for 2 hours, Ruben ate a banana split containing 650 calories and a fudge brownie containing 250 calories. Playing tennis uses 720 calories per hour. Did the banana split and the fudge brownie contain more or fewer calories than Ruben burned off playing tennis?

- **Translate the information in the word problem to an algebraic equation.** Remember that the unknown will appear on one side of the equation. Examine the equation and conduct a memory search to see if the equation is similar to other equations or prototypes you have studied.

- **Mentally talk or explain to yourself the steps you will use to solve the problem.** Shift your focus to the mathematical operations you need to use to solve the problem.

- **Apply the steps to solve the problem.** Show your work for each problem-solving step.

- **Use strategies to check the accuracy of your answer.** (See Strategy 44.)

STRATEGY 41   Use RSTUV to Read and Solve Problems

The **RSTUV Problem-Solving Method** is a five-step approach to solve math word problems. Each letter of RSTUV represents one step of this problem-solving approach.

- **R = READ** the problem, not once or twice, but until you understand it. Pay attention to key words or instructions such as *compute, draw, write, construct, make, show, identify, state, simplify, solve,* and *graph*.

- **S = SELECT** the unknown; that is, find out what the problem asks for. One good way to look for the unknown is to look for the question mark (?) and carefully read the material preceding it. Try to determine what information is given and what is missing.

- **T = THINK** of a plan to solve the problem. Problem solving requires many skills and strategies. Some of them are *look for a pattern; examine a related problem; make tables, pictures, and diagrams; write an equation; work backward;* and *make a guess.*

- **U = USE** the techniques you are studying to carry out the plan. Look for procedures that can be used to solve specific problems. Then carry out the plan. Check each step.

- **V = VERIFY** the answer. Look back and check the results of the original problem. *Is the answer reasonable? Can you find it some other way?*

Source: Bello and Britton, *Topics in Contemporary Mathematics,* 6th ed.

Avoid Getting Stuck on One Problem

- When you feel stuck and unsure how to solve a problem, shake your head a few times, look away from the problem, take a few deep breaths, and ask yourself a few questions to help change your thought processes.

  Why does this problem look familiar?

  What prototype do I know that looks similar?

  What processes are we studying that apply here?

- To solve math problems often requires your mind to shift back and forth rapidly and multiple times between the problem and the information in your long-term memory. Reread the problem, shift your eyes away a few seconds, do a memory search to scan memory for possible ways to solve a specific problem, and then look back at the problem.

- If you have tried a variety of strategies without success, or if you have spent too much time on one individual problem, place a check mark next to the question and move on.

- After completing as many questions on the test as possible, return to the questions with the check marks. Sometimes working on other problems will trigger associations that will make it possible for you to see the problem differently and recall a strategy to use to complete the problem-solving steps.

Check Accuracy of Steps and Answers

Checking the accuracy of your work leads to getting the most points possible on your test. Rather than hurry to exit the classroom after a test, use all of the test time to check your work and your accuracy. Following are four methods for checking your work.

- **Logical Method:** Ask yourself, *Is this answer reasonable? Does it make sense?* Sometimes when you look back at an answer, you realize it does not make sense. Perhaps the number in the answer is too large because you misplaced the decimal point. Perhaps you forgot to complete a final step to reach a reasonable answer. Reexamine your processes and steps if the answer is not logical.

- **Estimation Method:** Use the given facts to estimate a reasonable answer. Round whole numbers. Use the mathematic operation (addition, subtraction, multiplication, or division) with the whole numbers to estimate a reasonable answer. Compare the estimate with your original answer. If there is a large discrepancy, return to the problem to identify errors.

- **Substitution Method:** Place the answer or the solution back in the original equation. Verify that each side of the equation equals the other side. If one side of the equation does not equal the other side, you need to rework the problem to find the correct solution.

- **Algorithm Method:** Use sequential math steps to rework the problem. Compare your original answer with the answer for the reworked problem. If you do not end up with the same answer, find the discrepancy. Use one of the previous methods to check the answers for both the first and the reworked problem.

| STRATEGY 44 | **Analyze Your Errors on Graded Tests** |

Math is a sequential set of skills, so understanding concepts and processes on one level is essential in order to understand and solve problems on the next higher levels. As soon as you receive a graded test, examine the questions you answered correctly as well as the ones you answered incorrectly. Reworking and correcting your thinking and processes for the incorrect answers are important and should be done as soon as the graded test is returned to you. Your goal is to eliminate common errors or error patterns on future tests. Learn from your tests and strengthen your test-taking skills by asking the following kinds of questions:

- *Did I use incorrect mathematical operations to solve problems?*

- *Did I forget the proper equation to use to solve the problem?*

- *Did I forget to label answers in word questions?*

- *Did I misunderstand the necessary processes to use in application questions?*

- *Did I apply an incorrect prototype to a question that did not have the same characteristics as the prototype?*

- *Did I forget to show all the steps to reach the solution?*

- *Did I stop before completing the final step to solve the problem?*

- *Did I make careless mistakes that I easily identified when reviewing the graded test?*

- *Did I forget to align numbers in place value columns when calculating?*

- *Did I experience test anxiety that reduced my ability to stay focused and think logically?*

- *Did I leave the test early instead of using the extra time to check my work?*

Essay Test Questions

Essay questions require an organized composition that develops several main ideas that are related to one thesis sentence. The thesis sentence directly states the main point of the entire essay. Following are additional points about essay test questions.

- Answering essay questions is demanding because it requires you to know information thoroughly, to be able to pull the information from your memory, and to know how to integrate facts to show relationships.

- The way you express the information and the relationships you show need to follow a logical line of thinking and include sufficient details to develop an effective essay answer.

- Essays also require a sound grasp of writing skills (grammar, syntax, and spelling) and a well-developed, expressive vocabulary.

- Review Chapter 7 for different kinds of essay questions and additional strategies.

Familiarize Yourself with Terminology for Essay Test Questions

The structure of essays involves key concepts that you will also encounter in composition classes. Carefully read through the following terms before focusing your attention on the specific strategies.

- **Thesis statement:** A thesis statement is a strong, focused sentence that states the main point of an entire essay. The thesis statement often appears as the first sentence of the essay, but it may appear other places in the introductory paragraph.

- **Direction words:** Direction words are words in test questions that signal a specific kind of answer that is required. *List, define, discuss, tell, describe, explain why,* and *when* are a few examples of direction words.

- **Organizational plan:** An organizational plan is an outline, a hierarchy, a visual mapping, or a list of main ideas the writer intends to use in an essay to develop the thesis of the essay.

- **Five-paragraph format:** The five-paragraph essay format consists of an introductory paragraph, three paragraphs in the body of the essay to develop three separate main ideas, and a concluding paragraph.

- **Main idea:** A main idea is the most important point in a paragraph that the writer wishes to make about a topic. Each paragraph has only one main idea. The main idea supports or helps develop the thesis statement.

- **Supporting details:** Supporting details are facts, examples, or definitions that are related to the subject of a paragraph. A paragraph has adequate development when sufficient details appear in the paragraph to support the main idea.

Eight Easy-to-Use Strategies for Essay Test Questions

Do your essay answers tend to be underdeveloped and lack sufficient supporting details? Do your essays wander off course by including irrelevant information? Do you have difficulty clearly organizing information and expressing your ideas? The following eight easy-to-use strategies will guide you through the process of developing strong answers for essay test questions.

Understand How to Read and Respond to Essay Test Questions

STRATEGY 45

- **Budget your time carefully.** Allow sufficient time to answer all questions or to at least write some information for each question. If you run short on time, turn in your outline or organizational plan to show the main points you intended to discuss.

- **Weigh the value of different questions.** If one question is worth more points, take more time to develop that answer or to return to that answer later and add more information to strengthen your answer.

- **Carefully select which questions to answer when you have a choice.** Examine the questions carefully. Do not automatically choose the questions that look the shortest or the easiest. They are usually more general and more difficult to answer than longer questions that tend to be more specific. Also, select the questions that contain the topics that you are most familiar with and topics for which you can recall specific and sufficient supporting details.

- **Begin with the most familiar question.** Developing an answer for the most familiar question first tends to boost your confidence level and puts you in the "essay writing mode."

- **Use complete sentences to express your ideas.** Short phrases, charts, or lists of information are not appropriate for an essay.

- **Include supporting details so your essay will not be underdeveloped.** Include facts such as names, dates, events, and statistics; include definitions, examples, or appropriate applications of the information you are presenting. Do not make the mistake of assuming that information is obvious or that your instructor knows what you are thinking or clearly sees the connection.

- **Include quotations for details.** For some courses, you may want to memorize important quotations that appear in your textbook and that you predict you may be able to use to develop an essay test answer. Remember to place quotation marks around the quoted material and cite the source.

- **Use key words in the question and course-specific terminology in your answers as much as possible.**

- **Strive to write as neatly as possible.** Illegible handwriting will hurt your grade. If you need to delete some of the information, delete it by crossing it out with one neat line or by using correction fluid.

STRATEGY 46 Understand the Questions and the Direction Words

- Read each question carefully and identify the question as a closed or an open-ended question.

- Underline key words in the question as a reminder to include these key words in your introductory paragraph and to emphasize these words throughout your essay.

- Be sure you understand the direction word as it signals the type of response required. Circle the direction word to maintain a focus on the direction of your answer.

- **Figure 13** shows direction words frequently used for essay questions.

STRATEGY 47 Write a Strong, Focused Thesis Sentence

A **thesis sentence** is a strong, focused sentence that states the main point of an entire essay. The thesis sentence for an essay test answer usually appears as the first sentence on your paper. The following points about your thesis statement are important to remember:

- Clearly state the topic of the essay. Include key words that are a part of the question. If you wish, you may indicate the number of points you plan to develop.

- Show that you understand the direction word and plan to focus your answer in the direction indicated by the direction word.

FIGURE 13 Direction Words for Essay Questions

Direction Word	What Is Required
Compare	Show the similarities and differences between two or more items.
Contrast	Present only the differences between two or more items.
Define	Give the definition and expand it with more examples and greater details.
Trace/Outline	Discuss the sequence of events in chronological order.
Summarize	Identify and discuss the main points or the highlights of a subject. Omit in-depth details.
Evaluate/Critique	Offer your opinion or judgment and then back it up with specific facts, details, or reasons.
Analyze	Identify the different parts of something. Discuss each part individually.
Describe	Give a detailed description of different aspects, qualities, characteristics, parts, or points of view.
Discuss/Tell	Tell about the parts or the main points. Expand with specific details.
Explain/Explain why	Give reasons. Tell why. Show logical relationships or cause-effect.
Explain how	Give the process, steps, stages, or procedures involved. Explain each.
Illustrate	Give examples. Explain each example with details.
Identify/What are	Identify specific points. Discuss each point individually. Include sufficient details.
When	Describe a time or a specific condition needed for something to happen, occur, or be used. Provide details and any relevant background information.

© Cengage Learning

- Your thesis statement serves as a guide for developing the rest of your essay. It suggests the basic outline of main ideas to develop with important supporting details.

- Your thesis statement serves as an immediate indicator for your instructor that you understand the question and know the answer.

- Because of the significance of the thesis statement, take time to create a strong, direct, confident opening sentence.

- **Figure 14** shows examples of two essay test questions, the meaning of the direction words, and examples of strong thesis statements.

FIGURE 14 Thesis Sentences

Question	Direction Words	Possible Thesis Statement
Discuss the characteristics of each of Howard Gardner's multiple intelligences.	**Discuss = tell about** What are the eight intelligences?	Each of Howard Gardner's eight intelligences has clearly recognizable characteristics.
Explain why elaborative rehearsal is more effective for college learning than rote memory strategies.	**Explain why = give reasons** What are the reasons? How many reasons?	Elaborative rehearsal is more effective than rote memory because more Memory Principles are used and information in memory is in a more usable form.

© Cengage Learning 2015

STRATEGY 48   Develop an Organizational Plan

- After you have developed a strong thesis statement, take the time to develop an organizational plan.

- Your organizational plan provides an overview of the main ideas you plan to include in your essay. Once you conceptualize and develop your plan, you will be able to write your response faster and avoid wandering off course or becoming confused about the next point to write in your answer.

- Your organizational plan becomes your step-by-step outline that guides the writing process.

- Your plan may be an outline, a visual mapping, a hierarchy, or a basic list of main ideas.

- **Figure 15** shows the four basic kinds of organizational plans you can use.

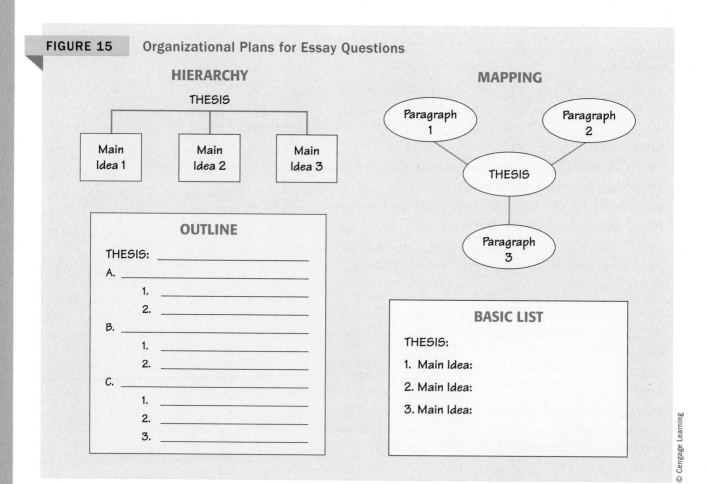

FIGURE 15   Organizational Plans for Essay Questions

© Cengage Learning

FIGURE 16	Key Elements in a Five-Paragraph Essay

Paragraph	Details
Introductory Paragraph (one paragraph)	• Includes the thesis statement • Indicates that you understand the direction word • Repeats key words from the essay test question
Body of the Essay (three paragraphs with three different main ideas)	• Expands *each category or section* of information in your organization plan into separate *paragraphs* • States a main idea in each paragraph and develops the main idea with details, such as facts, examples, reasons, or definitions • Limits one main idea per paragraph
Concluding Paragraph (one paragraph)	• Briefly summarizes your essay or draws a conclusion • Leaves a clear picture in your reader's mind of the main points • Repeats key words from the essay test question

© Cengage Learning

Use the Five-Paragraph Format

STRATEGY 49

- For many essay test questions, the five-paragraph essay is an effective format to use to write your essay answers.

- The five-paragraph essay format consists of an introductory paragraph, three paragraphs in the body of the essay to develop three separate main ideas, and a concluding paragraph.

- If you have more than three main ideas to develop, you can expand this format by adding additional paragraphs to the body of the essay.

- **Figure 16** shows the key elements of each part of the five-paragraph essay.

Create a Pre-Writing Chart to Guide Your Writing

STRATEGY 50

Many students waste too much precious test-taking time trying to "get started" on an essay. A systematic approach helps you gather your thoughts and move into action. Use the following steps to organize yourself and your thoughts before writing the actual essay.

- Circle the direction word. Underline key words in the question to use in your essay answer.

- Use this information to write a strong thesis sentence that will appear in the introductory paragraph. Quickly sketch a chart with five rows. (See **Figure 17**.) Write the thesis statement in the first box of your chart.

- In the second, third, and fourth rows, write the topic that you will develop for each paragraph.

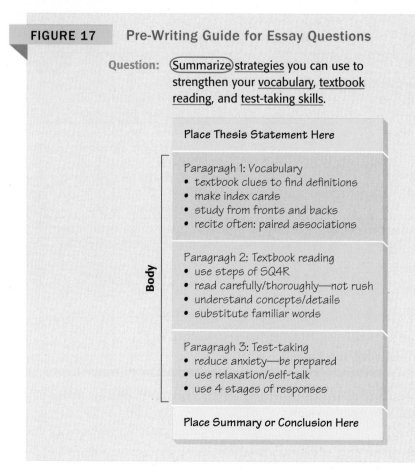

FIGURE 17   Pre-Writing Guide for Essay Questions

Question: Summarize strategies you can use to strengthen your vocabulary, textbook reading, and test-taking skills.

Place Thesis Statement Here

Body

Paragragh 1: Vocabulary
- textbook clues to find definitions
- make index cards
- study from fronts and backs
- recite often: paired associations

Paragragh 2: Textbook reading
- use steps of SQ4R
- read carefully/thoroughly—not rush
- understand concepts/details
- substitute familiar words

Paragragh 3: Test-taking
- reduce anxiety—be prepared
- use relaxation/self-talk
- use 4 stages of responses

Place Summary or Conclusion Here

© Cengage Learning

- Under each topic, which will become the main idea for the paragraph, briefly list the details you plan to use to develop the topic or main idea.

- After you write the essay, plan to summarize it in a short concluding paragraph (last row).

- If you run out of time on the test and are not able to complete your essay answer, turn in your organizational plan or notes showing the above information. You may receive partial points for your work.

- Figure 17 shows how much information you can generate and organize before you even begin writing your essay answer.

STRATEGY 51   Strengthen and Revise if You Have Time

Writing effective essays involves understanding and using effective vocabulary, writing, and spelling skills. Following are revisions you can make in your essays if you have time available during the testing period. If you do not have time to revise, familiarize yourself with the following writing tips so you can strive to implement them the next time you face an essay test.

- Replace slang or informal language with formal language or course terminology.

- Reword to avoid using the word *you*. Replace the word *you* with the word it represents, the specific noun, such as *students*.

- Replace vague pronouns such as *it* with the name of the specific item.

- Reword sentences to avoid weak "sentence starters" such as *There is ...*, *There are ...*, *Here is ...*, or *Here are ... .*

- Use sentence variety in your essay: simple, compound, complex, and compound-complex sentences. Knowing how to combine short sentences into compound, complex, or compound-complex sentences is an economical way to develop ideas. Using effective sentence variety results in an essay that is interesting to read and understand.

Learn from Your Tests

STRATEGY 52

- Writing strong essay answers becomes easier with practice.

- When you get your essay tests back, read the comments and suggestions.

- Analyze your essays and ask yourself questions: *Did I predict this question? Did I answer questions directly and in an organized way? Did I include sufficient details? How could I have strengthened my answer?*

- Adjust your studying and test-taking skills as needed to improve your performance on the next essay test.

Conclusion

This Essential Test-Taking Skills guide is designed to equip you with essential skills and strategies to improve your test-taking skills and performance. Using the fifty-two specific test-taking strategies will strengthen your ability to read, understand, interpret, and respond appropriately to a variety of test questions. Becoming an effective test-taker requires practice and attention to details. Each time you receive a graded test, take time to examine your answers and learn from your tests. Return to this guide to prepare for upcoming tests as well as refresh and refine your skills so your tests more truly reflect how well you have mastered the content of your courses.

Appendix B

Answer Keys

Master Profile Chart

Beginning-of-the-Term Profiles

1. As you begin a new chapter, complete the chapter profile chart in your textbook or online in the College Success CourseMate where your answers will be scored for you.

2. Score your profile. (See Chapter 1, page 4.) Find the chapter number below. Circle your score to show the number of correct responses.

3. Connect the circles on your Master Profile Chart with lines to create a graph.

	Learning Styles	Powerful Mindset	Using Time Effectively	Achieving Goals	Processing Information	Rehearsing and Retrieving	Upcoming Tests	Reading System	Reading and Notetaking	Organizing Content	Listening and Lecture Notes	Technology
Chapter	1	2	3	4	5	6	7	8	9	10	11	12
100%	10	10	10	10	10	10	10	10	10	10	10	10
90%	9	9	9	9	9	9	9	9	9	9	9	9
80%	8	8	8	8	8	8	8	8	8	8	8	8
70%	7	7	7	7	7	7	7	7	7	7	7	7
60%	6	6	6	6	6	6	6	6	6	6	6	6
50%	5	5	5	5	5	5	5	5	5	5	5	5
40%	4	4	4	4	4	4	4	4	4	4	4	4
30%	3	3	3	3	3	3	3	3	3	3	3	3
20%	2	2	2	2	2	2	2	2	2	2	2	2
10%	1	1	1	1	1	1	1	1	1	1	1	1
0%	0	0	0	0	0	0	0	0	0	0	0	0

Profile Answer Keys

CHAPTER 1: Learning Styles

1. Y	2. Y	3. N	4. N	5. Y
6. Y	7. Y	8. Y	9. Y	10. Y

CHAPTER 2: Powerful Mindset

1. Y	2. N	3. Y	4. N	5. Y
6. Y	7. N	8. Y	9. Y	10. Y

CHAPTER 3: Using Time Effectively

1. Y	2. N	3. Y	4. Y	5. N
6. N	7. N	8. Y	9. Y	10. Y

CHAPTER 4: Achieving Goals

1. Y	2. N	3. N	4. Y	5. N
6. Y	7. N	8. N	9. Y	10. Y

CHAPTER 5: Processing Information

1. Y	2. Y	3. N	4. Y	5. Y
6. Y	7. Y	8. N	9. N	10. Y

CHAPTER 6: Rehearsing and Retrieving

1. Y	2. N	3. Y	4. Y	5. Y
6. Y	7. N	8. Y	9. N	10. Y

CHAPTER 7: Upcoming Tests

1. Y	2. N	3. Y	4. N	5. Y
6. N	7. Y	8. N	9. Y	10. Y

CHAPTER 8: Reading System

1. N	2. Y	3. Y	4. Y	5. N
6. Y	7. N	8. N	9. Y	10. Y

CHAPTER 9: Reading and Notetaking

1. N	2. Y	3. Y	4. N	5. N
6. Y	7. Y	8. Y	9. Y	10. Y

CHAPTER 10: Organizing Content

1. N	2. Y	3. Y	4. N	5. Y
6. Y	7. Y	8. N	9. Y	10. Y

CHAPTER 11: Listening and Lecture Notes

1. Y	2. N	3. Y	4. Y	5. N
6. N	7. Y	8. N	9. Y	10. Y

CHAPTER 12: Technology

1. Y	2. Y	3. Y	4. Y	5. N
6. N	7. N	8. Y	9. Y	10. Y

End-of-the-Term Profiles

1. Redo all the profile questions so you can see the changes that you have made this term. Cut a two-inch-wide strip of paper to cover the original answers on the profile questions at the beginning of each chapter. Write Y or N *next to the number of each profile question*. If you prefer, you may complete the profile questions in the CourseMate website for this textbook where your responses will be scored for you.

2. Score your profile answers using the answer key listed at the beginning of Appendix B.

3. Chart your scores on the Master Profile Chart. Use a different color of ink so that you can compare these scores with your original scores.

Chapter Answer Keys

CHAPTER 1: Learning Styles

CHECK POINT 1.1

True or False

1. F	2. F	3. T	4. F
5. T	6. F	7. F	8. F

CHECK POINT 1.2

True or False

1. T	2. F	3. F	4. T	5. F

Fill-in-the-Blanks

1. core abilities
2. naturalist; logical-mathematical
3. linguistic

CHECK POINT 1.3

Matching

1. g	2. f	3. h	4. a
5. b	6. e	7. i	8. c

CHAPTER 1 REVIEW QUESTIONS

True or False

1. F	2. T	3. F	4. T	5. F

Multiple Choice

1. b	2. a	3. c	4. d

Definitions:

Answers will vary.*

CHAPTER 2: Powerful Mindset

CHECK POINT 2.1

Multiple Choice

1. b	2. d	3. c	4. d

Listing

Answers will vary.*

CHECK POINT 2.2

True or False

1. T	2. F	3. T	4. F
5. F	6. F	7. T	

CHECK POINT 2.3

Definitions

Answers will vary.*

Listing

1. remembering
2. understanding
3. applying
4. analyzing
5. evaluating
6. creating

Short Answer

Answers will vary.*

CHAPTER 2 REVIEW QUESTIONS

True or False

1. F	2. T	3. T	4. F	5. F
6. F	7. T	8. T	9. T	10. T

*Answers will vary. Check your answer with the textbook, another student, or with your instructor.

Multiple Choice

1. c	2. d	3. b	4. c	5. d
6. a	7. b	8. d	9. c	10. c

CHAPTER 3: Using Time Effectively

CHECK POINT 3.1
True or False

1. T	2. F	3. F
4. F	5. F	6. T

CHECK POINT 3.2
Matching

1. g	2. i	3. d	4. b	5. j
6. a	7. h	8. c	9. e	10. f

CHECK POINT 3.3
True or False

1. T	2. T	3. F	4. F

CHAPTER 3 REVIEW QUESTIONS
Multiple Choice

1. b	2. b	3. c	4. a
5. b	6. d	7. d	8. c

Fill-in-the-Blanks

1. studying
2. massed
3. distributed
4. internal
5. chunking
6. Take Charge

CHAPTER 4: Achieving Goals

CHECK POINT 4.1
True or False

1. T	2. F	3. T
4. F	5. F	6. F

CHECK POINT 4.2
True or False

1. F	2. T	3. T
4. T	5. T	6. T

CHECK POINT 4.3
Multiple Choice

1. b	2. d	3. b

CHECK POINT 4.4
True or False

1. T	2. F	3. T
4. F	5. F	6. T

CHAPTER 4 REVIEW QUESTIONS
Fill-in-the-Blanks

1. Success
2. Intrinsic
3. motivation
4. coping
5. breathing

Multiple Choice

1. c	2. c	3. d	4. b
5. d	6. c	7. d	8. d

Short Answers

Answers will vary.*

CHAPTER 5: Processing Information

CHECK POINT 5.1
Fill-in-the-Blanks

1. Metacognition
2. encoding
3. long-term
4. Retrieval

True or False

1. F	2. F	3. F	4. T
5. T	6. T	7. F	8. T

CHECK POINT 5.2
Multiple Choice

1. d	2. a	3. d	4. d

CHECK POINT 5.3
True or False

1. T	2. F	3. T	4. F
5. F	6. F	7. T	8. T

CHAPTER 5 REVIEW QUESTIONS
True or False

1. F	2. T	3. T	4. T	5. T
6. F	7. F	8. T	9. T	10. T

Matching

1. g	2. h	3. f	4. i	5. a
6. b	7. d	8. c	9. j	10. e

Recall

Compare to Figure 5.6.

CHAPTER 6: Rehearsing and Retrieving

CHECK POINT 6.1
Multiple Choice

1. d	2. a	3. c	4. b	5. a

CHECK POINT 6.2
True or False

1. F	2. T	3. T	4. T	5. F

CHECK POINT 6.3
Definitions

Answers will vary.*

CHAPTER 6 REVIEW QUESTIONS
True or False

1. F	2. F	3. F	4. T
5. T	6. F	7. F	8. F

Listings

1. Answers will vary.*
2. Decay Theory; Displacement Theory; Interference Theory; Incomplete Encoding Theory; Retrieval Failure Theory; Emotional Blocks Theory

CHAPTER 7: Upcoming Tests

CHECK POINT 7.1
True or False

1. T	2. F	3. F	4. T
5. T	6. T	7. F	8. F

CHECK POINT 7.2
Fill-in-the-Blanks

1. Recall
2. closed
3. definition

Listings

1. fill-in-the-blanks; listings; definitions; short answers
2. true-false; multiple-choice; matching

CHECK POINT 7.3
True or False

1. T	2. F	3. T	4. F	5. T

CHECK POINT 7.4
Definitions

Answers will vary.*

Essay

Answers will vary.* Include an organizational plan.

CHAPTER 7 REVIEW QUESTIONS
True or False

1. T	2. T	3. F
4. F	5. F	6. F

Multiple Choice

1. d	2. d	3. b	4. a	5. d

*Answers will vary. Check your answer with the textbook, another student, or with your instructor.

Definitions
Answers will vary.*
Short Answer
Answers will vary.*
Take-Home Essay
Answers will vary.*

CHAPTER 8: Reading System

CHECK POINT 8.1
Multiple Choice
1. d   2. d   3. d   4. b

CHECK POINT 8.2
True or False
1. T   2. F   3. T   4. F

Listings
Answers will vary.*

CHECK POINT 8.3
Fill-in-the-Blanks
1. read – record– recite – review
2. surveying
3. headings
Short Answer
Answers will vary.*

CHECK POINT 8.4
Short Answers
Answers will vary.*

CHAPTER 8 REVIEW QUESTIONS
True or False
1. T   2. F   3. T   4. T
5. T   6. F   7. F   8. F
Multiple Choice
1. a   2. d   3. d   4. c   5. d
Short Answers
Answers will vary.*
Essay
Answers will vary.*

CHAPTER 9: Reading and Notetaking

CHECK POINT 9.1
True or False
1. F   2. T   3. F   4. T   5. T

CHECK POINT 9.2
Multiple Choice
1. c   2. d   3. a   4. b   5. d

CHECK POINT 9.3
Short Answers
Answers will vary.*

CHECK POINT 9.4
Fill-in-the-Blanks
1. Index
2. Definition
3. Category
4. Question

CHECK POINT 9.5
True or False
1. F   2. F   3. T   4. T   5. T
Matching
1. d   2. f   3. b   4. c
5. h   6. g   7. a

CHAPTER 9 REVIEW QUESTIONS
True or False
1. F   2. F   3. T   4. F   5. F
6. T   7. T   8. F   9. F   10. T
Multiple Choice
1. a   2. d   3. d

CHAPTER 10: Organizing Content

CHECK POINT 10.1
True or False
1. T   2. T   3. F   4. T

CHECK POINT 10.2
True or False
1. T   2. F   3. T   4. T

CHECK POINT 10.3
True or False
1. F   2. T   3. F   4. F

CHECK POINT 10.4
1. a   2. d   3. d   4. a

CHAPTER 10 REVIEW QUESTIONS
Multiple Choice
1. a   2. d   3. b   4. d   5. d
6. b   7. d   8. a   9. d

CHAPTER 11: Listening and Lecture Notes

CHECK POINT 11.1
True or False
1. F   2. T   3. T   4. F   5. F

Matching
1. b   2. c   3. a
4. d   5. a   6. a

CHECK POINT 11.2
True or False
1. F   2. T   3. T
4. F   5. T   6. F

CHECK POINT 11.3
True or False
1. F   2. T   3. F
4. F   5. T   6. F

CHECK POINT 11.4
Short Answer
Answers will vary.*

CHAPTER 11 REVIEW QUESTIONS
Multiple Choice
1. b   2. d   3. a   4. d   5. b
6. d   7. b   8. d   9. c
Short Answers
Answers will vary.*

CHAPTER 12: Technology

CHECK POINT 12.1
True or False
1. T   2. T   3. T   4. F   5. T

CHECK POINT 12.2
Listings
Answers will vary.*

CHECK POINT 12.3
Multiple Choice
1. c   2. d   3. a

CHECK POINT 12.4
Application
Answers will vary.*

CHAPTER 12 REVIEW QUESTIONS
Definitions
Answers will vary.*
Short Answers
Answers will vary.*

*Answers will vary. Check your answer with the textbook, another student, or with your instructor.

Appendix C

Exercises, Inventories, and Checklists

Learning Styles Inventory

PURPOSE: Identify your learning style preference and the strength of your modalities. Understanding your learning style preference can guide your selection of study and learning strategies to use to be more effective and successful.

DIRECTIONS: Complete the Learning Styles Inventory by reading each statement carefully. Check YES if the statement relates to you all or most of the time. Check NO if the statement seldom or never relates to you. There is no in-between option, so you must check YES or NO. Your first, quick response to a question is usually the best response to use.

	YES	NO
1. I like to listen to and discuss information with another person.	X	
2. I could likely learn or review information effectively by hearing my own voice on a recording.		X
3. I prefer to learn something new by reading about it.		X
4. I often write down directions someone gives me so I do not forget them.		X
5. I enjoy physical sports and exercise.	X	
6. I learn best when I can see new information in picture or diagram form.		X
7. I can easily visualize or picture things in my mind.	X	
8. I learn best when someone talks or explains something to me.		X
9. I usually write things down so that I can look back at them later.	X	
10. I pay attention to the rhythm and patterns of notes I hear in music.	X	
11. I have a good memory for the words and melodies of old songs.	X	
12. I like to participate in small-group discussions.	X	
13. I often remember the sizes, shapes, and colors of objects when they are no longer in sight.		X
14. I often repeat out loud verbal directions that someone gives me.	X	
15. I enjoy working with my hands.	X	
16. I can remember the faces of actors, settings, and other visual details of movies I have seen.		X

(continued)

Exercise 1.1 (continued)

	YES	NO
17. I often use my hands and body movements when explaining something to someone else.	X	
18. I prefer standing up and working on a chalkboard or flip chart to sitting down and working on paper.	X	
19. I often seem to learn better if I can get up and move around while I study.	X	
20. I often refer to pictures or diagrams to assemble or install something new.	X	
21. I remember objects better when I have touched them or worked with them.	X	
22. I learn best by watching someone else first.	X	
23. I tend to doodle when I think about a problem or situation.	X	
24. I speak a foreign language.		X
25. I am comfortable building or constructing things.	X	
26. I can follow the plot of a story when I listen to an audio book.		X
27. I often repair things at home.	X	
28. I can understand information when I hear it on a recording.		X
29. I am good at using machines or tools.	X	
30. I enjoy role-playing or participating in skits.	X	
31. I enjoy acting or doing pantomimes.	X	
32. I can easily see patterns in designs.		X
33. I often know how to assemble, install, or fix something without referring to written directions.	X	
34. I like to recite or write poetry.	X	
35. I can usually understand people with foreign accents or dialects.		X
36. I can hear many different pitches or melodies in music.	X	
37. I like to dance and create new movements or steps.	X	
38. I enjoy participating in activities that require physical coordination.	X	
39. I follow written directions better than oral ones.	X	
40. I can easily recognize differences between similar sounds.		X
41. I like to create or use jingles or rhymes to learn things.		X
42. I prefer classes with hands-on experiences.	X	
43. I can quickly tell if two geometric shapes are identical.	X	
44. I remember best things that I have seen in print, in diagrams, or in pictures.		X
45. I follow oral directions better than written ones.		X

(continued)

Exercise 1.1 (continued)

		YES	NO
46.	I could learn the names of fifteen medical instruments more easily if I could touch and examine them.	X	
47.	I remember details better when I say and repeat them aloud.		X
48.	I can look at a shape and copy it correctly on paper.	X	
49.	I can usually read a map without difficulty.		X
50.	I can "hear" a person's exact words and tone of voice days after he or she has spoken to me.		X
51.	I remember directions best when someone gives me landmarks, such as specific buildings and trees.	X	
52.	I have a good eye for colors and color combinations.		X
53.	I like to paint, draw, sculpt, or be creative with my hands.	X	
54.	I can vividly picture the details of a meaningful past experience.		X

SCORING YOUR PROFILE:

1. Ignore the NO answers. Work only with the questions that have a YES answer.

2. For every YES answer, look at the number of the question. Find the number in the following chart and circle that number.

3. When you finish, not all the numbers in the following boxes will be circled. Your answers will very likely not match anyone else's.

4. Count the number of circles for the Visual box and write the total on the line. Do the same for the Auditory box and Kinesthetic box.

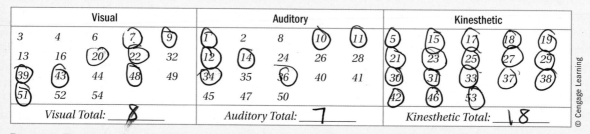

Visual					Auditory					Kinesthetic				
3	4	6	(7)	(9)	(1)	2	8	(10)	(11)	(5)	(15)	(17)	(18)	(19)
13	16	(20)	(22)	32	(12)	(14)	24	26	28	(21)	(23)	(25)	(27)	(29)
(39)	(43)	44	(48)	49	(34)	35	(36)	40	41	(30)	(31)	(33)	(37)	(38)
(51)	52	54			45	47	50			(42)	(46)	(53)		
Visual Total: ___8___					*Auditory Total:* ___7___					*Kinesthetic Total:* ___8___				

Return to Exercise 1.1 on page 6 in your textbook to record your scores and learn the meaning of your scores.

Time-Management Inventory

DIRECTIONS: Read each statement carefully. Answer YES or NO to each statement to show how you use or feel about time. This is a nongraded inventory, so answer honestly. Follow the directions at the end to score your inventory.

SENSE OF CONTROL

		YES	NO
1.	I feel time slips by quickly without anything important getting done.		X
2.	I lose sense of time so do not get things done that are on my to-do list.	X	
3.	I run out of time to get assignments or tasks done on time.	X	
4.	I am aware of times I need to buckle down and plan my use of time.		X
5.	I feel in control of time and use time to my benefit.		X
6.	I take charge and use new strategies when I feel I am unproductive.		X

STRATEGIES

		YES	NO
7.	I waste quite a bit of time trying to figure out how to start a task.	X	
8.	I am used to chaos and confusion in the way I do things.	X	
9.	I experience stress and frustration because I do not meet deadlines.		X
10.	I am more productive when I set aside and use time to work on a project.		X
11.	I finish projects on time, which boosts my sense of confidence.	X	
12.	I organize priorities and dedicate sufficient time to work on priorities.		X

SCHEDULES

		YES	NO
13.	I work without a schedule because I like the flexibility.	X	
14.	I do not have sufficient time to read and review notes each week.		X
15.	I am a spontaneous person so I study when I am in the mood.	X	
16.	I procrastinate less when I work with an organized schedule and plan.		X
17.	I create a structure for my daily and weekly routines.		X
18.	I am punctual and meet deadlines because I follow my plans of action.	X	

BALANCE

		YES	NO
19.	I do not have time to spend with family or friends.		X
20.	I turn assignments in late because I forget about them or don't finish them.		X
21.	I lack a satisfactory sense of balance in my life.		X
22.	I sufficiently plan use of my time to fulfill most obligations and deadlines.	X	
23.	I am comfortable with the amount of time I spend with family and friends.	X	
24.	I manage the demands of time by organizing time using schedules.		X

SCORING:

If you are using time management effectively, the first three statements in <u>each section</u> are *NO* statements, and the last three statements in each section are *YES* statements. Highlight all the statements in each section that do not match the above pattern (N, N, N, Y, Y, Y). What personal patterns do you see in this inventory?

EXERCISE 3.1

EXERCISE 3.2

How You Use Time: Three-Day Time Log

DAY 1

Time	Activity	Time	Activity
MIDNIGHT		NOON	
12:30 A.M.		12:30 P.M.	
1:00 A.M.		1:00 P.M.	
1:30 A.M.		1:30 P.M.	
2:00 A.M.		2:00 P.M.	
2:30 A.M.		2:30 P.M.	
3:00 A.M.		3:00 P.M.	
3:30 A.M.		3:30 P.M.	
4:00 A.M.		4:00 P.M.	
4:30 A.M.		4:30 P.M.	
5:00 A.M.		5:00 P.M.	
5:30 A.M.		5:30 P.M.	
6:00 A.M.		6:00 P.M.	
6:30 A.M.		6:30 P.M.	
7:00 A.M.		7:00 P.M.	
7:30 A.M.		7:30 P.M.	
8:00 A.M.		8:00 P.M.	
8:30 A.M.		8:30 P.M.	
9:00 A.M.		9:00 P.M.	
9:30 A.M.		9:30 P.M.	
10:00 A.M.		10:00 P.M.	
10:30 A.M.		10:30 P.M.	
11:00 A.M.		11:00 P.M.	
11:30 A.M.		11:30 P.M.	

DAY 2

Time	Activity	Time	Activity
MIDNIGHT		NOON	
12:30 A.M.		12:30 P.M.	
1:00 A.M.		1:00 P.M.	
1:30 A.M.		1:30 P.M.	
2:00 A.M.		2:00 P.M.	
2:30 A.M.		2:30 P.M.	
3:00 A.M.		3:00 P.M.	
3:30 A.M.		3:30 P.M.	
4:00 A.M.		4:00 P.M.	
4:30 A.M.		4:30 P.M.	
5:00 A.M.		5:00 P.M.	
5:30 A.M.		5:30 P.M.	
6:00 A.M.		6:00 P.M.	
6:30 A.M.		6:30 P.M.	
7:00 A.M.		7:00 P.M.	
7:30 A.M.		7:30 P.M.	
8:00 A.M.		8:00 P.M.	
8:30 A.M.		8:30 P.M.	
9:00 A.M.		9:00 P.M.	
9:30 A.M.		9:30 P.M.	
10:00 A.M.		10:00 P.M.	
10:30 A.M.		10:30 P.M.	
11:00 A.M.		11:00 P.M.	
11:30 A.M.		11:30 P.M.	

Exercise 3.2 (continued)

DAY 3			
Time	**Activity**	**Time**	**Activity**
MIDNIGHT		**NOON**	
12:30 A.M.		12:30 P.M.	
1:00 A.M.		1:00 P.M.	
1:30 A.M.		1:30 P.M.	
2:00 A.M.		2:00 P.M.	
2:30 A.M.		2:30 P.M.	
3:00 A.M.		3:00 P.M.	
3:30 A.M.		3:30 P.M.	
4:00 A.M.		4:00 P.M.	
4:30 A.M.		4:30 P.M.	
5:00 A.M.		5:00 P.M.	
5:30 A.M.		5:30 P.M.	
6:00 A.M.		6:00 P.M.	
6:30 A.M.		6:30 P.M.	
7:00 A.M.		7:00 P.M.	
7:30 A.M.		7:30 P.M.	
8:00 A.M.		8:00 P.M.	
8:30 A.M.		8:30 P.M.	
9:00 A.M.		9:00 P.M.	
9:30 A.M.		9:30 P.M.	
10:00 A.M.		10:00 P.M.	
10:30 A.M.		10:30 P.M.	
11:00 A.M.		11:00 P.M.	
11:30 A.M.		11:30 P.M.	

THREE-DAY TIME LOG			
Activity	**Day 1**	**Day 2**	**Day 3**
School: Classes, labs, studying, test preparation			
School: Meetings, practices			
Work: Job			
Work: Parenting, chores, other work			
Leisure: Family			
Leisure: Friends			
Leisure: Personal time; recreation			
Naps, Sleep			
Snacks, Meals			
Other/Unaccounted for Hours			
	TOTAL HOURS:	**TOTAL HOURS:**	**TOTAL HOURS:**

EXERCISE 3.5

Part I: Weekly Time-Management Schedule

FOR THE WEEK OF			NAME				
TIME	MONDAY	TUESDAY	WEDNESDAY	THURSDAY	FRIDAY	SATURDAY	SUNDAY
12–6 A.M.							
6–7:00							
7–8:00							
8–9:00							
9–10:00							
10–11:00							
11–12 NOON							
12–1:00 P.M.							
1–2:00							
2–3:00							
3–4:00							
4–5:00							
5–6:00							
6–7:00							
7–8:00							
8–9:00							
9–10:00							
10–11:00							
11–12 A.M.							

Exercise 3.5 (continued)

Part II: Time-Management Self-Assessment Checklist

Name _____ Date _____

Check only the statements that are true for your weekly time-management schedule.

STUDY BLOCKS

My schedule shows:

_____ Sufficient study blocks set aside for each class using the 2:1 ratio.

_____ Each study block labeled with the subject to be studied at that time.

_____ Study blocks spread throughout the week (spaced practice).

_____ Two or more study blocks scheduled on the weekend.

_____ No marathon studying (no more than 3 study hours in a row).

_____ The majority of study hours are during the day or early evening hours.

_____ Two or more FLEX blocks scheduled throughout the week.

_____ Study times for most difficult classes scheduled earlier in the day.

_____ Study blocks for lecture and math classes scheduled shortly after class.

FIXED ACTIVITIES

My schedule shows:

_____ Sufficient hours of sleep each night.

_____ A fairly regular sleep schedule throughout the week.

_____ Time set aside for three meals a day.

_____ My work schedule.

_____ Specific meetings or appointments that occur on a weekly basis.

BALANCING YOUR LIFE

My schedule shows:

_____ Time set aside to spend with family and friends.

_____ Time set aside for exercise, hobbies, or recreation.

_____ Time set aside for necessary errands, chores, or personal responsibilities.

_____ Time set aside to work on specific goals.

GENERAL GUIDELINES

Check only the statements that apply to you or your schedule.

_____ I walked through each day in my mind and believe it is realistic.

_____ As much as is possible, I used my peak energy times during the day to study.

_____ I color-coded my schedule so different activities are easier to identify.

_____ Using a schedule will help me have a more organized week.

_____ Using a schedule will help me achieve more tasks during the week.

_____ I will strive to follow this schedule to my greatest abilities this week.

_____ I will note problem areas on the schedule and use this information to adjust next week's schedule.

_____ I will use a "star system" to track the blocks of time I follow successfully.

QUESTIONS/COMMENTS/EXPLANATIONS

EXERCISE 4.1

Goal-Setting Inventory

DIRECTIONS: Are you a skillful goal setter? For each statement, circle the response that best characterizes you.

1 = never or seldom   2 = sometimes   3 = always or almost always

1. I find sufficient time to complete goals that I write.   1 2 3
2. I use the GPS goal-setting strategy to write goals that are clear and specific.   1 2 3
3. I start term-long assignments shortly after they are assigned.   1 2 3
4. I am confident and not afraid to try to achieve new goals.   1 2 3
5. The purpose or importance of my goals is clear to me.   1 2 3
6. I take time to create short-term goals for things I need to achieve within the next week, several weeks, or the month.   1 2 3
7. I use a checklist process to keep track of steps I complete in achieving my goals.   1 2 3
8. I use goal setting to organize tasks, assignments, and obligations.   1 2 3
9. I break larger goals into smaller steps or subgoals.   1 2 3
10. I use positive self-talk, affirmations, and visualization to help me stay motivated and productive.   1 2 3
11. I use rewards as incentives to complete goals.   1 2 3
12. I analyze my goal-setting processes and make adjustments when necessary to improve my goal-setting skills.   1 2 3
13. I begin working on my goals expecting to achieve the goal successfully.   1 2 3
14. Using goal-setting strategies results in less stress for me.   1 2 3
15. When I use goal-setting strategies, I reduce or eliminate procrastination.   1 2 3

TOTAL SCORE: _____

SCORING:

40–45   Congratulations! You are a skillful goal setter!

30–39   You are an effective goal setter who frequently benefits from setting goals.

20–29   You are on your way to becoming an effective goal setter; identify ways you can strengthen or expand your skills to become a more effective goal setter.

0–19   You have not yet learned the benefits of setting goals. Get ready for an exciting new journey! Begin using goal-setting strategies to achieve your desired outcomes and increase your performance.

Social Adjustment Scale (Stress Test)

PURPOSE: Good and bad events in one's life can increase stress levels. Knowing how to manage stress reduces the chances that stress will take a negative toll on your health and emotional well-being. In 1967, Dr. Thomas H. Holmes and Dr. Richard H. Rahe developed the following "stress test" to help individuals identify their stress levels. By knowing stress levels, people can make an even greater asserted effort to use strategies to manage stress effectively.

DIRECTIONS:

1. In the following list of events, circle every experience that you have had in the *past twelve months*.

2. Total the point values next to each of the experiences you circled. Use that total to find your stress level in the scoring section that follows.

Event	Point Value	Event	Point Value
Death of a Spouse	100	Change in Responsibilities at Work	29
Divorce	73	Son or Daughter Leaving Home	29
Marital Separation	65	Trouble with In-Laws	29
Jail Term	63	Outstanding Personal Achievements	28
Death of a Close Family Member	63	Partner Begins/Stops Work	28
Personal Injury or Illness	53	Begin or End School	26
Marriage	50	Change in Living Conditions	25
Fired at Work	47	Revision of Personal Habits	24
Marital Reconciliation	45	Trouble with Boss	23
Retirement	45	Change in Work Hours or Conditions	20
Change in Health of a Family Member	44	Change in Residence	20
Pregnancy	40	Change in School	20
Sex Difficulties	39	Change in Recreation	19
Gain of a New Family Member	39	Change in Religious Activities	19
Business Readjustments	39	Change in Social Activities	18
Change in Financial State	38	Loan Less than $50,000	17
Death of a Close Friend	37	Change in Sleeping Habits	16
Change to a Different Line of Work	36	Change in Number of Family Gatherings	15
Change in Number of Arguments with Spouse	35	Change in Eating Habits	15
Mortgage over $50,000	31	Vacation	13
Foreclosure of Mortgage	30	Holidays	12
		Minor Violation of Laws	11
		TOTAL SCORE	

SCORING:

Low Stress Level <149

Mild Stress Level 150–200

Moderate Stress Level 200–299

Major Stress Level >300

Source: Reprinted from *Journal of Psychosomatic Research*, 11 (2), Holmes, T. H. & Rahe, R. H., "The social readjustment rating scale," pp. 213–218. © 1967 with permission from Elsevier.

Working Memory Inventory

DIRECTIONS: Think back to the last time you sat down to study. Answer the following questions.

Circle **1** if you did not use the working memory strategy during the study block.

Circle **2** if you used the working memory strategy occasionally during the study block.

Circle **3** if you used the working memory strategy consistently during the study block.

1. As I studied, I was aware of different ways I encoded the information. — 1 2 3
2. I used selective attention to focus on important stimuli and ignore the unimportant stimuli and distractions. — 1 2 3
3. I changed my approach to more active learning when I realized I was shifting into using rote memory. — 1 2 3
4. I studied without the interference of visual or auditory stimuli from a television or background music. — 1 2 3
5. To avoid information dropping out of my short-term memory, I started thinking about or working with information as soon as I read it. — 1 2 3
6. I limited the number of items I studied at one time by using the Magic 7 ± 2 Theory. — 1 2 3
7. I rehearsed or repeated the information in some form at least one time. — 1 2 3
8. I worked slowly to give my working memory time to process information. — 1 2 3
9. I broke large chunks of information in my notes or in the textbook into smaller units to study. — 1 2 3
10. I used elaborative rehearsal to study factual information and multiple repetition to study process (procedural) information. — 1 2 3
11. I paid attention to categories of information or schemas connected to the new information I was studying. — 1 2 3
12. I maintained a positive attitude toward studying and toward the subject matter and materials. — 1 2 3
13. I used visualization and recitation when I studied and rehearsed information. — 1 2 3
14. I intentionally created new retrieval cues so I could recall the information more quickly at later times. — 1 2 3
15. I avoided overloading working memory by using selectivity to identify important ideas to focus on learning. — 1 2 3
16. I used some form of self-quizzing and feedback during the study process. — 1 2 3
17. I created clear associations to work as retrieval cues for me. — 1 2 3
18. I either felt a natural interest or created an interest in studying. — 1 2 3
19. I set a learning goal when I studied so I knew what I wanted to accomplish. — 1 2 3
20. I used multisensory strategies to work with the information. — 1 2 3

TOTAL SCORE: _____

YOUR SCORE:

20–35   You can make better use of your working memory. Look at all the items that received a **1**, indicating you do not use these strategies. Adjusting the way you study to include these strategies will strengthen your working memory and academic performance level.

36–50   You are making average use of your working memory, but there is room to improve. Strive to include the strategies marked with a **1** or a **2** on a more consistent basis when you study.

51–60   You are using your working memory effectively. Continue to use all of the strategies consistently when you study.

Memory Principles Inventory

EXERCISE 6.4

DIRECTIONS: Complete the following inventory by answering YES or NO to each question. Be honest with your answers so they reflect your *current* use of the principles.

SELECTIVITY
	YES	NO
1. Do you spend a lot of time studying but seem to study the "wrong information" for tests?		
2. Do you get frustrated when you read because everything seems important?		
3. Do you tend to highlight too much when you read textbooks?		
4. Do your notes seem excessively long and overly detailed?		
5. Do you avoid making study tools such as flashcards because you are not sure what information to put on the study tools?		

ASSOCIATION
	YES	NO
1. Do you tend to memorize facts or ideas in isolation?		
2. When you try to recall information you have studied, do you sometimes feel "lost" because there is no direct way to access the information in your memory?		
3. Do you feel that you are memorizing numerous lists of information but not really understanding what they mean or how they are connected?		
4. Do you "go blank" on tests when a question asks for information in a form or context different from the way you studied it?		
5. Do you lack sufficient time to link difficult information to familiar words or pictures?		

VISUALIZATION
	YES	NO
1. When you finish reading, do you have difficulty remembering what the paragraphs were even about?		
2. Do you have difficulty remembering information that appeared in a chart your instructor presented on the chalkboard or on a screen?		
3. Do you find it difficult to recall a visual image of printed information?		
4. When you try to recall information, do you rely mainly on words rather than pictures?		
5. When your instructor explains a new concept by giving a detailed example or anecdote (story), do you have difficulty recalling the example or anecdote after you leave class?		

ELABORATION
	YES	NO
1. Do you learn individual facts or details without thinking about the schema in which they belong?		
2. Do you frequently attempt to use rote memory to memorize facts, definitions, or rules?		
3. Do you complete a math problem and immediately move on to the next problem?		
4. Do you study information in the same order and in the same form in which it was presented?		
5. Do you avoid creating new study tools that involve reorganizing information?		

(continued)

Exercise 6.4 (continued)

CONCENTRATION

	YES	NO

1. Do you often experience divided attention because too many unrelated thoughts disrupt your thinking?

2. Do you have so many interruptions when you study that you are not quite sure what you have accomplished at the end of a study block?

3. Do you miss important information during a lecture because your mind tends to wander or daydream?

4. When you are reading, do you find it difficult to keep your mind focused on the information in the textbook?

5. Do you study with the television, radio, or stereo turned on?

RECITATION

	YES	NO

1. When you review for a test, do you do all or most of your review work silently?

2. Do you have difficulty defining new terminology out loud?

3. Do you have difficulty clearly explaining textbook information to another person?

4. When you rehearse information out loud, do you often feel that your explanations are "fuzzy," unclear, or incomplete?

5. Do you feel awkward or uncomfortable talking out loud to yourself?

INTENTION

	YES	NO

1. When you sit down to study, do you set a goal to complete the assignment as quickly as possible?

2. Do you always have the same purpose in mind when you sit down to study?

3. Do you lack curiosity, interest, or enthusiasm in the course content for one or more of your classes?

4. When you begin learning new information, do you find setting a specific learning goal difficult to do?

5. Do you study facts, details, or concepts in the same way that you study steps or processes for a procedure?

BIG AND LITTLE PICTURES

	YES	NO

1. Do you have problems distinguishing between main ideas and individual details in textbook passages?

2. Do you understand general concepts but oftentimes have difficulty giving details that relate to the concept?

3. Do you grasp specific details but oftentimes have difficulty connecting them together to form a larger picture or a concept?

4. Do your lecture notes capture main ideas but lack details?

5. Do your notes include running lists of details without a clear method of showing main ideas?

FEEDBACK

	YES	NO

1. Do you use tests as your main means of getting feedback about what you have learned?

2. Do you keep taking in new information without stopping to see whether or not you are trying to learn too much too fast?

Exercise 6.4 (continued)

3. When you are rehearsing, do you "keep on going" even if you sense that you have not clearly understood something?

4. Do you tend to use self-quizzing only when you are preparing for a test?

5. If you get feedback that you did not complete a math problem correctly, do you ignore your original work and try working the problem again?

ORGANIZATION   YES   NO

1. Does information from lectures often seem to be one continuous stream of information without any apparent organization or structure?

2. Do you have difficulty remembering the sequence of important events or the steps of a process?

3. When you try to do a "memory search" to locate information in your memory, are you usually unable to find the information?

4. Do you spend most of your time trying to learn information in the exact order in which it is presented?

5. Do you feel unsure about rearranging, reorganizing, or regrouping information so that it is easier to learn and recall?

TIME ON TASK   YES   NO

1. When your assignment is to read and study a specific chapter, do you spend a lot of time on the assignment but not make contact with it again for several weeks?

2. When you are studying, do you often feel as though you are trying to study too much information too quickly?

3. When you study, do you change to a second subject as soon as you complete the assignments for the first subject?

4. Are some of your study blocks more than three hours long?

5. In at least one of your courses, do you spend less time studying that subject than most other students in class do?

ONGOING REVIEW   YES   NO

1. Once you have completed an assignment, do you put it aside until close to the time of the next test?

2. Do you have problems remembering or recalling information that you know you learned several weeks earlier?

3. Do you need to add more review time to your weekly study schedule?

4. Do you study fewer than two hours per week for every one hour in class?

5. Do you sit down to study and feel that you are all caught up and have nothing to study?

ASSESSING YOUR CURRENT USE OF THE PRINCIPLES OF MEMORY:

1. A NO answer indicates you are already using the Principle of Memory when you study. If you gave NO answers to all the questions within one Memory Principle section, you are using the Principle of Memory consistently and effectively.

2. A YES answer indicates that you will benefit by learning to use this Principle of Memory more effectively when you study. The more YES answers you have, the greater the need to add this Principle of Memory to your learning strategies or study techniques.

Academic Preparation Inventory

DIRECTIONS: After identifying a specific class and the most recent test grade you received in that class, think back to the days prior to that test. Check **YES** or **NO** for each statement.

What is the specific class you are using for this inventory? _____

What was the last test grade you received in this class? _____

		YES	NO
1.	I had all the reading assignments and homework assignments done on time.	_____	_____
2.	I attended class regularly and was prepared for each class.	_____	_____
3.	I reviewed comments and my responses on my homework assignments when they were returned.	_____	_____
4.	I asked questions about information I did not understand.	_____	_____
5.	I worked with a tutor, with a study partner, or in a review group to prepare for the test.	_____	_____
6.	I participated in class discussions, asked questions, and responded to questions during class.	_____	_____
7.	I followed my time-management schedule and used the 2:1 ratio.	_____	_____
8.	I was an active learner and created a variety of study tools to rehearse and review information.	_____	_____
9.	I spent time each week reviewing information that I had previously studied.	_____	_____
10.	I knew the definitions for all the textbook terminology.	_____	_____
11.	I used study techniques that gave me feedback; I used both positive and negative feedback constructively.	_____	_____
12.	I read my textbook carefully and took notes on important textbook information.	_____	_____
13.	I was able to stay fairly motivated about the class and the work.	_____	_____
14.	I was organized, understood assignments, and had the materials necessary to study and review.	_____	_____
15.	I created a specific plan of action to prepare for the test.	_____	_____
16.	I avoided cramming the night before the test.	_____	_____
17.	I felt confident that I was prepared for the test.	_____	_____
18.	I can honestly say that I gave it my best.	_____	_____

All the **YES** responses for the above strategies indicate you are using those strategies effectively.

All the **NO** responses indicate strategies that you could use more effectively to achieve better test results.

Test Anxiety Inventory

DIRECTIONS: Check the responses that seem to best describe you this term.

	NEVER	SOMETIMES	ALWAYS
1. I have trouble sleeping the night before a test.	___	___	___
2. I can feel a lot of tension in my shoulders, arms, or face on the day of a test.	___	___	___
3. My heart beats fast during a test, and I feel hot, clammy, or downright sick during a test.	___	___	___
4. I am irritable, snappy, impatient, and sometimes even rude right before a test.	___	___	___
5. I try to find excuses not to go to school on the day of a test.	___	___	___
6. I prepare for tests by cramming the day or the night before the test.	___	___	___
7. I read my textbook, but when I start to review for tests, I get worried about how much I do not remember.	___	___	___
8. I procrastinate so much about studying that I am always behind in my assignments.	___	___	___
9. I find myself blaming the teacher, my family, or my friends for the fact that I am not prepared for tests.	___	___	___
10. I run short on time to study and do not make summary notes or review effectively.	___	___	___
11. My negative voice is quick to remind me that I never do well on tests.	___	___	___
12. I cannot seem to forget how disappointed I was with my last grade on a test; I really blew it.	___	___	___
13. It is difficult for me to get motivated to study for tests because the results are always discouraging.	___	___	___
14. I fear the consequences of failing a test because so much is riding on getting good grades.	___	___	___
15. I get so nervous about tests because anything less than my personal standards deflates my self-esteem.	___	___	___
16. I get stuck on one question and do not want to move on until I remember the answer.	___	___	___
17. I get distracted and annoyed by the littlest things others do in class during a test.	___	___	___
18. I am so anxious to get out of the classroom that I seldom check my answers or proofread.	___	___	___
19. I turn in tests that are incomplete even when I have more time.	___	___	___
20. Without knowing why, I panic and start changing answers right before I turn the test in.	___	___	___
21. I make careless mistakes on tests. Sometimes I can't believe the answers that I marked.	___	___	___
22. My mind goes blank, but as soon as I leave the classroom after taking a test, I remember the answers.	___	___	___

Answers in the **NEVER** column = Not major indicators of test anxiety.

Answers in the **SOMETIMES** column = Possible indicators of text anxiety; seek ways to alter your approach.

Answers in the **ALWAYS** column = Strong indicators of test anxiety; use strategies to reduce test anxiety.

Reading Process Inventory

DIRECTIONS: Reading is a complex process that involves many thinking and comprehension processes and functions. In the following inventory, circle **1, 2,** or **3** to show the processes you use or do not use when you read your college textbooks. Use the following information to select your answer 1, 2, or 3.

1 = use seldom or never   2 = use sometimes   3 = use on a regular basis

1. I am interested and eager to start new chapters and learn new information.   1 2 3

2. I use spaced practice to read textbooks so I can avoid engaging in marathon reading.   1 2 3

3. I read slowly and carefully to allow sufficient time to understand, process, and integrate new information.   1 2 3

4. I stay with a difficult paragraph until I figure out a way to understand the information.   1 2 3

5. I adjust my reading rate depending on my level of familiarity with the material and the complexity or the level of difficulty of the content.   1 2 3

6. I use thorough reading strategies, not recreational reading strategies, when I read college textbooks.   1 2 3

7. I use overview reading to skim a chapter or difficult sections of information before I begin the process of careful, thorough reading.   1 2 3

8. I verbalize, recite, visualize, and use feedback when I read my textbooks.   1 2 3

9. I immediately change my strategies when I realize I have shifted to the automatic pilot mode and am not focusing my attention on reading.   1 2 3

10. I chunk up or chunk down as needed to grasp information in meaningful ways.   1 2 3

11. I begin a new chapter by reading the headings and subheadings, the marginal notes, bold print, graphic materials, and summary materials.   1 2 3

12. On separate paper or next to the headings or in the margins of the textbook, I write questions for sections of information in a chapter.   1 2 3

13. I use a method of notetaking that is appropriate for each textbook.   1 2 3

14. I use the Read-Record-Recite Cycle when I read college textbooks.   1 2 3

15. I recite key information by explaining information out loud, in my own words, and without looking at printed text.   1 2 3

16. I can explain a specific reading process that I use for each textbook, but the process is not always the same for each textbook.   1 2 3

ANALYZING YOUR RESULTS:

- Processes marked with **1** are processes you lack that may weaken your reading skills and textbook reading success. Consider adding these strategies to your reading systems.

- Processes marked with **2** are used sometimes but not consistently. Using these processes more consistently strengthens your reading skills and comprehension.

- Processes marked with **3** are strategies that contribute to your success as an effective critical reader of your college textbooks. Continue using these processes consistently.

Active Reading Inventory

DIRECTIONS: Think about the way you read your college textbooks. Answer the following questions.

Circle **1** if you do not use this strategy when you read your textbooks.

Circle **2** if you use this strategy occasionally when you read your textbooks.

Circle **3** if you use this strategy consistently when you read your textbooks.

1. I create a plan of action before I begin reading a new textbook chapter.	1 2 3
2. I highlight and mark main ideas and the important supporting details in every paragraph.	1 2 3
3. I use word, punctuation, definition, word structure, and context clues to identify definitions of terminology and unfamiliar words.	1 2 3
4. I circle vocabulary terms and highlight their definitions.	1 2 3
5. I interact with printed materials by taking notes, copying diagrams, and creating study tools.	1 2 3
6. I read out loud or verbalize as I read.	1 2 3
7. I visualize information as I read.	1 2 3
8. I recite and check my accuracy throughout the reading process.	1 2 3
9. I make brief marginal notes next to important paragraphs.	1 2 3
10. I use a notetaking system to capture the important information in the chapter.	1 2 3
11. I ask questions and create study questions throughout the reading process.	1 2 3
12. I carefully examine charts, tables, illustrations, and graphs, and attach notes or brief summaries next to the graphic materials.	1 2 3
13. I use available resources and online materials that are available for the textbook.	1 2 3
14. I stay with a paragraph until I understand its meaning or content.	1 2 3
15. I use active reading strategies to avoid slipping into the automatic pilot mode.	1 2 3
16. I adjust my reading rate based on the difficulty and complexity of the material.	1 2 3
17. I create definition flashcards or vocabulary sheets to study terminology.	1 2 3
18. I push myself to analyze, evaluate, and use critical thinking skills.	1 2 3
19. I identify and label organizational patterns in paragraphs.	1 2 3
20. I am an active reader, not a passive reader.	1 2 3

SCORE: ☐ ☐ ☐

TOTAL SCORE: _____

YOUR SCORE:

20–35 You need to apply more effort to using active reading strategies to understand your college textbook material more thoroughly. Look at all the items that received a **1**. Strive to increase comprehension by adding these strategies to your textbook reading strategies.

36–50 You are using many active reading strategies effectively, but there is room to improve. Strive to include the strategies marked with a **1** or a **2** on a more consistent basis when you read your textbooks.

51–60 You are using active reading strategies effectively. Continue to use all of the strategies consistently when you study.

Annotation Checklist

DIRECTIONS: After annotating a passage, use the following checklist to assess your work.

	NO	SOMEWHAT	YES
1. I completely highlighted only one sentence, the topic sentence, in every paragraph.	_____	_____	_____
2. I selectively highlighted key words or phrases to show details that support the topic sentence.	_____	_____	_____
3. I avoided highlighting excessively to the point that most of the paragraph is highlighted.	_____	_____	_____
4. I circled all terminology that appeared in special print.	_____	_____	_____
5. I highlighted only the key words or phrases that define the terminology.	_____	_____	_____
6. I avoided highlighting every example; instead, I highlighted selective examples that can work as memory cues.	_____	_____	_____
7. I numbered details in the paragraphs that appear with ordinals.	_____	_____	_____
8. I wrote brief notes in the margins.	_____	_____	_____
9. I used abbreviations for some of the information that I wrote in the margins.	_____	_____	_____
10. To avoid highlighting too much, I sometimes use brackets to remind me about larger blocks of important text.	_____	_____	_____
11. For important graphic materials, I marked them and their captions in some meaningful way.	_____	_____	_____
12. At a glance, I can quickly pick out the important points when I review each paragraph.	_____	_____	_____
13. I used colors effectively.	_____	_____	_____
14. I reread my annotations by first reading out loud only the information that was highlighted or marked.	_____	_____	_____
15. I practiced stringing ideas together by adding my own words to explain the annotated information.	_____	_____	_____
16. I recited the annotated information without looking at the printed materials.	_____	_____	_____

Part I: Cornell Notetaking Self-Assessment Checklist

EXERCISE 9.8

Name _____   Date _____

Topic of Notes _____   Assignment _____

RECORD STEP	YES	NO
1. Did you clearly show headings in your notes so you can see the main topics?	_____	_____
2. Did you underline the headings and avoid putting numbers or letters in front of the headings?	_____	_____
3. Did you leave a space between headings or larger groups of information so that your notes are not cluttered or crowded?	_____	_____
4. Did you include sufficient details so that you do not need to return to the textbook to study this information?	_____	_____
5. Did you use numbering for the different details under the headings?	_____	_____
6. Did you indent and use dashes or other symbols to show minor supporting details?	_____	_____
7. Did you use meaningful phrases or shortened sentences that will be clear at a later time?	_____	_____
8. Did you paraphrase or shorten the information so that your notes are not too lengthy?	_____	_____
9. Did your notes refer to important charts, diagrams, or visual materials in the chapter, or did you make reference to the textbook pages in your notes?	_____	_____
10. Did you write on only one side of the paper, leaving the back side blank?	_____	_____
11. Did you label the first page of your notes (course, chapter number, and date) and use page numbers on the other pages?	_____	_____
12. Did you write your notes so that they are neat and easy to read?	_____	_____

RECALL COLUMN (REDUCE STEP)	YES	NO
1. Did you move each heading into the recall column and underline it?	_____	_____
2. Did you use a two-and-one-half-inch margin on the left for the recall column?	_____	_____
3. Did you include study questions in the recall column for the key points in your notes?	_____	_____
4. Did you include enough information in the recall column to guide you when you recite your notes?	_____	_____
5. Did you include in the recall column some key words that you need to define or explain?	_____	_____
6. Did you write the questions and the key words directly across from the corresponding information in your notes column?	_____	_____
7. Did you avoid writing too much information or giving yourself all of the information in the recall column, thus leaving you with little to recite from memory?	_____	_____
8. Did you try using the recall column?	_____	_____
9. Did you add or delete information in the recall column after you tried using that column for reciting?	_____	_____

Exercise 9.8 (continued)

Part II: Cornell Notetaking Instructor Assessment Form

Name _____   Date _____

Notes for _____

Check the statements that apply to a specific set of Cornell notes.

YOUR NOTES COLUMN

_____ You clearly showed and underlined the headings.

_____ Your notes will be easier to study because you left a space between new headings or sections of information.

_____ Your notes show accurate and sufficient details.

_____ You used meaningful phrases or shortened sentences effectively so that the information is clear and understandable.

_____ You shortened information effectively and captured the important ideas.

_____ Your notes are well organized. You effectively used numbering and indentations for supporting details.

_____ You included important visual graphics from the textbook.

_____ Your notes are neat and easy to read.

_____ You used notetaking standards effectively: you wrote on one side of the paper, you included a heading on the top of the page, and you numbered pages.

YOUR RECALL COLUMN

_____ You used a 2½-inch column.

_____ You placed your headings, questions, and key words directly across from the information in your notes.

_____ Your questions and key words are effective.

_____ You may need to add more self-quizzing questions, visual cues, or hints to guide reciting and create an effective recall column.

_____ You need to use a 2½-inch recall column on the left.

_____ You need to place the headings, questions, and key words directly across from the information in your notes.

_____ You need more meaningful questions and key words in the recall column.

_____ You are giving yourself too much information in the recall column; use questions without answers so that you will have more to recite.

AREAS FOR IMPROVEMENT IN YOUR NOTES

_____ Strive to identify and underline headings.

_____ Leave a space before you begin a new heading or section of information so your notes will be less crowded or cluttered.

_____ Include more information in your notes. Your notes lack some important details.

_____ Short phrases or isolated words lose meaning over time. Use more sentences or more detailed phrases to capture important ideas.

_____ Use shortened sentences to capture the important ideas. Your notes are unnecessarily lengthy.

_____ Strive for clearer organization. Number and indent supporting details.

_____ Include graphic information in your notes.

_____ Strive for neater penmanship and readability.

_____ Write on one side of the paper. Include a heading on the first page. Number all the pages of your notes.

OTHER COMMENTS

Photocopy this form before you use it.

EXERCISE 10.2

Organizational Patterns

1. NEWSPAPERS AND LENDING LIBRARIES   *Chronological?   Process?*

In addition to novels, newspapers and political pamphlets became increasingly available in the eighteenth century, especially in Britain and the Dutch Republic where censorship laws were relaxed or abolished. Reading newspapers had often been a collective activity in which one person read aloud to a group, but increasingly newspapers were read privately and silently, like novels, and passed along until the next day's newspaper was available. As the variety of reading material expanded, it is likely that Europeans received more information about the world and, often lost in the contents of the page in front of them, had a wider range of imaginative reading experiences than people had ever had before.

Source: Kidnet et al., *Making Europe: The Story of the West*, 2e, p. 516.

2. GLOBAL WARMING   *Chronological?   Process?*

Many scientists believe that global warming is already producing serious climate change, for as temperatures rise, more water evaporates, causing more rainfall and bigger storms, which lead to more flooding and soil erosion. People suffer and die all along the causal chain. This was tragically evident in 2005, when Hurricanes Katrina and Rita delivered knockout punches to coastal Louisiana, Alabama, Mississippi, and Texas, killing an estimated 2,300 people and causing many billions of dollars of damage (Brym, 2009: 53-81).

Source: Bryme, Lie. *Sociology*, 3e, © p. 377-378.

3. COASTS   *Comparison-Contrast?   Whole-and-Parts?*

Because coasts are influenced by so many factors, perhaps the most useful scheme for classifying a coast is based on the predominant events that occur there: erosion and deposition. **Erosional coasts** are new coasts in which the dominant processes are those that *remove* coastal material. **Depositional coasts** are *steady or growing* because of their rate of sediment accumulation or the action of living organisms (such as corals).

Source: Garrison. *Oceanography: An Invitation to Marine Science*, 8e, p. 12.

4. GREENHOUSE EFFECT   *Definition?   Examples?   Cause-Effect?*

Glass in a greenhouse is transparent to light but not to heat. The light is absorbed by objects inside the greenhouse, and its energy is converted into heat. The temperature inside a greenhouse rises because the heat is unable to escape. On Earth, **greenhouse gases**—water vapor, carbon dioxide, methane, chlorofluorocarbons, and others—take the place of glass. Heat that would otherwise radiate away from the planet is absorbed and trapped by these gases, causing a surface temperature to increase.

Source: Garrison. *Oceanography: An Invitation to Marine Science*, 8e, p. 533.

Visual Notes Checklist

Name _____ Date _____

Topic _____ Check one: _____ Visual mapping _____ Hierarchy

ORGANIZATION   YES   NO

1. The skeleton with level-one and level-two information is clear and easy
   to identify.   _____   _____

2. The lines connecting levels of information are clear and easy to follow.   _____   _____

3. The visual notes are uncluttered and easy to read.   _____   _____

4. Headings and supporting details are well spaced.   _____   _____

5. Only key words or short phrases appear on the visual notes and show use
   of selectivity.   _____   _____

VISUAL EFFECTS   YES   NO

1. I used colors or color-coding to emphasize different information or levels
   of information.   _____   _____

2. I used borders, shapes, or pictures for some information.   _____   _____

3. I wrote all of the information on a horizontal plane.   _____   _____

STUDYING FROM VISUAL NOTES   YES   NO

1. I have mentally imprinted the image of the skeleton.   _____   _____

2. I can visualize the skeleton without looking at the notes.   _____   _____

3. I have practiced reciting level-three and level-four information without
   referring to my notes.   _____   _____

4. I have completed at least one reflect activity with my notes.   _____   _____

5. I have reviewed my notes at least one additional time.   _____   _____

Classroom Listening Factors Inventory

EXERCISE 11.1

DIRECTIONS: Read each set of statements carefully. Check the statement that most reflects your behavior or attitude in a typical lecture class in which you are enrolled.

1. Interest Level

_____ A. I am not interested in the topic; in fact, it bores me.

_____ B. I do not have a genuine interest in the topic, but I know it is important to learn.

_____ C. I find ways to expand my interest in the topic, such as discussing it with others.

2. Seating Location

_____ A. I sit in the back of the classroom so I can see everything that goes on.

_____ B. I sit in the middle of the classroom so I can see the screen or chalkboard clearly.

_____ C. I sit in the front of the classroom so I have fewer distractions and a clearer view of visual materials.

3. Materials and Preparedness

_____ A. I often arrive to the classroom just as the lecture begins; I am seldom tardy.

_____ B. I arrive with sufficient time to select a good seat and "settle in."

_____ C. I arrive a few minutes early and prepared with sufficient paper, pens, my textbook, and class work.

4. Familiarity with the Topic

_____ A. I am curious at the beginning of each class about the topic for that day's lecture.

_____ B. I use the course syllabus to identify the topic for the day's lecture; then I survey the corresponding pages in the textbook.

_____ C. I read the textbook section or chapter for the lecture before class so I am familiar with the topic, definitions, and the kind of information I can find in the textbook.

5. Focused Attention

_____ A. I tend to "tune out" when the information is too technical or difficult to follow.

_____ B. I am aware that my concentration fades in and fades out multiple times during the lecture; I refocus as quickly as possible.

_____ C. I block out distractors so my concerted effort can be directed toward following the instructor's thinking and explanations.

6. Emotional Responses

_____ A. I immediately let an instructor know if I disagree with or dislike something he or she says during a lecture.

_____ B. I am aware during a lecture of the times when I do not agree with the instructor's information or point of view.

_____ C. I put my personal opinions aside so I can listen carefully to the information presented by an instructor before questioning or disagreeing with the information.

(continued)

Exercise 11.1 (continued)

7. Asking Questions

_____ A. I like to challenge the instructor by asking any questions as they pop into my mind.

_____ B. I jot down questions during a lecture and then ask them at an appropriate time.

_____ C. I ask open-ended clarifying questions to learn more about the topic; for example, I might ask: *What are some ways this could be used?* or *Why is it important to…?*

8. Checking Understanding

_____ A. I wait until after class to look at my notes to see what I understand.

_____ B. I ask questions or show my confusion at the point during a lecture when I do not understand what the instructor is presenting.

_____ C. At an appropriate time, I rephrase or paraphrase information that I do not understand clearly; for example, I might ask: *Do you mean that…? Is it correct then to say that…?*

9. Levels of Information

_____ A. I know that everything the instructor presents is important to remember.

_____ B. I use verbal and nonverbal clues to identify the main points of a lecture.

_____ C. I use verbal, nonverbal, and visual clues, such as information the instructor writes on an overhead or presents on a slide, to identify important information.

SCORING YOUR INVENTORY:

How many responses did you have in each category? Write the number of responses:

A_____   B_____   C_____

RESPONSES FOR A represent ineffective listening behaviors and attitudes.

RESPONSES FOR B represent adequate listening behaviors and attitudes that you can further strengthen.

RESPONSES FOR C indicate effective active learning behaviors and attitudes to use during lectures.

Lecture Notetaking Checklist

DIRECTIONS: Select any set of lecture notes you have for any one of your courses. Rank the quality of each of the following items in your notes, with **3** representing the highest quality.

1.	The notetaking system I used was effective for the lecture.	1	2	3
2.	The headings or main ideas are clear in my notes.	1	2	3
3.	I paraphrased the instructor's words.	1	2	3
4.	I used shortened sentences but did not lose the meaning.	1	2	3
5.	I used abbreviations and/or symbols in my notes.	1	2	3
6.	I used a combination of printing and cursive writing.	1	2	3
7.	I left a gap or shifted to paragraph form when I started falling behind taking notes.	1	2	3
8.	My notes include definitions for important terminology.	1	2	3
9.	My notes include supporting details: dates, names, facts, or statistics.	1	2	3
10.	My notes summarize examples without including every detail.	1	2	3
11.	I numbered individual details so they are easy to identify.	1	2	3
12.	I used the instructor's verbal, visual, and nonverbal clues to help identify important information for my notes.	1	2	3
13.	My notes include explanations for details or for steps in a process.	1	2	3
14.	My notes either include visual materials or references to textbook pages that have those visual materials.	1	2	3
15.	My notes are well-organized and have sufficient details so I will be able to use them for studying and review.	1	2	3

TOTAL SCORE: _____

SCORING YOUR RESPONSES: Total all the circled numbers for your final score.

15–20 Strive to use more effective strategies; your notes may lack sufficient information to be effective as a study tool to review lecture content.

21–40 Continue developing your notetaking skills for the areas ranked 1 and 2; your notes include adequate information for studying, but they could be stronger.

41–45 Continue using your notetaking skills; you have quality notes that you can use to study and review.

Exercise 11.5 (continued)

DIRECTIONS TO THE INSTRUCTOR:

In the _____ course, students are developing their lecture notetaking skills. One of your students, _____, chose to use your lecture class to practice notetaking skills. Your feedback on the student's notes would be greatly appreciated. Please take a few minutes to review the student's notes and answer the following questions. Students are asked to turn in this questionnaire with their practice notes.

Instructor's Name _____

Class _____

1. Do the notes appear to include the important information presented in the lecture?

    _____ Yes   _____ No   _____ Somewhat

    Comments:

2. Do the notes also show information that was presented on the overhead projector, blackboard, PowerPoint slides, or other form of visual presentation?

    _____ Yes   _____ No   _____ Somewhat

    Comments:

3. In what way could this student improve his or her notes for your lecture?

Appendix D
Excerpts

Understanding Stress and Stressors

HOW DO PSYCHOLOGICAL STRESSORS AFFECT PHYSICAL HEALTH?

You have probably heard that death and taxes are the only two things guaranteed in life. If there is a third, it surely must be stress. Stress is woven into the fabric of life. No matter how wealthy, powerful, attractive, or happy you might be, stress happens.

It comes in many forms: a difficult exam, an automobile accident, standing in a long line, reading about frightening world events, or just having a day when everything goes wrong. Some stress experiences, such as waiting to be with that special person, can be stimulating, motivating, and even desirable, but when circumstances begin to exceed our ability to cope with them, the result can be stress that creates physical, psychological, and behavioral problems. Stress in the workplace, for example, costs U.S. businesses more than $150 billion each year as a result of employee absenteeism, reduced productivity, and health care costs (Chandola, Brunner, & Marmot, 2006; Sauter et al., 1999; Schwartz, 2004; Spector, 2002).

Stress is the negative emotional and physiological process that occurs as individuals try to adjust to or deal with stressors. *Stressors*, in turn, are environmental circumstances (such as exams or accidents) that disrupt or threaten to disrupt people's daily functioning and cause people to make adjustments. *Stress reactions* are the physical, psychological, and behavioral responses (such as nervousness, nausea, or fatigue) that occur in the face of stressors (Taylor, 2002).

Some of us are more strongly affected by stressors than others, and we may be more strongly affected on some occasions than on others. Why? As described in more detail later, several *mediating factors* influence the relationship between people and their environments. These mediating factors include (1) the extent to which we can *predict* and *control* our stressors; (2) how we *interpret* the threat involved; (3) the *social support* we get; and (4) our *skills* for coping with stress. Mediating factors can either minimize or magnify a stressor's impact. In other words, as shown in **Figure 10.1**, stress is not a specific event but a transaction between people and their environments. It is a *process* in which the nature and intensity of our responses depend on what stressors occur and how they are affected by factors such as the way we think about them and how much confidence we have in our coping skills and resources.

Stress The process of adjusting to circumstances that disrupt or threaten to disrupt a person's daily functioning.

Stressors Events or situations to which people must adjust.

Stress reactions Physical and psychological responses to stressors.

FIGURE 10.1   The Process of Stress

Stressful events, stress reactions, and stress mediators are all important components of the stress process. Notice that the process involves many two-way relationships. For example, if a person has effective coping skills, stress responses will be less severe. Having milder stress responses can act as a "reward" that strengthens those skills. Further, as coping skills (such as refusing unreasonable demands) improve, certain stressors (such as a boss's unreasonable demands) may become less frequent.

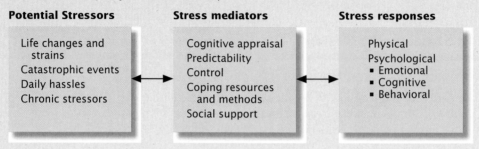

Source: Bernstein. *Essentials of Psychology,* 5e © 2011 Cengage Learning.

Practice Visualization

Sometimes, when we imagine giving a speech, we see the worst-case scenario. We see ourselves trembling, forgetting what we planned to say, dropping our notes, tripping on the way to the podium, and so on. Although a speech rarely goes this badly, these negative images stay in our minds. They increase our anxiety and often set up what is called a self-fulfilling prophecy: If you see yourself doing poorly in your mind before your speech, you set yourself up to do so in the speech. There are two solutions to this negative dynamic: visualization and affirmations.

Visualization. Visualization is a process in which you construct a mental image of yourself giving a successful speech. Research on the benefits of visualization before giving a speech suggests that one session of visualization (about fifteen minutes) has a significant positive effect on communication apprehension. The techniques of visualization are used by a wide range of people—athletes, performers, executives—and can range from elaborate to quite simple processes. For public speakers, the most effective process works as follows:

Find a quiet, comfortable place where you can sit in a relaxed position for approximately fifteen minutes. Close your eyes and breathe slowly and deeply through your nose, feeling relaxation flow through your body. In great detail, visualize the morning of the day you are to give your speech.

You get up filled with confidence and energy, and you choose the perfect clothing for your speech. You drive, walk, or ride to campus filled with this same positive, confident energy. As you enter the classroom, you see yourself relaxed, interacting with your classmates, full of confidence because you have thoroughly prepared for your speech. Your classmates are friendly and cordial in their greetings and conversations with you. You are *absolutely* sure of your material and your ability to present that material in the way you would like.

Next, visualize yourself beginning your speech. You see yourself approaching the place in your classroom from which you will speak. You are sure of yourself, eager to begin, and positive in your abilities as a speaker. You know you are organized and ready to use all your visual aids with ease. Now you see yourself presenting your speech. Your introduction is wonderful. Your transitions are smooth and interesting. Your main points are articulated brilliantly. Your evidence is presented elegantly. Your organization is perfect. Take as much time as you can in visualizing this part of your process. Be as specific and positive as you can.

Visualize the end of the speech: It could not have gone better. You are relaxed and confident, the audience is eager to ask questions, and you respond with the same talent as you gave your speech. As you return to your seat, you are filled with energy and appreciation for the job well done. You are ready for the next events of your day, and you accomplish them with success and confidence.

Now take a deep breath and return to the present. Breathe in, hold it, and release it. Do this several times as you return to the present. Take as much time as you need to make this transition.

Research on visualization for public speakers suggests that the more detail we are able to give to our visualizations (what shoes we wear, exactly how we feel as we see ourselves, imagining the specifics of our speech), the more effective the technique is in reducing apprehension. Visualization has a significant effect on reducing the nervousness we feel because it systematically replaces negative images with positive ones.

From Griffin. *Invitation to Public Speaking*, 3e. © 2009 Cengage Learning.

EXCERPT 3   ## Adopting a Healthy Lifestyle

A basic look at your lifestyle patterns begins by looking specifically at your lifestyle choices in the areas of nutrition, exercise, and sleep. These three areas tend to influence your level of stress, the ways you respond to a variety of stressors, and the degree to which you achieve your goals. Adopting a healthy lifestyle for many is a lifelong goal and not something you can check off as having completely achieved. The following sections provide you with healthy lifestyle choices to use for the areas of nutrition, sleep, and exercise.

NUTRITION

You are what you eat. Unfortunately, people experiencing stress frequently turn to fast foods and snacks that are high in fat and sugar, which produce an energy surge as blood sugar in the body increases and then is followed by a quick drop in energy as the blood sugar decreases. Foods high in sugar may lead to diabetes, obesity, heart disease, and other health issues. Foods high in fat contribute to health problems such as heart problems, high cholesterol, and increased blood pressure. Using the following nutritional guidelines can help you begin making healthier lifestyle choices:

- **Complex carbohydrates:** Instead of eating foods loaded with sugar, choose foods that break sugars down more slowly and release energy over a more sustained period of time. Complex carbohydrates, such as those found in grains, cereals, rice, pasta, bread, and potatoes, protect blood levels from the roller coaster effect of highs and lows.

- **Fruit and vegetables:** Consume three to four helpings of fruits and vegetables each day. In addition to providing you with essential vitamins and minerals, these foods increase your brain's production of serotonin, a brain chemical that stabilizes mood swings and promotes a sense of happiness. Multivitamins can supplement your dietary needs for vitamins and minerals, but they are not a substitute for good eating.

- **Items to avoid:** Limit your use of nicotine, caffeine, and alcohol; avoid nonprescription drugs. People often use more of these products when under stress, but they are not effective ways to cope with stress, and their health consequences may lead to more serious problems.

EXERCISE

Physical activity reduces the physiological effects of stress. Plan twenty to thirty minutes a day, a minimum of three times a week, for exercise—at a gym, running, or through a physical education course, a yoga class, an intramural sport, or a community exercise program. In addition to reducing your stress level and giving yourself a mental break from thinking about a stressor, the benefits of regular exercise are many:

- **Mental break:** Exercising not only reduces your stress level, but it provides you with a mental break by shifting your attention away from the stressor.

- **Oxygen to the brain:** Exercise gets oxygen moving more smoothly to your brain. Your concentration level increases, and information enters and moves through your memory system more efficiently.

- **Healthy heart:** Exercise improves your cardiovascular system, thus reducing your risk of more serious health conditions that may result from prolonged stress.

- **Stronger body:** Exercise strengthens your body, making it more resistant to the physical and emotional effects of stress. A healthy body becomes better equipped to handle stress, resist illnesses, and feel less fatigue.

SLEEP

Stress can disrupt your regular sleep patterns, and sleep deprivation can cause stress, creating a vicious cycle of fatigue of the body and diminished cognitive functioning. Under stress, some people sleep too little, while others sleep too much. People who sleep too little may experience symptoms of *insomnia*, the inability to fall asleep. People who sleep too much may be using excessive sleep to avoid feeling overwhelmed or helpless, to escape from the world, and to avoid dealing with their sources of stress. The following guidelines can help you obtain a healthy lifestyle that includes adequate sleep:

- **Eight hours of sound sleep:** On your weekly time-management schedule, plan to get eight hours of sound sleep per night.

- **Sleep pattern:** Strive to achieve a regular, predictable pattern of sleep throughout the week. Sleeping eight hours during the week and then five hours per night on the weekends, or sleeping six hours during the week and ten hours during the weekend creates the need for your body to keep adjusting to an irregular schedule. You will find that your days become more productive, your body more resilient, and your mind sharper on a more consistent basis when you have an established sleep pattern.

- **Relaxation strategies:** When faced with a night of tossing and turning, the inability to fall asleep has the tendency to create more stress and anxiety as you are fully aware of your need for sleep but are not able to fall asleep. When restless or stressed, shift your focus away from the stressor by relaxing in a prone position, engaging yourself in a relaxation technique, listening to soft music, visualizing pleasant scenes or memories, or practicing progressive relaxation techniques.

- **Professional advice:** If your inability to fall asleep and get a good night's sleep, or your inability to limit your nightly sleep to eight hours, persists for more than one month, underlying medical conditions, medications, or more deep-seated issues may be affecting your sleep patterns. Consult a counselor or a physician to discuss your sleep disorder.

Semantic Networks

Of course, not all information fits neatly into conceptual hierarchies or schemas. Much knowledge seems to be organized into less systematic frameworks, called semantic networks (Collins & Loftus, 1975). A **semantic network consists of nodes representing concepts, joined together by pathways that link related concepts.** A small semantic network is shown in **Figure 7.13**. The ovals are the nodes, and the words inside the ovals are the interlinked concepts. The lines connecting the nodes are the pathways. The length of each pathway represents the degree of association between two concepts. Shorter pathways imply stronger associations.

Semantic networks have proven useful in explaining why thinking about one word (such as *butter*) can make a closely related word (such as *bread*) easier to remember (Meyer & Schvaneveldt, 1976). According to Collins and Loftus (1975), when people think about a word, their thoughts naturally go to related words. These theorists call this process *spreading activation* within a semantic network. They assume that activation spreads out along the pathways of the semantic network surrounding the word. They also theorize that the strength of this activation decreases as it travels outward, much as ripples decrease in size as they radiate outward from a rock tossed into a pond. Consider again the semantic network shown in **Figure 7.13**. If subjects see the word *red*, words that are closely linked to it (such as *orange*) should be easier to recall than words that have longer links (such as *sunrises*).

From Weiten. *Psychology*, 9e. © 2011 Cengage Learning.

FIGURE 7.13   A semantic network.

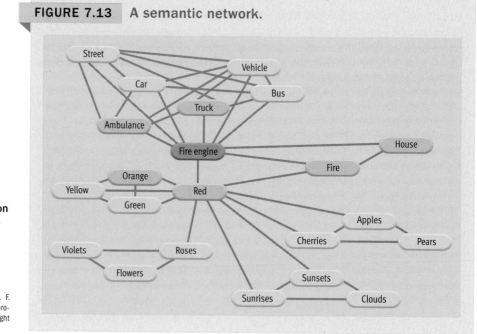

Much of the organization of long-term memory depends on networks of associations among concepts. In this highly simplified depiction of a fragment of a semantic network, the shorter the line linking any two concepts, the stronger the association between them. The coloration of the concept boxes represents activation of the concepts. This is how the network might look just after a person hears the words *fire engine*.

Source: Adapted from Collins, A. M., & Loftus, E. F. (1975). A spreading activation theory of semantic processing. *Psychological Review, 82*, 407–428. Copyright © 1975 by the American Psychological Association.

Building Blocks of Medical Language

Medical terms are composed of several parts, referred to as "elements." Each element has its own meaning and location in the term. Like building blocks, they can be combined to create thousands of different words. Learning the meaning of commonly used word elements and applying this knowledge to decipher medical terms is much more efficient than trying to memorize each new word as it is encountered.

The three principle elements that make up medical terms are roots, prefixes, and suffixes.

ROOTS AND COMBINING FORMS

The **root** is the part of the medical term that gives the main meaning. It usually, but not always, refers to the structure and function of the body. All medical terms have at least one root. The following are examples of roots:

- *gastr–* stomach
- *enter–* small intestine
- *cardi–* heart

Combining forms consist of roots plus a vowel, usually the letter "o," separated from the root with a slash mark:

- gastr/o
- enter/o
- cardi/o

SUFFIXES

Suffixes are word elements that are attached to the end of the roots and combining forms to add to or change their meaning. All medical terms have a suffix. Some common meanings of suffixes include:

- Pathological (disease) conditions
- Diagnostic procedures
- Surgical procedures
- Pertaining to
- Produced by
- Resembling

Recall that the combining form is used when the suffix begins with a consonant, as in the following example:

- cardi/o + megaly = cardiomegaly
- heart + enlarged = enlarged heart

Notice that the slash mark is dropped when the suffix is attached to the combining form.

When the suffix begins with a vowel, it is attached to the root word, as in the following example:

- gastr + itis = gastritis
- stomach + inflammation = inflammation of the stomach

Each suffix can be added to many roots. Knowing that *-itis* means "inflammation" enables the learner to know that the following words all indicate an inflammation of the body part indicated in the root:

1. Appendicitis: Inflammation of the appendix
2. Arthritis: Inflammation of the joint
3. Gastritis: Inflammation of the stomach

Another common suffix is *-ectomy*, which means "surgical removal." Like *-itis*, it can be combined with many root words. In each case, it means removal of the part indicated by the root word:

1. Appendectomy: Removal of the appendix

2. Gastrectomy: Removal of all or part of the stomach

3. Lumpectomy: Removal of a lump

When suffixes are listed in medical dictionaries and word lists, they are positioned alphabetically with other entries, preceded by a dash, and identified as a word element. Dictionary entries typically include the language of origin, as in the following sample dictionary entries:

- *-megaly*: word element (Gr.) enlargement

- *-itis*: word element (Gr.) inflammation

- *-ectomy*: word element (Gr.) surgical removal

PREFIXES

Prefixes are word elements that are attached to the beginning of roots and combining forms to add to or change their meaning. Many, but not all, medical terms have a prefix. Some common meanings of prefixes include the following:

- Location
- Position
- Direction
- Time
- Number
- Negation, absence of
- Color

Just as with suffixes, the same prefixes can be attached to many root words, resulting in thousands of variations. Knowing that the prefix *hyper-* means "abnormally increased" or "excessive" gives a clue to the meaning of the hundreds of words that contain this element, including the following examples:

1. Hyperacid: Abnormally or excessively acidic

2. Hyperactive: Exhibiting abnormally increased activity

3. Hypertension: Persistently high blood pressure

In the same way, knowing that *poly-* means "many" or "much" helps decipher the following examples:

1. Polyatomic: Made up of many atoms

2. Polyglandular: Pertaining to or affecting many glands

3. Polyphobia: Irrational fear of many things

When prefixes are listed in medical dictionaries and word lists, they are located alphabetically, followed by a dash, and identified as a word element, as in the following sample dictionary entries:

- *epi–* word element (Gr.) over

- *hyper–* word element (Gr.) abnormally increased; excessive

- *poly–* word element (Gr.) many; much

DECIPHERING MEDICAL TERMS

Learning the meanings of commonly used word elements and understanding how they combine enable the health care worker to decipher thousands of medical terms. When confronted with a new term, start at the far right, with the suffix. Think of each word as a combination of building blocks, fitted together to create a precise meaning. Work from right to left, identifying and defining each element, as in the following examples:

Example #1: cardiology

1. Starting from the right, find element –*logy*

2. Determine meaning: study of

3. Moving left, find element *cardio*

4. Determine meaning: heart

5. Combine elements: study of the heart

Example #2: polyarthritis

1. Starting from the right, find element –*itis*

2. Determine meaning: inflammation

3. Moving left, find element *arthr*

4. Determine meaning: joint

5. Moving left, find element *poly*

6. Determine meaning: many, much

7. Combine elements: inflammation of many joints

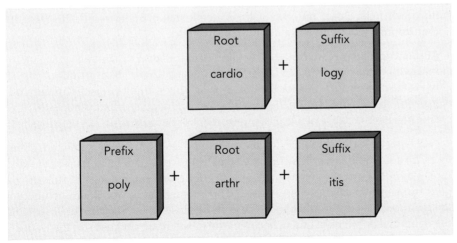

From Mitchell, Haroun. *Introduction to Health Care*, 2e © 2007 Cengage Learning.

EXCERPT 6   ## Professional Leadership

Leadership is an important concept in health occupations. **Leadership** is the skill or ability to encourage people to work together and do their best to achieve common goals. A **leader** is frequently defined as an individual who leads or guides others, or who is in charge or in command of others. A myth exists that leaders are born. In fact, leaders develop by their own efforts. Leaders combine visions of excellence with the ability to inspire others. They promote positive changes that benefit their professions and the people they serve. Anyone can learn to be a leader by making an effort to understand the principles of leadership. In a group, every member who makes a contribution to an idea can be considered a leader. The leadership in the group passes from person to person as each individual contributes to the achievement of the group's goals.

Leaders can often be classified into broad categories. Some of the categories include: religious, political, club or organizational, business, community, expertise in a particular area, and even informal or peer group. Leaders in these categories often develop based on their involvement with the particular category. An individual who joins a club or organization may become a leader when the group elects the individual to an office or position of leadership within the group.

Leaders are frequently classified as one of three types based on how they perform their leadership skills. The three main types of leader are *democratic, laissez-faire,* and *autocratic.*

- **Democratic leader:** encourages the participation of all individuals in decisions that have to be made or problems that have to be solved. This leader listens to the opinions of others, and then bases decisions on what is best for the group as a whole. By guiding the individuals to a solution, the leader allows the group to take responsibility for the decision.

- **Laissez-faire leader:** more of an informal type of leader. This leader believes in noninterference in the affairs of others. A laissez-faire leader will strive for only minimal rules or regulations, and allow the individuals in a group to function in an independent manner with little or no direction. This leader almost has a "hands-off" policy, and usually avoids making decisions until forced by circumstances to do so. The term *laissez-faire* comes from a French idiom meaning "to let alone" and can be translated to mean "allow to act"; therefore, it is an appropriate term to use for this type of leader.

- **Autocratic leader** often called a "dictator." This individual maintains total rule, makes all of the decisions, and has difficulty delegating or sharing duties. This type of leader seldom asks for the opinions of others, emphasizes discipline, and expects others to follow directions at all times. Individuals usually follow this type of leader because of a fear of punishment or because of an extreme loyalty.

All types of leadership have advantages and disadvantages. In some rare situations, an autocratic leader may be beneficial. However, the democratic leader is the model frequently presented as most effective for group interactions. By allowing a group to share in deciding what, when, and how something is to be done, members of the group will usually do what has to be done because they want to do it. Respecting the rights and opinions of others becomes the most important guide for the leader.

From Simmers, et. al. *Introduction to Health Science Technology,* 2e © 2009 Cengage Learning.

The Scientific Method

The **scientific method** of inquiry is based on three main concepts: observation, experimentation, and the development of theories or natural laws (**Table 1-2**). The first step in the scientific method is the actual observation and recording of facts. Much of the work of a scientist involves **observation** and the collection of data. This helps scientists to gain as much information as they can about the natural phenomena they are studying and then record that information in an organized way. Observation also involves conducting experiments. **Experiments** are controlled observations that help to answer questions about what scientists are trying to discover. The next step in the scientific method is the formulation of a **theory** that might explain how or why the natural phenomenon that is being studied is occurring. This is also called a **hypothesis**, which is an explanation that is supported by a set of facts. The final step in the scientific process is the formulation of a natural law that explains the phenomenon that is being studied. The formulation of a natural or a physical law helps to explain how certain aspects of the natural world operate and, more importantly, how they can be used to make predictions. Scientists often use observations they have made in the past to make inferences about what might occur in the future. An **inference** is a prediction or conclusion that is made about a future event based on previous scientific observations. The scientific method is a formal and organized procedure that scientists around the world use to make accurate investigations of the natural world.

TABLE 1-2   The scientific method is a formal procedure that scientists use to answer questions

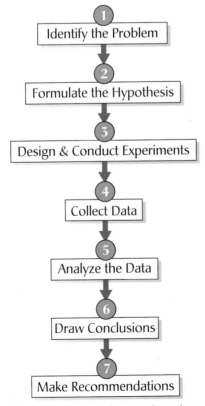

1. Identify the Problem
2. Formulate the Hypothesis
3. Design & Conduct Experiments
4. Collect Data
5. Analyze the Data
6. Draw Conclusions
7. Make Recommendations

From Butz. *Science of Earth Systems*, 2e © 2004 Cengage Learning.

EXCERPT 8   ## How to Listen Critically

When you listen to a speech critically, you mentally check it for accuracy, comparing what the speaker says with what you personally know and what your own research tells you. You also listen to assess the strengths and weaknesses of the reasoning and supporting materials presented in a speech. Note that listening critically is different from listening to judge or find fault with a message. Rather, **critical listeners** listen for the accuracy of a speech's content and the implications of a **speaker's message**. Critical listeners benefit by remaining open to new ideas, but they also listen carefully to how speakers develop those ideas into arguments. Additionally, they consider the impact of a speaker's ideas and how they may affect immediate audiences as well as larger communities.

To help you listen to speeches critically, ask yourself the questions in Table 3.1 and then follow the suggested guidelines. Asking these questions will help you assess a speaker's claims and arguments before you make decisions about their value or strength.

When we listen critically, we allow for dialogue because we avoid making quick decisions about good and bad, right and wrong. Listening critically encourages us to ask questions about ideas so we are better able to respond to claims and explore issues with others.

TABLE 3.1   Guidelines for Critical Listening

Question	Guideline
• How fully has the speaker developed an idea? Is something left out, exaggerated, or understated? Does the speaker use sound reasoning? Are claims based on fact or opinion?	• Speakers must develop all major arguments fully rather than present them without explanation and development. Speakers should not exaggerate arguments or understate their importance. Major ideas should be supported by evidence in the form of examples, statistics, testimony, and the like.
• What sources does the speaker rely on? Are they credible? How are they related to the speaker's topic? Will the sources benefit if facts are presented in a certain way? For example, is the tobacco industry arguing that smoking isn't harmful?	• Speakers must use credible sources that are as unbiased as possible. Speakers must cite sources for all new information. Sources should be cited carefully and with enough detail so the audience knows why the source is acceptable.
• Are the claims the speaker makes realistic? What are the implications of those claims? Who is affected by them? In what way? Has the speaker acknowledged these effects, or are they left unstated? Are there other aspects of the issue the speaker should address?	• Speakers must make realistic and logical claims and acknowledge different perspectives. They must also acknowledge those affected by their arguments and acknowledge the effects of their proposed solutions. When speakers take a position, they must not present their position as absolute or the only one possible.
• How does this speech fit with what I know to be true? What is new to me? Can I accept this new information? Why or why not?	• When speakers make claims that go against your personal experience, see if you can discover why. Sometimes, the answer lies in cultural differences or in a speaker's research. Try to be open to different views of the world while at the same time assessing the speaker's evidence and reasoning objectively. Before you reject a speaker's claims, engage the speaker in a civil discussion to find out why your perspective differs.
• What is at stake for the speaker? How invested is the speaker in the topic and the arguments being made? How will the speaker be affected if the audience disagrees?	• All speakers are invested in some way in their topics and arguments. However, some arguments benefit a speaker more than anyone else. Identify the speaker's motives so you can better understand why she or he is making particular claims.

From Griffin. *Invitation to Public Speaking*, 3e. © 2009 Cengage Learning.

Index